gale
e-commerce
sourcebook

ISSN 1542-1120

gale
e-commerce
sourcebook

volume 2

Directory of E-Commerce
   Associations, Consultants, and
   Other Organizations, continued

Directory of Leading
   E-Commerce Companies

General Index

Deborah J. Baker, Project Editor

GALE®

THOMSON
GALE

Detroit • New York • San Diego • San Francisco • Cleveland • New Haven, Conn. • Waterville, Maine • London • Munich

THOMSON

GALE

Gale E-Commerce Sourcebook

Project Editor
Deborah J. Baker

Editorial
Jason Baldwin, Eric Hoss, Amanda C. Quick,
Mike Weaver

Editorial Support Services
Magdalena Cureton, Edward J. David, Jr.,
Wayne Wilbur Fong

Product Design
Michelle DiMercurio, Michael Logusz

Composition and Electronic Capture
Evi Seoud

Manufacturing
NeKita McKee

This publication is a creative work fully protected by all applicable copyright laws, as well as by misappropriation, trade secret, unfair competition, and other applicable laws. The authors and editors of this work have added value to the underlying factual material herein through one or more of the following: unique and original selection, coordination, expression, arrangement, and classification of the information.

For permission to use material from this product, submit your request via Web at http://www.gale-edit.com/permissions, or you may download our Permissions Request form and submit your request by fax or mail to:

The Gale Group, Inc.
Permissions Department
27500 Drake Rd.
Farmington Hills, MI 48331-3535
Permissions Hotline:
248-699-8006 or 800-877-4253 ext. 8006
Fax: 248-699-8074 or 800-762-4058

While every effort has been made to ensure the reliability of the information presented in this publication, The Gale Group, Inc. does not guarantee the accuracy of the data contained herein. The Gale Group, Inc. accepts no payment for listing; and inclusion in the publication of any organization, agency, institution, publication, service, or individual does not imply endorsement of the editors or publisher. Errors brought to the attention of the publisher and verified to the satisfaction of the publisher will be corrected in future editions.

ISBN 0-7876-5750-6 (Set)
ISBN 0-7876-5751-4 (Vol. 1)
ISBN 0-7876-5752-2 (Vol. 2)
ISSN 1542-1120

Printed in the United States of America
10 9 8 7 6 5 4 3 2 1

▌2073

PUBLIC SECTOR CONSULTING

5718 Barlow Rd.
Sherman, IL 62684
PH: (217)629-9869
FX: (217)629-9732
E-mail: TEH@gotoPSC.com
URL: http://www.gotoPSC.com
Contact: Terry Edward Hornbacker, Principal

Description: Financial, managerial, and technological services and products for businesses and professionals. Special e-commerce packages for independent retail and service businesses. Search engine registration with track record of success. **Special Seminars:** CAD CAM Systems, Realestate Photoquick System, web sites, mobile computing. E-Commerce. **Geographic Area Served:** Worldwide.

▌2074

PYRAMID

110-64 Queens Blvd., Ste.260
Forest Hills, NY 11375
PH: (718)268-3884
FX: (718)897-6801
E-mail: info@pyramidupdate.com
URL: http://www.pyramidupdate.com
Contact: Nanette Cuccia, President

Description: Pyramid assists companies in retaining their business and retail customers. They provide online customer research (consumer research and business-to-business research), industry benchmarking and customer relationship management strategies and processes that are web-based and non-web-based.

▌2075

PYXIS INTERNATIONAL

1286 N Milwaukee Ave.
Chicago, IL 60622
PH: (773)394-0799
TF: 800-627-8202
E-mail: solutions@pyxis.net
URL: http://www.pyxis.net
Contact: Mr. Samuel Harper, Chief Executive Officer

Founded: 1998. **Description:** Internet consultants experienced with Microsoft Site Server, SQL Server, Oracle, and the latest web technologies. Specializing in web-based Internet/Intranet/Extranet systems, and strategic E-Commerce and Case Management solutions for competing in the new economy.

▌2076

QCIA LTD.

34-35 Station Approach
West Byfleet
Surry KT146NF, United Kingdom

PH: 44 1932 252993
FX: 44 1932 253273
URL: http://www.qci.co.uk

Description: QCi provides a range of solutions for CRM challenges and opportunities in all types of organizations. These solutions include strategic consultancy, proposition development, segmentation framework development, Senior Management Stop-Gap Resource, CRM Technical Architecture Design, software selection and implementation partner selection.

▌2077

QUAERO

13010 Morris Rd., 6th Fl.
Alpharetta, GA 30004
PH: (770)576-2056
E-mail: connardb@quaero.com
URL: http://www.quaero.com
Contact: Brad Connard

Description: Quaero's services help clients strengthen their customer relationships by helping them build an effective infrastructure, analyze their customer base and design smart customer communications. They can help build and analyze customer knowledge and increase customer value to increase a client's quality of customer service.

▌2078

QUAI INC.

44 School St., PMB 313
Boston, MA 02108
PH: (781)924-1211
TF: (866)782-4663
E-mail: curious@quai.com
URL: http://www.quai.com
Contact: Mr. Kirk Hill, Chief Executive Officer

Founded: 1996. **Description:** Internet Consulting and implementation services enabling companies to create additional business opportunities in the culmination of technology, development, project management and design. Provides services to industry-leading positions in the Finance, Education, Aeronautical, Healthcare and Technology industries. **Geographic Area Served:** United States.

▌2079

QUALDATA

13206 SE 57th St.
Bellevue, WA 98006
PH: (425)865-8339
E-mail: sales@qualdata.com
URL: http://www.qualdata.com

Description: A full service Web developer experienced in designing, developing, and managing the Internet for customers. Services include consultations, site design and architecture, modification of materials into HTML code, graphic design and development, programming, site hosting, upgrades, and maintenance. Also provides Web site management, e-mail and database management.

∎ 2080
QUALI-TECH BUSINESS MANAGEMENT CONSULTANTS

4151 Garnetwood Chase, Ste. 700
Mississauga, ON, Canada
PH: (905)624-2362
FX: (905)624-2728
E-mail: info@quali-tech.com
URL: http://www.quali-tech.com/
Contact: Mr. Thomas Duyck, President and Chief Executive Officer

Founded: 1985. **Description:** Quali-tech Management Consultants helps business to apply computer technology to ther business. Their services included businesses analysis, e-business, and e-commerce. QUALI-TECH engineers and specialists have worked in both small companies and in Fortune 500 companies, in business fields such as, electronics, finance, human resources, information systems, logistics, marketing, manufacturing, materials, quality to ISO-9000 and training. QUALI-TECH has access to over 30 different kinds of specialists, so they can compose a team specific to each client and their needs.

∎ 2081
QUALISOFT INC.

275 E South Temple, Ste. 100
Salt Lake City, UT 84111-1242
PH: (801)355-9043
FX: (801)355-9558
E-mail: admin@qsoft.com
URL: http://www.qsoft.com
Contact: Keith T. Kitterman, President

Staff: 4. **Description:** Specializes in custom programming for small and mid-range IBM systems (PCs and PC networks, Novell, Windows NT/2000, S/36, S/38, AS/400). Offers expertise in manufacturing and distribution systems, city/state government, purchase/leasing consultation, and software selection and customization. General business accounting systems, telecommunications expertise, and performance tuning. IBM partner in development of AS/400. Internet e-business set-up and development. Intranet setup & development. LAN/WAN EXTRANET setup & development. Industries served: medical, manufacturing, distribution, insurance, and government agencies in the United States. Web design & programming. **Special Seminars:** Develops computer software and customizes existing software; provide other I.S.-related servives. **Geographic Area Served:** United States.

∎ 2082
QUALISTICS INC.

5850 Oberlin Dr., Ste. 230
San Diego, CA 92121
PH: 888-775-4307
TF: 888-775-4307
FX: (858)404-7060
E-mail: info@qualistics.com
URL: http://www.surveyexpress.com

Founded: 1996. **Description:** Qualistics uses voice and Internet technologies to provide clients with a new-generation solution to improve customer service.

∎ 2083
QUALITY SERVICE INTL. (QSI)

2552 Britannia Rd.
Milton, ON, Canada L9T2X6
PH: (905)332-8095
FX: (905)332-3920
E-mail: info@qualityservice.ca
URL: http://www.qualityservice.ca

Description: Quality Service International is a full-service online and offline consulting firm that helps to improve service to customers through strategic planning, performance improvement, training programs and analysis over the web.

∎ 2084
QUALITY SOLUTIONS INC.

PO Box 40147
Cleveland, OH 44140
PH: (440)933-9946
TF: 800-471-1646
FX: (440)933-7077
E-mail: results@qualitysolutions.com
URL: http://www.qualitysolutions.com

Description: Quality Solutions Inc. provides a full range of management consulting services for companies seeking excellence in performance. One of the ways they help organizations achieve market leadership is by assisting them in the area customer satisfaction measurement and management systems through customer surveys that provide their clients with reports on information such as customer profiles, repurchase intentions, detailed competitive analysis, customer's buying criteria and more.

∎ 2085
QUBE CONSULTING LTD.

Willowbank House
84 Station Rd.
Marlow
Buckinghamshire SL71NX, United Kingdom

PH: 44 1628 681088
FX: 44 1628 681077
E-mail: info@qube.co.uk
URL: http://www.qube.co.uk

Description: Qube Consulting provides expertise in both consumer and business-to-business markets with consulting directed at effective Customer Relationship Marketing strategies to increase customer value. They offer custom-made consultancy projects for clients in all aspects of customer driven marketing with projects completed in CRM strategy, CRM infrastructure design and specification, financial feasibility models, customer retention strategies, devising referral programs, improving cost-effectiveness of customer acquisition, and specifying and implementing marketing databases solutions to support customer acquisition and retention programs.

∎ 2086
QUEST COMPUTING

68 Queen St.
Sheffield S11WR, United Kingdom
PH: 44 114 275 0006
FX: 44 114 276 1312
E-mail: info@questcomputing.co.uk
URL: http://www.questcomputing.co.uk

Description: Quest Computing are authorised Sage dealers and provide IT and website solutions for businesses throughout the UK. They offer a full range of computing expertise, from installation of IT systems to software support and web design, all backed up by a team of highly experienced advisors. Quest also provides independent and impartial advice on the selection of hardware and software, as well as hands-on help and guidance for existing installations.

∎ 2087
QUIDNUNC

218 W 40th St.
New York, NY 10018-1509
PH: (212)981-1900
FX: (212)981-1910
E-mail: nyinfo@quidnunc.com
URL: http://www.quidnunc.com
Contact: Mr. Bob Burke, Chief Executive Officer

Founded: 1988. **Description:** E-business consultant that helps build technology solutions that enhance interactions with corporate customers and intermediaries, whether the business goal is to improve customer understanding, increase loyalty and retention, build incremental or new revenue streams, or produce cost savings.

∎ 2088
QUILLIS INC.

10960 N Stallard Pl.
Tucson, AZ 85737
PH: (520)742-7747

TF: 800-443-7993
FX: (520)223-0139
E-mail: sales@quillis.com
URL: http://www.quillis.com

Description: Global provider of strategic information services, technology, and custom software solutions for businesses of all sizes. Specializes in consulting, creation, development, and deployment of business-critical solutions spanning the entire enterprise.

∎ 2089
QUOCIRCA LTD.

Mountbatten House
Fairacres
Windsor
Berkshire SL44LE, United Kingdom
PH: 44 1753 754 838
FX: 44 1753 857 612
E-mail: inquiries@quocirca.com
URL: http://www.quocirca.com

Description: Quocirca is an independent business analyst organization focusing on Customer Relationship Management, Mobility, eSolutions and hosted solutions in the technology marketplace. Their CRM services include helping clients with issues, such as integration of customer information and personalization to enhance a company's customer service.

∎ 2090
RA BROWN II

PO Box 12608
Fort Wayne, IN 46864-2608
PH: (219)479-1007
FX: (219)478-6577
E-mail: rab2@rab2.com
URL: http://www.rab2.com
Contact: Mr. Rick Brown, Consultant

Description: R A Brown II e-business management and consulting is a network of business and technology professionals organized and directed by Rick Brown. They offer their clients the flexibility and financial benefits of contract labor, while still maintaining the quality and professionalism of a large development firm.

∎ 2091
RADCLYFFE GROUP LLC

695 Rte. 46 W, Ste. 103
Fairfield, NJ 07004
PH: (973)276-0522
FX: (973)276-0529
URL: http://www.radclyffegroup.com

Description: The Radclyffe Group is a performance improvement consulting firm that assists call center organizations with strategic planning. Consulting services include management and trainer coaching, benchmarking, customer satisfaction and loyalty studies, call center start-up and more.

▌ 2092
RAINCITY TECHNOLOGY GROUP LLC

6012 Seaview Ave. NW
Seattle, WA 98107
PH: (206)781-0267
E-mail: info@raincitytech.com
URL: http://www.raincitytech.com
Contact: Mr. Dave Bly, President

Description: Technology consultants that focus on business-to-business e-commerce and project management. A systems integrator that specializes in content management solutions that improve business productivity. Helps companies select, implement, and customize commercial software that is used to manage, maintain, and deploy content. **Major Partners:** Microsoft; OnSite Technical Services; ICR Network; Blink Interactive Architects; Propoganza; Eagle Executive

▌ 2093
RAM ASSOCIATES

2662 Paden Pl.
Vestavia Hills, AL 35226-2823
PH: (202)543-3635
FX: (202)543-3610
E-mail: info@ramassociates.com
URL: http://www.ramassociates.com
Contact: Russell Mawn, President/CEO

Founded: 1983. **Description:** An e-commerce consulting company that specializes in developing electronic environments. Designs web sites that sell goods and services across the Internet. Custom internet products and services including Application Service Provider(ASP), web site hosting, server hosting, subscription and payment gateways, web, CD and network products, specialists in creating electronic environments, regulatory integration for proprietary products (CFR/FR).

▌ 2094
RAMBLER SYSTEMS LTD.

Cairncross House
25 Union St.
Edinburgh EH13LR, United Kingdom
PH: 44 131478 8200
FX: 44 131478 8221
E-mail: mail@.rambler.co.uk
URL: http://www.rambler.co.uk
Contact: Steve Rooney, Managing Director

Description: Rambler specializes in the development of applications software for self-service banking, customer information kiosk systems, EFTPOS, e-Commerce and m-Commerce.

▌ 2095
RAMCO SYSTEMS CORP.

Crossroads Corporate Center
3150 Brunswick Pike, Ste. 100
Lawrenceville, NJ 08648
PH: (609)620-4800
TF: 800-472-6261
FX: (609)620-4860
E-mail: infocrm@rsi.ramco.com
URL: http://www.ramco.com

Description: Ramco's eCRM initiatives can help clients prosper in the age of eBusiness by aligning their people, processes and technology into an integrated system with their customers as the central focus. Their service offerings include strategic consulting, turn-key implementation of eCRM applications, systems implementation, application integration and CRM outsourcing services. **Major Partners:** Siebel Systems.

▌ 2096
RAPIDIGM INC.

4400 Campbells Run Rd.
Pittsburgh, PA 15205
PH: (412)494-9800
FX: (412)494-9890
URL: http://www.rapidigm.com
Contact: Lew Wheeler, CEO & Co-Chairperson

Founded: 1968. **Description:** Rapidigm create e-business solutions that serve the needs of their clients and their users. At Rapidigm Solutions Centers, they employ a very simple Development Methodology: Architect, Construct, and Deliver. With their integrated teams of strategic, technical, and creative talent, their clients get the benefit of working with one e-business solutions provider that can deliver comprehensive solutions and robust web-centric applications with strong design execution founded upon a sound, strategic sensibility.

▌ 2097
RAY & BERNDTSON

301 Commerce St., Ste. 2300
Fort Worth, TX 76102
PH: (817)334-0500
FX: (817)334-0779
E-mail: marketing@rayberndtson.com
URL: http://www.rayberndtson.com
Contact: Paul R. Ray, Jr., Co-Managing Partner

Revenue: US$140,400,000. **Staff:** 740. **Description:** The 6th largest retained executive search and management consulting firm serving clients throughout the Americas, Europe, and Asia with a minimum compensation level of $150,000. Industries served: e-business, technology, financial services, healthcare and life sciences, business and professional services, consumer products and services, industrial products and services, energy and utilities. **Geographic Area Served:** North, Latin, and South America, Europe, Asia, and the Pacific Rim.

■ 2098
RCMS LTD.

Drake House
Homestead Road
Rickmansworth
Herts WD31FX, United Kingdom
PH: 44 1923 890 606
FX: 44 1923 890 607
E-mail: info@rcms.com
URL: http://www.rcms.com

Description: RCMS is an experienced web application builder helping clients with web-based applications including customer complaint systems that help them turn dissatisfied customers into satisfied customers. By using their web-based customer complaint system clients can turn their organization into a customer-oriented company by recording every customer complaint and controlling the way they deal with each complaint to become more customer focused. **Major Partners:** Business Objects; Informatica; Sun; Plumtree; Altio; BEA.

■ 2099
RDI GLOBAL

265 Notre Dame Ave.
Winnipeg, MB, Canada R3B1N9
PH: (204)943-5661
FX: (204)926-8302
E-mail: info@rdiglobal
URL: http://www.rdiglobal.com
Contact: Grant Barkman, General Manager & VP

Founded: 1994. **Description:** E-Business consulting company that specializes in providing innovative and advanced IT solutions to both public and private sector organizations. Provide business solutions for the digital marketplace including networking and application development services. **Major Partners:** IBM; TRIM-IT Development; Navision; Microforum; Microsoft; Beamstream.com; LearnLinc; Serenic **Awards:** Listed as the fourth fastest growing company in Manitoba by Manitoba Business Magazine, March 1999.

■ 2100
READYWEBGO

1770 W State St., Ste.146
Boise, ID 83702
PH: (208)345-5439

E-mail: info@readywebgo.com
URL: http://readywebgo.com

Description: Readywebgo is a group of Internet consultants and e-commerce developers with a focus on user-centered design methods to help clients reach their target audience.

■ 2101
REAL TECHNOLOGIES INC (RTI)

265 Rimrock Rd., Ste. 205
Toronto, ON, Canada M3J3C6
PH: (416)630-5577
FX: (416)630-6850
E-mail: info@realtechnologies.com
URL: http://www.realtechnologies.com

Description: Real Technologies provides e-commerce solutions for companies seeking to complete business to business organization transactions. Real Technologies provides core technologies that enable business-to-business transactions. They use backend database structures and fully integrated front-end custom applications to create, host, and maintain web sites.

■ 2102
RED TRAIN INC.

110-27 72nd Dr., 2nd Fl.
New York, NY 11375
PH: (859)466-3042
FX: (305)489-2241
E-mail: info@redtrain.com
URL: http://www.redtrain.com
Contact: Mr. Chris Greaves, Chief Executive Officer

History: In 2000, Red Train Inc. tripled in size, growing from a single-project association of programmers to a multimillion dollar IT consulting firm. **Description:** Developers and managers of custom solutions in Internet commerce, systems integration, and wireless applications. Services include E-commerce, systems integration, executive decisions support systems, and Intranet/Extranet. **Major Partners:** Cosmic Blender; Clearway; Lumasis

■ 2103
REDNETTLE

1c Beach Rd., Emsworth
Hampshire PO107JS, United Kingdom
PH: 44 124 337 0071
E-mail: info@rednettle.com
URL: http://www.rednettle.demon.co.uk

Description: Provides e-commerce and IT consultancy, web design and software development, and graphic design services.

▌2104

REGENERATOR LTD.

31 Great Marlborough St.
London W1F7JA, United Kingdom
PH: 44 207 4949456
FX: 44 207 4949567
E-mail: mail@regenerator.co.uk
URL: http://www.regenerator.co.uk
Contact: Mr. Steve Hinchliffe, Founder

Description: Regenerator is a UK based strategic consultancy, developing multi-channel ecommerce strategies for the boards of corporations.

▌2105

REMEDI ELECTRONIC COMMERCE GROUP

96 Northwoods Blvd.
Columbus, OH 43235
PH: (614)436-4040
FX: (614)436-7902
E-mail: sales@remedi.net
URL: http://www.remedi.net

Founded: 1994. **Description:** Specializes exclusively in Electronic Commerce (EC), Electronic Data Interchange (EDI), and Enterprise Application Integration (EAI) consulting. Perform both strategic and technical consulting services.

▌2106

RENTAWEBMASTER.NET
DCAS SOFTWARE SOLUTIONS

5720 LBJ Fwy, Ste. 325
Dallas, TX 75380
PH: (972)239-2327
FX: (972)385-2905
E-mail: webmaster@dcas.net
URL: http://www.rentawebmaster.net

Description: Rentawebmaster.com offers consulting for businesses to get on the Internet. The company helps their clients to get on the internet and have many ways to can help clients make this transition.

▌2107

RESEARCH TRIANGLE COMMERCE INC. (RTCI)

201 Shannon Oaks Cir.
Cary, NC 27511-5570
PH: (919)657-1500
FX: (919)657-1501
E-mail: sales@rtci.com
URL: http://www.rtci.com
Contact: Phil King, Group VP & General Manager

Description: Infrastructure solutions provider serving the B2B e-commerce market. RTCI facilitates the development and operations of comprehensive business-to-business Electronic Commerce (EC) solutions. Specializes in EC solutions involving EDI (Electronic Data Interchange) and EAI (Enterprise Application Integration) by providing mission critical EC consulting, EC software, outsourced EC services, and technical resource management. **Awards:** Inc. Magazine "Inc. 500" 1997, 1998, 1999; Deloitte & Touche "Technology Fast 500" 1997, 1998, 1999 and "Technology Fast 50" 1996, 1997,1998,1999; Mercator Software, Inc "Most Valuable Consulting Partner" 1998; Ernst & Young "Entrepreneur of the Year" 1998 "Technology Group"; KPMG Peat Marwick, LLP "Triangle Fast 50" 1996, 1997, 1998, 1999

▌2108

RESOURCE

343 N Front St.
Columbus, OH 43215
PH: (614)621-2888
TF: 800-550-5815
FX: (614)621-2873
E-mail: businessdevelopment@resource.com
URL: http://www.resource.com
Contact: Christopher Celeste, President

Revenue: US$200,000. **Staff:** 175. **Description:** Internet strategic marketing services. **Geographic Area Served:** United States. **Publications:** Resource E-Commerce Watch.

▌2109

THE RESOURCE CENTER FOR CUSTOMER SERVICE PROFESSIONALS

PO Box 401
Western Springs, IL 60558
PH: (708)246-0320
FX: (708)246-0251
E-mail: librarian@the-resource-center.com
URL: http://www.the-resource-center.com
Contact: Nina Kawalek, Founder

Founded: 1995. **Description:** The Resource Center is an online company where products from publishers all over the world have been assembled in one place for the convenience of help desk, customer service, technical support, and call center professionals.

▌2110

RESPONSIVE DESIGNS INC.

318 Diablo Rd., Ste. 240
Danville, CA 94526
PH: (925)743-1132
FX: (925)743-8450
E-mail: RDI@bigfoot.com
Contact: Karen T. Woolley-Stewart

Description: Provides systems analysis, requirements definition, development, documentation, testing, training for Unix/MS-DOS-based applications. Specializations include relational databases (Oracle, Unify, Informix, Ingres), electronic commerce/EDI (marketing, sales, lead tracking systems; Gentran:Server, Gentran:Mentor, Connect:Direct, Connect:Mailbox) and software engineering (automated Q/A regression test suites; system utilities). Industries served: insurance, banking, credit, billing, medical/healthcare, manufacturing, biological products. **Geographic Area Served:** Worldwide, but primarily California and continental United States.

∎ 2111
REYMONT ASSOCIATES

PO Box 114-Cooper Sta.
New York, NY 10276-0114
PH: (212)473-8031
E-mail: copyhawk@aol.com
URL: http://www.copyhawk.com
Contact: Daniel J. Scherer

Staff: 4. **Description:** Internet website content editing (offline) for e-business, goverment agencies and non-profit/civic groups; service for websites which are up and running, or in pre-launch phase (with NDA-non-disclosure aggrement). **Special Seminars:** Press release preparation. **Geographic Area Served:** United States and Canada.

∎ 2112
THE RICHARDSON CO. TRAINING MEDIA

13 Creekwood Ln. SW
Lakewood, WA 98499
PH: (253)582-2911
TF: 800-488-0319
FX: (253)588-0815
E-mail: rctm@rctm.com
URL: http://www.rctm.com

Founded: 1992. **Description:** The Richardson Company offers training programs to enhance customer service through video-based, audio-based and web-based programs.

∎ 2113
RIDENOUR & ASSOCIATES

1 E Wacker Dr., Ste. 3500
Chicago, IL 60601
PH: (312)644-1888
FX: (312)644-1883
E-mail: ssridenour@aol.com
URL: http://www.ridenourassociates.com
Contact: Suzanne S. Ridenour, President & CEO

Staff: 5. **Description:** International executive search consultancy which specializes in the recruitment of direct marketing, e-commerce and integrated communications professionals. **Geographic Area Served:** United States, Europe, Asia, Latin America and Australia.

∎ 2114
RIGHT ANSWER INC.

162 Bryant St. NW, Ste. 2C
Washington, DC 20001
PH: (202)667-6842
FX: (202)667-6843
E-mail: information@therightanswer.com
URL: http://www.therightanswer.com
Contact: Ms. Donna Hall, President

Description: The Right Answer Inc. strives to help educate individuals and organizations on how to build and develop successful customer relationships through effective communications. They help adapt training practices and procedures to meet the needs and unique aspects of each type of business. They also help clients determine the needs of their individual company and help formulate the training methods required to meet those needs.

∎ 2115
RIGHTNOW TECHNOLOGIES INC.

40 Enterprise Blvd.
PO Box 9300
Bozeman, MT 59718
PH: (406)522-4200
TF: 877-363-5678
FX: (406)522-4227
E-mail: info@rightnow.com
URL: http://www.rightnow.com
Contact: Greg Gianforte, Chief Executive Officer and Founder

Founded: 1995. **Description:** RightNow Technologies is a provider of eService solutions for the Internet and Intranet environments. They offer tools to support Web site operations with fully automated, online customer service, including online surveys, data analysis, and marketing.

∎ 2116
RJR COMPUTING SOLUTIONS INC.

12102 S 70th Ct.
Palos Heights, IL 60463
PH: (708)361-6510
FX: (708)876-0741
E-mail: bob@rjrcomputing.com
URL: http://www.rjrcomputing.com
Contact: Robert Regnerus, Principal

Description: Help businesses increase revenue and gain exposure through the Internet. **Geographic Area Served:** Worldwide.

■ 2117
RLK CONSULTING S.R.L.

Via del Corso, 112
00186 Rome, Italy
PH: 39 067009469
E-mail: info@rlkconsulting.com
URL: http://www.rlkconsulting.com
Contact: Mr. Raffaello Palandri, Owner/Consultant

Founded: 1999. **Description:** E-commerce, web development consulting and business intermediation services.

■ 2118
ROBERT E. NOLAN COMPANY

90 Hopmeadow St.
Simsbury, CT 06070
PH: 800-653-1941
TF: 800-653-1941
FX: (860)651-3465
URL: http://www.renolan.com
Contact: Dennis Sullivan, Chief Executive Officer

Founded: 1973. **Description:** The Robert E. Nolan Company is a management consulting firm specializing in the insurance, healthcare and banking industries. They can help clients achieve improvement in customer service, quality, productivity and costs. With an emphasis on customers and service process integration, they can help clients focus their operations to serve customers better. They begin with strategy and process design and will help select and integrate technologies to support their CRM process.

■ 2119
KEN ROBERTS COMPUTER CONSULTANTS INC.

148 York St., 2nd Fl.
London, ON, Canada N6A1A9
PH: (519)672-8844
FX: (519)672-3528
E-mail: ken@mirror.org
URL: http://www.mirror.org/krcc.html
Contact: Ken Roberts

Staff: 3. **Description:** Offers custom application development, systems administration and special project services for UNIX, Linux, AIX and related systems. Develops mostly in the Appgen databse language, C language, Perl scripts, and Unix shell scripts, and work on both stand-alone and network/Internet application services. Typical projects are 50 to 500 man-hours. Work is client business task centered, not product centered. Focus is on systems with above-normal

requirements for accuracy, reliability, security or auditability. Industries served include newspaper publishing, air and bus transportation, government documents search/filing, and network operations. **Geographic Area Served:** Southwestern Ontario directly, and anywhere in Canada and the United States working through clients' support staff, who provide first-call support and use our firm as a secondary resource.

■ 2120
ROCKWELL FIRST POINT CONTACT

300 Bauman Ct.
Wood Dale, IL 60191
PH: (630)227-8000
TF: 800-416-8199
FX: (630)227-8165
URL: http://www.ec.rockwell.com
Contact: Terry Murphy, President

Description: Rockwell FirstPoint Contact develops web-based contact center solutions based upon an open and integrated interaction infrastructure that provides high availability while facilitating rapid response, centralized management and access to in-depth information from multiple resources.

■ 2121
ROME TECHNOLOGY LTD.

PO Box 1716
Lansdale, PA 19446
PH: (215)631-1581
E-mail: info@rometechnology.com
URL: http://www.rometechnology.com

Description: Rome Technology Ltd. is a Web Services Firm who designs eBusiness products and solutions to enhance businesses. They develop solutions that are always thoroughly tested, debugged, and designed to meet customer expectations. They offer businesses Internet solutions ranging from eCommerce to Web Site Management to Complete Web Development. They create solutions that improve customer service and strengthen communication channels with customers, employees, and vendors. They design web components for Portals / Intranets / Extranets / and Internet web sites.

■ 2122
ROSE INTERNATIONAL

16401 Swingley Ridge Rd., Ste. 200
Chesterfield, MO 63017
PH: (636)532-3126
TF: 888-430-7673
FX: (636)532-6106
E-mail: development@roseint.com
URL: http://www.roseint.com
Contact: Ms. Himanshu Bhatia, Chief Executive Officer

Founded: 1993. **Staff:** 300. **Description:** Rose International provides information technology consulting and services for both commercial clients and government agencies. Rose is an e-business and e-commerce solutions provider. Himanshu and Gulab Bhatia founded Rose International in 1993. In 1995, St. Louis-based Rose committed to becoming a world-class IT provider.

▌2123
RSA TELESERVICES

14 Marie-Curie
Kirkland, PQ, Canada H9J3V9
PH: (514)575-7424
URL: http://www.offshore-callcenters.com
Contact: Robert Acoca

Description: RSA Teleservices is a strategic partner for both Offshore Call Center operators and for North American corporations looking to outsource their call center requirements to third-party service providers to better serve their customers. RSA specializes in strategic planning for contact center outsourcers and in-house call centers with expertise in technology assessments, human resources, training, business process re-engineering and performance management.

▌2124
A RUBY IMAGE

Sylvester, GA
PH: (912)776-2030
FX: (912)776-4733
E-mail: Consultant@RubyImage.com
URL: http://rubyImage.com

Description: Specializing in web site maintenance and design and Internet marketing.

▌2125
RUECKGAUER SYSTEMS ASSOCIATES INC.

2130 P St. NW, Ste. 711
Washington, DC 20037-1012
PH: (202)223-2872
URL: http://

Founded: 1981. **Description:** Rueckgauer Systems provides Full Life Cycle software development services for Microsoft Windows NT/2000 and Internet platforms. They specialize in advanced database driven solutions for any corporate need - from task-focused and departmental objectives to mission-critical enterprise and e-business applications. They also offer extensive IT management consulting, operational and strategic planning, and related knowledge assets. Rueckgauer Systems builds custom technology solutions that are based on their clients specific business requirements and objectives.

▌2126
RUFAN-REDI SOLUTIONS

PO Box 75
Manly, NSW 1655, Australia
PH: 61 096 271 180
URL: http://www.rufan-redi.com
Contact: Mr. Jeremy Cath

Description: rufan-redi provide consultancy and development services in the convergent media arena. They apply technology to business needs for advertising, marketing, media, tv and event companies, or work with clients who need to establish a presence on the web. Their projects are not limited to web. They are involved in all aspects of interactive marketing and development.

▌2127
RUNTIME LTD.

Unit 20 BDC, Stafford Pk. 4
Telford TF33BA, United Kingdom
PH: 44 800 018 2128
FX: 44 070 613 0865
E-mail: info@runtimeuk.com
URL: http://www.runtimeuk.com

Description: Runtime Ltd. is a consulting group who can develop a whole host of solutions to meet your business needs. They have developed on line shops and content managed sites for a wide variety of business to business and business to consumer operations.

▌2128
SAA CONSULTANTS LTD.

The Computer Complex
Somerset Pl.
Plymouth PL34BB, United Kingdom
PH: 44 1752 606000
FX: 44 1752 606838
E-mail: marketing@saaconsultants.com
URL: http://www.saaconsultants.com/

Description: SAA Consultants is an e-business software developer and professional services provider. Their experience and expertise are within business and government communications, and in meeting the e-business requirements of our substantial corporate customer base. This experience has been harnessed to develop world-class e-business enabling products, based on Internet standards, XML and open, multi-platform technologies.

▌2129
SAFINA INC.

955 N Plum Grove Rd., Ste. A-1
Schaumburg, IL 60173
PH: (847)605-8319

495

FX: (847)605-8331
Contact: Sanjiv Pillai, General Manager

Staff: 5. **Description:** Experts in performing environmental due diligence and environmental insurance claim investigations. Software division includes Web site development, custom software Java and e-commerce applications.

∎ 2130
SAGE MARKETING & CONSULTING ONLINE

300 E 34 St., Ste. 21K
New York, NY 10016-4909
PH: (212)889-1794
FX: (212)504-3243
E-mail: info@sagemarketing.com
URL: http://www.sagemarketing.com
Contact: Sandra L. Gassmann, President

Description: A marketing consulting firm providing strategic planning advice for the use of the Internet. Offers training in the use of Internet resources, Web site development and planning, and support sources. Provides a needs and cost analysis of your Internet use full promotional & marketing services. Multi and cross channel synchronzation and commreations strategy. **Geographic Area Served:** Worldwide.

∎ 2131
SAGE SOFTWARE CONSULTING INC.

5080 Meadville St.
Excelsior, MN 55331
PH: (612)396-7779
TF: 888-457-0000
E-mail: info@sagesw.com
URL: http://www.sagesw.com

Description: Sage Software Consulting is a Twin Cities based firm specializing in e-commerce, database design and development, and information technology staffing. Sage Consulting simplify e-business challenges with clear, concise answers to their clients' questions. Their consultants work with their clients to take their e-business ideas from strategy to design, and from design to implementation. They provide web design, copy writing, graphic development and strategic planning services.

∎ 2132
SAGE TECHNICAL SOLUTIONS

PO Box 5404
Fort Wayne, IN 46895
PH: (219)426-3462
E-mail: questions@sagetek.net
URL: http://www.sagetek.net

Description: Sage Technical Solutions specializes in web development both Intranet and Internet, database design and

deployment for Oracle, application development specializing in Delphi, Visual Basic, C and networking. They also provide consulting services on a contract basis as well as permanent placement.

∎ 2133
SAKSON & TAYLOR INC.

4300 Auroa Ave., N, Ste. 100
Seattle, WA 98103
PH: (206)632-6931
FX: (206)632-6927
E-mail: info@sakson.com
URL: http://www.sakson.com
Contact: Donna M. Sakson, President

Description: An information design and development consulting firm. Specializes in developing quality Internet and intranet web sites, online help, software and hardware documentation, training, and electronic performance support systems. Intranet web system services Expert information design, HTML coding, graphic design and illustration, CGI scripting, database interactivity, and writing and editing services.

∎ 2134
SALES TRAINING INTL.

2204 Timberloch Pl., Ste. 150
The Woodlands, TX 77380
PH: (281)367-5599
TF: 800-551-7355
E-mail: info@saleshelp.com
URL: http://www.saleshelp.com

Description: Sales Training Intl. provides various customer service training courses and customer service training online. Their customer service excellence series is a two-day course that links five of the most critical customer service skills modules into one course. These skills modules include telephone etiquette, trust and rapport building, active listening skills, problem solving and defusing anger.

∎ 2135
SALESPEAK INC.

5579B Chamblee Dunwoody Rd. 498
Atlanta, GA 30338
PH: (678)587-9911
E-mail: sales@salespeak.com
URL: http://www.salespeak.com

Description: SalesPeak Inc. provides customized sales and customer service seminars and skills training for companies who want to increase sales and customer satisfaction. They also offer customer service consulting and coaching services, with topics ranging from telephone customer service to generating customer loyalty. Some of their clients have included the BellSouth Corporation, CNN Interactive, The Coca-Cola

Company, Electronic Commerce System and Hewlett Packard.

∎ 2136
SALTZER, SUTTON & ENDICOTT

3205 Talbot St.
San Diego, CA 92106
PH: (619)222-2545
FX: (619)222-4211
E-mail: bsaltzer@consultsse.com
Contact: Benjamin A. Saltzer, President

Description: Works with management on the strategy and operations of their information systmes and technologies: getting the maximum benefit out of existing systems-increased profit, improved strategic advantage; taking advantage of new technologies to maintain and gain new profits and strategic advantages. Works with a wide variety of technologies and techniques, matched to our clients' requirements: internet, electronic commerce, data processing, telecommunications, document/record management; needs assessment, feasibility analysis, business system improvement and redesign. **Seminars:** Change Management (Strategic Planning, Systems Analysis, Project Management); "Transition to Management: Everything You Needed to Know When You Got Promoted, But Nobody Told You." Seminars/Workshops on Telecommunications: Entire curriculum and Certificate Programs on telecommunications. Seminars on Consulting: Entire curriculum and Certificate Programs on consulting as a profession. **Special Seminars:** Full range of computer, software, and information system development; complete documentation and training materials development; document design, development, and publication; training program desing, development, and presentation; bar coding applications for inventory management. **Geographic Area Served:** Worldwide.

∎ 2137
SAN JOSE FOCUS

3032 Bunker Hill Ln., Ste. 105
Santa Clara, CA 95054
PH: (408)988-4800
FX: (408)988-4866
E-mail: josh@sjfocus.com
URL: http://www.sjfocus.com

Description: San Jose Focus is a market research firm that facilitates web-based focus groups for research groups. Their focus groups specialize in taste tests, auto drive tests, product development, and software development.

∎ 2138
SANDRA STEEN & ASSOCIATES INC.

1777 NE Loop 410, Ste. 1009
San Antonio, TX 78217
PH: (210)804-0655
FX: (210)804-0658
E-mail: sales@sandrasteen.com
URL: http://www.sandrasteen.com
Contact: Ms. Sandra Steen, President and Chief Executive Officer

Description: Sandra Steen and Associates is a training and consulting firm specializing in the call center industry. They offer a variety of classes including bridging sales and service, first class customer service and telephone etiquette.

∎ 2139
SAPIENT CORPORATION

1 Memorial Dr.
Cambridge, MA 02142
PH: (617)621-0200
FX: (617)621-1300
E-mail: e-business@sapient.com
URL: http://www.sapient.com
Contact: Jerry A. Greenberg, Co-Chairman and Co-CEO

Founded: 1991. **Revenue:** US$503,000,000. **Staff:** 2615. **Description:** An innovative e-services consultancy providing Internet strategy consulting and sophisticated Internet-based solutions to Global 1000 companies and startup businesses.

∎ 2140
SATYAM COMPUTER SERVICES LTD.

Mayfair Centre, 1-8-303/36, S. P. Rd.
Secunderabad 500003, India
PH: 91407843222
FX: 91407840058
E-mail: svl@satyam.com
URL: http://www.satyam.com
Contact: Mr. B. Ramalinga Raju, Chairman

Founded: 1987. **Staff:** 8500. **Description:** Satyam Computer Services provides a wide range of information technology services, including software development, systems implementation and maintenance, application integration, and engineering design support. Services provided include: Software Development Services, Engineering Services, Systems Integration, ERP Solutions, Customer Relationship Management, Supply Chain Management, Product Development, Electronic Commerce, IT Outsourcing and Consulting.

∎ 2141
SAUERBRUN TECHNOLOGY GROUP LTD.

7979 E Princess Dr., Ste. 5
Scottsdale, AZ 85255-5878
PH: (602)502-4950
FX: (602)502-4292
E-mail: info@sauerbrun.com
URL: http://www.sauerbrun.com

Description: consultants are specialists in working within an organization to plan and implement various management and technology improvements. Specializes in strategic planning, business planning, financial planning, project management, organizing and structuring financial statements, and team building; Internet marketing programs, and site design, development and maintenance; and office automation consulting.

▌2142
SBA.NET.WEB

2711 Bellmore Ave.
Bellmore, NY 11710-4319
PH: (516)221-3306
FX: (516)221-7129
E-mail: info@sbaconsulting.com
URL: http://www.sbanetweb.com
Contact: Wayne Spivak, President

Revenue: US$800,000. **Staff:** 10. **Description:** Experienced in MIS, management, marketing and manufacturing. Works to empower clients with management and executive information systems to better manage their businesses. Specializes in implementation (planning and project management) of integrated accounting systems on PC-based computers. Industries served: professional, retail, distribution, and manufacturing. Provides consultation on the business and practical aspects of the Internet, from E-mail to E-commerce, from a dial-up account to direct connectivity, our consultants can plan and implement the project. **Seminars:** Presented Planning and Project Management, Columbia University; and LI Law Seminars: Time Billing Receivable in a Law Firm; Networking the Law Firm; and Office Automation in a Law Firm; Practicing Law Institute and the Law Journal Extra on Internet issues. Contact firm for list of additional seminars. **Special Seminars:** Specializes in LAN (local area network) based accounting systems, the Macola Accounting System and Navision Financials. Fluent in Financial, Distribution, and Manufacturing software system and have installed all its phases. Association of Internet Professionals, Internet Society, (where Prof. Spivak is President of the NY Chapter) and the HTML Writers Guild. **Geographic Area Served:** United States, Canada, England, France.

▌2143
SBT ACCOUNTING SYSTEMS

1401 Los Gamos Dr.
San Rafael, CA 94903
PH: (415)444-9900
TF: 800-944-1000
FX: (415)444-9901
E-mail: sbt@sbt.com
URL: http://www.sbt.com/
Contact: William Mills, Chairman & CEO

Description: Develops modifiable database accounting software. Products are available through authorized resellers and Internet business consultants. Resellers provide installation, training, and customization services. **Seminars:** Exectuive Series, Pro Series 5.0; Pro Series 3.0i, VisionPoint, the Small Business Accountant, Internet Accounting WebSeries.

▌2144
SCALAR CONSULTING GROUP

2540 Shaughnessy St., Ste. 200
Port Coquitlam, BC, Canada V3C3W4
PH: (604)552-3685
FX: (604)552-3685
E-mail: solutions@scalar.com
URL: http://www.scalar.com/

Description: Company specializes in customized Internet applications. Offers systems support that includes PC LAN administration, LAN hardware and software support, and systems hardware installations. Also provides WWW development services, technical documentation, document conversions to HTML format, and training seminars.

▌2145
SCB COMPUTER TECHNOLOGY, INC.

3800 Forest Hill-Irene Rd., Ste. 100
Memphis, TN 38125
PH: (901)754-6577
TF: 800-221-1640
FX: (901)754-1647
URL: http://www.scb.com
Contact: Mr. Jack Blair, Chairman

Founded: 1976. **Staff:** 1000. **Description:** Since 1976, SCB has been a provider of management and information systems consulting. Initially, the firm concentrated on providing strategic planning for data processing or information technology organizations. Evolving to meet both client demands and industry trends, SCB has broadened its activities to more than just consulting services. Now, SCB offers a full array of IT management consulting and development services. SCB Computer Technology provides a variety of information technology (IT) services to government agencies and FORTUNE 500 companies throughout the US. SCB's offerings include consulting (systems design and implementation), outsourcing (systems development and maintenance), and professional IT staffing.

▌2146
SCIENT CORPORATION

79 5th Ave., 4th Fl.
New York, NY 10003
PH: (212)500-4900
FX: (212)500-5032
URL: http://www.scient.com
Contact: Eric Greenberg, Chairman Emeritus

Revenue: US$300,000,000. **Staff:** 964. **Description:** Provides Internet and technology consulting services, from designing Web sites to developing e-commerce applications. It also helps clients integrate emerging technology into existing business systems to help increase efficiency and cut costs. In addition, Scient offers system maintenance, security management, and technology upgrade assistance.

∎ 2147
SDG CORP.

65 Water St.
Norwalk, CT 06854
PH: (203)866-8886
FX: (203)866-8887
URL: http://www.sdgc.com
Contact: Mr. Ajay Gupta, Chief Executive Officer

Staff: 39. **Description:** SDG offers information technology consulting and services from its US headquarters and international offices in Egypt, India, and the UK. SDG is led and managed by principals with a combined corporate and consulting experience of over 50 years in various IT disciplines. Their area of expertise include creating digital strategy to integrating legacy and enterprise applications across today's Internet and distributed processing technologies, SDG provides custom-tailored solutions to help businesses make the change to a dynamic, digital enterprise. SDG leverages pre-built, reusable software components supporting the industry's widest array of tested solutions for e.Business and distributed applications.

∎ 2148
SEA BASS SOFTWARE LTD.

Abbots Tower
Goring Heath
Oxon RG87RZ, United Kingdom
PH: 44 149 1682585
FX: 44 149 1682586
E-mail: sarah.bell@seabass.co.uk
URL: http://www.seabass.co.uk
Contact: Ms. Sarah Bell, Business Manager

Founded: 1998. **Description:** Sea Bass is a UK based company which provides internet products and services from E-Commerce to application hosting. Sea Bass provide a full range of professional services assisting in the entire development process from training to development and even technical support.

∎ 2149
SECURE SOLUTION INC.

482 W 300 N Mail Stop 61
Mount Pleasant, UT 84647-1142
PH: (435)426-2175
E-mail: rasmusoftwares@42.com
URL: http://www.4secure.order.com

Description: Provides a variety of World Wide Web and Internet services. These services include Web page design and maintenance, Web storage, domain registration services, email, and interactive Web pages. Offers traffic reports showing the number of visitors who access the Web page, FTP and mailing list services, and searching capabilities.

∎ 2150
SECURENET LTD.

Level 18/60 Albert Road
South Melbourne, VIC 3205, Australia
PH: 61 3 8696 9400
FX: 61 3 8696 9500
E-mail: securenet@securenet.com.au
URL: http://www.securenet.com.au
Contact: Geoffrey Ross, Managing Director & CEO

Founded: 1996. **History:** SecureNet's operations began in 1982, as Randata, and grew through a series of acquisitions and mergers. **Description:** SecureNet Ltd. is a global provider of secure solutions for Internet applications, remote banking, virtual private networks (VPNs) and e-commerce activities. A broad-based security business, SecureNet's expertise ranges from smart card technology, public key infrastructure (PKI) and firewalls to secure payments and security consultancy. **Awards:** SecureNet's export achievement to 27 countries was awarded the 1999 Australian Export Award in the category of ''Emerging Exporter''.

∎ 2151
SEDLAK MANAGEMENT CONSULTANTS INC.

4020 Kinross Lakes
Richfield, OH 44286
PH: (330)908-2100
FX: (330)587-2160
E-mail: info@jasedlak.com
URL: http://www.jasedlak.com
Contact: Jeffrey B. Graves, President

Staff: 72. **Description:** Offers strategic logistics planning; information systems integration; facilities layout; productivity improvement; materials handling and systems optimization. Serves mail order, e-commerce manufacturing, and retail industries in the U.S. and worldwide. **Seminars:** Distribution Centers of the 21st Century; Planning for a New or Expanded Distribution Center Facility; The Nuts and Bolts of Fulfillment Facilities; Planning for Growth; How Do You Improve Productivity in a Non-Automated Warehouse?; Techniques for successful selection and implementation of a WMS (Warehouse Management System) with automated material handling equipment; Lessons learned from implementing warehouse management systems; How Automated Materials Handling Systems Impact Operational Efficiency. **Special Seminars:** Provides informations systems integration consulting services. **Geographic Area Served:** Worldwide.

▌ 2152
SEI INFORMATION TECHNOLOGY

212 E Ohio St., Ste. 500
Chicago, IL 60611-3244
PH: 888-734-7343
FX: (312)440-8373
URL: http://www.sei-it.com
Contact: Mr. John Jasper, President and Chief Executive
Officer

Description: SEI help clients invent, develop, support, and deploy the technologies to meet their customers' needs. Their consultants have created successful business applications on virtually every major platform. They help companies conceive and define the technical solutions to meet their challenges. Their consultants work to understand their clients business to plan a customized integrated business solution.

▌ 2153
SENTO CORP.

808 E Utah Valley Dr.
American Fork, UT 84003
PH: (801)492-2000
TF: 800-868-8448
FX: (801)492-2100
URL: http://www.sento.com
Contact: Mr. Gary Filler, Chairman and Chief Financial
Officer

Founded: 1986. **Staff:** 557. **Description:** Sento customizes Customer Relationship Management (CRM) with integrated, multi-channel communications to provide high-tech, high-touch solutions. In addition to traditional telephone support, Sento offers self-help websites, express e-mail, chat/co-browsing and collaboration, and Web call back. This powerful contact medium is changing the way we do business across the globe.

▌ 2154
SERVICE 800

2190 W Wayzata Blvd.
PO Box 800
Minneapolis, MN 55356
PH: (952)475-3747
TF: 800-475-3747
FX: (952)475-3773
E-mail: info@service800.com
URL: http://www.service800.com

Founded: 1989. **Description:** Service 800 was founded to provide resources and tools to help service oriented organizations measure the quality of customer service they deliver. They provide a customer follow-up program in which they contact a client's customers and send "hot sheets" to their managers when a customer describes a situation that requires immediate attention. This real-time customer feedback helps measure the performance levels of individual technicians, service processes, customer perceptions and helps to reduce costs.

▌ 2155
THE SERVICE CENTER INC.

5670 Guhn Rd.
Houston, TX 77040
PH: (713)690-8175
TF: 800-634-6549
FX: (713)895-8683
E-mail: GaleP@calltsc.com
URL: http://www.calltsc.com
Contact: Randy Musgrove, President

Founded: 1983. **Description:** The Service Center Inc. provides storage, distribution, fulfillment, direct mail marketing, sweepstakes, refunds, rebates, information technology catalogs and promotional products for e-commerce businesses.

▌ 2156
SERVICE QUALITY INSTITUTE

9201 E Bloomington Fwy.
Minneapolis, MN 55420
PH: (952)884-3311
TF: (952)884-8901
E-mail: quality@servicequality.com
URL: http://www.customer-service.com
Contact: John Tschohl, Founder and President

Founded: 1972. **Description:** Service Quality Institute helps organizations improve the performance of their workforce through workshops for managers and supervisors. They also encourage instructionally based learning using video, user-friendly facilitator guides and participant material.

▌ 2157
PATRICIA SEYBOLD GROUP INC.

85 Devonshire St., 5th Fl.
Boston, MA 02109-3504
PH: (617)742-5200
TF: 800-826-2424
FX: (617)742-1028
E-mail: feedback@psgroup.com
URL: http://www.psgroup.com
Contact: Ms. Patricia Seybold, Chief Executive Officer

Founded: 1978. **Description:** World-wide consultants in conceptual designs for strategic e-business and technology, product and marketing positioning and e-business processes. Offers customized consulting services, an online strategic research service, executive workshops, and in-depth research reports.

∎ 2158
SHARED MEMORY

5 Gannon Ter.
Framingham, MA 01702
PH: (508)875-6525
FX: (508)875-3735
E-mail: sales@sharedmemory.com
URL: http://www.sharedmemory.com

Founded: 1997. **Description:** Shared Memory can help clients select and implement the appropriate software system and provide them with business process consulting improve customer retention with a focus on customer relationship management.

∎ 2159
SHASTA MARKETING CONSULTANTS

PO Box 649
Mount Shasta, CA 96067
PH: (530)926-1619
TF: 800-798-7318
FX: (530)926-6830
E-mail: sales@shastamarketing.com
URL: http://www.shastamarketing.com

Founded: 1995. **Description:** Shasta Marketing Consultants is a team of professionals specializing in search engine marketing, graphic design, web design and development, Flash, full E-commerce solutions, database development and special programming needs, as well as dynamic business hosting plans. They work with businesses and corporations throughout the United States to design and develop, host, maintain, and market their business website. They strive to develop a successful Internet strategy for businesses from large corporations to small home-based businesses. Shasta Marketing offer clients security on the web and setup business E-commerce by putting together a shopping cart system, online catalog, secure order form, or a major storefront.

∎ 2160
SHEARWATER ALLIANCE INC

PO Box 157
Dennis, MA 02638
PH: (508)385-3673
FX: (508)385-2246
E-mail: info@shearwateralliances.com
URL: http://shearwateralliances.com/HomePage.htm
Contact: Mr. Thomas Moran, Co-Founder

Description: Shearwater Alliances provide strategies and business/corporate development initiatives to start-ups, early stage, and mature technology companies. They work with firms in a variety of stages of growth to help them identify, develop and leverage technology. Shearwater Alliances designs tailored programs to identify, develop and establish valuable strategic alliances, corporate development initiatives and industry relationships. They design programs which may include: product/technology licensing agreements, joint product development initiatives, worldwide distribution agreements, bundling agreements, run time licensing agreements, corporate and business development alliances, lead generation programs, strategic alliances sourcing, and market opportunity evaluation.

∎ 2161
SHOPCREATOR LTD.

No. 6 Mortec Pk., York Rd.
Leeds LS154TA, United Kingdom
PH: 44 845 1211 400
FX: 44 113 201 8182
URL: http://www.shopcreator.com

Description: Shopcreator has a portfolio of E-Commerce tools that are used by a range of companies, from small SME's to large corporates.Shopcreator's philosophy has been to reduce the complexity of E-Commerce and produce an E-Commerce environment that is easy to use and manage. The software Ste. has a wide range of features together with the facility to integrate additional functionality. It has been used to produce highly sophisticated E-Commerce solutions.

∎ 2162
SIEMENS BUSINESS SERVICES, INC. (SBS)

101 Merritt 7
Norwalk, CT 06851
PH: (203)642-2300
FX: (203)642-2399
E-mail: Corporate.Communications@sbs.siemens.com
URL: http://www.sbs-usa.siemens.com
Contact: Mr. John McKenna, Chief Executive Officer

Founded: 2000. **Staff:** 3600. **Description:** Siemens Business Services (SBS) offers information technology and consulting services. The company (a unit of Siemens' Information and Communications division) provides a variety of information technology services, including consulting, systems management, network design, and security assessment services. SBS also offers managed services such as desktop problem resolution, remote network monitoring, help desk support, and infrastructure management.

∎ 2163
SILICON SPACE

401 B St.
San Diego, CA 92101
PH: (619)696-8820
FX: (619)696-0521
E-mail: dzlotin@siliconspace.com
URL: http://www.siliconspace.com
Contact: Dema Zlotin, Sales

Founded: 1996. **Description:** Silicon Space is a Web system integrator that provides e-Business strategic consulting and implementation services. They have pioneered solutions that enable clients to cut costs, create new revenue opportunities, generate measurable return on investment and foster collaborative relationships with customers, partners, vendors and employees. One of their areas of expertise is eSupport, which can reduce support costs while increasing customer loyalty and retention using Web-based support systems.

∎ 2164
SIMCOM TECHNOLOGIES INC.

325 E Eisenhower, Ste. 300
Ann Arbor, MI 48108
PH: (313)998-5526
FX: (313)332-5299
E-mail: simcom@simcom
URL: http://www.simcom.net/simcom

Description: A software consulting firm specializing in the areas of electronic commerce, automotive, transportation logistics, banking, and manufacturing.

∎ 2165
KATHLEEN SINDELL, PH.D. CONSULTANTS

200 N Columbus St.
Alexandria, VA 22314
PH: (703)299-1700
FX: (703)299-6026
E-mail: ksindell@kathleensindell.com
URL: http://www.kathleensindell.com
Contact: Dr. Kathleen Sindell

Description: Provides consulting and authoritative publications about management, marketing, finance, and real estate in the e-commerce environment. Specializes in assisting large and small businesses in building customer loyalty, transforming and positioning products and services for the emerging electronic economy. **Publications:** Loyalty Marketing for the Internet Age.

∎ 2166
SIRIUS IMAGES INC.

6006 N Mesa, Ste. 902
El Paso, TX 79912
PH: (915)587-7074
TF: (866)587-7074
FX: (915)832-0135
E-mail: sirius@sirius-images.com
URL: http://www.sirius-images.com

Founded: 1994. **Description:** Provides consulting for Intranet/Extranet solutions, system integration, and networking solutions for ecommerce. Helps analyze networking needs, maintain computer base, and implement a wide business strategy for online enterprises.

∎ 2167
SITCUR

7916 Melrose Ave., Ste. 2
Los Angeles, CA 90046
PH: (323)653-0311
FX: (323)653-8024
E-mail: roger@sitcur.com
URL: http://www.sitcur.com
Contact: Roger Curtis, President & CEO

Staff: 5. **Description:** Specializes in evaluating and providing e-business solutions to businesses, then implements, trains and supports these solutions. Acts as a liaison with management to assess specific Electronic Data Interchange (EDI), XML, Electronic Commerce and Business Process Reengineering needs. Also writes, implements and supports software applications for a variety of PC, LAN, WAN, UNIX, AX/400, and midrange systems. Designs, implementations and supports Web Site development on the Internet. **Special Seminars:** Specializes in EDI and EDI implementation, XML, UNIX, NT, Windows, Novell, and AS/400 systems; authorized integrator for softshare e-commerce software solutions, specialists in communications Gateway and Data Transmission. Offers practical solutions. **Geographic Area Served:** United States.

∎ 2168
SITEFUSION

6310 Windsor Ave.
Alexandria, VA 22315
PH: (703)921-9458
TF: 888-748-3522
FX: (703)719-9564
E-mail: info@sitefusion.com
URL: http://www.sitefusion.com

Description: SiteFusion is a small regional consulting group headquartered in Alexandria Virginia. SiteFusion design customized solutions for each of their clients. They provide full service Internet and web consulting specializing in website design, website content creation, website development, ecommerce website solutions, and PHP web applications design. Their consulting team has experience with many popular internet development languages and design tools that include: C, Perl 5, Java, Java Servlets, Web/Database integration, SQL/ODBC, DHTML/JavaScript, CGI, MySQL, Cold Fusion, PHP, Adobe Premier, Photoshop, Macromedia Flash, Macromedia Fireworks, 3D modeling and more.

∎ 2169
SITEL CORP.

111 S Calvert St., Ste. 1900
Baltimore, MD 21202
PH: (410)246-1505
URL: http://www.sitel.com

Description: SITEL offers contact center outsourcing solutions for their clients with more than 84 customer contact centers in 20 countries dedicated to strengthening their clients customer relationships whether the contact be by phone, email, web, fax or traditional mail while supporting the highest CRM standards.

∎ 2170
SKY SERVICES LTD.

41 Village Rd.
London N31TJ, United Kingdom
PH: 44 208 346 0831
E-mail: info@skyservices.co.uk
URL: http://www.skyservices.co.uk

Founded: 1990. **Description:** E-commerce strategy consultants. Their primary focus is e-business for small and medium enterprises (SMEs). We are a team of IT consultants, providing a number of e-commerce and general project services.

∎ 2171
SMALL BUSINESS CONSULTANTS

5602 Dumfries Dr.
Houston, TX 77096-3920
PH: (713)721-2109
FX: (713)723-1892
E-mail: info@computer-productivity.com
URL: http://www.small-business-consultants.net

Description: Small Business Consultants.net is a complete resource for personal, professional and experienced small business and technology consulting services. They apply big business knowledge and experience to a small business owner's unique needs. From providing short-term small business advice to becoming a long-term consulting partner, a consultant can increase productivity and allow clients to concentrate on what they do best.

∎ 2172
SMCONSULTING, INC.

1306 Concourse Dr., Ste. 200
Baltimore, MD 21090
TF: 888-476-2937
URL: http://www.smcteam.com
Contact: Ms. Sheila Courtney Heinze, Chief Executive Officer

Staff: 13. **Description:** SMConsulting was founded in Baltimore in 1996 and has since expanded into Florida, New York, and Virginia. The information technology consulting and services company provides network staffing, project management, systems implementation, security, and programming services for a variety of corporate customers. The company also provides Internet consulting and design

services, including Web site design, legacy system integration, and Web-based distributed application development, through its Silverlake division.

∎ 2173
BARBARA J. SMITH CONSULTING

10752 Amherst Way
Inver Grove Heights, MN 55077
PH: (651)365-0822
FX: (651)365-0823
E-mail: barb@bjsconsulting.com
URL: http://www.visi.com/bjscons/index.html
Contact: Barbara Smith

Description: Barbara J. Smith is an independent business and technology consultant who offers a variety of services that increase productivity while increasing sales. Background includes extensive experience in the areas of finance, accounting, store operations, and systems.

∎ 2174
SNEAKERLABS INC.

5001 Baum Blvd., Ste.650
Pittsburgh, PA 15213
PH: (412)687-7100
TF: 888-397-5227
FX: (412)687-4615
E-mail: info@sneakerlabs.com
URL: http://www.sneakerlabs.com

Description: SneakerLabs is a provider of live-interaction software solutions for the Web, enabling real-time person-to-person communication over the Internet.

∎ 2175
SODAN

20 Mead Rd.
Uxbridge UB81AU, United Kingdom
PH: 44 189 523 3194
FX: 44 189 523 3194
E-mail: info@sodan.co.uk
URL: http://www.sodan.co.uk/main.html

Description: SODAN is an independent consultancy that specializes in providing independent advice and assistance in the areas of workflow management, business processes and ecommerce. They act as consultants to both suppliers and users of workflow and e-commerce software and systems.

∎ 2176
SOFTPROS INC.

1 Dunwoody Park, Ste. 230
Atlanta, GA 30338
PH: (678)443-0703

FX: (678)443-0730
URL: http://www.softprosinc.com

Description: Softpros Inc. is a consultancy company with an application development background combined with web technology expertise. They are equipped to offer all encompassing Internet related solutions and services. These services include: portal development, management and hosting, web site design, web application development, web site hosting, web enabling legacy applications, and Internet development tools.

∎ 2177
SOFTWARE FOLKS INC.

120 Wood Ave. S, Ste. 300
Iselin, NJ 08830
PH: (732)603-7778
FX: 800-419-1908
E-mail: info@softwarefolks.com
URL: http://www.softwarefolks.com

Description: Offers e-commerce consulting and custom software development. Services include on-site consulting and project based custom software development in the e-commerce, e-business and multimedia technology areas. **Major Partners:** IBM; Lotus; Ramco Systems; eGrabber

∎ 2178
SOFTWARE LOGISTICS CORP.

48301 Lakeview Blvd.
Fremont, CA 94538
PH: (510)656-8000
TF: 800-999-9989
FX: (510)438-9486
E-mail: info@ilogistix.com
URL: http://www.ilogistix.com
Contact: Bill Downey, CFO & VP, Administration and HR

Founded: 1974. **Staff:** 2000. **Description:** Software Logistics Corporation which does business as iLogistix, provides supply chain consulting, management, and outsourcing services to the computing, medical, and electronics industries. iLogistix is an integrated value chain design, implementation and management company providing a complete line of traditional and eCommerce turnkey services through its global network of world class operation centers. From development to distribution, Software Logistics handles every step of the hardware and software implementation process, including product assembly, packaging, testing, and support. Other services include CD duplication, call center support, and inventory control.

∎ 2179
SOFTWARE PERFORMANCE SYSTEMS, INC. (SPS)

2011 Crystal Dr., Ste. 710
Arlington, VA 22202
PH: (703)797-7800
FX: (703)746-0160
E-mail: sps@gosps.com
URL: http://www.gosps.com
Contact: Mr. Greg Dorsett, President and Chief Executive Officer

Founded: 1995. **Description:** Software Performance Systems provides a variety of information technology consulting services for both government and corporate clients. Since 1995, Software Performance Systems has provided E-Business services to government and commercial clients both in the U.S. and internationally. Their core business is implementing enterprise-wide software systems

∎ 2180
SOFTWARE STUDIOS

15-A 1010 Polytek Ct.
Gloucester, ON, Canada K1J9H9
PH: (613)742-5453
FX: (613)748-5772
E-mail: info@ottowaonline.com
URL: http://www.softwarestudios.com

Description: Provides internet business strategizing and consulting, assisting in the design, development and deployment of superior electronic solutions by addressing a company's online needs. **Major Partners:** H.R. Software Tools; Prevue Resource Group Inc.; Xtreme Worlds; Chips & Bits

∎ 2181
SOFTWORLD CORP.

PO Box 8249
1 Apple Hill Dr., Ste. 301
Natick, MA 01760
PH: 888-827-6699
FX: (508)647-0345
E-mail: webmaster@softworld.com
URL: http://www.softworld.com

Description: Company offers computer consulting services in the areas of programming, the Internet, and local area networks.

∎ 2182
SOFTWRIGHT

The Langley Business Centre
11-49 Station Road, Langley
Berkshire SL38YT, United Kingdom

PH: 44 17 5381 1833
FX: 44 17 5381 1834
E-mail: request@softwright.co.uk
URL: http://www.softwright.co.uk

Description: Softwright consultants provide electronic business solutions specializing in content management, community and electronic commerce solutions. Offers full end-to-end service including project management, solution architecture, web design, solution development, deployment and ongoing support. **Major Partners:** Esual; BEA; IBM; Easynet; Borland; Oracle; Tridion; Open Market; Media Surface

▌2183
SOFTWRITE COMPUTER SYSTEMS INC.

Welsh Commons
1364 Welsh Rd.
North Wales, PA 19454
PH: (215)540-8048
TF: 800-538-9081
FX: (215)542-8898
E-mail: mailbox@softwrite.com
URL: http://www.softwrite.com
Contact: Mark S. Talaba, CEO

Revenue: US$3,000,000. **Staff:** 24. **Description:** An information technology consulting firm providing custom e-business solutions. Our mission is to assist clients in gaining a competitive edge, reducing operating costs, improving customer satisfaction and/or improving overall operations through the use of strategic technologies. **Seminars:** Business to Business E-Commerce, seminars to corporate management and information technology audiences. **Special Seminars:** Software and systems consulting specializing in IBM A/S 400 and Microsoft NT environments, including LAN-to-AS/400 communications. Also, enterprise client/server solutions for the manufacturing, warehouse/distribution, financial/insurance and service industries. **Geographic Area Served:** Northeast.

▌2184
SOJOURN CONSULTING INC.

1900 Spring Rd., Ste. 503
Oak Brook, IL 60523
PH: (630)574-2000
TF: 800-832-4331
FX: (630)574-2134
E-mail: info@sojournconsulting.com
URL: http://www.sojurnconsulting.com

Description: Provides information systems, software/hardware, and networking professionals on a contract basis. Services include staff augmentation, project execution, and outsourcing of distributed support systems. Also provides Internet Web site services which include server set-up and maintenance, technical assistance, disk storage, e-mail, and e-mail and telephone technical support. **Geographic Area Served:** Great Lakes and Ohio valley, including Illinois, Wisconsin, Indiana, Michigan, Ohio, Kentucky, Missouri.

▌2185
SOLONIS INC.

One Meridian Crossings, Ste. 810
Minneapolis, MN 55423
PH: (612)798-2100
TF: 877-798-2100
FX: (612)798-2101
E-mail: info@solonis.com
URL: http://www.solonis.com

Founded: 1991. **Description:** Solonis can help clients build customer loyalty and improve profitability through their customer relationship management service. They provide customized CRM solutions from the initial strategy, design, configuration and implementation to training and ongoing support. **Major Partners:** Microsoft; Onyx; Lexign; SeeBeyond; IBM; MindArrow; Paciolan.

▌2186
SOLUTION 6 HOLDINGS LTD.

Level 21, Town Hall House, 456 Kent St.
Sydney, NSW 2000, Australia
PH: 61292780666
FX: 61292780555
E-mail: info@solution6.com
URL: http://www.solution6.com
Contact: Mr. Peter Ritchie, Chairman

Staff: 1600. **Description:** The Solution 6 Group is a provider of software and services for professional services organizations globally, and a supplier of Information Technology (IT) services for business and government in the Asia Pacific region. Solution 6 Holdings provides information technology consulting and services, primarily to the legal and accounting industries. Their IT Services offering includes e-solutions (portals and software), infrastructure (enterprise systems, storage and security), information management solutions (content, document and records management), and managed services (onsite outsourcing, hosting and disaster recovery solutions).

▌2187
THE SOLUTION ASSOCIATES (TSA)

PO Box 292803
Tampa, FL 33687
PH: (813)984-1836
FX: (813)984-1613
E-mail: sales@the-solution.com
URL: http://www3.the-solution.com

Description: Consulting company that provides E-commerce and Intranet solutions for business-to-business transactions, including integration of accounting and other database applications.

▌2188
SOLUTION SPECIALISTS

9809 Cherry Valley SE, Ste. H
Caledonia, MI 49316
PH: (616)891-9114
FX: (616)891-9462
E-mail: isogroup@iserv.net
URL: http://www.9000.com

Staff: 35. **Description:** E-commerce, computer based training, video sales and production consultants for ISO 9000, QS-9000 (including the Tooling and Equipment Supplement of QS-9000), or ISO 14000. **Geographic Area Served:** Worldwide.

▌2189
SOLUTIONS CONSULTING GROUP

35-11 85 St., Ste. 3D
Jackson Heights, NY 11372-5561
PH: (718)457-3246
FX: (718)457-7433
E-mail: info@solcon.com
URL: http://www.solcon.com
Contact: Brian Caffrey, Founder, President

Description: A management consulting practice that specializes in electronic commerce and in the re-engineering and continuous improvement of supply chain management processes.

▌2190
SOLUTIONS CONSULTING LLC

370 Southpointe Blvd.
Canonsburg, PA 15317
PH: (724)514-5000
FX: (724)514-5050
URL: http://www.solutionsconsulting.com

Description: Provides IT consulting and systems implementation services involving enterprise resource planning, supply chain management, customer relationship management and e-commerce applications. **Major Partners:** IBM; Microsoft; Novell; Oracle; SAP Services; PeopleSoft; Siebel; JD Edwards; Optum; SCT; BAAN; IMI; Onyx Software; MindMatters Technologies Inc.; Crossworlds; Cisco Systems; EMC2; Dell; Hewlett Packard; f5; Sun Microsystems

▌2191
SOLUTIONS, STAFFING, AND EDUCATION INC. (SSE)

77 West Port Plaza, Ste. 500
St. Louis, MO 63146
PH: (314)439-4700
FX: (314)439-4799
E-mail: info@sseinc.com
URL: http://www.sseinc.com
Contact: Ms. Susan Elliot, Chairman and CEO

Description: Solutions, Staffing, and Education, Inc. (SSE) are E-commerce consultants in the St. Louis area. SSE is an Information Technology Solutions Provider that brings together business, technology and people to deliver complete solutions. SSE provides end-to-end application development, network design, eLearning, custom training and technical staffing services.

▌2192
SONATA SOFTWARE LTD.

1/4 APS Trust Bldg.
Bull Temple Rd.
N.R. Colony
Bangalore 560019, India
PH: 91806610330
TF: (866)276-6282
FX: 91806610972
E-mail: suku@sonata-software.com
URL: http://www.sonata-software.com
Contact: Shyam Ghia

Founded: 1986. **Description:** Sonata Software offers a host of technology consulting services through its offices in India, the UK, and the US. Since it's inception in 1986, Sonata Software Ltd. has been harnessing the power of Information Technology to help its customers gain a competitive edge in the business they operate in. Sonata focuses on long-term relationship with the customers by providing high quality, contemporary and cost effective Software Development and IT Consulting services. Sonata Software Limited is a professionally managed company.

▌2193
SONY NETSERVICES

Schipholweg 275
1171 PK Badhoevedorp
Amsterdam, Netherlands
PH: 31 20 658 5950
E-mail: amsterdam@sonynetservices.com
URL: http://www.sonynetservices.com/home.go

Founded: 1946. **Staff:** 100. **Description:** Sony NetServices provide clients with consulting, design and implementation of network business solutions across a multi-access platform via Internet, mobile telephone, PlayStation and Digital TV. Their services include multimedia design, e-commerce solutions, application software development and implementation. Sony NetServices focuses on empowering businesses by providing optimized, digital communications between our client and his customers. Their capabilities range from setting the strategic direction to building businesses. They have diversified practice areas in B2B, business to business to businesses, and B2C, business to business to consumer initiatives.

❚ 2194

SOPHRON PARTNERS

25 The Coda Centre
189 Munster Rd.
London SW66AW, United Kingdom
PH: 44 20 7385 8825
FX: 44 20 7385 7001
E-mail: info@sophron.co.uk
URL: http://www.sophronpartners.com

Description: Sophron Partners work with organizations to provide an understanding of the value of their customers and realize the value of using customer differentiated marketing, sales and service in a multi-channel environment. They help clients use customer relationship management by utilizing several stages including opportunity assessment; customer strategy development; designing, building and implementing business and IT technology including contact management and call centers; and operational improvement.

❚ 2195

SOPRA GROUP

9 bis, rue de Presbourg
75016 Paris Cedex, France
PH: 331 40 67 29 29
FX: 331 40 67 29 29
URL: http://www.sopra.com
Contact: Pierre Pasquier, Chairman, President & CEO

Description: The Sopra Group is an information technology support company that specializes in online and computer systems integration, consulting, and application development and hosting, among other services. Sopra, founded in 1968, caters to the telecommunications, banking and finance, manufacturing, government, and human resources markets. The company continues to expand its presence throughout Europe, focusing primarily on front-office, e-business, and customer resource management application implementation and administration.

❚ 2196

SOUND CONCEPTS

15 E 400 S
Orem, UT 84058
TF: 800-544-7044
FX: (801)437-0612
E-mail: Colby@soundconcepts.com
URL: http://www.soundconcepts.com

Description: Sound Concepts has been servicing the Network Marketing/Direct Selling industry for over 20 years. They provide customer care solutions for traditional, wired, and Internet business needs. The latest technologies are used for inbound and outbound services.

❚ 2197

SOUTH WEST CONSULTANTS

45 Cotehele Dr.
Paignton TQ33GN, United Kingdom
PH: 44 1803 556025
FX: 44 1803 556025
E-mail: southwestconsultants@hotmail.com
URL: http:///ww.n-uk.freeserve.co.uk

Description: South West consultants we provide our clients with top line support for, computer hardware, software, networking, exchange servers, e-commerce, and web-design. They produce a complete e-commerce package to enable clients to trade from a professional online shop and keep their customers up to date about your products and services.

❚ 2198

SOUTHERN EXPOSURE

313 S Lakeside Dr.
Lake Worth, FL 33460
PH: (561)547-6177
FX: (561)547-6177
E-mail: hwl@magg.net
URL: http://www.hway.net/expo/
Contact: Howard W. Lee, Owner

Description: Internet advertising, web page design, and consultation for businesses.

❚ 2199

SPARTAN INTERNET CONSULTING CORP.

4990 Northwind Dr., Ste. 240
East Lansing, MI 48823-5091
TF: 800-239-8181
URL: http://www.spartaninternet.com

Founded: 1997. **Description:** Spartan Internet provides a broad range of Internet and e-commerce related services including programming and development, hosting, and a complete set consulting services.

❚ 2200

SPHERION TECHNOLOGY GROUP, BUSINESS SOLUTIONS

823 Commerce Dr.
Oak Brook, IL 60523
PH: (630)574-3030
FX: (630)949-1026
URL: http://www.spherion.com/technology
Contact: Stuart Emanuel, President

Revenue: US$750,000,000. **Staff:** 6000. **Description:** Provides services in the areas of client server design and development, system and network administration, software engineering and programming, project management, software quality assurance and testing, and multimedia, World Wide Web and Internet design. **Geographic Area Served:** United States; Asia; Europe & Australia.

∎ 2201
SPIRIAN TECHNOLOGIES, INC.

NBC Tower, 23rd Fl.
455 N Cityfront Plaza Dr.
Chicago, IL 60611
PH: (312)895-3800
TF: 877-774-7426
FX: (312)895-3900
E-mail: sales@spirian.com
URL: http://www.spirian.com
Contact: Alan G. (Al) Wasserberger, Chairman and Chief Executive Officer

Founded: 1996. **Description:** Founded in 1996, Spirian specializes in process automation solutions that help enterprise IT departments, software companies (ISVs) and IT services providers deploy, manage and support software more effectively at lower costs. Spirian combines software with highly specialized expertise and services to create customized, reliable and scalable solutions that are delivered with guaranteed results and predictable costs The company provides infrastructure management services that enable customers to rapidly deploy and install software throughout their entire networks, regardless of geographic location or technology platforms. Spirian also offers desktop management services that companies including Cisco and Lotus subscribe to on a monthly basis to manage PC reliability, track inventory and assets, and provide maintenance services (freeing up internal IT staff for more important, complex projects).

∎ 2202
SPLASHDOT INC.

Pacific Plz., Ste. 705
238 Alvin Narod Mews
Vancouver, BC, Canada V6B5Z3
PH: (604)899-0597
FX: (604)608-9880
E-mail: info@splashdot.com
URL: http://www.splashdot.com
Contact: Patrick Watson, Chief Executive Officer

Description: SplashDot designs and builds web-based business solutions that enable organizations to leverage the Internet as part of their customer relationship strategy.

∎ 2203
STAN ADAMS AND ASSOCIATES

6-2400 Dundas St. W, Ste. 364
Mississauga, ON, Canada L5K2R8
PH: (905)608-0888
FX: (905)608-0889
E-mail: info@salesprevention.com
URL: http://www.salesprevention.com
Contact: Stan Adams, President

Founded: 1983. **Description:** Stan Adams and Associates is an e-commerce organization that specializes in programs dealing with time management, leadership development, empowerment training and customer service and customer relationship management.

∎ 2204
STANNET WWW DESIGNING & PUBLISHING CO.

Division of Danielle's Marketing Co.
37 Oxford Rd.
East Rockaway, NY 11518
PH: (516)593-1772
FX: (516)593-0824
URL: http://www.tccmweb.com/index.html

Description: Services include designing and publishing, establishing World Wide Web locations, customizing Web sites, creating graphics, providing server name, building interactive forms, and maintaining and upgrading sites.

∎ 2205
STAR INFORMATION TECHNOLOGY

266 Main St., Ste. 39
Medfield, MA 02052
TF: 800-711-5068
FX: (508)359-6888
E-mail: reach@starit.com
URL: http://www.starit.com

Description: Provides strategic e-business solutions, offering management consulting, systems integration, training, and support. Clients range in industry from high-tech, e-commerce, retail, government agencies, utilities, and manufacturing businesses to educational, healthcare, and financial institutions. **Major Partners:** Cognos; IBM; Microsoft; Microsoft Great Plains; Onyx Software

∎ 2206
STARPOINT SOLUTIONS

115 Broadway
New York, NY 10006
PH: (212)962-1550
FX: (212)962-7175

URL: http://www.starpoint.com
Contact: Mr. Jeffrey Najarian, Chairman

Staff: 922. **Description:** Starpoint Solutions (formerly TIS Worldwide) builds the systems for its clients' information transactions. At its Financial Lab for Interactive Technologies (FLITE) idea incubator, Starpoint works with clients to develop systems that process online transactions using software from vendors like Ariba, Lotus, and Mercury Interactive. Other Starpoint services include e-business planning, software implementation, systems design, information technology recruiting, and interactive marketing.

∎ 2207
STERLING CONSULTING GROUP INC. (SCG)

180 Harbor Dr., Ste. 221
Sausalito, CA 94965
PH: (415)331-5200
E-mail: service@scgtraining.com
URL: http://www.quality-service.com
Contact: Karen Leland, Founder

Description: Sterling Consulting Group Inc. is an online customer service consulting and training organization that uses training workshops, service management for supervisors, problem prevention and problem free production to help businesses with customer care.

∎ 2208
STERLING RESOURCES INC.

6 Forest Ave.
Paramus, NJ 07652
PH: (201)843-6444
FX: (201)843-3934
E-mail: steinbachr@sterlingnet.com
URL: http://www.sterlingnet.com

Founded: 1990. **Description:** Sterling Resources Inc. is an e-commerce company specializing in supporting ERP implementations that impact users in geographically dispersed locations, with web-based and instructor-led training and online coaching

∎ 2209
STEVENS AND STEVENS LLC

6315 N Delaware St.
Indianapolis, IN 46220-1726
PH: (317)726-0788
TF: 800-685-1248
FX: (317)726-1175
E-mail: info@stevens-stevens.com
URL: http://www.associationecommerce.com

Description: Provides consulting, marketing, and communications services using e-commerce strategies to help associations increase membership, revenues, attendance and participation. Focuses on trade associations, societies, fraternal organizations, and association management companies as clients.

∎ 2210
STEWART/LAURENCE ASSOCIATES INC.

Atrium Executive Park
PO Box 1156
Englishtown, NJ 07726
PH: (732)972-8000
FX: (732)972-8003
E-mail: mel@stewartlaurence.com
URL: http://www.stewartlaurence.com
Contact: Shelley Miller, Vice President, Marketing Communications

Staff: 6. **Description:** International Executive search and management consultants for all high tech industries: information technology, data processing, telecommunications, graphic communications, cable television, and work on a national and international level. Also arranges business development and joint marketing agreements between small to medium-sized companies and large multi-national corporations. Heavy emphasis on sales management, marketing and Internet executives worldwide.

∎ 2211
STRAFFORD TECHNOLOGY, INC.

7 Wall St., Ste. 200
Windham, NH 03087
PH: (603)434-2550
TF: 800-983-2443
E-mail: sales@strafford.com
URL: http://www.strafford.com
Contact: Mr. Steven Berry, President and Chief Executive Officer

Founded: 1995. **Staff:** 35. **Description:** Strafford Technology provides a variety of information technology consulting services, including software development and training. They specialize in providing clients with the tools and skill sets necessary to extract information hidden in complex databases, enabling our clients to conduct analysis and effectively manage their organizations.

∎ 2212
STRATAMAR INC.

5661 Seapine Rd.
Hilliard, OH 43026
PH: (614)539-2945
FX: (614)539-2945
E-mail: neilbrown@stratamar.com
URL: http://www.stratamar.com

Contact: Neil Brown, President

Revenue: US$1,000,000. **Staff:** 2. **Description:** A full-spectrum strategic marketing consulting company. Areas of concentration include product development, product management, strategic planning, development and implementation of tactical marketing plans, and internet marketing. The primary focus is upon maximizing the benefit/cost ratio of promotions through the use of direct marketing, low cost media, and the like. **Special Seminars:** Includes web page designing and hosting services via an affiliate, Designing Web. **Geographic Area Served:** United States and Canada.

▌2213
STRATEGIC INITIATIVES

12209 Jonathan's Glen Way
Herndon, VA 20170-2352
PH: (703)450-5255
FX: (703)404-2287
E-mail: stratinit@aol.com
URL: http://www.strategicinitiatives.com

Description: Strategic planning, marketing, and organizational transformation. Realignment of products, services, and experiences to e-business. New market-driven programs and high-tech, mixed-use facilities to support them.

▌2214
STRATEGIC INTERNET BUSINESS SOLUTIONS
SV MEDIA

940 South Ave. W, Ste. D
Westfield, NJ 07090
PH: (908)789-4200
FX: (908)789-4266
URL: http://www.svmedia.com

Description: Strategic Internet Business Solutions (SV Media) is a provider of strategic Internet business solutions that allow companies to leverage the Web to streamline business communication, facilitate collaboration with internal team members and external partners, and conduct commerce on-line. Consultants design and develop the applications, database systems, and network architecture to support the online business extension. SVMedia's services also include: application development, interactive design, and web site management.

▌2215
STRATEGIC VISIONS INC.

337 Turnberry Rd.
Birmingham, AL 35244
PH: (205)995-8495
FX: (205)995-8495
E-mail: jomalley@mindspring.com
URL: http://www.strategicvisionsinc.com
Contact: John O'Malley, President

Description: Strategic Visions Inc. is a national strategic consulting company specializing in growing businesses by providing specialized services and programs for professionals, executives and organizations. In the area of customer service, they offer an interactive customer service program called "Golden Baton" that focuses on the team approach to delivering customer service, comprehensive customer service planning, on-site supportive customer service training and auditing of a company's current customer service program.

▌2216
STRATEGIM CORP.

110 Main St., 4th Fl.
Burlington, VT 05401
PH: (802)846-2200
FX: (802)846-2205
E-mail: marketinginfo@strategim.com
URL: http://www.strategim.com
Contact: Farley Blackman, CEO & Chairman/Founder

Description: Provides strategic information management consulting, IT staffing and remote software development, offering clients integrated solutions for a full range of information management needs. StrategIM provides expert guidance and support for companies that are growing their IT departments and expanding their use of Web-based technology.

▌2217
STRATEGOS

2460 Sand Hill Rd., Ste. 202
Menlo Park, CA 94025
PH: (650)233-1100
FX: (650)233-1112
E-mail: info@strategos.com
URL: http://www.strategos.com
Contact: Gary Hamel, Chairman

Description: Service offerings from complete strategy innovation solutions through the total approach, an accelerated approach or along new business models, to more focused customized offerings of architecture development, e-commerce, interactive technology, and training. Offerings address innovation, strategy, and growth at all levels of an organization. **Seminars:** Innovation Academy, Innovation Summit. **Geographic Area Served:** Worldwide.

▌2218
STRATEGY CONSULTING LTD.

21 Dapps Hill
Keynsham BS311ES, United Kingdom
PH: 44 117 907 8034
FX: 44 870 136 9549
E-mail: strategy@nildram.co.uk

URL: http://www.strategy.nildram.co.uk/
internet_strategy.htm
Contact: Mr. John Courtney, Managing Director

Description: Strategy Consulting Limited is a management consultancy located in the UK. They work with clients in manufacturing, services, retailing, wholesaling, importing and exporting as well as the fields of agriculture, sporting goods, insurance, hotels, computer software and hardware, design, and chemicals. Their services include corporate strategy advice, strategic planning and implementation, business funding, business plans, marketing strategies and implementation, public relations, Internet strategies, web design, market research, business development, financial planning, corporate recovery, purchasing strategies, importing strategies, exporting strategies, and total quality management.

▌ 2219
STREAM INTL.

85 Dan Rd.
Canton, MA 02021
PH: (781)575-6800
FX: (781)575-6988
URL: http://www.stream.com
Contact: Stephen D.R. Moore, CEO & Chairman of the Board

Description: Stream International is an e-commerce company that works with clients to develop creative customer care services to meet the needs of online customers. They specialize in transaction director services, lead referral services, customer relations, customer retention, save and winback programs, warranty and RMA services and customer feedback programs.

▌ 2220
STYLECLICK INC.

111 E Wacker Dr., Ste. 500
Chicago, IL 60601
URL: http://www.styleclick.com

Description: Styleclick, Inc. provides e-commerce technologies and services to companies interested in expanding their online sales channels. Styleclick designs, builds, operates and hosts destination stores on the Web, assisting companies to increase sales, grow their customer base and extend their brands via the Internet.

▌ 2221
SUMMERHOUSENET

55 Charterhouse St.
London EC1M6HA, United Kingdom
PH: 44 207 490 4575
FX: 44 207 490 4307
E-mail: graham.smith@summcomm.co.uk

URL: http://www.summerhousenet.com/html/
website_framed.shtml
Contact: Mr. Graham Smith

Description: SummerhouseNet Professionals provide project management responsible for co-coordinating all aspects of a project, controlling schedules and costs and minimizing their clients' own investment of time. They offer design and construction including building online databases and the complex perl, php, asp and java scripting of websites with back-end administration screens and content management as necessary.

▌ 2222
SUPPLYWORKS INC.

24 Crosby Dr.
Bedford, MA 01730
PH: (781)301-7000
FX: (781)301-7010
URL: http://www.supplyworks.com
Contact: Mr. Jeff Herrman, President and Chief Executive Officer

Founded: 1996. **Description:** SupplyWorks, Inc. manufactures Supplier Relationship Management (SRM) solutions, helps discrete manufacturers manage their direct procurement, including their relationships with key suppliers, to lower costs and improve supply chain performance. The company was founded by pioneers in B2B eCommerce, and SupplyWorks has a management team with expertise in enterprise applications, supply chain management, Internet technology, and developing reliable software for the demanding discrete manufacturing environment

▌ 2223
SURREX SOLUTIONS CORP.

400 Continental Blvd., Ste. 600
El Segundo, CA 90245
PH: (310)426-2300
FX: (310)426-2001
E-mail: elsegundo@surrex.com
URL: http://www.surrex.com

Description: Surrex Solutions is an extension of the client's IT organization and include project management consultant services with a focus on customer service.

▌ 2224
SURVEYSITE

49 Sheppard Ave. E
Toronto, ON, Canada M2N2Z8
PH: (416)642-1002
FX: (416)642-1007
E-mail: sales@surveysite.com
URL: http://www.surveysite.com

Description: SurveySite is a provider of online market research. Services include customer relationship management research, Web site evaluation, e-commerce shopping cart analysis and, customer and employee surveys.

■ 2225

SWORD MICROSYSTEMS INC.

1525 Perimeter Pkwy., Ste. 410
Huntsville, AL 35806
PH: (256)704-1400
TF: 888-772-7545
FX: (256)704-1404
E-mail: info@swordmicro.com
URL: http://www.swordmicro.com
Contact: Steve Wakefield, President & CEO

Founded: 1992. **Description:** Sword Microsystems Inc. combines their eBusiness suite, YourCyberSolution.com, with their consulting and systems integration services to help build a connected enterprise to capture more market share, operate competitively, and communicate effectively with customers and partners.

■ 2226

SYNERGY CONSULTING INC.

1500 NE Irving St., Ste. 410
Portland, OR 97232
PH: (503)234-1095
FX: (503)234-1195
E-mail: ccryan@synergyhq.com
URL: http://www.synergyhq.com
Contact: Christine Chin Ryan, Pres.

Description: Offers client/server and database applications design, development, and implementation; systems integration; and network engineering and support. Internet/Intranet. Design & Development. Web-based and E-Business Solutions. Microsoft Ceritfied Partner.

■ 2227

SYNSTAR

Synstar House
1 Bracknell Ln. W
Bracknell RG127QX, United Kingdom
PH: 44 1344 662700
FX: 44 1344 662743
E-mail: enquiries@synstar.com
URL: http://www.synstar.com
Contact: Mr. John Leighfield, Chairman

Description: Synstar offers information technology consulting and services from its offices throughout Europe. From desktop configuration, installation and management to the design and detailed implementation of an IT risk management strategy. From simple software support for a confused end-user to restoring an entire crisis-struck organization at one of our dedicated business recovery centers. From a printer lead to a complex, state-of-the-art, integrated voice and data network. Synstar has expertise in all of these areas

■ 2228

SYNTEL INC.

525 E Big Beaver Rd., Ste. 300
Troy, MI 48083
PH: (248)619-2800
FX: (248)619-2888
E-mail: info@syntelinc.com
URL: http://www.syntelinc.com
Contact: Bharat Desai, Chairman, President & CEO

Founded: 1997. **Staff:** 2691. **Description:** Syntel rescues businesses from technology overload. The company provides applications outsourcing, e-business, and information technology (IT) consulting services for large companies and government agencies. The company's e-Business division specializes in Web applications and data warehousing, and its Team Sourcing division offers short-term IT consulting.

■ 2229

SYSTEMAXX

Madison Centre Bldg.
4950 Yonge St., Ste. 2200
Toronto, ON, Canada M2N6K1
PH: (416)218-5558
FX: (416)221-7426
E-mail: noel@systemaxx.com
URL: http://www.systemaxx.com
Contact: Noel Azucena, Principal

Description: Focuses on Internet/Intranet systems implementation; e-commerce systems development; corporate messaging and workflow; ISO 9000 systems implementation. **Geographic Area Served:** Canada.

■ 2230

SYSTEMS RESOURCES CONSULTING

700 E Butterfield Rd., Ste. 350
Lombard, IL 60148
PH: (630)515-1234
FX: (630)515-1282
URL: http://www.srcinc.com

Description: Firm has expertise in technical systems. JAVA, DD2, Peoplesoft, E-Commerce, E-Procurement, and Systems Integration. **Geographic Area Served:** Chicago Land area.

▌2231
SYSTEMS SERVICE ENTERPRISES INC. (SSE)

77 West Port Plz., Ste. 500
St. Louis, MO 63146
PH: (314)439-4700
FX: (314)439-4799
E-mail: info@sseinc.com
URL: http://www.sseinc.com
Contact: Susan Elliott, Chairman/Founder & CEO

Founded: 1996. **Description:** Provides all levels of information technology consulting services from e-Commerce, network design and application development to custom courseware, classroom training and e-Learning solutions. **Awards:** Five-time winner of St. Louis Regional Fast 50 Technology Award (1996-2000); Second largest software training company (2001); Fifteenth largest computer consultants (2000); Honorable mention in the People Development category of the Best Places to Work Laclede Awards (2000)

▌2232
A AND T SYSTEMS, INC. (ATS)

12520 Prosperity Dr., Ste. 300
Silver Spring, MD 20904
PH: (301)384-1425
FX: (301)384-1405
E-mail: robert.martins@ats.com
URL: http://www.ats.com

Founded: 1984. **Description:** AandT Systems serves the technology needs of government and business clients. Founded in 1984, the company provides its customers with a variety of technology products and services. Its services divisions offer software development and information technology (IT) services; systems and network management; and Internet and e-commerce services.

▌2233
TACPOINT TECHNOLOGIES INC.

1160 Chess Dr., Ste. 2
Foster City, CA 94404
PH: (650)577-3140
FX: (650)577-3141
E-mail: info@tacpoint.com
URL: http://www.tacpoint.com
Contact: Mr. John Tong, CEO

Founded: 1999. **Description:** Tacpoint Technologies is a technology services firm, focused on building scalable distributed enterprise solutions. Tacpoint is an Internet consulting firm specializing in integration and software development. Tacpoint is a team of senior system architects, engineers and consultants.

▌2234
TAJ TECHNOLOGIES INC.

1168 Northland Dr.
Mendota Heights, MN 55120
PH: (651)688-2801
FX: (651)688-8321
E-mail: webmaster@tajtech.com
URL: http://www.tajtech.com

Staff: 150. **Description:** A minority owned software consulting firm. Provides services in software development, project management, systems integration, network implementation and support, and management consulting, Internet/Intranet development and e-commerce. **Geographic Area Served:** United States, Europe, India.

▌2235
TAMCO INC.

POBox 2025
Palestine, TX 75802-2025
PH: 800-657-2235
TF: 800-657-2235
E-mail: tamco@tamcoinc.com
URL: http://www.tamcoinc.com
Contact: Ken Bratz, President

Description: TAMCO is a full-service training organization that provides training products and consulting services in the areas of management, communication, leadership, customer service and team building.

▌2236
THE TAPPING INSTITUTE INC.

160 Pine St., Ste. 10
Newton, MA 02466
PH: (617)969-3148
FX: (617)332-0292
E-mail: mjt@mediaone.net
URL: http://allergybuyersclub.com
Contact: Mercia J. Tapping, President

Staff: 3. **Description:** Firm offers expertise in management and marketing consulting. Internet marketing and Internet business planning and launch. **Geographic Area Served:** United States.

▌2237
TARGET MARKETING

211 E Victoria St., Ste. E
Santa Barbara, CA 93101
PH: (805)965-3184
FX: (805)965-8687
E-mail: jsterne@targeting.com
URL: http://www.targeting.com

Contact: Jim Sterne

Description: Target Marketing offers Internet Marketing Consulting including a customer service improvement workshop. The one-day, Online Customer Service Improvement Workshop includes a review of a client's current online customer service offerings and help in refocusing their efforts for improved customer service on their website.

▌2238
TARGETSURF

315 W 36th St., Ste. 1001
New York, NY 10018
PH: (212)268-9197
E-mail: info@targetsurf.com
URL: http://www.targetsurf.com
Contact: Anthony Cospito, Founder

Description: TargetSurf is a business-to-business e-commerce service that provides sites with feedback from hundreds of users within their target audience on navigation, purchasing and customer service.

▌2239
TARP

1655 N Fort Myer Dr., Ste.200
Arlington, VA 22209
PH: (703)524-1456
FX: (703)524-6374
E-mail: info@trap.com
URL: http://www.e-satisfy.com

Founded: 1972. **Description:** TARP's purpose is to assist web-based clients in increasing customer loyalty and corporate profitability through improved e-commerce customer service and product quality.

▌2240
TATA CONSULTANCY SERVICES

101 Park Ave., 26th Fl.
New York, NY 10178
PH: (212)557-8038
FX: (212)867-8652
E-mail: sidd@usa-tcs.com
URL: http://www.tcs.com
Contact: Arup Gupta, President

Revenue: US$489,000,000. **Staff:** 14500. **Description:** Information processing specialists offer expertise in custom software, product development, case tools, conversions/migrations, quality assurance support, and facilities management and training. Industries served: finance, insurance, manufacturing, banking, distribution, healthcare and hospitality. Also offers expertise in web building, e-commerce, e-business, CRIT, SCOTT, EAI, etc. **Special Seminars:**

Software services can be provided from offshore. **Geographic Area Served:** Worldwide.

▌2241
TAURUS INFOTEK

16/1, Siddharth Chambers, Behind Hotel Aditya
Pune 411004, India
PH: 20 542 3220
E-mail: info@taurusinfotek.com
URL: http://www.taurusinfotek.com

Description: Taurus Infotek is a team of engineers, designers, and e-commerce consultants offering web-related solutions. Taurus Infotek help clients leverage the Internet for their business. The solutions they provide are based on e-business strategies. Taurus Infotek combines web technology with database-Dr.n applications to help clients reach new customers, improve service, and increase efficiency throughout their operation. They combine a data-centric approach with proven skills to field efficient, secure, and successful e- commerce and enterprise applications.

▌2242
TCF CONSULTING GROUP

PO Box 109
Lookout Mountain, TN 37350
PH: (706)820-2698
TF: 800-498-9648
FX: (706)820-7229
E-mail: tcf@tcfgroup.com
URL: http://tcfgroup.com
Contact: T. Cartter Frierson, CMC

Staff: 2. **Description:** Using information technology to strengthen organizations. Helps exploit breakthroughs in information technology to transform the way firms work and even the work itself. Established an affiliate, MCNI, in 1995 to support consultants worldwide on the Internet (www.mcninet.com). Cartter Frierson is a creative, articulate strategist with thirty years experience in bringing senior and systems managers together. **Special Seminars:** Designing and publishing web pages and developing web strategy for business clients. **Geographic Area Served:** United States.

▌2243
TEAMLOG

9, Ave. Matignon
75009 Paris, France
PH: 330145631212
FX: 330145630526
URL: http://www.teamlog.fr
Contact: Robert Morin, President, CEO & CFO

Staff: 1236. **Description:** TEAMLOG offers information technology (IT) consulting services feature database management, network implementation, and Web site design.

Other areas of expertise include software development, systems integration, network security, call center and messaging systems, and applications for digital TV and smart cards.

■ 2244
TECH SUPERPOWERS, INC.

252 Newbury St.
Boston, MA 02116
PH: (617)267-9716
FX: (617)267-8927
E-mail: sales@techsuperpowers.com
URL: http://www.techsuperpowers.com
Contact: Mr. Michael Oh, President

Description: Tech Superpowers provides information technology consulting and maintenance services for Apple computers.

■ 2245
TECHNICA CORP.

45245 Business Ct., Ste. 300
Dulles, VA 20166
PH: (703)662-2000
FX: (703)662-2001
E-mail: info@technicacorp.com
URL: http://www.technicacorp.com
Contact: Mr. Miguel Collado, Founder

Founded: 1991. **Description:** Technica provides information technology (IT) consulting services, specializing in voice and data network design, installation, and performance testing. Other services include on-site support, order management, network security, and large-scale systems integration. Technica caters primarily to the telecommunications, government, and finance markets.

■ 2246
TECHNO MARKETING PTY. LTD.

44 McKean St.
North Fitzroy, VIC 3068, Australia
PH: 61 3 9482 9111
FX: 61 3 9482 9122
E-mail: info@technomarketing.com.au
URL: http://www.technomarketing.com.au

Description: Techno Marketing is a specialist marketing and management consulting company focused on providing services to promote technological advantage. Many of their clients are information technology or telecommunications companies. They provide a range of services designed to deliver business growth through the development and implementation of effective marketing programs.

■ 2247
TECHNOLOGY PARTNERZ LTD. (TP)

1235 Beranard St. W, Ste. 6
Outremont, PQ, Canada H2V1V7
PH: (514)278-2221
FX: (514)278-5060
E-mail: info@technologypartnerz.com
URL: http://www.technologypartnerz.com

Description: Technology Partnerz Ltd. is a Montreal based consulting firm whose primary focus is to facilitate organizations' interaction with technology. Their mission is to help organizations learn the new techniques, skills and processes associated with new e-commerce, e-business and Internet marketing initiatives. They help clients sustain and increase profitability through the balancing of effective strategic thinking, technology and human interaction.

■ 2248
TECOM RESOURCES CORP.

47 Meadow Bluff Rd.
Morris Plains, NJ 07950
PH: (973)326-1820
E-mail: team11@hotmail.com
Contact: Dr. Pravin V. Ajmera, Pres.

Staff: 6. **Description:** Firm specializes in planning, designing, and implementing information systems and networks, including Internet systems and services. High speed internet access, brochure, web, e-commerce systems.

■ 2249
TELEPHONE DOCTOR

30 Hollenberg Ct.
Saint Louis, MO 63044
PH: (314)291-6363
TF: 800-882-9911
FX: (314)291-3710
E-mail: nancy@telephonedoctor.com
URL: http://www.telephonedoctor.com
Contact: Nancy Friedman, President

Founded: 1983. **Description:** Telephone Doctor is a customer service web based training company offering solutions that improve the communication skills of staff members. Through the use of the internet, they supply organizations with the curriculum they need to improve the performance of their customer contact employees.

■ 2250
TELESIS LLC

50 Founders Plaza, Ste. 207
East Hartford, CT 06108
PH: (860)289-4504

515

FX: (860)289-4512
E-mail: contactus@telesisllc
URL: http://www.telesisllc.com

Description: TELESIS, LLC addresses the full range of testing challenges facing enterprise infrastructures for both production software code and e-Commerce network performance behavior. They improve the software testing and quality assurance process through functional testing tools; while at the same time utilize load testing tools to predict system performance under real-life conditions.

▮ 2251
TELESOLUTIONS CONSULTING INC.

136 Main St.
Metuchen, NJ 08840
PH: (732)767-1421
FX: (509)756-1896
E-mail: solutions@tsc-online.com
URL: http://www.tsc-online.com
Contact: Bill Gessert, President

Description: TeleSolutions Consulting is a full service training and consulting organization serving both business-to-business and business-to-consumer call center operations will expertise covering a wide range of customer contact operations including customer service, help desk, technical support, inside sales, sales support and telemarketing. They provide clients help in the areas of consulting, training and coaching solutions, customer service, start-ups, re-engineering and process improvement.

▮ 2252
TELTRUST.COM

6322 S 3000 E
Salt Lake City, UT 84121
PH: (801)535-2200
TF: 800-826-4666
FX: (801)535-2210
E-mail: info@teltrust.com
URL: http://www.teltrust.com

Description: Company provides Internet services.

▮ 2253
TEMPO2 LLC

917 Salt Ct.
Redwood City, CA 94065
PH: (530)690-7566
FX: (530)604-6660
E-mail: info@tempo2.com
URL: http://www.tempo2.com

Description: Offers consulting services and provides access to funding to help build internet business activities and related investment opportunities worldwide.

▮ 2254
TENACITY INC.

550 Oakhaven Dr., Suite 2-B
Roswell, GA 30075
PH: (770)642-0701
TF: 888-550-1900
E-mail: info@tenacity.com
URL: http://www.retentionseminars.com
Contact: John Gamble, Founder and Principle

Founded: 1986. **Description:** Tenacity Inc. is an e-commerce consulting firm specializing in internet based client management processes leading to improved client retention and loyalty.

▮ 2255
TERN CONSULTANCY

69 High St.
Wem SY45DR, United Kingdom
PH: 44 1939 235555
FX: 44 1939 236666
E-mail: office@ternconsultancy.co.uk
URL: http://www.ternconsultancy.co.uk

Founded: 1989. **Description:** Tern Consultancy works with web-based retailers to improve and track customer service. Their services include developing corporate standards and providing mystery shopping.

▮ 2256
TGT ASSOCIATES LTD.

Brooklands House
6 Hatherell Rd.
Chippenham SN153ST, United Kingdom
PH: 44 707 484 8277
FX: 44 870 321 4167
E-mail: k.fletcher@tgt-associates.com
URL: http://www.tgt-associates.com
Contact: Mr. Keith Fletcher, Chief Operating Officer

Founded: 1999. **Description:** TGT provides their clients with experienced consultants, contract resources and interim managers throughout the UK.TGT was formed in January 1999 to provide specialistbusiness and IT consultancy, contract resourcing and interim managementservices. Their mission isto enable their clients to maximize the business value and benefits achieved from their investment in Information Technology and to minimize the risks within their business and IT operations.

▮ 2257
THACKER NETWORK TECHNOLOGIES INC.

5338 51st Ave.
Lacombe, AB, Canada T4L1N5
PH: (403)782-5432

FX: (403)782-1794
E-mail: tnt@thackernet.com
URL: http://www.thackernet.com/public/dthacker/

Description: Firm offers LAN consulting, Internet consulting, BBS and online service consulting, custom software development, and general business and home computer consulting. Also offers ISDN consulting. **Geographic Area Served:** Central Alberta.

∎ 2258
THINKING AUSTRALIA

401 St. Kilda Rd., Ste. 1
Melbourne, VIC 3004, Australia
PH: 61 3 9821 5055
FX: 61 3 9821 5588
E-mail: info@thinking.com.au
URL: http://www.thinking.com.au
Contact: Mr. Mark Bergin, Managing Director

Description: Thinking Australia is a wholly owned Australian communications and internet management company focused on providing businesses with the increased capacity to utilize and realize the benefits of the Information Economy. Thinking provides streamlined online production services delivering everything from banner ads and CD-ROMS to Flash and e-commerce sites. Specializes in guiding organizations through development and implementation of online communication strategies and e-commerce risk management.

∎ 2259
TIS WORLDWIDE

115 Broadway, 20th Fl.
New York, NY 10006
PH: (212)962-1550
TF: 877-847-9983
FX: (212)962-7175
E-mail: tismarketing@tisny.com
URL: http://www.tisworldwide.com
Contact: Jeff Najarian, CEO

Revenue: US$83,000,000. **Staff:** 800. **Description:** An e-business solutions integrator specializing in delivering Internet based applications that help corporations increase sales and improve customer service. Focuses on e-business strategy, solutions development, interactive marketing, and recruiting/placing of technology specialists. **Seminars:** Visit website for event listings. **Geographic Area Served:** United States.

∎ 2260
TJ GROUP

15770 N Dallas Tollway, Ste. 600
Dallas, TX 75248
PH: (972)980-8032

FX: (972)980-4574
E-mail: craig.berry@tjgroup.com
URL: http://www.tjgroup.com
Contact: Craig Berry, U.S. Manager

Staff: 500. **Description:** TJ Group is a provider of extended Customer Relationship Management solutions. Their offerings include solutions for CRM, Digital Content and Communications Management, and Electronic Finance and Commerce with services including consulting, hosting, training, extensive customer support and systems integration. They deliver a variety of solutions from a single solution to consulting and development of an entire electronic business structure covering customer relationship management, digital communication management and customer interaction management.

∎ 2261
TMA RESOURCES INC.

8201 Greensboro Dr., Ste. 900
McLean, VA 22102
PH: (703)847-2800
TF: 888-878-8627
FX: (703)847-2899
E-mail: info@tmaresources.com
URL: http://www.tmaresources.com
Contact: Edi Dor, President and Chief Executive Officer

Founded: 1996. **Staff:** 200. **Description:** TMA Resources, Inc. is a web-based provider of Association Management Software products and services designed to help cost, reliability and performance of businesses and their employees.

∎ 2262
TMS CONSULTING SERVICES INC.

90 Park Ave, Ste. 1700, No.135
New York, NY 10016
PH: (212)984-0759
E-mail: Margaret@TMSConsultinginc.com
URL: http://www.tmsconsultinginc.com
Contact: J.R. Turi

Founded: 1988. **Description:** TMS provides commercial companies and government agencies with a single source for their IT solutions. TMS's E-commerce Solutions prepare businesses to enter the age of digital commerce with a strategic business plan and a deep understanding of the numerous benefits of the Internet. TMS provides information systems organizations with services related to all phases of System Development Life Cycle SDLC including surveys, fact finding, cost/benefit analysis, detailed studies, specifications, implementation, documentation and training. Extensive user interfacing and employment of CASE, prototyping and application generators is also provided.

▌2263
TOTAL MERCHANT SERVICES

5251-C Hwy. 153, PMB 266
Hixson, TN 37341
TF: 888-871-4558
FX: (423)326-1764
E-mail: info@21cr.com
URL: http://www.totalmerchandiser.com
Contact: Mr. Mark Kenyon

Description: Total Merchandiser Services offers solutions to businesses seeking an economical way to enter in function in the digital economy. Total Merchandiser Services provides a complete e-commerce software solution, The Total Merchandiser, which allows clients to easily create a web site right from their own web browser with full e-commerce shopping cart functionality.

▌2264
TOTAL SYSTEMS APPROACH, INC. (TSA)

14817 Sutton St.
Sherman Oaks, CA 91403
PH: (818)789-2824
URL: http://www.tsasoft.com/index1.html

Founded: 1983. **Description:** Total Systems Approach was founded by computer consultants to provide a total business application software solution through the integration of sales, distribution, accounting systems interface, e-commerce solution and custom applications.

▌2265
TOTALITY CORPORATION

44 Montgomery St., Ste. 500
San Francisco, CA 94104
PH: (415)402-3000
FX: (415)402-7978
URL: http://www.totality.com
Contact: Mr. Michael Carrier, Chief Executive Officer

Founded: 1999. **Staff:** 110. **Description:** Totality goes in through the outsource. The application and infrastructure management services company, formerly MimEcom, configures and operates e-commerce sites for FORTUNE 2000 businesses and high-growth Internet companies. Totality's services include integrating hardware and software, securing transactions, managing customer responses, and maintaining Web sites.

▌2266
TOUCH WORLD INC.

26913 Northwestern Hwy., Ste. 490
Southfield, MI 48034
PH: (248)386-0006
FX: (248)386-1399
E-mail: info@touchworld.com
URL: http://www.touchworld.com

Description: Touch World's solutions are scaleable, innovative and employ the latest technology, enabling customers to continually modify and improve their processes and systems. Specializes in e-commerce applications development and EDI consulting and training.

▌2267
TQINET INC. (TQI)

1165 Beargrass Way
Maineville, OH 45039
PH: (513)899-9581
TF: 877-774-4918
FX: (513)899-3769
E-mail: e-commerce@tqinet.com
URL: http://www.tqinet.com
Contact: Mr. Dana Dunmyer, President

Description: TQINET Inc. specializes in the development of B2B Internet solutions and B2E Intranet solutions, provides site maintenance, security, employee training, database development, site optimization and hit generation. **Major Partners:** Amazon.com; Snippets Software; Compaq; X.com PayPal; Cisco Systems; e-Softonline; 3COM; RHI Consulting; DB Pro Database Specialist; iBoost; Mimeo.com; TMC

▌2268
TR COMPUTING SOLUTIONS INC

9396 S Princeton Cir.
Highlands Ranch, CO 80126
PH: (303)346-8791
E-mail: info@trcs.com
URL: http://www.trcs.com

Founded: 1994. **Description:** Offers consulting solutions for the Internet and e-commerce. Provides support for a variety of companies in markets including large format printing, telecommunications, and health care. Offers technical expertise in a variety of areas, including Unix, NT, C, C, Java, XML, Motif, device drivers, embedded systems and Internet related technologies.

▌2269
TRAINING STATION

PO Drawer 170536
Arlington, TX 76003
PH: (817)683-2650
TF: 800-594-8181
E-mail: rferrell@thetrainers.com
URL: http://www.thetrainers.com
Contact: Reginald Ferrell

Description: The Training Station offers a variety of employee training solutions or systems to meet performance management needs for sales training, management training, customer service training, sexual harassment training and custom designed employee training programs. They offer three programs for customer service training, which includes the ACES program for all employees who have customer contact of any kind, especially customer care or customer service representatives; the STOP program designed for service personnel or technicians; and the PRO program for all employees.

▌2270
THE TRAINING STATION INC.

PO Drawer 170536
Arlington, TX 76003
PH: (817)572-4616
TF: 800-594-8181
E-mail: rferrell@thetrainers.com
URL: http://www.thetrainers.com
Contact: Reginald P. Ferrell, Owner and President

Founded: 1982. **Description:** The Training Station Inc. is an e-commerce firm specializing in sales and management consulting, training, and human resource development for the retention of online customers and employees.

▌2271
TRANQUILITY SYSTEMS ASSOCIATES INC.

2 Misty Ln., Ste. 100
Andover, NJ 07821
PH: (973)383-1279
FX: (973)383-6429
E-mail: ed@tranquilityinc.com
URL: http://www.tranquilityinc.com
Contact: Edward Youngberg, President/CEO

Description: Tranquility Systems Associates, inc. is an international information technology consulting firm focusing on IBM mainframe applications that are complex and difficult to maintain. Specializes in project management of large and complex information technology projects. Develops multi-tier client server and internet E-Commerce/E-Government applications using tools such as MIVA, Visual Age and Visual Basic 6. Tranquility is an expert network engineering firm with large Fortune 500 company experience in SNA and TCP/IP networks and the latest Telephony PBX and Software Defined Network technology.

▌2272
TRANSOFT INC.

2000 RiverEdge Pkwy., Ste. 450
Atlanta, GA 30328
PH: (770)933-1965
FX: (770)933-3464
E-mail: comments@transoft.com
URL: http://www.transoft.com
Contact: Mr. Mike Edwards, Chairman

Description: Transoft is an international provider of application assembly, transformation and integration products and services. The Transoft Intelligent Adapter family of products provides a wide range of solutions enabling organizations to quickly and easily integrate new e-business and client-server applications with existing core business systems in a scalable and seamless way.

▌2273
TRANSPARENT SOLUTIONS L.L.C.

14014 Ash Dr.
Overland Park, KS 66224-3538
PH: (913)897-5019
FX: (913)897-1666
E-mail: mark@transparentsolutions.com
URL: http://www.transparentsolutions.com
Contact: Mark J. Short, Managing Partner

Staff: 3. **Description:** An Internet development company. Using strategic partnerships, able to take on projects of any size, ranging from troubleshooting a current site to total development of a corporate web site.

▌2274
TRANSTECH CONSULTING INC.

630 Morrison, Ste. 100
Columbus, OH 43230
PH: (614)751-0575
FX: (614)751-0576
E-mail: facts@transtechconsulting.com
URL: http://www.transtechconsulting.com
Contact: Jeff Cook, Senior Vice President

Staff: 18. **Description:** A management consulting firm, specializing in strategic planning, design and implementation of fulfillment operations and information systems as a part of Supply Chain Management for manufacturing, mail order, wholesale and retail clients. Our process extends beyond the warehouse operations into purchasing, logistics, site selection, facility selection, transportation analyses, and productivity improvements. **Geographic Area Served:** Worldwide.

▌2275
TRANSWORLD INC.

1515 Woodfield Rd., Ste. 660
Schaumburg, IL 60173
PH: (847)240-1000
FX: (847)240-2002
E-mail: selva.durai@transwld.com
URL: http://www.transwld.com
Contact: Selva Durai, Director, Midwest Region

Founded: 1989. **Description:** Transworld is a Customer Relationship Management strategy and solutions integration firm with services including CRM Strategy and CRM Solution. Their CRM Strategy practice defines the framework for clients in helping them achieve higher profitability, improved client satisfaction and better customer retention. They also help clients implement solutions to help identify, attain, retain and evaluate customers. **Major Partners:** Siebel Systems; Amdocs; Oracle; PeopleSoft; Tibco.

▌2276
TRENDSOURCE

111 Elm St., Ste.100
San Diego, CA 92101
PH: (619)239-2543
FX: (619)239-2525
URL: http://www.trendsource.com
Contact: Rodney Moll, Founder

Founded: 1989. **Description:** Trendsource is a company that offers e-commerce award programs, mystery shops, competition shops, market intelligence reports and compliance audits for online and offline businesses.

▌2277
TRI-FORCE CONSULTING SERVICES INC.

109 Henning Dr.
North Wales, PA 19454
PH: (215)740-6806
FX: (267)200-0026
E-mail: mgorawala@icca.org
URL: http://www.triforce-Inc.com
Contact: Manish Gorawala, Principal

Revenue: US$250,000. **Staff:** 2. **Description:** A specialized consulting services firm focusing exclusively on providing e-Business application development and project management services for the web and e-Commerce projects. Offers both project and time and material based services. Applies Internet/ intranet and e-commerce technologies to real-world business problems. Offer consulting, programming and integration services in Internet/ intranet, e-commerce and client-server application development. Firm provides consulting services in the areas of architecture, design, development, integration and training for the leading edge Web related technologies and products. **Geographic Area Served:** United States.

▌2278
TRIARCHE RESEARCH GROUP (TRG)

38 Rice St., Ste. 2-0/2-2
Cambridge, MA 02140
PH: (617)491-2952
FX: (815)364-3002
E-mail: info@triarche.com
URL: http://www.triarche.com/ecommerce.html

Contact: Rodney Thayer, Dir., E-Commerce Deployment Strategies

Description: Triarche Research Group E-Commerce Strategies practice makes assessments for enterprises seeking a change in technological or organizational direction that includes development of Internet-mediated applications. Their consultants can provide e-commerce deployment strategies for internal applications, business-to-business processes and develop workable customer service applications for retail enterprises.

▌2279
TRINETRATECH

Flat No. 6, Vigneswara Apartments
49 W Mada St., Nungambakkam
Madras 600034, India
PH: 91 44 8220452
E-mail: sankar@jagaddhatri.com
URL: http://www.jagaddhatri.com
Contact: Sankar Viswanathan

Description: A Senior Executive and Software Developer started TrinetraTech, specializing in web development and E-Commerce consulting. They provide Ecommerce solutions for medium and small companies.

▌2280
TRUSTED INFORMATION SYSTEMS INC.

3060 Washington Rd.
Glenwood, MD 21738
PH: (301)854-6889
FX: (301)854-5363
E-mail: hrdept@tis.com
URL: http://www.tis.com
Contact: Stephen T. Walker, President/CEO

Staff: 250. **Description:** Provider of comprehensive security solutions for protection of computer networks, including global Internet-based systems, internal networks, and individual workstations and laptops. Firm will develop, market, license, and support the Gauntlet(r) family of firewall products and other network security products. Supports both civilian and military agencies with: security analysis, threat and vulnerability studies, policy development, security modeling, system security designs, system security design reviews, certification and accrediitation support. Industries served: healthcare, financial, pharmaceutical, universities, state, local, and federal government agencies, international organizations, and military organizations. **Seminars:** Interactive information system security training courses on the threats, vulnerabilities and security solutions for computer systems, networks, and data. **Special Seminars:** Produced Gauntlet(tm), the Internet firewall product that allows users to control access between their corporate networks and the Internet.

▌2281
TWIN MOONS LLC

2152 Dupont Dr., Ste. 218
Irvine, CA 92612
PH: (714)745-0888
FX: (714)827-7553
E-mail: service@twinmoons.com
URL: http://www.twinmoons.com
Contact: Mr. Tamim Azizadah, Founder

Description: Twin Moons, LLC is a multimedia development and consulting firm. They provide a broad spectrum of services to meet their clients interactive communication needs. They offer the following services: web design (concept, design, implementation), web site renovation, web site optimization, web site maintenance, web hosting, e-commerce, banner design, Intranet design and implementation, Computer Based Training (CBT) solutions, software prototyping, Graphical User Interface (GUI) design, corporate videos and presentations, and CD-ROM production.

▌2282
TWO CROWS CORP.

10500 Falls Rd.
Potomac, MD 20854
PH: (301)983-9550
FX: (301)983-3554
E-mail: herb@twocrows.com
URL: http://www.twocrows.com
Contact: Herb Edelstein, President

Description: A data warehousing and mining consultancy specializing in Internet consulting and client/server architecture computing.

▌2283
UBICS, INC.

333 Technology Dr., Ste. 210
Canonsburg, PA 15317
PH: (724)746-6001
TF: 800-441-0077
FX: (724)746-9597
URL: http://www.ubics.com
Contact: Mr. Vijay Mallya, Chairman

Staff: 250. **Description:** UBICS, Inc. is a provider of information technology professional services to large and mid-sized organizations. UBICS provides its clients with a wide range of professional services in areas such as client- server design and development, e-commerce applications design and development, enterprise resource planning package implementation and customization, applications maintenance programming, database administration and customer relationship management. UBICS information technology (IT) services include applications maintenance, client/server development, database and systems administration, e-commerce systems design, and enterprise resource planning.

▌2284
UNDERWIRED LTD.

1 Bermondsey St.
London SE12ER, United Kingdom
PH: 44 207 089 8666
E-mail: info@underwired.com
URL: http://www.underwired.com

Description: Underwired designs and builds web sites, interactive TV microsites and multimedia. They develop direct customer relationships, online communities and loyal brand advocates.

▌2285
UNICOMP, INC.

1850 Parkway Pl., Ste. 925
Marietta, GA 30067
PH: (770)424-3684
FX: (770)424-5558
E-mail: info@unicomp.com
URL: http://www.unicomp.com
Contact: Mr. Stephen Hafer, President and Chief Executive Officer

Staff: 231. **Description:** UniComp offers a wide variety of products and services, including platform migration software, human resources management applications, electronic payment products, and Web site design and hosting services. UniComp also furnishes hardware and software for the retail market, including customer-actived devices for reading bar codes, as well as interactive graphics display devices and point of sale terminals.

▌2286
UNIFIED TECHNOLOGIES INC.

Rensselaer Technology Park
105 Jordan Rd.
Troy, NY 12180
PH: (518)283-1003
TF: 888-538-6439
FX: (518)283-1189
E-mail: info@unifiedtech.com
URL: http://www.unifiedtech.com
Contact: Mr. Jo Raquel, Chief Executive Officer

Founded: 1995. **Description:** UNIFIED offers a line of professional services called: e-Business Readiness, e-Business Intelligence, and e-Business Engineering. Combined, these service offerings provide business guidance and engineering excellence that help guide organizations' through the e-transformation process. **Major Partners:** Sun Microsystems; Microsoft; Oracle; Citrix; iPlanet; Cisco Systems; Check Point Software Technologies Ltd.; Veritas; OpenConnect Systems; Hewlett Packard **Awards:** Named one of 1999's Fastest Growing Companies by INC. 500.

2287

UNILOG

97-99 Boulevard Pereire
75017 Paris, France
PH: 33140684000
FX: 33140684005
URL: http://www.unilog.fr

Description: Unilog specializes in IT consulting, systems engineering and integration, and training. Unilog's customers come primarily from the financial services, manufacturing, telecommunications, pharmaceuticals, and government sectors

2288

UNIPRESS SOFTWARE INC.

2025 Lincoln Hwy.
Edison, NJ 08817
PH: (732)287-2100
TF: 800-222-0550
FX: (732)287-4929
E-mail: info@unipress.com
URL: http://www.unipress.com
Contact: Mark Krieger, President

Founded: 1983. **Description:** Unipress Software Inc. develops the FootPrints product line. First released in 1996, FootPrints features 100% web-based help desk and customer problem management software tools without high costs and complex administration.

2289

UNIQURE COMPUTING SOLUTIONS

1661 Worcester Rd.
Framingham, MA 01701-5401
PH: (508)598-6000
FX: (508)598-6199
E-mail: info@uniquecomputing.com
URL: http://www.uniquecomputing.com
Contact: Krishna Nangegadda, Chairman & President

Founded: 1995. **Staff:** 185. **Description:** Unique Computing Solutions offers information technology consulting services through its offices in India and the US. As an information technology consulting company, Unique offers a full range of IT services. The Services include: IT Consulting and Outsourcing. Unique works with members of user groups and management teams to determine technologies and skills which will meet business objectives.

2290

UNITED CUSTOMER MANAGEMENT
SOLUTIONS

80 Dorcas St.
South Melbourne, VIC 3205, Australia
PH: 61 03 9256 5555

FX: 61 03 9256 5015
URL: http://www.ucms.net

Staff: 1000. **Description:** United Customer Management Solutions is an international provider of essential Electronic Customer Relationship Management (eCRM) solutions. They offer end-to-end, full service eCRM solutions that span the customer life-cycle from acquisition to retention and their service range has extended beyond the customer management solutions to include delivery of CRM technology and professional service offerings.

2291

U.S. INTERACTIVE INC.

2012 Renaissance Blvd.
King of Prussia, PA 19406
PH: (610)313-9700
FX: (610)382-8908
URL: http://www.usinteractive.com
Contact: Eric Pulier, Chairman

Revenue: US$35,300,000. **Staff:** 700. **Description:** U.S. Interactive provides a road map to help companies do business on the Internet. Through its proprietary e-Roadmap development plan, which can be customized, the consulting firm focuses on four areas: e-commerce, digital marketing, enterprise relationship managmenet, and knowledge management. U.S. Interactive also provides client-specific exranets, which provide work plans, project updates, new proposals, and other project information.

2292

UNITEK INFORMATION SYSTEMS INC.

39465 Paseo Padre Pkwy., Ste. 2900
Fremont, CA 94538
PH: (510)249-1060
FX: (510)249-9125
E-mail: info@unitek.com
URL: http://www.unitek.com
Contact: Mr. Paul Afshar, President

Staff: 150. **Description:** Unitek Information Systems offers information technology consulting, technical education, and contracting services. Founded in 1992 as a high-technology network and systems integrator, Unitek Information Systems is dedicated to IT/IS integration and support solutions utilizing various technologies. Unitek provides IT consulting, contracting and training to clients that represent a wide gamut of firms in terms of size and industry background.

2293

UNITY SOLUTIONS LTD.

PO Box 249
Banbury
Oxon OX171UY, United Kingdom
PH: 44 1295 690793

522

FX: 44 1295 690243
E-mail: info@unity-solutions.co.uk
URL: http://www.unity-solutions.co.uk

Description: Unity Solutions offers Customer Value Management, which is based primarily on customer profitability. They also offer customer analysis support for customer relationship management programs, presentations and workshops and training in the fields of customer profitability for the client's sales team and customer value management for managers at all levels in various company functions.

▌ 2294
UNIVERSAL SOFTWARE CORP.

100 Apollo Dr.
Chelmsford, MA 01824
PH: (978)677-2600
FX: (978)244-9511
E-mail: info@universal-sw.com
URL: http://www.universal-sw.com
Contact: Krishore Deshpande, President and Chief Executive Officer

Founded: 1992. **Staff:** 130. **Description:** Universal Software provides information technology services, including software consulting and staffing. Founded in 1992 as a small Massachusetts based IT services company, Universal Software Corporation their goal is to provide software staffing and consulting services in leading-edge technologies.

▌ 2295
UNIVERSALDIALOG INC.

4909 Murphy Canyon Rd., Ste. 301
San Diego, CA 92123
PH: (858)503-0010
FX: (858)503-1935
URL: http://www.universaldialog.com
Contact: Sasha Briskin, Principal

Description: An information technology and globalization services provider. Offers multilingual e-business solutions, such as development of multilingual web sites/portals, multimedia presentations and multilingual e-commerce systems.

▌ 2296
US BUSINESS PLAN INC.

1200 Barrett Pky., Ste. 4-400
Kennesaw, GA 30144
PH: (770)794-8000
FX: (770)423-9444
E-mail: consulting@usbusinessplan.com
URL: http://www.usbusinessplan.com
Contact: George F. Culler, President

Description: Develops high quality business plans for technology ventures, especially technology transfer, Internet,

software, telecommunications, biomedical, and other technologies. Clients in U.S. and Canada include investment intermediaries, entrepreneurs, experienced angel investors, major start-ups, established companies, and Fortune 500. Extensive experience including Big 5 management consulting. **Special Seminars:** Proficient in all major PC-based business software packages. **Geographic Area Served:** Worldwide.

▌ 2297
UTR

2 Duncan Mill Rd.
Toronto, ON, Canada M3B1Z4
PH: (416)445-3222
TF: 888-737-7667
FX: (416)445-2325
E-mail: sales@utr.com
URL: http://www.utr.com

Description: UTR is a multi-faceted Call Center Service Bureau. Their clients want to improve customer support or maintain contact with customers and prospects and UTR uses both human and technical resources to make this happen. They assist clients with customer support and retention programs via phone, web and email customer support 24 hours a day, seven days a week, 365 days a year.

▌ 2298
VALTECH

Grande Arche de La Defense
92044 La Defense, France
PH: 33141882300
FX: 33141882301
URL: http://www.valtech.com
Contact: Mr. Jean-Yves Hardy, Chairman and Chief Executive Officer

Description: For Valtech, e-business is the only business. The company helps its clients build, implement, and maintain Internet and intranet applications relating to electronic commerce, process automation, and supply chain management. Other services include Web site marketing (site ergonomics, audience measurement, customer retention programs), legacy system integration, and Web site technology training. Valtech targets large companies primarily in the finance and communications industries.

▌ 2299
VANGUARD COMMUNICATIONS CORP.

100 American Rd.
Morris Plains, NJ 07950
PH: (973)605-8000
FX: (973)605-8329
E-mail: dvandoren@vanguard.net
URL: http://www.vanguard.net
Contact: Don Van Doren, President

Founded: 1980. **Description:** Vanguard Communications Corp. offers contact center expertise in the areas of technology, process, operations and self-service. Their call center consulting service offers assistance in helping clients find the solution that fits; call center process improvement, assessment and consolidation or decentralization; and call center education. They also offer help with self service customer contact by helping clients design and manage eCommerce, IVR and speech recognition, email and other contact automation applications. This service includes assistance with self-service strategy, self-service design and implementation and channel review and self-service assessments.

▌2300
VAPOR

237 Noblestown Rd.
Carnegie, PA 15106
PH: (412)722-1500
FX: (412)722-1504
URL: http://www.vaporbiz.com

Description: Vapor is a consulting firm that specializes in empowering their clients with total utilization of the Internet. They build brands and business solutions to meet client and customer technological needs.

▌2301
VENCON MANAGEMENT INC.

301 W 53rd St.
New York, NY 10019
PH: (212)581-8787
FX: (212)397-4126
URL: http://www.venconinc.com
Contact: Irvin Barash, President

Staff: 6. **Description:** Venture capital firm and management consultants to corporations and entrepreneurs. Specializes in the areas of mergers and acquisitions evaluation and negotiation, and the preparation of marketing and business plans. Assists small or new businesses in expansion plans and financing. Also involved in new enterprise planning with industry and communities for rural economic analysis. Industries served: environment, semiconductor, electronics, chemicals, alternative energy, and e-commerce. **Seminars:** Holds venture capital forums. **Geographic Area Served:** United States, Canada, Mid-East, Korea, Japan, India, Southeast Asia.

▌2302
VENTERA

1600 International Dr., Ste. 100
McLean, VA 22102
PH: (703)760-4600
FX: (703)760-9494
E-mail: info@ventera.com
URL: http://www.ventera.com

Contact: Mr. Robert Acosta, Chief Executive Officer

Founded: 1996. **Description:** A project-based information technology consulting company that focuses on application development and integration using Internet technology. Provider of ecommerce solutions including business plan development, strategic direction, assessment of site and system requirements, technology architecture and software development. **Awards:** 2001 Deloitte and Touche Fast 50 No. 7 in Virginia; 2001 ComputerWorld Top 100 Places to Work in IT; 2001 Inc 500 list No. 60; 2001 Washington Business Journal Philanthropy Award; 2000 Deloitte and Touche Fast 50 Rising Star.

▌2303
VENTURENET PARTNERS LTD.

70 Old Brompton Rd.
London SW73LQ, United Kingdom
PH: 44 207 589 0803
FX: 44 207 589 2458
E-mail: enquiries@venturenetpartners.com
URL: http://www.venturenetpartners.com
Contact: Mr. Paul Dale, Managing Director

Description: VentureNet Partners is a 50/50 joint venture between Price Bertram Dale, an international business information and strategy consultancy and Paradigm RedShift, an Internet strategy and project management consultancy. As well as writing the business plan, they conduct market research, identify key executives to support the business, and provide ongoing support in technical implementation and business management. VentureNet act as an intermediary between entrepreneurs and investment. They have the expertise to support both large and small e-commerce business initiatives.

▌2304
VERISIGN INC.

487 E Middlefield Rd.
Mountain View, CA 94043
PH: (650)961-7500
TF: 800-361-8319
FX: (650)961-7300
E-mail: websitesales@verisign.com
URL: http://www.verisign.com
Contact: Stratton Sclavos, Chairman, President & CEO

Founded: 1995. **Description:** VeriSign Inc. is a provider of digital trust services. They enable businesses and consumers to engage in e-commerce and communications through web presence services, security services, payment services, and telecommunications services.

▌2305
VERITY INC.

894 Ross Dr.
Sunnyvale, CA 94089
PH: (408)541-1500

FX: (408)541-1600
E-mail: info@verity.com
URL: http://www.verity.com

History: Verity was one of the first companies to recognize the value of and deliveery of full-text search solutions for intranet, e-commerce and business portals. **Description:** Provides consulting and software solutions that power business portals, including corporate portals that share information within enterprises, e-commerce portals that sell products and services online, and B2B market exchange portals. **Awards:** Best Practice Award 2001 for Technology Inovation from eWEEK Magazine; Crossroads 2001 A-List Award for Knowledge Retrieval in Business Portals from Open Systems Advisors Inc.; Software Magazine's Software 500; Inter@ctive Week Fast 50; Best Core Compentency from Software Business Magazine.

■ 2306
VERTEX CUSTOMER MANAGEMENT

Vertex House
Greencourts Business Park
Styal Rd.
Manchester M225TX, United Kingdom
PH: 44 161 493 2200
FX: 44 161 493 2360
E-mail: marketing@vertex.co.uk
URL: http://www.vertex.co.uk

Description: Vertex offers outsourcing to help clients manage their customer-facing activities, to achieve excellence in customer service and build profitable relationships with their customers. They provide call center, billing and customer relationship management services. Their CRM outsourcing solution is a fully integrated system that links together marketing activities, such as customer segmentation, and campaign management, with customer-facing operations, such as contact center management, which frees up a client's in-house customer service agent to up-sell or cross-sell and increase the profitability of each customer.

■ 2307
VIANT CORP.

89 South St., 2nd Fl.
Boston, MA 02111
PH: (617)531-3700
FX: (617)531-3803
E-mail: info@viant.com
URL: http://www.viant.com
Contact: Willian H. Davidow, Chairman

Revenue: US$102,200,000. **Staff:** 737. **Description:** An Internet consulting firm that helps diverse clients in a broad range of industries plan, build and launch digital businesses. Provides digital business strategy, marketing and brand consulting, and web design and project management.

■ 2308
VIGORD CORP.

182 Kingsberry Dr.
Somerset, NJ 08873-4312
PH: (732)545-9756
FX: (732)545-9756
E-mail: info@vigord.com
URL: http://www.vigord.com

Founded: 1998. **Description:** Vigord provides a full range of web services to its customers including web hosting, web design and development, e-commerce, e-mail and domain name registration services. Vigord helps individual customers as well as small to medium size businesses with computing tasks such as network and Internet hookup, software and hardware installations and upgrades. They also provide nationwide dial-up Internet access.

■ 2309
VILLAGE PRINCIPLE CORP. (VP)

760 Cabin Dr.
Mill Valley, CA 94941
PH: (415)888-3108
FX: (415)888-3107
E-mail: welcomevp@villageprinciple.com
URL: http://www.villageprinciple.com
Contact: James Harrington, President & Principle Partner

Description: Provides consulting that focuses on next generation online, beginning with conception to rollout and beyond. Offers expertise in the following areas: Strategic Planning; Electronic Commerce; Project Management; Web Strategies and Implementations; Portal Centric for Marketing, Sales, Purchasing, Financial, and Human Resources Divisions; Technology Areas and Recommendations; Partnerships; Web Centric Enterprise-The Complete Competitive Advantage; Breakdown and Recommendations of Products and Services for Online Implementation

■ 2310
VINE TECHNOLOGY

10746 Linda Vista Dr.
Cupertino, CA 95014
PH: (408)996-1294
FX: (408)973-0310
E-mail: webmaster@vine.com
URL: http://www.vine.com

Description: Web services include providing system administration (Windows NT, Macintosh, UNIX), custom hardware/software design and implementation, network security, HTML construction, firewalls, supervisory control and data acquisition via the Internet, graphic art design, scanning, Web audio, CD-ROM creation, animation and 3D modeling, and large format darkroom facilities.

▌2311
VIP COMMUNIQUE

2-76 Cassandra Blvd.
Mississauga, ON, Canada M3A1S6
PH: (954)443-1844
FX: (416)445-8983
E-mail: vipcomm@hotmail.com
Contact: Valerie Whittaker, Principal

Description: Specializes in e-commerce and information technology in the travel and tourism industry. **Geographic Area Served:** Canada.

▌2312
VIRTUAL COMMUNICATIONS

35 Lincoln Dr.
Sausalito, CA 94965
PH: (415)257-9503
E-mail: virtual@virtualcommunications.com
URL: http://www.virtualcommunications.com
Contact: Don Wieneke, Manager

Description: Company provides computer and communication support, including Internet design and management.

▌2313
VIRTUAL TRIBES INC.

1025 Connecticut Ave. NW, Ste. 1012
Washington, DC 20036
PH: (202)857-9792
FX: (202)478-1950
E-mail: info@virtualtribes.com
URL: http://virtualtribes.com
Contact: Christian Brulhart, Principal

Description: Firm helps small- to medium-sized companies and organizations without internal IT capabilities to use electronic business to succeed in the digital marketplace. Provides a single gateway to commercial, financial, legal and technical expertise in e-business.

▌2314
VIRTUALREP INC.

21710 NE 199th Ct.
Battle Ground, WA 98604
PH: (360)687-5800
FX: (360)684-6456
E-mail: virtualrep@virtualrep.com
URL: http://www.virtualrep.com

Description: A full service Internet solution provider specializing in e-commerce. Provides an affordable launching pad to establish an E-commercepresence on the Internet.

Develops, designs, publishs, hosts and maintains e-commerce websites. The company's focus is consulting for online shopping systems.

▌2315
VISIONFACTORY INC.

15300 Weston Pkwy.
Cary, NC 27513
PH: (919)253-2500
TF: 888-564-7006
FX: (919)253-2525
E-mail: businessinquiries@visionfactory.com
URL: http://www.visionfactory.com
Contact: Mr. Deven Spear, President and CEO

Description: VisionFactory help their clients market their products and services more effectively by creating engaging, informative experiences in physical spaces, virtual spaces, and the intersection of the two. VisionFactory seeks to create these experiences by relying on their expertise in four principal disciplines: consulting, rich media design and development, Web-based technology systems, and Customer Experience Management.

▌2316
VISIONONE INC.

6781 N. Palm Ave., Ste. 120
Fresno, CA 93704
PH: (559)432-8000
FX: (559)431-5082
E-mail: Management@v-1.com
URL: http://www.visionone.ws/main.asp

Description: VisionOne is an e-business solutions provider. They are able to leverage resources critical to the success of e-business initiatives our clients engage us in. Their core team of business, technical, and functional professionals are assembled in teams fitting the task and provide Internet-based solutions in the areas of: Customer Relationship Management (CRM), Electronic Commerce (B2B/ B2C),employee relationship management, and Supply-Chain Management (SCM). Their industry-focused solutions include custom developed Web applications in healthcare, retail and manufacturing, agriculture, and services.

▌2317
VISIONPARTNER

3404 Garner Ln., Ste. 100
Plano, TX 75023-7325
PH: (972)516-9743
FX: (866)271-1085
E-mail: wilten.haynes@visionpartner.com
URL: http://www.visionpartner.com
Contact: Wilten Haynes, President

Founded: 2001. **Description:** VisionPartner is a sales and marketing consulting firm delivering Fortune 500-quality guidance and counseling services to small and medium sized businesses. They help clients increase and optimize profits, manage their sales cycle, expand their client bases, define customer relationships, improve customer satisfaction, increase customer loyalty, decrease customer acquisition costs and remain competitive for the long-term.

▌2318
VISTA 7 WEST INC.

5696 Peachtree Pwy., Ste. K1
Norcross, GA 30092
PH: (678)966-9274
TF: 888-421-6383
E-mail: sales@vista7west.com
URL: http://www.vista7west.com
Contact: Ms. Lisa Anglese, Founder

Description: Vista 7 West provides web development and marketing services to companies throughout the United States. Their service line includes: electronic commerce applications for use in business-to-business and business-to-consumer Internet environments; specialized, individualized applications for on-line enterprises; database integration; custom graphic design and imagery; web-based marketing and advertising.

▌2319
VISTA TRAK INC.

4615 First St., Ste. 230
Pleasanton, CA 94566
PH: (925)600-7060
FX: (925)600-7066
E-mail: information@vistatrak.com
URL: http://www.vistatrak.com
Contact: Alexander White, President/CEO

Description: VistaTrak is a systems integration and IT services firm focused on integrating new and existing enterprise applications for effective and profitable e-business solutions. Their team of professionals has extensive industry experience and a proven success record in e-business and IT projects. **Major Partners:** Arc 7; InterShop; Arcadia One; Kassner; Documentun; Manex; Inte; Microsoft; UUNet; Verisign; webMethods; Xerox

▌2320
VISTRONIX INC.

1970 Chain Bridge Rd., Ste. 1200
McLean, VA 22102
PH: (703)734-2270
TF: 800-483-2434
FX: (703)734-2271
E-mail: Info@vistronix.com
URL: http://www.vistronix.com

Contact: Mr. Deepak Hathiramani, President and Chief Executive Officer

Description: The Vistronix practice areas include the eSolutions Consulting Group, focused on Internet Solutions and Strategies, Application Integration, Education Accountability Solutions, and Portal and Enterprise Content Management (ECM). The Enterprise Systems Management group focuses on Help-Desk management and Network Management services; and the Information Management Solutions group, which provides document and records management solutions, and digital imaging solutions.

▌2321
VISUAL PERSPECTIVES INTERNET INC.

23181 Verdugo Dr., Ste. 105-B
Laguna Hills, CA 92653
PH: (949)595-8622
E-mail: info@vpi.net
URL: http://www.vpi.net

Founded: 1995. **Description:** Visual Perspectives Internet, Inc. (VPI.Net) has created a collection of E-Commerce tools to help their clients do business online. Their E-Commerce offerings ensure a complete, end-to-end solution, taking you from the initial design phases, through management, to E-Marketing capabilities.

▌2322
VOICECENTRAL

PO 31064
Laguna Hills, CA 92654-1064
PH: (949)598-0900
FX: (949)598-3258
E-mail: sales@voicecentral.com
URL: http://www.voicecentral.com
Contact: Robert P. Bosche', Jr., President

Staff: 10. **Description:** Full service telecommunications service bureau, firm offers Internet Billing Services, Internet/Telephony Customer Services connectivity, helps businesses reduce advertising and promotional costs and improve capabilities through computer telephony. Audiotext consulting, including Interactive Voice Response (IVR) and audiotext consulting; development of voice systems solutions as alternatives to manual processing, information distribution, and order fulfillment; and ''Free'' and ''Pay-per-Call'' (900 number) consulting. Firm assists businesses and organizations in establishing a national presence for family and business-oriented information, services, and information products, without the high ongoing cost of advertising. **Seminars:** Various material and training related to voice-based delivery of family and business-oriented information and services. **Special Seminars:** Computer telephony. Telecommunications Service Bureau. Internet Customer Service Billing. **Geographic Area Served:** United States.

▌2323
VOYAGER STRATEGY CONSULTANTS

97 Chobham Rd. Sunningdale
Berkshire SL5OHQ, United Kingdom
PH: 44 1344 876339
E-mail: info@voyagergb.com
URL: http://www.voyagergb.com

Description: Voyager Strategy Consultants is a European strategic consultancy in digital media. They provide an integrated, objective strategic consultancy for clients within the European Digital TV, Internet, Streaming Media and E-commerce market sectors. Voyager will deliver solutions for clients looking to create new media ventures, assess proposed business models and provide guidance on bringing new digital products to market. From assisting with new digital TV channel ventures, Content Management, Streaming Media, E-commerce security and Corporate Services such as Interim Management, Regulatory Compliance and Executive Search, Voyager provides a one stop solution for companies in digital media.

▌2324
VOYUS CANADA INC.

3602 Gilmore Way, Ste. 302
Burnaby, BC, Canada V5G4W9
PH: (604)320-6566
TF: 888-225-1157
FX: (604)320-6568
E-mail: schute@voyus.com
URL: http://www.velocityit.com
Contact: Mr. Shawn Chute, President and CEO

Founded: 1998. **Staff:** 75. **Description:** Voyus is a technology services organization. Their consultants help clients manage their IT environment, provide predictability, and reliability.

▌2325
WALKER INFORMATION

3939 Priority Way S Dr.
PO Box 40972
Indianapolis, IN 46240-0972
PH: (317)843-3939
TF: 800-334-3939
FX: (317)843-8897
E-mail: info@walkerinfo.com
URL: http://www.walkerinfo.com

Founded: 1939. **Description:** Walker Information is a research firm with offices throughout the U.S. and Canada who conduct research and measurement in the areas of customer satisfaction, employee commitment, corporate reputation and business ethics. They serve clients of all sizes around the world by helping them measure and understand the attitudes and perceptions of their customers so they may utilize this customer feedback to improve their customer service.

▌2326
WAS INC.

1233 S Gene Autry Trl.
Palm Springs, CA 92264
PH: (760)864-7400
TF: 888-625-5429
FX: (760)864-7498
E-mail: info@was-inc.com
URL: http://www.was-inc.com
Contact: Walter Schwarz, President

Description: WAS Inc. offers web-based businesses complete service from initial consultation through fulfillment and customer care providing a one-source solution to help them profit.

▌2327
WATERS COMPUTER CONSULTANTS

PO BOX 286CP
MILDURA, VIC 3501, Australia
PH: 61 350 246 279
FX: 61 350 246 279
E-mail: richard@waterscc.com.au
URL: http://www.waterscc.com.au

Founded: 1996. **Description:** Waters Computer Consultants are a web design company located in Mildura, Victoria, Australia. They also provide other services, such as intranet design consultation and implementation, especially for local government. Established in 1996, Waters Computer Consultants is primarily a web design company, but also provide networking, programming, GIS Mapping and IT management. They provide total site solutions to customers with advanced programming, encryption, e-commerce and database integration.

▌2328
WD NET INC.

100 Avenue J
Lake Charles, LA 70615
PH: (337)436-7481
E-mail: info@wd-net.com
URL: http://www.wd-net.com

Description: WD Net Inc. is an application service provider (ASP) offering electronic bill presentment and payment (EBPP) to businesses, financial institutions and municipal utilities. Offers consulting services to commercial clients so that they can successfully enter e-commerce while reducing billing costs and increasing revenue. **Major Partners:** VeriSign; Sun Microsystems; iPlanet; Cisco

▌2329
WEB-CONSULTANTS

Sisters of St Josephs
Workhouse Ln.
Greetland HX48BS, United Kingdom

PH: 44 7779169715
E-mail: enquiries@web-consultants.co.uk
URL: http://www.web-consultants.co.uk

Description: The Web-consultants are a team of independent Internet Consultants and Project Managers. They have industry experience in a variety of areas, which will benefit their clients when planning and implementing their Web / E-Commerce Strategy.

▌2330
WEB DATA ACCESS

6 Montgomery Village Ave., Ste 622
Gaithersburg, MD 20879
PH: (301)926-8323
FX: (301)417-0508
E-mail: sales@webdataaccess.com
URL: http://www.webdataaccess.com

Founded: 1978. **Description:** Helps industrial enterprises strategize, build and deploy e-business systems that improve productivity and business performance. Consults clients in customer relationship management, business intelligence, supply chain collaboration, and research and executive education.

▌2331
WEB MARKETING NOW

210 West 200 North Ste. 101
Provo, UT 84601
PH: (801)356-3321
FX: (801)356-2715
E-mail: info@webmarketingnow.com
URL: http://www.webmarketingnow.com/
Contact: Mr. Jerry West, Founder

Founded: 1999. **Description:** WebMarketingNow.com is comprised of professionals in the fields of: web design, search engine placement, ad copy writing, web programming, professional web site reviewing, directory listings and marketing consulting.

▌2332
WEB PERFORMANCE INC.

9207 Baileywick Rd., Ste 203
Raleigh, NC 27615
PH: (919)845-7601
FX: (919)845-7603
E-mail: sales@webperformanceinc.com
URL: http://www.webperformanceinc.com

Founded: 1999. **Description:** Web Performance Inc. develops easy to use web testing software that is appropriate to use on projects of all sizes, especially during the early development stages.

▌2333
WEB SERVICES GROUP INTERNET CONSULTING

14055 Cedar Rd., Ste. 309
Cleveland, OH 44118
PH: (216)932-7119
FX: (216)932-7120
E-mail: info@wbsq.com
URL: http://www.websg.com

Description: An Internet consulting firm that assists business with web site development and maintenance. Services include site design, custom graphics, web site publicity, market research, scheduled updates, multiple links to other web sites, site maintenance, E-mail, customer feedback forms, and online catalogs and sales.

▌2334
WEBB CONSULTING INC.

2485 Lexington St.
Lafayette, CO 80026
PH: (303)926-7990
FX: (303)926-7991
E-mail: laurie@webb-consult.com
URL: http://www.webb-consult.com
Contact: Laurie Webb-DesJardins, President/CEO

Founded: 1996. **Description:** E-consulting company that offers services such as web site design, development, management, content development and site operational support. Provides Internet professional services to small businesses, as well as, Fortune 500 companies globally, specializing in providing web solutions and services to support on-line business.

▌2335
THE WEBB PARTNERSHIP

1212 Hancock St.
Quincy, MA 02169
PH: (617)376-0595
FX: (617)769-0555
E-mail: info@thewebbpartership.com
URL: http://www.thewebbpartnership.com

Description: Provides e-commerce consulting and education services to co-ordinate concept development, market research, operations design, service development and technology integration. Helps clients innovate and transform how they serve their customers and how they accelerate the delivery of new product and services. Offices in London, Kenilworth, France, and Boston

▌2336
WEBCENTRICITY

208 Aspetuck Ridge Road
New Milford, CT 06776
PH: (860)354-4748

FX: (603)372-5872
E-mail: tjtrujillo@webcentricity.com
URL: http://www.webcentricity.com

Description: With multiple facilities and Internet technology expertise, Webcentricity is positioned to provide clients with a reliable, fully outsourced e-operations solution capable of supporting the full range of marketing and sales programs in the direct channels. With a national, coast-to-coast network of over 20 customer contact centers, fulfillment facilities, and data centers, Webcentricity offers clients the broadest possible range of solutions to demand-side needs such as order management and sales and marketing support, and supply-side needs such as purchasing procurement and transportation.

∎ 2337
WEBINTENTION SERVICES

109 6th St.
Lynden, WA 98264-1912
PH: (360)354-7964
E-mail: info@webintention.com
URL: http://www.webintention.com

Description: Webintention Services offers Internet consulting services such as performing mission critical strategic Internet analysis. Helps determine product content, design and direction, while focusing on customer requirements, installation, implementation, and support service for e-commerce.

∎ 2338
WEBLINX INC.

4777 Route 71
Oswego, IL 60543
PH: (630)551-0334
FX: (630)554-5872
E-mail: support@weblinxinc.com
URL: http://www.weblinxinc.com

Description: In addition to standard marketing services, WebLink Inc. also offers a broad range of information technology services. These include: Networks, Computer Upgrades, Troubleshooting, Database Design, Web Site Consulting, New Personal Computers, and Information Technology.

∎ 2339
THE WEBMACHINE

108 Fore St.
Kingsbridge TQ71AW, United Kingdom
PH: 44 01548 852282
FX: 44 01548 853550
E-mail: info@webmachine.co.uk
URL: http://www.webmachine.co.uk
Contact: Stephen Oggelsby, Founder

Description: The WebMachine is an Internet Design and Business Solutions provider, dedicated to providing tailor made Internet and database systems and consulting for business seeking to engage in digital enterprise. The WebMachine offers a wide range of services to help businesses make the most from the latest Internet technologies, range of E-commerce, site management tools and bespoke back-office systems. Their consultants can review internal IT business systems and evaluate their performance. They can then suggest how the latest technologies could streamline business operations to work faster and more profitably.

∎ 2340
WEBMASTERS INC.

2260 S Northwest Pky.
Marietta, GA 30067
PH: (770)953-2261
FX: (770)977-3006
E-mail: postermaster@webmastersinc.com
URL: http://www.webmastersinc.com
Contact: Mark K. Lane, President

Revenue: US$350,000. **Staff:** 4. **Description:** Provides Internet consulting and Web site development services. Provides customized Internet services in the areas of highspeed vector graphics and real-time video, database access, human resource functions, and virtual retail shopping. **Special Seminars:** Experience with SAP accounting, Sybase, and Access databases. **Geographic Area Served:** Southeastern United States.

∎ 2341
WEBMETRO INC.

2 North Lake Ave. Ste. 100
Pasadena, CA 91101
PH: (626)793-8047
TF: (866)922-4632
FX: (626)793-8051
E-mail: webmetro@webmetro.com
URL: http://www.webmetro.com
Contact: Mr. Carlos Ugalde, President and CEO

Founded: 1995. **Description:** WebMetro is a California based, full Internet resource company, providing training, development, e-commerce, and much more. They were formed to help businesses capitalize on the growth and potential available via the World Wide Web. WebMetro provides services through Internet-based technologies, namely: e-Planning, Web development, Programming/Applications and Online Marketing.

∎ 2342
@WEBO

17 Torrey Pines
Coto de Caza, CA 92679
PH: (530)348-8800

FX: (530)348-8800
E-mail: atwebo@atwebo.com
URL: http://www.atwebo.com

Description: Provides e-commerce consulting to traditional small businesses. Expertise ranges from Web application development and integration to implementation and maintenance of enterprise applications. Offers comprehensive services, encompassing the entire application lifecycle, from business process consulting, through design and development, to integration and ongoing management.

▌ 2343
WEBPAGE DESIGN HAWAII

1019 Mokapu Blvd.
Kailua, HI 96734
PH: (808)254-0176
E-mail: heinz@wpd-hawaii.com
URL: http://www.wpd-hawaii.com/ecommerce.html

Description: WebPage Design Hawaii is an independent web designer company based in Kailua Hawaii (Oahu). They work from their home office to produce affordable web sites on the island. They do the research to provide advice and solutions to fit their clients business needs.

▌ 2344
WEBSITE CREATIONS

22 W Bryan St., Ste. 220
Savannah, GA 31401
PH: (912)727-3242
FX: (912)727-3248
E-mail: info@websitecreations.net
URL: http://www.websitecreations.net

Founded: 1997. **Description:** WebSite Creations was created as a firm devoted to web development, design and promotion.They produced Dapper Desk, an online help desk tool that companies can utilize to provide faster and better support to their customers.

▌ 2345
WEBSITEHELP

1155 Lola St., Ste. 100
Ottawa, ON, Canada K1K4C1
PH: (613)564-6565
TF: 800-461-0957
FX: (613)842-4176
E-mail: info@websitehelp.com
URL: http://www.websitehelp.com
Contact: David Hayes, President and Chief Executive Officer

Description: WebSiteHelp is a provider of web-based customer service solutions for eCommerce, eBusiness and corporate web sites. They help clients acquire more customers,

increase sales and build customer loyalty through their live and automated solutions.

▌ 2346
WEBSTARPRISES

159-30 Colonial Park
New York, NY 10039
PH: (212)926-8328
FX: (914)840-2244
E-mail: admin@webstarprises.8m.com
URL: http://www.webstarprises.8m.com

Description: Offers consulting, web page creation, web site packages, e-commerce, hosting, promotions and site administration. Also, provides consulting and training on how to setup and operate a successful e-commerce web site.

▌ 2347
WESTEND NEW MEDIA

224 W 30th St., Ste. 809
New York, NY 10001
PH: (212)417-9130
FX: (212)417-9131
E-mail: info@westendnow.com
URL: http://www.westendmedia.com
Contact: Jim Sherman, Founder/CEO

Founded: 1998. **Description:** An Internet strategy consulting firm providing services in business strategy, product development, consumer research, project management/general contractor supervision, marketing, technology planning, and strategic architecture. Focuses on companies in the new media market space, including on-line and off-line companies seeking to develop an Internet presence.

▌ 2348
WESTLAKE SOLUTIONS INC.

4445 Wisconsin Ave. NW, 2nd Fl.
Washington, DC 20016-2141
PH: (202)237-6600
TF: 800-357-2320
FX: (202)237-8649
E-mail: info@wlcg.com
URL: http://www.wlcg.com
Contact: Greg Eoyang, Pres./Dir. of Web Development

Revenue: US$1,500,000. **Staff:** 12. **Description:** WestLake Solutions offers a complete range of service for Internet and Intranet Website development, including page design and construction; CGI script, JavaScript and Java authoring; Web-to-database and Web-to-fax integration; on-site Internet/Web server setup and maintenance, and Internet market analysis and site promotion. **Seminars:** Offers hands-on, full-day training classes in its Internet training facility in Washington, D.C.: Navigating the Internet with Netscape; World Wide Web Publishing with HTML; Intermediate

HTML: Frames, Columns and Enhanced Layout; Advanced HTML/Introduction to CGI Scripting; Graphic Design for the World Wide Web; CGI Scripting with Perl (for programmers); CGI Scripting with Perl for New Programmers (2 days); JavaScript for Interactive Web Design; and Introduction to Java Programming (2 days). **Special Seminars:** Internet and Intranet Website development and hosting; Shell, CGI, Perl, JavaScript, Java, C and C programming; Web-to-fax and Web-to-database integration; and Internet and Website development training courses.

▌2349
WHEEL MEDIA

1008 10th St., Ste. 100
Sacramento, CA 95814
PH: (916)599-4335
E-mail: info@wheelmedia.com
URL: http://www.wheelmedia.com
Contact: Mr. Michael Rolph, President

Description: Strategic planning Internet company providing e-commerce consulting, online advertising and marketing, search engine optimization, email marketing, web design and development, and content management solutions.

▌2350
WHITE WHALE LTD.

Hill House
1 Little New St.
London EC4A3TR, United Kingdom
PH: 44 08 000 568 158; 44 12 52 84 96 13
E-mail: customers@whitewhale.co.uk
URL: http://www.whitewhale.co.uk

Description: White Whale is a consultancy offering services to multiple business sectors with help in the Customer Relationship Management field covering general business consultancy, organizational development and change management services and help with the application of information technology to support enhanced customer relationships.

▌2351
WHITECAP CANADA INC.

235 Yorkland Blvd., Ste. 904
North York, ON, Canada M2J4Y8
PH: (416)490-9900
FX: (416)490-9334
E-mail: sales@whitecapcanada.com
URL: http://www.whitecapcanada.com
Contact: Robb Carmichael, President/CEO

Description: Develops strategic plans for e-business through the design, development, implementation and on-going operation of professional e-business environments. Expertise in the design and implementation of premier on-line shopping environments. Understands how to securely integrate direct payment gateways with banks and credit card institutions. **Major Partners:** IBM; Apple; Microsoft; Oracle; Hewlett Packard; Macromedia; Adobe

▌2352
WICK HILL GROUP

Bradstone Brook, Christmas Hill
Guildford GU48HR, United Kingdom
PH: 44 1483 466500
FX: 44 1483 466638
E-mail: info@wickhill.co.uk
URL: http://www.wickhill.com

Description: Wick Hill Group are consultants in enterprise connectivity and e-commerce. Wick Hill is an international value added distributor specializing in secure infrastructure solutions for ebusiness. Their portfolio includes a comprehensive range of security solutions, as well as web access and web management products.

▌2353
WINTERGREEN ASSOCIATES

517 W Pelham Rd.
Amherst, MA 01002
PH: (413)259-1720
FX: (413)259-1720
E-mail: info@wintergreen.com
URL: http://www.wintergreen.com

Description: Offers commercial Web site design and maintenance services. Also provides database management, CGI programming, forms processing, graphics and videoprocessing, and technical writing services.

▌2354
WIPRO TECHNOLOGIES

137 Euston Rd.
London NW12AA, United Kingdom
PH: 44 207 3870606
FX: 44 207 3870605
E-mail: info@wipro.com
URL: http://www.wipro.com
Contact: Mr. Azim Premji, Chairman

Staff: 14000. **Description:** Wipro Technologies is the global technology services E-Commerce business partner in the global markets. Wipro consultants use technology solutions to provide services for business transformation and product realization.

▌2355
TINA WISSEN'S DESIGN CENTER LLC

4624 Mallard Crest
Portsmouth, VA 23703
PH: (757)638-9326

FX: (757)638-9325
E-mail: tina@wissendesign.com
URL: http://www.wissendesign.com
Contact: Ms. Tina Wissen, Owner

Founded: 1996. **Description:** Freelance e-commerce consultant provides web site design and marketing services. Also offers web consulting for the development and marketing of online business.

▮ 2356
WMB GROUP

131 Union Ave.
Komoka, ON, Canada N0L1R0
PH: (519)657-7011
E-mail: info@wmbgroup.com
URL: http://www.wmbgroup.com

Description: WMB Group are "Knowledge Management Consultants" specializing in helping small and medium-sized businesses in the areas of benchmarking, customer relationship management (systems development, implementation and training), business intelligence, integrated eBusiness, data mining and more.

▮ 2357
WOGOS.COM

11657 Doverwood Dr.
Riverside, CA 92505-3216
TF: 877-214-8008
FX: 877-214-8008
E-mail: sales@wogos.com
URL: http://www.wogos.com
Contact: Mr. Greg Short

Founded: 2000. **Description:** WOGOS.com provides their clients with logo design, web design, Flash animations, multimedia presentations, eCommerce, hosting and domain name registration. They offer consulting services in advertising and promotion, web site improvement, and online business setup. Consultations can be conducted via email or by phone.

▮ 2358
WOHLDORF SYSTEMS INC.

25 San Miguel Ave., Ste. 2204
MPO Building
Ortigas Center
1600 Pasig City, Philippines
PH: 632 633 1855
FX: 632 638 5646
E-mail: info@wohldorf.com
URL: http://www.wohldorf.com
Contact: Mr. B. Nicolaus Wohldorf, Managing Director

Founded: 1999. **Description:** Wohldorf Systems, Inc., is a Philippines based information technology and management consultancy. They advise corporate clients on all aspects of mission critical enterprise systems. Their service offerings include project management, workshops, business process re-engineering, system migration, etc.

▮ 2359
WOLFBLAST INTERACTIVE

5900 West Dry Creek Rd.
Healdsburg, CA 95448
PH: (707)431-1891
E-mail: info@wolfblast.com
URL: http://www.wolfblast.com

Description: WolfBlast is an Interactive Advertising and Design Agency. They utilize proprietary software and processes to create interactive marketing campaigns that enable their clients to get to market quickly, with maximum ROI on their advertising expenditures.

▮ 2360
WOMEN'S GLOBAL BUSINESS ALLIANCE

501 Westport Ave., Ste. 205
Norwalk, CT 06851
PH: (203)454-1540
FX: (203)938-7475
E-mail: administration@wgba-business.com
URL: http://wgba-business.com
Contact: Nancy May, Principal and Managing Partner

Description: Fax-on-demand, disk-based marketing and custom training, interactive voice, audiotex or telephone services, CD-ROM, etc. Industries served: consumer products and services; and business-to-business products and services. Business information for senior executives-Distribution via electronic media/interactive media- business focus on improving operational and financial performance for companies run and managed by executive women. **Seminars:** Business Performance. **Special Seminars:** Mac, PC, and UNIX systems and software. **Geographic Area Served:** Worldwide.

▮ 2361
WORLDMACHINE TECHNOLOGIES CORP.

355 Congress
South Boston, MA 02127
PH: (617)357-4040
FX: (617)492-1953
E-mail: info@worldmachine.com
URL: http://www.worldmachine.com
Contact: Eric Hansen, Principal

Description: Provides Web site engineering, software development, and system installation and administration. Web site services include design of HTML pages, server installation,

533

creation of graphic, sound, and video media for Web site, and development of server-side and client-side functional components. Software development expertise in relational database design and analysis, inter-process communication and networking under TCP/IP, and release engineering and configuration management. System installation and administration services offer management of users and system resources, troubleshooting, database administration, and shell scripting.

∎ 2362

WORLDWIDE ADVERTISING CONSULTANTS CORP.

69 Luisa St., Condado
San Juan, PR 00907
PH: (787)648-3435
FX: (787)287-0896
E-mail: info@wwacc.net
URL: http://www.wwacc.net

Description: Worldwide Advertising Consultants provide dozens of services, in which the small, medium, and large business can competitively compete in the Internet market. They provide solutions for publicity, marketing, public relations, promotions, direct marketing, and Internet and E-Commerce Solutions.

∎ 2363

WORLDWIDE IMPACT INC.

30 Boltwood Walk
Amherst, MA 01002
TF: 877-857-6700
FX: (413)253-6701
E-mail: info@worldwideimpact.com
URL: http://www.worldwideimpact.com
Contact: Mr. William Carr, President

Description: Worldwide Impact, Inc. is a full service Internet content developer. They assist their clients in building their business on the web. Worldwide Impact has systems for design and ongoing support of e-commerce solutions.

∎ 2364

WRQ INC.

1500 Dexter Ave. N
Seattle, WA 98109
PH: (206)217-7100
TF: 800-872-2829
FX: (206)217-7515
E-mail: info@wrq.com
URL: http://www.wrq.com

Founded: 1981. **Description:** WRQ offers a variety of services including consulting services, support programs and training courses. Consulting services include integrating customer relationship management systems and automating business processes.

∎ 2365

XAMAX CONSULTANCY PTY. LTD.

78 Sidaway St.
Chapman, ACT 2611, Australia
PH: 61 2 6288 1472
FX: 61 2 6288 6916
E-mail: roger.clarke@xamax.com.au
URL: http://www.xamax.com.au
Contact: Roger Clarke, Consultant & Owner

Founded: 1982. **Description:** Performs consulting assignments in the areas of information management and information technology management, with particular reference to - electronic commerce, information infrastructure and the information economy, and privacy.

∎ 2366

XANSA

Campus 300, Maylands Ave.
Hemel Hempstead HP27TQ, United Kingdom
PH: 448702416181
FX: 441442434242
E-mail: information@xansa.com
URL: http://www.xansa.com
Contact: Ms. Hilary Cropper

Staff: 5120. **Description:** Xansa provides information technology (IT) services to banking, pharmaceuticals, telecommunications, utilities, government, and retail markets in Asia, Europe, and North America. It specializes in large-scale integrated software, particularly applications management. It also offers business consulting, training, IT staffing, and e-commerce services.

∎ 2367

XISOURCE

505 Montgomery St.
San Francisco, CA 94111
PH: (415)887-3456
TF: 877-482-4370
FX: (415)887-3001
E-mail: info@xisource.com
URL: http://www.xisource.com
Contact: Mr. Navin Nagiah, President and CEO

Founded: 2000. **Description:** Xixource is an end to end outsourcing solution for e-commerce services. Xisource solutions empower companies to manage sourcing practices for purchases and optimize supplier relationships.

∎ 2368
XOR INC.

5718 Central Ave.
Boulder, CO 80301
PH: (303)448-4800
TF: 800-XOR-4404
FX: (303)448-4890
E-mail: info@xor.com
URL: http://www.xor.com/index.html
Contact: John Oltman, CEO and Chairman

Description: A provider fo customized eBusiness application and systems management services that help established companies leverage the Internet to measurably reduce costs and increase revenues.

∎ 2369
XORIANT CORP.

165 Nortech Pkwy.
San Jose, CA 95134
PH: (408)635-4400
TF: 888-835-3129
E-mail: info@xoriant.com
URL: http://www.xoriant.com
Contact: Girish Gaitonde Gaitonde, President and Chief Executive Officer

Founded: 1990. **Description:** Xoriant Corporation is a provider of integrated business solutions to the manufacturing and financial services industries. Their suite of products, packaged solutions, training and consulting services assist global clients enhance customer, partner, and value chain relationships. Xoriant delivers e-business solutions through technology strategy, business integration and lifecycle management of systems and applications.

∎ 2370
XPAND CORP

464 Herndon Pkwy.
Herndon, VA 20170
PH: (703)742-0900
FX: (703)742-0935
E-mail: info@xpandcorp.com
URL: http://www.xpandcorp.com

Founded: 1991. **Description:** XPAND Corporation was founded in 1991 to provide consulting, system engineering, integration, and support for distributive and telecommunications systems. XPAND Corporation provides innovative solutions employing cutting edge technology. XPAND's technical staff develops and implements mission critical solutions using the core disciplines that are reshaping the computing landscape now and into the next century.

∎ 2371
XPEDIOR INC.

1 N Franklin, Ste. 1500
Chicago, IL 60606
PH: (312)251-2000
TF: 877-973-3467
FX: (312)251-2999
E-mail: info@xpedior.com
URL: http://www.xpedior.com
Contact: James W. Crownover, Chairman

Revenue: US$8,400,000. **Staff:** 1317. **Description:** Provides comprehensive eBusiness solutions to Global 2000 companies and emerging Internet businesses. eBusiness solutions integrate one or more of the following services, customized to fit a client's needs: digital business strategy, electronic commerce, digital branding and user experience design, ebusiness applications and integration, ebusiness technology management, ebusiness networks, ebusiness intelligence, and enterprise portals and knowledge management.

∎ 2372
XPORTA

275 Saratoga Ave., Ste. 260
Santa Clara, CA 95050
PH: (408)556-1414
TF: (866)490-0853
FX: (408)556-1401
E-mail: contact@xporta.com
URL: http://www.xporta.com
Contact: Antony Awaida, Chairman, CEO & Co-Founder

Founded: 1999. **Description:** XPORTA devlivers universal landed cost solutions to B2B exchanges and e-marketplaces, purchasing and procurement departments, and sales and marketing professionals. XPORTA solutions enable companies to maximize their competitive advantage in global trade., analyzing the impact of origin on all transactions. XPORTA provides assistance to product design teams to select products targeted at selected markets.XPORTA is led by an executive team experienced in e-business, international logistics, transportation, world trade and the high-technology industries.

∎ 2373
XPRAGMA

Mechelsesteenweg 254
2820 Bonheiden, Belgium
PH: 32 015 340845
FX: 32 015 340845
E-mail: info@xpragma.com
URL: http://www.xpragma.com

Description: Xpragma is an independent IT research, analysis and consulting firm. Xpragma provides advice and assistance to companies that want to achieve business excellence, by working towards the successful alignment of IT with their business strategy and objectives. Xpragma provides management and advisory services for organisations that are deploying or planning to deploy strategic initiatives in the domain of e-business.

▮ 2374

XYST MARKETING LTD.

Business and Innovation Centre
Sunderland Enterprise Pk.
Sunderland SR52TA, United Kingdom
PH: 44 191 5166 308
FX: 44 191 5166 309
E-mail: mark@xyst.biz
URL: http://www.xyst.co.uk
Contact: Mr. Mark Irvine, Founder

Description: Xyst Marketing offers a range of consultancy and strategic planning services as well as a full range of marketing services with particular focus and expertise in the Internet.

▮ 2375

YELLOWZONE INC.

16055 Ventura Blvd., Ste. 600
Encino, CA 91436
PH: (818)788-7810
TF: 800-518-9505
FX: (818)788-7845
E-mail: info@yellowzone.com
URL: http://www.yellowzone.com

Founded: 1997. **Description:** The YellowZone company is a full service Internet and software company dedicated to providing solutions to online business demands. Their knowledge of software and web technologie and their inter-active architects and business consultants help clients max-imize their online business opportunity. The YellowZone marketing team will works closely with their clients market-ing staff to provide the best approach for their online needs.

▮ 2376

YOUSH CONSULTING

17 Ebony Gate
Richmond Hill, ON, Canada L4S2C1
PH: (905)508-8377
E-mail: sales@yoush.com
URL: http://www.yoush.com
Contact: Ms. Madeline Sansi, Vice President, Sales and Marketing

Description: Yoush consultants offer solutions to customer contact management, web presence, sales force automation and customer care with consulting in assessment, planning and design and implementation.

▮ 2377

ZEFER CORP.

119 Beach St.
Boston, MA 02111
PH: (617)292-7888
TF: 888-820-8454
FX: (617)292-7880
URL: http://www.zefer.com
Contact: William A. ''Bill'' Seibel, Chairman, President, and CEO

Revenue: US$25,300,000. **Staff:** 481. **Description:** A stra-tegic Internet consulting and services firm. We work with both leading corporations and dot-com startups to design and build new business models for the digital economy-models with the power to fundamentally reshape business dynamics, reinvent whole industries and redefine the nature of competition.

▮ 2378

ZERO DEFECTS SOFTWARE INC.

3741 Walnut St., No. 415
Philadelphia, PA 19104
PH: (215)684-2267
FX: (215)790-2971
E-mail: contact@zerodefect.com
URL: http://www.zerodefect.com

Description: Provides creative and technical services for new media projects, including Internet and multimedia appli-cations. A full service website development company, offer-ing design, hosting, programming, and technical consulting services. Also offers comprehensive creative services, in-cluding graphic design, animation, digital photography, mu-sic composition, sound design, and audio engineering.

▮ 2379

ZOETICS INC.

270 Lafayette St., Ste. 1202
New York, NY 10012-3327
PH: (212)941-8344
FX: (212)941-8348
E-mail: general@zoetics.com
Contact: Joel D. Tucciarone, President, Strategy and Planning

Staff: 12. **Description:** Company provides business market-ing strategy, new product development, Relationship Mar-keting services, Customer Relationship Management, direct marketing, market research, and Internet/e-commerce enter-prise architecture services. **Geographic Area Served:** Worldwide. **Publications:** Journal of Advertising Research.

▌2380

ZYNERGY

215 Celebration Pl., Ste. 500
Celebration, FL 34747
PH: (407)566-2323
E-mail: info@zynergy.com
URL: http://www.zynergy.com
Contact: Mr. James Zimbardi, President

Founded: 1997. **Description:** Zynergy is a traditional marketing and advertising agency and an Internet technology company working to create innovative ways for their clients to increase sales and develop stronger relationships with their existing customers. Zynergy has been working on Internet projects since its creation. Zynergy's efforts are now focused on the area of Marketing Research over the Internet. They offer clients a more cost-effective and faster way to collect and aggregate data through providing Real-Time Web-Based Marketing Research administered through a PDA, website, and/or email.

EDUCATIONAL PROGRAMS

▌2381

THE ABC'S OF E-COMMERCE

JIM WORLD
28432 Via Alfonse
Laguna Niguel, CA 92677
PH: (949)360-9915
E-mail: jim@jimworld.com
URL: http://www.virtualpromote.com/guest5.html

Description: Jim World offers a free online tutorial called ''The A B C's of E-Commerce.'' This tutorial covers topics such as setting up a profitable web site, budgeting, and web site design.

▌2382

THE ABC'S OF E-COMMERCE

EAST TENNESSEE STATE UNIVERSITY
COLLEGE OF BUSINESS, E-COMMERCE
PO Box 70710
Johnson City, TN 37614
E-mail: bergg@etsu.edu
URL: http://ecommerce.etsu.edu/
Contact: Dr. Gary G. Berg

Description: E-Commerce at East Tennessee State University provides traditional coursework focusing on business topics as well as providing resource information which covers E-Commerce topics ranging from website design and security to E-Commerce How To's and a glossary of commonly used terms. The Web site offers a tutorial called ''The ABC's of E-Commerce'' which gives a brief overview of how and when to establish a Web site for entrepreneurs.

▌2383

ACCESSING APPLICATIONS OVER THE INTERNET

NOTRE DAME DE NAMUR UNIVERSITY
1500 Ralston Ave.
Belmont, CA 94002-1997
PH: (650)508-3782
FX: (650)508-3660
E-mail: ebusiness@ndnu.edu
URL: http://www.ndnu.edu

Description: Notre Dame de Namur University offers a graduate course called Accessing Applications Over the Internet. This course researches changes in network based services such as email and video conferencing, and hosted services such as Enterprise Resource Planning and Supply Chain Management. Students will analyze successful hosting and applications services.

▌2384

ACCOUNTING FOR ELECTRONIC BUSINESS

UNIVERSITY OF SCRANTON
Kania School of Management
Brennan Hall, Ste. 438
Scranton, PA 18510
PH: (570)941-7746
E-mail: kakumanu@scranton.edu
URL: http://www.scranton.edu
Contact: Dr. Parsed Kakumanu, Chair, Operation & Info. Mgmt. Dept.

Description: Accounting for Electronic Business is intended to introduce e-commerce students to the role of accounting in today's business environment. Students will examine how technology has impacted the techniques of accounting and reporting and Internet business and traditional business transactions will be evaluated in regards to global markets. Student must complete accounting courses ACC252 or ACC 254 and have junior standing before attempting this course.

▌2385

ADVANCE ELECTRONIC COMMERCE

WEST CHESTER UNIVERSITY OF PENNSYLVANIA
GRADUATE SCHOOL
McKelvie Hall
102 Rosedale Ave.
West Chester, PA 19383-2600
PH: (610)436-2943
E-mail: gradstudy@wcupa.edu
URL: http://www.wcupa.edu/

Description: West Chester University of Pennsylvania offers a graduate level course called Advance Electronic Commerce. In this course students will learn about the concepts, tools, technologies, and strategies connected with the creation and maintenance of an Electronic Commerce business. E-commerce is changing the way organizations conduct business, including how they manufacture, market, and manage their products and services.

■ **2386**

ADVANCED E-BUSINESS APPLICATION DEVELOPMENT

BRIGHAM YOUNG UNIVERSITY

ROLLINS CENTER FOR E-BUSINESS

510 N. Tanner Bldg
PO Box 23068
Provo, UT 84602-3068
PH: (801)422-2815
FX: (801)422-5933
E-mail: ebusiness@byu.edu
URL: http://ebusiness.byu.edu/ebus.cfm
Contact: J. Owen Cherrington, Director

Description: Brigham Young University's Rollins Center for E-Business offers a course called "Advanced E-Business Application Development." This course looks at Unix, PHP, JavaScript, Java, and databases (mySql).

■ **2387**

ADVANCED E-BUSINESS: B2B

UNIVERSITY OF WEST FLORIDA

COLLEGE OF BUSINESS

11000 University Pky.
Pensacola, FL 32514-5752
PH: (850)474-2348
E-mail: ebiz@uwf.edu
URL: http://ebiz.uwf.edu/

Description: The University of West Florida provides a course called "Advanced E-Business: B2B." This course focuses on current trends in B2B, design and implementation issues, customer relationship management, selling chain management, enterprise resource planning, supply chain management, e-procurement, knowledge-tone applications, agents, bots, virtual corporations with virtual employees, global issues, security concerns, and legal implications.

■ **2388**

ADVANCED E-BUSINESS: B2C

UNIVERSITY OF WEST FLORIDA

COLLEGE OF BUSINESS

11000 University Pky.
Pensacola, FL 32514-5752
PH: (850)474-2348
E-mail: ebiz@uwf.edu
URL: http://ebiz.uwf.edu/

Description: The University of West Florida provides an E-business course called "Advanced E-Business: B2C" which addresses the manner in which e-Business is changing the way that firms market their products and services. The course will explore the issues of advertising and selling on the Internet, the use of web sites to provide service and support to customers, consumer decision making when shopping on the Internet, the development of databases which allow customization of products and services to specific customers, and payment and transaction processes.

■ **2389**

ADVANCED ELECTRONIC COMMERCE

WEST CHESTER UNIVERSITY

Office of Graduate Studies
McKelvie Hall
102 Rosedale Ave.
West Chester, PA 19383-2300
PH: (610)436-2943; (610)436-2608
FX: (610)436-2763
E-mail: gradstud@wcupa.edu
URL: http://www.tecmba.org
Contact: Dr. Paul Christ, Director, TEC MBA Program

Description: The primary focus of the Advanced Electronic Commerce course is on the concepts, tools, technologies and strategies connected with the creation and maintenance of an e-commerce business model. The course will show how e-commerce is making it possible to change the way organizations conduct business, including how it manufactures, markets, transacts and manages its product and service. Prerequisites of taking the course include completion of course number TEC501 and ECO501.

■ **2390**

ADVANCED ELECTRONIC COMMERCE

UNIVERSITY OF MEMPHIS

Graduate Admissions Office
216 Administration Bldg.
Memphis, TN 38152-3370
PH: (901)678-2531
E-mail: mgarzon@memphis.edu
URL: http://www.memphis.edu
Contact: Dr. Max Garzon, Program Coordinator

Description: Advanced Electronic Commerce picks up where Contemporary Electronic Commerce leaves off covering marketing related topics and related technology infrastructure.

■ **2391**

ADVANCED GRADUATE STUDIES IN ELECTRONIC COMMERCE

NORWICH UNIVERSITY

158 Harmon Dr.
Northfield, VT 05663
PH: (802)485-2001
TF: 800-468-6679
E-mail: nuadm@norwich.edu
URL: http://www.norwich.edu

Description: Norwich University offers a Certificate of Advanced Graduate Studies in Electronic Commerce. This program offers a more focused look at E-commerce by exploring existing advanced models, reviewing past cases of success and failure, and exploring future technologies.

▌2392

ADVANCED INFORMATION TECHNOLOGIES FOR ELECTRONIC COMMERCE

OKLAHOMA STATE UNIVERSITY

Center for Academic Services
324 Student Union
Stillwater, OK 74078-1012
PH: (405)744-6858
E-mail: admit@okstate.edu
URL: http://www.okstate.edu

Description: Advanced Information Technologies for Electronic Commerce covers information technologies that enable e-commerce including database and web technologies and infrastructure, web software, transaction security, business web models and applications

▌2393

ADVERTISING AND ELECTRONIC COMMERCE

NEW YORK UNIVERSITY
SCHOOL OF CONTINUING AND PROFESSIONAL STUDIES VIRTUAL COLLEGE

10 Astor Pl., 5th Fl.
New York, NY 10003
PH: (212)998-7080
TF: 877-998-7080
E-mail: scpsinfo@nyu.edu
URL: http://www.scps.nyu.edu/dyncon/virt/

Description: NYU's Virtual College offers a course called ''Advertising and Electronic Commerce.'' In this class students will gain understanding of the interrelationships between internet technologies and advertising, as well as look at outlines for different technical options for advertising, and obtain guidelines on how to use internet technologies to develop effective campaigns.

▌2394

ADVERTISING ON THE INTERNET

AMERICAN UNIVERSITY
KOGOD SCHOOL OF BUSINESS

4400 Massachusetts Ave., NW
Washington, DC 20016-8044
PH: (202)885-1900
E-mail: askkogod@american.edu
URL: http://www.kogod.american.edu
Contact: Myron Roomkin, Dean

Description: The American University offers a graduate level course titled ''Advertising on the Internet.'' This course focuses on the creation of an Internet advertising strategy, as well as the use of banners, e-mail advertising, Web sponsorships and media placement decisions. It also looks at controversies surrounding advertisement effectiveness measurement and reviews legal issues.

▌2395

AFFILIATE MASTER COURSE

COMPUTER BASED TRAINING

19 Nations Hill, Kings Worthy
Winchester, Hants SO237QY, United Kingdom
PH: 44 0 1962 883754
FX: 44 0 1962 889177
E-mail: freecourses@computerbasedtraining.co.uk
URL: http://www.computerbasedtraining.co.uk

Description: Computer Based Training offers a free online course called ''Affiliate Master Course.'' Topics covered in this course include developing a product or service, building a web site that sells, and attracting targeted traffic to your site.

▌2396

ANDERSON EXECUTIVE EDUCATION (CMIE)

UNIVERSITY OF CALIFORNIA LOS ANGELES
ANDERSON SCHOOL OF BUSINESS
CENTER FOR MANAGEMENT IN THE INFORMATION ECONOMY

110 Westwood Plz., Ste. C310
Los Angeles, CA 90068
PH: (310)206-0937
FX: (310)794-7053
E-mail: cmie@anderson.ucla.edu
URL: http://www.anderson.ucla.edu/research/cmie/
Contact: Bob Foster, Executive Director

Description: The Center for Management in the Information Economy focuses on current management processes and practices being used in businesses and organizations involved in the creation, management and delivery of digital information. It encompasses all aspects of the information economy including electronic commerce and the Internet. The Center develops and conduct educational conferences, seminars, programs and graduate courses that are directed to students, and industry executives. The Anderson Executive Education program includes courses on managing information and marketing strategy.

▌2397

APPLICATION DEVELOPMENT

MCGILL UNIVERSITY
FACULTY OF MANAGEMENT

1001 Sherbrooke St. W
Montreal, PQ, Canada H3A1G5
PH: (514)398-4000
FX: (514)398-3876
E-mail: gagnon@management.mcgill.ca
URL: http://www.intranet.management.mcgill.ca/course/mis/273434/CO273690_W00.htm

Description: McGill University in Montreal offers a course titled ''Application Development.'' This course looks at the whole range of Web Information Technologies: suites, scripting, multimedia, security, payment, agents, data mining

539

▌2398

ARCHITECTURES FOR THE NEW E-CONOMY

BENTLEY COLLEGE

175 Forest St.
Waltham, MA 02452-4705
PH: (781)891-2000
URL: http://www.bentley.edu

Description: Bentley College offers a graduate level course entitled Architectures for the New E-conomy. This course focuses on how to build, acquire and modify new systems and components; integrate e-business systems; ensure 24/7 reliability and security; identify and assimilate appropriate new information technologies; and deploy IT talent. The course addresses these IT challenges in the context of emerging e-business models.

▌2399

THE ART AND SCIENCE OF ELECTRONIC COMMERCE

UNIVERSITY OF TEXAS AT ARLINGTON

DEPARTMENT OF INFORMATION SYSTEMS AND OPERATIONS MANAGEMENT

Box 19437
Arlington, TX 76019-0437
PH: (817)272-5235
FX: (817)272-5801
E-mail: reimann@uta.edu
URL: http://www.uta.edu/infosys/e_comm/
Contact: Dr. Mike Reimann

Description: "The Art and Science of Electronic Commerce" offered for both undergraduates and graduate students at the University of Texas at Arlington will explore the use of electronic media as an innovative approach for marketing. In this course the area of electronic commerce will be viewed from multiple perspectives. A variety of readings, lectures, guest speakers, and presentations will occur throughout the semester. These are intended to give an overview of elements essential for creating persuasive multi-media presentations.

▌2400

ASSOCIATE OF ARTS DEGREE IN E-COMMERCE

KEISER COLLEGE

1500 NW 49th St.
Fort Lauderdale, FL 33309
PH: (954)776-4476
TF: 800-749-4456
E-mail: admissions@keisercollege.cc.fl.us
URL: http://www.keisercollege.edu

Description: Founded in 1977, Keiser college offers specialized courses in e-commerce. They emphasize Internet marketing strategies, secure transactions, and realistic expectations for Internet business. The history and culture of the Internet are also explored. Students learn basic business, management, and marketing skills. Course work introduces computer fundamentals, including technical language, software choices, and hardware. Students learn the basics of web site design, management, and analysis and are introduced to the legal and ethical issues that pertain to multimedia use, copyrights, and privacy concerns.

▌2401

ASSOCIATES CERTIFICATE IN ELECTRONIC BUSINESS (BCIT)

BRITISH COLUMBIA INSTITUTE OF TECHNOLOGY

ADMINISTRATIVE MANAGEMENT

3700 Willingdon Ave.
Burnaby, BC, Canada V5G3H2
PH: (604)432-8860
E-mail: jean_covell@bcit.ca
URL: http://programs.bcit.ca/program.php3?program=
pt_cert_busi_01
Contact: Jean Covell

Description: The British Columbia Institute of Technology (BCIT) offers an Associates Certificate in Electronic Business. This program can be completed online and offers a curriculum designed to prepare students for conducting business using information technology and the Internet.

▌2402

B2B COMMERCE

CREIGHTON UNIVERSITY

JOE RICKETTS CENTER EXECUTIVE EDUCATION PROGRAMS

2500 California Plz.
Omaha, NE 68178
PH: (402)280-2439
FX: (402)280-5565
E-mail: rnath@creighton.edu
URL: http://www.creighton.edu
Contact: Dr. Ravi Nath, Director, Joe Ricketts Center

Description: Creighton University's Joe Ricketts Center offers an executive education course called B2B Commerce. This course examines e-commerce business-to-business issues such as quality service, management, and communication that are important components for the further development of B2B markets.

▌2403

B2B E-COMMERCE

CARDEAN UNIVERSITY

500 Lake Cook Rd.
Deerfield, IL 60015-5609
TF: (866)948-1289
E-mail: inquires@cardean.edu
URL: http://www.cardean.edu
Contact: Dr. Geoffrey M. Cox, Cardean University President

Description: Cardean University is an accredited online University which offers a course called "B2B E-Commerce." This suite of four two-hour courses provides a look at the role of the Internet in business to business Ecommerce and identifies the major B2B business markets and models. These courses offer professionals an overview of B2B e-commerce, looking at both global purchasing/distribution and the way new customers and suppliers can be gained.

▌2404
B2B E-COMMERCE SUITE
NETG

1751 W Diehl Rd, 2nd Fl.
Naperville, IL 60563-9099
PH: (630)369-3000
TF: 877-561-6384
FX: (630)983-4877
E-mail: info@netg.com
URL: http://www.netg.com

Description: NETg offers a course called B2B E-Commerce Suite. This suite of courses covers the broad area of business-to-business e-commerce. Some topics addressed include supply chain management, the Internet's effect on business, business models and critical success factors.

▌2405
B2B E-COMMERCE (VALUE CHAIN INTEGRATION)
NEW YORK UNIVERSITY
SCHOOL OF CONTINUING AND PROFESSIONAL STUDIES VIRTUAL COLLEGE

10 Astor Pl., 5th Fl.
New York, NY 10003
PH: (212)998-7080
TF: 877-998-7080
E-mail: scpsinfo@nyu.edu
URL: http://www.scps.nyu.edu/dyncon/virt/

Description: NYU's Virtual College offers a course called "B2B E-Commerce (Value Chain Integration)." This course provides understanding of ERP and how it works; how the Internet and ERP function together to produce b2b e-commerce; the place of EDI in the process; electronic catalogs; approval and procedural processes; and integration of master contracts.

▌2406
BACHELOR OF SCIENCE WITH E-COMMERCE CONCENTRATION
OLD DOMINION UNIVERSITY
COLLEGE OF BUSINESS AND PUBLIC ADMINISTRATION

49th St. and Hampton Blvd., Hughes Hall
Norfolk, VA 23529
PH: (757)683-3585
FX: (757)683-5750
E-mail: admit@odu.edu
URL: http://www.odu.edu

Description: Old Dominion University offers a Bachelor of Science degree with a concentration in E-Commerce. Coursework in this program will provide students with training and education in all facets of using technology to manage a business.

▌2407
A BANKER'S GUIDE TO SEARCHING THE INTERNET
DIGITALTHINK INC

601 Brannan St.
San Francisco, CA 94107
PH: (415)625-4000
TF: 888-686-8817
FX: (415)625-4100
E-mail: info@digitalthink.com
URL: http://www.digitalthink.com
Contact: Mr. Pete Goettner, Chairman

Founded: 1996. **Staff:** 450. **Description:** DigitalThink provides an online course entitled "A Banker's Guide to Searching the Internet." Geared towards financial professionals, this class teaches students effective techniques for finding information on the World Wide Web. Students will visit various services, compare their ease of use and the quantity and quality of their results, and perform increasingly complex searches using simple and advanced search queries. This course will provide students with ideas on how to use the Internet to accomplish some of the tasks they face as a banker, such as shopping the competition, gathering information about specific financial services markets, and gathering information about a prospective business customer.

▌2408
THE BASICS
ANITA ROSEN CONSULTING

1798 Vassar Ave.
Mountain View, CA 94043
PH: (650)960-2959
FX: (650)960-2958
E-mail: question@anitarosen.com
URL: http://www.anitarosen.com/E-Commerce-Training.html
Contact: Anita Rosen, Founder

Description: Anita Rosen Consulting offers a free online tutorial called The Basics. In this tutorial students will learn the basics of creating an e-business web site and look at current trends in e-commerce.

▌2409
BASICS OF THE INTERNET (SBA)
U.S. SMALL BUSINESS ADMINISTRATION

409 3rd St. SW
Washington, DC 20416
PH: 800-827-5722
E-mail: classroom@sba.gov
URL: http://www.sba.gov/classroom

Description: The Small Business Administration (SBA) in partnership with Cisco Systems offers a free online course called Basics of the Internet. This course looks at how the Internet works. Students will learn why the Internet could be important to them, as well as learning about technologies and services available.

▪ 2410

BEST PRACTICES KNOWDULE
LOUSIANA STATE UNIVERSITY
CENTER FOR VIRTUAL ORGANIZATION AND COMMERCE
Ourso College of Business
3190 CEBA Bldg.
Baton Rouge, LA 70803
PH: (225)578-2126
E-mail: bives@lsu.edu
URL: http://isds.bus.lsu.edu/cvoc/

Description: The Center for Virtual Organization and Commerce is a global partnership between individual centers at Louisiana State University (USA), University College Dublin (Ireland), and the University of Melbourne in Australia. Its purpose is to create and research worldwide virtual organizations, particularly those involved in electronic commerce and the dissemination of knowledge. One project through the Center, called Best Practices ''Knowdule,'' is designed to give a broad audience foundational knowledge of best practices and technology-enabled best practices.

▪ 2411

BRIDGING ECM TECHNOLOGY AND BUSINESS
SAN JOSE STATE UNIVERSITY
PROFESSIONAL DEVELOPMENT CENTER
3031 Tisch Way, Ste. 200 Plz. E
San Jose, CA 95128
PH: (408)257-3000
E-mail: mitchell.levy.sjsupd@ecnow.com
URL: http://ecmtraining.com/sjsu/
Contact: Mitchell Levy, Program Founder and Coordinator

Description: San Jose State University offers an executive education course called ''Bridging ECM Technology and Business.'' This class looks at key technologies being developed that facilitate networked business processes, and is designed for the business professional and manager who needs to advise, choose, and or implement Internet technology into business flow.

▪ 2412

BUILDING E-BUSINESSES: CRAFTING E-BUSINESS MODELS
HARVARD BUSINESS ONLINE
Harvard Business School Publishing
60 Harvard Way
Boston, MA 02163
PH: (617)783-7600
TF: 800-545-7685
FX: (617)783-7666
E-mail: custserv@hbsp.harvard.edu
URL: http://www.elearning.hbsp.org

Description: Building E-Businesses: Crafting E-Business Models is an online course that explores 17 different online strategies, plus interactive online tools help students put new ideas to work. These include customer experience, e-business models, idea generation and business plan assessment tools.

▪ 2413

BUILDING E-BUSINESSES: CREATING E-BUSINESS VALUE
HARVARD BUSINESS ONLINE
Harvard Business School Publishing
60 Harvard Way
Boston, MA 02163
PH: (617)783-7600
TF: 800-545-7685
FX: (617)783-7666
E-mail: custserv@hbsp.harvard.edu
URL: http://www.elearning.hbsp.org

Description: Building E-Businesses: Creating E-Business Value is an online course that explores how to analyze both short-term and long-term opportunities and how to measure corporate value in the Internet economy, plus interactive online tools help students put new ideas to work. These include e-business value, e-business financial and defining e-business offerings tools.

▪ 2414

BUILDING E-BUSINESSES: DEVELOPING E-BUSINESS CAPABILITIES
HARVARD BUSINESS ONLINE
Harvard Business School Publishing
60 Harvard Way
Boston, MA 02163
PH: (617)783-7600
TF: 800-545-7685
FX: (617)783-7666
E-mail: custserv@hbsp.harvard.edu
URL: http://www.elearning.hbsp.org

Description: Building E-Businesses: Developing E-Business Capabilities is an online that explores new approaches to management, new ways of working with alliance partners and new operating models that harness the power of an Internet-based digital infrastructure, plus interactive online tools help students put new ideas to work. These include capability assessment, entrepreneurial mindset and business plan assessment tools.

▌2415
BUILDING AN E-COMMERCE BUSINESS CASE

NETG

1751 W Diehl Rd, 2nd Fl.
Naperville, IL 60563-9099
PH: (630)369-3000
TF: 877-561-6384
FX: (630)983-4877
E-mail: info@netg.com
URL: http://www.netg.com

Description: NETg offers a course called Building an E-Commerce Business Case. In this course students will learn about consumer transactions, online customer relations, the virtual value chain and how to build online revenues.

▌2416
BUILDING AN E-COMMERCE BUSINESS CASE

UNIVERSITY OF FLORIDA

Office of the University Registrar
Cruiser Hall
PO Box 114000
Gainesville, FL 32611-4000
PH: (352)392-3261; (352)392-1374
URL: http://www.ufl.edu

Description: Building an E-Commerce Business Case provides students with information addressing the relationship between costs and benefits. The intended audience is managers and technical staff who are in a position to provide e-commerce recommendations to executives and will teach them about online revenues, business-to-business transactions, sales and service, online customer relationships and the virtual value chain.

▌2417
BUILDING AN INTERNET-BASED INTERACTIVE ORDER FORM

ELEMENTK

500 Canal View Blvd.
Rochester, NY 14623
PH: (585)240-7500
TF: 800-434-3466
FX: (585)240-7760
URL: http://www.elementk.com

Description: Element K offers an online seminar called "Building an Internet-Based Interactive Order Form." This self-study seminar shows students how to use Visual Basic 6.0 and Internet Information Server applications to build a product order form. Students will create the order page, code the form, build an HTML page and write data into a database.

▌2418
BUSINESS TO BUSINESS INTERNET SYSTEMS

MERCY COLLEGE

555 Broadway
Dobbs Ferry, NY 10522
PH: (914)674-7306
FX: (914)674-7518
E-mail: jdielsi@mercy.edu
URL: http://www.mercy.edu
Contact: John DiElsi, Program Dir.

Description: Mercy College offers a graduate level course called Business to Business Internet Systems. This course examines the use of the Internet in business to business interactions. Topics covered include developing an Internet supply chain, integrating information systems, and creating systems for overseeing business relationships.

▌2419
BUSINESS ENGINEERING FOR E-COMMERCE

UNIVERSITY OF CALIFORNIA EXTENSION ONLINE

2000 Center St., Ste. 400
Berkeley, CA 94704
PH: (510)642-4124
E-mail: askus@ucxonline.berkeley.edu
URL: http://learn.berkely.edu/

Description: The University of California Extension Online offers "Business Engineering for E-Commerce." Taught from a business perspective, this course introduces students to concepts, models, and processes businesses use to develop e-commerce applications. Technology will be emphasized for implementation.

▌2420
BUSINESS ON THE INTERNET

MARSHALL UNIVERSITY

1 John Marshall Dr.
Huntington, WV 25755
PH: (304)696-2314
E-mail: webmaster@marshall.edu
URL: http://www.marshall.edu/muonline/

Description: Marshall University offers an online course called Business on the Internet. This course will teach students about marketing methods available electronically as well as principles of conducting business on the Internet.

▌2421
BUSINESS ISSUES IN ELECTRONIC COMMERCE

CHRISTOPHER NEWPORT UNIVERSITY
CENTER FOR COMMUNITY LEARNING

1 University Place
Newport News, VA 23606-2998
PH: (757)594-7158

FX: (757)594-8736
E-mail: ccl@cnu.edu
URL: http://ec.seva.net/

Description: Christopher Newport University and the Virginia Electronic Commerce Technology Center offer a course called Business Issues in Electronic Commerce. This course gives students an introduction to principles and practices of doing business online using the Internet. Students will learn about e-commerce hardware and software, discuss e-commerce marketing, and develop an e-commerce business plan.

■ **2422**

BUSINESS ISSUES FOR ELECTRONIC COMMERCE

DALHOUSIE UNIVERSITY

Faculty of Computer Science
6050 University Ave.
Halifax, NS, Canada B3H1W5
PH: (902)494-2740
FX: (902)492-1517
E-mail: mec@cs.dal.ca
URL: http://www.ecomm.dal.ca
Contact: Dr. Kori Inkpen, Dir., Master of E-Commerce Program

Description: Business Issues for Electronic Commerce examines the recent and rapid growth of e-commerce from four approaches including an introduction to e-commerce, EDI and re-engineering, e-commerce and the Internet and organizational issues in implementing e-commerce.

■ **2423**

BUSINESS ISSUES IN ELECTRONIC COMMERCE

THE UNIVERSITY OF CALIFORNIA, RIVERSIDE
ANDERSON GRADUATE SCHOOL OF
MANAGEMENT

209 Anderson Hall
Riverside, CA 92521
PH: (909)787-4493
FX: (909)787-3970
E-mail: john.gerdes@ucr.edu
URL: http://condor.ucr.edu/class/gerdes/mgt280f99/index.html
Contact: Dr. John H. Gerdes

Description: The course Business Issues in Electronic Commerce is offered at the University of California Riverside and provides the student with an understanding of the issues and strategic implications of electronic commerce. It investigates different facets of electronic commerce, various business strategies, management issues and pertinent technologies.

■ **2424**

BUSINESS LAW AND PUBLIC POLICY FOR ELECTRONIC COMMERCE

RUTGERS, THE STATE UNIVERSITY OF NEW JERSEY

CENTER FOR INFORMATION MANAGEMENT,
INTEGRATION & CONNECTIVITY

180 University Ave.
Newark, NJ 07102
PH: (973)353-1014
FX: (973)353-5808
E-mail: ec-certificate@cimic.rutgers.edu
URL: http://www.rutgers.edu

Description: Business Law and Public Policy for Electronic Commerce includes information on establishing an Internet business presence, legal elements of e-commerce, Internet activities, public policy issues, electronic contracts, intellectual property protection, tax issues, online crime, Internet speech, E-mail and data privacy, liability for Internet service failures and International Internet issues.

■ **2425**

THE BUSINESS MANAGER'S GUIDE TO E-BUSINESS TECHNOLOGY

HYPERSMITH CONSULTANTS

1020 Mainland St., Ste. 101
Vancouver, BC, Canada V6B2T4
PH: (604)684-7728
E-mail: info@hypersmith.com
URL: http://www.hypersmith.com
Contact: John Foster, President

Description: Hypersmith offers a variety of courses including the The Business Manager's Guide to E-Business Technology. This series of courses addresses topics including databases, web design, networks, security, e-business systems, and knowledge management.

■ **2426**

BUSINESS OPPORTUNITIES (STRATEGY)

MCGILL UNIVERSITY
FACULTY OF MANAGEMENT

1001 Sherbrooke St. W
Montreal, PQ, Canada H3A1G5
PH: (514)398-4000
FX: (514)398-3876
E-mail: gagnon@management.mcgill.ca
URL: http://www.intranet.management.mcgill.ca/course/mis/273434/CO273690_W00.htm

Description: McGill University in Montreal offers a course titled "Business Opportunities (Strategy)" which focuses on analyzing various segments of the Internet to compare the profitability of business models and better appreciate the potential of various technologies.

■ **2427**

BUSINESS-ORIENTED RESOURCE ALLOCATION POLICIES

GEORGE MASON UNIVERSITY

E-CENTER FOR EXCELLENCE IN RESEARCH AND EDUCATION FOR E-BUSINESS

4400 University Dr.
Fairfax, VA 22030-4444
PH: (703)993-1661
E-mail: kersch@gmu.edu
URL: http://eceb.gmu.edu/
Contact: Dr. Larry Kerschberg, Co-Director

Description: The George Mason University E-Center for Excellence in Research and Education for E-Business works with industry and government to establish research and educational programs to generate and share e-business knowledge regionally, nationally and internationally. Conferences and symposiums for executives, as well as traditional coursework for university students are offered on E-Business topics. Research topics include Business-oriented Resource Allocation Policies, which studies how resources of an e-commerce site affect earnings.

▮ 2428
BUSINESS STRATEGY IN THE DIGITAL AGE
ILLINOIS INSTITUTE OF TECHNOLOGY
STUART GRADUATE SCHOOL OF BUSINESS

565 W Adams St.
Chicago, IL 60661
PH: (312)906-6500
FX: (312)906-6549
E-mail: degrees@stuart.iit.edu
URL: http://www.stuart.iit.edu

Description: The Illinois Institute of Technology Stuart Graduate School of Business offers a course entitled Business Strategy in the Digital Age. This capstone course of the E-Commerce program examines case studies and theories of business strategy that allow students to appreciate running a business from the executive's point of view, and what criteria for decision-making are faced daily by senior business and technology executives.

▮ 2429
BUSINESS STRATEGY IN THE NEW ECONOMY
BRIGHAM YOUNG UNIVERSITY
ROLLINS CENTER FOR E-BUSINESS

510 N. Tanner Bldg
PO Box 23068
Provo, UT 84602-3068
PH: (801)422-2815
FX: (801)422-5933
E-mail: ebusiness@byu.edu
URL: http://ebusiness.byu.edu/ebus.cfm
Contact: J. Owen Cherrington, Director

Description: Brigham Young University's Rollins Center for E-Business offers a course titled "Business Strategy in the New Economy." This MBA level course explores structure and economics of the new economy, Internet infrastructure and business strategy, and organizing for change.

▮ 2430
BUSINESS TRANSFORMATION IN THE DIGITAL AGE
ILLINOIS INSTITUTE OF TECHNOLOGY
STUART GRADUATE SCHOOL OF BUSINESS

565 W Adams St.
Chicago, IL 60661
PH: (312)906-6500
FX: (312)906-6549
E-mail: degrees@stuart.iit.edu
URL: http://www.stuart.iit.edu

Description: The Illinois Institute of Technology Stuart Graduate School of Business offers a course entitled Business Transformation in the Digital Age. This course undertakes to understand human behavior embedded in contemporary corporate culture in order to develop effective business teams that achieve results.

▮ 2431
CASE STUDIES
UNIVERSITY OF MINNESOTA EXTENSION SERVICE

240 Coffey Hall
1420 Eckles Ave.
St. Paul, MN 55108-6068
PH: (612)624-1222
E-mail: mainstreet@extension.umn.edu
URL: http://www.extension.umn.edu/mainstreet/curriculum/index.html

Description: The University of Minnesota Extension Service offers a course called Case Studies. This course focuses on case studies of e-commerce businesses as a way to learn about effective strategies in web site design and other aspects of e-commerce.

▮ 2432
CASE STUDIES IN ELECTRONIC COMMERCE (BCIT)
BRITISH COLUMBIA INSTITUTE OF TECHNOLOGY
ADMINISTRATIVE MANAGEMENT

3700 Willingdon Ave.
Burnaby, BC, Canada V5G3H2
PH: (604)451-7134
E-mail: wendy_lee@bcit.ca
URL: http://online.bcit.ca/de/Ecomm.htm
Contact: Wendy Lee

Description: The British Columbia Institute of Technology (BCIT) offers an online course called "Case Studies in Electronic Commerce." This course looks at events in Internet trade and e-Business. Case studies will include successes, failures and new and evolving business. The course is based on team participation and case studies.

■ 2433
CASE STUDY: E-BUSINESS STRATEGY
WALDEN UNIVERSITY

155 5th Ave. S
Minneapolis, MN 55401
PH: (612)338-7224
TF: 800-925-3368
FX: (612)338-5092
E-mail: info@waldenu.edu
URL: http://www.waldenu.edu

Description: Walden University offers an MBA course called "Case Study: E-Business Strategy." This class looks at business-to-business (B2B) issues and business strategies. This course also analyzes case studies of business fundamentals and improvements. A business plan outline, strategy for the Internet, and insights into the criteria used by investors to make funding decisions for new companies are also included in this course.

■ 2434
CENTER FOR TECHNOLOGY AND ADVANCED COMMERCE
UNIVERSITY OF NORTH CAROLINA AT CHAPEL HILL

KENAN INSTITUTE OF PRIVATE ENTERPRISE

Campus Box No. 3440
Chapel Hill, NC 27599-3440
PH: (919)962-0500
FX: (919)962-8202
E-mail: ctac@unc.edu
URL: http://www.kenaninstitute.unc.edu/Centers/CTAC/ctac.cfm
Contact: Dr. Albert Segars, Director

Description: Providing educational programs for business leaders, the community, and university students, the Center for Technology and Advanced Commerce at the University of North Carolina at Chapel Hill works to create and disseminate knowledge to help organizations prosper in the digital marketplace. Outreach programs are offered for public schools and business attempting to develop new technologies.

■ 2435
CERTIFICATE IN E-BUSINESS
CAPELLA UNIVERSITY

222 S 9th St., 20th Fl.
Minneapolis, MN 55402
PH: (612)339-8650
TF: 888-227-3552
FX: (612)339-8022
URL: http://www.capella.edu

Description: The Certificate in E-Business helps prepare professionals for leadership roles in their organizations by strengthening their ability to design, develop and manage e-business strategies including those that leverage e-commerce and online communities as part of their overall business plan. To earn certification a total of 16 credits must be obtained, four of which must be from the Intro to E-Business course with the remaining 12 from any combination of MBA approved e-commerce courses.

■ 2436
CERTIFICATE IN E-COMMERCE
E-LEARNING CENTER.COM

4308 Heather Ln.
Tyler, TX 75703
PH: (903)245-4669
TF: 877-437-5265
E-mail: learn@e-learningcenter.com
URL: http://www.e-learningcenter.com/e-commerce.htm

Description: The E-Learning Center provides online courses for the CEC, Certificate in E-Commerce. In partnership with Mindleaders, the E-Learning Center's program will provide students with a solid understanding of the fundamentals of e-commerce.

■ 2437
CERTIFICATE IN E-COMMERCE
MINDLEADERS

851 W 3rd Ave., Bldg. 3
Columbus, OH 43212
PH: (614)781-7300
TF: 800-223-3732
FX: (614)781-6510
E-mail: webrequest@mindleaders.com
URL: http://www.mindleaders.com

Description: MindLeaders provides online learning courses, including a certificate in E-Commerce. This certificate (the Cec) is earned after the completion of 13 interactive courses which will give the student competency in a variety of e-commerce skills. The CeC is recognized by the American E-Commerce Association, as well as by many other associations in the United States, Europe, Canada, and Asia.

■ 2438
CERTIFICATE IN E-COMMERCE
UNIVERSITY OF CALIFORNIA EXTENSION ONLINE

2000 Center St., Ste. 400
Berkeley, CA 94704
PH: (510)642-4124
E-mail: askus@ucxonline.berkeley.edu
URL: http://learn.berkely.edu/

Description: The University of California Extension Online offers a range of online e-commerce courses which can be taken individually or to earn a Certificate in E-Commerce. Current courses cover topics such as marketing for e-commerce, e-commerce business and technology, e-commerce Internet strategies, business engineering for e-commerce, e-commerce systems design, integration and deployment, and crafting the e-business model.

■ **2439**

CERTIFICATE IN E-COMMERCE-3 COURSE SEQUENCE WITH SOFTWARE

JER GROUP INC.

ONLINEWORKSHOPS.COM

56 Seabreeze Way
Dawsonville, GA 30534
PH: (706)216-3406
FX: (706)216-3979
E-mail: drjer@jergroup.com
URL: http://www.onlineworkshops.com
Contact: Dr. John E. Reid, Jr., President

Description: JER Group Inc. offers an online E-Commerce Certificate course series called ''Certificate in E-Commerce-3 Course Sequence with Software.'' This three-course series will provide students with skills to set up a business on the Internet. Onlineworkshops.com has combined three workshops that offer the beginner the needed tools and information to achieve success. Online facilitators are professionals in the field and will deliver techniques and methods that students can apply in an interactive web-based environment.

■ **2440**

CERTIFICATE IN E-COMMERCE MANAGEMENT

DREXEL UNIVERSITY

LEBOW COLLEGE OF BUSINESS

3141 Chestnut St.
Matheson Hall, Rm. 105
Philadelphia, PA 19104
PH: (215)895-6070
FX: (215)895-1012
E-mail: marcos@drexel.edu.
URL: http://www.drexel.edu/academics/lebow/ecomm/

Description: Drexel University offers a Certificate in E-Commerce Management. This program is designed for middle and upper management, and entrepreneurs who want to help their organization with its e-commerce business. In this program students will learn about new electronic commerce technologies and how to use them, identify new e-commerce opportunities, and learn to understand the legal and regulatory climate for e-commerce.

■ **2441**

CERTIFICATE PROGRAM IN ELECTRONIC COMMERCE

CHRISTOPHER NEWPORT UNIVERSITY ONLINE

1 University Pl.
Newport News, VA 23606
PH: (757)594-7607
E-mail: online@cnu.edu
URL: http://ec.seva.net/

Description: Christopher Newport University and the Virginia Electronic Commerce Technology Center offer a Certificate Program in Electronic Commerce. Designed for business managers and executives, this program allows students an opportunity to increase their skills and knowledge in the theory, practices, and processes of electronic commerce.

■ **2442**

CERTIFICATE PROGRAM IN ELECTRONIC COMMERCE

NEW YORK UNIVERSITY

SCHOOL OF CONTINUING AND PROFESSIONAL STUDIES VIRTUAL COLLEGE

10 Astor Pl., 5th Fl.
New York, NY 10003
PH: (212)998-7080
TF: 877-998-7080
E-mail: scpsinfo@nyu.edu
URL: http://www.scps.nyu.edu/dyncon/virt/

Description: NYU's Virtual College offers a certificate program in Electronic Commerce. Students completing the 4 course requirement will gain an overview of applications and services provided on the Internet as well as being able to focus on particular areas of e-business such as B2B, customer relationship management (CRM), security and advertising.

■ **2443**

CERTIFICATE PROGRAM IN ELECTRONIC COMMERCE (ECC)

UNIVERSITY OF TEXAS AT ARLINGTON

DIGITAL SOCIETY ALLIANCE

7300 Jack Newell Blvd. S
Ft. Worth, TX 76118
PH: (817)272-5914
E-mail: reimann@uta.edu
URL: http://www2.uta.edu/ecomm/
Contact: Dr. Michael Reimann, Director

Description: The University of Texas at Arlington Digital Society Alliance offers a certificate program in Electronic Commerce (eCC) which is targeted at individuals who want to expand their expertise in technologies for creating state-of-the-art eCommerce websites. This certificate requires that entering students are proficient in information technology. The eCC familiarizes students with new eCommerce concepts and web development.

■ **2444**

CERTIFIED E-COMMERCE CONSULTANT

BRIGHAM YOUNG UNIVERSITY

ROLLINS CENTER FOR E-BUSINESS

510 N. Tanner Bldg
PO Box 23068
Provo, UT 84602-3068
PH: (801)422-2815
FX: (801)422-5933
E-mail: e.education@byu.edu
URL: http://ebiz.byu.edu/~jsd47/3
Contact: J. Owen Cherrington, Director

547

Description: Brigham Young University's Rollins Center for E-Business offers Extended Education Programs, with the opportunity to earn certification as a Certified E-Commerce Consultant. This certification is a validation of e-business skills, experience and education.

▌2445
CERTIFIED INTERNET MARKETER WORKSHOP
JER GROUP INC.
ONLINEWORKSHOPS.COM
56 Seabreeze Way
Dawsonville, GA 30534
PH: (706)216-3406
FX: (706)216-3979
E-mail: drjer@jergroup.com
URL: http://www.onlineworkshops.com
Contact: Dr. John E. Reid, Jr., President

Description: JER Group Inc. offers an online course called "Certified Internet Marketer Workshop." This workshop is designed to help students expand and apply their understanding of Internet Marketing techniques. Topics this workshop covers include arranging a functional database and communicating to it via email marketing campaigns, as well as improving your sales positioning and managing client expectations.

▌2446
CHANGE MANAGEMENT FOR E-BUSINESS SUCCESS
UNIVERSITY OF WISCONSIN-MADISON
CONSORTIUM FOR GLOBAL ELECTRONIC COMMERCE
Room 266D Mechanical Engineering Bldg.
1513 University Ave.
Madison, WI 53706
PH: (608)262-0861
FX: (608)262-8454
E-mail: raj@engr.wisc.edu
URL: http://cgec.engr.wisc.edu
Contact: Dr. Raj Veeramani, Director

Description: The University of Wisconsin Consortium for Global Electronic Commerce is a "university-industry collaborative initiative to create, integrate, transfer and apply knowledge of e-commerce and e-business technologies, business processes and organizational strategies to enhance the competitiveness of industry." Focus areas include eMarketing, Electronic Security, and Outsourcing. The Consortium offers an interactive seminar titled Change Management for E-Business Success with panel presentations covering basic concepts as well as more specific issues.

▌2447
CHARACTERIZING ELECTRONIC COMMERCE SITES
MICHIGAN STATE UNIVERSITY
Telecommunication
409 Communication Arts Bldg.
East Lansing, MI 48824

PH: (517)355-8372
URL: http://www.msu.edu

Description: Characterizing Electronic Commerce Sites gives students an introductory working level of knowledge of several aspects of e-commerce including the main players involved in e-commerce, technological fundamentals of web-based commerce, design of e-commerce sites, basic legal and policy issues raised by the development of e-commerce, factors associated with the success or failure of an e-commerce, components of e-commerce transactions, marketing and advertising strategies that can support e-commerce and organizational impacts of e-commerce.

▌2448
COMMERCE IN THE DIGITAL AGE
CREIGHTON UNIVERSITY
COLLEGE OF BUSINESS ADMINISTRATION
2500 California Plz.
Omaha, NE 68178
PH: (402)280-2602
FX: (402)280-2172
E-mail: ghafer@creighton.edu
URL: http://www.creighton.edu
Contact: Ms. Gail Hafer, Graduate Coordinator

Description: Creighton University offers a graduate level course called Commerce in the Digital Age. This course introduces the concepts of electronic commerce as facilitated by the Internet, World Wide Web, and other technologies. Topics covered include: the catalysts for e-commerce (business-to-business and business-to-customer), convergence of technologies and capabilities, legal and regulatory framework, behavior and educational challenges, and strategies for e-commerce success.

▌2449
COMMUNICATION TECHNOLOGIES FOR E-COMMERCE
UNIVERSITY OF WISCONSIN-MADISON
SCHOOL OF BUSINESS
975 University Ave.
Madison, WI 53706
PH: (608)262-1550
E-mail: uwmadmba@bus.wisc.edu
URL: http://instruction.bus.wisc.edu/courses/op_listings/765.htm

Description: The University of Wisconsin provides a course titled "Communication Technologies for E-Commerce." This course looks at basic concepts of data communications, networking, internetworking and telecommunication strategies for modern business.

▌2450
COMPETITION IN ELECTRONIC COMMERCE
KRANNERT SCHOOL OF MANAGEMENT
Purdue University
1310 Krannert Bldg.
West Lafayette, IN 47907

PH: (765)496-3384
FX: (765)494-9841
E-mail: jdietz@mgmt.purdue.edu
URL: http://www.mgmt.purdue.edu
Contact: Joy Dietz, Manager of Advising and Student Services

Description: Competition in Electronic Commerce focuses on identifying and highlighting issues pertaining to business models that firms employ in e-commerce, organizational challenges and transitions in Internet commerce, sustaining value in cyberspace and entry into cyberspace by new and established firms.

∎ 2451
COMPETITIVE STRATEGIES FOR E-BUSINESS
BELLEVUE UNIVERSITY

1000 Galvin Rd. S
Bellevue, NE 68005
PH: (402)293-2000
TF: 800-756-7920
FX: (402)293-2020
URL: http://www.bellevue.edu

Description: Bellevue University offers a course called "Competitive Strategies for E-Business." Topics covered in this course that looks at technological and economic change include: strategic planning and management, fast-cycle management, gathering market intelligence, corporate restructuring, and global business strategy.

∎ 2452
COMPUTER SECURITY FOR E-BUSINESS
BELLEVUE UNIVERSITY

1000 Galvin Rd. S
Bellevue, NE 68005
PH: (402)293-2000
TF: 800-756-7920
FX: (402)293-2020
URL: http://www.bellevue.edu

Description: Bellevue University offers a course called "Computer Security for E-Business." This course will look at methods of assuring secure and confidential transmission of information. Topics include: secure hardware; intrusion detection and countermeasures, digital signatures, encryption, password attacks, public key certificates, firewalls, virus detection and removal, and copy and counterfeit detection.

∎ 2453
COMPUTER SECURITY, PRIVACY AND POLICY
BENTLEY COLLEGE

175 Forest St.
Waltham, MA 02452-4705
PH: (781)891-2000
URL: http://www.bentley.edu

Description: Bentley College offers a graduate level course called Computer Security, Privacy and Policy. This course focuses on online privacy and security from the legal, ethical, and organizational perspectives. Other topics addresses include using technology to manage privacy and management issues relating to online security.

∎ 2454
CONTEMPORARY ELECTRONIC COMMERCE
UNIVERSITY OF MEMPHIS

Graduate Admissions Office
216 Administration Bldg.
Memphis, TN 38152-3370
PH: (901)678-2531
E-mail: mgarzon@memphis.edu
URL: http://www.memphis.edu
Contact: Dr. Max Garzon, Program Coordinator

Description: Contemporary Electronic Commerce focuses on Business-to-Consumer aspects of e-commerce. Its main components are marketing related topics and related technology infrastructure.

∎ 2455
CRAFTING THE E-BUSINESS MODEL
UNIVERSITY OF CALIFORNIA EXTENSION ONLINE

2000 Center St., Ste. 400
Berkeley, CA 94704
PH: (510)642-4124
E-mail: askus@ucxonline.berkeley.edu
URL: http://learn.berkely.edu/

Description: The University of California Extension Online's class "Crafting the E-Business Model" encourages students to analyze and rethink existing business models. Students will also build new models that produce quantifiable results to grow businesses. This course focuses on e-commerce business strategies. Students will be confronted with the issues that companies face when creating an e-business or moving an existing business into the e-world.

∎ 2456
CREATING COMMUNICATION SYNERGY IN THE EWORLD
CALIFORNIA STATE UNIVERSITY, FULLERTON
UNIVERSITY EXTENDED EDUCATION

800 N State College Blvd.
Fullerton, CA 92834-6870
PH: (714)278-2611
FX: (714)278-2088
URL: http://www.takethelead.fullerton.edu/Classes/

Description: Cal State Fullerton offers a course called "Creating Communication Synergy in the eWorld." This course looks at building the team of marketing, general business management, IT, and customer service, and combining ideas with technology to increase profitability.

549

▌ 2457

CREATING THE E-BUSINESS

UNIVERSITY OF PHOENIX

3201 E Elwood St.
Phoenix, AZ 85034
PH: (480)966-5394
TF: 800-366-9699
URL: http://www.uoponline.com

Description: As the capstone course for its MBA in E-Business, the University of Phoenix offers a course entitled Creating the E-Business. This course integrates skills learned in previous e-business courses. Students will develop a design for all elements of an e-business, either creating an original e-business or converting an existing business. A convincing argument for why the business will be financially successful will be a vital part of the course.

▌ 2458

CREATING THE E-BUSINESS STRATEGY

SAN JOSE STATE UNIVERSITY

PROFESSIONAL DEVELOPMENT CENTER

3031 Tisch Way, Ste. 200 Plz. E
San Jose, CA 95128
PH: (408)257-3000
E-mail: mitchell.levy.sjsupd@ecnow.com
URL: http://ecmtraining.com/sjsu/
Contact: Mitchell Levy, Program Founder and Coordinator

Description: San Jose State University offers an executive education class called ''Creating the E-Business Strategy.'' This course will give students understanding of the e-business strategic planning process and techniques for achieving alignment across the business. Topics discussed include building successful strategies for e-marketing, e-selling, e-support, e-supply chain, and e-workforce.

▌ 2459

CREATING AN EFFECTIVE WEB USER INTERFACE

ECNOW.COM

21265 Stevens Creek Blvd., Ste. 205
Cupertino, CA 95014
PH: (408)257-3000
FX: (603)843-0769
E-mail: info@ecnow.com
URL: http://ecnow.com/courses/mgt04.htm

Description: ECnow.com offers a course called Creating an Effective Web User Interface. This course uses a cross-disciplinary approach to user interface. It looks at how visual designers, information architects and database engineers collaborate to build a user interface for websites and web applications.

▌ 2460

CREATING AND IMPLEMENTING THE ECRM MASTER PLAN

CALIFORNIA STATE UNIVERSITY, FULLERTON

UNIVERSITY EXTENDED EDUCATION

800 N State College Blvd.
Fullerton, CA 92834-6870
PH: (714)278-2611
FX: (714)278-2088
URL: http://www.takethelead.fullerton.edu/Classes/

Description: Cal State Fullerton offers a course called ''Creating and Implementing the eCRM Master Plan.'' In this course students will work on a simulated project using case studies as a basis. Students will develop implement an eCRM strategic plan, and develop techniques for measuring the success of their plan.

▌ 2461

CREATING INTERNET-BASED APPLICATIONS

UNIVERSITY OF MICHIGAN SCHOOL OF BUSINESS

E-LAB

701 Tappan Street
Ann Arbor, MI 48109-1234
PH: (734)763-5796
E-mail: samoore@umich.edu
URL: http://elab-unix1.bus.umich.edu/index.php
Contact: Scott Moore, Faculty Director, E-Lab

Description: The University of Michigan School of Business offers courses such as Creating Internet-based Applications, which is geared to entry-level students and covers the design and implementation of a Web site. The School of Business also provides the E-Lab as a technology incubator for faculty and students. Testing Internet-based projects or products in the hope of developing a business, as well as providing coursework online are some of the functions of the E-lab.

▌ 2462

CREATING AND MANAGING YOUR E-COMMERCE INITIATIVES

ECNOW.COM

21265 Stevens Creek Blvd., Ste. 205
Cupertino, CA 95014
PH: (408)257-3000
FX: (603)843-0769
E-mail: info@ecnow.com
URL: http://ecnow.com/courses/mgt04.htm

Description: ECnow.com offers a course called Creating and Managing Your E-Commerce Initiatives. This tutorial provides information on how to effectively deploy, manage, and utilize technology in business. Topics covered include the business case for e-commerce, enlisting management support, and communicating and measuring results.

▌2463

CREATING A WINNING E-BUSINESS

NETG

1751 W Diehl Rd, 2nd Fl.
Naperville, IL 60563-9099
PH: (630)369-3000
TF: 877-561-6384
FX: (630)983-4877
E-mail: info@netg.com
URL: http://www.netg.com

Description: NETg offers a course called Creating a Winning E-Business. This course serves as a guide to getting an online business off the ground. It begins with idea generation and progresses through business plans to creating and maintaining an e-business site.

▌2464

CRM AND CALL CENTER INTEGRATION IN THE E-BUSINESS ENTERPRISE

GW CENTER FOR PROFESSIONAL DEVELOPMENT

2029 K Street NW, Ste. 600
Washington, DC 20006
PH: (202)973-1150
FX: (202)973-1165
E-mail: cpd@gwu.edu
URL: http://www.gwu.edu/~cpd/programs/CWEC/

Description: The GW Center for Professional Development offers a course called "CRM and Call Center Integration in the E-Business Enterprise." This course looks at the processes in CRM by which sales and support teams work together, multiple sales channels are supported, and business processes are integrated.

▌2465

CUSTOMER RELATIONSHIP MANAGEMENT

SOLOMON D. TRUJILLO CENTER FOR E.BUSINESS

University of Wyoming
College of Business
PO Box 3275
Laramie, WY 82071
PH: (307)766-6902
E-mail: e-biz@uwyo.edu
URL: http://www.uwyo.edu
Contact: Dr. Kenton Walker, Director

Description: Customer Relationship Management deals with the requirement of electronic assistance in e-commerce and the methods for helping customers electronically to ensure that they have questions answered promptly, obtain help when needed and can complain if dissatisfied.

▌2466

CUSTOMER RELATIONSHIP MANAGEMENT

UNIVERSITY OF DELAWARE
E-COMMERCE PROGRAM

206 John M. Clayton Hall
Newark, DE 19716-7410
PH: (302)831-2741
E-mail: continuing-ed@udel.edu
URL: http://www.continuingstudies.udel.edu/it/ecomm/index.shtml

Description: The University of Delaware's Continuing Studies Program offers a course entitled "Customer Relationship Management." This course teaches effective Customer Relationship Management (CRM) techniques, and examines getting, keeping and growing customers.

▌2467

CYBER LAW

PURDUE UNIVERSITY
KRANNERT GRADUATE SCHOOL OF MANAGEMENT

1310 Krannert Bldg.
West Lafayette, IN 47907
PH: (765)494-9700
FX: (765)494-9658
E-mail: krannert_ms@mgmt.purdue.edu
URL: http://www.mgmt.purdue.edu/centers/ceer/

Description: Purdue University's Krannert Graduate School of Management offers a course entitled Cyber Law. This course covers topics including regulation of cyberspace, legal jurisdiction over cyberspace, intellectual property, copyrights, on-line contracts, taxation, and on-line securities offerings.

▌2468

CYBER LAW

FOX SCHOOL-TEMPLE UNIVERSITY

Speakman Hall, Rm. 5
Philadelphia, PA 19122
PH: (215)204-7678
E-mail: foxmbams.info@temple.edu
URL: http://www.sbm.temple.edu

Description: Cyber Law focuses on the legal issues surrounding the world of Electronic Commerce and will examine the needs of business managers in the online environment. Topics include business uses of Internet technology, intellectual property issues in Cyberspace, contract creation and enforcement, taxation, online security offerings, privacy, obscenity, defamation and computer crimes. The course will address these issues in a practical, business-oriented fashion and also includes a discussion of relevant laws and judicial decisions.

■ 2469

CYBER LAW

KRANNERT SCHOOL OF MANAGEMENT

Purdue University
1310 Krannert Bldg.
West Lafayette, IN 47907
PH: (765)496-3384
FX: (765)494-9841
E-mail: jdietz@mgmt.purdue.edu
URL: http://www.mgmt.purdue.edu
Contact: Joy Dietz, Manager of Advising and Student Services

Description: Cyber Law covers the laws affecting e-commerce and covers such topics as the regulations of cyberspace, intellectual property rights, copyrights, online contracts, taxation and online security. This is an eight-week course with Phillip Scaletta as the current instructor.

■ 2470

DATA COMMUNICATIONS

THE UNIVERSITY OF TEXAS AT AUSTIN
CENTER FOR RESEARCH IN ELECTRONIC COMMERCE

Department of MSIS, CBA 5.202
Austin, TX 78712
PH: (512)471-7962
FX: (512)471-0587
E-mail: abw@uts.cc.utexas.edu
URL: http://crec.bus.utexas.edu
Contact: Dr. Andrew B. Whinston, Director

Description: Offering courses both online and in a traditional university setting, the University of Texas Center for Research in Electronic Commerce also sponsors multidisciplinary research programs and encourages collaboration with industry leaders. The Center offers a course titled Data Communications which aims to train IS professionals in techincal, managerial, and economic issues related to data communication and distributed processing.

■ 2471

DATA FOR EBUSINESS

TEXAS CHRISTIAN UNIVERSITY

The Neeley School of Business
TCU Box 298530
Fort Worth, TX 76129
PH: (817)257-7540
E-mail: j.mackay@tcu.edu
URL: http://www.tcu.edu
Contact: Dr. Jane Mackay, Program Director

Description: The Data for eBusiness (EBUS 30823) course teaches students solid database principles. Students will also be exposed to how data relates to eBusiness through such topics as data warehousing, use of consumer data for marketing, financial data available on the Internet and data and information reporting. Students must complete EBUS 20813 with a grade of C or better before taking this course.

■ 2472

DATA MINING

UNIVERSITY OF MARYLAND
SMITH SCHOOL OF BUSINESS

Van Munching Hall
College Park, MD 20742
PH: (301)405-2278
E-mail: info@hsmith.umd.edu
URL: http://ecommerce.umd.edu/

Description: The University of Maryland Smith School of Business offers an MBA seminar course entitled ''Data Mining.'' This seminar will focus on methods and tools for turning large quantities of data into information useful for managerial decision making.

■ 2473

DATA MINING TECHNIQUES FOR BUSINESS

CREIGHTON UNIVERSITY
COLLEGE OF BUSINESS ADMINISTRATION

2500 California Plz.
Omaha, NE 68178
PH: (402)280-2602
FX: (402)280-2172
E-mail: ghafer@creighton.edu
URL: http://www.creighton.edu
Contact: Ms. Gail Hafer, Graduate Coordinator

Description: Creighton University offers a graduate level course called Data Mining Techniques for Business. This course focuses on extracting information and knowledge from large databases. Methods of using this data, such as uncovering factors that affect purchasing patterns and identifying potential profitable investments and opportunities, are also explored.

■ 2474

DATABASE MANAGEMENT FOR ELECTRONIC BUSINESS

UNIVERSITY OF SCRANTON

Kania School of Management
Brennan Hall, Ste. 438
Scranton, PA 18510
PH: (570)941-7746
E-mail: kakumanu@scranton.edu
URL: http://www.scranton.edu
Contact: Dr. Parsed Kakumanu, Chair, Operation & Info. Mgmt. Dept.

Description: Database Management for Electronic Business deals with database design, implementation and use of Database Management Systems to support e-commerce. Covered topics will include data modeling and structured query language, distributed database management system, open database connectivity, integration of web server and backend database server, data warehousing and mining, online analytical processing and database application and management. Students must complete Intro to E-Business before taking this class.

■ 2475

DATABASE WAREHOUSING, MINING AND BUSINESS INTELLIGENCE

NOTRE DAME

COLLEGE OF BUSINESS

276 Mendoza College of Business
Notre Dame, IN 46556
PH: (219)631-8488
TF: 800-631-8488
FX: (219)631-8800
E-mail: mba.1@nd.edu
URL: http://www.nd.edu/~mba
Contact: Carolyn Woo, Dean

Description: The Notre Dame MBA Program offers a course called ''Database Warehousing, Mining and Business Intelligence.'' This course involves discussion of the administration of the data warehouse including transaction management, data management, information supply chain and the data warehouse interface using the Web as a delivery system. Data mining enabling technologies and data mining methods will be discussed using management perspectives.

■ 2476

DATABASES AND DATA MINING FOR ELECTRONIC COMMERCE

DALHOUSIE UNIVERSITY

Faculty of Computer Science
6050 University Ave.
Halifax, NS, Canada B3H1W5
PH: (902)494-2740
FX: (902)492-1517
E-mail: mec@cs.dal.ca
URL: http://www.ecomm.dal.ca
Contact: Dr. Kori Inkpen, Dir., Master of E-Commerce Program

Description: Databases and Data Mining for Electronic Commerce covers key issues in data warehouse architecture; design of data warehouses; creation, development and maintenance of warehouses; and tools and techniques for querying, analyzing and mining the warehouse data.

■ 2477

DECISION TECHNOLOGIES FOR E-BUSINESS

UNIVERSITY OF MINNESOTA

CARLSON SCHOOL OF MANAGEMENT

321 19th Ave. S.
Minneapolis, MN 55455
PH: (612)624-8030
FX: (612)626-1316
E-mail: mbawebmaster@csom.umn.edu
URL: http://www.csom.umn.edu/

Description: The Carlson School of Management at the University of Minnesota offers a graduate level course called ''Decision Technologies for E-Business.'' This course covers technologies as well as business applications in areas such as revenue yield management in the hospitality and travel industries, e-business intelligence in supply chain management, and support of consumer decision making for Web-based purchasing.

■ 2478

DESIGNING FOR DOLLARS: DISCOVERING HOW PEOPLE BUY ONLINE

USER INTERFACE ENGINEERING

242 Neck Rd.
Bradford, MA 01835
PH: (978)374-8300
FX: (978)374-9175
E-mail: uie@uie.com
URL: http://world.std.com/~uieweb/courses.htm

Description: User Interface Engineering offers a course called Designing for Dollars: Discovering How People Buy Online. This course is offered at User Interface's sites in Boston, Austin, Seattle, and San Francisco; or can be offered at an individual company's place of business. In this course students will learn to turn visitors into customers. This course will discuss many common problems that stop visitors from completing purchases on e-commerce sites, and provide sound ideas for solutions.

■ 2479

DESIGNING EFFECTIVE WEBSITES: A MARKETING PERSPECTIVE

HARVARD UNIVERSITY

HARVARD EXTENSION SCHOOL

51 Brattle St.
Cambridge, MA 02138
PH: (617)495-4005
E-mail: css@hudce7.harvard.edu
URL: http://www.extension.harvard.edu/

Description: Harvard University's Extension School offers a course called Designing Effective Websites: A Marketing Perspective. This course looks at what makes a site beneficial to the visitor, encouraging return visits. It also examines the problem of measuring the site's effectiveness from the marketer's perspective.

■ 2480

DESIGNING AND PLANNING E-COMMERCE SOLUTIONS

BAKER COLLEGE

1116 W Bristol Rd.
Flint, MI 48507-9843
PH: (810)766-4390
TF: 800-469-3165
FX: (810)766-4399
E-mail: gradschl@baker.edu
URL: http://www.baker.edu

Description: Baker College offers an online course called Designing and Planning E-Commerce Solutions. This course

553

examines the decisions and processes involved in creating an e-commerce web site.

∎ 2481

DESIGNING WEB SITES FOR INTERACTIVITY

MERCY COLLEGE

555 Broadway
Dobbs Ferry, NY 10522
PH: (914)674-7306
FX: (914)674-7518
E-mail: jdielsi@mercy.edu
URL: http://www.mercy.edu
Contact: John DiElsi, Program Dir.

Description: Mercy College offers a graduate level course called Designing Web Sites for Interactivity. This course covers topics including creating appropriate forms for gathering information, improving site navigation, animated graphics, and using customer service tools.

∎ 2482

DEVELOPING E-COMMERCE MODELS

HARVARD UNIVERSITY
HARVARD EXTENSION SCHOOL

51 Brattle St.
Cambridge, MA 02138
PH: (617)495-4005
E-mail: css@hudce7.harvard.edu
URL: http://www.extension.harvard.edu/

Description: Harvard University's Extension School offers a course called Developing E-Commerce Models. In this course E-business models will be presented, and students will examine how an electronic commerce platform for the Internet affects costs, customer response time, and quality across a variety of industries.

∎ 2483

DEVELOPING INTERNET BUSINESS STRATEGIES

CARDEAN UNIVERSITY

500 Lake Cook Rd.
Deerfield, IL 60015-5609
TF: (866)948-1289
E-mail: inquires@cardean.edu
URL: http://www.cardean.edu
Contact: Dr. Geoffrey M. Cox, Cardean University President

Description: Cardean University is an accredited online university offering a suite of courses called "Developing Internet Business Strategies." This series of 4 two hour courses addresses the difference between traditional companies moving into the information economy and Internet start-ups. It helps students assess the readiness and strategic position of a company looking at developing its Internet business.

∎ 2484

DEVELOPING AN INTERNET BUSINESS STRATEGY

MASSACHUSETTS INSTITUTE OF TECHNOLOGY
SLOAN SCHOOL OF MANAGEMENT
OFFICE OF EXECUTIVE EDUCATION

E52-126, 50 Memorial Dr.
Cambridge, MA 02142-1347
PH: (617)253-7166
FX: (617)252-1200
E-mail: sloanexeced@mit.edu
URL: http://mitsloan.mit.edu/
Contact: Marie T. Eiter, Executive Director

Description: The Executive Education program at MIT's Sloan School of Management offers "Developing an Internet Business Strategy" designed to help senior executives understand and manage the new ways of marketing and doing business in the digital economy. It draws on MIT's leadership in developing Internet technologies and innovations, in addressing how you can successfully bring your business onto the Internet to bridge the gap between current business strategies and Internet-based business models.

∎ 2485

DEVELOPING AND MANAGING YOUR E-COMMERCE CONTENT

SAN JOSE STATE UNIVERSITY
PROFESSIONAL DEVELOPMENT CENTER

3031 Tisch Way, Ste. 200 Plz. E
San Jose, CA 95128
PH: (408)257-3000
E-mail: mitchell.levy.sjsupd@ecnow.com
URL: http://ecmtraining.com/sjsu/
Contact: Mitchell Levy, Program Founder and Coordinator

Description: San Jose State University offers a course called "Developing and Managing Your E-Commerce Content." This management course will teach students about systems for efficient content delivery and storage, maintaining style, assessing the content's success and adapting to changing markets. From concept to creation, archiving and assessing success, you discover what makes content compelling, easy for users to navigate and easy for Web teams to work with.

∎ 2486

DEVELOPING YOUR INTERNET BUSINESS PLAN

UNIVERSITY OF MINNESOTA EXTENSION SERVICE

240 Coffey Hall
1420 Eckles Ave.
St. Paul, MN 55108-6068
PH: (612)624-1222
E-mail: mainstreet@extension.umn.edu
URL: http://www.extension.umn.edu/mainstreet/curriculum/index.html

Description: The University of Minnesota Extension Service offers a course called Developing Your Internet Business Plan. This course will guide the student through the process of creating a business plan. Topics covered include setting goals, building a team, creating a budget, and locating resources.

∎ 2487

DEVELOPMENT TECHNOLOGIES FOR THE WEB

CREIGHTON UNIVERSITY

COLLEGE OF BUSINESS ADMINISTRATION

2500 California Plz.
Omaha, NE 68178
PH: (402)280-2602
FX: (402)280-2172
E-mail: ghafer@creighton.edu
URL: http://www.creighton.edu
Contact: Ms. Gail Hafer, Graduate Coordinator

Description: Creighton University offers a graduate level course called Development Technologies for the Web. This course will explore new programming languages and environments such as CGI, JavsScript and flash, in order to improve functionality in commercial web sites.

∎ 2488

DEVELOPMENT TECHNOLOGY FOR E-COMMERCE

REGIS UNIVERSITY

GRADUATE PROGRAMS

3333 Regis Boulevard, L-16
Denver, CO 80221-1099
PH: (303)458-4080
TF: 800-667-9270
FX: (303)964-5538
E-mail: masters@regis.edu
URL: http://www.regis.edu

Description: Regis University offers a course called Development Technology for E-Commerce. This course examines HTML insufficiency and its resulting nEED for better features. Students will also look at alternate programming languages and environments.

∎ 2489

DIGITAL DISTRIBUTION AND PROTECTING YOUR PROPERTY ONLINE

MARLBORO COLLEGE TECHNOLOGY CENTER

PO Box A
Marlboro, VT 05344
PH: (802)257-4333
FX: (802)257-4154
E-mail: lmchrist@marlboro.edu
URL: http://www.marlboro.edu/techcenter/programs/

Description: Marlboro College Technology Center offers a variety of community and professional programs, including Digital Distribution and Protecting Your Property Online. This seminar examines issues in protecting intellectual and creative property in the age of digital distribution.

∎ 2490

DIGITAL SOCIETY CERTIFICATE

UNIVERSITY OF TEXAS AT ARLINGTON

DIGITAL SOCIETY ALLIANCE

7300 Jack Newell Blvd. S
Ft. Worth, TX 76118
PH: (817)272-5914
E-mail: reimann@uta.edu
URL: http://www2.uta.edu/ecomm/
Contact: Dr. Michael Reimann, Director

Description: The University of Texas at Arlington Digital Society Alliance offers the Digital Society Certificate (dSC). This program utilizes education to immerse students in the realities of a complex world. An interdisciplinary perspective of society, business, industry, and technology is approached in this program. Students benefit from exposure to organizations that are experts in the digital society.

∎ 2491

DIRECT MARKETING

UNIVERSITY OF WASHINGTON

COLLEGE OF BUSINESS

E-BUSINESS PROGRAM

Box 353200
Seattle, WA 98195-3200
PH: (206)543-8749
E-mail: uwebiz@u.washington.edu
URL: http://depts.washington.edu/ebiz/
Contact: Jim Jiambalvo, Faculty Director

Description: As a part of its MBA E-Business program, the University of Washington offers ''Direct Marketing.'' This class will explore how direct marketing, in its principles and practices, is uniquely suited to take advantage of the Internet. The course will revolve around case study and in-class discussion. An exercise in best case/worst case analysis of Internet direct marketing ventures will offer the opportunity to study extended topics such as direct marketing to children on the Internet, classic direct marketing on the Internet, catalog marketing and the Internet, services and B2B direct marketing on the Internet, and non-for-profit marketing on the Internet.

∎ 2492

DIRECT MARKETING AND E-COMMERCE

BABSON COLLEGE

F.W. OLIN GRADUATE SCHOOL OF BUSINESS

231 Forest St.
Babson Park, MA 02457-0310
PH: (781)235-1200
URL: http://faculty.babson.edu/isaacson/dmec/syldm00s1.htm
Contact: Larry Isaacson, Professor

Description: Direct Marketing and E-Commerce is the title of this Babson College course which focuses on how firms are using new e-business technologies to market and deliver a wide range of products and services to their B2B and B2C customers.

▌2493
DIRECT MARKETING MANAGEMENT
MARQUETTE UNIVERSITY
COLLEGE OF BUSINESS ADMINISTRATION

PO Box 1881
Milwaukee, WI 53201-1881
PH: (414)288-7142
FX: (414)288-1660
E-mail: jeanne.simmons@marquette.edu
URL: http://www.busadm.mu.edu/mba
Contact: Jeanne Simmons, Assistant Dean of Graduate Programs

Description: Marquette University's College of Business Administration offers a course called Direct Marketing Management. This graduate level course will give an overview of direct marketing (database marketing) fundamentals and issues of ethics and privacy. Students will develop an e-commerce marketing plan for direct marketing via the Internet.

▌2494
DOING BUSINESS ON THE INTERNET
YALE UNIVERSITY
DEPT. OF COMPUTER SCIENCE

PO Box 208285
New Haven, CT 06520-8285
PH: (203)432-1246
FX: (203)432-0593
E-mail: judi.paige@yale.edu
URL: http://zoo.cs.yale.edu/classes/cs155/fall01/
Contact: Joan Feigenbaum, Instructor

Description: Yale University offers an undergraduate course called "Doing Business on the Internet." Topics covered include internet basics; online content distribution and digital copyright; web searching, as a technology and as a business; B2B, B2C, and C2C technology and business models; user privacy, information ownership, and related policy issues.

▌2495
E-BUSINESS
CARDEAN UNIVERSITY

500 Lake Cook Rd.
Deerfield, IL 60015-5609
TF: (866)948-1289
E-mail: inquires@cardean,edu
URL: http://www.cardean.edu
Contact: Dr. Geoffrey M. Cox, Cardean University President

Description: Cardean University is an accredited online university which provides business education coursework for working professionals, including an online MBA degree. Cardean offers a complete E-Business curriculum, consisting of over a dozen courses developed with Columbia Business School, Stanford University and others. Some coursework is designed to give an overview of various E-Business topics, while other courses cover the subject in depth.

▌2496
E-BUSINESS
ELEMENTK

500 Canal View Blvd.
Rochester, NY 14623
PH: (585)240-7500
TF: 800-434-3466
FX: (585)240-7760
URL: http://www.elementk.com

Description: Element K offers a coursework curriculum in E-Business, with classes offered both online and in their Rochester learning center. Online classes can be either self-paced or instructor led. Element K has more than 20 years experience in adult learning, and provides a variety of accessible coursework authored by experts. The Element K E-Business concentration is designed to introduce students to the world on online business and e-commerce.

▌2497
E-BUSINESS
TEMPLE UNIVERSITY
THE FOX SCHOOL

Speakman Hall, Rm. 5
Philadelphia, PA 19122
PH: (215)204-7678
E-mail: tschumac@surfer.sbm.temple.edu
URL: http://www.sbm.temple.edu/ebi/
Contact: Otto W. K. Lee, Managing Director

Description: The Temple University E-Business Institute at the Fox School offers technology-based, business-focused degree programs. Some of the programs offered are MBA in E-business or information systems, MS in E-business, and BBA in E-marketing. The Institute also offers certificate and non-credit programs for executives and mid-level managers. Workshops and seminars study subjects such as Strategy and Policy, Information Technology Integration, and Marketing and Distribution.

▌2498
E-BUSINESS
UNIVERSITY OF PHOENIX

3201 E Elwood St.
Phoenix, AZ 85034
PH: (480)966-5394
TF: 800-366-9699
URL: http://www.uoponline.com

Description: The University of Phoenix offers a course called E-Business. In this course students will gain an overview of e-business strategic management, business-to-business and business-to-consumer transactions, effective e-marketing, and the legal and ethical issues of e-business.

2499

E-BUSINESS

GEORGETOWN UNIVERSITY

MCDONOUGH SCHOOL OF BUSINESS

310 Old North
Washington, DC 20057
PH: (202)687-3802
E-mail: culnanm@msb.edu
URL: http://www.msb.edu/faculty/culnanm/TKM/syllabus.html

Description: The course E-Business will address issues related to developing an Internet strategy for existing brick and mortar organizations. These include the ways organizations gain advantage or reduce their costs by using electronic commerce. The majority of these issues are also relevant to the entrepreneur planning to start a new.com company.

2500

E-BUSINESS

EAST TENNESSEE STATE UNIVERSITY

Box 70267
Johnson City, TN 37614-0054
PH: (423)429-1000
E-mail: moffitt@etsu.edu
URL: http://www.etsu.edu

Description: This E-business course will cover the design and implementation of a typical e-business system. The student will gain insight into technologies and procedures that makeup e-business.

2501

E-BUSINESS ARCHITECTURE

RED HAT

1801 Varsity Dr.
Raleigh, NC 27606
PH: (919)754-3700
TF: 888-733-4281
FX: (919)754-3701
E-mail: customerservice@redhat.com
URL: http://www.redhat.com

Description: Red Hat, the largest provider of open source technology, offers an online course called "E-Business Architecture." This course examines the methods for creating a solid, scalable e-business architecture. Topics include a discussion of how e-business is being shaped by technology and telecommunications, as well as a look at e-business models, business-to-business (B2B) and business-to-consumer (B2C) relationships.

2502

E-BUSINESS ARCHITECTURE

DIGITALTHINK INC

601 Brannan St.
San Francisco, CA 94107
PH: (415)625-4000
TF: 888-686-8817
FX: (415)625-4100
E-mail: info@digitalthink.com
URL: http://www.digitalthink.com
Contact: Mr. Pete Goettner, Chairman

Founded: 1996. **Staff:** 450. **Description:** Founded in 1996, DigitalThink offers a course entitled "E-Business Architecture" which examines the components and process for creating a solid e-business architecture. It begins with a discussion about how e-business is being shaped by technology, and then covers e-business models, business-to-business (B2B) and business-to-consumer (B2C) relationships, how to prepare an organization for e-business, and the technology that is needed.

2503

E-BUSINESS ARCHITECTURES

UNIVERSITY OF OKLAHOMA

PRICE COLLEGE OF BUSINESS

307 W Brooks, Room 307E
Norman, OK 73019-4006
PH: (405)325-0768
FX: (405)325-7482
E-mail: rzmud@ou.edu
URL: http://www.ou.edu/business/mis/courses.html
Contact: Robert W. Zmud, MIS Division Director

Description: The University of Oklahoma offers a course titled "E-Business Architectures." This course looks at the basic concepts of telecommunications and distribution processing and their applications to e-business. This course focuses on managerial issues.

2504

E-BUSINESS BACHELOR OF SCIENCE DEGREE

UNIVERSITY OF PHOENIX ONLINE

3157 E. Elwood St.
Phoenix, AZ 85034
PH: (480)966-5394
TF: 800-366-9699
URL: http://www.uoponline.com

Description: The University of Phoenix Online offers a Bachelor of Science degree in E-Business. This degree program provides fundamental knowledge in both business and information technology. The coursework is designed to produce graduates ready to work in e-Business positions.

▌2505

E-BUSINESS BASICS (SBA)

U.S. SMALL BUSINESS ADMINISTRATION

409 3rd St. SW
Washington, DC 20416
PH: 800-827-5722
E-mail: classroom@sba.gov
URL: http://www.sba.gov/classroom

Description: The Small Business Administration (SBA) in partnership with Cisco Systems offers a free online course called E-Business Basics. This course gives information about the technologies, software and products students will nEED for a successful Internet strategy and shows them how to work with third-party resources, such as resellers and Internet Service Providers (ISPs) to determine and implement an e-business strategy.

▌2506

E-BUSINESS BBA

TEXAS CHRISTIAN UNIVERSITY

The Neeley School of Business
TCU Box 298530
Fort Worth, TX 76129
PH: (817)257-7540
E-mail: j.mackay@tcu.edu
URL: http://www.tcu.edu
Contact: Dr. Jane Mackay, Program Director

Description: The BBA with a major in E-Business program gives students the ability to develop, implement and manage an infrastructure of information technology, data and organization-wide systems. The program also gives the skills to manage, analysis and develop applications dealing with e-business, and they will be able to assist in incorporating information technology into the organization's strategy, planning and practices. To obtain a degree students must complete 30 semester hours of the Business Core and all required E-Business courses.

▌2507

E-BUSINESS: BUSINESS DEVELOPMENT FOR THE WEB

CAPELLA UNIVERSITY

222 S 9th St., 20th Fl.
Minneapolis, MN 55402
PH: (612)339-8650
TF: 888-227-3552
FX: (612)339-8022
URL: http://www.capella.edu

Description: E-Business: Business Development for the Web builds on the Intro to E-Business course and deals with topics such as business models, staffing and finance for businesses that operate partially or entirely on the web.

▌2508

E-BUSINESS CERTIFICATE

RENSSELAER POLYTECHNIC INSTITUTE

RENSSELAER PROFESSIONAL AND DISTANCE EDUCATION

CII Ste. 4011, 110 8th St.
Troy, NY 12180-3590
PH: (518)276-7787
FX: (518)276-8495
E-mail: rsvp@rpi.edu
URL: http://rsvp.rpi.edu/

Description: Rensselaer's Lally School of Management and Technology offers a certificate in E-Business. This certificate is designed to prepare working professionals for operating in the new E-Business environments. The certificate program includes courses at the intersection of Management and Technology. Students can choose from a variety of courses in E-Business topics.

▌2509

E-BUSINESS CERTIFICATE PROGRAM

ILLINOIS INSTITUTE OF TECHNOLOGY
STUART GRADUATE SCHOOL OF BUSINESS

565 W. Adams St.
Chicago, IL 60661
PH: (312)906-6500
E-mail: bariff@stuart.iit.edu
URL: http://www.stuart.iit.edu/

Description: The Illinois Institute of Technology offers an E-Business Certificate program designed for managers and professionals. In this graduate level program, students will learn about supply chain management, marketing on the Internet, data communications, customer relationship management and web site design.

▌2510

E-BUSINESS CERTIFICATE PROGRAM

MANHATTAN INSTITUTE OF MANAGEMENT

99 Hudson St., 3rd Fl.
New York, NY 10013
PH: (212)625-9483
FX: (212)431-0420
E-mail: mim@mimusa.org
URL: http://mimusa.org

Description: The Manhattan Institute of Management offers an E-Business Certificate Program. This short term program (6-12 months) includes coursework and an internship at an American company. Both the courses and the internship can be provided online or on-site.

▌2511

E-BUSINESS CONCENTRATION

BELLEVUE UNIVERSITY

1000 Galvin Rd. S
Bellevue, NE 68005
PH: (402)293-2000
TF: 800-756-7920
FX: (402)293-2020

URL: http://www.bellevue.edu

Description: Bellevue University offers a B.S. degree with a concentration in E-Business. This degree is a 36-credit hour program. The courses cover many topics related to E-Business including E-commerce technology, marketing, computer security, electronic payment systems, competitive strategies, Web programming and design, emerging technologies, and legal and ethical issues.

∎ 2512

E-BUSINESS CONSULTING
BRIGHAM YOUNG UNIVERSITY
ROLLINS CENTER FOR E-BUSINESS

510 N. Tanner Bldg
PO Box 23068
Provo, UT 84602-3068
PH: (801)422-2815
FX: (801)422-5933
E-mail: ebusiness@byu.edu
URL: http://ebusiness.byu.edu/ebus.cfm
Contact: J. Owen Cherrington, Director

Description: Brigham Young University's Rollins Center for E-Business offers a course titled "E-Business Consulting." In this course students will complete professional consulting projects with industry partners.

∎ 2513

E-BUSINESS CURRICULUM
NETG

1751 W Diehl Rd, 2nd Fl.
Naperville, IL 60563-9099
PH: (630)369-3000
TF: 877-561-6384
FX: (630)983-4877
E-mail: info@netg.com
URL: http://www.netg.com

Description: NETg provides an E-Business curriculum which consists of eight courses. Topics covered include building and securing infrastructure, choosing tools and technologies, understanding applications, working with employees and customers.

∎ 2514

E-BUSINESS E-COMMERCE CERTIFICATE PROGRAM
UNIVERSITY OF ILLINOIS AT CHICAGO
COLLEGE OF BUSINESS ADMINISTRATION
PROFESSIONAL DEVELOPMENT PROGRAM (MC077)

815 W Van Buren St., Ste. 220
Chicago, IL 60607-3525
PH: (312)413-2404
FX: (312)413-0338
E-mail: pdp@uic.edu
URL: http://www.uic.edu/cba/pdp/online/ebiz/

Description: The University of Illinois at Chicago offers an online E-Business E-Commerce Certificate Program. This 12 week course will enable students to become e-business proficient, and gain understanding of where E-Business can fit in their organizations. The course consists of 6 modules which cover topics such as an e-business overview, marketing and the Internet, and technology architecture.

∎ 2515

E-BUSINESS: E-LEADERSHIP FOR E-BUSINESS
CAPELLA UNIVERSITY

222 S 9th St., 20th Fl.
Minneapolis, MN 55402
PH: (612)339-8650
TF: 888-227-3552
FX: (612)339-8022
URL: http://www.capella.edu

Description: E-Business: E-Leadership for E-Business focuses on an analysis of leadership issues in e-business, including mentoring in the virtual organization, long-range thinking on Internet time, e-business ethics and diversity awareness. Students will look beyond today's e-commerce mentality to envision the future of work and business in an interconnected world.

∎ 2516

E-BUSINESS ECONOMICS
UNIVERSITY OF WASHINGTON
COLLEGE OF BUSINESS
E-BUSINESS PROGRAM

Box 353200
Seattle, WA 98195-3200
PH: (206)543-8749
E-mail: uwebiz@u.washington.edu
URL: http://depts.washington.edu/ebiz/
Contact: Jim Jiambalvo, Faculty Director

Description: As a part of its MBA program, the University of Washington provides a course entitled "E-Business Economics." This course will use economic principles to help students to see the implications of evolving Internet technology for business decision-making, market prices and market structure. The course will also develop theoretical extensions of the models already covered to enable students to more deeply analyze the questions that the Internet poses.

∎ 2517

E-BUSINESS: ENTERPRISE WIDE PLANNING
ELEMENTK

500 Canal View Blvd.
Rochester, NY 14623
PH: (585)240-7500
TF: 800-434-3466
FX: (585)240-7760
URL: http://www.elementk.com

Description: Element K offers an online course entitled "E-Business: Enterprise Wide Planning." In this self study course students will learn to write vision and mission statements for their E-Business and select planning strategies to carry out those statements, perform a market analysis to help shape your plan, select an E-Business model, Web site model, and Web strategies for their own E-Business, evaluate and make decisions regarding the internal operation functions, create a marketing strategy, develop a financial plan, and write an E-Business plan using the components of a traditional business plan.

▌ 2518

E-BUSINESS: ENTERPRISE WIDE PLANNING

SMARTPLANET

CNET Networks Inc.
235 Second St.
San Francisco, CA 94105
PH: 800-449-2738
TF: 800-449-2738
URL: http://www.smartplanet.com

Description: E-Business: Enterprise Wide Planning is an online independent study course that will teach students to write vision and mission statements for their e-business, select planning strategies to carry out those statements, perform a market analysis to help shape their e-business plan, select an e-business model, select website model, select Web strategies for their e-business, evaluate and make decisions regarding the internal operation functions for their e-business, create a marketing strategy for their e-business, develop a financial plan for their e-business and write an e-business plan using the components of a traditional business plan.

▌ 2519

E-BUSINESS: ETHICS

CAPELLA UNIVERSITY

222 S 9th St., 20th Fl.
Minneapolis, MN 55402
PH: (612)339-8650
TF: 888-227-3552
FX: (612)339-8022
URL: http://www.capella.edu

Description: E-Business: Ethics covers the ethical topics that are presently of concern to electronic commerce businesses and their customers. Covered topics include the proper use of information about customers, censorship verses free speech, responsibility for site security and promoting consumer trust of Internet transactions, access to websites by minors and website conduct that may be legal in one state and illegal in another.

▌ 2520

E-BUSINESS FOUNDATIONS AND APPLICATIONS

UNIVERSITY OF DELAWARE
E-COMMERCE PROGRAM

206 John M. Clayton Hall
Newark, DE 19716-7410
PH: (302)831-2741

E-mail: continuing-ed@udel.edu
URL: http://www.continuingstudies.udel.edu/it/ecomm/index.shtml

Description: The University of Delaware's Continuing Studies Program offers a course titled "E-Business Foundations and Applications." This course serves as an introduction to e-commerce, and examines the latest trends and directions in e-commerce applications. It also helps students to begin using the Internet for business purposes.

▌ 2521

E-BUSINESS: FUNDAMENTALS OF E-COMMERCE

SMARTPLANET

CNET Networks Inc.
235 Second St.
San Francisco, CA 94105
PH: 800-449-2738
TF: 800-449-2738
URL: http://www.smartplanet.com

Description: E-Business: Fundamentals of E-Commerce is an online instructor-led introductory-level course designed to provide students with a basic understanding of some of the fundamental concepts related to e-commerce. Some objectives of the course includes clearly understanding the fundamental aspects of e-commerce including a knowledge of the history of the Internet and its influence on e-commerce; understanding e-commerce customer relationship management, resource planning, supply chain management and procurement; locating and interpreting e-commerce marketing statistics in order to effectively plan e-commerce marketing strategies; and researching information about software, hardware and service providers.

▌ 2522

E-BUSINESS: FUNDAMENTALS OF ECOMMERCE

ELEMENTK

500 Canal View Blvd.
Rochester, NY 14623
PH: (585)240-7500
TF: 800-434-3466
FX: (585)240-7760
URL: http://www.elementk.com

Description: Element K offers an online course called "E-Business: Fundamentals of eCommerce." This course is instructor-led and is designed to provide students with a basic understanding of some of the fundamental concepts related to eCommerce, Some of the topics covered include the history of the Internet and its influence on eCommerce, understanding eCommerce customer relationship management, resource planning, supply chain management and procurement, and knowledge management.

∎ 2523

E-BUSINESS: FUNDAMENTALS OF ENTERPRISE WIDE INFRASTRUCTURE

ELEMENTK

500 Canal View Blvd.
Rochester, NY 14623
PH: (585)240-7500
TF: 800-434-3466
FX: (585)240-7760
URL: http://www.elementk.com

Description: Element K offers a course intended for both managers and developers called ''E-Business: Fundamentals of Enterprise Wide Infrastructure.'' This course will provide students with an understanding of both the strategic models and enabling technologies that underpin business to business (B2B) eCommerce, which is an important segment of the broader category of eBusiness. The course focuses on the ways in which Internet technologies can be used to build an end-to-end value chain, facilitating the management of supply chains, selling chains, enterprise resources, and relationships with both customers and partners.

∎ 2524

E-BUSINESS: FUNDAMENTALS OF ENTERPRISE WIDE INFRASTRUCTURE

SMARTPLANET

CNET Networks Inc.
235 Second St.
San Francisco, CA 94105
PH: 800-449-2738
TF: 800-449-2738
URL: http://www.smartplanet.com

Description: E-Business: Fundamentals of Enterprise Wide Infrastructure is an online independent study course that will discuss the main differences between e-commerce and e-business, review several e-business trends, discuss Customer Relationship Management core competencies, CRM implementation trends, common CRM implementation planning strategies, discuss e-procurement business drivers, operating resource procurement, common e-procurement business problems, common e-procurement implementation planning strategies, and discuss core knowledge management application classes.

∎ 2525

E-BUSINESS: FUNDAMENTALS OF SMALL BUSINESS SITE PLANNING AND DEVELOPMENT

ELEMENTK

500 Canal View Blvd.
Rochester, NY 14623
PH: (585)240-7500
TF: 800-434-3466
FX: (585)240-7760
URL: http://www.elementk.com

Description: Element K offers an online self-study course called ''E-Business: Fundamentals of Small Business Site Planning and Development.'' This class will examine E-Commerce planning ideas, and E-Commerce equipment requirements. Students will also search the Web to get help for your small business needs such as selecting an Internet Service Provider (ISP), Web hosting service and E-commerce solutions. They will also examine how to create a secure E-Commerce environment, review legal issues involved in creating an E-Commerce business, register with search engines, identify Internet marketing tools, and use Customer Relationship Management (CRM) to establish and maintain relationships with their customers.

∎ 2526

E-BUSINESS I: SYSTEMS FUNDAMENTALS

UNIVERSITY OF WEST FLORIDA

11000 University Pky.
Pensacola, FL 32514-5752
PH: (850)474-2317
E-mail: rplatt@uwf.edu
URL: http://ebiz.uwf.edu/
Contact: Dr. Richard Platt, Instructor

Description: The University of West Florida provides a course called ''E-Business I: Systems Fundamentals'' which is designed to be an informative course on the fundamental technologies and systems used to conduct electronic business. The course presents the theory and practice involved with organization-wide application of technology to e-nable improved business processes and decisions

∎ 2527

E-BUSINESS INFRASTRUCTURES

NEW YORK UNIVERSITY
SCHOOL OF CONTINUING AND PROFESSIONAL STUDIES VIRTUAL COLLEGE

10 Astor Pl., 5th Fl.
New York, NY 10003
PH: (212)998-7080
TF: 877-998-7080
E-mail: scpsinfo@nyu.edu
URL: http://www.scps.nyu.edu/dyncon/virt/

Description: NYU's Virtual College offers a certificate program in E-business Infrastructures. This 4 course certificate will introduce students to Internet applications, web application servers, and further study strategy and structure of e-business.

∎ 2528

E-BUSINESS INTERFACE DESIGN

DEPAUL UNIVERSITY
KELLSTADT GRADUATE SCHOOL OF BUSINESS

1 E Jackson, Ste. 7900
Chicago, IL 60604-2287
PH: (312)362-8810
FX: (312)362-6677
E-mail: mbainfo@depaul.edu
URL: http://commerce.depaul.edu/
Contact: Felicia Richardson-McGee, Assistant Director

Description: DePaul University's Kellstadt School of Business offers a "E-Business Interface Design" which is an MBA web design class. This class will study web design, tools, and techniques, and we apply them to building web interfaces.

▌2529

E-BUSINESS FOR IT MANAGEMENT: FROM STRATEGY TO INTERNET MARKETING TECHNIQUES

ECNOW.COM

21265 Stevens Creek Blvd., Ste. 205
Cupertino, CA 95014
PH: (408)257-3000
FX: (603)843-0769
E-mail: info@ecnow.com
URL: http://ecnow.com/courses/mgt04.htm

Description: ECnow.com offers a course called E-Business for IT Management: From Strategy to Internet Marketing Techniques. This course explores e-business topics including strategic planning, business models, business processes and tools.

▌2530

E-BUSINESS LECTURE SERIES

BRIGHAM YOUNG UNIVERSITY
ROLLINS CENTER FOR E-BUSINESS

510 N. Tanner Bldg
PO Box 23068
Provo, UT 84602-3068
PH: (801)422-2815
FX: (801)422-5933
E-mail: ebusiness@byu.edu
URL: http://ebusiness.byu.edu/ebus.cfm
Contact: J. Owen Cherrington, Director

Description: Brigham Young University's Rollins Center for E-Business offers a course titled "E-Business Lecture Series." Taught by the director of the Rollins Center, and beginning with information on the fundamentals of e-business, this course consists of lectures from e-business leaders on important e-business subjects.

▌2531

E-BUSINESS: MANAGING IN THE TECHNICAL ENVIRONMENT

CAPELLA UNIVERSITY

222 S 9th St., 20th Fl.
Minneapolis, MN 55402
PH: (612)339-8650
TF: 888-227-3552
FX: (612)339-8022
URL: http://www.capella.edu

Description: The E-Business: Managing in the Technical Environment course surveys the manager's role and function within an electronic business environment. The course will develop an understanding and practical skills in management issues that bridge technical and non-technical sides of the business. Covered topics include virtual team management, project management and considerations for hardware and software development and/or purchasing.

▌2532

E-BUSINESS FOR MANUFACTURING ENTERPRISES

PURDUE UNIVERSITY
KRANNERT GRADUATE SCHOOL OF MANAGEMENT

1310 Krannert Bldg.
West Lafayette, IN 47907
PH: (765)494-9700
FX: (765)494-9658
E-mail: krannert_ms@mgmt.purdue.edu
URL: http://www.mgmt.purdue.edu/centers/ceer/

Description: Purdue University's Krannert Graduate School of Management offers a course entitled E-Business for Manufacturing Enterprises. This course will give an overview of the opportunities and challenges of implementing e-business within an established corporate environment.

▌2533

E-BUSINESS AND MARKETING

YALE SCHOOL OF MANAGEMENT

135 Prospect St.
PO Box 208200
New Haven, CT 06520-8200
PH: (203)432-5932
FX: (203)432-7004
E-mail: mba.admissions@yale.edu
URL: http://www.mba.yale.edu
Contact: James Stevens, Director

Description: The E-business and Marketing course is designed to link the opportunities and challenges offered by the Internet with the theory and practice of marketing. The course aims to understand how these principles will have to change in order to create and capture value online and students will be actively engaged in critically evaluating online business ideas.

▌2534

E-BUSINESS MARKETING

SENECA COLLEGE OF APPLIED ARTS AND TECHNOLOGY, NEWNHAM CAMPUS
FACULTY OF BUSINESS

1750 Finch Ave. E
Toronto, ON, Canada M2J2X5
PH: (416)491-5050
FX: (416)493-4144
E-mail: tim.richardson@senecac.on.ca
URL: http://www.witiger.com/senecacollege/IEC812.htm
Contact: Tim Richardson, Professor

562

Description: Seneca College, Toronto offers a course called "E-Business Marketing." This course looks at e-business topics such as business models, strategy and acquisition, new product development, promotion and pricing issues.

▮ 2535
E-BUSINESS MARKETING
WALDEN UNIVERSITY

155 5th Ave. S
Minneapolis, MN 55401
PH: (612)338-7224
TF: 800-925-3368
FX: (612)338-5092
E-mail: info@waldenu.edu
URL: http://www.waldenu.edu

Description: Walden University offers an MBA course titled "E-Business Marketing." This course focuses on customer relationship management (CRM) for digital startups. Traditional and e-marketing practices are compared and contrasted.

▮ 2536
E-BUSINESS MARKETING
UNIVERSITY OF WASHINGTON
COLLEGE OF BUSINESS
E-BUSINESS PROGRAM

Box 353200
Seattle, WA 98195-3200
PH: (206)543-8749
E-mail: uwebiz@u.washington.edu
URL: http://depts.washington.edu/ebiz/
Contact: Jim Jiambalvo, Faculty Director

Description: The University of Washington offers the graduate course "E-Business Marketing" which will critically analyze current strategies for Internet Marketing and explore new frontiers. Topics covered include examining the history, culture and design of the Internet and the resulting impact on Internet Marketing; Web-based business models; consumer demographics and Web usage behavior; personalization versus privacy invasion; reputation and brand loyalty on the Net; virtual communities; and the marketing mix for cyberspace.

▮ 2537
E-BUSINESS: MARKETING, CUSTOMERS AND VIRTUAL COMMUNITY
CAPELLA UNIVERSITY

222 S 9th St., 20th Fl.
Minneapolis, MN 55402
PH: (612)339-8650
TF: 888-227-3552
FX: (612)339-8022
URL: http://www.capella.edu

Description: E-Business: Marketing, Customers and Virtual Community focuses on development and management of a virtual community, including financial considerations, community-building, developing and managing content, aligning online and offline marketing with virtual community goals, developing partnerships and vendor relationships.

▮ 2538
E-BUSINESS MBA
CAPELLA UNIVERSITY

222 S 9th St., 20th Fl.
Minneapolis, MN 55402
PH: (612)339-8650
TF: 888-227-3552
FX: (612)339-8022
URL: http://www.capella.edu

Description: The MBA with specialization in E-Business program can prepare professionals for leadership roles in their organizations by strengthening their skills to plan, develop and manage e-business strategies. A total of 52 credits must be obtained to fulfill the requirements for an MBA with E-Business specialization.

▮ 2539
E-BUSINESS MBA
UNIVERSITY OF PHOENIX ONLINE

3157 E. Elwood St.
Phoenix, AZ 85034
PH: (480)966-5394
TF: 800-366-9699
URL: http://www.uoponline.com

Description: The University of Phoenix Online offers an MBA in E-Business. This degree program emphasizes the identification, analysis, and solution of management problems that require technical understanding and effective decision making.

▮ 2540
E-BUSINESS MINOR
UNIVERSITY OF WEST FLORIDA
COLLEGE OF BUSINESS

11000 University Pky.
Pensacola, FL 32514-5752
PH: (850)474-2348
E-mail: ebiz@uwf.edu
URL: http://ebiz.uwf.edu/

Description: The University of West Florida College of Business offers an e-business minor for undergraduates. The school recognizes that e-Business is a discipline whose foundations bridge technology and business policies. Different from any of the areas that support technology and business, the e-Business minor is an interdisciplinary undergraduate program consisting of three foundation courses and two electives.

▌2541

E-BUSINESS: MODELS AND APPLICATIONS FOR E-COMMERCE
THE WHARTON SCHOOL
FT KNOWLEDGE EXECUTIVE EDUCATION
80 Strand
London WC2R0RL, United Kingdom
PH: 44 20 7010 2751
FX: 44 20 7010 6616
E-mail: executive.education@ftknowledge.com
URL: http://www.ftknowledge-wharton.com/ftk_war_mainframeset.html

Description: The Wharton School at the University of Pennsylvania's FT Knowledge offers an executive education program called "E-Business: Models and Applications for E-Commerce." These 30 hour 5 week self-paced online seminars led by Wharton faculty will help students understand e-business trends, analyze e-business options for your company and plan your e-business strategy.

▌2542

E-BUSINESS MODELS FOR THE NEW ECONOMY
UNIVERSITY OF DELAWARE
E-COMMERCE PROGRAM
206 John M. Clayton Hall
Newark, DE 19716-7410
PH: (302)831-2741
E-mail: continuing-ed@udel.edu
URL: http://www.continuingstudies.udel.edu/it/ecomm/index.shtml

Description: The University of Delaware's Continuing Studies Program offers a course titled "E-Business Models for the New Economy." This course looks at how new business models are evolving and provides information on how to identify and evaluate strategies for the new economy.

▌2543

E-BUSINESS OPERATIONS
UNIVERSITY OF PHOENIX
3201 E Elwood St.
Phoenix, AZ 85034
PH: (480)966-5394
TF: 800-366-9699
URL: http://www.uoponline.com

Description: The University of Phoenix offers a graduate level course entitled E-Business Operations. This course looks at the integration of business processes and technology for companies conducting e-business. Business processes included are Enterprise Resource Planning, Customer Relationship Management, Selling Chain Management, Supply Chain Management, e-procurement, and Knowledge Management.

▌2544

E-BUSINESS OPTION
UNIVERSITY OF NORTH CAROLINA AT WILMINGTON
CAMERON SCHOOL OF BUSINESS
601 S College Rd.
Wilmington, NC 28403
PH: (910)962-3777
FX: (910)962-3815
E-mail: howe@uncw.edu
URL: http://www.csb.uncwil.edu/indexie.htm
Contact: Lawrence S. Clark, Dean

Description: the University of North Carolina at Wilmington Cameron School of Business offers an "E-Business Option" for business majors interested in study of the application of information technology to business processes. Students gain understanding of business fundamentals as well as the technology enabling E-Business.

▌2545

E-BUSINESS PRACTICAL APPLICATIONS
UNIVERSITY OF CALGARY
FACULTY OF CONTINUING EDUCATION
COMPUOFC
Education Tower, Rm. 126
2500 University Dr. NW
Calgary, AB, Canada T2N1N4
PH: (403)220-2866
FX: (403)289-7287
E-mail: compuofc@ucalgary.ca
URL: http://www.computer.ucalgary.ca
Contact: Theresa Ferguson, Program Director

Description: The University of Calgary offers online learning through its Faculty of Continuing Education. Courses include "E-Business Practical Applications" which examines e-business case studies. These case studies demonstrate how Web sites have been created or improved upon based on problems unique to each case. Students will then access the Web sites for each company, with the intention of generating ideas for your own e-commerce site and identifying common issues.

▌2546

E-BUSINESS: PRACTICAL APPLICATIONS
ELEMENTK
500 Canal View Blvd.
Rochester, NY 14623
PH: (585)240-7500
TF: 800-434-3466
FX: (585)240-7760
URL: http://www.elementk.com

Description: Element K offers an instructor-led online course called "E-Business: Practical Applications." This course is designed as a laboratory study of 4 successful or not so successful eCommerce enterprises currently in place on the Internet. These are actual case studies of four businesses that have been operating in the eCommerce arena for a number of years. It is designed to expose students to the practical application of technology that may be used in their own eCommerce endeavor, and to aid them with successful decision making regarding their eCommerce project.

∎ 2547
E-BUSINESS: PRACTICAL APPLICATIONS
SMARTPLANET

CNET Networks Inc.
235 Second St.
San Francisco, CA 94105
PH: 800-449-2738
TF: 800-449-2738
URL: http://www.smartplanet.com

Description: E-Business: Practical Applications is an online instructor-led course designed as a laboratory study of four successful or unsuccessful e-commerce initiatives currently in place on the Internet. These are actual case studies of four businesses that have been operating in the e-commerce arena for a number of years. The course is designed to expose students to the practical application of technology elements that may be used in their own e-commerce endeavor. During the course students will develop an e-business model of a fictitious company as a practical exercise to reinforce the information learned in the course

∎ 2548
E-BUSINESS PRACTICE AND PROJECTS
KRANNERT SCHOOL OF MANAGEMENT

Purdue University
1310 Krannert Bldg.
West Lafayette, IN 47907
PH: (765)496-3384
FX: (765)494-9841
E-mail: jdietz@mgmt.purdue.edu
URL: http://www.mgmt.purdue.edu
Contact: Joy Dietz, Manager of Advising and Student Services

Description: E-Business Practice and Projects is an E-Business consulting course with included topics covering consulting and e-consulting project management, e-supply chain management, e-customer relationship management and overviews of e-business trends in manufacturing, financial services and consumer packaged goods industry. This is a 16 week course offered each year from October to February and is currently taught by Patrick Duparcq.

∎ 2549
E-BUSINESS PRACTICUM
BELLEVUE UNIVERSITY

1000 Galvin Rd. S
Bellevue, NE 68005
PH: (402)293-2000
TF: 800-756-7920
FX: (402)293-2020
URL: http://www.bellevue.edu

Description: Bellevue University offers a course called ''E-Business Practicum.'' This is one of the final courses in the B.S. degree in E-Commerce, and is an opportunity for students to complete and fine tune their E Business website and submit an analysis of the process. Students will also be asked to critique a variety of websites and E Business models.

∎ 2550
E-BUSINESS PRINCIPLES AND PRACTICES
UNIVERSITY OF PHOENIX

3201 E Elwood St.
Phoenix, AZ 85034
PH: (480)966-5394
TF: 800-366-9699
URL: http://www.uoponline.com

Description: The University of Phoenix offers a graduate level course called E-Business Principles and Practices. This course introduces models for conducting business-to-business and business-to-consumer electronic transactions. Other topics covered include the application of e-business strategic management, leveraging technology to enhance business processes, and unique characteristics of e-marketing.

∎ 2551
E-BUSINESS PROCESS FOUNDRY
STANFORD UNIVERSITY
GRADUATE SCHOOL OF BUSINESS

518 Memorial Way
Stanford, CA 94305-5015
PH: (650)725-5663
FX: (650)723-3950
E-mail: cebc@gsb.stanford.edu
URL: http://www.gsb.stanford.edu/cebc/

Description: Stanford University's MBA program offers a course titled ''E-Business Process Foundry.'' This is a project-based course in which multi-disciplinary teams create prototypes of business processes that take advantage of World Wide Web technologies.

∎ 2552
E-BUSINESS PRODUCTIVITY
SMARTPLANET

CNET Networks Inc.
235 Second St.
San Francisco, CA 94105
PH: 800-449-2738
TF: 800-449-2738
URL: http://www.smartplanet.com

Description: E-Business Productivity is a complete library of online courses. These courses will teach students how to develop an e-business from writing a business plan to managing an e-commerce website, students will gain a variety of practical skills to launch their business. The complete library contains more than 20 courses, which students will have access to for over 12 months.

∎ 2553

E-BUSINESS PROGRAM

HYPERSMITH CONSULTANTS

1020 Mainland St., Ste. 101
Vancouver, BC, Canada V6B2T4
PH: (604)684-7728
E-mail: info@hypersmith.com
URL: http://www.hypersmith.com
Contact: John Foster, President

Description: Hypersmith offers a variety of courses including the E-Business Program. This curriculum includes course modules on topics including e-business systems and strategies, management, legal issues, security, marketing and e-business policy.

∎ 2554

E-BUSINESS: PROJECT IMPLEMENTATION AND MANAGEMENT

SMARTPLANET

CNET Networks Inc.
235 Second St.
San Francisco, CA 94105
PH: 800-449-2738
TF: 800-449-2738
URL: http://www.smartplanet.com

Description: E-Business: Project Implementation and Management is an online independent study course that will teach students how to evaluate the benefits of sub-dividing an e-business implementation to manage scope, recognize and discuss how trends impacting e-business affect implementing and managing e-business projects, define what to consider when getting ready for an e-business project, define approaches for e-business implementations, identify and define needed skills and knowledge for a winning e-business project manager and team, and discuss technology tools that contribute to successful e-business project management.

∎ 2555

E-BUSINESS: PROJECT IMPLEMENTATION AND MANAGEMENT

ELEMENTK

500 Canal View Blvd.
Rochester, NY 14623
PH: (585)240-7500
TF: 800-434-3466
FX: (585)240-7760
URL: http://www.elementk.com

Description: Element K offers an online course entitled "E-Business: Project Implementation and Management." This is a self study course which will teach students how to evaluate the benefits of sub-dividing an E-Business to manage it, recognize and discuss how trends impacting E-Business affect E-Business projects, define what to consider when getting ready for an E-Business project, as well as define approaches for E-Business implementations, identify and define needed skills and knowledge for a winning E-Business project manager and team, and discuss technology

tools that contribute to successful E-Business project management.

∎ 2556

E-BUSINESS: SECURITY TECHNIQUES

ELEMENTK

500 Canal View Blvd.
Rochester, NY 14623
PH: (585)240-7500
TF: 800-434-3466
FX: (585)240-7760
URL: http://www.elementk.com

Description: Element K offers an online class called "E-Business: Security Techniques" which explores security technique fundamentals involved in E-Business. This course introduces students to concepts such as securing Web clients, servers, and communications. It also investigates the use of firewalls and digital certificates, and takes a look at legal issues including appropriate responses when security has been breached.

∎ 2557

E-BUSINESS: SECURITY TECHNIQUES

SMARTPLANET

CNET Networks Inc.
235 Second St.
San Francisco, CA 94105
PH: 800-449-2738
TF: 800-449-2738
URL: http://www.smartplanet.com

Description: E-Business: Security Techniques is an online independent study course that will explore the security technique fundamentals involved in minimizing e-business security risks, introduce students to concepts such as securing Web clients, servers and communications, investigates the use of firewalls and digital certificates, and look at legal issues including how to respond when security has been breached.

∎ 2558

E-BUSINESS SEMINAR - WINNERS AND SURVIVORS

UNIVERSITY OF VIRGINIA

DARDEN GRADUATE SCHOOL OF BUSINESS
ADMINISTRATION

PO Box 6550
Charlottesville, VA 22906-6500
PH: (434)924-7281
TF: 800-882-6221
E-mail: darden@virginia.edu
URL: http://www.darden.edu/mba/index.htm

Description: The University of Virginia's Darden School of Business MBA program offers a course called "E-Business Seminar - Winners and Survivors." This course will look at the business models and strategies of both survivors and established firms to understand the keys to successfully exploiting the Internet and other new technologies.

▌2559
E-BUSINESS SERVICE AND LEARNING PROJECTS
BRIGHAM YOUNG UNIVERSITY
ROLLINS CENTER FOR E-BUSINESS
510 N. Tanner Bldg
PO Box 23068
Provo, UT 84602-3068
PH: (801)422-2815
FX: (801)422-5933
E-mail: ebusiness@byu.edu
URL: http://ebusiness.byu.edu/ebus.cfm
Contact: J. Owen Cherrington, Director

Description: Brigham Young University's Rollins Center for E-Business offers a course titled ''E-Business Service and Learning Projects.''

▌2560
E-BUSINESS: SMALL BUSINESS SITE PLANNING AND DEVELOPMENT
SMARTPLANET
CNET Networks Inc.
235 Second St.
San Francisco, CA 94105
PH: 800-449-2738
TF: 800-449-2738
URL: http://www.smartplanet.com

Description: E-Business: Small Business Site Planning and Development is an online independent study course that will examine e-commerce planning ideas and e-commerce equipment requirements. Students will search the Internet to get help for their small business needs, such as selecting an Internet Service Provider, Web-hosting service and e-commerce solutions. They will also learn how to create a secure e-commerce environment, review legal issues involved in creating an e-commerce business, register with search engines, identify Internet marketing tools and use Customer Relationship Management to establish and maintain relationships with their customers.

▌2561
E-BUSINESS SPECIALIZATION
MARQUETTE UNIVERSITY
COLLEGE OF BUSINESS ADMINISTRATION
Holthusen Hall 305, PO Box 1881
Milwaukee, WI 53201-9702
PH: (414)288-7137
FX: (414)288-1902
URL: http://www.busadm.mu.edu/

Description: Marquette University provides an MBA degree with an E-Business specialization. Geared toward business managers, this program offers interdisciplinary exposure to

e-business. The coursework focuses on a managerial approach for those who develop business strategy and provide input to Web design.

▌2562
E-BUSINESS STRATEGY
BRIGHAM YOUNG UNIVERSITY
ROLLINS CENTER FOR E-BUSINESS
510 N. Tanner Bldg
PO Box 23068
Provo, UT 84602-3068
PH: (801)422-2815
FX: (801)422-5933
E-mail: ebusiness@byu.edu
URL: http://ebusiness.byu.edu/ebus.cfm
Contact: J. Owen Cherrington, Director

Description: Brigham Young University's Rollins Center for E-Business offers a course titled ''E-Business Strategy.'' This graduate level course looks at key issues and problems facing managers in start-up e-businesses and in mature companies transitioning to e-business. Topics covered include successful business models for e-businesses, raising and acquiring capital necessary to finance the e-business, as well as strategies and methods to acquire and protect intellectual property.

▌2563
E-BUSINESS STRATEGY AND POLICY
UNIVERSITY OF TEXAS
MCCOMBS SCHOOL OF BUSINESS
GSB 2.104
Austin, TX 78712-1178
PH: (512)471-5921
FX: (512)471-7725
E-mail: Sirkka.jarvenpaa@bus.utexas.edu
URL: http://www.bus.utexas.edu/faculty/Sirkka.Jarvenpaa/spring2002/strategy/stratandpolicy.htm
Contact: Dr. Sirkka Jarvenpaa, Instructor

Description: The course at the University of Texas entitled ''E-Business Strategy and Policy'' is a seminar course on new business models emerging in e-commerce. These new models are being deployed by both traditional firms moving to the Internet and by Internet-born firms. The models are driven by new technologies, new marketing philosophies, business innovations, and policies from around the world. This course will examine these models from business, technology, and policy perspectives.

▌2564
E-BUSINESS AND SUPPLY CHAINS
UNIVERSITY OF CALIFORNIA LOS ANGELES
ANDERSON SCHOOL OF MANAGEMENT
Box 951481
110 Westwood Plz.
Los Angeles, CA 90095-1481
PH: (310)825-6121
FX: (310)206-9830

E-mail: ageoffri@agsm.ucla.edu
URL: http://www.anderson.ucla.edu

Description: E-Business and Supply Chains is the title of a course offered at UCLA's Anderson business school. This course begins with a broad overview of e-business, surveying such topics as customer relationship management (CRM), dynamic pricing, e-business models, e-markets including auctions and exchanges, intellectual property, mass customization, security, and Web data mining

▌2565
E-BUSINESS: TECHNICAL INFRASTRUCTURE
CAPELLA UNIVERSITY

222 S 9th St., 20th Fl.
Minneapolis, MN 55402
PH: (612)339-8650
TF: 888-227-3552
FX: (612)339-8022
URL: http://www.capella.edu

Description: E-Business: Technical Infrastructure helps students discover the opportunities, technical platforms and technical limitations of electronic commerce over the Internet. Covered topics include e-commerce technologies focusing on modes of operation, an introduction to security issues, the technology of secure transactions and issues related to establishing websites to support e-commerce.

▌2566
E-BUSINESS TECHNOLOGIES
NOTRE DAME
COLLEGE OF BUSINESS

276 Mendoza College of Business
Notre Dame, IN 46556
PH: (219)631-8488
TF: 800-631-8488
FX: (219)631-8800
E-mail: mba.1@nd.edu
URL: http://www.nd.edu/~mba
Contact: Carolyn Woo, Dean

Description: The Notre Dame MBA Program offers a course called "E-Business Technologies." This course provides an overview of the technologies relevant to electronic commerce, including operating systems, networking, the Internet, computer security, and electronic transaction processing. The course also involves hands-on work in developing e-commerce applications.

▌2567
E-BUSINESS TECHNOLOGY
WALDEN UNIVERSITY

155 5th Ave. S
Minneapolis, MN 55401
PH: (612)338-7224
TF: 800-925-3368
FX: (612)338-5092

E-mail: info@waldenu.edu
URL: http://www.waldenu.edu

Description: Walden University offers an MBA course called "E-Business Technology." This course will give students an understanding of how to integrate an E-business technology plan into an enterprise infrastructure and how to determine its value. Issues examined in this course include system planning and management, performance, and testing.

▌2568
E-BUSINESS TECHNOLOGY
BELLEVUE UNIVERSITY

1000 Galvin Rd. S
Bellevue, NE 68005
PH: (402)293-2000
TF: 800-756-7920
FX: (402)293-2020
URL: http://www.bellevue.edu

Description: Bellevue University offers a course called "E-Business Technology." This course consists of an overall look at the technologies of electronic business. This course examines web systems, the attributes of a good web-site, data interchange, search engines, data mining, profile building, customer management, and intelligent agents.

▌2569
E-BUSINESS TECHNOLOGY AND ENTERPRISE MANAGEMENT I
GW CENTER FOR PROFESSIONAL DEVELOPMENT

2029 K Street NW, Ste. 600
Washington, DC 20006
PH: (202)973-1150
FX: (202)973-1165
E-mail: cpd@gwu.edu
URL: http://www.gwu.edu/~cpd/programs/CWEC/

Description: The GW Center for Professional Development offers a course called "E-Business Technology and Enterprise Management I." This course will provide an overview of e-commerce, and look at the process of mapping traditional business processes to new models. Some topics included will be the foundations of electronic commerce, retailing and marketing in electronic commerce, and B2B e-commerce.

▌2570
E-BUSINESS TECHNOLOGY FOR ENTERPRISE MANAGEMENT II
GW CENTER FOR PROFESSIONAL DEVELOPMENT

2029 K Street NW, Ste. 600
Washington, DC 20006
PH: (202)973-1150
FX: (202)973-1165
E-mail: cpd@gwu.edu
URL: http://www.gwu.edu/~cpd/programs/CWEC/

Description: The GW Center for Professional Development provides a course called "E-Business Technology for Enterprise Management II." This course will cover topics such as public policy issues, legal and privacy, infrastructure planning, economic issues and global expansion. Web site design will also be covered.

▌2571

E-BUSINESS TRAINING
ANITA ROSEN CONSULTING

1798 Vassar Ave.
Mountain View, CA 94043
PH: (650)960-2959
FX: (650)960-2958
E-mail: question@anitarosen.com
URL: http://www.anitarosen.com/E-Commerce-Training.html
Contact: Anita Rosen, Founder

Description: Anita Rosen Consulting offers a course called E-Business Training. This course is designed for business people who want to integrate e-business into their current business. Topics students will learn about include trends, strategies, creating infrastructure to support e-business, and maximizing effectiveness of web sites and services.

▌2572

E-BUSINESS: VIRTUAL TEAMS
CAPELLA UNIVERSITY

222 S 9th St., 20th Fl.
Minneapolis, MN 55402
PH: (612)339-8650
TF: 888-227-3552
FX: (612)339-8022
URL: http://www.capella.edu

Description: E-Business: Virtual Teams is intended for anyone who works in or leads virtual teams. Through team exercises, students will explore the groundwork, agreements, process and technical infrastructure that facilitate smooth teamwork and make appropriate use of online technology.

▌2573

E-COMMERCE
UNIVERSITY OF ALASKA FAIRBANKS

PO Box 757520
Fairbanks, AK 99775
PH: (907)474-7581
URL: http://www.uaf.edu

Description: The E-Commerce course explores the trends in Internet commerce and provides and analysis of the elements needed to build and manage a successful e-commerce business. Website planning and creation including information design, navigation design and site presentation will also be covered.

▌2574

E-COMMERCE
IDAHO STATE UNIVERSITY

College of Business
921 S 8th Ave.
Pocatello, ID 83209-8020
PH: (208)236-2915
E-mail: balsrona@isu.edu
URL: http://www.isu.edu
Contact: Dr. Ronald Balsley, Course Instructor

Description: E-Commerce (MBA 637) is a study of Internet market opportunities, business models, customer interfaces and communication issues and includes issues of planning, implementation and evaluation of online enterprises.

▌2575

E-COMMERCE
UNIVERSITY OF TOLEDO

2801 W Bancroft
Toledo, OH 43606-3390
PH: (419)530-2987
E-mail: tle2@utnet.utoledo.edu
URL: http://www.utoledo.edu
Contact: Dr. Thuong Le

Founded: 1872. **Description:** The University of Toledo's E-Commerce program offers students both an e-commerce major and minor and enables students to pursue a wide range of career options, in e-commerce or in more "traditional" fields. Students specializing in e-commerce can broaden their career horizon by combining it with a minor in another field, such as marketing, information systems, financial services, international business and supply management. Those specializing in other fields can gain a competitive edge in their future careers with a minor in e-commerce. A minimum of 18 hours is required to major in this area of specialization.

▌2576

E-COMMERCE
UNIVERSITY OF MARYLAND
SMITH SCHOOL OF BUSINESS

Van Munching Hall
College park, MD 20742
PH: (301)405-2278
E-mail: sfaraj@rhsmith.umd.edu
URL: http://ecommerce.umd.edu/faraj/
Contact: Dr. Samer Faraj, Instructor

Description: The University of Maryland Smith School of Business offers a course titled "E-Commerce." This course it taught from a business perspective and covers both the strategic and technical essentials of what a manager needs to know in order to manage and lead an electronic commerce initiative. We will focus on assessing the marketing and strategic impact of EC on areas such as: publishing, retailing, entertainment, and travel.

▌ 2577

E-COMMERCE

RUTGERS UNIVERSITY

ACCOUNTING AND INFO. SYS.

180 University Ave.
Newark, NJ 07102
PH: (973)353-5002
FX: (973)353-1283
E-mail: miklosv@andromeda.rutgers.edu
URL: http://raw.rutgers.edu/ecommerce/
Contact: Miklos Vasarhelyi, Professor

Description: The course titled "E-Commerce" at Rutgers University covers such topics as Electronic Commerce: evolving business towards an electronic future, business to business e-commerce, creating strategy for e-business, and predicting technology.

▌ 2578

E-COMMERCE

UNIVERSITY OF TEXAS AT SAN ANTONIO

COLLEGE OF BUSINESS

6900 N Loop 1604 W
San Antonio, TX 78249-0631
PH: (210)458-4313
FX: (210)458-4308
E-mail: jstory@utsa.edu
URL: http://www.business.utsa.edu/faculty/jstory/mkt6973/mkt6973.htm
Contact: Dr. John Story, Instructor

Description: The University of Texas at San Antonio offers "E-Commerce" which will introduce students to the concepts, theories, and strategies of marketing on the Internet in a global marketplace. Students will develop an understanding of what the Internet is and how it is affecting marketing; learn to understand the role information technology plays in establishing competitive advantages; as well as develop strategies and tactics for successful e-commerce

▌ 2579

E-COMMERCE

UNIVERSITY OF CENTRAL FLORIDA

COLLEGE OF BUSINESS ADMINISTRATION

4000 Central Florida Blvd.
Orlando, FL 32816
PH: (407)823-4138
E-mail: jim.courtney@bus.ucf.edu
URL: http://www.bus.ucf.edu/jcourtney/Ecomm/ec-Frames.htm
Contact: James Courtney, Instructor

Description: The University of Central Florida offers a course "E-Commerce" which is taught about 50% online, and 50% in the classroom. This class will introduce the concept of electronic commerce, and help students understand how electronic commerce is affecting business enterprises, governments, consumers and people in general. In addition, the class will study the development of websites using software such as HTML, the extensible markup language (XML), Frontpage 2000, FrontPage Express (available with MS Windows 98) or Netscape Composer.

▌ 2580

E-COMMERCE

NORTHWESTERN OKLAHOMA STATE UNIVERSITY

DIVISION OF E-COMMERCE

709 Oklahoma Blvd.
Alva, OK 73717-2399
PH: (580)213-3109
FX: (580)213-3115
E-mail: kharris@nwosu.edu
URL: http://www.nwosu.edu/ecom/

Description: The Division of E-Commerce at Northwestern Oklahoma State University is dedicated to the education of students in e-commerce. The program offers a Bachelor of Science degree in electronic commerce. The e-commerce degree at Northwestern Oklahoma State University has been designed with a strong emphasis on theory, along with rigorous laboratory requirements. Students will graduate with skills in designing, developing and deploying a full scale e-commerce venture.

▌ 2581

E-COMMERCE AND ACCOUNTING

KRANNERT SCHOOL OF MANAGEMENT

Purdue University
1310 Krannert Bldg.
West Lafayette, IN 47907
PH: (765)496-3384
FX: (765)494-9841
E-mail: jdietz@mgmt.purdue.edu
URL: http://www.mgmt.purdue.edu
Contact: Joy Dietz, Manager of Advising and Student Services

Description: E-Commerce and Accounting discusses the effect that the increase in e-commerce and the growth of information available on the Internet has on financial and managerial accounting.

▌ 2582

E-COMMERCE ADMINISTRATION

BAKER COLLEGE

1116 W Bristol Rd.
Flint, MI 48507-9843
PH: (810)766-4390
TF: 800-469-3165
FX: (810)766-4399
E-mail: gradschl@baker.edu
URL: http://www.baker.edu

Description: Baker College offers an online course entitled E-Commerce Administration. This graduate level course looks at administrative issues such as payment systems, maintenance, privacy and security, legal and marketing aspects, and social and political issues.

▌2583

E-COMMERCE: ADVANCED TOPICS

THE STUDENT CENTER

STUDENT.COM

9A Main St.
Irvington, NY 10533
PH: (914)591-3080
FX: (914)591-3264
E-mail: info@student.com.sg
URL: http://broadbeans.com/vibenet/Training/E-Commerce_Courses/index.html

Description: Student.com and Vibenet offer an online course called E-Commerce: Advanced Topics. This online course looks at the advanced technical and business aspects of e-commerce, including case studies of both successful and unsuccessful companies.

▌2584

E-COMMERCE: ADVERTISING ON THE INTERNET

MINDLEADERS

851 W 3rd Ave., Bldg. 3
Columbus, OH 43212
PH: (614)781-7300
TF: 800-223-3732
FX: (614)781-6510
E-mail: webrequest@mindleaders.com
URL: http://www.mindleaders.com

Description: MindLeaders provides online learning courses, including a class titled "E-Commerce: Advertising on the Internet." In this course some topics students will look at are Internet promotion, attracting customers to your site, and designing your ads.

▌2585

E-COMMERCE: AN INTRODUCTION

BERKMAN CENTER FOR INTERNET AND SOCIETY

Pound Hall 511
1563 Massachusetts Ave.
Cambridge, MA 02138
PH: (617)495-7547
FX: (617)495-7641
E-mail: dcabell@law.harvard.edu
URL: http://www.cyber.law.harvard.edu
Contact: Diane Cabell, Director, Clinical Program in Cyberlaw

Description: E-Commerce: An Introduction is an online education opportunity that will cover the major legal issues related to establishing and maintaining an e-commerce enterprise. This is a beginner's level series for practitioners new to e-commerce. The program runs for two weeks and participants can choose to either read the text online or listen to an audio recording of the syllabus material.

▌2586

E-COMMERCE ANALYSIS AND STRATEGY DECISIONS

BAKER COLLEGE

1116 W Bristol Rd.
Flint, MI 48507-9843
PH: (810)766-4390
TF: 800-469-3165
FX: (810)766-4399
E-mail: gradschl@baker.edu
URL: http://www.baker.edu

Description: Baker College offers an online course called E-Commerce Analysis and Strategy Decisions. This graduate level course gives managers an introduction to e-commerce and examines action to be taken in the development of an e-business. This course includes an evaluation of services or products to be sold on the Internet.

▌2587

E-COMMERCE APPLICATION DEVELOPMENT

ST. LOUIS UNIVERSITY

COOK SCHOOL OF BUSINESS

3674 Lindell Blvd.
St. Louis, MO 63108
PH: (314)977-3864
FX: (314)977-3897
E-mail: katzja@slu.edu
URL: http://eweb.slu.edu/e-com_courses.htm

Description: St. Louis University offers a course called "E-Commerce Application Development." This graduate level course looks at an approach to the principles of design and implementation for electronic commerce systems. Issues in project management are also covered.

▌2588

E-COMMERCE ARCHITECTURE AND APPLICATIONS

REGIS UNIVERSITY

GRADUATE PROGRAMS

3333 Regis Boulevard, L-16
Denver, CO 80221-1099
PH: (303)458-4080
TF: 800-667-9270
FX: (303)964-5538
E-mail: masters@regis.edu
URL: http://www.regis.edu

Description: Regis University offers a course called E-Commerce Architecture and Applications. In this course students will learn about the architectural components of a successful E-Commerce business site (telecom, web server, user interface, management) through case histories. This course focuses on telecom and management.

571

▌2589

E-COMMERCE/ASP

INTERNET TECHNOLOGY TRAINING CENTER

156 E Milton Ave.
Rahway, NJ 07065
PH: (732)574-9595
TF: 800-481-4142
FX: (732)574-9599
E-mail: training@getontheworldwideweb.com
URL: http://www.getontheworldwideweb.com/ecommerce.htm

Description: The Internet Technology Training Center offers a course called E-Commerce/ASP. This course focuses on Microsoft Active Server Pages Technology to create an e-commerce site. Students learn how to build an e-commerce site including a shopping cart system, Check Out, Payment, Order Status Fulfillment and Online Store Management Facilities.

▌2590

E-COMMERCE BASIC IT INFRASTRUCTURE

GEORGE MASON UNIVERSITY

DEPARTMENT OF COMPUTER SCIENCE

MSN 4A5
4400 University Dr.
Fairfax, VA 22030
PH: (703)993-1530
FX: (703)993-1710
E-mail: csadmin@cs.gmu.edu
URL: http://ite.gmu.edu/msecomm/description.htm

Description: George Mason University offers a course called ''E-Commerce Basic IT Infrastructure.'' This course looks at the basic networking infrastructure used in E-commerce environments as well as typical multi-tiered E-commerce architectures of E-commerce sites.

▌2591

E-COMMERCE BASICS (SBA)

U.S. SMALL BUSINESS ADMINISTRATION

409 3rd St. SW
Washington, DC 20416
PH: 800-827-5722
E-mail: classroom@sba.gov
URL: http://www.sba.gov/classroom

Description: The Small Business Administration (SBA) in partnership with Cisco Systems offers a free online course called E-Commerce Basics. This course will help students learn about the basics of e-commerce and the various different kinds of e-commerce.

▌2592

E-COMMERCE BASICS

THE STUDENT CENTER

STUDENT.COM

9A Main St.
Irvington, NY 10533
PH: (914)591-3080
FX: (914)591-3264
E-mail: info@student.com.sg
URL: http://broadbeans.com/vibenet/Training/E-Commerce_Courses/index.html

Description: Student.com and Vibenet offer an online course called E-Commerce Basics. This course covers basic topics including how to choose a service provider and register a domain name, as well as managing and promoting a web site, and measuring its effectiveness.

▌2593

E-COMMERCE BEST PRACTICES

24/7 UNIVERSITY, INC.

16980 Dallas Pky., Ste. 247
Dallas, TX 75248
PH: (972)248-2470
E-mail: info@247university.com
URL: http://www.247university.com

Description: 24/7 University offers an online course called E-Commerce Best Practices. This course shows students best practices for planning, project management, and security. While looking at both business-to-business and consumer transactions, the course program also explores areas such as required technical infrastructure and the future direction of e-commerce.

▌2594

E-COMMERCE AND BEYOND

NOTRE DAME

COLLEGE OF BUSINESS

276 Mendoza College of Business
Notre Dame, IN 46556
PH: (219)631-8488
TF: 800-631-8488
FX: (219)631-8800
E-mail: mba.1@nd.edu
URL: http://www.nd.edu/~mba
Contact: Carolyn Woo, Dean

Description: The Notre Dame MBA Program offers a course called ''E-Commerce and Beyond.'' This course introduces students to issues in E-commerce. Topics addressed include Business-to-Consumer e-tailing, Business-to-Business relationships, Supply Chain Management, Data Warehousing and Mining, Internet Security, Valuation and assessment of e-businesses.

▌ 2595

E-COMMERCE: BUILDING MARKETING STRATEGY

MINDLEADERS

851 W 3rd Ave., Bldg. 3
Columbus, OH 43212
PH: (614)781-7300
TF: 800-223-3732
FX: (614)781-6510
E-mail: webrequest@mindleaders.com
URL: http://www.mindleaders.com

Description: MindLeaders provides online learning courses, including a class titled "E-Commerce: Building Marketing Strategy." In this course students will gain an overview of online marketing options including data mining and external promotion. Students will also look at investor and public relations.

▌ 2596

E-COMMERCE BUSINESS ANALYST CERTIFICATE PROGRAM

UNIVERSITY OF DELAWARE

192 South Chapel St.
Newark, DE 19716
PH: (302)831-2000
FX: (302)831-2970
E-mail: registrar@udel.edu
URL: http://www.udel.edu

Description: In addition to courses offered on campus in a traditional college setting, the University of Delaware offers the online E-Commerce Business Analyst Certificate Program. The E-Commerce Certificate is a sequence of six related courses built around a specific e-commerce functional role and can be completed within about 12 months on a part-time basis. There is no formal prerequisite for admission, but the material is presented at an advanced undergraduate level.

▌ 2597

E-COMMERCE BUSINESS AND TECHNOLOGY: AN INTRODUCTION

UNIVERSITY OF CALIFORNIA EXTENSION ONLINE

2000 Center St., Ste. 400
Berkeley, CA 94704
PH: (510)642-4124
E-mail: askus@ucxonline.berkeley.edu
URL: http://learn.berkely.edu/

Description: The University of California Extension Online offers an E-Commerce course called "E-Commerce Business and Technology: An Introduction." This online course looks at a range of e-commerce business and technology concepts, using case studies and demonstrations. It is intended to allow e-commerce managers and other professionals to visualize and experience planning and executing of an e-commerce project.

▌ 2598

E-COMMERCE BUSINESS TRACK CERTIFICATE PROGRAM

NATIONAL CENTER FOR MANUFACTURING SCIENCES

3025 Boardwalk
Ann Arbor, MI 48108-3266
PH: (734)995-0300
FX: (734)995-4004
E-mail: training@ncms.org
URL: http://wwww.ncms.org

Description: The National Center for Manufacturing Sciences offers an E-Commerce Business Track Certification program. The coursework in this program includes information on e-business fundamentals, JAVA business basics, and e-commerce business models and processes. These classes are offered at the NCMS headquarters in Ann Arbor, Michigan.

▌ 2599

E-COMMERCE C/F

INTERNET TECHNOLOGY TRAINING CENTER

156 E Milton Ave.
Rahway, NJ 07065
PH: (732)574-9595
TF: 800-481-4142
FX: (732)574-9599
E-mail: training@getontheworldwideweb.com
URL: http://www.getontheworldwideweb.com/ecommerce.htm

Description: The Internet Technology Training Center offers a course called E-Commerce C/F. This course uses Allaire's ColdFusion Application Server to create an e-commerce site. Students will learn how to build a functional e-commerce site.

▌ 2600

E-COMMERCE CAPSTONE IMPLEMENTATION PROJECT

UNIVERSITY OF CALIFORNIA EXTENSION ONLINE

2000 Center St., Ste. 400
Berkeley, CA 94704
PH: (510)642-4124
E-mail: askus@ucxonline.berkeley.edu
URL: http://learn.berkely.edu/

Description: The University of California Extension Online's "E-Commerce Capstone Implementation Project" is designed to provide students with a hands-on, project-based introduction to building an e-commerce systems implementation. Students will learn how to plan, develop, deploy and manage an e-commerce business that is focused on direct marketing, selling, and service, or corporate business to business applications.

▌2601

E-COMMERCE CERTIFICATE

GEORGIA TECH

DUPREE COLLEGE OF MANAGEMENT

IXL CENTER FOR ELECTRONIC COMMERCE

755 Ferst Dr.
Atlanta, GA 30332-0250
PH: (404)385-0138
E-mail: michelle.graham@mgt.gatech.edu
URL: http://www.dupree.gatech.edu/ebus/
Contact: Michelle Graham

Description: Georgia Tech iXL Center for Electronic Commerce offers opportunities for both learning and research. The research and teaching activities of the Center focus on these key areas: online marketing, strategic uses of business-to-business inter-organizational systems, information security, information technology-enabled entrepreneurship, business intelligence, and business models for Internet-based ventures.

▌2602

E-COMMERCE CONCENTRATION

ILLINOIS INSTITUTE OF TECHNOLOGY

STUART GRADUATE SCHOOL OF BUSINESS

565 W. Adams St.
Chicago, IL 60661
PH: (312)906-6500
E-mail: bariff@stuart.iit.edu
URL: http://www.stuart.iit.edu/

Description: The Illinois Institute of Technology offers an MBA with a concentration in E-Commerce. This program teaches students how to attract new customers and business partners as well as strengthening existing relationships through the use of the Internet. Courses address business strategy in the network economy, marketing, managing a web-enabled supply chain, and security and privacy issues.

▌2603

E-COMMERCE: CUSTOMER SERVICE AND PAYMENT

MINDLEADERS

851 W 3rd Ave., Bldg. 3
Columbus, OH 43212
PH: (614)781-7300
TF: 800-223-3732
FX: (614)781-6510
E-mail: webrequest@mindleaders.com
URL: http://www.mindleaders.com

Description: MindLeaders provides online learning courses, including a class titled "E-Commerce: Customer Service and Payment." This course examines various types of customer payment resources and different methods of serving customers, such as call centers.

▌2604

E-COMMERCE DESIGN AND DEVELOPMENT

UNIVERSITY OF DALLAS

GRADUATE SCHOOL OF MANAGEMENT

1845 E Northgate Dr.
Irving, TX 75062
PH: (972)721-5000
E-mail: msavoie@udallas.edu
URL: http://gsmweb.udallas.edu/concentrations/
e_business.html

Description: The University of Dallas Graduate School of Management provides a course called E-Commerce Design and Development. This course examines various processes necessary to successfully integrate a web site into the strategic plan of an organization.

▌2605

E-COMMERCE: DEVELOPING YOUR E-BUSINESS

MINDLEADERS

851 W 3rd Ave., Bldg. 3
Columbus, OH 43212
PH: (614)781-7300
TF: 800-223-3732
FX: (614)781-6510
E-mail: webrequest@mindleaders.com
URL: http://www.mindleaders.com

Description: MindLeaders provides online learning courses, including "E-Commerce: Developing Your E-Business." This course provides students with an overview of the virtual corporation and looks at pitfalls in the process of creating one.

▌2606

E-COMMERCE FOR THE E-ENTREPRENEUR WITH MICROSOFT FRONTPAGE

UNIVERSITY OF COLORADO AT DENVER

Campus Box 165
PO Box 173364
Denver, CO 80217-3364
PH: (303)556-5826
FX: (303)556-6276
E-mail: pdp@carbon.cudenver.edu
URL: http://www.cudenver.edu

Description: E-Commerce for the E-entrepreneur with Microsoft FrontPage is an introductory course that combines one day of fundamentals for promoting and marketing your business online with two days of hands-on Microsoft FrontPage training. The course is designed for Small Business Owners, Computer Technology Professionals, Marketing and Sales Consultants, Executives and Managers.

▌2607

E-COMMERCE AND E-MARKETING

VALPARAISO UNIVERSITY

COLLEGE OF BUSINESS ADMINISTRATION

104 Urschel Hall
Valparaiso, IN 46383
PH: (219)465-7952
TF: 800-599-0840
FX: (219)464-5789
E-mail: mba@valpo.edu
URL: http://www.valpo.edu/mba/

Description: Valparaiso University offers a course titled "E-Commerce and E-Marketing." This graduate level course looks at using the Internet as an integral component of a firm's marketing communications strategy. Internet only as well as 'bricks and mortar' companies will be studied.

▌2608

E-COMMERCE ENTREPRENEURIAL START-UP PROJECT

FOX SCHOOL-TEMPLE UNIVERSITY

Speakman Hall, Rm. 5
Philadelphia, PA 19122
PH: (215)204-7678
E-mail: foxmbams.info@temple.edu
URL: http://www.sbm.temple.edu

Description: E-Commerce Entrepreneurial Start-up Project can be taken only by MBA/MS Day Cohort Program Students and integrates material from the previous courses in the MBA/MS program. The course provides an opportunity for students to explore the creation of an idea for a new e-business, as well as the planning and research involved in moving from the idea stage to the startup stage. This course involves preparation of a business plan on the new e-business idea and provides students with an on-going platform to develop and integrate concepts presented in previous and concurrent seminars.

▌2609

E-COMMERCE ENTREPRENEURSHIP

UNIVERSITY OF DALLAS

GRADUATE SCHOOL OF MANAGEMENT

1845 E Northgate Dr.
Irving, TX 75062
PH: (972)721-5000
E-mail: msavoie@udallas.edu
URL: http://gsmweb.udallas.edu/concentrations/e_business.html

Description: The University of Dallas Graduate School of Management provides a course called E-Commerce Entrepreneurship. This course explores value-based management and the metrics required to analyze and direct an e-company as it grows from start-up to a publicly-traded company.

▌2610

E-COMMERCE IN THE FINANCIAL SERVICES INDUSTRY

UNIVERSITY OF MINNESOTA

CARLSON SCHOOL OF MANAGEMENT

321 19th Ave. S.
Minneapolis, MN 55455
PH: (612)624-8030
FX: (612)626-1316
E-mail: mbawebmaster@csom.umn.edu
URL: http://www.csom.umn.edu/
Contact: Larry Benveniste, Dean

Description: The Carlson School of Management at the University of Minnesota offers a graduate level course called "E-Commerce in the Financial Services Industry." This course covers organizational, strategic and technology-focused consideration of e-commerce and traditional systems in the financial services. IT-focused business models of financial firms; industry and firm technology infrastructures, applications (e.g., data mining of financial data on the Web) and in-firm control technologies (risk management and payment security) are other topics addressed.

▌2611

E-COMMERCE FUNDAMENTALS

SEREBRA LEARNING CORP.

7565 132nd St., Unit 119
Surrey, BC, Canada V3W1K5
PH: (604)592-0552
TF: 800-567-7766
FX: (604)592-0553
E-mail: info@serebra.com
URL: http://www.serebra.com
Contact: Mr. Bruce Stewart, President

Founded: 1987. **Description:** Serebra Learning Corporation offers an online course called, "E-Commerce Fundamentals." Designed for business managers who want to incorporate ecommerce into their businesses, this class will provides students with an introduction to the technologies and concepts of e-commerce. It will also provide students with the knowledge of different e-commerce system architectures and help them in planning the implementation of an e-commerce system.

▌2612

E-COMMERCE FUNDAMENTALS

DIGITALTHINK INC

601 Brannan St.
San Francisco, CA 94107
PH: (415)625-4000
TF: 888-686-8817
FX: (415)625-4100
E-mail: info@digitalthink.com
URL: http://www.digitalthink.com
Contact: Mr. Pete Goettner, Chairman

Founded: 1996. **Staff:** 450. **Description:** DigitalThink offers online courses, one of which is ''E-Commerce Fundamentals.'' This course, which is also offered in an international version, is designed to teach students the basics of conducting business online. This course covers the similarities and differences between traditional and electronic commerce and the technologies used to place orders and process payments. Students will also address the legal issues surrounding this new medium, and the security protections offered for Web-based businesses and their customers.

▌2613

E-COMMERCE FUNDAMENTALS

RED HAT

1801 Varsity Dr.
Raleigh, NC 27606
PH: (919)754-3700
TF: 888-733-4281
FX: (919)754-3701
E-mail: customerservice@redhat.com
URL: http://www.redhat.com

Description: Red Hat, the largest provider of open source technology, offers an online course called ''E-Commerce Fundamentals.'' In this course students will learn the basics of conducting business online. Students will look at technologies, legal issues and security issues of doing business on the Internet.

▌2614

E-COMMERCE FUNDAMENTALS FOR BANKERS

DIGITALTHINK INC

601 Brannan St.
San Francisco, CA 94107
PH: (415)625-4000
TF: 888-686-8817
FX: (415)625-4100
E-mail: info@digitalthink.com
URL: http://www.digitalthink.com
Contact: Mr. Pete Goettner, Chairman

Founded: 1996. **Staff:** 450. **Description:** DigitalThink provides an online course entitled ''E-Commerce Fundamentals for Bankers.'' Geared towards financial professionals, this class is designed to teach students the basics of conducting business online. The course begins with a discussion about commerce and how it impacts traditional business models. It then discusses the similarities and differences between traditional and electronic commerce, and how to prepare a business for e-business. Students also address the legal issues surrounding this new medium. After discussing the technologies used to place orders and process payments, this course covers security offered for Web-based banking, as well as for businesses and their customers.

▌2615

E-COMMERCE: GETTING STARTED

MINDLEADERS

851 W 3rd Ave., Bldg. 3
Columbus, OH 43212
PH: (614)781-7300
TF: 800-223-3732
FX: (614)781-6510
E-mail: webrequest@mindleaders.com
URL: http://www.mindleaders.com

Description: MindLeaders provides online learning including a course called ''E-Commerce: Getting Started.'' This course looks at the benefits of e-commerce, defining e-commerce, domains, Internet mechanics and operations issues.

▌2616

E-COMMERCE IN A GLOBAL ENVIRONMENT

UNIVERSITY OF LOUISVILLE
COLLEGE OF BUSINESS AND PUBLIC
ADMINISTRATION

College of Business and Public Administration
Louisville, KY 40292
PH: (502)852-4787
E-mail: bldoss01@acm.org
URL: http://dossantos.cbpa.louisville.edu/courses/Imba/index.html
Contact: Brian L. Dos Santos, Instructor

Description: The course E-Commerce in a Global Environment offered by the University of Louisville's College of Business will provide you with an understanding of what the information revolution means to you and to industries. Our emphasis will be on how business models are changing in a digital world and how global business environments are affected by and affect these changes.

▌2617

E-COMMERCE IMPLEMENTATION ISSUES

NETG

1751 W Diehl Rd, 2nd Fl.
Naperville, IL 60563-9099
PH: (630)369-3000
TF: 877-561-6384
FX: (630)983-4877
E-mail: info@netg.com
URL: http://www.netg.com

Description: NETg offers a course called E-Commerce Implementation Issues. This course uses case studies to explore the issues of implementing an e-commerce business. Topics covered include web sites, online storefronts, access control, and features and functions of shopping carts.

■ 2618
E-COMMERCE IMPLEMENTATION ISSUES
UNIVERSITY OF FLORIDA

Office of the University Registrar
Cruiser Hall
PO Box 114000
Gainesville, FL 32611-4000
PH: (352)392-3261; (352)392-1374
URL: http://www.ufl.edu

Description: E-Commerce Implementation Issues provides students with information and case studies highlighting the issues associated with e-commerce implementation. The intended audience is managers and technical staff who are in a position to provide e-commerce recommendations to executives and will teach them about the scale of implementation and other implementation issues.

■ 2619
E-COMMERCE: INFLUENCES ON E-COMMERCE
MINDLEADERS

851 W 3rd Ave., Bldg. 3
Columbus, OH 43212
PH: (614)781-7300
TF: 800-223-3732
FX: (614)781-6510
E-mail: webrequest@mindleaders.com
URL: http://www.mindleaders.com

Description: MindLeaders provides an online course called "E-Commerce: Influences on E-Commerce." This course takes a look at Internet stock and the influences that raise stock value. Other topics covered include building an online presence and approaching the market.

■ 2620
E-COMMERCE: INTERNET BUSINESS STRATEGIES
GESTALT PARTNERS LLC

2070 Chain Bridge Rd., Ste. G40
Vienna, VA 22182
PH: 888-844-4549
FX: (703)748-1553
E-mail: courseware@gestalt-sys.com
URL: http://www.gestalt-courseware.com/outlines/html/ecom1d.htm

Description: Gestalt Partners LLC offers a course called E-Commerce: Internet Business Strategies. This course is designed to give students an overview of e-business concepts and strategies. In this course students will learn about the evolution of e-commerce, the benefits and effects of e-commerce, and elements of creating and deploying a successful e-commerce business.

■ 2621
E-COMMERCE INTERNET TECHNOLOGIES
UNIVERSITY OF CALIFORNIA EXTENSION ONLINE

2000 Center St., Ste. 400
Berkeley, CA 94704
PH: (510)642-4124
E-mail: askus@ucxonline.berkeley.edu
URL: http://learn.berkely.edu/

Description: The University of California Extension Online offers online coursework titled "E-Commerce Internet Technologies." This course focuses on e-commerce network design, integration, and deployment concepts, and technologies, through case studies, class exercises, and illustrations. Students will gain a working knowledge of how to effectively use the Internet networking infrastructure for e-business networks.

■ 2622
E-COMMERCE ISSUES
NORWICH UNIVERSITY

158 Harmon Dr.
Northfield, VT 05663
PH: (802)485-2001
TF: 800-468-6679
E-mail: nuadm@norwich.edu
URL: http://www.norwich.edu

Description: Norwich University offers a seminar called "E-Commerce Issues." This course is offered through Norwich University's online MBA program and covers e-business structures, strategies, operations and marketing.

■ 2623
E-COMMERCE ISSUES AND TOOLS
BAKER COLLEGE

1116 W Bristol Rd.
Flint, MI 48507-9843
PH: (810)766-4390
TF: 800-469-3165
FX: (810)766-4399
E-mail: gradschl@baker.edu
URL: http://www.baker.edu

Description: Baker College offers an online course entitled E-Commerce Issues and Tools. This course helps students evaluate various methods for implementing an e-commerce plan. Some of the tools investigated are web servers, HTML, web page editors, and programming options.

■ 2624
E-COMMERCE: KILLER APPS
MINDLEADERS
851 W 3rd Ave., Bldg. 3
Columbus, OH 43212
PH: (614)781-7300
TF: 800-223-3732
FX: (614)781-6510

E-mail: webrequest@mindleaders.com
URL: http://www.mindleaders.com

Description: MindLeaders provides an online course titled ''E-Commerce: Killer Apps.'' This course defines 'killer apps' and teaches students how to build them. It also looks at avoiding potential problems and protecting yourself.

▌ 2625
E-COMMERCE LAW
ILLINOIS INSTITUTE OF TECHNOLOGY
STUART GRADUATE SCHOOL OF BUSINESS

565 W Adams St.
Chicago, IL 60661
PH: (312)906-6500
FX: (312)906-6549
E-mail: degrees@stuart.iit.edu
URL: http://www.stuart.iit.edu

Description: The Illinois Institute of Technology Stuart Graduate School of Business offers a course entitled E-Commerce Law. This course explores the legal framework governing electronic commerce in the United States. Students will look at potential problems and their solutions, as well as some aspects of international law.

▌ 2626
E-COMMERCE LAW
NORTHWESTERN OKLAHOMA STATE UNIVERSITY
DIVISION OF E-COMMERCE

709 Oklahoma Blvd.
Alva, OK 73717-2399
PH: (580)327-8440
FX: (580)327-8167
E-mail: kharris@nwosu.edu
URL: http://www.nwosu.edu/ecom/curriculum/cdesc.html

Description: Northwestern Oklahoma State University's Division of E-Commerce offers a course called ''E-Commerce Law.'' This course takes an in-depth look at electronic commerce law, policy and regulations.

▌ 2627
E-COMMERCE LAW AND REGULATION
FOX SCHOOL-TEMPLE UNIVERSITY

Speakman Hall, Rm. 5
Philadelphia, PA 19122
PH: (215)204-7678
E-mail: foxmbams.info@temple.edu
URL: http://www.sbm.temple.edu

Description: E-Commerce Law and Regulation integrates material from the previous courses in the MBA/MS program and is only available to MBA/MS students. This is a graduate course that highlights the legal concerns that an educated consumer or business professional must know when dealing with the world of e-commerce. Issues discussed will include

the law of Internet transactions, intellectual property protection, contract creation and enforcement, potential tort liability and police powers.

▌ 2628
E-COMMERCE: LOWERING YOUR BUSINESS COSTS
MINDLEADERS

851 W 3rd Ave., Bldg. 3
Columbus, OH 43212
PH: (614)781-7300
TF: 800-223-3732
FX: (614)781-6510
E-mail: webrequest@mindleaders.com
URL: http://www.mindleaders.com

Description: MindLeaders provides online learning courses, including ''E-Commerce: Lowering Your Business Costs.'' This course provides an overview of how you can lower your e-business costs by using virtual employees and automating the vendor and customer flow.

▌ 2629
E-COMMERCE MAJOR
UNIVERSITY OF DENVER
DANIELS COLLEGE OF BUSINESS

2101 S University Blvd.
Denver, CO 80208
PH: (303)871-3416
FX: (303)871-4466
E-mail: dcb@du.edu
URL: http://www.dcb.du.edu/itec/mbaec.asp

Description: The University of Denver Daniels College of Business offers an undergraduate degree program, BS in Business with an E-Commerce major. The electronic commerce (EC) major is designed to prepare students for a career in strategic marketing in an EC environment. Careers for graduates may include consulting firms, with internal systems or electronic commerce groups, or with technology-intensive firms such as software developers or providers of information services.

▌ 2630
E-COMMERCE MANAGEMENT
UNIVERSITY OF DALLAS
GRADUATE SCHOOL OF MANAGEMENT

1845 E Northgate Dr.
Irving, TX 75062
PH: (972)721-5000
E-mail: msavoie@udallas.edu
URL: http://gsmweb.udallas.edu/concentrations/e_business.html

Description: The University of Dallas Graduate School of Management provides a course called E-Commerce Management. This course uses Harvard Business School cases and other reports to present an overview of the E-commerce environment. Other topics covered include telecommunications, information technology and marketing.

∎ 2631

E-COMMERCE MANAGEMENT

CARNEGIE MELLON UNIVERSITY

GRADUATE SCHOOL

GSIA, Tech & Frew Sts., Rm. 206
Pittsburgh, PA 15213
PH: (412)268-1322
FX: (412)268-6837
E-mail: msecinfo@andrew.cmu.edu
URL: http://www.ecom.cmu.edu

Description: Carnegie Mellon University offers a graduate level course called E-Commerce Management. In this course, students will address how marketing and service, business-to-business commerce and supply chain management are affected by new technologies. In addition, students will examine Internet strategies of today and tomorrow.

∎ 2632

E-COMMERCE MANAGEMENT: THE BIG PICTURE

SAN JOSE STATE UNIVERSITY

PROFESSIONAL DEVELOPMENT CENTER

3031 Tisch Way, Ste. 200 Plz. E
San Jose, CA 95128
PH: (408)257-3000
E-mail: mitchell.levy.sjsupd@ecnow.com
URL: http://ecmtraining.com/sjsu/
Contact: Mitchell Levy, Program Founder and Coordinator

Description: San Jose State University offers an executive education course called "E-Commerce Management: The Big Picture." This course focuses on the big picture of e-commerce, examining both effective and non-effective strategies that companies have used. Students will gain a good understanding of what e-commerce is and learn about some of the approaches necessary to make it an asset to companies' long-term survival.

∎ 2633

E-COMMERCE FOR MANAGERS

INTERNET TECHNOLOGY TRAINING CENTER

156 E Milton Ave.
Rahway, NJ 07065
PH: (732)574-9595
TF: 800-481-4142
FX: (732)574-9599
E-mail: training@getontheworldwideweb.com
URL: http://www.getontheworldwideweb.com/ecommerce.htm

Description: The Internet Technology Training Center offers a course called E-Commerce for Managers. This course

examines e-commerce concepts, software and hardware architecture, including outsourcing your e-commerce infrastructure.

∎ 2634

E-COMMERCE: MANAGING YOUR E-BUSINESS

MINDLEADERS

851 W 3rd Ave., Bldg. 3
Columbus, OH 43212
PH: (614)781-7300
TF: 800-223-3732
FX: (614)781-6510
E-mail: webrequest@mindleaders.com
URL: http://www.mindleaders.com

Description: MindLeaders provides online learning courses, including a class titled "E-Commerce: Managing Your E-Business." This course looks at ways to reduce costs, to leverage your assets, encouraging repeat customers, and other issues important to ensure continued success of an E-business.

∎ 2635

E-COMMERCE AND MARKETING

CREIGHTON UNIVERSITY

COLLEGE OF BUSINESS ADMINISTRATION

2500 California Plz.
Omaha, NE 68178
PH: (402)280-2602
FX: (402)280-2172
E-mail: ghafer@creighton.edu
URL: http://www.creighton.edu
Contact: Ms. Gail Hafer, Graduate Coordinator

Description: Creighton University offers a graduate level course called E-Commerce and Marketing. This course looks at the way e-commerce and the Internet is changing the way businesses market their products and services. Topics covered include advertising and selling on the Internet, the use of web sites to provide customer service and support, consumer decision making when shopping online, and the development of databases which allow customization of products and services.

∎ 2636

E-COMMERCE MARKETING

UNIVERSITY OF DALLAS

GRADUATE SCHOOL OF MANAGEMENT

1845 E Northgate Dr.
Irving, TX 75062
PH: (972)721-5000
E-mail: msavoie@udallas.edu
URL: http://gsmweb.udallas.edu/concentrations/e_business.html

Description: The University of Dallas Graduate School of Management provides a course called E-Commerce Marketing. This course focuses on the basic principles of marketing to create and retain customers. Using Harvard Business School cases and team projects, students will also learn about mass customization.

■ 2637
E-COMMERCE MARKETING
NORTHWESTERN OKLAHOMA STATE UNIVERSITY
DIVISION OF E-COMMERCE

709 Oklahoma Blvd.
Alva, OK 73717-2399
PH: (580)327-8440
FX: (580)327-8167
E-mail: kharris@nwosu.edu
URL: http://www.nwosu.edu/ecom/curriculum/cdesc.html

Description: Northwestern Oklahoma State University's Division of E-Commerce offers a course called "E-Commerce Marketing." This class examines marketing concepts with specific attention to electronic commerce. The course will cover topics including customer support and quality of service in the online setting, and methods of personalization.

■ 2638
E-COMMERCE: MARKETING YOUR E-BUSINESS
MINDLEADERS

851 W 3rd Ave., Bldg. 3
Columbus, OH 43212
PH: (614)781-7300
TF: 800-223-3732
FX: (614)781-6510
E-mail: webrequest@mindleaders.com
URL: http://www.mindleaders.com

Description: MindLeaders provides online learning courses, including a class titled "E-Commerce: Marketing Your E-Business." This course will look at marketing plans, marketing models, affiliate marketing, and identifying your customers.

■ 2639
E-COMMERCE MASTER OF SCIENCE
GOLDEN GATE UNIVERSITY
CYBERCAMPUS

536 Mission St.
San Francisco, CA 94105-2968
PH: (415)369-5250
TF: 888-874-2923
FX: (415)227-4502
E-mail: cybercampus@ggu.edu
URL: http://cybercampus.ggu.edu/

Description: Golden Gate University's online university, CyberCampus, offers an M.S. degree in E-commerce. This program will help students learn the skills essential to advance a career or transition into e-commerce. Learn to make money on the web, redesign businesses to function online, and improve storefront operation. Students will graduate

with understanding of all aspects of evaluating, operating and managing an e-commerce business.

■ 2640
E-COMMERCE MBA
GOLDEN GATE UNIVERSITY
CYBERCAMPUS

536 Mission St.
San Francisco, CA 94105-2968
PH: (415)369-5250
TF: 888-874-2923
FX: (415)227-4502
E-mail: cybercampus@ggu.edu
URL: http://cybercampus.ggu.edu/

Description: Golden Gate University's online university, CyberCampus, is fully accredited and offers an MBA in E-Commerce. The program is designed for professionals and students who are interested in learning about the electronic commerce technologies and associated managerial techniques. This MBA program includes courses specifically e-commerce focused.

■ 2641
E-COMMERCE MBA
CARDIFF UNIVERSITY

Cardiff Business School
Aberconway Bldg, Colum Dr.
Cardiff CF103EU, United Kingdom
PH: 44 29 2087 4000
FX: 44 29 2087 4419
URL: http://www.cf.ac.uk

Description: The Master of Business Administration E-Commerce program covers topics such as the business benefits of electronic trading, technology platforms, financial security and legal issues, e-commerce applications within the supply chain, global developments, e-commerce implementation strategies and practical examples of good business practice

■ 2642
E-COMMERCE MBA CONCENTRATION
DEPAUL UNIVERSITY
KELLSTADT GRADUATE SCHOOL OF BUSINESS

1 E Jackson, Ste. 7900
Chicago, IL 60604-2287
PH: (312)362-8810
FX: (312)362-6677
E-mail: mbainfo@depaul.edu
URL: http://commerce.depaul.edu/
Contact: Felicia Richardson-McGee, Assistant Director

Description: DePaul University's Kellstadt Graduate School of Business offers an MBA program with a concentration in E-Commerce. The focus of this concentration is to study the impact of digital economy on businesses. This program plans on graduating business professionals, who are literate with technological trends, technology, and social and public implications of technological evolution.

▌2643

E-COMMERCE MBA CONCENTRATION
UNIVERSITY OF NORTH CAROLINA AT CHAPEL HILL
THE KENAN-FLAGLER BUSINESS SCHOOL

Campus Box 3490
McColl Bldg.
Chapel Hill, NC 27599-3490
PH: (919)962-8301
FX: (919)962-0898
E-mail: mba_info@unc.edu
URL: http://www.kenanflagler.unc.edu/
Contact: Albert H. Segars, Chair, Information Tech. & E-Commerce

Description: The Kenan-Flagler School of Business at North Carolina University at Chapel Hill offers an MBA with a concentration in E-Commerce. The curriculum exposes students to real-world examples of how information technology is used to gain sustainable e-business advantage. A number of technologies are dealt with: enterprise integration, customer relationship management software, interorganizational process linking technologies, and knowledge management systems. Industry speakers are invited to give presentations on how various technologies are being leveraged by their companies. Students can create a customized curricula for themselves with electives.

▌2644

E-COMMERCE MBA CONCENTRATION
DUQUESNE UNIVERSITY
SCHOOL OF BUSINESS

704 Rockwell Hall
Pittsburgh, PA 15282
PH: (412)396-6276
TF: 800-456-0590
FX: (412)396-5304
E-mail: grad-bus@duq.edu
URL: http://www.bus.duq.edu/grad/programs/default.htm

Description: Duquesne University's School of Business offers an MBA program with a concentration in E-commerce. Courses include, Electronic Business I and II, as well as courses that focus on marketing, purchasing and systems analysis and design.

▌2645

E-COMMERCE MBA PROGRAM CONCENTRATION
UNIVERSITY OF MARYLAND
SMITH SCHOOL OF BUSINESS

Van Munching Hall
College Park, MD 20742
PH: (301)405-2278
E-mail: info@hsmith.umd.edu

URL: http://ecommerce.umd.edu/

Description: The University of Maryland Smith School of Business offers an MBA program concentration in E-Commerce. The curriculum consists of cross-functional concentration consisting of EC courses offered by the faculty specializing in Decision and Information Technologies, Marketing, Economics, and Supply Chain Management.

▌2646

E-COMMERCE MBA SPECIALIZATION
UNIVERSITY OF DENVER
DANIELS COLLEGE OF BUSINESS

2101 S University Blvd.
Denver, CO 80208
PH: (303)871-3416
FX: (303)871-4466
E-mail: dcb@du.edu
URL: http://www.dcb.du.edu/itec/mbaec.asp

Description: The University of Denver Daniels College of Business offers an MBA degree with a specialization in E-Commerce. This degree program is designed to prepare students for a career in strategic marketing in an EC environment. Students focus on marketing concepts and techniques while learning about the technological aspects of E-Commerce.

▌2647

E-COMMERCE: NEW MODELS FOR A CHANGING ECONOMY
STEVENS INSTITUTE OF TECHNOLOGY
HOWE SCHOOL OF TECHNOLOGY MANAGEMENT

Kidde Bldg., Rm. 324-A
Hoboken, NJ 07030
PH: (201)216-5381
FX: (201)216-5385
E-mail: howe_grad@stevens-tech.edu
URL: http://attila.stevens-tech.edu/stmm/e-comm/certificate.htm

Description: Stevens Institute of Technology's School of Technology Management offers a course called E-Commerce: New Models for a Changing Economy. This graduate level course will give students knowledge of the basic components of the Internet; an understanding of how to build a business model that integrates e-commerce; and techniques for adapting existing systems to work with e-commerce.

▌2648

E-COMMERCE AND ONLINE TRADING SEMINAR
HIGHLANDECOM
NESS HORIZONS CENTRE

Kintail House
Beechwood Business Park
Inverness IV33BW, United Kingdom
PH: 01463 732556

FX: 01463 732501
E-mail: info@highlandecom.com
URL: http://www.highlandecom.com

Description: Highlandecom offers a course called E-Commerce and Online Trading Seminar. This seminar will help students define e-commerce, target a client base, analyze successful web sites, and use e-commerce tools.

∎ 2649

E-COMMERCE PRACTICUM
ILLINOIS INSTITUTE OF TECHNOLOGY
STUART GRADUATE SCHOOL OF BUSINESS

565 W Adams St.
Chicago, IL 60661
PH: (312)906-6500
FX: (312)906-6549
E-mail: degrees@stuart.iit.edu
URL: http://www.stuart.iit.edu

Description: The Illinois Institute of Technology Stuart Graduate School of Business offers a course entitled E-Commerce Practicum. This course involves teams of students working on real world e-commerce challenges given by industry executives, who will then evaluate the students' projects.

∎ 2650

E-COMMERCE PROCUREMENT: VENDORS, PROCESSES AND STANDARDS
SAN JOSE STATE UNIVERSITY
PROFESSIONAL DEVELOPMENT CENTER

3031 Tisch Way, Ste. 200 Plz. E
San Jose, CA 95128
PH: (408)257-3000
E-mail: mitchell.levy.sjsupd@ecnow.com
URL: http://ecmtraining.com/sjsu/
Contact: Mitchell Levy, Program Founder and Coordinator

Description: San Jose State University offers a course titled ''E-Commerce Procurement: Vendors, Processes and Standards.'' This executive education course is designed for purchasing, financial and Internet systems managers, and will help them to assess opportunities, evaluate alternatives and develop a plan for streamlining their requisitioning and purchasing processes through Web-based purchasing systems.

∎ 2651

E-COMMERCE, PUBLIC POLICY AND THE LAW
SAN JOSE STATE UNIVERSITY
PROFESSIONAL DEVELOPMENT CENTER

3031 Tisch Way, Ste. 200 Plz. E
San Jose, CA 95128
PH: (408)257-3000
E-mail: mitchell.levy.sjsupd@ecnow.com

URL: http://ecmtraining.com/sjsu/
Contact: Mitchell Levy, Program Founder and Coordinator

Description: San Jose State University offers an executive education class called ''E-Commerce, Public Policy and the Law.'' This course will introduce students to important models, resources, and practical steps to take. Topics include: taxation, copyright, privacy, the European Union's privacy requirements, digital signatures, cyber squatting, encryption, SPAM, cyber crime, and criminal liability issues.

∎ 2652

E-COMMERCE READINESS
UNIVERSITY OF CALIFORNIA EXTENSION ONLINE

2000 Center St., Ste. 400
Berkeley, CA 94704
PH: (510)642-4124
E-mail: askus@ucxonline.berkeley.edu
URL: http://learn.berkely.edu/

Description: The University of California Extension Online offers an E-Commerce course called ''E-Commerce Readiness.'' This online course offers an overview of concepts for e-commerce business and technology through case studies and demonstrations. It is designed to help potential e-commerce managers get started with the E-Commerce Business Certificate Program. This course covers both the technological and business aspects needed to gain understanding of E-Commerce.

∎ 2653

E-COMMERCE: REAL TIME AND DATA MINING
MINDLEADERS

851 W 3rd Ave., Bldg. 3
Columbus, OH 43212
PH: (614)781-7300
TF: 800-223-3732
FX: (614)781-6510
E-mail: webrequest@mindleaders.com
URL: http://www.mindleaders.com

Description: MindLeaders provides online learning courses, including ''E-Commerce: Real Time and Data Mining.'' This course provides an introduction to both real time systems and collecting and analyzing data, as well as looking at the benefits of data mining.

∎ 2654

E-COMMERCE: RESOURCE PLANNING
MINDLEADERS

851 W 3rd Ave., Bldg. 3
Columbus, OH 43212
PH: (614)781-7300
TF: 800-223-3732
FX: (614)781-6510
E-mail: webrequest@mindleaders.com

URL: http://www.mindleaders.com

Description: MindLeaders provides online learning courses, including a class titled "E-Commerce: Resource Planning." This course looks at e-commerce risks and strategy, knowledge management and changes in technology.

■ 2655

E-COMMERCE SECURITY

NETG

1751 W Diehl Rd, 2nd Fl.
Naperville, IL 60563-9099
PH: (630)369-3000
TF: 877-561-6384
FX: (630)983-4877
E-mail: info@netg.com
URL: http://www.netg.com

Description: NETg offers a course called E-Commerce Security. This course examines aspects of Internet security including firewalls, encryption, and payment security.

■ 2656

E-COMMERCE SECURITY

UNIVERSITY OF FLORIDA

Office of the University Registrar
Cruiser Hall
PO Box 114000
Gainesville, FL 32611-4000
PH: (352)392-3261; (352)392-1374
URL: http://www.ufl.edu

Description: E-Commerce Security is for students wanting to consider the impact of security issues on e-commerce implementation. The intended audience is managers and technical staff who are in a position to provide e-commerce recommendations to executives and will teach them how to identify the features of a security firewall, information encryption, authentication and authorization and e-commerce payment security.

■ 2657

E-COMMERCE SECURITY AND PAYMENT SYSTEMS

ILLINOIS INSTITUTE OF TECHNOLOGY
STUART GRADUATE SCHOOL OF BUSINESS

565 W Adams St.
Chicago, IL 60661
PH: (312)906-6500
FX: (312)906-6549
E-mail: degrees@stuart.iit.edu
URL: http://www.stuart.iit.edu

Description: The Illinois Institute of Technology Stuart Graduate School of Business offers a course entitled E-Commerce Security and Payment Systems. This course looks at policies, procedures, and technology to provide appropriate data security and privacy will be discussed. Topics

to be covered include databases, web sites, intranets, extranets, and the Internet.

■ 2658

E-COMMERCE SEMINAR SERIES

NORTH CAROLINA STATE UNIVERSITY
BUSINESS MANAGEMENT DEPARTMENT
COLLEGE OF MANAGEMENT

Campus Box 7229
Raleigh, NC 27695-7229
PH: (919)513-2694
E-mail: ecommerce@ncsu.edu
URL: http://ecommerce.ncsu.edu/seminar/
Contact: Dr. Michael Rappa

Description: This series of lectures at North Carolina State University is free and open to the public. Unless otherwise indicated lectures are held from 11:30 AM-12:30 PM, in the Engineering Graduate Research Center (EGRC), Room 313, on the NC State University Centennial Campus. Video taped lectures are made available over the web. Topics include: new business models for Web services, and technology readiness and e-service quality.

■ 2659

E-COMMERCE: SETTING UP SHOP AND MAKING THE SALE

GESTALT PARTNERS LLC

2070 Chain Bridge Rd., Ste. G40
Vienna, VA 22182
PH: 888-844-4549
FX: (703)748-1553
E-mail: courseware@gestalt-sys.com
URL: http://www.gestalt-courseware.com/outlines/html/ecom1d.htm

Description: Gestalt Partners LLC offers a course called E-Commerce: Setting Up Shop and Making the Sale. This 2 day course will give students information on how to choose an Internet Service Provider, secure a domain, find a host, write a business plan, raise funds, buy software, market products and services, and sell them on the Web.

■ 2660

E-COMMERCE FOR SMALL BUSINESS

MCMASTER UNIVERSITY
MICHAEL G. DEGROOTE SCHOOL OF BUSINESS
MCMASTER EBUSINESS RESEARCH CENTRE

1280 Main St. W
Hamilton, ON, Canada L8S4M4
PH: (905)525-9140
E-mail: essch@mcmaster.ca
URL: http://merc.mcmaster.ca/
Contact: Dr. Elliot Schreiber, Director

Description: McMaster University eBusiness Research Centre has developed e-commerce programs for students and business offered both online and onsite. Programs include E-Commerce for Small Business, as well as courses addressing other e-commerce topics.

▌2661

E-COMMERCE FOR SMALL AND MEDIUM SIZED BUSINESSES
UNIVERSITY OF DELAWARE
E-COMMERCE PROGRAM

206 John M. Clayton Hall
Newark, DE 19716-7410
PH: (302)831-2741
E-mail: continuing-ed@udel.edu
URL: http://www.continuingstudies.udel.edu/it/ecomm/index.shtml

Description: The University of Delaware's Continuing Studies Program offers a course titled "E-Commerce for Small and Medium Sized Businesses." This course is designed for Small- and Mid-sized enterprises (SMEs), the fastest growing segment of the U.S. economy. Topics covered include developing Internet strategies, marketing and branding strategies, creating web site content and increasing web site traffic.

▌2662

E-COMMERCE SOCIAL CHANGES AND THE INTERNET
NORTHWESTERN OKLAHOMA STATE UNIVERSITY
DIVISION OF E-COMMERCE

709 Oklahoma Blvd.
Alva, OK 73717-2399
PH: (580)327-8440
FX: (580)327-8167
E-mail: kharris@nwosu.edu
URL: http://www.nwosu.edu/ecom/curriculum/cdesc.html

Description: Northwestern Oklahoma State University's Division of E-Commerce offers a course called "E-Commerce Social Changes and the Internet." This course looks at social and business Internet trends, and teaches students how to develop an in-depth business plan.

▌2663

E-COMMERCE SOFTWARE SERVICES
GEORGE MASON UNIVERSITY
DEPARTMENT OF COMPUTER SCIENCE

MSN 4A5
4400 University Dr.
Fairfax, VA 22030
PH: (703)993-1530
FX: (703)993-1710
E-mail: csadmin@cs.gmu.edu
URL: http://ite.gmu.edu/msecomm/description.htm

Description: George Mason University offers a course called "E-Commerce Software Services." This graduate level course examines E-commerce transactions and the role

of the various software servers (web, application, and database servers) in executing E-commerce transactions.

▌2664

E-COMMERCE SOLUTIONS: THINKING OUTSIDE THE BOX
SAN JOSE STATE UNIVERSITY
PROFESSIONAL DEVELOPMENT CENTER

3031 Tisch Way, Ste. 200 Plz. E
San Jose, CA 95128
PH: (408)257-3000
E-mail: mitchell.levy.sjsupd@ecnow.com
URL: http://ecmtraining.com/sjsu/
Contact: Mitchell Levy, Program Founder and Coordinator

Description: San Jose State University offers an executive education class titled "E-Commerce Solutions: Thinking Outside the Box." In this course students work in self-supervised workgroups to solve a problem or issue which demonstrates the knowledge you have learned in the ECM program. Students will also be taught about brainstorming techniques.

▌2665

E-COMMERCE SPECIALIZATION
NEW JERSEY INSTITUTE OF TECHNOLOGY
SCHOOL OF MANAGEMENT

University Heights
Newark, NJ 07102-1982
PH: (973)596-3254
FX: (973)596-3074
E-mail: wachspress@admin.njit.edu
URL: http://www.njit.edu/BETA/ecomm/
Contact: David Wachspress, Dir., Undergrad. & E-Commerce Programs

Description: The New Jersey Institute of Technology offers a B.S. degree in Management with a specialization in E-Commerce. This program's graduates will have skills and knowledge required to conduct business successfully online.

▌2666

E-COMMERCE SPECIALIZATION PROGRAM
LOYOLA UNIVERSITY CHICAGO

Graduate School of Business
25 E. Pearson, 14th Fl.
Chicago, IL 60611
PH: (312)915-6120
FX: (312)915-7207
E-mail: ayoung3@luc.edu
URL: http://www.luc.edu
Contact: Alan Young, Director of Enrollment & Recruitment

Description: The E-Commerce Specialization program provides an emphasis on the opportunities for integrating e-commerce with business processes from functional areas of operations, marketing, finance, and economics and presents the telecommunications technologies used to support e-commerce.

■ 2667

E-COMMERCE STRATEGY

YALE SCHOOL OF MANAGEMENT

135 Prospect St.
PO Box 208200
New Haven, CT 06520-8200
PH: (203)432-5932
FX: (203)432-7004
E-mail: mba.admissions@yale.edu
URL: http://www.mba.yale.edu
Contact: James Stevens, Director

Description: E-Commerce Strategy will apply microeconomic concepts to both e-commerce stand-alone ventures and e-commerce initiatives inside traditional corporations to help students understand the reasons for profitability and success. The course will include distinguishing between value creation and value capture and involve presenting a series of models of value capture that are appropriate for e-commerce and evaluating the choice and use of these strategies in a range of e-commerce applications.

■ 2668

E-COMMERCE STRATEGY

LOYOLA UNIVERSITY CHICAGO

Graduate School of Business
25 E. Pearson, 14th Fl.
Chicago, IL 60611
PH: (312)915-6120
FX: (312)915-7207
E-mail: ayoung3@luc.edu
URL: http://www.luc.edu
Contact: Alan Young, Director of Enrollment & Recruitment

Description: The E-Commerce Strategy course focuses on the use of information and information technology to create competitive advantage via e-commerce. The management of information as a resource and the relation of information systems to strategic planning are discussed with cases used to illustrate how information systems can be used to enable e-commerce strategies.

■ 2669

E-COMMERCE STRATEGY AND MARKETING

DREXEL UNIVERSITY
LEBOW COLLEGE OF BUSINESS

3141 Chestnut St.
Matheson Hall, Rm. 105
Philadelphia, PA 19104
PH: (215)895-6070

FX: (215)895-1012
E-mail: marcos@drexel.edu.
URL: http://www.drexel.edu/academics/lebow/ecomm/

Description: Drexel University offers a course called E-Commerce Strategy and Marketing. This executive education course will teach students how to develop e-Commerce web sites using the online and offline strategies now being implemented by Internet marketing professionals.

■ 2670

E-COMMERCE STRATEGY AND POLICY

GEORGETOWN UNIVERSITY
MCDONOUGH SCHOOL OF BUSINESS

BOX 571148
Washington, DC 20057-1221
PH: (202)687-3802
E-mail: mba@georgetown.edu
URL: http://www.msb.edu/mba/mba.htm
Contact: Robert Wheeler, Assistant Dean

Description: Georgetown University's McDonough School of Business offers a graduate level course called "E-Commerce Strategy and Policy." This MBA course examines various facets of electronic commerce strategy and policy.

■ 2671

E-COMMERCE AND SUPPLY CHAIN MANAGEMENT

KRANNERT SCHOOL OF MANAGEMENT

Purdue University
1310 Krannert Bldg.
West Lafayette, IN 47907
PH: (765)496-3384
FX: (765)494-9841
E-mail: jdietz@mgmt.purdue.edu
URL: http://www.mgmt.purdue.edu
Contact: Joy Dietz, Manager of Advising and Student Services

Description: E-Commerce and Supply Chain Management focuses on the logistics aspects of e-commerce and discusses strategic issues, tactical choices and operational details.

■ 2672

E-COMMERCE SYSTEMS

UNIVERSITY OF PENNSYLVANIA
PENN ENGINEERING
EXECUTIVE MASTER'S IN TECHNOLOGY MANAGEMENT

119 Towne Bldg.
Philadelphia, PA 19104-6391
PH: (215)898-5241
FX: (215)573-9673
E-mail: emtm@seas.upenn.edu
URL: http://www.seas.upenn.edu/profprog/emtm/news/stories/ecommerce-courses.html

Description: The University of Pennsylvania Executive Master's in Technology Management program offers a course titled "E-Commerce Systems." This course reviews the concepts, principles and technologies important to developing reliable E-Commerce systems.

∎ 2673

E-COMMERCE SYSTEMS

UNIVERSITY OF GEORGIA

TERRY COLLEGE OF BUSINESS

346 Brooks Hall
Athens, GA 30602-6264
PH: (706)542-8100
FX: (706)542-3835
E-mail: mcrask@terry.uga.edu
URL: http://www.terry.uga.edu
Contact: Dr. Mel Crask, Director, MBA Programs

Description: The University of Georgia Terry College of Business Executive MBA program offers a course called E-Commerce Systems. This course examines Internet base technologies that support e-commerce. Topics covered include virtual integration, B2B systems, customer service, business intelligence technology, mass customization technology, mobile commerce, e-government, and virtual communities.

∎ 2674

E-COMMERCE SYSTEMS DESIGN, INTEGRATION AND DEPLOYMENT

UNIVERSITY OF CALIFORNIA EXTENSION ONLINE

2000 Center St., Ste. 400
Berkeley, CA 94704
PH: (510)642-4124
E-mail: askus@ucxonline.berkeley.edu
URL: http://learn.berkely.edu/

Description: The University of California Extension Online provides an E-Commerce course called "E-Commerce Systems Design, Integration and Deployment." This online course for managers studies a full range of e-commerce systems design, integration, and deployment concepts through case studies, class exercises, and demonstrations. The course is designed to help students develop and deploy an e-commerce system that includes integration.

∎ 2675

E-COMMERCE SYSTEMS SECURITY AND FIREWALL

UNIVERSITY OF CALIFORNIA EXTENSION ONLINE

2000 Center St., Ste. 400
Berkeley, CA 94704
PH: (510)642-4124
E-mail: askus@ucxonline.berkeley.edu
URL: http://learn.berkely.edu/

Description: The University of California Extension Online provides a course entitled "E-Commerce Systems Security

and Firewall." This introductory security course explores a full range of e-commerce security issues, including technology solutions and examples. It is designed to help e-commerce managers with planning and executing the security aspects of an e-commerce project, including firewalls.

∎ 2676

E-COMMERCE TECHNOLOGIES

SEREBRA LEARNING CORP.

7565 132nd St., Unit 119
Surrey, BC, Canada V3W1K5
PH: (604)592-0552
TF: 800-567-7766
FX: (604)592-0553
E-mail: info@serebra.com
URL: http://www.serebra.com
Contact: Mr. Bruce Stewart, President

Founded: 1987. **Description:** Serebra Learning Corporation offers a course entitled "E-Commerce Technologies." Designed for business managers and technical staff who need to determine whether e-commerce is suitable for their company and if so how best to provide it, this class will introduce the students to the technologies used in implementing e-commerce.

∎ 2677

E-COMMERCE TECHNOLOGIES

UNIVERSITY OF DALLAS

GRADUATE SCHOOL OF MANAGEMENT

1845 E Northgate Dr.
Irving, TX 75062
PH: (972)721-5000
E-mail: msavoie@udallas.edu
URL: http://gsmweb.udallas.edu/concentrations/ e_business.html

Description: The University of Dallas Graduate School of Management offers a course called E-Commerce Technologies. This course examines e-commerce technologies including email, telnet, ftp, chat, and business application of the Internet. Information on the history of the Internet is also presented.

∎ 2678

E-COMMERCE TECHNOLOGIES

NEW JERSEY INSTITUTE OF TECHNOLOGY

SCHOOL OF MANAGEMENT, GRADUATE PROGRAMS

323 Martin Luther King Jr. Blvd.
Newark, NJ 07102-1982
PH: (973)596-6378
FX: (973)596-3074
E-mail: lipper@njit.edu
URL: http://www.njit.edu/SOM/MBA/index.html
Contact: Stuart Lipper, Director of Graduate Programs

Description: The New Jersey Institute of Technology School of Management MBA program offers a course called

"E-Commerce Technologies." In this course, students will gain understanding of the Internet and its underlying technologies as a foundation for e-commerce with an introduction to E-Commerce applications. Data communication and networking, EDI, Intranets and Extranets, bandwidth and security issues are also covered.

▌2679
E-COMMERCE TECHNOLOGY
E-COMMERCE LEARNING CENTER

NC State University
Business Management Dept.
College of Management
Campus Box 7229
Raleigh, NC 27695-7229
PH: (919)515-5584
E-mail: ecommerce@ncsu.edu
URL: http://www.ecommerce.ncsu.edu
Contact: Dr. Michael Rappa

Description: E-Commerce Technology is an introductory graduate level e-commerce course in Computer Science first taught in January 2000 and is required for students concentrating in e-commerce. The course content is entirely web-enabled.

▌2680
E-COMMERCE TECHNOLOGY CERTIFICATE
GW CENTER FOR PROFESSIONAL DEVELOPMENT

2029 K Street NW, Ste. 600
Washington, DC 20006
PH: (202)973-1150
FX: (202)973-1165
E-mail: cpd@gwu.edu
URL: http://www.gwu.edu/~cpd/programs/CWEC/

Description: The GW Center for Professional Development offers an E-Commerce Technology Certificate program. This program is designed to give students an overview of the e-commerce business model and an opportunity to focus on specific aspects of its technology.

▌2681
E-COMMERCE-TECHNOLOGY COMPETENCY FOR E-COMMERCE MARKETING
GW CENTER FOR PROFESSIONAL DEVELOPMENT

2029 K Street NW, Ste. 600
Washington, DC 20006
PH: (202)973-1150
FX: (202)973-1165
E-mail: cpd@gwu.edu
URL: http://www.gwu.edu/~cpd/programs/CWEC/

Description: The GW Center for Professional Development offers a course called "E-Commerce-Technology Competency for E-Commerce Marketing." This course focuses on

one-to-one—personalizing and customizing the interface to develop a relationship with each customer (CRM). Other topics covered include branding, company image, channel and alliance partnering, web advertising, email communications, search engines and indexes.

▌2682
E-COMMERCE TECHNOLOGY SYSTEM DESIGN
NORTHWESTERN OKLAHOMA STATE UNIVERSITY
DIVISION OF E-COMMERCE

709 Oklahoma Blvd.
Alva, OK 73717-2399
PH: (580)327-8440
FX: (580)327-8167
E-mail: kharris@nwosu.edu
URL: http://www.nwosu.edu/ecom/curriculum/cdesc.html

Description: Northwestern Oklahoma State University's Division of E-Commerce offers a course called "E-Commerce Technology System Design." This course focuses on technologies for electronic commerce. The course will cover the design, development, implementation and management of e-commerce solutions.

▌2683
E-COMMERCE TECHNOLOGY TRACK CERTIFICATE PROGRAM
NATIONAL CENTER FOR MANUFACTURING SCIENCES

3025 Boardwalk
Ann Arbor, MI 48108-3266
PH: (734)995-0300
FX: (734)995-4004
E-mail: training@ncms.org
URL: http://wwww.ncms.org

Description: The National Center for Manufacturing Sciences offers an E-Commerce Technology Track Certificate Program. This program includes courses such as E-Commerce Fundamentals, and JAVA Programming and Business Fundamentals. Coursework in this program track focuses on the technological aspects of e-business.

▌2684
E-COMMERCE: TRANSACTIONAL SITE DESIGN
UNITED DIGITAL ARTISTS

186 Fifth Ave., 4th Fl.
New York, NY 10010
PH: (212)777-7200
TF: 800-227-4935
FX: (212)777-7222
E-mail: info@uda.com
URL: http://www.uda.com/training/categories.php?course_id=40

587

Description: United Digital Artists offers a course entitled E-Commerce: Transactional Site Design. This workshop focuses on sites that sell. Students look at successful e-commerce sites and outline winning strategies for compelling online transactions.

▮ 2685
E-COMMERCE TUTORIAL
NET NATION COMMUNICATIONS, INC.

Ste. 1410, Harbour Center
555 W Hastings St.
Vancouver, BC, Canada V6B4N6
PH: (604)688-8946
TF: 888-277-0000
FX: (604)688-8934
E-mail: webmaster@online-commerce.com
URL: http://www.online-commerce.com/

Description: Net Nation Communications offers an online E-Commerce Tutorial. This course gives information on how to get started in e-commerce. Topics addressed include different online payment options, web hosting and e-commerce software.

▮ 2686
E-COMMERCE TUTORIAL
INTERNATIONAL ENGINEERING CONSORTIUM

549 West Randolph St., Ste. 600
Chicago, IL 60661-2208
PH: (312)559-4100
FX: (312)559-4111
E-mail: info@iec.org
URL: http://www.iec.org

Description: The E-Commerce online tutorial's objective is to provide an overview of how e-commerce works, the challenges of hosting complex e-commerce environments and the importance of e-commerce capabilities that enhance the services and core competencies of the service provider.

▮ 2687
E-COMMERCE TUTORIAL
WEBSITE 101

1275 4th St. No. 308
Santa Rosa, CA 95404
PH: (707)836-1826
FX: (707)924-0940
E-mail: learn@website101.com
URL: http://www.website101.com
Contact: Mike Banks Valentine, Founder

Description: WebSite 101 provides an online E-commerce Tutorial designed for small businesses. The coursework includes resources to help small business managers learn how to get established online without great funding. Topics addressed include incorporation online, e-health insurance, business software, and time management.

▮ 2688
E-COMMERCE TUTORIAL
CNET.COM

235 2nd St.
San Francisco, CA 94105
PH: (415)344-2000
E-mail: lizb@cnet.com
URL: http://builder.cnet.com/webbuilding/pages/Business/Tutorial/
Contact: Liz Brooks

Description: CNET.com offers a free online tutorial on E-Commerce. This tutorial covers topics such as software options, cataloging your product, adding image support, publishing your catalog and supporting transactions.

▮ 2689
E-COMMERCE TUTORIAL
TERRA LYCOS
WEBMONKEY

400-2 Totten Pond Rd.
Waltham, MA 02451
PH: (781)370-2700
FX: (781)370-2600
E-mail: khakman@emergingmedia.com
URL: http://hotwired.lycos.com/webmonkey/e-business/tutorials/tutorial3.html?tw=eg199908
Contact: Kevin Hackman

Description: This free online E-commerce tutorial is taught in 5 sections which cover how to generate a realistic e-business plan, create a site design, deal with credit cards, tax, shipping, and security; and decide whether you should build, buy, or rent an e-commerce solution to manage your site. Students will also learn how to attract new customers by refining their marketing programs.

▮ 2690
E-COMMERCE USING THE INTERNET
SUNY INSTITUTE OF TECHNOLOGY

PO Box 3050
Utica, NY 13504-3050
PH: (315)792-7158
E-mail: sgay@sunyit.edu
URL: http://www.sunyit.edu/~sgay/
Contact: Gene Yelle, Instructor

Description: SUNY at Utica offers a course entitled ''E-Commerce Using the Internet.'' This course explores the topic of doing business on the World Wide Web. It covers entry strategies, emerging web-based business models, web site design strategies, payment systems employed, as well as contemporary marketing, legal, regulatory, technological, social and ethical issues.

▮ 2691
E-COMMERCE, YOUR E-BUSINESS
MINDLEADERS

851 W 3rd Ave., Bldg. 3
Columbus, OH 43212
PH: (614)781-7300

TF: 800-223-3732
FX: (614)781-6510
E-mail: webrequest@mindleaders.com
URL: http://www.mindleaders.com

Description: MindLeaders provides online learning, including a course called "E-Commerce, Your E-Business." This course is an introduction to e-commerce and includes topics such as future directions, building resources, and marketing and management.

▌ 2692
E-CONOMY PROJECT(TM)
BERKELEY ROUNDTABLE ON THE INTERNATIONAL ECONOMY

2234 Piedmont Avenue
Berkeley, CA 94720-2322
PH: (510)642-3067
FX: (510)643-6617
E-mail: e-conomy@uclink4.berkeley.edu
URL: http://e-conomy.berkeley.edu/

Description: The new E-conomy Project(tm) is a collaborative undertaking of the Berkeley Roundtable on the International Economy (BRIE), the College of Engineering, the Haas School of Business and the School of Information Management and Systems (SIMS), at the University of California, Berkeley, and the UC Institute on Global Conflict and Cooperation (IGCC). Participating faculty represent a range of UC Berkeley departments as well as faculty from other UC campuses. The project fuses research with knowledge and concerns of industry leaders and policy makers, creating resources to focus on changes brought about by new digital technologies. The project aims to develop business models, and more effective policies, legal frameworks and corporate strategies. Many conferences and publications are offered toward this end.

▌ 2693
E-CUSTOMER SERVICE: OBTAINING AND MAINTAINING CUSTOMERS ON THE INTERNET
UNIVERSITY OF COLORADO AT DENVER

Campus Box 165
PO Box 173364
Denver, CO 80217-3364
PH: (303)556-5826
FX: (303)556-6276
E-mail: pdp@carbon.cudenver.edu
URL: http://www.cudenver.edu

Description: E-Customer Service: Obtaining and Maintaining Customers on the Internet teaches students what determines customer satisfaction in an online environment with a focus on identifying the reasons why customers switch online businesses and the negative impact switching could have on long-term profits. Covered topics include the impact of positive interpersonal communication on product success,

the impact of negative interpersonal communication on product failure, customer satisfaction strategies, positioning strategies to reduce replacement, profiling dissatisfied individuals and service recovery and other retention-oriented strategies.

▌ 2694
E-ENTERPRISE TECHNOLOGIES AND APPLICATIONS
NEW YORK UNIVERSITY
SCHOOL OF CONTINUING AND PROFESSIONAL STUDIES VIRTUAL COLLEGE

10 Astor Pl., 5th Fl.
New York, NY 10003
PH: (212)998-7080
TF: 877-998-7080
E-mail: scpsinfo@nyu.edu
URL: http://www.scps.nyu.edu/dyncon/virt/

Description: NYU's Virtual College offers a course called "E-Enterprise Technologies and Applications." This overview course provides a look at fundamental protocols, technologies, applications, and services of the Internet.

▌ 2695
E-ENTREPRENEURSHIP
NOTRE DAME
COLLEGE OF BUSINESS

276 Mendoza College of Business
Notre Dame, IN 46556
PH: (219)631-8488
TF: 800-631-8488
FX: (219)631-8800
E-mail: mba.1@nd.edu
URL: http://www.nd.edu/~mba
Contact: Carolyn Woo, Dean

Description: The Notre Dame MBA Program offers a course called "E-Entrepreneurship." This course is designed for the student who is interested in starting his or her e-business. In addition to the technology know-how, the students learn how to create a business plan and develop a prototype of their e-business.

▌ 2696
E-LAW AND RISK MANAGEMENT
UNIVERSITY OF PHOENIX

3201 E Elwood St.
Phoenix, AZ 85034
PH: (480)966-5394
TF: 800-366-9699
URL: http://www.uoponline.com

Description: The University of Phoenix offers a graduate course called E-Law and Risk Management. This course examines the process of risk management in an e-business context. Students will analyze operational, financial, legal, strategic, and technical aspects of risk management, and be exposed to global issues in e-commerce risk management.

■ 2697

E-LEADERSHIP

BINGHAMTON UNIVERSITY
SCHOOL OF MANAGEMENT

PO Box 6000
Binghamton, NY 13902
PH: (607)777-2000
E-mail: sivasub@binghamton.edu
URL: http://bingweb.binghamton.edu/~eleader/

Description: Binghamton University's School of Management offers a course entitled "E-Leadership." This course will enable students to be familiar with e-business architecture and vocabulary, as well as develop skills to analyze e-business strategies and processes.

■ 2698

E-MARKETING

PENN STATE UNIVERSITY
SMEAL COLLEGE OF BUSINESS

106 Business Administration Bldg.
University Park, PA 16802-3000
PH: (814)865-1907
E-mail: arvindr@psu.edu
URL: http://www2.smeal.psu.edu/courses/mktg597d.rangaswamy/csobj.html

Description: Penn State University offers a course entitled "E-Marketing." E-Marketing refers to the use of the Internet and related technologies to transform marketing processes. This course was created to help students learn to design and deploy marketing strategies that will help their organizations in a global digital economy. The course will cover such topics as market exchanges, online relationships with various downstream stakeholders, and new marketing tools and techniques.

■ 2699

E-MARKETING: BUSINESS-TO-BUSINESS MARKETING ON THE INTERNET

UNIVERSITY OF COLORADO AT DENVER

Campus Box 165
PO Box 173364
Denver, CO 80217-3364
PH: (303)556-5826
FX: (303)556-6276
E-mail: pdp@carbon.cudenver.edu
URL: http://www.cudenver.edu

Description: E-Marketing: Business-to-Business Marketing on the Internet shows students the impact of business-to-business marketing on the Internet. Covered topics include outsourcing efficiencies, finding the best suppliers, online

purchasing of raw materials, online quotes, decision processes in choosing suppliers, acquisition of timely and pertinent information regarding competitor and consumer trends and improved targeting of business and consumers.

■ 2700

E-MARKETING: CONSUMER MARKETING ON THE INTERNET

UNIVERSITY OF COLORADO AT DENVER

Campus Box 165
PO Box 173364
Denver, CO 80217-3364
PH: (303)556-5826
FX: (303)556-6276
E-mail: pdp@carbon.cudenver.edu
URL: http://www.cudenver.edu

Description: E-Marketing: Consumer Marketing on the Internet examines the differences in effective consumer marketing, market segmentation, marketing research and product positioning while teaching students the differences and similarities between internet-based and conventional product marketing. Topics covered include determining the main reasons more online businesses than conventional businesses fail, analyzing online shopping verses conventional shopping, targeting and segmenting online consumers, positioning online businesses, collecting data online and direct marketing over the web.

■ 2701

E-MARKETING THEORY AND APPLICATION

UNIVERSITY OF PHOENIX

3201 E Elwood St.
Phoenix, AZ 85034
PH: (480)966-5394
TF: 800-366-9699
URL: http://www.uoponline.com

Description: As a part of its MBA in E-Business, the University of Phoenix offers a graduate level course called E-Marketing Theory and Application. This course provides a look at the theory and application of electronic marketing. In addition to looking at the way the Internet applies to traditional marketing functions of products, price, distribution, and promotion, students will evaluate Web sites and determine how different industries can use the Internet in creating new markets.

■ 2702

E-MBA

NOTRE DAME
COLLEGE OF BUSINESS

276 Mendoza College of Business
Notre Dame, IN 46556
PH: (219)631-8488
TF: 800-631-8488
FX: (219)631-8800

E-mail: mba.1@nd.edu
URL: http://www.nd.edu/~mba
Contact: Carolyn Woo, Dean

Description: The Notre Dame MBA Program offers an E-MBA. This concentration includes courses in E-Commerce, E-Consulting, and E-Entrepreneurship.

■ **2703**

E-OPERATIONS
BELLEVUE UNIVERSITY
1000 Galvin Rd. S
Bellevue, NE 68005
PH: (402)293-2000
TF: 800-756-7920
FX: (402)293-2020
URL: http://www.bellevue.edu

Description: Bellevue University offers ''E-Operations'', a course designed to look at business management, process sustainability, online ordering systems, telephone ordering, record keeping, inventory control and management, order fulfillment, delivery assurance, delivery methods, electronic bills of lading, as well as other aspects of daily E-business.

■ **2704**

E-PEOPLE
PURDUE UNIVERSITY
KRANNERT GRADUATE SCHOOL OF MANAGEMENT
1310 Krannert Bldg.
West Lafayette, IN 47907
PH: (765)494-9700
FX: (765)494-9658
E-mail: krannert_ms@mgmt.purdue.edu
URL: http://www.mgmt.purdue.edu/centers/ceer/

Description: Purdue University's Krannert Graduate School of Management offers a course entitled E-People. This course is designed to introduce students to the human side of e-business. Students will gain an understanding of how e-business affects both customers and employees.

■ **2705**

E-PROCESS MANAGEMENT
UNIVERSITY OF PITTSBURGH
CENTER FOR EXECUTIVE EDUCATION
Mellon Financial Corp. Hall, 5th Fl.
4227 Fifth Ave.
Pittsburgh, PA 15260
PH: (412)648-1600
E-mail: exeducation@katz.pitt.edu
URL: http://www.execed.pitt.edu/

Description: The Executive Education Program at the University of Pittsburgh offers a seminar entitled E-Process Management. This seminar should be of interest to middle-level managers in organizations who wish to improve their

organization's processes to support eBusiness. The techniques learned here are useful not only for dot com firms, but also for manufacturing and service firms making the transition to the eBusiness.

■ **2706**

E-PROJECTS
NOTRE DAME
COLLEGE OF BUSINESS
276 Mendoza College of Business
Notre Dame, IN 46556
PH: (219)631-8488
TF: 800-631-8488
FX: (219)631-8800
E-mail: mba.1@nd.edu
URL: http://www.nd.edu/~mba
Contact: Carolyn Woo, Dean

Description: The Notre Dame MBA Program offers a course called ''E-Projects.'' This course is for MBA students who have developed a preliminary design for an e-commerce product, and have sufficient technical skills and interest to pursue its implementation. General topics such as e-project management and best practices for project development, as well as technical topics as appropriate for the projects, will complement the goal of getting the projects up and running.

■ **2707**

E-PROMOTIONS: COMMUNICATIONS FOR GROWTH ON THE INTERNET
UNIVERSITY OF COLORADO AT DENVER
Campus Box 165
PO Box 173364
Denver, CO 80217-3364
PH: (303)556-5826
FX: (303)556-6276
E-mail: pdp@carbon.cudenver.edu
URL: http://www.cudenver.edu

Description: E-Promotions: Communications for Growth on the Internet focuses on distinction between online and conventional promotion with discussion on advertising media, interactivity, advertising strategy, ad design, sales promotion strategy, direct marketing, personal selling and publicity. Covered topics include product life cycle; communication models and their applicability to Internet promotion; Internet verses conventional advertising characteristics; types of Internet ads including web pages and banners; reach and frequency in internet promotion; advertising costs; media design and scheduling; sales promotion on the Internet and the absence of coupons; and what to avoid with online promotions.

■ **2708**

E-RETAIL: SALES ON THE INTERNET
UNIVERSITY OF COLORADO AT DENVER
Campus Box 165
PO Box 173364
Denver, CO 80217-3364

PH: (303)556-5826
FX: (303)556-6276
E-mail: pdp@carbon.cudenver.edu
URL: http://www.cudenver.edu

Description: E-Retail: Sales on the Internet explores the changes in pricing and distribution of products on the Internet and compares how marketing through online channels is different from traditional channels of distribution. Covered topics include pricing tactics; the Internet's effect of channel length, channel facilitation and price escalation; inventory control; types of products and stores most conducive to Internet retailing; the lack of a physical location factor; and the retail life cycle and the wheel of retailing.

▌2709
E-SECURITY
REGIS UNIVERSITY
GRADUATE PROGRAMS

3333 Regis Boulevard, L-16
Denver, CO 80221-1099
PH: (303)458-4080
TF: 800-667-9270
FX: (303)964-5538
E-mail: masters@regis.edu
URL: http://www.regis.edu

Description: Regis University offers a course entitled E-Security. In this course Students learn to analyze concepts related to Internet and e-commerce security. They will look at risk and threat analysis, authentication, encryption, payment systems, intrusion pathology, vulnerability assessment, and defensive strategies, tactics and countermeasures.

▌2710
E-SECURITY ESSENTIALS TOOLS AND TECHNIQUES
NEW YORK UNIVERSITY
SCHOOL OF CONTINUING AND PROFESSIONAL
STUDIES VIRTUAL COLLEGE

10 Astor Pl., 5th Fl.
New York, NY 10003
PH: (212)998-7080
TF: 877-998-7080
E-mail: scpsinfo@nyu.edu
URL: http://www.scps.nyu.edu/dyncon/virt/

Description: NYU's Virtual College offers a summer intensive program called ''E-Security Essentials Tools and Techniques.'' This course covers antivirus defense strategies, key concepts of cryptography and encryption, comprehensive security policies, including password policy, and network traffic and log files analysis using freely available tools. This course gives strategies and tools to students, helping them master the essentials of Information Security.

▌2711
E-STRATEGY FORMULATION AND IMPLEMENTATION
UNIVERSITY OF PHOENIX

3201 E Elwood St.
Phoenix, AZ 85034
PH: (480)966-5394
TF: 800-366-9699
URL: http://www.uoponline.com

Description: The University of Phoenix offers a graduate level course entitled E-Strategy Formulation and Implementation. This course addresses the concepts of strategy as applied to an e-business environment. Students formulate, implement, and evaluate global e-business solutions. This capstone course for the e-business curriculum integrates strategy and policy formulation, e-business architecture, marketing strategy, and legal and ethical considerations.

▌2712
E-SUPPLY CHAIN MANAGEMENT AND LOGISTICS
UNIVERSITY OF DALLAS
GRADUATE SCHOOL OF MANAGEMENT

1845 E Northgate Dr.
Irving, TX 75062
PH: (972)721-5000
E-mail: msavoie@udallas.edu
URL: http://gsmweb.udallas.edu/concentrations/
e_business.html

Description: The University of Dallas Graduate School of Management provides a course called E-Supply Chain Management and Logistics. This course gives information on the latest concepts for using technology to improve logistics efficiency.

▌2713
EBUSINESS CONSULTANCY I
TEXAS CHRISTIAN UNIVERSITY
The Neeley School of Business
TCU Box 298530
Fort Worth, TX 76129
PH: (817)257-7540
E-mail: j.mackay@tcu.edu
URL: http://www.tcu.edu
Contact: Dr. Jane Mackay, Program Director

Description: The eBusiness Consultancy I (EBUS 40813) course is the first of a two-course sequence. This first course starts the consultancy phases and completes the eBusiness analysis phase. This two-semester approach will allow students the extra time needed to complete the entire process of creating a Web presence from beginning to end. Students work in teams that last the entire two semesters with a focus on creativity, entrepreneurship and using a team approach to develop creative ideas and observe the processes and factors crucial to a successful eBusiness. Students must complete EBUS 30813, EBUS 30833 and EBUS 30843 with a grade of C or better before taking this course.

▌2714
EBUSINESS CONSULTANCY II
TEXAS CHRISTIAN UNIVERSITY

The Neeley School of Business
TCU Box 298530
Fort Worth, TX 76129
PH: (817)257-7540
E-mail: j.mackay@tcu.edu
URL: http://www.tcu.edu
Contact: Dr. Jane Mackay, Program Director

Description: The eBusiness Consultancy II (EBUS 40823) course provides a more advanced inquiry into Electronic Business and is a continuation of EBUS 40813. Students must complete EBUS 40813 with a grade of C or better before taking this course.

▌2715
EBUSINESS DEVELOPMENT
TEXAS CHRISTIAN UNIVERSITY

The Neeley School of Business
TCU Box 298530
Fort Worth, TX 76129
PH: (817)257-7540
E-mail: j.mackay@tcu.edu
URL: http://www.tcu.edu
Contact: Dr. Jane Mackay, Program Director

Description: The eBusiness Development (EBUS 3833) course teaches students to use the results of the eBusiness analysis to design and implement a Web presence. Students will learn traditional project management techniques in this process. Team building, conflict, diversity, conflict resolution and other team issues are also components of this course. Students must complete EBUS 30813 and EBUS 30823 with a grade of C or better before taking this course.

▌2716
EBUSINESS FUNDAMENTALS
SOUTHERN METHODIST UNIVERSITY

HART E-CENTER

PO Box 750309
Dallas, TX 75275-0309
PH: (214)768-4278
E-mail: ebiz@smu.edu
URL: http://www2.smu.edu/ecenter/
Contact: Dr. Peter E. Raad, Director

Description: The eCenter delivers innovative educational programs (both degree and professional) on emerging technology issues delivered on-campus, on-site, online, and remote. The eCenter offers a course called eBusiness Fundamentals, which explores basic concepts of electronic business including challenges, opportunities, and legal issues.

▌2717
EBUSINESS I
TEXAS CHRISTIAN UNIVERSITY

The Neeley School of Business
TCU Box 298530
Fort Worth, TX 76129
PH: (817)257-7540
E-mail: j.mackay@tcu.edu
URL: http://www.tcu.edu
Contact: Dr. Jane Mackay, Program Director

Description: The eBusiness I (EBUS 20253) course examines the history, basic tools and other important issues surrounding the many forms of e-commerce through lecture, hands-on experience and interactive activities. During the course, students will develop skills and gain knowledge and experience with a networked community designed for business functions and transactions. Students must have a sophomore standing before taking this course.

▌2718
EBUSINESS II
TEXAS CHRISTIAN UNIVERSITY

The Neeley School of Business
TCU Box 298530
Fort Worth, TX 76129
PH: (817)257-7540
E-mail: j.mackay@tcu.edu
URL: http://www.tcu.edu
Contact: Dr. Jane Mackay, Program Director

Description: The eBusiness II (EBUS 20813) course covers topics such as security, privacy and legal issues. During the course, students will learn to start their own e-business and build a site for their own business, compare businesses in various industries and learn how an eBusiness compares to traditions businesses. Students must complete EBUS 20253 with a grade of B or better before taking this course.

▌2719
EBUSINESS PLANNING
TEXAS CHRISTIAN UNIVERSITY

The Neeley School of Business
TCU Box 298530
Fort Worth, TX 76129
PH: (817)257-7540
E-mail: j.mackay@tcu.edu
URL: http://www.tcu.edu
Contact: Dr. Jane Mackay, Program Director

Description: The eBusiness Planning (EBUS 30813) course teaches students how to analyze a business, division or department for a Web presence. Students will investigate how the eBusiness fits into the traditional roles for a business or industry and consider how the Internet can impact the business. Return on Investment, funding, Internet stock valuation and development of communication skills are also components of this course. Students must complete EBUS 20813 with a grade of B or better before taking this course.

▌2720

ECM ORGANIZATIONAL ALIGNMENT

SAN JOSE STATE UNIVERSITY

PROFESSIONAL DEVELOPMENT CENTER

3031 Tisch Way, Ste. 200 Plz. E
San Jose, CA 95128
PH: (408)257-3000
E-mail: mitchell.levy.sjsupd@ecnow.com
URL: http://ecmtraining.com/sjsu/
Contact: Mitchell Levy, Program Founder and Coordinator

Description: San Jose State University offers a course called "ECM Organizational Alignment." This course looks at organizational alignment and efficiency in e-businesses, especially focusing on vision, mission, values, strategy, structure, process, leadership, and people.

▌2721

ECOMMERCE BACHELOR OF SCIENCE

EVERGLADES COLLEGE

1500 NW 49th St., Ste. 600
Ft. Lauderdale, FL 33309
PH: (954)772-2655
TF: 888-772-6077
FX: (954)772-2695
E-mail: evadmissions@evergladescollege.edu
URL: http://www.evergladescollege.edu

Description: Everglades College offers a B.S. degree with an E-Commerce major. This degree prepares students to be successful doing business on the Internet. Students take business and Internet courses as well as classes on web design and analysis. They also look at relationships between customers and suppliers as well as legal and ethical issues unique to doing business over the Internet.

▌2722

ECONOMIC ANALYSIS AND E-COMMERCE MANAGEMENT

DREXEL UNIVERSITY

LEBOW COLLEGE OF BUSINESS

3141 Chestnut St.
Matheson Hall, Rm. 105
Philadelphia, PA 19104
PH: (215)895-6070
FX: (215)895-1012
E-mail: marcos@drexel.edu.
URL: http://www.drexel.edu/academics/lebow/ecomm/

Description: Drexel University offers an executive education course called Economic Analysis and E-Commerce Management. In this course students will gain understanding of the rapidly changing Internet / e-Commerce economy. The effects of this new technology infrastructure on consumer and producer behavior will also be explored.

▌2723

ECONOMICS OF E-COMMERCE MARKETS

NORTHWESTERN UNIVERSITY

KELLOGG SCHOOL OF MANAGEMENT

2001 Sheridan Rd
Evanston, IL 60208
PH: (847)491-8684
E-mail: reiley@vanderbilt.edu
Contact: David Lucking-Reiley, Instructor

Description: Northwestern University offers a "Economics of E-Commerce Markets" which will include topics such as the economics of information goods, the theory of the firm, the economics of intermediation, price competition, price discrimination, and auction theory. It will also provide necessary background on relevant Internet technologies, such as compression, encryption, and collaborative filtering, when relevant to understanding of the economic problems.

▌2724

ECONOMICS OF ELECTRONIC COMMERCE

LOYOLA UNIVERSITY CHICAGO

Graduate School of Business
25 E. Pearson, 14th Fl.
Chicago, IL 60611
PH: (312)915-6120
FX: (312)915-7207
E-mail: ayoung3@luc.edu
URL: http://www.luc.edu
Contact: Alan Young, Director of Enrollment & Recruitment

Description: Economics of Electronic Commerce will present the microeconomic principles that guides information technology. Covered topics will include value maximizing methods, pricing strategies, product lines of information goods, managing intellectual property rights, dynamics of technological positive feedback, compatibility choices and standardization efforts, government policies and regulation, firm strategies and Global issues of e-commerce.

▌2725

ECONOMICS OF ELECTRONIC COMMERCE

UNIVERSITY OF MEMPHIS

Graduate Admissions Office
216 Administration Bldg.
Memphis, TN 38152-3370
PH: (901)678-2531
E-mail: mgarzon@memphis.edu
URL: http://www.memphis.edu
Contact: Dr. Max Garzon, Program Coordinator

Description: Economics of Electronic Commerce teaches students about the market characteristics of e-commerce, economic impact of e-commerce on traditional commerce, and broader issues of property rights, government regulation, information infrastructure maintenance and business cycles.

▌2726

ECRM - THE CUSTOMER COMES FIRST

CALIFORNIA STATE UNIVERSITY, FULLERTON

UNIVERSITY EXTENDED EDUCATION

800 N State College Blvd.
Fullerton, CA 92834-6870
PH: (714)278-2611
FX: (714)278-2088
URL: http://www.takethelead.fullerton.edu/Classes/

Description: Cal State Fullerton offers a course called "eCRM - The Customer Comes First." This course explores eCRM by discussing customer lifetime value as it relates to acquisition and retention campaigns, technology, business processes, and increased profitability.

▌2727

EFFECTIVE E-MARKETING

CARDEAN UNIVERSITY

500 Lake Cook Rd.
Deerfield, IL 60015-5609
TF: (866)948-1289
E-mail: inquires@cardean.edu
URL: http://www.cardean.edu
Contact: Dr. Geoffrey M. Cox, Cardean University President

Description: Cardean University is an accredited online university offering a suite of courses entitled "Effective E-Marketing." This suite of 5 two hour courses helps experienced marketers to recognize the advantages and obstacles of the Internet and utilize them for improved sales, reach, products, and customer satisfaction.

▌2728

EFFECTIVE E-MARKETING SUITE

NETG

1751 W Diehl Rd, 2nd Fl.
Naperville, IL 60563-9099
PH: (630)369-3000
TF: 877-561-6384
FX: (630)983-4877
E-mail: info@netg.com
URL: http://www.netg.com

Description: NETg provides an E-Business course called Effective E-Marketing Suite. This suite of 5 courses analyzes the effect of the Internet on marketing strategies and highlights many ways in which the Internet can be used to make information more valuable for customers. These courses also include specific information on personalization, traffic building, and customer collaboration.

▌2729

ELAB POSTDOCTORAL FELLOWSHIP PROGRAM

VANDERBILT UNIVERSITY

ELAB, OWEN GRADUATE SCHOOL OF MANAGEMENT

401 21st Ave. S
Nashville, TN 37203
PH: (615)343-6904
FX: (615)343-7177
E-mail: elab@owen.vanderbilt.edu
URL: http://ecommerce.vanderbilt.edu/about/
Contact: Professor Donna L. Hoffman, Co-Director

Description: Founded in 1994, Vanderbilt University's eLab is one of the nation's first academic research centers dedicated to the study of the Internet. eLab was recognized by the New York Times as "one of the premiere research centers in the world for the study of electronic commerce." Since its founding, the center has applied the results of its research to help corporate sponsors integrate the Internet into their business strategies. eLab consists of virtual experiments and surveys, web sites, and an online consumer panel that provides an extensive subject pool for Web-based surveys and experiments fielded in the virtual lab. The School of Management offers a two-year postdoctoral fellowship program designed to bridge the gap between scholarship and electronic commerce in the areas of marketing, organization studies, economics, and strategy.

▌2730

ELECTRONIC BUSINESS

DUQUESNE UNIVERSITY

SCHOOL OF BUSINESS

600 Forbes Ave.
Pittsburgh, PA 15282
PH: (412)396-6000
TF: 800-456-0590
E-mail: peace@duq.edu
URL: http://www.drpeace.com/G670/g670.html
Contact: Dr. A. Graham Peace

Description: "Electronic Business" is the title of a course offered at Duquesne University. This course focuses on the managerial side of ebusiness and electronic commerce, as opposed to the technical side. This course is recommended for MBA students who wish to undertake the Graduate School of Business' concentration in ebusiness.

▌2731

ELECTRONIC BUSINESS

UNIVERSITY OF SOUTH CAROLINA

DARLA MOORE SCHOOL OF BUSINESS

1705 College St.
Columbia, SC 29208
PH: (803)777-2940
FX: (803)777-7044
E-mail: bill@sc.edu
URL: http://dmsweb.badm.sc.edu/imd/imdsylEC.htm-Course%20Overview
Contact: Bill Kettinger, Instructor

Description: The University of South Carolina's MBA program offers a course called "Electronic Business." This course looks at is creating both opportunities and uncertainties created by the internet for business leaders who question the potential impact, cost, and applicability of eCommerce to transform business processes and improve performance. This short course will introduce students to these topics and begin to address important eCommerce issues that managers face in the real world.

∎ 2732

ELECTRONIC BUSINESS

CAPITOL COLLEGE

11301 Springfield Rd.
Laurel, MD 20708
PH: (301)369-2800
TF: 800-950-1992
FX: (301)953-1442
E-mail: gradschool@capitol-college.edu
URL: http://www.capitol-college.edu

Description: Capitol College offers a course called Electronic Business. This graduate level course is the capstone of the MS in Electronic Commerce program. Students will cover the entire e-commerce process, from start-up to promotion and investor relations.

∎ 2733

ELECTRONIC BUSINESS CERTIFICATE (EBC)

UNIVERSITY OF TEXAS AT ARLINGTON
DIGITAL SOCIETY ALLIANCE

7300 Jack Newell Blvd. S
Ft. Worth, TX 76118
PH: (817)272-5914
E-mail: reimann@uta.edu
URL: http://www2.uta.edu/ecomm/
Contact: Dr. Michael Reimann, Director

Description: The University of Texas at Arlington Digital Society Alliance provides coursework for students and business people to earn an Electronic Business Certificate (eBC). This program is oriented toward those who want to use digital solutions in government, business, and commercial areas. Business principles and functional knowledge about digital technology form the basis upon which current and emerging applications are studied.

∎ 2734

ELECTRONIC BUSINESS COMMUNICATION NETWORKS

UNIVERSITY OF SCRANTON

Kania School of Management
Brennan Hall, Ste. 438
Scranton, PA 18510
PH: (570)941-7746
E-mail: kakumanu@scranton.edu
URL: http://www.scranton.edu
Contact: Dr. Parsed Kakumanu, Chair, Operation & Info. Mgmt. Dept.

Description: Electronic Business Communication Networks is designed to provide students with networking and telecommunications fundamentals necessary to develop enterprise networks to conduct business on the Internet. Covered topics include communication network media, processors and protocols, multimedia transmission, wireless networks, network design and management and security. As prerequisite of taking this course, students must have already completed the Introduction to Electronic Business course.

∎ 2735

ELECTRONIC BUSINESS AND ENTREPRENEURSHIP

UNIVERSITY OF SCRANTON

Kania School of Management
Brennan Hall, Ste. 438
Scranton, PA 18510
PH: (570)941-7746
E-mail: kakumanu@scranton.edu
URL: http://www.scranton.edu
Contact: Dr. Parsed Kakumanu, Chair, Operation & Info. Mgmt. Dept.

Description: Electronic Business and Entrepreneurship links e-commerce with entrepreneurship and will examine the issues related to the starting and establishment of new businesses based on e-commerce. It's a three part course including issues related to the establishment of a new business and entrepreneurship, issues related to e-commerce including the development of business models and plans and a practical sections where students break into groups and develop and establish small e-commerce businesses from start to finish. Students must complete Electronic Commerce courses EC 361 and EC 362 before taking this course.

∎ 2736

ELECTRONIC BUSINESS FUNDAMENTALS

DEPAUL UNIVERSITY
KELLSTADT GRADUATE SCHOOL OF BUSINESS

1 E Jackson, Ste. 7900
Chicago, IL 60604-2287
PH: (312)362-8810
FX: (312)362-6677
E-mail: mbainfo@depaul.edu
URL: http://commerce.depaul.edu/
Contact: Felicia Richardson-McGee, Assistant Director

Description: DePaul University's Kellstadt Graduate School of Business offers ''Electronic Business Fundamentals'' which explores the business implications of evolving Internet technologies. Students will acquire basic skills for navigating the Internet and creating personal and business electronic presence on the World Wide Web

∎ 2737

ELECTRONIC BUSINESS SECURITY CONTROLS AND ETHICS

UNIVERSITY OF SCRANTON

Kania School of Management
Brennan Hall, Ste. 438
Scranton, PA 18510

PH: (570)941-7746
E-mail: kakumanu@scranton.edu
URL: http://www.scranton.edu
Contact: Dr. Parsed Kakumanu, Chair, Operation & Info. Mgmt. Dept.

Description: Electronic Business Security Controls and Ethics is designed to provide students with an understanding of the technical, managerial, legal and ethical issues involved in building, operating and managing e-commerce solutions. Covered topics will include web server and client security, secure transactions and payments, information security, digital certificates and practices, civil and criminal legal issues, morality and ethical issues, intellectual property and patents, governmental regulations and policies and emerging technologies and standards. Students must complete Electronic Commerce courses EC 361 and EC 362 before attempting this course.

▌2738
ELECTRONIC COMMERCE
REGIS UNIVERSITY
GRADUATE PROGRAMS

3333 Regis Boulevard, L-16
Denver, CO 80221-1099
PH: (303)458-4080
TF: 800-667-9270
FX: (303)964-5538
E-mail: masters@regis.edu
URL: http://www.regis.edu

Description: Regis University offers a course entitled Electronic Commerce. This course introduces concepts of electronic commerce as facilitated by the Internet, and by other technologies. It looks at business-to-business (B2B) and business-to-customer (B2C), convergence of technologies and capabilities, technological challenges, as well as the legal and regulatory framework.

▌2739
ELECTRONIC COMMERCE
KRANNERT SCHOOL OF MANAGEMENT

Purdue University
1310 Krannert Bldg.
West Lafayette, IN 47907
PH: (765)496-3384
FX: (765)494-9841
E-mail: jdietz@mgmt.purdue.edu
URL: http://www.mgmt.purdue.edu
Contact: Joy Dietz, Manager of Advising and Student Services

Description: Electronic Commerce is an Internet Marketing course. Covered topics include getting started, Internet marketing strategies, Internet security, distributing and retailing strategies on the Internet and communications on the Internet. The course is an eight-week module taught every year in the spring since 1996 with Patrick Duparcq as the current instructor.

▌2740
ELECTRONIC COMMERCE
UNIVERSITY OF NEW BRUNSWICK-SAINT JOHN
FACULTY OF BUSINESS

PO Box 5050
Saint John, NB, Canada E2L4L5
PH: (506)648-5570; (506)648-5806
TF: 800-508-6275
FX: (506)648-5574
E-mail: business@unbsj.ca
URL: http://www.unbsj.ca/business
Contact: Shelley Rinehart, Dean, Faculty of Business

Description: UNBSJ's Electronic Commerce program examines all aspects of business as they relate to online commerce. Students explore the role e-commerce can play in all dimensions of business and will acquire a full range of business skills and specific expertise in the business models of e-commerce. Students are not expected to be technical experts, but will leave the program with a level of technical familiarity that will enable them to work in the development and implementation of e-commerce solutions in a wide range of organizations.

▌2741
ELECTRONIC COMMERCE
STANFORD UNIVERSITY
GRADUATE SCHOOL OF BUSINESS

518 Memorial Way
Stanford, CA 94305-5015
PH: (650)725-5663
FX: (650)723-3950
E-mail: cebc@gsb.stanford.edu
URL: http://www.gsb.stanford.edu/cebc/

Description: Stanford University's MBA program offers a course titled "Electronic Commerce." This course focuses on ways in which firms can use electronic commerce to create value. Other topics covered include web-based and multi-channel retailing, and how electronic commerce is likely to change logistics and payment systems and supply chains.

▌2742
ELECTRONIC COMMERCE
UNIVERSITY OF DENVER
DANIELS COLLEGE OF BUSINESS

2101 S University Blvd.
Denver, CO 80208
PH: (303)871-3416
FX: (303)871-4466
E-mail: dcb@du.edu
URL: http://www.dcb.du.edu/itec/mbaec.asp

Description: The University of Denver Daniels College of Business offers a course taught at both the undergraduate and graduate level called "Electronic Commerce." This course gives students an overview of electronic commerce trends and techniques including the underlying technical infrastructure, and traditional EC techniques such as electronic data interchange (EDI). Other topics covered include Internet use for EC, business models for business-to-business and business-to-consumer EC, marketing on the Internet, and security and regulatory issues.

■ 2743

ELECTRONIC COMMERCE

INDIANA UNIVERSITY

COLLEGE OF LIBRARY AND INFORMATION SCIENCE

1320 E 10th St., LI 011
Bloomington, IN 47405-3907
PH: (812)855-2018
TF: 888-335-7547
FX: (812)855-6166
E-mail: hrosenba@indiana.edu
URL: http://www.slis.indiana.edu/hrosenba/www/L561/syll/syll7.html
Contact: Howard Rosenbaum, Instructor

Description: Indiana University offers a course called ''Electronic Commerce.'' In this course will learn about the history, development, and economics of ecommerce. The class will discuss current policy documents and research reports that are attempting to shape ecommerce. Students will also design, create, and manage their own internet business and operate it in a virtual economy (VE) during the course.

■ 2744

ELECTRONIC COMMERCE

UNIVERSITY OF OKLAHOMA

PRICE COLLEGE OF BUSINESS

307 W Brooks, Room 307E
Norman, OK 73019-4006
PH: (405)325-0768
FX: (405)325-7482
E-mail: rzmud@ou.edu
URL: http://www.ou.edu/business/mis/courses.html
Contact: Robert W. Zmud, MIS Division Director

Description: The University of Oklahoma offers a course entitled ''Electronic Commerce.'' This course studies the application of electronic communication to achieve business objectives. Explores the use of such information technologies and concepts as virtual firms, EDI, electronic funds transfer, the Internet and the World Wide Web.

■ 2745

ELECTRONIC COMMERCE

NOTRE DAME UNIVERSITY

COLLEGE OF BUSINESS ADMINISTRATION

Main Bldg.
Notre Dame, IN 46556-5612
PH: (574)631-8613
E-mail: ballou.1@nd.edu
URL: http://www.nd.edu/~mgtnet/ballou/Mgt643/643SYL.HTML
Contact: Deborah Ballou, Instructor

Description: ''Electronic Commerce'' is the name of a course taught at Notre Dame's College of Business Administration. This course will examine how managers can effectively use technology to enhance their organization's competitive position. Students will gain understanding of the fundamentals of Electronic Commerce.

■ 2746

ELECTRONIC COMMERCE

UNIVERSITY OF CALGARY

FACULTY OF CONTINUING EDUCATION

COMPUOFC

Education Tower, Rm. 126
2500 University Dr. NW
Calgary, AB, Canada T2N1N4
PH: (403)220-2866
FX: (403)289-7287
E-mail: compuofc@ucalgary.ca
URL: http://www.computer.ucalgary.ca
Contact: Theresa Ferguson, Program Director

Description: The University of Calgary offers online learning through its Faculty of Continuing Education. Courses include ''Electronic Commerce'', which will teach students basics and infrastructure of Electronic Commerce, and Electronic Businesses. Topics covered include electronic commerce business opportunities and establishing an electronic business.

■ 2747

ELECTRONIC COMMERCE

UNIVERSITY OF CALGARY

FACULTY OF MANAGEMENT MBA PROGRAM

2500 University Dr. NW
Calgary, AB, Canada T2N1N4
PH: (403)220-5685
FX: (403)282-0095
E-mail: mbarequest@mgmt.ucalgary.ca
URL: http://www.acs.ucalgary.ca/~marcolin/eccalgary.html

Description: The University of Calgary offers ''Electronic Commerce'' as a part of its MBA program. The course covers topics relating to electronic commerce and information technologies.

■ 2748

ELECTRONIC COMMERCE

UNIVERSITY OF ILLINOIS AT URBANA-CHAMPAIGN

COLLEGE OF COMMERCE AND BUSINESS ADMINISTRATION

260 Wohlers Hall
1206 S Sixth
Champaign, IL 61820
PH: (217)333-2747
FX: (217)244-3118
E-mail: gebauer@uiuc.edu

URL: http://www.staff.uiuc.edu/~gebauer/BADM457/Orga/syllabus.html
Contact: Dr. Judith Gebauer, Instructor

Description: the University of Illinois at Urbana-Champaign offers ''Electronic Commerce.'' This course covers main topics in electronic commerce, including understanding technology, defining e-commerce, history of the Internet, and e-business infrastructure.

■ 2749

ELECTRONIC COMMERCE
NEW YORK UNIVERSITY
STERN SCHOOL OF BUSINESS

44 W Fourth St.
New York, NY 10012
PH: (212)998-0100
E-mail: admissions@nyu.edu
URL: http://oz.stern.nyu.edu/ec2001/

Description: New York University's Stern School of Business offers a course entitled ''Electronic Commerce.'' This course teaches future business leaders how to handle the new business world of e-commerce, and gives them the concepts and principles necessary to separate the value from the hype.

■ 2750

ELECTRONIC COMMERCE
UNIVERSITY OF MISSOURI-ST. LOUIS
COLLEGE OF BUSINESS ADMINISTRATION

8001 Natural Bridge Rd.
St. Louis, MO 63121-4499
PH: (314)516-5888
E-mail: Vicki.Sauter@umsl.edu
Contact: Dr. Vicki L. Sauter, Professor

Description: The University of Missouri-St. Louis offers ''Electronic Commerce,'' a course which examines critical information technologies that provide the basis for electronic commerce, and their application in a variety of sectors and industries. It will begin with coverage of the tools, skills and business concepts that surround electronic commerce and the consequences of applying these information technologies to different commercial processes.

■ 2751

ELECTRONIC COMMERCE
AUBURN UNIVERSITY
COLLEGE OF BUSINESS

415 W Magnolia Ave.
Auburn, AL 36849-5247
PH: (334)844-6545
E-mail: knock@business.auburn.edu
URL: http://www.business.auburn.edu/~knock/MNGT4880-Ecommerce/MNGT4880.html

Description: ''Electronic Commerce'' at Auburn University will help students explore fundamental technical aspects that are required to build e-business Web sites. They will gain a general understanding of the business aspects that are necessary to conduct effective Web sites.

■ 2752

ELECTRONIC COMMERCE
BOSTON COLLEGE

140 Commonwealth Ave.
Chestnut Hill, MA 02467
PH: (617)552-2519
E-mail: john.gallaugher@bc.edu
URL: http://www2.bc.edu/~gallaugh/
Contact: John Gallaugher, Professor

Description: Boston College offers ''Electronic Commerce,'' a course which has objectives of providing a managerial overview of the technologies supporting and enabling electronic commerce, and examining current strategies, issues, and trends in electronic commerce

■ 2753

ELECTRONIC COMMERCE
UNIVERSITY OF MINNESOTA
CARLSON SCHOOL OF MANAGEMENT

321 19th Ave. S., CSOM 4-327
Minneapolis, MN 55455
PH: (612)624-1874
FX: (612)626-1316
E-mail: lwanning@umn.edu
URL: http://ids.csom.umn.edu/faculty/wanninger/IDSc4441/right4441.html
Contact: Dr. Lester A. Wanninger, Instructor

Description: The Carlson School of Management at the University of Minnesota offers ''Electronic Commerce.'' This course will introduce students to the world of electronic commerce applications. It will give students an appreciation for the roles of people, infrastructure, business processes and technologies to develop successful electronic commerce applications.

■ 2754

ELECTRONIC COMMERCE
MCGILL UNIVERSITY
FACULTY OF MANAGEMENT

1001 Sherbrooke St. W
Montreal, PQ, Canada H3A1G5
PH: (514)398-4000
FX: (514)398-3876
E-mail: gagnon@management.mcgill.ca
URL: http://www.intranet.management.mcgill.ca/course/mis/273434/CO273690_W00.htm

Description: The course called ''Electronic Commerce'' at McGill University in Montreal is focused on identifying business opportunities and analyzing how new Internet technologies can enhance profitability. It can be seen as an advanced introduction to e-commerce, and is the first of a series of 5 courses which make up an E-Commerce major.

▌2755

ELECTRONIC COMMERCE
INDIANA STATE UNIVERSITY
SCHOOL OF BUSINESS

217 N Sixth St.
Terre Haute, IN 47809
PH: (812)237-3232
FX: (812)237-8720
E-mail: sdharper@befac.indstate.edu
URL: http://misnt.indstate.edu/harper/690_syllabus.htm

Description: Indiana State University School of business offers a course entitled "Electronic Commerce" as a part of their MBA program. This course is intended to give MBA students an overview of the electronic commerce phenomenon currently sweeping through the global economy. The course introduces contemporary management philosophies as used for the marketing, selling, and distribution of goods and services through the Internet, World-Wide-Web, and other electronic media.

▌2756

ELECTRONIC COMMERCE
UNIVERSITY OF MARYLAND
INSTITUTE FOR GLOBAL ELECTRONIC COMMERCE

1000 Hilltop Cir.
Baltimore, MD 21250
PH: (410)455-3522
FX: (410)455-3969
E-mail: igec@igec.umbc.edu
URL: http://www.igec.umbc.edu/
Contact: Tim Finin, Director

Description: The Institute for Global Electronic Commerce at the University of Maryland has a multidisciplinary educational and research program designed to promote the electronic transmission of commercial transactions through the connection of companies and universities and through the creation of new entities. It covers areas of Computer and Information Sciences and Technology, Law, and Business with curriculum and degree programs to train students, industrial and government leaders in the area of Electronic Commerce.

▌2757

ELECTRONIC COMMERCE
VANDERBILT UNIVERSITY
OWEN SCHOOL OF MANAGEMENT

401 21st Ave. S
Nashville, TN 37203
PH: (615)322-4064
E-mail: kelly.Christie@owen.vanderbilt.edu
URL: http://mba.vanderbilt.edu/
Contact: Kelly Christie, Director of Academic Programs

Description: The Owen School of Management at Vanderbilt University offers a concentration in Electronic Commerce for graduate study. Course titles include Consumer Behavior in Online Environments, Information Tech and Electronic Commerce, and Management of Intellectual

Assets. An Executive MBA program as well as Executive conferences and seminars are also offered.

▌2758

ELECTRONIC COMMERCE
UNIVERSITY OF PITTSBURGH
KATZ SCHOOL OF BUSINESS

372 Mervis Hall
Pittsburgh, PA 15260
PH: (412)648-1699
FX: (412)648-1693
E-mail: galletta@katz.pitt.edu
URL: http://www.pitt.edu/~galletta/ecommerce/index.html
Contact: Dennis Galletta

Description: University of Pittsburgh's course Electronic Commerce is offered on campus and will help students understand a broad range of Internet tools, gain skills in developing basic Internet applications (HTML reviewed by studying image maps, tables, and forms), and create business models while studying the benefits and risks involved.

▌2759

ELECTRONIC COMMERCE BASICS
UNIVERSITY OF MINNESOTA EXTENSION SERVICE

240 Coffey Hall
1420 Eckles Ave.
St. Paul, MN 55108-6068
PH: (612)624-1222
E-mail: mainstreet@extension.umn.edu
URL: http://www.extension.umn.edu/mainstreet/curriculum/index.html

Description: The University of Minnesota Extension Service offers a course called Electronic Commerce Basics. This course explores the definition of electronic commerce, looks at changing demographics, examines security issues and provides information on e-commerce's potential effects on business.

▌2760

ELECTRONIC COMMERCE CONCEPTS
NOTRE DAME
COLLEGE OF BUSINESS

276 Mendoza College of Business
Notre Dame, IN 46556
PH: (219)631-8488
TF: 800-631-8488
FX: (219)631-8800
E-mail: mba.1@nd.edu
URL: http://www.nd.edu/~mba
Contact: Carolyn Woo, Dean

Description: The Notre Dame MBA Program offers a course called "Electronic Commerce Concepts." This course looks at how managers can effectively use technology to enhance their organization's competitive position. Specific topics covered include use of the Web for commerce, electronic payment systems, and the role of extranets in supply-chain management.

■ 2761
ELECTRONIC COMMERCE: CREATING GLOBAL PARTNERSHIPS
LOYOLA UNIVERSITY CHICAGO

Graduate School of Business
25 E. Pearson, 14th Fl.
Chicago, IL 60611
PH: (312)915-6120
FX: (312)915-7207
E-mail: ayoung3@luc.edu
URL: http://www.luc.edu
Contact: Alan Young, Director of Enrollment & Recruitment

Description: The Electronic Commerce: Creating Global Partnerships course teaches students how e-commerce is helping companies establish global partnerships that create new markets and establish new supply chains with cases of successful alliances and the competitive advantages of these alliances studied. Students will work in teams to analyze and present cases that represent global partnerships in a variety of service and manufacturing industries.

■ 2762
ELECTRONIC COMMERCE IN THE GLOBAL ECONOMY
BENTLEY COLLEGE

175 Forest St.
Waltham, MA 02452-4705
PH: (781)891-2000
URL: http://www.bentley.edu

Description: Bentley College offers a graduate course entitled Electronic Commerce in the Global Economy. This course looks at opportunities and strategies involved in maintaining e-commerce. Students use case studies of e-commerce firms to study current technologies and issues.

■ 2763
ELECTRONIC COMMERCE GRADUATE CERTIFICATE PROGRAM
RUTGERS, THE STATE UNIVERSITY OF NEW JERSEY
CENTER FOR INFORMATION MANAGEMENT, INTEGRATION & CONNECTIVITY

180 University Ave.
Newark, NJ 07102
PH: (973)353-1014
FX: (973)353-5808
E-mail: ec-certificate@cimic.rutgers.edu
URL: http://www.rutgers.edu

Description: The Electronic Commerce Graduate Certificate Program has been designed for students interested in acquiring the knowledge and skills and understanding the

concepts in the technology aspects of e-commerce. Currently, the certificate program is offered only in the technology track.

■ 2764
ELECTRONIC COMMERCE I
PURDUE UNIVERSITY
KRANNERT SCHOOL OF MANAGEMENT

1310 Krannert Bldg.
West Lafayette, IN 47907
PH: (765)494-9700
FX: (765)494-9658
E-mail: webmaster@mgmt.purdue.edu
URL: http://courses.mgmt.purdue.edu/duparcq/ecommerce/

Description: Purdue University's Krannert School of Management offers ''Electronic Commerce I'' which will discuss how interactive technologies will reshape industries and the structure of companies. Discussions will cover what its implications are for business in general, and for Marketing specifically. After a discussion on E-Business Strategies and Online Consumer Behavior, students will focus on the e-enabled Marketing Mix.

■ 2765
ELECTRONIC COMMERCE: INTEGRATING BUSINESS FUNCTIONS
LOYOLA UNIVERSITY CHICAGO

Graduate School of Business
25 E. Pearson, 14th Fl.
Chicago, IL 60611
PH: (312)915-6120
FX: (312)915-7207
E-mail: ayoung3@luc.edu
URL: http://www.luc.edu
Contact: Alan Young, Director of Enrollment & Recruitment

Description: The Electronic Commerce: Integrating Business Functions course uses an integrated approach to e-commerce and includes discussions on how e-commerce can be used to reengineer business processes. Plus, representatives from firms that have successfully employed e-commerce in their business will discuss technical, legal, economic, social and business issues related to e-commerce.

■ 2766
ELECTRONIC COMMERCE INTEGRATION
CHRISTOPHER NEWPORT UNIVERSITY ONLINE

1 University Pl.
Newport News, VA 23606
PH: (757)594-7607
E-mail: online@cnu.edu
URL: http://ec.seva.net/

Description: Christopher Newport University and the Virginia Electronic Commerce Technology Center offer an online course called ''Electronic Commerce Integration.'' This course looks at the benefits and issues involved with integrating an EC system into a company's business process, including electronic integration with trading partners.

▌2767

ELECTRONIC COMMERCE AND INTERACTIVE MARKETING
OKLAHOMA STATE UNIVERSITY

Center for Academic Services
324 Student Union
Stillwater, OK 74078-1012
PH: (405)744-6858
E-mail: admit@okstate.edu
URL: http://www.okstate.edu

Description: Electronic Commerce and Interactive Marketing is for people who want to understand how digital interactive tools are changing the way we manage markets. The course examines the development and impact of e-commerce on businesses and use of interactive (electronic) marketing for building a one-to-one relationship with customers. This is a hands-on course that focuses on understanding how to use the web for building a dialogue with customers, managing relationships with customers and improving effectiveness of marketing functions.

▌2768

ELECTRONIC COMMERCE ON THE INTERNET
NOVA SOUTHEASTERN UNIVERSITY
GRADUATE SCHOOL OF COMPUTER AND INFORMATION SCIENCES

3301 College Ave.
Ft. Lauderdale, FL 33314-7796
PH: (954)262-2000
TF: 800-986-2247
E-mail: manningr@nova.edu
URL: http://www.nova.edu/~manningr/syl654f00.htm
Contact: Dr. Richard Manning, Instructor

Description: Electronic Commerce on the Internet is a course offered at Nova Southeastern University. This class examines the foundation, operation and implications of the Internet economy. Topics include Internet technologies, online market mechanisms, interactive customers, knowledge-based products, smart products and services, pricing in the internet economy, online auctions and e-marketplaces, digital governance, and policies for the internet economy.

▌2769

ELECTRONIC COMMERCE: LAW AND BUSINESS IN CYBERSPACE
STANFORD LAW SCHOOL

Crown Quadrangle
559 Nathan Abbott Way
Stanford, CA 94305-8610
PH: (650)723-2465
FX: (650)725-0253

E-mail: mradin@stanford.edu
URL: http://www.law.stanford.edu/faculty/radin/ecommerce/index.shtml

Description: Stanford Law School offers a course entitled ''Electronic Commerce: Law and Business in Cyberspace'' which explores the rapidly evolving legal environment in Cyberspace, in the context of Internet business models and strategies. Guest speakers with a variety of perspectives on business and legal issues will be invited to share their information.

▌2770

ELECTRONIC COMMERCE MANAGEMENT
SAN JOSE STATE UNIVERSITY
PROFESSIONAL DEVELOPMENT CENTER

3031 Tisch Way, Ste. 200 Plz. E
San Jose, CA 95128
PH: (408)257-3000
E-mail: mitchell.levy.sjsupd@ecnow.com
URL: http://ecmtraining.com/sjsu/
Contact: Mitchell Levy, Program Founder and Coordinator

Description: San Jose State University offers an executive education certificate program ''Electronic Commerce Management.'' This program is designed to help students deploy, manage and expand e-commerce within organizations, helping them grow into the Internet age. Courses in this program are taught by industry professionals who daily are focused on electronic commerce.

▌2771

ELECTRONIC COMMERCE: MARKETS AND NETCENTRIC SYSTEMS
UNIVERSITY OF MARYLAND
SMITH SCHOOL OF BUSINESS

Van Munching Hall
College Park, MD 20742
PH: (301)405-2278
E-mail: info@hsmith.umd.edu
URL: http://ecommerce.umd.edu/

Description: The University of Maryland Smith School of Business offers an MBA course entitled ''Electronic Commerce: Markets and Netcentric Systems'' This course focuses on a business perspective, and course examines the use of the web for the marketing and distribution of goods and services. The course will look at the three market mechanisms most typically employed: brokers, dealers, and auctions and study the role of intermediaries in making these markets function.

▌2772

ELECTRONIC COMMERCE MBA
SAN FRANCISCO STATE UNIVERSITY

1600 Holloway Ave.
San Francisco, CA 94132-4013
PH: (415)338-1935

FX: (415)338-6237
E-mail: mba@sfsu.edu
URL: http://www.sfsu.edu

Description: San Francisco State University offers an MBA in Electronic Commerce. This program focuses on business management while allowing each student to develop an understanding of particular areas of electronic commerce. Students may choose to emphasize either technical or marketing aspects e-commerce, or combinations of these or other business areas.

▌2773

ELECTRONIC COMMERCE MBA
DREXEL UNIVERSITY
COLLEGE OF BUSINESS

32nd and Chestnut Sts.
Philadelphia, PA 19104
PH: (215)895-6070
E-mail: admissions@drexel.edu
URL: http://www.lebow.drexel.edu/

Description: Drexel University offers an MBA in Electronic Commerce. This curriculum provides information on various aspects of e-commerce including the economic, legal, marketing, managerial, strategic, operational, and technical.

▌2774

ELECTRONIC COMMERCE MSBA
SAN FRANCISCO STATE UNIVERSITY

1600 Holloway Ave.
San Francisco, CA 94132-4013
PH: (415)338-1935
FX: (415)338-6237
E-mail: mba@sfsu.edu
URL: http://www.sfsu.edu

Description: San Francisco State University offers an MSBA in Electronic Commerce. This degree program gives students an understanding of the planning, development, and management of e-commerce applications. Students learn both the technical and marketing aspects of e-commerce as well as how e-commerce functions with an overall business strategy.

▌2775

ELECTRONIC COMMERCE PROGRAM
UNIVERSITY OF SCRANTON

Kania School of Management
Brennan Hall, Ste. 438
Scranton, PA 18510
PH: (570)941-7746
E-mail: kakumanu@scranton.edu
URL: http://www.scranton.edu
Contact: Dr. Parsed Kakumanu, Chair, Operation & Info. Mgmt. Dept.

Founded: 1938. **Description:** The Electronic Commerce Program offers students hands-on experience designing and building an interactive e-commerce site and an understanding of how electronic commerce is transforming business and industry, including the supply of related strategic issues and business models. The E-Commerce major is interdisciplinary and consists of eight courses beyond the general education and business core courses. The student will take five required courses and choose three elective courses from a selection of six.

▌2776

ELECTRONIC COMMERCE PROJECT
UNIVERSITY OF MEMPHIS

Graduate Admissions Office
216 Administration Bldg.
Memphis, TN 38152-3370
PH: (901)678-2531
E-mail: mgarzon@memphis.edu
URL: http://www.memphis.edu
Contact: Dr. Max Garzon, Program Coordinator

Description: Electronic Commerce Project allows students majoring in e-commerce to be immersed in a real-world experience. The course places students into groups and arranges for them to go out and complete e-commerce projects for local businesses with the objective of applying classroom knowledge in a real-life situation.

▌2777

ELECTRONIC COMMERCE SECURITY ISSUES
SEREBRA LEARNING CORP.

7565 132nd St., Unit 119
Surrey, BC, Canada V3W1K5
PH: (604)592-0552
TF: 800-567-7766
FX: (604)592-0553
E-mail: info@serebra.com
URL: http://www.serebra.com
Contact: Mr. Bruce Stewart, President

Founded: 1987. **Description:** Serebra Learning Corporation presents an online course entitled "Electronic Commerce Security Issues." This course describes the technologies of electronic commerce, including e-commerce security issues and electronic payment systems. Also presented are business strategies for electronic commerce, including branding and technology-enabled relationship management. The course ends with a discussion of project planning and management issues.

▌2778

ELECTRONIC COMMERCE STRATEGIES
SEREBRA LEARNING CORP.

7565 132nd St., Unit 119
Surrey, BC, Canada V3W1K5
PH: (604)592-0552
TF: 800-567-7766
FX: (604)592-0553
E-mail: info@serebra.com

URL: http://www.serebra.com
Contact: Mr. Bruce Stewart, President

Founded: 1987. **Description:** Serebra Learning Corporation offers a class for those with no previous knowledge of electronic commerce called "Electronic Commerce Strategies." This course presents business strategies for electronic commerce, including branding, technology-enabled relationship management, purchasing, electronic data interchange, supply-chain management, auction sites, virtual communities, and Web portals. Also discussed are international, legal, ethics, and tax issues.

▌2779
ELECTRONIC COMMERCE STRATEGIES
UNIVERSITY OF PITTSBURGH
CENTER FOR EXECUTIVE EDUCATION

Mellon Financial Corp. Hall, 5th Fl.
4227 Fifth Ave.
Pittsburgh, PA 15260
PH: (412)648-1600
E-mail: exeducation@katz.pitt.edu
URL: http://www.execed.pitt.edu/

Description: The Executive Education Program at the University of Pittsburgh offers a course called Electronic Commerce Strategies. Five basic areas are covered: technologies, opportunities, cautions, strategies, and tactics. Coverage of both technological and strategic content helps provide understanding of both what is possible for designing not only your web site, and your overall approach to internet strategy.

▌2780
ELECTRONIC COMMERCE - STRATEGY AND IMPLEMENTATION
IDAHO STATE UNIVERSITY
COLLEGE OF BUSINESS

921 S 8th Ave.
Pocatello, ID 83209
PH: (208)282-0211
E-mail: cobsupport@cob.isu.edu
URL: http://cob.isu.edu/mba691/
Contact: Kregg Aytes, Instructor

Description: Idaho State University College of Business offers a course entitled "Electronic Commerce - Strategy and Implementation." Objectives of this course include learning to have a broad understanding of the technology architecture necessary to implement ecommerce, being familiar with the vocabulary to evaluate internet strategies and offerings

▌2781
ELECTRONIC COMMERCE TECHNOLOGY
RUTGERS, THE STATE UNIVERSITY OF NEW JERSEY

CENTER FOR INFORMATION MANAGEMENT, INTEGRATION & CONNECTIVITY
180 University Ave.
Newark, NJ 07102
PH: (973)353-1014
FX: (973)353-5808
E-mail: ec-certificate@cimic.rutgers.edu
URL: http://www.rutgers.edu

Description: Electronic Commerce Technology is an introduction to e-commerce technologies, Internet, Networking Technologies, HTML, JavaScript, CGI, Perl and XML.

▌2782
ELECTRONIC COMMERCE AND TELECOMMUNICATIONS
OLD DOMINION UNIVERSITY

Hampton Blvd.
Norfolk, VA 23529
PH: (757)683-3000
E-mail: admit@odu.edu
URL: http://www.odu.edu

Description: Old Dominion University offers a course called Electronic Commerce and Telecommunications. This course looks at electronic commerce and telecommunications in the global business environment, and also gives students a broad introduction to the Internet.

▌2783
ELECTRONIC COMMUNITIES IN ORGANIZATIONS
NEW JERSEY INSTITUTE OF TECHNOLOGY
SCHOOL OF MANAGEMENT, GRADUATE PROGRAMS

323 Martin Luther King Jr. Blvd.
Newark, NJ 07102-1982
PH: (973)596-6378
FX: (973)596-3074
E-mail: lipper@njit.edu
URL: http://www.njit.edu/SOM/MBA/index.html
Contact: Stuart Lipper, Director of Graduate Programs

Description: The New Jersey Institute of Technology School of Management MBA program offers a course called "Electronic Communities in Organizations." This course looks at the dynamics of electronic communities, emphasizing on their role in work organizations. Students will also learn how to evaluate learning communities and to examine their relationship to important processes in organizations.

▌2784
ELECTRONIC CUSTOMER RELATIONSHIP MANAGEMENT (ECRM)
CALIFORNIA STATE UNIVERSITY, FULLERTON
UNIVERSITY EXTENDED EDUCATION

800 N State College Blvd.
Fullerton, CA 92834-6870
PH: (714)278-2611

FX: (714)278-2088
URL: http://www.takethelead.fullerton.edu/Classes/

Description: Cal State Fullerton offers a certificate program in Electronic Customer Relationship Management (eCRM). Designed for business managers and other professionals, the eCRM combines business strategies with technology that closes the gaps between an organization's current and potential performance in customer acquisition, growth, and retention. Students in this program learn about technology alternatives for customer relationship management and how to develop a strategy to focus on cultivating and retaining valuable customers.

▌ 2785
ELECTRONIC DATA INTERCHANGE (BCIT)
BRITISH COLUMBIA INSTITUTE OF TECHNOLOGY
ADMINISTRATIVE MANAGEMENT

3700 Willingdon Ave.
Burnaby, BC, Canada V5G3H2
PH: (604)451-7134
E-mail: wendy_lee@bcit.ca
URL: http://online.bcit.ca/de/Ecomm.htm
Contact: Wendy Lee

Description: The British Columbia Institute of Technology (BCIT) offers a course titled "Electronic Data Interchange." This online course gives a management overview of Electronic Data Interchange (EDI), including the history of EDI, Implementing EDI systems, EDI on the internet, and data communications. The course combines a series of lectures and research projects and provides students with the skills necessary to utilize EDI and Electronic Business.

▌ 2786
THE ELECTRONIC ECONOMY
CLAREMONT GRADUATE UNIVERSITY
SCHOOL OF INFORMATION SCIENCE

130 E 9th St.
Claremont, CA 91711
PH: (909)621-8209
E-mail: infosci@cgu.edu
URL: http://is.cgu.edu

Description: Claremont Graduate University offers a course called The Electronic Economy. This course looks at conducting business over the Internet from the perspective of the individual consumer as well as from a business-to-business point of view.

▌ 2787
ELECTRONIC ENTERPRISE CERTIFICATE
UNIVERSITY OF TEXAS AT ARLINGTON
DIGITAL SOCIETY ALLIANCE

7300 Jack Newell Blvd. S
Ft. Worth, TX 76118
PH: (817)272-5914

E-mail: reimann@uta.edu
URL: http://www2.uta.edu/ecomm/
Contact: Dr. Michael Reimann, Director

Description: The University of Texas at Arlington Digital Society Alliance offers an Electronic Enterprise Certificate (eEC) for executives and students. It is designed for those interested in implementing digital technologies in industry and engineering environments. Foundational knowledge about enterprise engineering and technology is complemented with current practices and real examples.

▌ 2788
ELECTRONIC MARKET PLACES OF THE FUTURE
YALE SCHOOL OF MANAGEMENT

135 Prospect St.
PO Box 208200
New Haven, CT 06520-8200
PH: (203)432-5932
FX: (203)432-7004
E-mail: mba.admissions@yale.edu
URL: http://www.mba.yale.edu
Contact: James Stevens, Director

Description: Electronic Market Places of the Future will address the current and future state of electronic commerce, with particular emphasis on business-to-business commerce, electronic marketplaces and the rapid increase in tempo. Topics will include basics of e-commerce technology, including networking, information protocols, security, standards and platform middleware; business-to-consumer commerce including personalization and privacy issues; business-to-business commerce including marketplaces, auctions, exchanges, intermediaries, business processes and optimization; new areas of e-commerce, including mobile commerce; dynamic commerce, intelligent agents and use of networked services, implications for the enterprise and the economy.

▌ 2789
ELECTRONIC MARKETING
CLEMSON UNIVERSITY

E-108 Martin Hall
Clemson, SC 29634-5713
PH: (864)656-3311
E-mail: ddiane@clemson.edu
URL: http://www.clemson.edu

Description: Clemson University offers a course called Electronic Marketing. This graduate level course applies the concepts and practices of marketing to e-commerce. Topics covered include business-to-business marketing and business-to-consumer marketing.

▌ 2790
ELECTRONIC MARKETING AND BUSINESS
RUTGERS, THE STATE UNIVERSITY OF NEW JERSEY

CENTER FOR INFORMATION MANAGEMENT,
INTEGRATION & CONNECTIVITY

180 University Ave.
Newark, NJ 07102
PH: (973)353-1014
FX: (973)353-5808
E-mail: ec-certificate@cimic.rutgers.edu
URL: http://www.rutgers.edu

Description: Electronic Marketing and Business has two modules included, formulating and implementing strategies for e-commerce and market failure and public policy toward e-commerce. Part of the course will be specifically tailored to the e-commerce industry and will cover the theoretical aspects of competing in hyper-competitive and technology-intensive environments.

▌2791
ELECTRONIC PAYMENTS AND SECURITY
DALHOUSIE UNIVERSITY

Faculty of Computer Science
6050 University Ave.
Halifax, NS, Canada B3H1W5
PH: (902)494-2740
FX: (902)492-1517
E-mail: mec@cs.dal.ca
URL: http://www.ecomm.dal.ca
Contact: Dr. Kori Inkpen, Dir., Master of E-Commerce Program

Description: Electronic Payments and Security covers the various methods of transferring money over the Internet in regards to e-commerce and compares their functionality. Covered topics include electronic cash, electronic checks, electronic credit cards, micro-payments, the encryption and digital signature techniques needed to support electronic cash, the technology available to support secure transactions on the Internet and comparison of the various payment systems.

▌2792
ELECTRONIC COMMERCE FOR SUPPLY CHAIN MANAGEMENT
ARIZONA STATE UNIVERSITY

Main Campus
PO Box 874706
Tempe, AZ 85287-4706
PH: (480)752-2277
FX: (480)965-8629
E-mail: pcarter@asu.edu
URL: http://www.asu.edu
Contact: Dr. Phillip Carter, Professor

Description: Electronic commerce for Supply Chain Management covers process automation systems, operations resources management, purchasing systems, buying on the Internet, electronic catalogs, electronic auctions, electronic markets, buyer/supplier interfaces, cost/benefit analysis, technical issues, international business issues, legal issues and company case studies.

▌2793
ELEMENTS OF THE E-BUSINESS SOLUTION
RED HAT

1801 Varsity Dr.
Raleigh, NC 27606
PH: (919)754-3700
TF: 888-733-4281
FX: (919)754-3701
E-mail: customerservice@redhat.com
URL: http://www.redhat.com

Description: Red Hat, the largest provider of open source technology, offers an online course called "Elements of the E-Business Solution." This course contains an overview of the history and significance of e-business and then teaches students how to build their own e-business solution. Students will learn which infrastructure and technologies are needed, which products and services can be used, and which issues to consider when purchasing or implementing the various elements of a solution.

▌2794
ELEMENTS OF THE E-BUSINESS SOLUTION
DIGITALTHINK INC

601 Brannan St.
San Francisco, CA 94107
PH: (415)625-4000
TF: 888-686-8817
FX: (415)625-4100
E-mail: info@digitalthink.com
URL: http://www.digitalthink.com
Contact: Mr. Pete Goettner, Chairman

Founded: 1996. **Staff:** 450. **Description:** Founded in 1996, DigitalThink created a student focused online learning experience. "Elements of the E-Business Solution" is the name of a course which introduces students to the tools and products needed to build an e-business solution from start to finish. It begins with an overview of the history and significance of e-business and then teaches students how to build their own e-business solution.

▌2795
EMARKETING 1.1
JER GROUP INC.
ONLINEWORKSHOPS.COM

56 Seabreeze Way
Dawsonville, GA 30534
PH: (706)216-3406
FX: (706)216-3979
E-mail: drjer@jergroup.com
URL: http://www.onlineworkshops.com
Contact: Dr. John E. Reid, Jr., President

Description: JER Group Inc. onlineworkshops.com offers an e-commerce marketing course called "eMarketing 1.1." This course is the eMarketing Association's complete basic emarketing course. Topics covered include Internet history, banner advertising strategies and design, writing styles for e-mail, use of HTML and text in e-mail, and integration of online and conventional marketing.

▌ 2796
EMERGING E-COMMERCE LAW AND POLICY
HARVARD UNIVERSITY
HARVARD EXTENSION SCHOOL

51 Brattle St.
Cambridge, MA 02138
PH: (617)495-4005
E-mail: css@hudce7.harvard.edu
URL: http://www.extension.harvard.edu/

Description: Harvard University's Extension School offers a course called Emerging E-Commerce Law and Policy. This course examines laws and regulations as they apply to the use of the new information technologies in a commercial context. Policy concerns are also addressed.

▌ 2797
EMERGING TECHNOLOGIES
CREIGHTON UNIVERSITY
COLLEGE OF BUSINESS ADMINISTRATION

2500 California Plz.
Omaha, NE 68178
PH: (402)280-2602
FX: (402)280-2172
E-mail: ghafer@creighton.edu
URL: http://www.creighton.edu
Contact: Ms. Gail Hafer, Graduate Coordinator

Description: Creighton University offers a graduate level course called Emerging Technologies. This course focuses on identifying, acquiring and using new technologies, and learning to capitalize early on emerging technologies to gain competitive advantage.

▌ 2798
EMERGING TECHNOLOGIES IN E-BUSINESS
BELLEVUE UNIVERSITY

1000 Galvin Rd. S
Bellevue, NE 68005
PH: (402)293-2000
TF: 800-756-7920
FX: (402)293-2020
URL: http://www.bellevue.edu

Description: Bellevue University offers a course called "Emerging Technologies in E-Business." This course takes a look at the possible future of E Business. Topics covered will include: gathering technological intelligence and developing electronic communities. Students will research other uses of the Internet and examine the ways this electronic medium can further change how we do business.

▌ 2799
ENHANCING YOUR CORPORATE REPUTATION ONLINE
UNIVERSITY OF PITTSBURGH
CENTER FOR EXECUTIVE EDUCATION

Mellon Financial Corp. Hall, 5th Fl.
4227 Fifth Ave.
Pittsburgh, PA 15260
PH: (412)648-1600
E-mail: exeducation@katz.pitt.edu
URL: http://www.execed.pitt.edu/

Description: The Executive Education Program at the University of Pittsburgh offers a two-day seminar called Enhancing Your Corporate Reputation Online. Participants learn the basics of managing reputation in an online world. Via theory, reviews of practice, hands-on exercises, and specially developed analytic tools, participants will learn the essentials of building and defending reputation on the web.

▌ 2800
ENTERPRISE ELECTRONIC BUSINESS STRATEGIES
COLORADO STATE UNIVERSITY
COLLEGE OF BUSINESS

029 Rockwell Hall
Fort Collins, CO 80523
PH: (970)491-7511
FX: (970)491-5205
E-mail: stephen.hayne@mail.biz.colostate.edu
URL: http://www.speedofheat.com/hayne/ecommerce/
Contact: Dr. Stephen Hayne, Instructor

Description: Colorado State University offers a course titled "Enterprise Electronic Business Strategies." This course will provide students with a general understanding of the Internet and related technologies, as well as teach them to be able to store/retrieve/build files on the Internet and examine obstacles for ebusiness.

▌ 2801
ENTREPRENEURIAL STRATEGY
BRIGHAM YOUNG UNIVERSITY
ROLLINS CENTER FOR E-BUSINESS

510 N. Tanner Bldg
PO Box 23068
Provo, UT 84602-3068
PH: (801)422-2815
FX: (801)422-5933
E-mail: ebusiness@byu.edu
URL: http://ebusiness.byu.edu/ebus.cfm
Contact: J. Owen Cherrington, Director

Description: Brigham Young University's Rollins Center for E-Business offers a course titled "Entrepreneurial Strategy." This course provides information on financing, marketing, organization, and strategy. Students will develop e-business strategies and models through the association with local businesses and entrepreneurs that will assist with student projects.

607

▌2802

EPEOPLE COURSE

KRANNERT SCHOOL OF MANAGEMENT

Purdue University
1310 Krannert Bldg.
West Lafayette, IN 47907
PH: (765)496-3384
FX: (765)494-9841
E-mail: jdietz@mgmt.purdue.edu
URL: http://www.mgmt.purdue.edu
Contact: Joy Dietz, Manager of Advising and Student Services

Description: The ePeople Course covers how the growth of e-commerce has implications on employees and customers and introduces students to the human side of e-business including staffing issues in regards to an e-commerce. This is an eight-week course currently being taught by Brad Alge.

▌2803

ESTABLISHING A WEB PRESENCE

NOTRE DAME DE NAMUR UNIVERSITY

1500 Ralston Ave.
Belmont, CA 94002-1997
PH: (650)508-3782
FX: (650)508-3660
E-mail: ebusiness@ndnu.edu
URL: http://www.ndnu.edu

Description: Notre Dame de Namur University offers a graduate course called Establishing a Web Presence. In this course students will build a web site and address issues and topics including the technology of the Internet, development tools, messaging strategies, design, security, scalability, and usability testing.

▌2804

ESTRATEGY

CARNEGIE MELLON UNIVERSITY

GRADUATE SCHOOL

GSIA, Tech & Frew Sts., Rm. 206
Pittsburgh, PA 15213
PH: (412)268-1322
FX: (412)268-6837
E-mail: msecinfo@andrew.cmu.edu
URL: http://www.ecom.cmu.edu

Description: Carnegie Mellon University offers a graduate level course called eStrategy. This course uses game theory to develop ways of thinking strategically about the challenges e-businesses face. Students develop their strategic thinking skills using an E-Strategy Game, a computer simulation of competition between e-businesses.

▌2805

ESTUDIO

NORTH CAROLINA STATE UNIVERSITY

E-COMMERCE STUDIO

Campus Box 7229
Raleigh, NC 27695-7229
PH: (919)513-4606
E-mail: ecommerce@ncsu.edu
URL: http://ecommerce.ncsu.edu/studio/
Contact: Dr. Annie Anton

Description: The eStudio is a practicum based on teams of computer science and business students working on industry-sponsored projects. Under the supervision of faculty members in both Business Management and Computer Science, students work in teams that blend technical and managerial skills.

▌2806

ETHICS IN ELECTRONIC COMMERCE

LOYOLA UNIVERSITY CHICAGO

Graduate School of Business
25 E. Pearson, 14th Fl.
Chicago, IL 60611
PH: (312)915-6120
FX: (312)915-7207
E-mail: ayoung3@luc.edu
URL: http://www.luc.edu
Contact: Alan Young, Director of Enrollment & Recruitment

Description: Ethics in Electronic Commerce explores the ethical dilemmas, problems and solutions presented by the use of cutting-edge communications and computer technology in doing business. Topics include the use and abuse of intellectual property law, electronic information gathering, online financial transactions and student suggested topics.

▌2807

ETHICS IN INFORMATION TECHNOLOGY

UNIVERSITY OF PHOENIX

3201 E Elwood St.
Phoenix, AZ 85034
PH: (480)966-5394
TF: 800-366-9699
URL: http://www.uoponline.com

Description: The University of Phoenix offers a course called Ethics in Information Technology. This course explores legal and ethical issues associated with the use and implementation of information systems in business and society.

▌2808

EVALUATING E-COMMERCE OPTIONS

NETG

1751 W Diehl Rd, 2nd Fl.
Naperville, IL 60563-9099
PH: (630)369-3000

TF: 877-561-6384
FX: (630)983-4877
E-mail: info@netg.com
URL: http://www.netg.com

Description: NETg offers a course called Evaluating E-Commerce Options. This course is designed to look at costs as well as the potential benefits of e-commerce. An overview of e-commerce strategies and implementation descriptions will help the student understand costs associated with e-commerce.

∎ 2809
EVALUATING E-COMMERCE OPTIONS
UNIVERSITY OF FLORIDA

Office of the University Registrar
Cruiser Hall
PO Box 114000
Gainesville, FL 32611-4000
PH: (352)392-3261; (352)392-1374
URL: http://www.ufl.edu

Description: Evaluating E-Commerce Options is intended for students wanting to consider some of the costs as well as the potential benefits of e-commerce with a survey of e-commerce strategies and an overview containing implementation descriptions to help them understand the basis of costs associated with e-commerce better. The intended audience is managers and technical staff who are in a position to provide e-commerce recommendations to executives and will teach them about the market environment, external factors, core developer technologies and programming paradigms.

∎ 2810
EXECUTIVE EDUCATION CERTIFICATE IN E-BUSINESS EXECUTIVE BRIEFINGS
CREIGHTON UNIVERSITY

JOE RICKETTS CENTER EXECUTIVE EDUCATION PROGRAMS

2500 California Plz.
Omaha, NE 68178
PH: (402)280-2439
FX: (402)280-5565
E-mail: rnath@creighton.edu
URL: http://www.creighton.edu
Contact: Dr. Ravi Nath, Director, Joe Ricketts Center

Description: Creighton University's Joe Ricketts Center offers an executive education certificate, E-Business Executive Briefings. The curriculum consists of 10 three-hour course sessions covering a key aspect of e-business. The certificate program is designed for managers and executives who want to gain more knowledge and understanding of e-business.

∎ 2811
EXECUTIVE MASTER OF ELECTRONIC COMMERCE
DALHOUSIE UNIVERSITY

Faculty of Computer Science
6050 University Ave.
Halifax, NS, Canada B3H1W5
PH: (819)956-2289
FX: (819)956-7223
E-mail: emec@pwgsc.gc.ca
URL: http://www.ecomm.dal.ca

Founded: 2000. **Description:** Dalhousie University initiated the Executive Master of Electronic Commerce program in partnership with the Institute for Government Information Professionals of Public Works and Government Services Canada in the summer of 2000. The EMEC is a multidisciplinary degree and a customized version of Dalhousie University's Master of Electronic Commerce. The program is for public sector executives and professionals employed in technology, law and policy or business who want to play a leadership role in the establishment of Government online. It's a part-time program that links the student's education and their working environment.

∎ 2812
EXPLORING E-COMMERCE WEB SITES
UNIVERSITY OF MINNESOTA EXTENSION SERVICE

240 Coffey Hall
1420 Eckles Ave.
St. Paul, MN 55108-6068
PH: (612)624-1222
E-mail: mainstreet@extension.umn.edu
URL: http://www.extension.umn.edu/mainstreet/curriculum/index.html

Description: The University of Minnesota Extension Service offers a course called Exploring E-Commerce Web Sites. This course looks at what makes a successful e-commerce web site, including customer support, virtual storefronts, and fee-based content providers.

∎ 2813
FINANCE AND ELECTRONIC PAYMENT SYSTEMS
BELLEVUE UNIVERSITY

1000 Galvin Rd. S
Bellevue, NE 68005
PH: (402)293-2000
TF: 800-756-7920
FX: (402)293-2020
URL: http://www.bellevue.edu

Description: Bellevue University offers "Finance and Electronic Payment Systems", a course designed to look at the financial fundamentals of setting up an electronic business and its day-to-day money operations. Topics covered are: capital budgeting and structure, and diversification, risk and return, e credit card transactions, cybercash, electronic banking, billing servers, secure check, negotiable electronic instruments and possible future electronic payment technologies.

▌2814

FINANCIAL MANAGEMENT FOR E-COMMERCE AND E-BUSINESS
GW CENTER FOR PROFESSIONAL DEVELOPMENT

2029 K Street NW, Ste. 600
Washington, DC 20006
PH: (202)973-1150
FX: (202)973-1165
E-mail: cpd@gwu.edu
URL: http://www.gwu.edu/~cpd/programs/CWEC/

Description: The GW Center for Professional Development provides a course called ''Financial Management for E-Commerce and E-Business.'' Using financial models, demonstrations and case studies, this course offers information on topics such as improved procurement practices, supply chain management, customer interaction, sales and marketing, billing and collections, and internal and external logistics.

▌2815

FINANCIAL STATEMENT ANALYSIS FOR E-BUSINESS
UNIVERSITY OF WASHINGTON
COLLEGE OF BUSINESS
E-BUSINESS PROGRAM

Box 353200
Seattle, WA 98195-3200
PH: (206)543-8749
E-mail: uwebiz@u.washington.edu
URL: http://depts.washington.edu/ebiz/
Contact: Jim Jiambalvo, Faculty Director

Description: As a part of its MBA program, the University of Washington offers ''Financial Statement Analysis for E-Business.'' This course covers topics like analyzing financial performance and estimating the value of various e-businesses. These skills include, fundamental analysis, preparation of pro-forma financial statements, and estimation of future cash flows. Various accounting issues related to financial analysis are considered. Insights into the usefulness of financial statement analysis for purposes of investment decisions, lending decisions, decisions related to selecting partners, and performance evaluation are also developed.

▌2816

FOUNDATIONS OF THE DIGITAL ECONOMY
NOTRE DAME DE NAMUR UNIVERSITY

1500 Ralston Ave.
Belmont, CA 94002-1997
PH: (650)508-3782
FX: (650)508-3660

E-mail: ebusiness@ndnu.edu
URL: http://www.ndnu.edu

Description: Notre Dame de Namur University offers a graduate course called Foundations of the Digital Economy. This course gives students an overview of the digital economy and the principles of e-business. Topics covered include electronic money, social issues, business models, and case studies of best and worst practices.

▌2817

FOUNDATIONS OF E-BUSINESS
UNIVERSITY OF WASHINGTON
COLLEGE OF BUSINESS
E-BUSINESS PROGRAM

Box 353200
Seattle, WA 98195-3200
PH: (206)543-8749
E-mail: uwebiz@u.washington.edu
URL: http://depts.washington.edu/ebiz/
Contact: Jim Jiambalvo, Faculty Director

Description: The University of Washington offers the graduate course ''Foundations of E-Business'' which covers the fundamental technologies associated with consumer-to-business and business-to-business interaction and delivery of content via the Internet. It contrasts client- versus server-side approaches to database processing and XML, as well as execution of business rules and logic.

▌2818

FROM BRICK AND MORTAR TO BRICK AND CLICK
CALIFORNIA STATE UNIVERSITY, FULLERTON
UNIVERSITY EXTENDED EDUCATION

800 N State College Blvd.
Fullerton, CA 92834-6870
PH: (714)278-2611
FX: (714)278-2088
URL: http://www.takethelead.fullerton.edu/Classes/

Description: Cal State Fullerton offers a course called ''From Brick and Mortar to Brick and Click.'' This course looks at the transition from the traditional business enterprise to the cyber world. Students learn how to take their companies beyond that of a Web ''storefront'' to create a competitive advantage, and generate significant value for the company, its partners and customers.

▌2819

FRONTIERS OF ELECTRONIC COMMERCE I
UNIVERSITY OF NEW BRUNSWICK-SAINT JOHN
FACULTY OF BUSINESS

PO Box 5050
Saint John, NB, Canada E2L4L5
PH: (506)648-5570; (506)648-5806
TF: 800-508-6275

FX: (506)648-5574
E-mail: business@unbsj.ca
URL: http://www.unbsj.ca/business
Contact: Shelley Rinehart, Dean, Faculty of Business

Description: Frontiers of Electronic Commerce I (BA 3126) is an introduction to current issues in e-commerce with emphasis on the management of these issues. Prerequisites include completing BA 2123 and BA 2663 before taking this course.

▋ 2820

FRONTIERS OF ELECTRONIC COMMERCE II

UNIVERSITY OF NEW BRUNSWICK-SAINT JOHN
FACULTY OF BUSINESS

PO Box 5050
Saint John, NB, Canada E2L4L5
PH: (506)648-5570; (506)648-5806
TF: 800-508-6275
FX: (506)648-5574
E-mail: business@unbsj.ca
URL: http://www.unbsj.ca/business
Contact: Shelley Rinehart, Dean, Faculty of Business

Description: Frontiers of Electronic Commerce II (BA 4126) is an in-depth examination of current issues in electronic commerce with emphasis on the management of these issues. Prerequisites include the completion of BA 2123, BA 2663 and BA 3718, BA 3126 or BA 3305 before a student can take this course.

▋ 2821

FUNDAMENTALS OF CUSTOMER RELATIONSHIP MANAGEMENT (CRM) AND PERSONALIZATION

NEW YORK UNIVERSITY
SCHOOL OF CONTINUING AND PROFESSIONAL STUDIES VIRTUAL COLLEGE

10 Astor Pl., 5th Fl.
New York, NY 10003
PH: (212)998-7080
TF: 877-998-7080
E-mail: scpsinfo@nyu.edu
URL: http://www.scps.nyu.edu/dyncon/virt/

Description: NYU's Virtual College offers a course entitled "Fundamentals of Customer Relationship Management (CRM) and Personalization." This course will provide students with a fundamental technical and practical background in CRM and personalization. Topics covered include: CRM implementation; e-customer service, e-support, call centers/help desk/knowledge base/internet integration; and costs and benefits of CRM.

▋ 2822

FUNDAMENTALS OF E-BUSINESS

AMERICAN UNIVERSITY
KOGOD SCHOOL OF BUSINESS

4400 Massachusetts Ave., NW
Washington, DC 20016
PH: (202)885-1900
E-mail: bizundergrad@american.edu
URL: http://www.kogod.american.edu
Contact: Myron Roomkin, Dean

Description: American University's Kogod School of Business offers an undergraduate course called "Fundamentals of E-Business." This course covers consumer-to-business and business to-business electronic commerce models, systems, and technical solutions. It includes student e-business projects.

▋ 2823

FUNDAMENTALS OF E-BUSINESS

SKILL SOFT

20 Industrial Park Dr.
Nashua, NH 03062
PH: (603)324-3000
TF: 877-631-7405
FX: (603)324-3009
E-mail: information@skillsoft.com
URL: http://www.skillsoft.com

Description: Skill Soft offers a course called Fundamentals of E-Business. This course ensures that students understand the major questions to ask regarding e-commerce. The course also reviews Internet vocabulary and examines the effect of adding e-business to an existing company.

▋ 2824

FUNDAMENTALS OF ELECTRONIC COMMERCE

NEW YORK UNIVERSITY
SCHOOL OF CONTINUING AND PROFESSIONAL STUDIES VIRTUAL COLLEGE

10 Astor Pl., 5th Fl.
New York, NY 10003
PH: (212)998-7080
TF: 877-998-7080
E-mail: scpsinfo@nyu.edu
URL: http://www.scps.nyu.edu/dyncon/virt/

Description: NYU's Virtual College offers a course called "Fundamentals of Electronic Commerce." This course examines emerging technologies and how we conduct business in a "wired" world. Topics include: ingredients of a commerce-enabled website; copyright, authentication, encryption, certification, and security; online payment strategies; companies offering e-business solutions; and e-commerce business models.

611

▌2825

FUNDAMENTALS OF INFORMATION TECHNOLOGY AND ELECTRONIC COMMERCE

NEW YORK UNIVERSITY
STERN SCHOOL OF BUSINESS

44 W Fourth St.
New York, NY 10012
PH: (212)998-0100
E-mail: admissions@nyu.edu
URL: http://oz.stern.nyu.edu/ec2001/

Description: New York University's Stern School of Business offers a course entitled "Fundamentals of Information Technology and Electronic Commerce." This course addresses the fundamentals of modern IT that must be understood to make an informed analysis of the effects of IT on business. Modern applications of IT to commerce and decision-making, and the impact of modern IT on organizations, markets, and strategy are also topics that will be covered.

▌2826

FUNDAMENTALS OF INTERNET ARCHITECTURE

NOTRE DAME DE NAMUR UNIVERSITY

1500 Ralston Ave.
Belmont, CA 94002-1997
PH: (650)508-3782
FX: (650)508-3660
E-mail: ebusiness@ndnu.edu
URL: http://www.ndnu.edu

Description: Notre Dame de Namur University offers a graduate course called Fundamentals of Internet Architecture. This course offers a basic look at technologies important to electronic business including networking, communications, security, databases, multimedia, transaction processing, and the Internet.

▌2827

GET THE NET

CARDEAN UNIVERSITY

500 Lake Cook Rd.
Deerfield, IL 60015-5609
TF: (866)948-1289
E-mail: inquires@cardean.edu
URL: http://www.cardean.edu
Contact: Dr. Geoffrey M. Cox, Cardean University President

Description: Cardean University is an accredited online university that offers a suite of courses called "Get the Net." This series of 5 two hour courses helps professionals understand, recognize, and analyze Internet business models using information gathered on the Internet. It explains key economic principles that underlie the Internet's transformation of business strategy and culture.

▌2828

GLOBAL EMANAGEMENT PROGRAM (GEM)

GEORGIA STATE UNIVERSITY
ROBINSON COLLEGE OF BUSINESS
ECOMMERCE INSTITUTE

University Plaza
Atlanta, GA 30303-3087
PH: (404)463-9301
E-mail: richard.welke@eci.gsu.edu
URL: http://www.eci.gsu.edu
Contact: Dr. Richard Welke, Director

Description: The Georgia State University eCommerce Institute's educational mission is "To equip professionals with the knowledge and skills they need to succeed in the digital economy." A variety of programs have been developed to fulfill this goal including public seminars, executive development programs, post-degree certification programs and distance/Internet programs.

▌2829

GLOBAL STRATEGY IN AN INTERNET ENVIRONMENT

HARVARD UNIVERSITY
HARVARD EXTENSION SCHOOL

51 Brattle St.
Cambridge, MA 02138
PH: (617)495-4005
E-mail: css@hudce7.harvard.edu
URL: http://www.extension.harvard.edu/

Description: Harvard University's Extension School offers a course called Global Strategy in an Internet Environment. This course gives students an understanding of operating a global business. The Internet will be used during business simulations to interact with students in other countries.

▌2830

GLOBAL SUPPLY CHAIN MANAGEMENT: CONCEPTS, STRATEGIES, AND MEASURES

ST. LOUIS UNIVERSITY
COOK SCHOOL OF BUSINESS

3674 Lindell Blvd.
St. Louis, MO 63108
PH: (314)977-3864
FX: (314)977-3897
E-mail: katzja@slu.edu
URL: http://eweb.slu.edu/e-com_courses.htm

Description: St. Louis University offers a course called "Global Supply Chain Management: Concepts, Strategies, and Measures." This course examines an integrated enterprise approach of flow of goods and services from suppliers to customers, including supplier relationship, procurement, operations management, inventory control, distribution, customer service and information technology.

▌2831
GRADUATE CERTIFICATE IN E-COMMERCE
WORCESTER POLYTECHNIC INSTITUTE

100 Institute Rd.
Worcester, MA 01609
PH: (508)831-5218
FX: (508)831-5720
URL: http://www.wpi.edu
Contact: McRae Banks, Department Head

Founded: 1865. **Description:** The Graduate Certificate in E-Commerce was developed for those students not yet ready to pursue a graduate degree, but want the rigor and depth in a particular area that graduate courses offer. To earn this certificate, students must complete the Supply Chain Management and Electronic Commerce, Marketing and Electronic Commerce and Telecommunications Management and Electronic Commerce courses, plus any combination of two of the Managing Organizational Change, Project Management or New Venture Management and Entrepreneurship courses.

▌2832
GRADUATE CERTIFICATE IN E-COMMERCE AND E-BUSINESS EXECUTIVE CERTIFICATE
CREIGHTON UNIVERSITY
COLLEGE OF BUSINESS ADMINISTRATION
JOE RICKETTS CENTER FOR E-COMMERRCE

2500 California Plz.
Omaha, NE 68178
PH: (402)280-2439
FX: (402)280-5565
E-mail: rnath@creighton.edu
URL: http://ecommerce.creighton.edu/
Contact: Dr. Ravi Nath, Director

Description: Offering both a Graduate Certificate in E-Commerce and an E-Business Executive Certificate, the Joe Ricketts Center for E-Commerce at Creighton University Provides coursework presented by Creighton's faculty and business executives. In addition to credit and non-credit courses the E-Commerce Center also sponsors an annual Information Technology in the Workplace conference.

▌2833
GRADUATE CERTIFICATE IN ELECTRONIC COMMERCE
HAWAII PACIFIC UNIVERSITY
DIVISION OF PROFESSIONAL STUDIES

1164 Bishop St., Ste. 911
Honolulu, HI 96813
PH: (866)472-3478
FX: (808)544-0280
E-mail: gradservctr@hpu.edu
URL: http://web2.hpu.edu/index.cfm?section=graduate464

Description: Hawaii Pacific University's Division of Professional Studies offers a Graduate Certificate in Electronic Commerce. This program is designed to teach professionals about the creation, operation, and management of online commercial ventures.

▌2834
GRADUATE CERTIFICATE PROGRAM IN E-COMMERCE
STEVENS INSTITUTE OF TECHNOLOGY
HOWE SCHOOL OF TECHNOLOGY MANAGEMENT

Kidde Bldg., Rm. 324-A
Hoboken, NJ 07030
PH: (201)216-5381
FX: (201)216-5385
E-mail: howe_grad@stevens-tech.edu
URL: http://attila.stevens-tech.edu/stmm/e-comm/certificate.htm

Description: Stevens Institute of Technology's School of Technology Management offers a Graduate Certificate Program in E-Commerce. This 4 course program is designed to help students learn how to create their own e-business, or be a successful professional in any e-business enterprise.

▌2835
GROUP PROJECT IN ELECTRONIC COMMERCE
GEORGE MASON UNIVERSITY
DEPARTMENT OF COMPUTER SCIENCE

MSN 4A5
4400 University Dr.
Fairfax, VA 22030
PH: (703)993-1530
FX: (703)993-1710
E-mail: csadmin@cs.gmu.edu
URL: http://ite.gmu.edu/msecomm/description.htm

Description: George Mason University offers a course called "Group Project in Electronic Commerce." This graduate course consists of group projects in electronic commerce designed to look at problems and solutions in development, design, and implementation of e-commerce systems.

▌2836
HIGH TECH MARKETING
BRIGHAM YOUNG UNIVERSITY
ROLLINS CENTER FOR E-BUSINESS

510 N. Tanner Bldg
PO Box 23068
Provo, UT 84602-3068
PH: (801)422-2815
FX: (801)422-5933
E-mail: ebusiness@byu.edu
URL: http://ebusiness.byu.edu/ebus.cfm
Contact: J. Owen Cherrington, Director

Description: Brigham Young University's Rollins Center for E-Business offers a course titled "High Tech Marketing." Offered at both the graduate and undergraduate level, this course examines e-marketing topics such as partnerships and customers, alliances and change, digital strategy, designing killer applications, information flow and commerce, and bringing insights to business.

■ 2837

HOW THE BEST RUN EBUSINESSES STAY IN BUSINESS

PENN STATE EBUSINESS RESEARCH CENTER

401 Business Administration Bldg.
University Park, PA 16802
PH: (814)863-7575
FX: (814)865-9119
E-mail: ebrc@psu.edu
URL: http://www.ebrc.psu.edu
Contact: Nirrmal Pal, Executive Director

Description: The Penn State eBusiness Research Center features conferences and seminars focusing on various ebusiness topics such as "How the Best Run Ebusinesses Stay in Business." Its goal is to expand and disseminate research in e-Business, and to bring research learning and insights to corporations and support them in shaping e-Business practice.

■ 2838

HOW TO BUILD AN E-COMMERCE BUSINESS PLAN

SAN JOSE STATE UNIVERSITY
PROFESSIONAL DEVELOPMENT CENTER

3031 Tisch Way, Ste. 200 Plz. E
San Jose, CA 95128
PH: (408)257-3000
E-mail: mitchell.levy.sjsupd@ecnow.com
URL: http://ecmtraining.com/sjsu/
Contact: Mitchell Levy, Program Founder and Coordinator

Description: San Jose State University offers a course called "How to Build an E-Commerce Business Plan." This executive education class looks at the elements of a successful e-commerce business plan, as well as the planning processes necessary to generate it. Class discussions examine sample business plans and other strategic topics.

■ 2839

HUMAN FACTORS IN E-BUSINESS

CREIGHTON UNIVERSITY
JOE RICKETTS CENTER EXECUTIVE EDUCATION PROGRAMS

2500 California Plz.
Omaha, NE 68178
PH: (402)280-2439
FX: (402)280-5565
E-mail: rnath@creighton.edu

URL: http://www.creighton.edu
Contact: Dr. Ravi Nath, Director, Joe Ricketts Center

Description: Creighton University's Joe Ricketts Center offers an executive education course called Human Factors in E-Business. This three-hour course looks at how human behavior affects interaction with computer systems. Students will learn about the principles and concepts which underlie interactions between humans and computers, as well as how to use this knowledge for designing and evaluating online information systems.

■ 2840

HYBRID AND TRANSITION STRATEGIES

CARDEAN UNIVERSITY

500 Lake Cook Rd.
Deerfield, IL 60015-5609
TF: (866)948-1289
E-mail: inquires@cardean.edu
URL: http://www.cardean.edu
Contact: Dr. Geoffrey M. Cox, Cardean University President

Description: Cardean University is an accredited online university which offers a course called "Hybrid and Transition Strategies." Developed with Stanford University, this course looks at methods for merging elements of Internet and traditional marketing. By looking at issues such as channel conflict and integration, automated versus human interaction with customers, and changing customer behavior, managers in this course can learn skills in maximizing market opportunities using the Internet.

■ 2841

IBM SOLUTION ADVISOR

BRIGHAM YOUNG UNIVERSITY
ROLLINS CENTER FOR E-BUSINESS

510 N. Tanner Bldg
PO Box 23068
Provo, UT 84602-3068
PH: (801)422-2815
FX: (801)422-5933
E-mail: e.education@byu.edu
URL: http://ebiz.byu.edu/~jsd47/3
Contact: J. Owen Cherrington, Director

Description: Brigham Young University's Rollins Center for E-Business Extended Education Programs offers a certification as an IBM Solution Advisor. This certification is for sales professionals who help their customers create successful e-business strategies.

■ 2842

IBM SOLUTION TECHNOLOGIST

BRIGHAM YOUNG UNIVERSITY
ROLLINS CENTER FOR E-BUSINESS

510 N. Tanner Bldg
PO Box 23068
Provo, UT 84602-3068

PH: (801)422-2815
FX: (801)422-5933
E-mail: e.education@byu.edu
URL: http://ebiz.byu.edu/~jsd47/3
Contact: J. Owen Cherrington, Director

Description: Brigham Young University's Rollins Center for E-Business Extended Education Programs offers a certification as an IBM Solution Technologist. This certification is for people who develop e-business solutions and already hold an IBM technical certificate such as Linux Professional Certification or the Java cross-vendor certification.

▌2843
IBM SOLUTIONS DESIGNER CERTIFICATE
BRIGHAM YOUNG UNIVERSITY
ROLLINS CENTER FOR E-BUSINESS

510 N. Tanner Bldg
PO Box 23068
Provo, UT 84602-3068
PH: (801)422-2815
FX: (801)422-5933
E-mail: e.education@byu.edu
URL: http://ebiz.byu.edu/~jsd47/3
Contact: J. Owen Cherrington, Director

Description: Brigham Young University's Rollins Center for E-Business Extended Education Program offers an IBM Solutions Designer Certificate. This Certificate is for technical specialists who translate customer's e-business strategies into the technical requirements for implementing solutions.

▌2844
IMPLEMENTATION TECHNOLOGIES FOR E-BUSINESS APPLICATIONS
BENTLEY COLLEGE

175 Forest St.
Waltham, MA 02452-4705
PH: (781)891-2000
URL: http://www.bentley.edu

Description: Bentley College offers a graduate level course called Implementation Technologies for E-Business Applications. This course looks at tools and technologies used to develop e-business applications, and addresses the effect of these technologies on e-business solutions. Topic covered include developing web applications that are database driven, support online inventory inquiry, deal with electronic cash and credit transactions, and provide data for supply chain management.

▌2845
IMPLEMENTING INTERNET APPLICATIONS
OLD DOMINION UNIVERSITY

Hampton Blvd.
Norfolk, VA 23529
PH: (757)683-3000

E-mail: admit@odu.edu
URL: http://www.odu.edu

Description: Old Dominion University offers a course called Implementing Internet Applications. In this course students will learn advanced design and implementation strategies to create e-commerce applications.

▌2846
INDUSTRY IMPACT OF ELECTRONIC COMMERCE
UNIVERSITY OF NEW BRUNSWICK-SAINT JOHN
FACULTY OF BUSINESS

PO Box 5050
Saint John, NB, Canada E2L4L5
PH: (506)648-5570; (506)648-5806
TF: 800-508-6275
FX: (506)648-5574
E-mail: business@unbsj.ca
URL: http://www.unbsj.ca/business
Contact: Shelley Rinehart, Dean, Faculty of Business

Description: Industry Impact of Electronic Commerce (BA 3125) addresses the implications of e-commerce with a broad industry level perspective. Students will develop the profile of e-commerce in a particular industry and identify e-commerce opportunities for the industry and its member organizations. As a prerequisite, classes BA 2123 and BA 2663 must first be completed before taking this course.

▌2847
INFORMATION NETWORKS AND ELECTRONIC COMMERCE
MICHIGAN STATE UNIVERSITY

Telecommunication
409 Communication Arts Bldg.
East Lansing, MI 48824
PH: (517)355-8372
URL: http://www.msu.edu

Description: Information Networks and Electronic Commerce is part of Michigan State University's Online Learning & Continuing Education courses and is available either on or off campus the fall of every year. Coursework includes the design and management of electronic commerce strategies, telecommunications infrastructure and the impact of e-commerce on organizations and society.

▌2848
INFORMATION PRODUCT MASTERS COURSE
COMPUTER BASED TRAINING

19 Nations Hill, Kings Worthy
Winchester, Hants SO237QY, United Kingdom
PH: 44 0 1962 883754
FX: 44 0 1962 889177
E-mail: freecourses@computerbasedtraining.co.uk
URL: http://www.computerbasedtraining.co.uk

Description: Computer Based Training offers a free online course called "Information Product Masters Course." This course will teach students how to create, publish market and sell their own information product.

▌2849

INFORMATION RULES - BUSINESS STRATEGY FOR THE INFORMATION ECONOMY

CARDEAN UNIVERSITY

500 Lake Cook Rd.
Deerfield, IL 60015-5609
TF: (866)948-1289
E-mail: inquires@cardean.edu
URL: http://www.cardean.edu
Contact: Dr. Geoffrey M. Cox, Cardean University President

Description: Cardean University is an accredited online university which offers a suite of courses called "Information Rules - Business Strategy for the Information Economy." This suite of 4 two hour courses for managers looks at the decisions that arise in information-based industries. It gives professionals ideas about how to succeed in this new environment, based on the best-selling book, Information Rules, by Carl Shapiro and Hal R. Varian.

▌2850

INFORMATION SECURITY AND ELECTRONIC COMMERCE

NEW YORK UNIVERSITY

SCHOOL OF CONTINUING AND PROFESSIONAL STUDIES VIRTUAL COLLEGE

10 Astor Pl., 5th Fl.
New York, NY 10003
PH: (212)998-7080
TF: 877-998-7080
E-mail: scpsinfo@nyu.edu
URL: http://www.scps.nyu.edu/dyncon/virt/

Description: NYU's Virtual College offers a course called "Information Security and Electronic Commerce." This course will provide information on securing data such as credit card numbers; firewalls as a device for securing data interchange; and keeping the intranet inaccessible to outsiders.

▌2851

INFORMATION SYSTEMS AND ELECTRONIC COMMERCE SECURITY

CLAREMONT GRADUATE UNIVERSITY

SCHOOL OF INFORMATION SCIENCE

130 E 9th St.
Claremont, CA 91711
PH: (909)621-8209
E-mail: infosci@cgu.edu
URL: http://is.cgu.edu

Description: Claremont Graduate University offers a course called Information Systems and Electronic Commerce Security. This course focuses on information systems security and threats. Solving potential security threats and examining the risks to information systems are also covered.

▌2852

INFORMATION SYSTEMS AND GLOBAL NETWORKS

BOSTON UNIVERSITY GLOBAL

755 Commonwealth Ave.
Boston, MA 02215
PH: (617)353-8429
FX: (617)353-7120
E-mail: global@bu.edu
URL: http://www.bu.edu/global/training.html
Contact: Elizabeth Nassar, Director

Description: Boston University Global offers a wide range of educational programs all over the world in subject areas that include Information Technology, Project Management, and E-commerce. BU Global also offers specific training programs to meet the challenges of organizations. Formats for customized training can include seminars, certificate and diploma programs, Faculty Executive Development Programs, and Distance Education Solutions. A diploma in Information Systems and Global Networks covers IT management in an intensive, four month program.

▌2853

INFORMATION TECHNOLOGIES FOR ELECTRONIC COMMERCE

OKLAHOMA STATE UNIVERSITY

Center for Academic Services
324 Student Union
Stillwater, OK 74078-1012
PH: (405)744-6858
E-mail: admit@okstate.edu
URL: http://www.okstate.edu

Description: The Information Technologies for Electronic Commerce course covers topics including an overview of e-commerce, security issues including firewall technology, web-based tools for design and implementation, electronic payment methods, the Internet and intranets and extranets.

▌2854

INFORMATION TECHNOLOGY FOR COMPETITIVE ADVANTAGE

BENTLEY COLLEGE

175 Forest St.
Waltham, MA 02452-4705
PH: (781)891-2000
URL: http://www.bentley.edu

Description: Bentley College offers a graduate level course called Information Technology for Competitive Advantage. This course in the Information Age MBA program allows students to learn how key leading-edge technologies such as enterprise systems database tools, systems modeling software, and e-business enablers influence a company's ability to compete in today's economy.

∎ 2855

INFORMATION TECHNOLOGY & E-BUSINESS MANAGEMENT

WAKE FORREST UNIVERSITY

BABCOCK GRADUATE SCHOOL OF MANAGEMENT

PO Box 7659
1834 Wake Forest Rd.
Winston-Salem, NC 27106
PH: (336)758-5255; (336)758-5421
TF: 800-722-1622
FX: (336)758-5830
URL: http://www.mba.wfu.edu

Founded: 1969. **Description:** The Information Technology & E-Business Management course allows students to explore the strategic implications of information technology and e-business trends.

∎ 2856

INFORMATION TECHNOLOGY FOR ELECTRONIC COMMERCE

KRANNERT SCHOOL OF MANAGEMENT

Purdue University
1310 Krannert Bldg.
West Lafayette, IN 47907
PH: (765)496-3384
FX: (765)494-9841
E-mail: jdietz@mgmt.purdue.edu
URL: http://www.mgmt.purdue.edu
Contact: Joy Dietz, Manager of Advising and Student Services

Description: The goal of Information Technology for Electronic Commerce is to help students develop an understanding of the relevant issues, advantages and disadvantages and specific techniques involved in using the Internet to assist in the production and marketing of goods and services while gaining hands-on experience developing an Internet-based business. This is an eight-week course offered every year in the spring since 1996 with Alok Chaturvedi as the current instructor.

∎ 2857

INFORMATION TECHNOLOGY AND MARKETING

UNIVERSITY OF GEORGIA

TERRY COLLEGE OF BUSINESS

346 Brooks Hall
Athens, GA 30602-6264
PH: (706)542-8100
FX: (706)542-3835
E-mail: mcrask@terry.uga.edu
URL: http://www.terry.uga.edu

Contact: Dr. Mel Crask, Director, MBA Programs

Description: The University of Georgia Terry College of Business offers a course called Information Technology and Marketing. This course explores the utilization of information technology in marketing. Topics covered include the World Wide Web, database marketing, frequency and relationship marketing programs, and direct marketing.

∎ 2858

INTEGRATIVE CASE STUDIES IN ELECTRONIC COMMERCE

GEORGE MASON UNIVERSITY

DEPARTMENT OF COMPUTER SCIENCE

MSN 4A5
4400 University Dr.
Fairfax, VA 22030
PH: (703)993-1530
FX: (703)993-1710
E-mail: csadmin@cs.gmu.edu
URL: http://ite.gmu.edu/msecomm/description.htm

Description: George Mason University offers a course called "Integrative Case Studies in Electronic Commerce." Students will learn to manage the complexity of e-commerce in specialized applications. Using case studies, they will look at the requirements for successful e-commerce program development and management.

∎ 2859

INTELLIGENT SUPPLY CHAINS: THE CHANGING FACE OF E-BUSINESS

24/7 UNIVERSITY, INC.

16980 Dallas Pky., Ste. 247
Dallas, TX 75248
PH: (972)248-2470
E-mail: info@247university.com
URL: http://www.247university.com

Description: 24/7 University offers an online course called Intelligent Supply Chains: The Changing Face of E-Business. This course program focuses on the process and technology for achieving the competitive advantages of an intelligent supply chain.

∎ 2860

INTERCHANGE E-COMMERCE PLATFORM

RED HAT

1801 Varsity Dr.
Raleigh, NC 27606
PH: (919)754-3700
TF: 888-733-4281
FX: (919)754-3701
E-mail: customerservice@redhat.com
URL: http://www.redhat.com

Description: Red Hat, the largest provider of open source technology, offers a program called ''Interchange E-Commerce Platform'' to train people in their enterprise-class open source e-commerce platform. Interchange training courses are designed to provide students with the knowledge and skills to create or manage e-commerce sites based on the Interchange platform.

■ **2861**

INTERDISCIPLINARY THEORIES OF E-COMMERCE
PURDUE UNIVERSITY
KRANNERT GRADUATE SCHOOL OF MANAGEMENT

1310 Krannert Bldg.
West Lafayette, IN 47907
PH: (765)494-9700
FX: (765)494-9658
E-mail: krannert_ms@mgmt.purdue.edu
URL: http://www.mgmt.purdue.edu/centers/ceer/

Description: Purdue University's Krannert Graduate School of Management offers a course called Interdisciplinary Theories of E-Commerce. This course explores pricing options in e-business. Topics covered include pricing the infrastructure of electronic commerce, bundling and pricing of information goods, and models of Web server pricing.

■ **2862**

INTERDISCIPLINARY THEORIES OF E-COMMERCE
KRANNERT SCHOOL OF MANAGEMENT

Purdue University
1310 Krannert Bldg.
West Lafayette, IN 47907
PH: (765)496-3384
FX: (765)494-9841
E-mail: jdietz@mgmt.purdue.edu
URL: http://www.mgmt.purdue.edu
Contact: Joy Dietz, Manager of Advising and Student Services

Description: Interdisciplinary Theories of E-commerce includes pricing the Infrastructure of Electronic Commerce, bundling of Information goods, pricing of these bundles and models of Web server pricing.

■ **2863**

INTERNATIONAL ELECTRONIC COMMERCE
AMERICAN UNIVERSITY
KOGOD SCHOOL OF BUSINESS

4400 Massachusetts Ave., NW
Washington, DC 20016-8044
PH: (202)885-1900
E-mail: askkogod@american.edu
URL: http://www.american.edu/academic.depts/ksb/mogit//ec/

Contact: Erran Carmel, Professor

Description: The American University offers a course titled ''International Electronic Commerce.'' This graduate level course explores what the Internet means to international trade and how well it has lived up to its promises. This course also looks at methods of payment, B2B e-commerce, security and regulations for e-commerce.

■ **2864**

INTERNET BUYING BEHAVIOR
UNIVERSITY OF DALLAS
GRADUATE SCHOOL OF MANAGEMENT

1845 E Northgate Dr.
Irving, TX 75062
PH: (972)721-5000
E-mail: msavoie@udallas.edu
URL: http://gsmweb.udallas.edu/concentrations/e_business.html

Description: The University of Dallas Graduate School of Management provides a course called Internet Buying Behavior. This course looks at techniques for creating customer value on-line. Students will evaluate new and evolving Internet marketing models, and participate in class marketing projects.

■ **2865**

THE INTERNET: CONCEPT AND APPLICATIONS
UNIVERSITY OF PHOENIX

3201 E Elwood St.
Phoenix, AZ 85034
PH: (480)966-5394
TF: 800-366-9699
URL: http://www.uoponline.com

Description: The University of Phoenix offers a course called The Internet: Concept and Applications. This course introduces the student to business use of the Internet, including the history, browsers, search engines, architecture and intranets. Also included is an overview of development tools and security. Students will be able to use the World Wide Web to research business problems and understand the role of the Internet in supporting business functions such as marketing.

■ **2866**

THE INTERNET ECONOMY (SBA)
U.S. SMALL BUSINESS ADMINISTRATION

409 3rd St. SW
Washington, DC 20416
PH: 800-827-5722
E-mail: classroom@sba.gov
URL: http://www.sba.gov/classroom

Description: The Small Business Administration (SBA) in partnership with Cisco Systems offers a free online course called The Internet Economy. This course is designed to help a growing business become more competitive by using the Internet.

▌2867

INTERNET AND ELECTRONIC COMMERCE

SENECA COLLEGE OF APPLIED ARTS AND TECHNOLOGY, NEWNHAM CAMPUS

FACULTY OF BUSINESS

1750 Finch Ave. E
Toronto, ON, Canada M2J2X5
PH: (416)491-5050
FX: (416)493-4144
E-mail: fred.clark@senecac.on.ca
URL: http://www.iec.senecac.on.ca/iec/index.html
Contact: Fred Clark, Program Coordinator

Description: Seneca College, Toronto offers a post graduate diploma program, Internet and Electronic Commerce. Graduates of this business oriented program will gain skills in business processes and be comfortable with the technology fundamentals related to conducting business over the Internet and/or other E-Commerce means.

▌2868

INTERNET ENABLED BUSINESS

UNIVERSITY OF MICHIGAN BUSINESS SCHOOL

701 Tappan Street
Ann Arbor, MI 48109-1234
PH: (734)763-5796
FX: (734)763-7804
E-mail: widmeyer@umich.edu
URL: http://www.umich.edu/~cisdept/mba/CIS518/

Description: Internet Enabled Business is the title of a course offered at the University of Michigan School of Business. The focus of this course is on technology and business issues surrounding the use of the Internet in business such as customer relationship management (CRM), enterprise management, and supply chain management (SCM). Other topics include: understanding the Internet, creating web pages with HTML, using XML for data interchange, describing Internet-enabled applications, the practical use of document encryption and digital signatures.

▌2869

INTERNET ISSUES AND FUTURE INITIATIVES

UNIVERSITY OF NORTH CAROLINA AT CHAPEL HILL

SCHOOL OF INFORMATION AND LIBRARY SCIENCE

CB No. 3360, 100 Manning Hall
Chapel Hill, NC 27599-3360
PH: (919)962-8366
E-mail: info@ils.unc.edu
URL: http://www.ils.unc.edu/

Description: The University of North Carolina offers a graduate level seminar course entitled "Internet Issues and Future Initiatives." Participants in this seminar discuss emerging Internet policy issues such as copyright, intellectual property, privacy, and security, and explore emerging Internet tools and applications.

▌2870

INTERNET FOR MANAGERS

NEW JERSEY INSTITUTE OF TECHNOLOGY

SCHOOL OF MANAGEMENT

University Heights
Newark, NJ 07102-1982
PH: (973)596-3254
FX: (973)596-3074
E-mail: wachspress@admin.njit.edu
URL: http://www.njit.edu/BETA/ecomm/
Contact: David Wachspress, Dir., Undergrad. & E-Commerce Programs

Description: The New Jersey Institute of Technology offers an undergraduate course called "Internet for Managers." Students will learn about the Internet, intranets and extranets and incorporating them into business planning and operations.

▌2871

INTERNET MARKETING

SOLOMON D. TRUJILLO CENTER FOR E.BUSINESS

University of Wyoming
College of Business
PO Box 3275
Laramie, WY 82071
PH: (307)766-6902
E-mail: e-biz@uwyo.edu
URL: http://www.uwyo.edu
Contact: Dr. Kenton Walker, Director

Description: Internet Marketing focuses on marketing issues that must be addressed when considering how to develop successful commercial strategies on the Internet and other emerging electronic media and changes strategic issues due to the Internet and using e-business to market to business-to-business customers and final consumers.

▌2872

INTERNET MARKETING

LOYOLA UNIVERSITY CHICAGO

Graduate School of Business
25 E. Pearson, 14th Fl.
Chicago, IL 60611
PH: (312)915-6120
FX: (312)915-7207
E-mail: ayoung3@luc.edu
URL: http://www.luc.edu
Contact: Alan Young, Director of Enrollment & Recruitment

Description: The Internet Marketing course uses an applied and a theory-based approach to leveraging the Internet and other electronic media in marketing efforts. Topics discussed

619

include how to formulate an effective Web marketing strategy, how to use the Internet in marketing and distribution and the role of the Internet in electronic commerce.

∎ 2873

INTERNET MARKETING
NEW JERSEY INSTITUTE OF TECHNOLOGY
SCHOOL OF MANAGEMENT ·

University Heights
Newark, NJ 07102-1982
PH: (973)596-3254
FX: (973)596-3074
E-mail: wachspress@admin.njit.edu
URL: http://www.njit.edu/BETA/ecomm/
Contact: David Wachspress, Dir., Undergrad. & E-Commerce Programs

Description: The New Jersey Institute of Technology offers an undergraduate level course called "Internet Marketing." This course looks at electronic markets, data collection and market research, and Internet-based marketing programs.

∎ 2874

INTERNET MARKETING
RICE UNIVERSITY
JESSE H. JONES GRADUATE SCHOOL OF MANAGEMENT

6100 Main St.
Houston, TX 77005-1892
PH: (713)348-4918
TF: 888-844-4773
FX: (713)348-5838
E-mail: cmiller@rice.edu
URL: http://www.owlnet.rice.edu/~mgmt692/
Contact: Lisa R. Klein, Instructor

Description: This Rice University course, "Internet Marketing", focuses on understanding consumer behavior online. Topics covered include promotion, outbound and inbound communication, and the website design.

∎ 2875

INTERNET MARKETING
UNIVERSITY OF NORTH CAROLINA AT WILMINGTON
CAMERON SCHOOL OF BUSINESS

601 S College Rd.
Wilmington, NC 28403
PH: (910)962-3777
FX: (910)962-3815
E-mail: clarkl@uncwil.edu
URL: http://www.csb.uncwil.edu/people/portert/533/schedule.htm
Contact: Lawrence S. Clark, Dean

Description: the University of North Carolina at Wilmington offers a course titled "Internet Marketing." Topics covered in this course include Internet business models and

strategy, direct and database marketing, supply chains, and understanding the e-customer.

∎ 2876

INTERNET MARKETING
AMERICAN UNIVERSITY
KOGOD SCHOOL OF BUSINESS

4400 Massachusetts Ave., NW
Washington, DC 20016-8044
PH: (202)885-1900
E-mail: askkogod@american.edu
URL: http://www.kogod.american.edu
Contact: Myron Roomkin, Dean

Description: The American University offers a course titled "Internet Marketing." This course explores Internet marketing strategy, electronic markets, customer purchase behavior, Internet marketing ethics, and the impact of the Internet on product development, promotion, pricing, and distribution strategies.

∎ 2877

INTERNET MARKETING
BRIGHAM YOUNG UNIVERSITY
ROLLINS CENTER FOR E-BUSINESS

510 N. Tanner Bldg
PO Box 23068
Provo, UT 84602-3068
PH: (801)422-2815
FX: (801)422-5933
E-mail: ebusiness@byu.edu
URL: http://ebusiness.byu.edu/ebus.cfm
Contact: J. Owen Cherrington, Director

Description: Brigham Young University's Rollins Center for E-Business offers a course titled "Internet Marketing." This course includes an introduction to the Internet and Internet customers. Then examines customer motivational analysis, HTML, Internet site types, looking at competition, success and sales strategies, headlines and copy, layout and design, interactive sites, promoting a site.

∎ 2878

INTERNET MARKETING MANAGEMENT
AMERICAN UNIVERSITY
KOGOD SCHOOL OF BUSINESS

4400 Massachusetts Ave., NW
Washington, DC 20016-8044
PH: (202)885-1900
E-mail: askkogod@american.edu
URL: http://www.kogod.american.edu
Contact: Myron Roomkin, Dean

Description: The American University offers a graduate level course entitled "Internet Marketing Management." This course examines the Internet as an implementation tool for business and marketing strategy. It also provides an overview of Web and commerce technologies, but focuses on marketing applications of the Internet, including distribution, commerce, advertising, public relations, and other "stake-holder" relations.

∎ 2879
INTERNET MARKETING PROJECT
AMERICAN UNIVERSITY
KOGOD SCHOOL OF BUSINESS

4400 Massachusetts Ave., NW
Washington, DC 20016-8044
PH: (202)885-1900
E-mail: askkogod@american.edu
URL: http://www.kogod.american.edu
Contact: Myron Roomkin, Dean

Description: The American University offers a graduate level course entitled "Internet Marketing Project." In this course, students analyze Internet marketing opportunities facing a client firm and develop a strategic marketing plan. Issues assessed include the firm's Internet and technological capabilities, as well as the stage of Internet development.

∎ 2880
INTERNET MARKETING STRATEGIES
NEW JERSEY INSTITUTE OF TECHNOLOGY
SCHOOL OF MANAGEMENT, GRADUATE
PROGRAMS

323 Martin Luther King Jr. Blvd.
Newark, NJ 07102-1982
PH: (973)596-6378
FX: (973)596-3074
E-mail: lipper@njit.edu
URL: http://www.njit.edu/SOM/MBA/index.html
Contact: Stuart Lipper, Director of Graduate Programs

Description: The New Jersey Institute of Technology School of Management MBA program offers a course called "Internet Marketing Strategies." This course consists of an introduction to the use of the Internet and Electronic Commerce in the development of marketing strategy. It will also examine the characteristics of electronic markets, and the use of Internet for data collection and market research.

∎ 2881
INTERNET MARKETING SYSTEMS
MERCY COLLEGE

555 Broadway
Dobbs Ferry, NY 10522
PH: (914)674-7306
FX: (914)674-7518
E-mail: jdielsi@mercy.edu
URL: http://www.mercy.edu
Contact: John DiElsi, Program Dir.

Description: Mercy College offers a graduate level course called Internet Marketing Systems. This course looks at Internet-centered marketing principles and practices. Emphasis is on one-on-one marketing rather than mass marketing. Students will learn about Internet advertising, portal

alliances, marketing research and database management and analysis.

∎ 2882
INTERNET PROGRAMMING
BRIGHAM YOUNG UNIVERSITY
ROLLINS CENTER FOR E-BUSINESS

510 N. Tanner Bldg
PO Box 23068
Provo, UT 84602-3068
PH: (801)422-2815
FX: (801)422-5933
E-mail: ebusiness@byu.edu
URL: http://ebusiness.byu.edu/ebus.cfm
Contact: J. Owen Cherrington, Director

Description: Brigham Young University's Rollins Center for E-Business offers a course called "Internet Programming." This course examines multiple aspects of programming for the Internet.

∎ 2883
INTERNET ROLE FOR MARKETING AND ADVERTISING
UNIVERSITY OF DELAWARE
E-COMMERCE PROGRAM

206 John M. Clayton Hall
Newark, DE 19716-7410
PH: (302)831-2741
E-mail: continuing-ed@udel.edu
URL: http://www.continuingstudies.udel.edu/it/ecomm/index.shtml

Description: The University of Delaware's Continuing Studies Program offers a course titled "Internet Role for Marketing and Advertising." This course covers new marketing models and strategies that can by used in an e-commerce business environment.

∎ 2884
INTERNET SECURITY
UNIVERSITY OF DELAWARE
E-COMMERCE PROGRAM

206 John M. Clayton Hall
Newark, DE 19716-7410
PH: (302)831-2741
E-mail: continuing-ed@udel.edu
URL: http://www.continuingstudies.udel.edu/it/ecomm/index.shtml

Description: The University of Delaware's Continuing Studies Program offers a course entitled "Internet Security." This course addresses security issues from both the server and the client side, and participants formulate strategies and look at alternative solutions for threats in a Web-enabled enterprise.

■ **2885**

INTERNET TECHNOLOGY

NEW JERSEY INSTITUTE OF TECHNOLOGY
SCHOOL OF MANAGEMENT

University Heights
Newark, NJ 07102-1982
PH: (973)596-3254
FX: (973)596-3074
E-mail: wachspress@admin.njit.edu
URL: http://www.njit.edu/BETA/ecomm/
Contact: David Wachspress, Dir., Undergrad. & E-Commerce Programs

Description: The New Jersey Institute of Technology offers an undergraduate level course called ''Internet Technology.'' This course will examine the current technologies behind E-commerce such as dynamic Web sites, database integration, server-side scripting, client-side scripting, and XML.

■ **2886**

INTERNET TECHNOLOGY AND STRATEGY

UNIVERSITY OF GEORGIA
TERRY COLLEGE OF BUSINESS

346 Brooks Hall
Athens, GA 30602-6264
PH: (706)542-8100
FX: (706)542-3835
E-mail: mcrask@terry.uga.edu
URL: http://www.terry.uga.edu
Contact: Dr. Mel Crask, Director, MBA Programs

Description: The University of Georgia Terry College of Business Executive MBA program offers a course called Internet Technology and Strategy. This course addresses the use of Internet technology to support goals and increase a company's performance. An executive's guide to Internet technology and computer networks is also provided.

■ **2887**

INTERNET USER EXPERIENCE

CARDEAN UNIVERSITY

500 Lake Cook Rd.
Deerfield, IL 60015-5609
TF: (866)948-1289
E-mail: inquires@cardean.edu
URL: http://www.cardean.edu
Contact: Dr. Geoffrey M. Cox, Cardean University President

Description: Cardean University is an accredited online university which offers a suite of courses for managers and website designers called ''Internet User Experience.'' This suite of 4 two hour courses is designed to show students how to produce a web site that meets the needs of a business and of a site's users. It offers ways to test web site usability, collect and implement user data, and integrate user experience into your design process. It also explores how the Internet user experience is evolving beyond the World Wide Web.

■ **2888**

INTRA/ENTREPRENEURSHIP

STEVENS INSTITUTE OF TECHNOLOGY
HOWE SCHOOL OF TECHNOLOGY MANAGEMENT

Kidde Bldg., Rm. 324-A
Hoboken, NJ 07030
PH: (201)216-5381
FX: (201)216-5385
E-mail: howe_grad@stevens-tech.edu
URL: http://attila.stevens-tech.edu/stmm/e-comm/certificate.htm

Description: Stevens Institute of Technology's School of Technology Management offers a course called Intra/Entrepreneurship. In this course students will use the knowledge and skills they have developed in preceding e-commerce courses to help them create their own prospective E-business.

■ **2889**

INTRODUCTION TO E-BUSINESS

CALIFORNIA STATE UNIVERSITY, CHICO

400 W 1st St.
Chico, CA 95929
PH: (530)898-4636
E-mail: publicaffairs@csuchico.edu
URL: http://www.csuchico.edu/~gregrose/mins298/

Description: California State University Chico offers a course called Introduction to E-Business. This course functions as an introduction to e-business topics including Internet, extranets, web based e-commerce applications.

■ **2890**

INTRODUCTION TO E-BUSINESS

CAPELLA UNIVERSITY

222 S 9th St., 20th Fl.
Minneapolis, MN 55402
PH: (612)339-8650
TF: 888-227-3552
FX: (612)339-8022
URL: http://www.capella.edu

Description: Introduction to E-Business deals with key ideas and practices in planning, marketing and operating in online business environments and is a good introduction to the diverse ways that organizations can use the web.

■ **2891**

INTRODUCTION TO E-COMMERCE

NETG

1751 W Diehl Rd., 2nd Fl.
Naperville, IL 60563-9099
PH: (630)369-3000

TF: 877-561-6384
FX: (630)983-4877
E-mail: info@netg.com
URL: http://www.netg.com

Description: NETg offers a course called Introduction to E-Commerce. This course gives an overview of e-commerce today. It defines electronic commerce and discusses electronic commerce elements including business-to-business and business-to-consumer e-commerce.

■ 2892
INTRODUCTION TO E-COMMERCE
PEIRCE COLLEGE

1420 Pine St.
Philadelphia, PA 19102
PH: (215)545-6400
TF: 877-670-9190
E-mail: info@peirce.edu
URL: http://www.peirce.edu

Description: Peirce College offers an online course called Introduction to E-Commerce. This undergraduate course gives an introduction to electronic commerce. Real world examples will be used to explain technical and business aspects, and their effect on traditional business models.

■ 2893
INTRODUCTION TO E-COMMERCE
UNIVERSITY OF FLORIDA
WARRINGTON COLLEGE OF BUSINESS

100 Bryan Hall
PO Box 117150
Gainesville, FL 32611-7150
PH: (352)392-2397
FX: (352)392-2086
E-mail: ufwcba@cba.ufl.edu
URL: http://www.cba.ufl.edu/index.asp

Description: Introduction to E-Commerce provides students with an overview of e-commerce today, defines e-commerce and discusses e-commerce elements. During the course, an overview of business-to-consumer and business-to-business e-commerce is given and issues and technologies available for companies wanting to engage in e-commerce is addressed. This course is intended for Managers and technical staff with little experience of e-commerce and will introduce them to e-commerce standards, e-commerce in enterprise and e-commerce technology building blocks.

■ 2894
INTRODUCTION TO E-COMMERCE
NORTHWESTERN OKLAHOMA STATE UNIVERSITY
DIVISION OF E-COMMERCE

709 Oklahoma Blvd.
Alva, OK 73717-2399
PH: (580)327-8440
FX: (580)327-8167
E-mail: kharris@nwosu.edu

URL: http://www.nwosu.edu/ecom/curriculum/cdesc.html

Description: Northwestern Oklahoma State University's Division of E-Commerce offers a course called "Introduction to E-Commerce." This overview course looks at computers, Internet technology and business transactions. Other topics covered include terminology, applications, and content for E-Commerce.

■ 2895
INTRODUCTION TO E-COMMERCE
WELLESLEY COLLEGE

106 Central St.
Wellesley, MA 02481
PH: (781)283-1000
E-mail: ltobin@wellesley.edu
URL: http://www.wellesley.edu/CS/cshome.html

Description: Wellesley offers a course titled "Introduction to E-Commerce." This course covers topics including Internet marketing applications, security issues, and web technology. Students will design and implement an e-business web site.

■ 2896
INTRODUCTION TO E-COMMERCE
SEREBRA LEARNING CORP.

7565 132nd St., Unit 119
Surrey, BC, Canada V3W1K5
PH: (604)592-0552
TF: 800-567-7766
FX: (604)592-0553
E-mail: info@serebra.com
URL: http://www.serebra.com
Contact: Mr. Bruce Stewart, President

Founded: 1987. **Description:** Serebra Learning Corp. offers a class called Introduction to E-Commerce. In this course, students will gain a basic understanding of the world of e-commerce. Some topics include: the World Wide Web and how it has become the infrastructure of e-commerce, programming languages of the Web, and choosing the best software for your e-commerce enterprise.

■ 2897
INTRODUCTION TO ELECTRONIC BUSINESS
BELLEVUE UNIVERSITY

1000 Galvin Rd. S
Bellevue, NE 68005
PH: (402)293-2000
TF: 800-756-7920
FX: (402)293-2020
URL: http://www.bellevue.edu

Description: Bellevue University offers an Introduction to Electronic Business course. This class is an overview of information processing using electronic techniques for business. Areas covered include: E Business terminology, the foundations of E Business, why E Business, retailing, customer service, advertising, managing, using Intranets and Extranets, and infrastructure for E Business. Students will apply their knowledge by building their own website during this course.

▌2898
INTRODUCTION TO ELECTRONIC BUSINESS
SOLOMON D. TRUJILLO CENTER FOR E.BUSINESS

University of Wyoming
College of Business
PO Box 3275
Laramie, WY 82071
PH: (307)766-6902
E-mail: e-biz@uwyo.edu
URL: http://www.uwyo.edu
Contact: Dr. Kenton Walker, Director

Description: Introduction to Electronic Business describes what e-business is, how it is being conducted and managed, and its major opportunities, limitations, issues, and risks. Covered topics include Business-to-Business and Business-to-Consumer, technological challenges, legal and regulatory framework, educational challenges, business barriers and strategies for e-business.

▌2899
INTRODUCTION TO ELECTRONIC BUSINESS
UNIVERSITY OF SCRANTON

Kania School of Management
Brennan Hall, Ste. 438
Scranton, PA 18510
PH: (570)941-7746
E-mail: kakumanu@scranton.edu
URL: http://www.scranton.edu
Contact: Dr. Parsed Kakumanu, Chair, Operation & Info. Mgmt. Dept.

Description: Introduction to Electronic Business is an introductory course in e-business and explores how the Internet has revolutionized the buying and selling of goods and services in the marketplace. Covered topics will include business-to-business and business-to-consumer e-commerce, designing and managing online storefronts, e-commerce infrastructure, payment acceptance and security issues, and the legal and ethical challenges of e-commerce.

▌2900
INTRODUCTION TO ELECTRONIC COMMERCE
CLAREMONT GRADUATE UNIVERSITY
SCHOOL OF INFORMATION SCIENCE

130 E 9th St.
Claremont, CA 91711
PH: (909)621-8209
E-mail: infosci@cgu.edu

URL: http://is.cgu.edu

Description: Claremont Graduate University offers a course called Introduction to Electronic Commerce. This course gives students an overview of commercial issues on the Internet. Strategy, security, and measuring performance are also discussed in this class.

▌2901
INTRODUCTION TO ELECTRONIC COMMERCE
UNIVERSITY OF MEMPHIS

Graduate Admissions Office
216 Administration Bldg.
Memphis, TN 38152-3370
PH: (901)678-2531
E-mail: mgarzon@memphis.edu
URL: http://www.memphis.edu
Contact: Dr. Max Garzon, Program Coordinator

Description: Introduction to Electronic Commerce includes exploring, understanding, organizing and effectively using a mix of technology, business, services and marketing in cyberspace.

▌2902
INTRODUCTION TO ELECTRONIC COMMERCE
UNIVERSITY OF NEW BRUNSWICK-SAINT JOHN
FACULTY OF BUSINESS

PO Box 5050
Saint John, NB, Canada E2L4L5
PH: (506)648-5570; (506)648-5806
TF: 800-508-6275
FX: (506)648-5574
E-mail: business@unbsj.ca
URL: http://www.unbsj.ca/business
Contact: Shelley Rinehart, Dean, Faculty of Business

Description: Introduction to Electronic Commerce (BA 2123) is an introductory course that examines all facets of Internet commerce with covered topics including marketing products on the Internet, electronic money and third party use of the Internet for creating management information systems. There is no prerequisite required to take this course.

▌2903
INTRODUCTION TO ELECTRONIC COMMERCE (BCIT)
BRITISH COLUMBIA INSTITUTE OF TECHNOLOGY
ADMINISTRATIVE MANAGEMENT

3700 Willingdon Ave.
Burnaby, BC, Canada V5G3H2
PH: (604)451-7134
E-mail: wendy_lee@bcit.ca
URL: http://online.bcit.ca/de/Ecomm.htm
Contact: Wendy Lee

Description: The British Columbia Institute of Technology (BCIT) offers an online course called "Introduction to Electronic Commerce." This course will provide an overview of all aspects of commerce on the Internet. Topics covered include marketing products on the Internet, systems integration, virtual organizations, electronic payment systems, privacy and security concerns, intellectual property, customs and excise issues, and Internet issues where regulation has been contemplated.

▌2904

INTRODUCTION TO ELECTRONIC COMMERCE

UNIVERSITY OF MINNESOTA

CARLSON SCHOOL OF MANAGEMENT

321 19th Ave. S.
Minneapolis, MN 55455
PH: (612)624-8030
FX: (612)626-1316
E-mail: smoidsdesk@csom.umn.edu
URL: http://ids.csom.umn.edu/undergraduate.htm
Contact: Larry Benveniste, Dean

Description: The Carlson School of Management at the University of Minnesota offers an undergraduate course called "Introduction to Electronic Commerce." This class covers the impact of the Internet on the disciplines of business, including information products and distribution channels, Internet-focused marketing, operational transformation, formation of electronic markets and digital economy.

▌2905

INTRODUCTION TO THE INTERNET FOR BANKERS

DIGITALTHINK INC

601 Brannan St.
San Francisco, CA 94107
PH: (415)625-4000
TF: 888-686-8817
FX: (415)625-4100
E-mail: info@digitalthink.com
URL: http://www.digitalthink.com
Contact: Mr. Pete Goettner, Chairman

Founded: 1996. **Staff:** 450. **Description:** Founded in 1996, DigitalThink offers an online course geared toward financial professionals called "Introduction to the Internet for Bankers." This class introduces students to the fundamentals of the Internet, and demonstrates what it can do for them. Student will learn about the technology behind the Internet, how to connect to it, and how to use email and the World Wide Web. As employees of financial institutions, a basic knowledge of the workings of the Internet will help improve service to their clients.

▌2906

INTRODUCTION TO INTERNET BUSINESS SYSTEMS

MERCY COLLEGE

555 Broadway
Dobbs Ferry, NY 10522
PH: (914)674-7306
FX: (914)674-7518
E-mail: jdielsi@mercy.edu
URL: http://www.mercy.edu
Contact: John DiElsi, Program Dir.

Description: Mercy College offers a graduate level course called Introduction to Internet Business Systems. This course is an overview of Internet business systems and how they function to create an Internet-based business. Students will also look at Internet business models and business plans for an Internet business.

▌2907

INTRODUCTION TO INTERNET MARKETING

CARDEAN UNIVERSITY

500 Lake Cook Rd.
Deerfield, IL 60015-5609
TF: (866)948-1289
E-mail: inquires@cardean.edu
URL: http://www.cardean.edu
Contact: Dr. Geoffrey M. Cox, Cardean University President

Description: Cardean University is an accredited online university which offers a course called "Introduction to Internet Marketing." This class was developed with Stanford University and looks at the economic and technological forces that are shaping Internet commerce. It also introduces the "DNI framework" for marketing in the Internet economy. This course makes use of real-world examples on the web to illustrate key Internet marketing concepts.

▌2908

INTRODUCTION TO INTERNET TECHNOLOGY

MERCY COLLEGE

555 Broadway
Dobbs Ferry, NY 10522
PH: (914)674-7306
FX: (914)674-7518
E-mail: jdielsi@mercy.edu
URL: http://www.mercy.edu
Contact: John DiElsi, Program Dir.

Description: Mercy College offers a graduate level course called Introduction to Internet Technology. This course introduces students to Internet concepts such as domain names, urls, and Internet service providers. Students will learn about the hardware and software nEEDed to create a client/server hosting system.

■ 2909

INTRODUCTION TO THE INTERNET AND WORLD WIDE WEB

NETG

1751 W Diehl Rd, 2nd Fl.
Naperville, IL 60563-9099
PH: (630)369-3000
TF: 877-561-6384
FX: (630)983-4877
E-mail: info@netg.com
URL: http://www.netg.com

Description: NETg offers a course called Introduction to the Internet and World Wide Web. This course provides knowledge and skills to select an Internet Service Provider, locate information on the web, and communicate with others using the Internet.

■ 2910

INTRODUCTION TO ONLINE PRIVACY

CARDEAN UNIVERSITY

500 Lake Cook Rd.
Deerfield, IL 60015-5609
TF: (866)948-1289
E-mail: inquires@cardean.edu
URL: http://www.cardean.edu
Contact: Dr. Geoffrey M. Cox, Cardean University President

Description: Cardean University is an accredited online university offering a suite of courses for marketing professionals called ''Introduction to Online Privacy.'' This series of 5 two hour courses will help students obtain an overview of the considerations that affect the development and implementation of online privacy policies, the relationship between online privacy policies and current technology, and global online privacy policies.

■ 2911

ISSUES IN PUBLIC POLICY

UNIVERSITY OF DELAWARE

E-COMMERCE PROGRAM

206 John M. Clayton Hall
Newark, DE 19716-7410
PH: (302)831-2741
E-mail: continuing-ed@udel.edu
URL: http://www.continuingstudies.udel.edu/it/ecomm/index.shtml

Description: The University of Delaware's Continuing Studies Program offers a course titled ''Issues in Public Policy.'' This course offers new perspectives on issues likely to affect an online business. Topics covered include consumer privacy, target marketing, electronic payment systems, and copyright/patent protection.

■ 2912

ISSUES IN TECHNOLOGY AND ELECTRONIC COMMERCE

WEST CHESTER UNIVERSITY

Office of Graduate Studies
McKelvie Hall
102 Rosedale Ave.
West Chester, PA 19383-2300
PH: (610)436-2943; (610)436-2608
FX: (610)436-2763
E-mail: gradstud@wcupa.edu
URL: http://www.tecmba.org
Contact: Dr. Paul Christ, Director, TEC MBA Program

Description: The purpose of the Issues in Technology and Electronic Commerce course is to provide a forum for the examination of current TEC issues that are not covered in great detail in other TEC or MBA courses. Prerequisites of taking the course include completion of course numbers TEC501, TEC502 and TEC503.

■ 2913

IT FOR E-COMMERCE

PURDUE UNIVERSITY

KRANNERT GRADUATE SCHOOL OF MANAGEMENT

1310 Krannert Bldg.
West Lafayette, IN 47907
PH: (765)494-9700
FX: (765)494-9658
E-mail: krannert_ms@mgmt.purdue.edu
URL: http://www.mgmt.purdue.edu/centers/ceer/

Description: Purdue University's Krannert Graduate School of Management offers IT for E-Commerce, a course that will help students understand how the Internet can be used to do business. This course will provide information on improving the way companies deal with stakeholders (customers, suppliers, owners, employees, etc.) and how the Internet can be used to develop and market new products and services.

■ 2914

IT ENABLED E-COMMERCE

UNIVERSITY OF OKLAHOMA

PRICE COLLEGE OF BUSINESS

307 W Brooks, Room 307E
Norman, OK 73019-4006
PH: (405)325-0768
FX: (405)325-7482
E-mail: rzmud@ou.edu
URL: http://www.ou.edu/zmud/MIS5403/
Contact: Robert W. Zmud, MIS Division Director

Description: The University of Oklahoma offers a course titled ''IT Enabled E-Commerce.'' This course covers topics including e-marketplace foundations, models and strategies, and B2B applications.

▌2915
KNOWLEDGE MANAGEMENT AND EFFECTIVE DECISION MAKING
UNIVERSITY OF PITTSBURGH
CENTER FOR EXECUTIVE EDUCATION

Mellon Financial Corp. Hall, 5th Fl.
4227 Fifth Ave.
Pittsburgh, PA 15260
PH: (412)648-1600
E-mail: exeducation@katz.pitt.edu
URL: http://www.execed.pitt.edu/

Description: The Executive Education Program at the University of Pittsburgh offers a course for managers entitled Knowledge Management and Effective Decision Making. This seminar will help managers learn to increase both their own and their organization's efficiency in making effective use of new and existing knowledge for decision-making, problem-solving, error-reduction and improved customer service.

▌2916
LAUNCHING E-COMMERCE VENTURES
NOTRE DAME
COLLEGE OF BUSINESS

276 Mendoza College of Business
Notre Dame, IN 46556
PH: (219)631-8488
TF: 800-631-8488
FX: (219)631-8800
E-mail: mba.1@nd.edu
URL: http://www.nd.edu/~mba
Contact: Carolyn Woo, Dean

Description: The Notre Dame MBA Program offers a course called "Launching E-Commerce Ventures." This course is focused on writing an effective business plan. All participants are required to write a business plan for their new e-business venture.

▌2917
LAW AND POLICY ISSUES FOR ELECTRONIC COMMERCE
DALHOUSIE UNIVERSITY

Faculty of Computer Science
6050 University Ave.
Halifax, NS, Canada B3H1W5
PH: (902)494-2740
FX: (902)492-1517
E-mail: mec@cs.dal.ca
URL: http://www.ecomm.dal.ca
Contact: Dr. Kori Inkpen, Dir., Master of E-Commerce Program

Description: Law and Policy Issues for Electronic Commerce will provide students with an overview of law and policy issues in relation to e-commerce, introduce students to Canadian, U.S. and international policy making institutions and processes, and illustrate these processes using examples from domestic and international law relating to e-commerce.

▌2918
LAW AND PUBLIC POLICY IN E-COMMERCE
GEORGE MASON UNIVERSITY
DEPARTMENT OF COMPUTER SCIENCE

MSN 4A5
4400 University Dr.
Fairfax, VA 22030
PH: (703)993-1530
FX: (703)993-1710
E-mail: csadmin@cs.gmu.edu
URL: http://ite.gmu.edu/msecomm/description.htm

Description: George Mason University offers a course called "Law and Public Policy in E-Commerce." This course explores the legal and policy framework of advanced communications and information technology. The basis for this course will be a rapid review of the history of electronic communications regulation in the United States.

▌2919
LEADING CHANGE IN INTERNET BUSINESS
MERCY COLLEGE

555 Broadway
Dobbs Ferry, NY 10522
PH: (914)674-7306
FX: (914)674-7518
E-mail: jdielsi@mercy.edu
URL: http://www.mercy.edu
Contact: John DiElsi, Program Dir.

Description: Mercy College offers a graduate level course called Leading Change in Internet Business. This course focuses on the complexity of the change process and analyzes barriers that nEED to be overcome. Other topics covered are organizational performance and Internet business collaboration along the value chain.

▌2920
LEADING TECHNICAL TEAMS
GW CENTER FOR PROFESSIONAL DEVELOPMENT

2029 K Street NW, Ste. 600
Washington, DC 20006
PH: (202)973-1150
FX: (202)973-1165
E-mail: cpd@gwu.edu
URL: http://www.gwu.edu/~cpd/programs/CWEC/

Description: The GW Center for Professional Development offers a course called "Leading Technical Teams." This course will enable students to better communicate with technical professionals by examining learning styles and problem-solving approaches of high tech professionals.

▌2921

LEARN TO SPEAK IT STRATEGY
CARDEAN UNIVERSITY

500 Lake Cook Rd.
Deerfield, IL 60015-5609
TF: (866)948-1289
E-mail: inquires@cardean.edu
URL: http://www.cardean.edu
Contact: Dr. Geoffrey M. Cox, Cardean University President

Description: Cardean University is an accredited online university offers a suite of courses called "Learn to Speak IT Strategy." This suite of 5 2 hour courses offers students basic principles to assist in understanding IT trends and to assist in planning, integrating, and managing IT within an organization to help give a company strategic advantage over its competitors.

▌2922

LEGAL ASPECTS OF E-COMMERCE
DREXEL UNIVERSITY
LEBOW COLLEGE OF BUSINESS

3141 Chestnut St.
Matheson Hall, Rm. 105
Philadelphia, PA 19104
PH: (215)895-6070
FX: (215)895-1012
E-mail: marcos@drexel.edu.
URL: http://www.drexel.edu/academics/lebow/ecomm/

Description: Drexel University offers an executive education course called Legal Aspects of E-Commerce. This course will look at many topics including electronic contracts, a review of the proposed Uniform Computer Information Transactions Act, online service providers agreements, Internet contract forms, intellectual property rights, changes in trademark and copyrights laws related to e-business, privacy and security issues, and computer crime.

▌2923

LEGAL ASPECTS OF ELECTRONIC COMMERCE
CHRISTOPHER NEWPORT UNIVERSITY ONLINE

1 University Pl.
Newport News, VA 23606
PH: (757)594-7607
E-mail: online@cnu.edu
URL: http://ec.seva.net/

Description: Christopher Newport University and the Virginia Electronic Commerce Technology Center offer an online course called "Legal Aspects of Electronic Commerce." Topics covered in this course include taxation and jurisdiction, principles of contract law, intellectual property, and privacy in the online environment.

▌2924

LEGAL AND ETHICAL INTERNET ISSUES
NOTRE DAME DE NAMUR UNIVERSITY

1500 Ralston Ave.
Belmont, CA 94002-1997
PH: (650)508-3782
FX: (650)508-3660
E-mail: ebusiness@ndnu.edu
URL: http://www.ndnu.edu

Description: Notre Dame de Namur University offers a graduate course called Legal and Ethical Internet Issues. This course addresses high technology, intellectual property and other legal issues in relationship to the Internet. Other topics covered include patents and copyrights, computer crime, and security.

▌2925

LEGAL AND ETHICAL ISSUES IN E-BUSINESS
BELLEVUE UNIVERSITY

1000 Galvin Rd. S
Bellevue, NE 68005
PH: (402)293-2000
TF: 800-756-7920
FX: (402)293-2020
URL: http://www.bellevue.edu

Description: Bellevue University offers a course called "Legal and Ethical Issues in E-Business." This course examines the legal and policy environment of E Business. Domain name registration, proposals and bids, the use of cookies, licenses, financial services, taxation, antitrust, trademarks and copyrights, criminal law, and international protection are some of the topics covered.

▌2926

LEGAL AND ETHICAL ISSUES IN INTERNET BUSINESS
MERCY COLLEGE

555 Broadway
Dobbs Ferry, NY 10522
PH: (914)674-7306
FX: (914)674-7518
E-mail: jdielsi@mercy.edu
URL: http://www.mercy.edu
Contact: John DiElsi, Program Dir.

Description: Mercy College offers a graduate level course called Legal and Ethical Issues in Internet Business. This course looks at legal issues in e-commerce, and covers topics such as jurisdiction in a 24/7 environment, intellectual property, taxation, security, and business transactions.

▌2927

LEGAL ISSUES IN E-COMMERCE

CREIGHTON UNIVERSITY

COLLEGE OF BUSINESS ADMINISTRATION

2500 California Plz.
Omaha, NE 68178
PH: (402)280-2602
FX: (402)280-2172
E-mail: ghafer@creighton.edu
URL: http://www.creighton.edu
Contact: Ms. Gail Hafer, Graduate Coordinator

Description: Creighton University offers a graduate level course called Legal Issues in E-Commerce. Developed in conjunction with the Creighton University Law School, this course will cover topics including copyright, trademark and trade secret laws, contract and jurisdictional concerns, internet payment systems and security, encryption and digital signature issues, and First Amendment concerns related to privacy and defamation.

▌2928

LEGAL ISSUES IN E-COMMERCE

STANFORD UNIVERSITY

GRADUATE SCHOOL OF BUSINESS

518 Memorial Way
Stanford, CA 94305-5015
PH: (650)725-5663
FX: (650)723-3950
E-mail: cebc@gsb.stanford.edu
URL: http://www.gsb.stanford.edu/cebc/

Description: Stanford University's MBA program offers a course titled "Legal Issues in E-Commerce." This course examines laws and regulations applying to businesses that operate on the Internet. Subjects covered include copyrights, patents, online privacy and security, domain name policies and liability concerns for e-commerce businesses.

▌2929

LEGAL ISSUES IN A WIRED WORLD

STEVENS INSTITUTE OF TECHNOLOGY

HOWE SCHOOL OF TECHNOLOGY MANAGEMENT

Kidde Bldg., Rm. 324-A
Hoboken, NJ 07030
PH: (201)216-5381
FX: (201)216-5385
E-mail: howe_grad@stevens-tech.edu
URL: http://attila.stevens-tech.edu/stmm/e-comm/certificate.htm

Description: Stevens Institute of Technology's School of Technology Management offers a course called Legal Issues in a Wired World. This course examines areas of law that have an impact on the world of electronic commerce.

▌2930

LEGAL, PRIVACY, AND SECURITY ISSUES IN ELECTRONIC COMMERCE

UNIVERSITY OF NEW BRUNSWICK-SAINT JOHN

FACULTY OF BUSINESS

PO Box 5050
Saint John, NB, Canada E2L4L5
PH: (506)648-5570; (506)648-5806
TF: 800-508-6275
FX: (506)648-5574
E-mail: business@unbsj.ca
URL: http://www.unbsj.ca/business
Contact: Shelley Rinehart, Dean, Faculty of Business

Description: Legal, Privacy, and Security Issues in Electronic Commerce (BA 3718) deals with the various systems that provide privacy and security on the Internet and the legal issues that arise in e-commerce. Topics will include an examination of encryption, firewalls, user authentication and copyright of intellectual property and contracts. Prerequisites include courses BA 2123 and BA 2663.

▌2931

LOCK-IN STRATEGIES FOR THE INFORMATION ECONOMY

CARDEAN UNIVERSITY

500 Lake Cook Rd.
Deerfield, IL 60015-5609
TF: (866)948-1289
E-mail: inquires@cardean.edu
URL: http://www.cardean.edu
Contact: Dr. Geoffrey M. Cox, Cardean University President

Description: Cardean University is an accredited online university offering a suite of courses called "Lock-in Strategies for the Information Economy." This suite of 5 two hour courses is geared towards managers in information-based companies who would like to know how lock-in strategies may increase profits from current customers, keep customers from switching to a competitor, and attract new customers. This course offers ideas about how to succeed in the information economy, based on the book, Information Rules, by Carl Shapiro and Hal R. Varian.

▌2932

MACROMEDIA E-COMMERCE EXPERT CERTIFICATE

STERLING LEDET AND ASSOCIATES, INC.

2200 Northlake Pky., Ste. 275
Tucker, GA 30084
PH: (770)414-5007
TF: 877-819-2665
FX: (770)414-5661
E-mail: sales@ledet.com
URL: http://www.ledet.com

Description: Sterling Ledet and Associates offer the Macromedia E-Commerce Expert Certificate. This curriculum

629

is based around Macromedia software products and is designed to give the student proficiency in Internet commerce technology. Coursework includes an Introduction to E-Commerce course as well as courses in Dreamweaver, Flash, HTML, and JavaScript.

▌ 2933

MAKING MONEY THROUGH B2C MARKETING

ECNOW.COM

21265 Stevens Creek Blvd., Ste. 205
Cupertino, CA 95014
PH: (408)257-3000
FX: (603)843-0769
E-mail: info@ecnow.com
URL: http://ecnow.com/courses/mgt04.htm

Description: ECnow.com offers a course called Making Money Through B2C Marketing. This interactive course covers topic such as guerilla marketing techniques, targeted email, banner advertising, and integrated marketing communications.

▌ 2934

MANAGEMENT CONTROL AND SECURITY OF E-COMMERCE

CREIGHTON UNIVERSITY

COLLEGE OF BUSINESS ADMINISTRATION

2500 California Plz.
Omaha, NE 68178
PH: (402)280-2602
FX: (402)280-2172
E-mail: ghafer@creighton.edu
URL: http://www.creighton.edu
Contact: Ms. Gail Hafer, Graduate Coordinator

Description: Creighton University offers a graduate level course called Management Control and Security of E-Commerce. In this course students will gain understanding of planning and security of e-commerce systems and applications, including an emphasis on electronic payment systems. Other topics covered include risk management, control systems, security measures, encryption, and performance evaluation.

▌ 2935

MANAGEMENT OF E-COMMERCE

CLEMSON UNIVERSITY

E-108 Martin Hall
Clemson, SC 29634-5713
PH: (864)656-3311
E-mail: ddiane@clemson.edu
URL: http://www.clemson.edu

Description: Clemson University offers a course called Management of E-Commerce. In this course students will learn about concepts of electronic commerce as conducted on the Internet and other related technologies.

▌ 2936

MANAGEMENT OF ELECTRONIC BUSINESS I AND II

NOTRE DAME DE NAMUR UNIVERSITY

1500 Ralston Ave.
Belmont, CA 94002-1997
PH: (650)508-3782
FX: (650)508-3660
E-mail: ebusiness@ndnu.edu
URL: http://www.ndnu.edu

Description: Notre Dame de Namur University offers graduate courses called Management of Electronic Business I and II. These two integrated courses look at the creation of an e-businesses comprehensive strategy. Students use case studies of successful business transformations that address management issues, business models, value chain analysis, technical strategy and technology.

▌ 2937

MANAGEMENT IN AN INFORMATION AGE

STANFORD UNIVERSITY

GRADUATE SCHOOL OF BUSINESS

518 Memorial Way
Stanford, CA 94305-5015
PH: (650)725-5663
FX: (650)723-3950
E-mail: cebc@gsb.stanford.edu
URL: http://www.gsb.stanford.edu/cebc/

Description: Stanford University's MBA program offers a course titled "Management in an Information Age." This course examines management issues surrounding the development and use of information technology in organizations. Its focus is on managerial and organizational aspects surrounding technologies such as the Internet.

▌ 2938

MANAGEMENT OF ONLINE BUSINESS

UNIVERSITY OF NEW BRUNSWICK-SAINT JOHN

FACULTY OF BUSINESS

PO Box 5050
Saint John, NB, Canada E2L4L5
PH: (506)648-5570; (506)648-5806
TF: 800-508-6275
FX: (506)648-5574
E-mail: business@unbsj.ca
URL: http://www.unbsj.ca/business
Contact: Shelley Rinehart, Dean, Faculty of Business

Description: Management of Online Business (BA 4109) is a project course in which students prepare a proposal for launching a new product or service on the Internet and will include a complete strategy for an online business. Students must complete BA 3424 and all required courses for the major in Electronic Commerce or receive permission from the instructor before taking this course.

∎ 2939

MANAGEMENT STRATEGIES FOR E-COMMERCE

NEW JERSEY INSTITUTE OF TECHNOLOGY
SCHOOL OF MANAGEMENT, GRADUATE
PROGRAMS

323 Martin Luther King Jr. Blvd.
Newark, NJ 07102-1982
PH: (973)596-6378
FX: (973)596-3074
E-mail: lipper@njit.edu
URL: http://www.njit.edu/SOM/MBA/index.html
Contact: Stuart Lipper, Director of Graduate Programs

Description: The New Jersey Institute of Technology School of Management MBA program offers a course called ''Management Strategies for E-Commerce.'' This course will help students understand the Internet from a management perspective. It will prepare them to become effective managers of internet-based businesses and electronic commerce,

∎ 2940

MANAGEMENT AND TECHNOLOGY OF ELECTRONIC COMMERCE

WEST VIRGINIA UNIVERSITY
COLLEGE OF BUSINESS AND ECONOMICS

PO Box 6025
Morgantown, WV 26506-6025
PH: (304)293-4092
FX: (304)293-5652
E-mail: bjchang@mail.wvu.edu
URL: http://www.be.wvu.edu/divmim/mgmt/kleist/MAN-G200Lspring01syllabus.htm
Contact: Virginia Kleist, Instructor

Description: West Virginia's College of Business and Economics offers a course called ''Management and Technology of Electronic Commerce.'' This course covers topics including the managerial and technical aspects of electronic commerce. The student will learn to think and act as an executive level manager, understanding technologies and new developments in Electronic Commerce.

∎ 2941

MANAGING COMPLEMENTS IN THE INFORMATION ECONOMY

CARDEAN UNIVERSITY

500 Lake Cook Rd.
Deerfield, IL 60015-5609
TF: (866)948-1289
E-mail: inquires@cardean.edu
URL: http://www.cardean.edu
Contact: Dr. Geoffrey M. Cox, Cardean University President

Description: Cardean University is an accredited online university which offers a suite of courses called ''Managing Complements in the Information Economy.'' This series of 4 two hour courses explores the issues surrounding whether a company should supply its own complements or allow other companies to produce them. It offers ideas about how to succeed in the information economy, based on the book, Information Rules, by Carl Shapiro and Hal R. Varian. This course is geared towards managers in information-based businesses, and may be especially useful for companies considering joint ventures, mergers or relationships with other companies.

∎ 2942

MANAGING THE DIGITAL ENTERPRISE

NORTH CAROLINA STATE UNIVERSITY
E-COMMERCE LEARNING CENTER

Campus Box 7229
Raleigh, NC 27695-7229
PH: (919)513-2694
E-mail: ecommerce@ncsu.edu
URL: http://ecommerce.ncsu.edu
Contact: Dr. Michael Rappa

Description: The E-Commerce Learning Center at North Carolina State University is a portal to web-based educational materials and scholarly research related to electronic commerce. While coursework is offered in a traditional setting, many classes can be completed on a self-study basis. Courses and seminars offered for both graduate and undergraduate students include Managing the Digital Enterprise, which covers topics such as digital design, Internet privacy, and Web ethics.

∎ 2943

MANAGING THE DIGITAL ENTERPRISE

E-COMMERCE LEARNING CENTER

NC State University
Business Management Dept.
College of Management
Campus Box 7229
Raleigh, NC 27695-7229
PH: (919)515-5584
E-mail: ecommerce@ncsu.edu
URL: http://www.ecommerce.ncsu.edu
Contact: Dr. Michael Rappa

Description: Managing the Digital Enterprise is an introductory graduate-level course in e-commerce first taught January 1999. The course content is entirely web-enabled and contains an online guide to the literature about e-commerce to be used in conjunction with the course taught at NC State University. The course relies solely on the web as the source of content and does not use a standard textbook.

∎ 2944

MANAGING THE DIGITAL FIRM

NEW JERSEY INSTITUTE OF TECHNOLOGY
SCHOOL OF MANAGEMENT, GRADUATE
PROGRAMS

323 Martin Luther King Jr. Blvd.
Newark, NJ 07102-1982
PH: (973)596-6378

FX: (973)596-3074
E-mail: lipper@njit.edu
URL: http://www.njit.edu/SOM/MBA/index.html
Contact: Stuart Lipper, Director of Graduate Programs

Description: The New Jersey Institute of Technology School of Management MBA program offers a course called "Managing the Digital Firm." This course looks at digital processes that are transforming organizations, and explores managing all aspects of the digital firm. Other topics covered include managing a virtual workforce, managing digital technologies, and protecting and leveraging digital assets.

▮ 2945

MANAGING IN AN E-BUSINESS ENVIRONMENT

AMERICAN UNIVERSITY
KOGOD SCHOOL OF BUSINESS, EXECUTIVE EDUCATION

4400 Massachusetts Ave., NW
Washington, DC 20016
PH: (202)885-1994
FX: (202)885-1030
E-mail: execed@american.edu
URL: http://
Contact: Ann Donahue, Director, Executive Education

Description: The American University Kogod School of Business Executive Education program offers a course called "Managing in an E-Business Environment." This 2 day course addresses the evolving role of the manager in e-businesses. It explores the expanding role of information systems and the use of technology as a management tool. It will address the benefits and challenges of e-commerce in today's marketplace.

▮ 2946

MANAGING E-COMMERCE IN THE DIGITAL ECONOMY

ILLINOIS INSTITUTE OF TECHNOLOGY
STUART GRADUATE SCHOOL OF BUSINESS

565 W Adams St.
Chicago, IL 60661
PH: (312)906-6500
FX: (312)906-6549
E-mail: degrees@stuart.iit.edu
URL: http://www.stuart.iit.edu

Description: The Illinois Institute of Technology Stuart Graduate School of Business offers a course entitled Managing E-Commerce in the Digital Economy. This course examines a variety of business models and industry examples. Economic, legal, organizational and technological factors will also be discussed.

▮ 2947

MANAGING THE E-COMMERCE LIFE CYCLE

UNIVERSITY OF DELAWARE
E-COMMERCE PROGRAM

206 John M. Clayton Hall
Newark, DE 19716-7410
PH: (302)831-2741
E-mail: continuing-ed@udel.edu
URL: http://www.continuingstudies.udel.edu/it/ecomm/index.shtml

Description: The University of Delaware's Continuing Studies Program offers a course entitled "Managing the E-Commerce Life Cycle." This course explores the e-commerce process and life cycle for various types of businesses, which are a part of the evolving world of e-commerce. Key success elements for e-commerce are identified.

▮ 2948

MANAGING ELECTRONIC COMMERCE

UNIVERSITY OF SOUTHERN CALIFORNIA
MARSHALL SCHOOL OF BUSINESS

HOH 800, MC 1421
Los Angeles, CA 90089
PH: (213)740-6422
FX: (213)740-5432
E-mail: rwesterfield@sba.usc.edu
URL: http://www-rcf.usc.edu/~sulin/iom540/
Contact: Randolph W. Westerfield, Dean

Description: The University of Southern California offers a course titled "Managing Electronic Commerce." This course covers topics including an overview of e-commerce, electronic payment systems, data security, B2C business models, and B2B electronic commerce.

▮ 2949

MANAGING THE ELECTRONIC COMMERCE ENTERPRISE

OKLAHOMA STATE UNIVERSITY

Center for Academic Services
324 Student Union
Stillwater, OK 74078-1012
PH: (405)744-6858
E-mail: admit@okstate.edu
URL: http://www.okstate.edu

Description: The Managing the Electronic Commerce Enterprise course explores organizational issues faced by e-commerce enterprises and traditional organizations as they navigate their worlds as the Internet evolves into click and mortar organizations. Special focus is on topics like strategic alliances, experimental organizational forms and human resource systems that organizations are adopting to succeed in this highly competitive arena.

▌2950
MANAGING ELECTRONIC COMMERCE IN THE KNOWLEDGE AGE
UNIVERSITY OF MARYLAND
SMITH SCHOOL OF BUSINESS

Van Munching Hall
College Park, MD 20742
PH: (301)405-2278
E-mail: info@hsmith.umd.edu
URL: http://ecommerce.umd.edu/

Description: The University of Maryland Smith School of Business offers an MBA course entitled "Managing Electronic Commerce in the Knowledge Age." This course examines the managerial challenges facing individuals running firms in the knowledge age. Identifies key managerial implications of electronic commerce on intra and interorganizational relationships, power, and strategy.

▌2951
MANAGING EMERGING TECHNOLOGIES
LOYOLA UNIVERSITY CHICAGO

Graduate School of Business
25 E. Pearson, 14th Fl.
Chicago, IL 60611
PH: (312)915-6120
FX: (312)915-7207
E-mail: ayoung3@luc.edu
URL: http://www.luc.edu
Contact: Alan Young, Director of Enrollment & Recruitment

Description: The Web and e-commerce will be the main focus of Managing Emerging Technologies with other emerging technologies studied, as well. Guest speakers from leading technology firms will discuss successful strategies for supporting creativity in their organizations and transforming technological innovations into marketable products.

▌2952
MANAGING THE INFORMATION RESOURCE PROGRAM
UNIVERSITY OF CALIFORNIA LOS ANGELES
COLLINS CENTER FOR EXECUTIVE EDUCATION

110 Westwood Plz., Ste. A101D
Los Angeles, CA 90095-1464
PH: (310)825-2001
FX: (310)206-7539
E-mail: execed@anderson.ucla.edu
URL: http://www.anderson.ucla.edu/programs/

Description: UCLA's Executive Education offers Managing the Information Resource Program. This curriculum for business executives is designed to help you and your organization meet the challenges of a continuously changing information technology environment, providing the tools and strategies you need to succeed in the competitive information environment.

▌2953
MANAGING INTERNET BUSINESS SYSTEMS
MERCY COLLEGE

555 Broadway
Dobbs Ferry, NY 10522
PH: (914)674-7306
FX: (914)674-7518
E-mail: jdielsi@mercy.edu
URL: http://www.mercy.edu
Contact: John DiElsi, Program Dir.

Description: Mercy College offers a graduate level course called Managing Internet Business Systems. This course explores the use of the Internet as a management resource. Topics covered include connecting an Internet channel with a sales network, using the Internet in supply chains, and understanding security issues.

▌2954
MANAGING INTERNET TECHNOLOGY
ILLINOIS INSTITUTE OF TECHNOLOGY
STUART GRADUATE SCHOOL OF BUSINESS

565 W Adams St.
Chicago, IL 60661
PH: (312)906-6500
FX: (312)906-6549
E-mail: degrees@stuart.iit.edu
URL: http://www.stuart.iit.edu

Description: The Illinois Institute of Technology Stuart Graduate School of Business offers a course entitled Managing Internet Technology. This course explores topics including Internet platform architecture, converging network technologies, enterprise and web process integration, and data mining. Students will use case studies and computer exercises.

▌2955
MANAGING THE REAL TIME SUPPLY CHAIN
UNIVERSITY OF MARYLAND
ROBERT H. SMITH SCHOOL OF BUSINESS
NETCENTRICITY

Van Munching Hall
College Park, MD 20742
PH: (301)405-2286
E-mail: info@rhsmith.umd.edu
URL: http://www.rhsmith.umd.edu/netcentricity/edu.htm

Description: University of Maryland's Netcentricity lab offers educational opportunities focused on a variety of E-commerce topics. Using real-time e-business transaction data, undergraduate, MBA, and doctoral students can experience the big picture of today's complex business environment. Courses, including Managing the Real Time Supply Chain, work to teach analycal skills needed for e-commerce. Other activities of Netcentricity include seminar series for business leaders.

▌2956
MANAGING VIRTUAL TEAMS
UNIVERSITY OF DELAWARE
E-COMMERCE PROGRAM

206 John M. Clayton Hall
Newark, DE 19716-7410
PH: (302)831-2741
E-mail: continuing-ed@udel.edu
URL: http://www.continuingstudies.udel.edu/it/ecomm/index.shtml

Description: The University of Delaware's Continuing Studies Program offers a course titled "Managing Virtual Teams." Students will explore the foundations of managing virtual teams. They will focus on the differences between traditional and online management, tools for online management, and developing virtual teams and e-training.

▌2957
MARKET LEADERSHIP IN AN E-COMMERCE AGE
JER GROUP INC.
ONLINEWORKSHOPS.COM

56 Seabreeze Way
Dawsonville, GA 30534
PH: (706)216-3406
FX: (706)216-3979
E-mail: drjer@jergroup.com
URL: http://www.onlineworkshops.com
Contact: Dr. John E. Reid, Jr., President

Description: JER Group Inc. offers an online course on E-Commerce entitled "Market Leadership in an E-Commerce Age." This course looks in detail at the principles of e-commerce. Students will begin to examine the mechanisms and process of the e-commerce environment that our society lives with daily.

▌2958
MARKETING FOR E-COMMERCE
UNIVERSITY OF CALIFORNIA EXTENSION ONLINE

2000 Center St., Ste. 400
Berkeley, CA 94704
PH: (510)642-4124
E-mail: askus@ucxonline.berkeley.edu
URL: http://learn.berkely.edu/

Description: The University of California Extension Online offers a course entitled "Marketing for E-Commerce." This online course provides an overview of e-commerce marketing. Students will look at market trends and case studies, discuss strategies for acquiring and retaining customers, and determine effective ways to launch an e-commerce solution. Students will also learn what it takes to maintain a successful e-commerce program and how to measure results.

▌2959
MARKETING AND ELECTRONIC COMMERCE
WORCESTER POLYTECHNIC INSTITUTE

100 Institute Rd.
Worcester, MA 01609
PH: (508)831-5218
FX: (508)831-5720
URL: http://www.wpi.edu
Contact: McRae Banks, Department Head

Founded: 1865. **Description:** The Marketing and Electronic Commerce course discusses the tools and techniques being used to harness the vast marketing potential of the Internet. It examines various web-based business models for effectively and efficiently using the Internet as a strategic marketing tool for new products, market research, direct and indirect distribution channels and marketing communications. The course considers both business-to-consumer and business-to-business applications and explores the major opportunities, limitations and issues of profiting from the Internet.

▌2960
MARKETING AND ELECTRONIC COMMERCE
ST. LOUIS UNIVERSITY
COOK SCHOOL OF BUSINESS

3674 Lindell Blvd.
St. Louis, MO 63108
PH: (314)977-3864
FX: (314)977-3897
E-mail: katzja@slu.edu
URL: http://eweb.slu.edu/e-com_courses.htm

Description: St. Louis University offers a course called "Marketing and Electronic Commerce." This graduate level course provides information on the marketing issues surrounding commercialization of the Web, and other emerging electronic media.

▌2961
MARKETING HIGH TECHNOLOGY
STANFORD UNIVERSITY
GRADUATE SCHOOL OF BUSINESS

518 Memorial Way
Stanford, CA 94305-5015
PH: (650)725-5663
FX: (650)723-3950
E-mail: cebc@gsb.stanford.edu
URL: http://www.gsb.stanford.edu/cebc/

Description: Stanford University's MBA program offers a course entitled "Marketing High Technology." This course offers guidelines for the development of marketing programs for high-technology firms. Topics covered include identifying and evaluating opportunities, the technology adoption life cycle, and building business models.

∎ 2962

MARKETING AND INFORMATION TECHNOLOGY

BENTLEY COLLEGE

175 Forest St.
Waltham, MA 02452-4705
PH: (781)891-2000
URL: http://www.bentley.edu

Description: Bentley College offers a graduate level course called Marketing and Information Technology. In this course students gain an understanding of technologies that may to affect marketing in the future, as well as the human implications of technology. Students will learn how to develop strategies for using the Internet as a marketing tool, to measure performance, and investigate the impact of e-marketing on the marketing function within a company.

∎ 2963

MARKETING AND THE INTERNET

NOTRE DAME DE NAMUR UNIVERSITY

1500 Ralston Ave.
Belmont, CA 94002-1997
PH: (650)508-3782
FX: (650)508-3660
E-mail: ebusiness@ndnu.edu
URL: http://www.ndnu.edu

Description: Notre Dame de Namur University offers a graduate course called Marketing and the Internet. This course examines managerial skills and marketing infrastructure for successful e-businesses. Students will create an Internet marketing plan addressing issues such as consumer behaviors, legal guidelines, ISPs, e-commerce portals, and product and service branding.

∎ 2964

MARKETING ON THE INTERNET

UNIVERSITY OF NEW BRUNSWICK-SAINT JOHN
FACULTY OF BUSINESS

PO Box 5050
Saint John, NB, Canada E2L4L5
PH: (506)648-5570; (506)648-5806
TF: 800-508-6275
FX: (506)648-5574
E-mail: business@unbsj.ca
URL: http://www.unbsj.ca/business
Contact: Shelley Rinehart, Dean, Faculty of Business

Description: Marketing on the Internet (BA 3305) examines the integration of the Internet in an organization's marketing strategy with topics including goals for online marketing, customer communications, interactive Internet pages and customer service issues. These topics can also be relevant in an e-commerce industry. Prerequisites include completion of courses BA 2123, BA 2303 and BA 2663.

∎ 2965

MARKETING ON THE INTERNET

AUGUSTA STATE UNIVERSITY

2500 Walton Way
Augusta, GA 30904-2200
PH: 800-341-4373
TF: 800-341-4373
E-mail: bcoleman@aug.edu
URL: http://www.aug.edu/~sbamdm/marketing/index.htm
Contact: Dr. Barbara Coleman, Instructor

Description: Augusta State University offers a course called ''Marketing on the Internet.'' This course looks at the way in which e-commerce is changing how firms market their products and services. The course explores topics including the basic issues of advertising and selling on the Internet, the use of web sites, and consumer decision making on the Internet.

∎ 2966

MARKETING ON THE INTERNET

NOTRE DAME
COLLEGE OF BUSINESS

276 Mendoza College of Business
Notre Dame, IN 46556
PH: (219)631-8488
TF: 800-631-8488
FX: (219)631-8800
E-mail: mba.1@nd.edu
URL: http://www.nd.edu/~mba
Contact: Carolyn Woo, Dean

Description: The Notre Dame MBA Program offers a course called ''Marketing on the Internet.'' This course explores various facets of marketing on the internet, including interactive marketing. Interactive marketing builds on experience with databases, online communications, mass marketing and supply chain management to effectively tie together marketers, customers, and vendors through the Internet.

∎ 2967

MARKETING ISSUES IN ELECTRONIC COMMERCE

CHRISTOPHER NEWPORT UNIVERSITY
CENTER FOR COMMUNITY LEARNING

1 University Place
Newport News, VA 23606-2998
PH: (757)594-7158
FX: (757)594-8736
E-mail: ccl@cnu.edu
URL: http://ec.seva.net/

Description: Christopher Newport University and the Virginia Electronic Commerce Technology Center offer a course called Marketing Issues in Electronic Commerce. This course explores the ways that marketing is being done on the Internet. Students will learn about promotion strategies, customer retention, search engine strategies, and branding and selling strategies.

▌2968
MARKETING IN THE NETWORKED ECONOMY
ILLINOIS INSTITUTE OF TECHNOLOGY
STUART GRADUATE SCHOOL OF BUSINESS

565 W Adams St.
Chicago, IL 60661
PH: (312)906-6500
FX: (312)906-6549
E-mail: degrees@stuart.iit.edu
URL: http://www.stuart.iit.edu

Description: The Illinois Institute of Technology Stuart Graduate School of Business offers a course entitled Marketing in the Networked Economy. This course examines consumer and business buying behavior on the Internet. Interactive marketing, value propositions, pricing, branding, promotion, and sales channels will also be covered.

▌2969
MARKETING ONLINE
STEVENS INSTITUTE OF TECHNOLOGY
HOWE SCHOOL OF TECHNOLOGY MANAGEMENT

Kidde Bldg., Rm. 324-A
Hoboken, NJ 07030
PH: (201)216-5381
FX: (201)216-5385
E-mail: howe_grad@stevens-tech.edu
URL: http://attila.stevens-tech.edu/stmm/e-comm/certificate.htm

Description: Stevens Institute of Technology's School of Technology Management offers a graduate level course called Marketing Online. This course looks at consumer demand, industry projections, delivery platforms, sources of materials, market research, and the product development process.

▌2970
MARKETING STRATEGY IN THE INFORMATION AGE
UNIVERSITY OF CALIFORNIA LOS ANGELES
COLLINS CENTER FOR EXECUTIVE EDUCATION

110 Westwood Plz., Ste. A101D
Los Angeles, CA 90095-1464
PH: (310)825-2001
FX: (310)206-7539
E-mail: execed@anderson.ucla.edu
URL: http://www.anderson.ucla.edu/programs/

Description: UCLA's Executive Education offers a program entitled Marketing Strategy in the Information Age. In this program you will learn how to combine proven strategies with new techniques to form an optimal marketing strategy for your organization. You will acquire the tools, applications, and frameworks to strategically market your products and services. You will gain innovative, profit-enhancing ways to use technology and information to make smarter marketing decisions.

▌2971
MARKETING AND TECHNOLOGY
WEST CHESTER UNIVERSITY OF PENNSYLVANIA
GRADUATE SCHOOL

McKelvie Hall
102 Rosedale Ave.
West Chester, PA 19383-2600
PH: (610)436-2943
E-mail: gradstudy@wcupa.edu
URL: http://www.wcupa.edu/

Description: West Chester University of Pennsylvania offers a graduate course called Marketing and Technology. This course emphasizes new technologies and examines how they fit within the marketing strategy of a company. A main focus is the role of the Internet in marketing.

▌2972
MASTER OF ARTS IN E-COMMERCE
VILLA JULIE COLLEGE
E-COMMERCE

1525 Greenspring Valley Rd.
Stevenson, MD 21153-0641
PH: (410)486-7001
E-mail: admissions@mail.vjc.edu
URL: http://www.vjc.edu

Description: Villa Julie College provides an MA degree in E-Commerce. This program takes a detailed look at new technologies and provides an opportunity for students to discover how these technologies are incorporated into a company's processes, and can lead to efficiencies and enhancements in business operations.

▌2973
MASTER OF ELECTRONIC COMMERCE
DALHOUSIE UNIVERSITY

Faculty of Computer Science
6050 University Ave.
Halifax, NS, Canada B3H1W5
PH: (902)494-2740
FX: (902)492-1517
E-mail: mec@cs.dal.ca
URL: http://www.ecomm.dal.ca
Contact: Dr. Kori Inkpen, Dir., Master of E-Commerce Program

Description: The Master of Electronic Commerce program is a full-time interdisciplinary program, however it is not an MBA, but an academic degree that blends coursework, research and an industrial internship to provide an overview of the field. The program can be completed in 16 months, including the industrial internship, is thematic rather than content driven and is the only Canadian Master of Electronic Commerce program.

▌ 2974

MASTER OF ELECTRONIC COMMERCE

CLEMSON UNIVERSITY

165 Sirrine Hall
Clemson, SC 29634
PH: (864)656-6371
E-mail: Grigsby@clemson.edu
URL: http://business.clemson.edu/ECommerce/Index.htm
Contact: Dr. David Grigsby

Description: Clemson University offers a Master of Electronic Commerce degree. This curriculum prepares students to understand trends in electronic commerce and to participate in analysis, design, implementation, and operation of e-commerce systems.

▌ 2975

MASTER OF SCIENCE IN COMPUTER INFORMATION TECHNOLOGY (MSCIT)

REGIS UNIVERSITY

GRADUATE PROGRAMS

3333 Regis Boulevard, L-16
Denver, CO 80221-1099
PH: (303)458-4080
TF: 800-667-9270
FX: (303)964-5538
E-mail: masters@regis.edu
URL: http://www.mscisonline.org/

Description: Regis University offers a Master of Science in Computer Information Technology (MSCIT) degree with a focus in E-Commerce. In this online degree program students will gain understanding in various areas including hardware, software, communications, and project management.

▌ 2976

MASTER OF SCIENCE IN E-BUSINESS

UNIVERSITY OF WISCONSIN

BUSINESS ADMINISTRATION

PO Box 742
Milwaukee, WI 53201
PH: (414)229-5403
FX: (414)229-2372
E-mail: uwmbusmasters@uwm.edu
URL: http://www.uwm.edu/Dept/Business

Description: The University of Wisconsin offers a Master of Science degree in E-Business. This program is designed to train executives in both the technology and business aspects of e-business. The program concludes with a practicum during which students work in multi-disciplinary teams with a faculty adviser to develop a working solution to a real e-business challenge provided by an industrial affiliate.

▌ 2977

MASTER OF SCIENCE DEGREE IN E-BUSINESS

UNIVERSITY OF WYOMING, LARAMIE

SOLOMON D. TRUJILLO CENTER FOR E.BUSINESS

PO Box 3275
Laramie, WY 82071
PH: (307)766-6902
E-mail: e-biz@uwyo.edu
URL: http://uwadmnweb.uwyo.edu/e-biz/
Contact: Dr. Kenton Walker, Director

Description: The University of Wyoming's Solomon D. Trujillo Center for e.Business offers a Master of Science degree in e-business. The program features an equal portion of computer science and business coursework. The program incorporates a team-based curriculum that is offered in Laramie, Wyoming. The students will learn to create new products, processes, and services that leverage technology to improve business, as well as to lead and manage technology based organizations.

▌ 2978

MASTER OF SCIENCE IN E-COMMERCE

NATIONAL GRADUATE SCHOOL OF QUALITY MANAGEMENT

PO Box 674
Falmouth, MA 02541
PH: (508)457-1313
TF: 800-838-2580
FX: (508)457-5347
E-mail: info@nationalgradschool.org
URL: http://www.nationalgradschool.org

Description: The National School of Quality Management offers a Master of Science degree in E-Commerce. This program focuses on comprehensive skills necessary to manage e-commerce organizations.

▌ 2979

MASTER OF SCIENCE WITH E-COMMERCE CONCENTRATION

OLD DOMINION UNIVERSITY

COLLEGE OF BUSINESS AND PUBLIC ADMINISTRATION

49th St. and Hampton Blvd., Hughes Hall
Norfolk, VA 23529
PH: (757)683-3585
FX: (757)683-5750
E-mail: admit@odu.edu
URL: http://www.odu.edu

Description: Old Dominion University offers a Master of Science degree with a concentration in E-Commerce. This degree will provide instruction in all facets of managing an e-business, including supply chain management, information systems, data mining, Internet marketing and legal issues.

▌2980

MASTER OF SCIENCE IN ELECTRONIC BUSINESS MANAGEMENT

NOTRE DAME DE NAMUR UNIVERSITY CALIFORNIA
BUSINESS AND MANAGEMENT

1500 Ralston Ave.
Belmont, CA 94002-1997
PH: (650)508-3782
FX: (650)508-3476
E-mail: grad.admit@ndnu.edu
URL: http://www.ndnu.edu

Description: Notre Dame de Namur University California offers a Master of Science in Electronic Business Management. This degree program is designed to develop managers who can manage new ways of doing business in the emerging digital economy. The program targets students who will take leadership positions in companies who are shifting into Electronic Business and Internet Marketing.

▌2981

MASTER OF SCIENCE IN ELECTRONIC COMMERCE

UNIVERSITY OF MEMPHIS

Graduate Admissions Office
216 Administration Bldg.
Memphis, TN 38152-3370
PH: (901)678-2531
E-mail: mgarzon@memphis.edu
URL: http://www.memphis.edu
Contact: Dr. Max Garzon, Program Coordinator

Description: In response to the need to educate people in the e-commerce field, the Master of Science in Electronic Commerce program was developed by the faculty of the University of Memphis to promote technology education and research support and make available the appropriate expertise to competitively enter the new digital age.

▌2982

MASTER OF SCIENCE IN ELECTRONIC COMMERCE

UNIVERSITY OF SAN DIEGO
SCHOOL OF BUSINESS, ELECTRONIC COMMERCE

5998 Alcala Park
San Diego, CA 92110
PH: (619)260-4524
FX: (619)260-4158
E-mail: grads@sandiego.edu
URL: http://www.sandiego.edu

Description: San Diego State University offers a Master of Science degree in Electronic Commerce. This program combines business and technology courses. The ten-course program includes three main elements. The tools element includes courses in Web site design, computer networking, and Web applications, while the breadth element includes information on law and ethics. The capstone element consists of students working with faculty members on a research project.

▌2983

MASTER OF SCIENCE IN ELECTRONIC COMMERCE

CLAREMONT GRADUATE UNIVERSITY
INFORMATION SCIENCE DEPT.

130 E 9th St.
Claremont, CA 91711-6190
PH: (909)621-8209
FX: (909)621-8564
E-mail: webmaster@cgu.edu
URL: http://www.cgu.edu

Description: Claremont Graduate University offers a MS in Electronic Commerce (MSEC). This degree program integrates technical, organizational and systems elements in the coursework to enable students to interact effectively with the technical specialists in their organization, and to understand the management of computer information systems.

▌2984

MASTER OF SCIENCE IN ELECTRONIC COMMERCE

CAPITOL COLLEGE
GRADUATE SCHOOL

11301 Springfield Rd.
Laurel, MD 20708
PH: (301)369-2800
TF: 800-950-1992
FX: (301)953-1442
E-mail: gradschool@capitol-college.edu
URL: http://www.capitol-college.edu

Description: Capitol College offers a MS in Electronic Commerce. In this degree program students will look at e-commerce as it pertains to enabling technologies and organization development. Other issues examined are technical and management.

▌2985

MASTER OF SCIENCE IN ELECTRONIC COMMERCE

BARRY UNIVERSITY
ANDREAS SCHOOL OF BUSINESS, ELECTRONIC COMMERCE

11300 NE 2nd Ave.
Miami Shores, FL 33161-6695
PH: (305)899-3535
TF: 800-289-1111
FX: (305)892-6412
E-mail: jpoza@mail.barry.edu
URL: http://www.barry.edu

Description: Barry University offers a MS in Electronic Commerce. This program will give students skills in marketing in the Internet environment, technical skills related to Internet projects, and general knowledge of business processes.

▪ 2986

MASTER OF SCIENCE IN ELECTRONIC COMMERCE

NATIONAL UNIVERSITY

11255 N Torrey Pines Rd
La Jolla, CA 92037
PH: 800-628-8648
TF: 800-628-8648
E-mail: rvainer@nu.edu
URL: http://www.online.nu.edu/
Contact: Renata Vainer, Advisor

Description: National University offers an online degree of Master of Science in Electronic Commerce. This degree prepares students to meet the demands of business over the Internet. This program offers students the educational opportunities that will prepare them for designing, managing, consulting and teaching Internet-based business and commerce.

▪ 2987

MASTER OF SCIENCE IN INTERNET BUSINESS SYSTEMS

MERCY COLLEGE
INTERNET BUSINESS SYSTEMS

555 Broadway
Dobbs Ferry, NY 10522
PH: (914)674-7306
TF: 800-637-2969
FX: (914)674-7518
E-mail: admissions@mercy.edu
URL: http://www.mercynet.edu

Description: Mercy College offers a Master of Science in Internet Business Systems. This degree program gives students the knowledge and skills necessary to be successful in the field of Internet business. The curriculum focuses on developing a strong background in business, technology and design while stressing collaborative processes and communication skills.

▪ 2988

MASTER OF SCIENCE DEGREE IN INTERNET ENGINEERING

MARLBORO COLLEGE GRADUATE CENTER

28 Vernon St., Ste. 120
Brattleboro, VT 05301
PH: (802)258-9200
TF: 888-258-5665
FX: (802)258-9201
E-mail: gradcenter@marlboro.edu
URL: http://www.gradcenter.marlboro.edu

Description: Marlboro College offers a Master of Science degree in Internet Engineering. This graduate degree program provides advanced programming and database training that employs state-of-the-art technological and business practices, and will enable students to create and maintain high-end web sites.

▪ 2989

MASTER OF SCIENCE IN INTERNET STRATEGY MANAGEMENT

MARLBORO COLLEGE
THE GRADUATE CENTER

28 Vermont St. Ste. 120
Brattleboro, VT 05301
PH: (802)258-9200
TF: 888-258-5665
FX: (802)258-9201
E-mail: gradcenter@marlboro.edu
URL: http://www.gradcenter.marlboro.edu/academics/academics.html

Description: Marlboro College offers a Master of Science in Internet Strategy Management degree. This program prepares students to lead the development and management of an organization's Internet and Intranet strategy, offering coursework that incorporates theoretical and strategic issues, technology, design, and marketing, utilizing up to date technological and business practices.

▪ 2990

MASTER OF SCIENCE DEGREE IN SYSTEMS INTEGRATION MANAGEMENT

MARLBORO COLLEGE GRADUATE CENTER

28 Vernon St., Ste. 120
Brattleboro, VT 05301
PH: (802)258-9200
TF: 888-258-5665
FX: (802)258-9201
E-mail: gradcenter@marlboro.edu
URL: http://www.gradcenter.marlboro.edu

Description: Marlboro College offers a Master of Science degree in Systems Integration Management. This degree program prepares students to lead complex systems integration projects that information technology companies face, offering training that incorporates conceptual and tactical issues, technology, information design, and leadership strategies.

▪ 2991

MASTER OF SCIENCE IN TECHNOLOGY MANAGEMENT

UNIVERSITY AT STONY BROOK (SUNY)
W. AVERELL HARRIMAN SCHOOL FOR MANAGEMENT AND POLICY

Harriman Hall
Stony Brook, NY 11794-3775
PH: (516)632-7744
FX: (516)632-9412
E-mail: ann.carvalho@sunysb.edu
URL: http://www.sunysb.edu/

Description: The University at Stony Brook offers a Master of Science in Technology Management. This degree program is an executive program designed for students with professional experience in technical fields who wish to improve managerial skills.

■ **2992**

MASTERS OF SCIENCE IN E-COMMERCE

GEORGE MASON UNIVERSITY
DEPARTMENT OF COMPUTER SCIENCE

MSN 4A5
4400 University Dr.
Fairfax, VA 22030
PH: (703)993-1530
FX: (703)993-1710
E-mail: csadmin@cs.gmu.edu
URL: http://ite.gmu.edu/msecomm/description.htm
Contact: Daniel A. Menasce, Program Director

Description: George Mason University offers a Masters of Science degree in E-Commerce. This degree program is designed to prepare graduates with the information they need to take advantage of electronic commerce opportunities in commercial and enterprise management in the "new economy." They will be able to understand management, public policy, and information technology aspects, and effectively integrate these in developing electronic commerce solutions.

■ **2993**

MASTERS OF SCIENCE IN ELECTRONIC COMMERCE

CARNEGIE MELLON INSTITUTE FOR E-COMMERCE

Tech and Frew Sts.
Pittsburgh, PA 15213
PH: (412)268-2307
TF: 877-544-3266
FX: (412)268-6837
E-mail: tridas@andrew.cmu.edu
URL: http://www.ecom.cmu.edu
Contact: Dr. Tridas Mukopadhyay, Director

Description: Offered by the Carnegie Mellon Institute for eCommerce, a joint program of two top graduate programs, the Masters of Science in Electronic Commerce offers a unique curriculum. World-renowned faculty from Carnegie Mellon's Graduate School of Industrial Administration and School of Computer Science teach a mix of business and technology courses. The final Practicum project gives student teams the opportunity to apply the coursework by working on a real world business problem with corporate sponsors.

■ **2994**

MBA CERTIFICATE PROGRAM IN E-BUSINESS

UNIVERSITY OF WASHINGTON
COLLEGE OF BUSINESS
E-BUSINESS PROGRAM

Box 353200
Seattle, WA 98195-3200
PH: (206)543-8749
E-mail: uwebiz@u.washington.edu
URL: http://depts.washington.edu/ebiz/
Contact: Jim Jiambalvo, Faculty Director

Description: The MBA Certificate Program in E-Business at the University of Washington prepares business leaders to think creatively, and critically about the strategic use of information technology to create value. To earn the Certificate, students complete a series of courses; participate in quarterly workshops, executive roundtables, and our annual e-business conference. They also work as a member of a team to complete an e-business research project, case study, consulting engagement, or business plan; and will participate in development of a prototype e-business system.

■ **2995**

MBA PROGRAM WITH A SPECIALIZATION IN E-BUSINESS

PURDUE UNIVERSITY
KRANNERT GRADUATE SCHOOL OF MANAGEMENT

1310 Krannert Bldg.
West Lafayette, IN 47907
PH: (765)494-9700
FX: (765)494-9658
E-mail: krannert_ms@mgmt.purdue.edu
URL: http://www.mgmt.purdue.edu/centers/ceer/

Description: Purdue University's Krannert Graduate School of Management offers an MBA degree with a specialization in E-Business. This degree program includes core management courses as well as coursework focused on e-business.

■ **2996**

MBA PROGRAM WITH AN E-COMMERCE CONCENTRATION

BAKER COLLEGE

1116 W Bristol Rd.
Flint, MI 48507-9843
PH: (810)766-4390
TF: 800-469-3165
FX: (810)766-4399
E-mail: gradschl@baker.edu
URL: http://www.baker.edu

Description: Baker College offers an MBA degree with an E-Commerce concentration. This program is designed to give students a managerial overview of e-commerce focusing on the processes involved in developing, creating and managing an e-business.

■ **2997**

MBA EBUSINESS TRACK AND EBUSINESS EXECUTIVE EDUCATION CURRICULUM

MASSACHUSETTS INSTITUTE OF TECHNOLOGY
SLOAN SCHOOL OF MANAGEMENT
CENTER FOR EBUSINESS@MIT

MIT NE20-336
Cambridge, MA 02142
PH: (617)253-7054
FX: (617)452-3231
E-mail: ebusiness@mit.edu

URL: http://ebusiness.mit.edu
Contact: Peter Metz, Executive Director

Description: Building on over 30 years of research on the internet, The MIT Sloan School of Management created the Center for eBusiness@MIT to provide leadership for faculty, students, and industry interested in Internet-enabled business. Both an MBA eBusiness track, and eBusiness executive education curriculum are offered, as well as large scale research programs funded by industry leaders.

■ **2998**

MBA IN ELECTRONIC COMMERCE

NEW YORK UNIVERSITY

STERN SCHOOL OF BUSINESS

DIGITAL ECONOMY INITIATIVE

Henry Kaufman Management Center

44 W Fourth St.

New York, NY 10012

PH: (212)998-0100

E-mail: dei@stern.nyu.edu

URL: http://www.stern.nyu.edu/dei/education.html1

Description: This MBA program offers a degree for students interested in specializing in the digital economy. Courses include Managing the Digital Firm, Information and Internet Technologies, Electronic Communities, and Marketing of High-Tech Products.

■ **2999**

MBA IN ELECTRONIC COMMERCE

UNIVERSITY OF DALLAS

GRADUATE SCHOOL OF MANAGEMENT

1845 E Northgate Dr.

Irving, TX 75062

PH: (972)721-5000

E-mail: msavoie@udallas.edu

URL: http://gsmweb.udallas.edu/e_commerce_mba.htm

Description: The University of Dallas Graduate School of Management offers an MBA in Electronic Commerce. This degree program provides students with information about the management of Electronic Commerce through marketing, web technology, and site design & development.This MBA program is offered online or onsite.

■ **3000**

MBA WITH AN ELECTRONIC COMMERCE CONCENTRATION

VIRGINIA TECH

PAMPLIN COLLEGE OF BUSINESS

CENTER FOR GLOBAL ELECTRONIC COMMERCE

Pamplin 28

Blacksburg, VA 24061

PH: (540)231-6720

E-mail: ecommerce@vt.edu/

URL: http://www.cob.vt.edu/cgec/

Contact: Dr. France Belanger, Director

Description: The Center for Global Electronic Commerce offers a MBA with an Electronic Commerce Concentration. Courses in the program explore technical aspects such as design of web-based systems and databases, as well as legal, regulatory, financial, managerial, and marketing aspects of e-commerce.

■ **3001**

MBA IN MANAGING ELECTRONIC COMMERCE

WHARTON SCHOOL-UNIVERSITY OF PENNSYLVANIA

Office of MBA Admissions

102 Vance Hall

3733 Spruce St.

Philadelphia, PA 19104-6361

PH: (215)898-6183

FX: (215)898-0120

E-mail: mba.admissions@wharton.upenn.edu

URL: http://www.wharton.upenn.edu

Staff: 199. **Description:** The MBA in Managing Electronic Commerce deals with the design and implementation of effective strategies related to the use of e-commerce and is intended to provide an in-depth foundation for those interested in pursuing ventures specifically focused on the Internet and traditional product/service firms that are attempting to define the appropriate role for e-commerce. It also provides a useful basis for consulting to both of these types of organizations. Non-majors interested in an overview of business and policy in the electronic commerce area should also find selected courses from this major of interest.

■ **3002**

MBA/MS IN E-BUSINESS

FOX SCHOOL-TEMPLE UNIVERSITY

Speakman Hall, Rm. 5

Philadelphia, PA 19122

PH: (215)204-7678

E-mail: foxmbams.info@temple.edu

URL: http://www.sbm.temple.edu

Description: Fox School's MBA/MS in E-Business is full-time program educating students for e-business enterprise. It combines advanced knowledge of management strategy with a solid understanding of information systems and e-business concepts and practices and provides intensive, practical coverage of applicable business and technology topics plus an entrepreneurial project for a Web-based start-up business and a summer integrative experience. Students can complete the course in two years with an optional 10-week business core over the summer.

■ **3003**

MBA/MS IN E-BUSINESS

TEMPLE UNIVERSITY

FOX SCHOOL OF BUSINESS AND MANAGEMENT

5 Speakman Hall

1810 N 13th St.

Philadelphia, PA 19122

PH: (215)204-7678
E-mail: foxmbams.info@temple.edu
URL: http://www.sbm.temple.edu/mbams/

Description: The MBA/MS in E-Business program educates students for e-business enterprises. The program combines advanced knowledge of management strategy with an understanding of information systems and e-business concepts and practices. The program will provide intensive, practical coverage of applicable business and technology topics.

∎ 3004

MBA PROGRAM IN ELECTRONIC COMMERCE

STANFORD BUSINESS SCHOOL
CENTER FOR ELECTRONIC BUSINESS AND COMMERCE

518 Memorial Way
Stanford, CA 94305-5015
PH: (650)725-5663
FX: (650)723-3950
E-mail: cebc@gsb.stanford.edu
URL: http://www.gsb.stanford.edu/CEBC/
Contact: Garth Saloner, Center Co-Director

Description: The Stanford Business School Center for Electronic Business and Commerce provides coursework for those interested in an MBA, as well as courses for practicing managers who wish to focus on electronic commerce. Course programs include The Electronic Business and Commerce Executive Program, Strategic Uses of Information Technology, Legal Issues in E-Commerce, and E-Business and Supply Chain Management.

∎ 3005

MBA SPECIALIZATION IN E-COMMERCE

WORCESTER POLYTECHNIC INSTITUTE

100 Institute Rd.
Worcester, MA 01609
PH: (508)831-5218
FX: (508)831-5720
URL: http://www.wpi.edu
Contact: McRae Banks, Department Head

Founded: 1865. **Description:** The Worchester Polytechnic Institute offers an MBA Specialization in E-Commerce program within their MBA program. The intent of the specialization is to educate MBA students in both the broad areas of business and to provide them with an understanding of the full range of opportunities for e-commerce within organizations. To satisfy the specialization requirements, students must complete the Supply Chain Management and Electronic Commerce, Marketing and Electronic Commerce, Telecommunications Management and Electronic Commerce and either Managing Organizational Change, Project Management or New Venture Management and Entrepreneurship courses.

∎ 3006

MEASURING AND EVALUATING E-BUSINESS PERFORMANCE

SOLOMON D. TRUJILLO CENTER FOR E.BUSINESS

University of Wyoming
College of Business
PO Box 3275
Laramie, WY 82071
PH: (307)766-6902
E-mail: e-biz@uwyo.edu
URL: http://www.uwyo.edu
Contact: Dr. Kenton Walker, Director

Description: Measuring and Evaluating E-Business Performance discusses performance reporting structure and content issues for different groups of stakeholders. Covered topics include budgets and variances, performance models, balanced scorecard reporting, financial statements, audits, concepts in efficiency and effectiveness, and customer satisfaction measures.

∎ 3007

METRICS: MEASURING THE EFFECTS OF ECM CHANGE

SAN JOSE STATE UNIVERSITY
PROFESSIONAL DEVELOPMENT CENTER

3031 Tisch Way, Ste. 200 Plz. E
San Jose, CA 95128
PH: (408)257-3000
E-mail: mitchell.levy.sjsupd@ecnow.com
URL: http://ecmtraining.com/sjsu/
Contact: Mitchell Levy, Program Founder and Coordinator

Description: San Jose State University offers a course called "Metrics: Measuring the Effects of ECM Change." In this course students will learn how to develop metrics that measure the changes in the business processes used for e-commerce and that are still linked to the overall measurements of the business.

∎ 3008

MIS MBA WITH A CONCENTRATION IN ELECTRONIC COMMERCE

UNIVERSITY OF GEORGIA
TERRY COLLEGE OF BUSINESS

346 Brooks Hall
Athens, GA 30602-6264
PH: (706)542-8100
FX: (706)542-3835
E-mail: mcrask@terry.uga.edu
URL: http://www.terry.uga.edu
Contact: Dr. Mel Crask, Director, MBA Programs

Description: The University of Georgia Terry College of Business offers a MIS MBA with a concentration in Electronic Commerce. This program is for those students who want to gain electronic commerce skills. The curriculum consists of coursework in marketing, information technology and strategy.

▌3009

MOBILE COMMERCE AND TECHNOLOGY

ILLINOIS INSTITUTE OF TECHNOLOGY
STUART GRADUATE SCHOOL OF BUSINESS

565 W Adams St.
Chicago, IL 60661
PH: (312)906-6500
FX: (312)906-6549
E-mail: degrees@stuart.iit.edu
URL: http://www.stuart.iit.edu

Description: The Illinois Institute of Technology Stuart Graduate School of Business offers a course entitled Mobile Commerce and Technology. This course looks at different wireless telecommunications industries, and approaches the subject from a business and stock market perspective with students following wireless companies as wireless, Internet, and e-commerce technologies merge.

▌3010

M.S. DEGREE IN INFORMATION AGE MARKETING

BENTLEY COLLEGE

175 Forest St.
Waltham, MA 02452-4705
PH: (781)891-2000
URL: http://www.bentley.edu

Description: Bentley College offers a M.S. degree in Information Age Marketing. This degree program prepares students for success in the technologically changing global marketplace. The curriculum includes strategic marketing for the information economy as well as fundamentals of marketing practice. Students learn about the latest technologies and practices in marketing.

▌3011

M.S. DEGREE IN INFORMATION TECHNOLOGY

BENTLEY COLLEGE

175 Forest St.
Waltham, MA 02452-4705
PH: (781)891-2000
URL: http://www.bentley.edu

Description: Bentley College offers a M.S. degree in Information Technology. In this degree program students will study programming, systems analysis and design, telecommunications, and data management, all with an e-business focus. This develops students' expertise in building, managing and using the systems that drive e-business. Graduates of this degree program are prepared for a variety of positions in e-business information technology.

▌3012

MSC DEGREE IN E-BUSINESS

ASTON UNIVERSITY
ASTON CENTRE FOR E-BUSINESS

Birmingham B47ET, United Kingdom
PH: 440121 359 7293
FX: 440121 359 5267
E-mail: a.j.broderick@aston.ac.uk
URL: http://www.abs.aston.ac.uk/ace.biz/

Description: The Aston Centre for E-Business offers an MSc degree in e-Business. The curriculum includes courses on e-marketing, e-business logistics and operations, and e-commerce law and ethics.

▌3013

NET AUCTION MASTERS COURSE

COMPUTER BASED TRAINING

19 Nations Hill, Kings Worthy
Winchester, Hants SO237QY, United Kingdom
PH: 44 0 1962 883754
FX: 44 0 1962 889177
E-mail: freecourses@computerbasedtraining.co.uk
URL: http://www.computerbasedtraining.co.uk

Description: Computer Based Training offers a free online course called "Net Auction Masters Course." This course will teach students how to utilize auctions to create an e-business.

▌3014

NET MARKET MAKER SUCCESS-CONTENT, TRAFFIC, AND REVENUE

SAN JOSE STATE UNIVERSITY
PROFESSIONAL DEVELOPMENT CENTER

3031 Tisch Way, Ste. 200 Plz. E
San Jose, CA 95128
PH: (408)257-3000
E-mail: mitchell.levy.sjsupd@ecnow.com
URL: http://ecmtraining.com/sjsu/
Contact: Mitchell Levy, Program Founder and Coordinator

Description: San Jose State University offers a course called "Driving Net Market Maker Success-Content, Traffic, and Revenue." This course focuses on keys to success for any Net Market Maker-appropriate content, traffic generation and the building of scalable revenue. Real world examples will be examined. Students will obtain an understanding of the variables required to guarantee the success of a Net Market Making opportunity.

▌3015

NET WRITING MASTER COURSE

SITE SELL

68 Cote St. Charles
Hudson Heights, PQ, Canada J0P1J0
PH: (450)458-1064

FX: (450)458-1068
E-mail: info@sitesell.com
URL: http://www.sitesell.com

Description: Site Sell offers an online course called "Net Writing Master Course." This course teaches students to write effectively for their web sites.

▌ 3016

NETCENTRICITY AND BUSINESS IN THE DIGITAL AGE
CREIGHTON UNIVERSITY
JOE RICKETTS CENTER EXECUTIVE EDUCATION PROGRAMS

2500 California Plz.
Omaha, NE 68178
PH: (402)280-2439
FX: (402)280-5565
E-mail: rnath@creighton.edu
URL: http://www.creighton.edu
Contact: Dr. Ravi Nath, Director, Joe Ricketts Center

Description: Creighton University's Joe Ricketts Center offers an executive education course called Netcentricity and Business in the Digital Age. This three-hour course serves as an introduction to electronic business. Students will also gain understanding of the convergence of technologies, organizational barriers and success factors.

▌ 3017

NETWORK EFFECTS IN THE INFORMATION ECONOMY
CARDEAN UNIVERSITY

500 Lake Cook Rd.
Deerfield, IL 60015-5609
TF: (866)948-1289
E-mail: inquires@cardean.edu
URL: http://www.cardean.edu
Contact: Dr. Geoffrey M. Cox, Cardean University President

Description: Cardean University is an accredited online university which offers a offers a suite of courses called "Network Effects in the Information Economy." This suite of 4 two hour courses is designed to help students understand what influences product compatibility, standards, "open" versus "closed" systems, interconnection, and interfaces. It explores the influence of these dynamics on consumers, and is based on the book, Information Rules, by Carl Shapiro and Hal R. Varian.

▌ 3018

NETWORK AND TELECOMMUNICATIONS CONCEPTS
UNIVERSITY OF PHOENIX

3201 E Elwood St.
Phoenix, AZ 85034
PH: (480)966-5394

TF: 800-366-9699
URL: http://www.uoponline.com

Description: The University of Phoenix offers a course called Network and Telecommunications Concepts. This course functions as an overview of telecommunication systems in a business. Topics examined include telecommunication applications, standards, transmission, networks, computer telephony and management.

▌ 3019

NETWORKING FOR ELECTRONIC COMMERCE
DALHOUSIE UNIVERSITY

Faculty of Computer Science
6050 University Ave.
Halifax, NS, Canada B3H1W5
PH: (819)956-2289
FX: (819)956-7223
E-mail: emec@pwgsc.gc.ca
URL: http://www.ecomm.dal.ca

Founded: 2000. **Description:** Networking for Electronic Commerce gives students a foundation in computer networks and the Internet, and current methods and practices in the use of computer networks to enable communication are examined.

▌ 3020

NETWORKING INFRASTRUCTURE FOR E-BUSINESS
NORTH CAROLINA STATE UNIVERSITY
COLLEGE OF MANAGEMENT

Campus Box 7229
Raleigh, NC 27695-7229
PH: (919)513-1707
E-mail: ecommerce@ncsu.edu
URL: http://
Contact: Julie Earp, Professor

Description: North Carolina State University offers a course called "Networking Infrastructure for E-Business." This graduate level course gives students an introduction to the network infrastructure necessary for electronic commerce as well as for general business needs. Topics covered in this course include network technologies, architectures, security and applications.

▌ 3021

NETWORKING AND SECURITY ISSUES IN ELECTRONIC COMMERCE
CHRISTOPHER NEWPORT UNIVERSITY ONLINE

1 University Pl.
Newport News, VA 23606
PH: (757)594-7607
E-mail: online@cnu.edu
URL: http://ec.seva.net/

Description: Christopher Newport University and the Virginia Electronic Commerce Technology Center offer a course titled "Networking and Security Issues in Electronic Commerce." This online course will give students an understanding of computer networks and how they can be used to facilitate and EC development at their company.

∎ 3022

NETWORKING TECHNOLOGY

UNIVERSITY OF GEORGIA

TERRY COLLEGE OF BUSINESS

346 Brooks Hall
Athens, GA 30602-6264
PH: (706)542-8100
FX: (706)542-3835
E-mail: mcrask@terry.uga.edu
URL: http://www.terry.uga.edu
Contact: Dr. Mel Crask, Director, MBA Programs

Description: The University of Georgia Terry College of Business offers a course called Networking Technology. This course will give students a basic understanding of business data communications and networking.

∎ 3023

NETWORKS AND E-COMMERCE

UNIVERSITY OF CALIFORNIA LOS ANGELES

ANDERSON SCHOOL OF MANAGEMENT

Box 951481
110 Westwood Plz.
Los Angeles, CA 90095-1481
PH: (310)825-6121
FX: (310)206-9830
E-mail: ageoffri@agsm.ucla.edu
URL: http://www.anderson.ucla.edu

Description: UCLA's Anderson School of Business offers a course entitled Networks and E-commerce. This course covers the network and communications technology, use of the Internet and intranets, trends in the technology, and business applications in electronic commerce and business processes. Specific topics include: electronic commerce, evaluating web sites, development of an Internet web, and using the web to gather business data.

∎ 3024

NETWORKS AND ELECTRONIC COMMERCE

UNIVERSITY OF SOUTHERN CALIFORNIA

MARSHALL SCHOOL OF BUSINESS

HOH 800, MC 1421
Los Angeles, CA 90089
PH: (213)740-6422
FX: (213)740-5432
E-mail: rwesterfield@sba.usc.edu
URL: http://www.usc.edu/dept/publications/cat2001/business/
Contact: Randolph W. Westerfield, Dean

Description: The University of Southern California offers a course titled "Networks and Electronic Commerce." This course looks at computer networks and the Internet, electronic commerce, and web application development.

∎ 3025

NEW PARADIGMS IN ELECTRONIC COMMERCE MARKETING AND DISTRIBUTION

DREXEL UNIVERSITY

LEBOW COLLEGE OF BUSINESS

3141 Chestnut St.
Matheson Hall, Rm. 105
Philadelphia, PA 19104
PH: (215)895-6070
FX: (215)895-1012
E-mail: marcos@drexel.edu.
URL: http://www.drexel.edu/academics/lebow/ecomm/

Description: Drexel University offers an executive education course called New Paradigms in Electronic Commerce Marketing and Distribution. This course looks at various models in the strategy of electronic commerce. Other topics examined include new value propositions created by e-Commerce, channel flows in cyberspace, delayed profit models, first mover advantage, brand equity, lifetime value of customers, micro marketing via the Internet, and customer service through the Internet space.

∎ 3026

NEXT GENERATION B2B E-COMMERCE TECHNOLOGIES

24/7 UNIVERSITY, INC.

16980 Dallas Pky., Ste. 247
Dallas, TX 75248
PH: (972)248-2470
E-mail: info@247university.com
URL: http://www.247university.com

Description: 24/7 University offers an online course called Next Generation B2B E-Commerce Technologies. This program explores the next generation of B2B e-commerce, including key areas of innovation, the impact on business processes, and core technologies.

∎ 3027

ONLINE BUSINESS MANAGEMENT (BCIT)

BRITISH COLUMBIA INSTITUTE OF TECHNOLOGY

ADMINISTRATIVE MANAGEMENT

3700 Willingdon Ave.
Burnaby, BC, Canada V5G3H2
PH: (604)451-7134
E-mail: wendy_lee@bcit.ca
URL: http://online.bcit.ca/de/Ecomm.htm
Contact: Wendy Lee

Description: The British Columbia Institute of Technology (BCIT) offers an online course titled "Online Business Management." This course will teach students skills in analysis of web sites. Topics include brainstorming and goal analysis, site host needs and transactions, security systems, advertising and promotion, and site and host measurements. This is a research course where students will prepare a business proposal for a new company.

▌3028

ONLINE COMMUNITIES TO DRIVE E-COMMERCE: WHAT, WHY AND HOW
SAN JOSE STATE UNIVERSITY
PROFESSIONAL DEVELOPMENT CENTER

3031 Tisch Way, Ste. 200 Plz. E
San Jose, CA 95128
PH: (408)257-3000
E-mail: mitchell.levy.sjsupd@ecnow.com
URL: http://ecmtraining.com/sjsu/
Contact: Mitchell Levy, Program Founder and Coordinator

Description: San Jose State University offers a course called "Online Communities to Drive E-Commerce: What, Why and How." This course looks at the business aspects of online communities. Topics covered include translating community needs into Web software and getting a good return on investment from the web community - how community drives e-commerce.

▌3029

OPERATIONAL EXCELLENCE IN THE INTERNET ENVIRONMENT
NOTRE DAME DE NAMUR UNIVERSITY

1500 Ralston Ave.
Belmont, CA 94002-1997
PH: (650)508-3782
FX: (650)508-3660
E-mail: ebusiness@ndnu.edu
URL: http://www.ndnu.edu

Description: Notre Dame de Namur University offers a graduate course called Operational Excellence in the Internet Environment. In this course students will research the role that technology plays in shaping the Internet and developing new practices. Students will also look at market data of trends, operational challenges, and the movement of information technology to the Internet.

▌3030

OPERATIONS MANAGEMENT: E-BUSINESS AND SUPPLY CHAIN MANAGEMENT
WAKE FORREST UNIVERSITY
BABCOCK GRADUATE SCHOOL OF MANAGEMENT

PO Box 7659
1834 Wake Forest Rd.
Winston-Salem, NC 27106

PH: (336)758-5255; (336)758-5421
TF: 800-722-1622
FX: (336)758-5830
URL: http://www.mba.wfu.edu

Founded: 1969. **Description:** Operations Management: E-Business and Supply Chain Management provides students with a background in supply chain management and its interface with Electronic Commerce

▌3031

ORGANIZATIONAL COMMUNICATIONS
UNIVERSITY OF PHOENIX

3201 E Elwood St.
Phoenix, AZ 85034
PH: (480)966-5394
TF: 800-366-9699
URL: http://www.uoponline.com

Description: The University of Phoenix offers a course called Organizational Communications. This undergraduate course focuses on communications issues in a global high tech environment. Students will gain understanding of the methods and processes necessary for effective communications in both physical and electronic situations.

▌3032

ORGANIZATIONS AND ELECTRONIC COMMERCE
UNIVERSITY OF NEW BRUNSWICK-SAINT JOHN
FACULTY OF BUSINESS

PO Box 5050
Saint John, NB, Canada E2L4L5
PH: (506)648-5570; (506)648-5806
TF: 800-508-6275
FX: (506)648-5574
E-mail: business@unbsj.ca
URL: http://www.unbsj.ca/business
Contact: Shelley Rinehart, Dean, Faculty of Business

Description: Organizations and Electronic Commerce (BA 4506) focuses on the internal changes that happen in an organization when it implements e-commerce with considerations in redesign of organizational structures, jobs, processes and workflow. Intranets, extranets and enterprise integration will also be explored. Prerequisites include completing courses BA 2123, BA 2663, BA 2672 and BA 3718, BA 3125 or BA 3305.

▌3033

ORGANIZATIONS AND TECHNOLOGY
UNIVERSITY OF PHOENIX

3201 E Elwood St.
Phoenix, AZ 85034
PH: (480)966-5394
TF: 800-366-9699
URL: http://www.uoponline.com

Description: The University of Phoenix offers a course called Organizations and Technology. This undergraduate course looks at organizational theory as it relates to technology. Included is an examination of the effects of technology on organizational structures; alignment of processes, and organizational management issues in cyberspace.

∎ 3034
OVERVIEW OF COMPUTER AND INTERNET TECHNOLOGY
DREXEL UNIVERSITY
LEBOW COLLEGE OF BUSINESS

3141 Chestnut St.
Matheson Hall, Rm. 105
Philadelphia, PA 19104
PH: (215)895-6070
FX: (215)895-1012
E-mail: marcos@drexel.edu.
URL: http://www.drexel.edu/academics/lebow/ecomm/

Description: Drexel University offers a course called Overview of Computer and Internet Technology. This course is geared towards those who have little or no background in computers or electronics. Students will be introduced to the terminology and concepts involved in modern electronics, telecommunications, networks, and the Internet.

∎ 3035
OVERVIEW OF ELECTRONIC COMMERCE
DALHOUSIE UNIVERSITY

Faculty of Computer Science
6050 University Ave.
Halifax, NS, Canada B3H1W5
PH: (902)494-2740
FX: (902)492-1517
E-mail: mec@cs.dal.ca
URL: http://www.ecomm.dal.ca
Contact: Dr. Kori Inkpen, Dir., Master of E-Commerce Program

Description: Overview of Electronic Commerce examines issues in global e-commerce and the impact of the interaction and interdependencies of technology, business, and policy on e-commerce.

∎ 3036
PLANNING AND DESIGNING E-COMMERCE PROJECTS
REGIS UNIVERSITY
GRADUATE PROGRAMS

3333 Regis Boulevard, L-16
Denver, CO 80221-1099
PH: (303)458-4080
TF: 800-667-9270
FX: (303)964-5538
E-mail: masters@regis.edu
URL: http://www.regis.edu

Description: Regis University offers a course called Planning and Designing E-Commerce Projects. This course gives students the opportunity to apply systems analysis principles and project management techniques to the planning and design of an E-Commerce project.

∎ 3037
PLANNING A WEBSITE
DIGITALTHINK INC

601 Brannan St.
San Francisco, CA 94107
PH: (415)625-4000
TF: 888-686-8817
FX: (415)625-4100
E-mail: info@digitalthink.com
URL: http://www.digitalthink.com
Contact: Mr. Pete Goettner, Chairman

Founded: 1996. **Staff:** 450. **Description:** Founded in 1996, DigitalThink offers an online course called ''Planning a Website.'' This class gives corporate professionals and interested individuals a survey of the practices and procedures for planning Web sites. It provides those new to website building with the foundation necessary to identify a site's goals, audience, content, and hardware and software requirements.

∎ 3038
PRICING DECISIONS IN THE INFORMATION ECONOMY
CARDEAN UNIVERSITY

500 Lake Cook Rd.
Deerfield, IL 60015-5609
TF: (866)948-1289
E-mail: inquires@cardean.edu
URL: http://www.cardean.edu
Contact: Dr. Geoffrey M. Cox, Cardean University President

Description: Cardean University is an accredited online university which offers a suite of courses entitled ''Pricing Decisions in the Information Economy.'' This series of 4 two hour courses is for managers who wish to explore pricing principles by demonstrating how companies can increase revenue by using personalized pricing techniques, versioning, and bundling. This course is based on the book, Information Rules, by Carl Shapiro and Hal R. Varian.

∎ 3039
PRICING MASTER COURSE
COMPUTER BASED TRAINING

19 Nations Hill, Kings Worthy
Winchester, Hants SO237QY, United Kingdom
PH: 44 0 1962 883754
FX: 44 0 1962 889177
E-mail: freecourses@computerbasedtraining.co.uk
URL: http://www.computerbasedtraining.co.uk

Description: Computer Based Training offers a free online course called "Pricing Master Course." This course looks at issues in finding the optimum price for your product or service, including information on checking your competitors pricing.

∎ 3040

PRINCIPLES OF E-MARKETING
OHIO STATE UNIVERSITY
FISHER COLLEGE OF BUSINESS

2100 Neil Ave.
Columbus, OH 43210-1144
PH: (614)292-8150
E-mail: hanser.3@osu.edu
URL: http://fisher.osu.edu/marketing/courses/au01/841-de-rosa-au01.htm
Contact: Joseph A. Alutto, Dean

Description: Ohio State University offers a graduate level course called "Principles of E-Marketing." This course focuses on marketing management and strategy, research, advertising and services as they relate to use of Internet technologies.

∎ 3041

PRINCIPLES OF EFFECTIVE E-COMMERCE
DUKE UNIVERSITY
DEPARTMENT OF COMPUTER SCIENCES

Box 90129
Durham, NC 27708
PH: (919)660-6524
E-mail: lucic@cs.duke.edu
URL: http://www.cs.duke.edu/education/courses/fall01/cps181s/
Contact: Richard Lucic, Instructor

Description: Duke University offers an undergraduate course entitled "Principles of Effective E-Commerce" which explores issues related to planning and deploying e-commerce business solutions. Using experience in web storefront development and basic principles of organization, strategic planning, and analysis, students will identify the skills all successful e-commerce developers need to know.

∎ 3042

PRINCIPLES OF INTERNET MARKETING
BELLEVUE UNIVERSITY

1000 Galvin Rd. S
Bellevue, NE 68005
PH: (402)293-2000
TF: 800-756-7920
FX: (402)293-2020
URL: http://www.bellevue.edu

Description: Bellevue University offers an E-Business course called "Principles of Internet Marketing." This course looks at marketing as applied to the Internet. Topics covered include the psychology of web marketing, strategies for building online brands and extending existing brands on the web, fundamentals of E-tailing, buyer motivation, as well as ideas for increasing web presence and activity.

∎ 3043

PRINCIPLES OF INTERNET MARKETING
STANFORD UNIVERSITY
GRADUATE SCHOOL OF BUSINESS

518 Memorial Way
Stanford, CA 94305-5015
PH: (650)725-5663
FX: (650)723-3950
E-mail: cebc@gsb.stanford.edu
URL: http://www.gsb.stanford.edu/cebc/

Description: Stanford University's MBA program offers a course entitled "Principles of Internet Marketing." This course combines theoretical approaches, and hands-on experience to give students an understanding of implementing marketing on the Internet. The course looks at how existing organizations should combine the Internet with their traditional marketing approaches.

∎ 3044

PRODUCT STRATEGY IN THE DIGITAL ECONOMY
UNIVERSITY OF CALIFORNIA LOS ANGELES
ANDERSON SCHOOL OF MANAGEMENT

Box 951481
110 Westwood Plz.
Los Angeles, CA 90095-1481
PH: (310)825-6121
FX: (310)206-9830
E-mail: ageoffri@agsm.ucla.edu
URL: http://www.anderson.ucla.edu

Description: UCLA's Anderson School of Business offers Product Strategy in the Digital Economy. This class deals with high-technology product strategy — particularly how product strategy changes as we go through stages of the technology adoption life cycle. It also addresses product strategy when a group of companies are required to create a compelling reason to buy a whole product offering. After progressing though the technology adoption life cycle, this course looks at how competitive advantage can change throughout the cycle.

∎ 3045

PRODUCT USABILITY: SURVIVAL TECHNIQUES
USER INTERFACE ENGINEERING

242 Neck Rd.
Bradford, MA 01835
PH: (978)374-8300
FX: (978)374-9175
E-mail: uie@uie.com
URL: http://world.std.com/~uieweb/courses.htm

Description: User Interface Engineering offers a course called Product Usability: Survival Techniques. This course is offered at User Interface's sites in Boston, Austin, Seattle, and San Francisco; or can be offered at an individual company's place of business. In this course students will learn to keep their product or web site on track with continuous measurements. This course will also discuss how to prevent common usability problems by focusing on design basics.

∎ 3046

PROFESSIONAL EBUSINESS INTERNSHIP
TEXAS CHRISTIAN UNIVERSITY

The Neeley School of Business
TCU Box 298530
Fort Worth, TX 76129
PH: (817)257-7540
E-mail: j.mackay@tcu.edu
URL: http://www.tcu.edu
Contact: Dr. Jane Mackay, Program Director

Description: The Professional eBusiness Internship (EBUS 40013) course is a full-time internship with a corporation, a non-profit or governmental agency allowing the student to gain professional experience that will help integrate the theory and practice of Information systems. Students must have a senior standing before taking this course.

∎ 3047

PROFESSIONAL PRACTICUM IN E-COMMERCE
GOLDEN GATE UNIVERSITY
CYBERCAMPUS

536 Mission St.
San Francisco, CA 94105-2968
PH: (415)369-5250
TF: 888-874-2923
FX: (415)227-4502
E-mail: cybercampus@ggu.edu
URL: http://cybercampus.ggu.edu/

Description: Golden Gate University's online university, CyberCampus, offers a course titled "Professional Practicum in E-Commerce." This course gives students the opportunity to learn how to integrate the skills and technologies of an e-commerce business into a coherent whole. Students will study the functions of senior management using advanced case analysis, focusing on analysis the analysis, planning, and implementation of an e-commerce solution; and will carry out a team-based professional project in electronic commerce.

∎ 3048

PROJECTS IN E-COMMERCE
PURDUE UNIVERSITY
KRANNERT GRADUATE SCHOOL OF MANAGEMENT

1310 Krannert Bldg.
West Lafayette, IN 47907
PH: (765)494-9700

FX: (765)494-9658
E-mail: krannert_ms@mgmt.purdue.edu
URL: http://www.mgmt.purdue.edu/centers/ceer/

Description: Purdue University's Krannert Graduate School of Management offers a course entitled Projects in E-Commerce. In this course, which builds on previous electronic commerce courses, students will work in teams to complete an e-commerce project.

∎ 3049

PROJECTS IN ELECTRONIC BUSINESS
UNIVERSITY OF SCRANTON

Kania School of Management
Brennan Hall, Ste. 438
Scranton, PA 18510
PH: (570)941-7746
E-mail: kakumanu@scranton.edu
URL: http://www.scranton.edu
Contact: Dr. Parsed Kakumanu, Chair, Operation & Info. Mgmt. Dept.

Description: Projects in Electronic Business allows students to develop an e-commerce project that will be used to conduct online business. The purpose of the course is to integrate the Internet related technologies and the business knowledge acquired in the different courses to develop a working e-commerce site. Students will work in teams under the guidance of the instructor and will design, develop, implement and operate a secure content-rich e-commerce website to attract and retain customers. Students must complete Electronic Commerce course EC 461 Internet Applications Development before taking this course.

∎ 3050

PROMOTING AN EZINE
JER GROUP INC.
ONLINEWORKSHOPS.COM

56 Seabreeze Way
Dawsonville, GA 30534
PH: (706)216-3406
FX: (706)216-3979
E-mail: drjer@jergroup.com
URL: http://www.onlineworkshops.com
Contact: Dr. John E. Reid, Jr., President

Description: JER Group Inc. onlineworkshops.com offers a course focused on the ezine. It is called "Promoting an Ezine." This course will provide students information and techniques on processes and sources available to promote an ezine.

∎ 3051

PROMOTING YOUR WEB SITE
UNIVERSITY OF MINNESOTA EXTENSION SERVICE

240 Coffey Hall
1420 Eckles Ave.
St. Paul, MN 55108-6068
PH: (612)624-1222

E-mail: mainstreet@extension.umn.edu
URL: http://www.extension.umn.edu/mainstreet/curriculum/index.html

Description: The University of Minnesota Extension Service offers a course called Promoting Your Web Site. This course covers topics including developing an Internet marketing plan, press releases, measuring progress, and considering affiliate programs.

■ **3052**

PROVEN SUCCESS IN BUILDING AN E-BUSINESS

JER GROUP INC.

ONLINEWORKSHOPS.COM

56 Seabreeze Way
Dawsonville, GA 30534
PH: (706)216-3406
FX: (706)216-3979
E-mail: drjer@jergroup.com
URL: http://www.onlineworkshops.com
Contact: Dr. John E. Reid, Jr., President

Description: JER Group Inc. offers an online course on E-Commerce called ''Proven Success in Building an E-Business.'' This course covers information students will need on how to control the costs associated with starting an Internet business, as well as the language and technological information students need to make informed and educated e-business decisions.

■ **3053**

PUBLIC POLICY

MCGILL UNIVERSITY

FACULTY OF MANAGEMENT

1001 Sherbrooke St. W
Montreal, PQ, Canada H3A1G5
PH: (514)398-4000
FX: (514)398-3876
E-mail: gagnon@management.mcgill.ca
URL: http://www.intranet.management.mcgill.ca/course/mis/273434/CO273690_W00.htm

Description: McGill University in Montreal, Canada provides a course called ''Public Policy'' which students will learn about leading issues affecting the internet: intellectual property, privacy, taxation, backbone, capital.

■ **3054**

PUBLISHING AN EZINE

JER GROUP INC.

ONLINEWORKSHOPS.COM

56 Seabreeze Way
Dawsonville, GA 30534
PH: (706)216-3406
FX: (706)216-3979
E-mail: drjer@jergroup.com
URL: http://www.onlineworkshops.com

Contact: Dr. John E. Reid, Jr., President

Description: JER Group Inc. onlineworkshops.com offers a course called ''Publishing an Ezine.'' This course will give students the information necessary to plan, design, promote and publish an ezine.

■ **3055**

REDUCING THE FAILURE RATE OF TECHNOLOGY START-UPS

UNIVERSITY OF PITTSBURGH

CENTER FOR EXECUTIVE EDUCATION

Mellon Financial Corp. Hall, 5th Fl.
4227 Fifth Ave.
Pittsburgh, PA 15260
PH: (412)648-1600
E-mail: exeducation@katz.pitt.edu
URL: http://www.execed.pitt.edu/

Description: The Executive Education Program at the University of Pittsburgh offers a course called Reducing the Failure Rate of Technology Start-Ups. Containing valuable information for anyone looking to create a new tech company, this seminar focuses on building the organization necessary to increase the odds of commercial success.

■ **3056**

RELATIONSHIP MARKETING ON THE INTERNET

AMERICAN UNIVERSITY

KOGOD SCHOOL OF BUSINESS

4400 Massachusetts Ave., NW
Washington, DC 20016-8044
PH: (202)885-1900
E-mail: askkogod@american.edu
URL: http://www.kogod.american.edu
Contact: Myron Roomkin, Dean

Description: The American University offers a graduate level course titled ''Relationship Marketing on the Internet.'' This course examines the process of building and maintaining relationships with customers, suppliers, employees and the public through the Internet.

■ **3057**

RESTRUCTURING FOR ELECTRONIC BUSINESS THROUGH OBJECT ORIENTED MODELS

CAPITOL COLLEGE

11301 Springfield Rd.
Laurel, MD 20708
PH: (301)369-2800
TF: 800-950-1992
FX: (301)953-1442
E-mail: gradschool@capitol-college.edu
URL: http://www.capitol-college.edu

Description: Capitol College provides a graduate level course entitled Restructuring for Electronic Business Through Object Oriented Models. This course analyzes the use of object-oriented technologies in business process engineering and modeling. Students will prepare an object-oriented business model as part of this class.

▌3058

SCALING TECHNOLOGY FOR E-BUSINESS

GEORGE MASON UNIVERSITY
DEPARTMENT OF COMPUTER SCIENCE

MSN 4A5
4400 University Dr.
Fairfax, VA 22030
PH: (703)993-1530
FX: (703)993-1710
E-mail: csadmin@cs.gmu.edu
URL: http://cs.gmu.edu/syllabus/syllabi-fall01/it809-menasce.html

Description: George Mason University offers a course called "Scaling Technology for E-Business." This course examines the most important technologies used to support e-business sites. Topics covered include hardware and software, architectures of e-business sites, authentication, payment services, and understanding customer behavior.

▌3059

SECURE ELECTRONIC COMMERCE

IBM

1133 Westchester Ave.
White Plains, NY 10604
PH: 800-IBM-4YOU
TF: 800-IBM-4YOU
URL: http://security.polito.it/doc/ecomm/ibmtut/

Description: IBM offers an online tutorial called "Secure Electronic Commerce." This tutorial covers topics such as cryptography, secure end-to-end transport, public key infrastructure, payment systems and secure transfer of digital originals.

▌3060

SECURITY FOR ELECTRONIC COMMERCE

RUTGERS, THE STATE UNIVERSITY OF NEW JERSEY
CENTER FOR INFORMATION MANAGEMENT,
INTEGRATION & CONNECTIVITY

180 University Ave.
Newark, NJ 07102
PH: (973)353-1014
FX: (973)353-5808
E-mail: ec-certificate@cimic.rutgers.edu
URL: http://www.rutgers.edu

Description: Security for Electronic Commerce introduces the area of e-commerce and the security challenges and threats involved in e-commerce. The course provides an understanding of the e-commerce security technologies and discusses security requirements for e-commerce such as identification and authentication, authorization and access control, data integrity, confidentiality, non-repudiation, trust and regulation.

▌3061

SEMINAR IN E-COMMERCE

UNIVERSITY OF WISCONSIN-MADISON
SCHOOL OF BUSINESS

975 University Ave.
Madison, WI 53706
PH: (608)262-1550
E-mail: uwmadmba@bus.wisc.edu
URL: http://instruction.bus.wisc.edu/oim765

Description: The University of Wisconsin offers a seminar in E-commerce. This seminar will look at business models, Internet Economy and IT infrastructure, supply chain management, business plans and venture capital.

▌3062

SEMINAR IN ECONOMICS: THE NEW ECONOMY

MARQUETTE UNIVERSITY
COLLEGE OF BUSINESS ADMINISTRATION

PO Box 1881
Milwaukee, WI 53201-1881
PH: (414)288-7142
FX: (414)288-1660
E-mail: jeanne.simmons@marquette.edu
URL: http://www.busadm.mu.edu/mba
Contact: Jeanne Simmons, Assistant Dean of Graduate Programs

Description: Marquette University's College of Business Administration offers a course called Seminar in Economics: The New Economy. This seminar looks at the current writings on e-commerce and the new economy. Students will create a business plan for the development of a new product or service related to e-commerce.

▌3063

SEMINAR IN INTERNET MARKETING

STANFORD UNIVERSITY
GRADUATE SCHOOL OF BUSINESS

518 Memorial Way
Stanford, CA 94305-5015
PH: (650)725-5663
FX: (650)723-3950
E-mail: cebc@gsb.stanford.edu
URL: http://www.gsb.stanford.edu/cebc/

Description: Stanford University's MBA program offers a course titled "Seminar in Internet Marketing." This seminar is geared towards those with previous experience in web-based marketing. Students will study emerging Web marketing trends, get hands-on experience with real-world marketing, and join a small group forum for active discussion.

■ 3064

SEMINAR IN IT: E-BUSINESS: INFORMATION TECHNOLOGY INFRASTRUCTURE

MARQUETTE UNIVERSITY

COLLEGE OF BUSINESS ADMINISTRATION

PO Box 1881
Milwaukee, WI 53201-1881
PH: (414)288-7142
FX: (414)288-1660
E-mail: jeanne.simmons@marquette.edu
URL: http://www.busadm.mu.edu/mba
Contact: Jeanne Simmons, Assistant Dean of Graduate Programs

Description: Marquette University's College of Business Administration offers a course called Seminar in IT: E-Business: Information Technology Infrastructure. This seminar is taught for managers to demystify e-business jargon and principles. Students will learn how to analyze, allocate, and use IT resources to maximize their company's e-business success.

■ 3065

SEMINAR IN IT: PRIVACY AND SECURITY

MARQUETTE UNIVERSITY

COLLEGE OF BUSINESS ADMINISTRATION

PO Box 1881
Milwaukee, WI 53201-1881
PH: (414)288-7142
FX: (414)288-1660
E-mail: jeanne.simmons@marquette.edu
URL: http://www.busadm.mu.edu/mba
Contact: Jeanne Simmons, Assistant Dean of Graduate Programs

Description: Marquette University's College of Business Administration offers a course called Seminar in IT: Privacy and Security. This course addresses technical safeguards that can prevent disruption of service, data tampering and theft. Other topics covered include risk assessment, management policies, authentication, encryption, digital signatures, authorization procedures, and government standards.

■ 3066

SEMINAR IN MARKETING: INTERNET MARKETING

MARQUETTE UNIVERSITY

COLLEGE OF BUSINESS ADMINISTRATION

PO Box 1881
Milwaukee, WI 53201-1881
PH: (414)288-7142
FX: (414)288-1660
E-mail: jeanne.simmons@marquette.edu
URL: http://www.busadm.mu.edu/mba
Contact: Jeanne Simmons, Assistant Dean of Graduate Programs

Description: Marquette University's College of Business Administration offers a course called Seminar in Marketing: Internet Marketing. This seminar will provide students with both a classroom and online learning environment for marketing on the Internet. The course will cover topics including database marketing;how the Internet differs from other marketing/advertising media, how.com businesses differ from brick and mortar businesses.

■ 3067

SEMINAR IN OPERATIONS MANAGEMENT: E-BUSINESS AND SUPPLY CHAIN

MARQUETTE UNIVERSITY

COLLEGE OF BUSINESS ADMINISTRATION

PO Box 1881
Milwaukee, WI 53201-1881
PH: (414)288-7142
FX: (414)288-1660
E-mail: jeanne.simmons@marquette.edu
URL: http://www.busadm.mu.edu/mba
Contact: Jeanne Simmons, Assistant Dean of Graduate Programs

Description: Marquette University's College of Business Administration offers a course called Seminar in Operations Management: E-Business and Supply Chain. This graduate level seminar will help students develop an integrated strategy of managing the supply chain, along with e-business, effectively and efficiently.

■ 3068

SOFTWARE ENGINEERING FOR E-COMMERCE

UNIVERSITY OF DELAWARE

E-COMMERCE PROGRAM

206 John M. Clayton Hall
Newark, DE 19716-7410
PH: (302)831-2741
E-mail: continuing-ed@udel.edu
URL: http://www.continuingstudies.udel.edu/it/ecomm/index.shtml

Description: The University of Delaware's Continuing Studies Program offers a course titled ''Software Engineering for E-Commerce.'' This course will help students obtain information on choosing tools and languages for application development, including requirements analysis, specification, system design, and integrated testing.

■ 3069

SPECIAL TOPICS IN E-COMMERCE MARKETING STRATEGY

UNIVERSITY OF PENNSYLVANIA

PENN ENGINEERING

EXECUTIVE MASTER'S IN TECHNOLOGY MANAGEMENT

119 Towne Bldg.
Philadelphia, PA 19104-6391
PH: (215)898-5241

FX: (215)573-9673
E-mail: emtm@seas.upenn.edu
URL: http://www.seas.upenn.edu/profprog/emtm/news/stories/ecommerce-courses.html

Description: The University of Pennsylvania Executive Master's in Technology Management program offers a course titled ''Special Topics in E-Commerce Marketing Strategy.'' This course covers an introduction to e-commerce and provides information on how business is being transformed by information, technology and the Web.

█ 3070

SPECIAL TOPICS IN TECHNOLOGY AND ELECTRONIC COMMERCE
WEST CHESTER UNIVERSITY

Office of Graduate Studies
McKelvie Hall
102 Rosedale Ave.
West Chester, PA 19383-2300
PH: (610)436-2943; (610)436-2608
FX: (610)436-2763
E-mail: gradstud@wcupa.edu
URL: http://www.tecmba.org
Contact: Dr. Paul Christ, Director, TEC MBA Program

Description: Special Topics in Technology and Electronic Commerce is a seminar or independent study course on selected TEC topics and includes research papers or projects, which examine contemporary TEC issues not available in the existing curriculum. Students must obtain permission of the course instructor to take this class.

█ 3071

STRATEGIC 8 PLANNING PROCESS
GREATER CINCINNATI CHAMBER OF COMMERCE
STRATEGIC 8 PLANNING PROGRAM

441 Vine St., Ste. 300
Cincinnati, OH 45202
PH: (513)579-3100
FX: (513)579-3101
E-mail: info@gccc.com
URL: http://www.gccc.com

Description: The Greater Cincinnati Chamber of Commerce offers an educational program called Strategic 8 Planning Process. This program will enable participants to compile a strategic plan, learn how to profitably manage their customer base, and formulate an e-business strategy for their business.

█ 3072

STRATEGIC E-BUSINESS ADVANTAGES
NOTRE DAME
COLLEGE OF BUSINESS, EXECUTIVE EDUCATION

126 Mendoza College of Business
Notre Dame, IN 46556
PH: (574)631-3622
TF: 800-631-3622

FX: (574)631-6783
E-mail: execprog@nd.edu
URL: http://www.nd.edu/~execprog/index.html
Contact: Leo Burke, Director

Description: Notre Dame's College of Business offers an Executive Education course titled ''Strategic E-Business Advantages.'' This course explains how changing business models, rethinking processes and forming new relationships with trading partners and customers can provide a competitive edge. This course also looks at technologies, applications, challenges and strategies of e-businesses.

█ 3073

STRATEGIC ENVIRONMENT OF INTERNET COMMERCE
YALE SCHOOL OF MANAGEMENT

135 Prospect St.
PO Box 208200
New Haven, CT 06520-8200
PH: (203)432-5932
FX: (203)432-7004
E-mail: mba.admissions@yale.edu
URL: http://www.mba.yale.edu
Contact: James Stevens, Director

Description: Strategic Environment of Internet Commerce presents a survey of major policy issues related to the growth and development of the Internet. Among the topics covered will be Internet governance, privacy, intellectual property and crime.

█ 3074

STRATEGIC ISSUES IN E-COMMERCE
CREIGHTON UNIVERSITY
COLLEGE OF BUSINESS ADMINISTRATION

2500 California Plz.
Omaha, NE 68178
PH: (402)280-2602
FX: (402)280-2172
E-mail: ghafer@creighton.edu
URL: http://www.creighton.edu
Contact: Ms. Gail Hafer, Graduate Coordinator

Description: Creighton University offers a graduate level course called Strategic Issues in E-Commerce. This course looks at business strategies for using e-commerce within a company. A review of key concepts of strategic management and consideration of various strategies and business models for e-commerce will also be included.

█ 3075

STRATEGIC ISSUES INVOLVING TECHNOLOGY
YALE SCHOOL OF MANAGEMENT

135 Prospect St.
PO Box 208200
New Haven, CT 06520-8200

PH: (203)432-5932
FX: (203)432-7004
E-mail: mba.admissions@yale.edu
URL: http://www.mba.yale.edu
Contact: James Stevens, Director

Description: Strategic Issues Involving Technology uses a mix of lecture and case discussion to explore economic and managerial issues involving technology. Among the topics covered will be the economics of research and development, patents, copyright and licensing rules, network industries and issues of standards.

∎ 3076
STRATEGIC PLANNING AND ANALYSIS FOR TECHNOLOGY AND ELECTRONIC COMMERCE
WEST CHESTER UNIVERSITY

Office of Graduate Studies
McKelvie Hall
102 Rosedale Ave.
West Chester, PA 19383-2300
PH: (610)436-2943; (610)436-2608
FX: (610)436-2763
E-mail: gradstud@wcupa.edu
URL: http://www.tecmba.org
Contact: Dr. Paul Christ, Director, TEC MBA Program

Description: Strategic Planning and Analysis for Technology and Electronic Commerce is designed to serve as the capstone course for the Technology and Electronic Commerce concentration and focuses on integrating the functional areas of business and technology issues. Prerequisites of this course include the completion of business core courses and completion of course numbers TEC501, TEC502, TEC503 and TEC505.

∎ 3077
STRATEGIES FOR E-COMMERCE SITE IMPLEMENTATION
DIGITALTHINK INC

601 Brannan St.
San Francisco, CA 94107
PH: (415)625-4000
TF: 888-686-8817
FX: (415)625-4100
E-mail: info@digitalthink.com
URL: http://www.digitalthink.com
Contact: Mr. Pete Goettner, Chairman

Founded: 1996. **Staff:** 450. **Description:** DigitalThink's online classes include "Strategies for E-Commerce Site Implementation." This course focuses on the technological issues associated with implementation of an e-commerce solution. It provides an overview of the various solutions available for building an e-commerce site so that students can select the best possible methods for their organizational needs.

∎ 3078
STRATEGY IN E-BUSINESS
E-COMMERCE LEARNING CENTER

NC State University
Business Management Dept.
College of Management
Campus Box 7229
Raleigh, NC 27695-7229
PH: (919)515-5584
E-mail: ecommerce@ncsu.edu
URL: http://www.ecommerce.ncsu.edu

Description: The Strategy in E-Business (BUS 500) course develops students' strategic management skills by providing them with an understanding of how company strategies are changing in today's technology economy.

∎ 3079
SUCCESSFULLY MANAGING AN E-COMMERCE PROJECT WITHIN YOUR COMPANY
SAN JOSE STATE UNIVERSITY
PROFESSIONAL DEVELOPMENT CENTER

3031 Tisch Way, Ste. 200 Plz. E
San Jose, CA 95128
PH: (408)257-3000
E-mail: mitchell.levy.sjsupd@ecnow.com
URL: http://ecmtraining.com/sjsu/
Contact: Mitchell Levy, Program Founder and Coordinator

Description: San Jose State University offers an executive education course called "Successfully Managing an E-Commerce Project Within Your Company." This course covers getting started, gaining support, and mobilizing your company to take action. Developing an e-commerce plan for a company is also covered.

∎ 3080
SUPPLY CHAIN MANAGEMENT AND ELECTRONIC COMMERCE
WORCESTER POLYTECHNIC INSTITUTE

100 Institute Rd.
Worcester, MA 01609
PH: (508)831-5218
FX: (508)831-5720
URL: http://www.wpi.edu
Contact: McRae Banks, Department Head

Founded: 1865. **Description:** The Supply Chain Management and Electronic Commerce course provides students with a managerial background in supply chain management and its interface with Electronic Commerce. The course discusses the role of each element of a supply chain in creating value for the business and the issues involved in integrating and coordinating the elements. Electronic data change, the Internet and E-commerce are introduced and their impacts on internal and external value chains are explored. Topics such as competitive operations strategies, outsourcing, purchasing and inbound logistics, inventory management, outbound logistics, types of electronic commerce, electronic data interchange, virtual integration and others are covered.

▌3081
SUPPLY CHAIN MANAGEMENT: END TO END
ILLINOIS INSTITUTE OF TECHNOLOGY
STUART GRADUATE SCHOOL OF BUSINESS

565 W Adams St.
Chicago, IL 60661
PH: (312)906-6500
FX: (312)906-6549
E-mail: degrees@stuart.iit.edu
URL: http://www.stuart.iit.edu

Description: The Illinois Institute of Technology Stuart Graduate School of Business offers a course entitled Supply Chain Management: End to End. This course provides a foundation for the E-Commerce MBA. Students examine the flow of goods, information and services in a global economy; and begin to look at the optimal supply chain.

▌3082
SUPPLY CHAIN MANAGEMENT AND INTEGRATION FOR E-COMMERCE
GW CENTER FOR PROFESSIONAL DEVELOPMENT

2029 K Street NW, Ste. 600
Washington, DC 20006
PH: (202)973-1150
FX: (202)973-1165
E-mail: cpd@gwu.edu
URL: http://www.gwu.edu/~cpd/programs/CWEC/

Description: The GW Center for Professional Development offers a course called "Supply Chain Management and Integration for E-Commerce." This course looks at the complexities involved in the implementation of a supply chain, the tools available, the issues involved and the various implementation models.

▌3083
TEC MBA DEGREE PROGRAM
WEST CHESTER UNIVERSITY OF PENNSYLVANIA
GRADUATE SCHOOL

McKelvie Hall
102 Rosedale Ave.
West Chester, PA 19383-2600
PH: (610)436-2943
E-mail: gradstudy@wcupa.edu
URL: http://www.wcupa.edu/

Description: West Chester University of Pennsylvania offers a TEC MBA degree program. This technology-focused curriculum also provides an emphasis on foundation business principles and concepts. Other areas of coursework include e-business, intellectual property, competitive intelligence, and technology project planning.

▌3084
TECHNICAL FOUNDATIONS OF ELECTRONIC COMMERCE
ARIZONA STATE UNIVERSITY

Main Campus
PO BOX 873606
Tempe, AZ 85287-3606
PH: (480)965-6191
FX: (480)965-8392
E-mail: uday.kulkarni@asu.edu
URL: http://www.asu.edu
Contact: Dr. Uday Kulkarni, Professor

Description: Technical Foundations of Electronic Commerce will expose students to technology that is essential for managing an e-business. A proper balance of conceptual and hands-on exposure is maintained throughout the course and addresses the issues in three modules including the infrastructure, the application of technologies and the transaction processing systems. This course is only available to students pursuing the Arizona State UniversityMBA/MSIM dual degree.

▌3085
TECHNOLOGIES FOR B2B E-COMMERCE
UNIVERSITY OF MINNESOTA
CARLSON SCHOOL OF MANAGEMENT

321 19th Ave. S.
Minneapolis, MN 55455
PH: (612)624-8030
FX: (612)626-1316
E-mail: mbawebmaster@csom.umn.edu
URL: http://www.csom.umn.edu/
Contact: Larry Benveniste, Dean

Description: The Carlson School of Management at the University of Minnesota offers a graduate level course called "Technologies for B2B E-Commerce." This course addresses strategies, process design principles and information technologies for business-to-business e-commerce. Coverage of traditional firms' planning process to establish e-business operational, sales and Web-based marketing capabilities are also covered.

▌3086
TECHNOLOGY AND ELECTRONIC COMMERCE
WEST CHESTER UNIVERSITY

Office of Graduate Studies
McKelvie Hall
102 Rosedale Ave.
West Chester, PA 19383-2300
PH: (610)436-2943; (610)436-2608
FX: (610)436-2763
E-mail: gradstud@wcupa.edu
URL: http://www.tecmba.org
Contact: Dr. Paul Christ, Director, TEC MBA Program

Description: The purpose of the Technology and Electronic Commerce course is to introduce students to the basics of technology and how it impacts today's business environment. The class material is a combination of classroom discussions and hands-on approaches in the computer lab. The main focus is on Information Technology, particularly on the Internet and e-commerce.

▌3087
TECHNOLOGY FUNDAMENTALS OF ELECTRONIC COMMERCE
UNIVERSITY OF NEW BRUNSWICK-SAINT JOHN
FACULTY OF BUSINESS

PO Box 5050
Saint John, NB, Canada E2L4L5
PH: (506)648-5570; (506)648-5806
TF: 800-508-6275
FX: (506)648-5574
E-mail: business@unbsj.ca
URL: http://www.unbsj.ca/business
Contact: Shelley Rinehart, Dean, Faculty of Business

Description: Technology Fundamentals of Electronic Commerce (BA 2663) examines the technological basis of e-commerce with the computer-based network enabling e-commerce as the focus. Data and voice networks, Internet and telephony, bandwidth, architecture, software strategies and World Wide Web supplier industries will be discussed with relevance to e-commerce implementation planning. As a prerequisite, either course BA2672 must be completed or students must seek permission from the instructor before taking this course.

▌3088
TECHNOLOGY ISSUES FOR ELECTRONIC COMMERCE
DALHOUSIE UNIVERSITY

Faculty of Computer Science
6050 University Ave.
Halifax, NS, Canada B3H1W5
PH: (902)494-2740
FX: (902)492-1517
E-mail: mec@cs.dal.ca
URL: http://www.ecomm.dal.ca
Contact: Dr. Kori Inkpen, Dir., Master of E-Commerce Program

Description: Technology Issues for Electronic Commerce examines the technologies and infrastructure required to support e-commerce and examines the major components of the infrastructure including networks, databases and data warehousing, electronic payment, security and human-computer interfaces.

▌3089
TECHNOLOGY SEMINAR: E-COMMERCE TECHNOLOGIES AND APPLICATIONS
REGIS UNIVERSITY
GRADUATE PROGRAMS

3333 Regis Boulevard, L-16
Denver, CO 80221-1099
PH: (303)458-4080

TF: 800-667-9270
FX: (303)964-5538
E-mail: masters@regis.edu
URL: http://www.regis.edu

Description: Regis University offers a course called Technology Seminar: E-Commerce Technologies and Applications. In this course students will examine the progression of the E-Commerce value proposition through specific concepts, applications, and tools used to implement E-Commerce programs.

▌3090
TELECOMMUNICATIONS MANAGEMENT
NEW JERSEY INSTITUTE OF TECHNOLOGY
SCHOOL OF MANAGEMENT, GRADUATE PROGRAMS

323 Martin Luther King Jr. Blvd.
Newark, NJ 07102-1982
PH: (973)596-6378
FX: (973)596-3074
E-mail: lipper@njit.edu
URL: http://www.njit.edu/SOM/MBA/index.html
Contact: Stuart Lipper, Director of Graduate Programs

Description: The New Jersey Institute of Technology School of Management MBA program offers a course called ''Telecommunications Management.'' This course will review current trends in telecommunications with an emphasis on the techniques required by non-technically trained managers to deal with hardware, software, and human interfaces.

▌3091
TELECOMMUNICATIONS MANAGEMENT AND ELECTRONIC COMMERCE
WORCESTER POLYTECHNIC INSTITUTE

100 Institute Rd.
Worcester, MA 01609
PH: (508)831-5218
FX: (508)831-5720
URL: http://www.wpi.edu
Contact: McRae Banks, Department Head

Founded: 1865. **Description:** The Telecommunications Management and Electronic Commerce course provides students with the technical and managerial background of telecommunications and its applications in e-commerce. This course will examine the role of telecommunications technology, especially the Internet, in e-commerce and survey current topics in e-commerce.

▌3092
TELECOMMUNICATIONS AND TECHNOLOGY POLICY: INTERNET ECONOMICS
UNIVERSITY OF MARYLAND
SMITH SCHOOL OF BUSINESS

Van Munching Hall
College Park, MD 20742
PH: (301)405-2278

E-mail: info@hsmith.umd.edu
URL: http://ecommerce.umd.edu/

Description: The University of Maryland Smith School of Business offers an MBA course entitled ''Telecommunications and Technology Policy: Internet Economics.'' This course covers topics in telecommunications, economics, and public policy. It is intended for students who have a particular interest in telecommunications, e-commerce, and information technology. The course describes how converging industries require telecommunications policy to be understood within the context of broader technology policy.

∎ 3093
THIRTY PLUS INTERNET MARKETING TECHNIQUES
ECNOW.COM

21265 Stevens Creek Blvd., Ste. 205
Cupertino, CA 95014
PH: (408)257-3000
FX: (603)843-0769
E-mail: info@ecnow.com
URL: http://ecnow.com/courses/mgt04.htm

Description: ECnow.com offers a course called 30 Plus Internet Marketing Techniques. This course provides information on many ways to market products and services on the Internet, as well as how to have an effective web site.

∎ 3094
TRAFFIC BUILDING
CARDEAN UNIVERSITY

500 Lake Cook Rd.
Deerfield, IL 60015-5609
TF: (866)948-1289
E-mail: inquires@cardean.edu
URL: http://www.cardean.edu
Contact: Dr. Geoffrey M. Cox, Cardean University President

Description: Cardean University is an accredited online university which offers a course called ''Traffic Building.'' This course examines strategies for acquiring and retaining customers through the Internet. By exploring issues of brand building, domain names, online advertising, dynamic and permission-based marketing, managers can learn to use the Internet to increase market share.

∎ 3095
TWELVE PRINCIPLES OF E-BUSINESS
THE ECADAMY

6 Glen House
Stag Place
Victoria
London SW1E5AQ, United Kingdom
PH: 44 20 8342 9460
FX: 44 870 139 4722
E-mail: webmaster@ecademy.com
URL: http://www.theecademy.com

Description: The Ecademy offers an free online e-business tutorial called The 12 Principles of E-Business. This tutorial includes a look at e-commerce planning, software, networks, security, payment methods, purchasing, and customer service.

∎ 3096
UNDERSTANDING THE E-AGE CONSUMER
UNIVERSITY OF DELAWARE
E-COMMERCE PROGRAM

206 John M. Clayton Hall
Newark, DE 19716-7410
PH: (302)831-2741
E-mail: continuing-ed@udel.edu
URL: http://www.continuingstudies.udel.edu/it/ecomm/index.shtml

Description: The University of Delaware's Continuing Studies Program offers a course titled ''Understanding the E-Age Consumer.'' In this course students will learn to know who consumers are and what they want, and how to develop and communicate information to them. This course also helps students understand consumer preferences and behaviors in electronic environments.

∎ 3097
UNDERSTANDING E-COMMERCE AND TECHNOLOGY FOR NON-TECHNICAL PROFESSIONALS
ECNOW.COM

21265 Stevens Creek Blvd., Ste. 205
Cupertino, CA 95014
PH: (408)257-3000
FX: (603)843-0769
E-mail: info@ecnow.com
URL: http://ecnow.com/courses/mgt04.htm

Description: ECnow.com offers a course called Understanding E-Commerce and Technology for Non-Technical Professionals. This course is designed for business managers and professionals who nEED to learn about Internet technology in order to incorporate it into their businesses. Wireless networks, middleware, and web application development are among topics discussed.

∎ 3098
UNDERSTANDING INTERNET TECHNOLOGIES
CARDEAN UNIVERSITY

500 Lake Cook Rd.
Deerfield, IL 60015-5609
TF: (866)948-1289
E-mail: inquires@cardean.edu
URL: http://www.cardean.edu
Contact: Dr. Geoffrey M. Cox, Cardean University President

Description: Cardean University is an accredited online university which offers a offers a suite of courses called "Understanding Internet Technologies." This series of 4 two hour courses shows students how effective e-commerce can connect businesses to suppliers, distributors, and customers. It offers an overview of terminology, basic concepts surrounding the Internet, and how the Internet can benefit a company or organization.

▍3099

USING TECHNOLOGY TO OPTIMIZE CUSTOMER RELATIONSHIPS

CALIFORNIA STATE UNIVERSITY, FULLERTON

UNIVERSITY EXTENDED EDUCATION

800 N State College Blvd.
Fullerton, CA 92834-6870
PH: (714)278-2611
FX: (714)278-2088
URL: http://www.takethelead.fullerton.edu/Classes/

Description: Cal State Fullerton offers a course called "Using Technology to Optimize Customer Relationships." This course examines design of customer-centric eCRM systems, and look at leading-edge technology strategies of customer life cycle management.

▍3100

VENTURE MANAGEMENT (ENTREPRENEURSHIP)

MCGILL UNIVERSITY

FACULTY OF MANAGEMENT

1001 Sherbrooke St. W
Montreal, PQ, Canada H3A1G5
PH: (514)398-4000
FX: (514)398-3876
E-mail: gagnon@management.mcgill.ca
URL: http://www.intranet.management.mcgill.ca/course/mis/273434/CO273690_W00.htm

Description: McGill University in Montreal offers a course titled "Venture Management (Entrepreneurship)" in which students will formulate a complete business plan for a new web site and learn the "tricks of the trade" in starting, financing, and growing a.com venture.

▍3101

WEB BUSINESS STRATEGY

UNIVERSITY OF IOWA

COLLEGE OF BUSINESS

21 E Market St.
Iowa City, IA 52242-1000
PH: (319)335-0862
E-mail: business-webmaster@uiowa.edu
URL: http://www.biz.uiowa.edu/class/6m105/

Description: The University of Iowa provides a course called "Web Business Strategy." In this course students will design and update their own websites and learn about what makes a successful Internet business.

▍3102

WEB COMMERCE SECURITY

UNIVERSITY OF MARYLAND

SMITH SCHOOL OF BUSINESS

Van Munching Hall
College Park, MD 20742
PH: (301)405-2278
E-mail: info@hsmith.umd.edu
URL: http://ecommerce.umd.edu/

Description: The University of Maryland Smith School of Business offers an MBA course entitled "Web Commerce Security." This class will explore security issues of Web Commerce and the Internet for conducting business over public and private networks. The main focus in this course is on security (authentication, authorization, encryption) which make web commerce sites successful in processing business transactions securely. Other topics that will be covered in this course include: Data security, encryption, infrastructure requirements, and electronic payment systems.

▍3103

WEB CONTENT DESIGN

ILLINOIS INSTITUTE OF TECHNOLOGY

STUART GRADUATE SCHOOL OF BUSINESS

565 W Adams St.
Chicago, IL 60661
PH: (312)906-6500
FX: (312)906-6549
E-mail: degrees@stuart.iit.edu
URL: http://www.stuart.iit.edu

Description: The Illinois Institute of Technology Stuart Graduate School of Business offers a course entitled Web Content Design. This course gives an overview of Principles of effective web site design. These principles will then be used to evaluate existing web sites. Student teams will develop a design and working prototype for an e-business web site.

▍3104

THE WEB: CURRENT TOPICS

UNIVERSITY OF PHOENIX

3201 E Elwood St.
Phoenix, AZ 85034
PH: (480)966-5394
TF: 800-366-9699
URL: http://www.uoponline.com

Description: The University of Phoenix offers a course called The Web: Current Topics. This course examines constantly changing web technologies. Topics covered include current programming languages, security developments, network and telecommunications, and business applications.

∎ 3105

WEB-DATABASE INTEGRATION WITH ASP

ELEMENTK

500 Canal View Blvd.
Rochester, NY 14623
PH: (585)240-7500
TF: 800-434-3466
FX: (585)240-7760
URL: http://www.elementk.com

Description: Element K offers an online course entitled "Web-Database Integration with ASP." This instructor led class examines one possible integration solution: Microsoft's Active Server Pages (ASP) technology. ASP is becoming popular as a web-database integration tool for developers using MS Internet Information Server (IIS) and either MS Access or MS SQL Server database management systems. In this class students will gain command of ASP, and will create a small e-business product catalog.

∎ 3106

WEB-DATABASE INTEGRATION FOR E-BUSINESS

ELEMENTK

500 Canal View Blvd.
Rochester, NY 14623
PH: (585)240-7500
TF: 800-434-3466
FX: (585)240-7760
URL: http://www.elementk.com

Description: Element K offers an online course called "Web-Database Integration for E-Business." This instructor led class is designed for eCommerce developers who wish to gain a better understanding both of the reasons for building integrated web-database applications, and of the various tools available to do the job. This course is geared toward students who have basic web development and administration skills.

∎ 3107

WEB DESIGN AND USABILITY

MERCY COLLEGE

555 Broadway
Dobbs Ferry, NY 10522
PH: (914)674-7306
FX: (914)674-7518
E-mail: jdielsi@mercy.edu
URL: http://www.mercy.edu
Contact: John DiElsi, Program Dir.

Description: Mercy College offers a graduate level course called Web Design and Usability. This course examines good web site design, and the use of site development tools including image editors and HTML editors.

∎ 3108

WEB, INTERNET AND E-COMMERCE

COLUMBIA UNIVERSITY

Information Center
303 Lewisohn
2970 Broadway
Mail Code 4110
New York, NY 10027-6902
PH: (212)854-9699; (212)854-9666
E-mail: sp-info@columbia.edu
URL: http://www.columbia.edu
Contact: Dennis Green, Program Director

Description: Web, Internet and E-Commerce surveys the design, development, management and promotion of Internet websites in today's rapidly expanding electronic economy. This course includes an overview of web business models, e-commerce industry structure and web specific project management. It also includes a lecture on web marketing and a tour of the premises of a web hosting facility with a final project of a web startup proposal.

∎ 3109

WEB MARKETING (SBA)

U.S. SMALL BUSINESS ADMINISTRATION

409 3rd St. SW
Washington, DC 20416
PH: 800-827-5722
E-mail: classroom@sba.gov
URL: http://www.sba.gov/classroom

Description: The Small Business Administration (SBA) in partnership with Cisco Systems offers a free online course called Web Marketing. This course provides students with an understanding of successful marketing using the Internet. Students will learn to create and promote their web presence, and ensure that it is effective.

∎ 3110

WEB PROGRAMMING AND DESIGN

BELLEVUE UNIVERSITY

1000 Galvin Rd. S
Bellevue, NE 68005
PH: (402)293-2000
TF: 800-756-7920
FX: (402)293-2020
URL: http://www.bellevue.edu

Description: Bellevue University offers an E-Business course titled "Web Programming and Design." This course gives students the opportunity to explore the languages and tools of building a website including HTML and Javascript. Students will practice these internet language skills by constructing their personal website.

∎ 3111

WEB SITE MANAGEMENT

MERCY COLLEGE

555 Broadway
Dobbs Ferry, NY 10522
PH: (914)674-7306

FX: (914)674-7518
E-mail: jdielsi@mercy.edu
URL: http://www.mercy.edu
Contact: John DiElsi, Program Dir.

Description: Mercy College offers a graduate level course called Web Site Management. This course discusses Internet business models, the evaluation of technologies, and implementing a user-centered focus for Internet business.

▌3112
WEB SITE SECURITY: MESSAGING, SERVERS AND VIRUSES
UNIVERSITY OF FLORIDA

Office of the University Registrar
Cruiser Hall
PO Box 114000
Gainesville, FL 32611-4000
PH: (352)392-3261; (352)392-1374
URL: http://www.ufl.edu

Description: Web Site Security: Messaging, Servers and Viruses is the second course in a two-part series on Web Site Security. This course will give students the knowledge and skills to identify and prevent tactical security risks and measures. Students will learn how to implement message security and identify and minimize security risks. They will also receive a detailed overview of Internet-transmitted viruses, virus prevention and anti-virus programs.

▌3113
WEB SITES THAT WORK: DESIGNING WITH YOUR EYES OPEN
USER INTERFACE ENGINEERING

242 Neck Rd.
Bradford, MA 01835
PH: (978)374-8300
FX: (978)374-9175
E-mail: uie@uie.com
URL: http://world.std.com/~uieweb/courses.htm

Description: User Interface Engineering offers a course called Web Sites That Work: Designing With Your Eyes Open. This course is offered at User Interface's sites in Boston, Austin, Seattle, and San Francisco; or can be offered at an individual company's place of business. In this course students will learn about making their web sites useful to customers, and will learn methods of testing web sites and drawing their own conclusions.

▌3114
WEB VALUE
CARDEAN UNIVERSITY

500 Lake Cook Rd.
Deerfield, IL 60015-5609
TF: (866)948-1289
E-mail: inquires@cardean.edu
URL: http://www.cardean.edu

Contact: Dr. Geoffrey M. Cox, Cardean University President

Description: Cardean University is an accredited online university which offers a course called "Web Value." Developed with Stanford University, this course helps managers understand how to use the Internet to create value for firms and their customers. By understanding how the Internet helps capture and enhance customer information, managers can change their marketing efforts to be more successful in the networked economy.

▌3115
WIRELESS DIRECTIONS
UNIVERSITY OF DALLAS
GRADUATE SCHOOL OF MANAGEMENT

1845 E Northgate Dr.
Irving, TX 75062
PH: (972)721-5000
E-mail: msavoie@udallas.edu
URL: http://gsmweb.udallas.edu/concentrations/e_business.html

Description: The University of Dallas Graduate School of Management provides a course called Wireless Directions. This course examines wireless enterprise, valuation methodologies, and business case development. Students will learn about wireless technologies, networks, protocols, standards, and trends in the marketplace.

▌3116
YOUR E-BUSINESS
APT LEARNING

PO Box 2
Hall, ACT 2618, Australia
PH: 61 2 6230 2848
FX: 61 2 6230 2865
E-mail: info@aptlearning.com
URL: http://www.aptlearning.com

Description: APT Learning provides a free online course called "Your E-Business." This course introduces students to e-commerce. They will learn how to plan a strategy for converting your current business to an e-business, or starting a new e-business.

GOVERNMENT REGULATORY AGENCIES

▌3117
ADVISORY COMMISSION ON ELECTRONIC COMMERCE

Internal Revenue Service
Department of the Treasury
1111 Constitution Ave. NW

Washington, DC 20224

History: Commission was established in 1999. It is a public advisory commission under the Internal Revenue Service, Department of the Treasury. Commission was established to discuss ways in which Internet sales can effectively be taxed. **Memberships:** Commission consists of nineteen members representing lawmakers and technology executives.

■ **3118**

ADVISORY COMMITTEE ON INTERNATIONAL COMMUNICATIONS AND INFORMATION POLICY

Bur. of Economic & Business Affairs
Department of State
2201 C St. NW, Rm. 4826
Washington, DC 20520
PH: (202)647-5385
FX: (202)647-0158
E-mail: ebba@state.gov
URL: http://www.state.gov/e/eb/adcom/c667.htm
Contact: Pamela Bates, Exec.Sec.

History: Committee was established in 1989 as a public advisory committee under the Bureau of Economic and Business Affairs, Department of State. Committee advises the Department of State concerning major economic, social, and legal issues and problems in international communications and information policy, especially as these issues involve users of information and communication services, providers of such services, technology research and development, foreign industrial and regulatory policy, the activities of international organizations with regard to communications and information, and developing country interests. Committee provides information and advice on both public and private aspects of current foreign affairs issues in these areas and provides advice in the formulation of United States communications and information policy, positions and proposals for multilateral and bilateral consultation, and negotiations on communications and information policy issues. **Memberships:** Committee consists of members from private industry, the academic community, labor, and other professionals who represent a diverse, dedicated group of individuals from industry and academia who have continued the process of presenting forward-thinking advice and recommendations on the future of the telecommunications and information technology sectors and their potential effects on U.S. Government foreign policy. The committee has a roster of 28 prominent members of the telecommunications and information technology industries with representatives of telephone companies (equipment manufacturers and services providers (both local and long distance)), computer companies (both hardware and software), content providers, and academia. The U.S. Coordinator for International Communications and Information Policy serves ex officio. Members serve for a period of two years or less. Edward J. Black, President and CEO, Computer and Communications Industry Association, chairs the Committee. **Meetings:** Committee meets quarterly.

■ **3119**

ADVISORY COMMITTEE ON PUBLIC INTERNATIONAL LAW

Office of the Legal Adviser
Department of State
2430 E. St.
South Bldg., Ste. 357
Washington, DC 20037-2800
PH: (202)647-2767
FX: (202)736-7028
Contact: Mary Catherine Malin, Designated Fed.Off.

History: Committee was established August 21, 1986, as a public advisory committee of the Department of State. Committee provides advice to the Department of State on formulating U.S. policy on key issues of international law. **Memberships:** Committee consists of twenty-eight persons who are outstanding academics and practitioners in the field of public international law and former State Department Legal Advisers who are appointed by the Legal Adviser of the Department of State. **Meetings:** Committee meets twice a year. Committee also known as Department of State Advisory Committee on Public International Law and the Advisory Committee on International Law.

■ **3120**

CHIEF INFORMATION OFFICERS COUNCIL (CIO)

Eisenhower Executive Office Bldg.
725 17th St. NW, Rm. 349
Washington, DC 20503
PH: (202)395-1095
FX: (202)395-4995
E-mail: ciocouncil.support@gsa.gov
URL: http://www.cio.gov
Contact: Mark Forman, Chairman

Founded: 1996. **Staff:** 25. **Members:** 35. **Description:** The Chief Information Officers Council (CIO) serves as the main interagency forum for improving practices in the design, modernization, use, sharing and performance of federal government agency information resources. The council develops recommendations for information technology management practices; procedures and standards; identifies opportunities to share information resources; and assesses and addresses the needs of the federal governments IT workforce

■ **3121**

CRITICAL INFRASTRUCTURE ASSURANCE OFFICE (CIAO)

1401 Constitution Ave. NW, Rm. 6095
Washington, DC 20230
PH: (202)482-7473
FX: (202)482-7498
E-mail: public.affairs@ciao.gov
URL: http://www.ciao.gov
Contact: John Tritak, Director

Founded: 1998. **Description:** Critical Infrastructure Assurance Office (CIAO) was created in response to a Presidential Decision Directive (PDD-63) in May 1998 to coordinate the Federal Governments initiatives on critical infrastructure assurance. CIAO raises issues that ensure a cohesive approach to achieving continuous delivery of critical infrastructure services.

∎ 3122

FEDERAL COMMUNICATIONS COMMISSION (FCC)

445 12th St. SW
Washington, DC 20554
PH: (202)418-2555
TF: 888-225-5322
FX: (202)418-0232
E-mail: fccinfo@fcc.gov
URL: http://www.fcc.gov
Contact: Michael K. Powell, Chairman

Founded: 1934. **Members:** 5. **Description:** The Federal Communications Commission (FCC) regulates interstate and international communities by radio, television, wire, satellite and cable.

∎ 3123

FEDERAL LIBRARY AND INFORMATION CENTER COMMITTEE (FLICC)

The Library of Congress
101 Independence Ave. SE
Adams Bldg., Rm. 217
Washington, DC 20540
PH: (202)707-4800
FX: (202)707-4818
E-mail: wtab@loc.gov
URL: http://www.loc.gov/flicc/
Contact: Winston Tabb, Associate Librarian

Founded: 1965. **Members:** 15. **Description:** The Federal Library and Information Center Committee (FLICC) is responsible for making recommendation on Federal library and information policies, programs, and procedures to others concerned with libraries and information centers.

∎ 3124

FEDERAL TRADE COMMISSION (FTC)

600 Pennsylvania Ave., NW
Washington, DC 20580
PH: (202)326-2222
TF: 877-382-4357
FX: (202)326-3197
URL: http://www.ftc.gov
Contact: Timothy J. Muris, Chairman

Description: The Federal Trade Commission enforces federal antitrust and consumer protection laws. The FTC works to ensure that the Nation's markets function competitively and are efficient and free of restrictions. The FTC also works to eliminate acts or practices that are unfair or deceptive.

∎ 3125

FIRSTGOV.GOV

Office of FirstGov c/o GSA
750 17th St. NW, Ste. 200
Washington, DC 20006
PH: (202)456-1111
TF: (202)456-2461
URL: http://www.firstgov.gov
Contact: Deborah Diaz, Deputy Associate Administrator

Description: FirstGov is a free-access web site, designed to give you a place to find information from U.S. local, state and federal government agency web sites.

∎ 3126

GLOBAL MARKETS ADVISORY COMMITTEE

Commodity Futures Trading Commission
3 Lafayette Ctr.
1155 21st St. NW, Rm. 9136
Washington, DC 20581
PH: (202)418-5070
FX: (202)418-5539
URL: http://www.cftc.gov/cftc/cftccommittees.htm
Contact: Barbara P. Holum, Designated Fed.Off.

History: Committee was established in March 1998. It is a public advisory committee of the Commodity Futures Trading Commission. The globalization of futures markets has been a principle development of the 1980s and 1990s. The recent volatility that has shaken world equity and currency markets has demonstrated more vividly than ever before that the markets are inextricably linked through common products and related market participants. Events that occur in one market can and frequently do cause global regulatory and business concerns. Increasingly sophisticated and low-cost communication technology such as the Internet has expanded access to markets and to market users. The CFT, as well as other U.S. and foreign regulators, is considering appropriate regulation of the use of such electronic cross-border vehicles for trading. These issues could profoundly affect the integrity and competitiveness of U.S. markets and U.S. firms engaged in providing financial services globally. Commission was established as a result to assist the CFT concerning the its role in working with foreign regulators to address global markets issues, including enhancing international supervisory cooperation and emergency procedures; establishing concrete standards of best practices that set international benchmarks for regulation of futures and derivatives markets; encouraging improved transparency in those markets; improving the quality and timeliness of international information sharing; and encouraging jurisdictions around the world to remove legal or practical obstacles to achieving these goals. **Memberships:** Committee members total thirty and include those U.S. markets, firms and market users most directly involved in and affected by global operations. They represent U.S. exchanges, regulators and self-regulators, financial intermediaries, end-users, traders, academics, the National Futures Association, the Futures Industry Association and the Managed Funds Association. Barbara P. Holum, Commissioner, Commodity Futures Trading Commission, serves as chair and designated federal official. **Meetings:** Committee meets several times a year, or as required by changing events.

∎ 3127
INDUSTRY FUNCTIONAL ADVISORY COMMITTEE ON ELECTRONIC COMMERCE FOR TRADE POLICY MATTERS

Industry Consultations Program, Rm. H2015B
Department of Commerce
14th and Constitution Ave., NW
Washington, DC 20230
PH: (202)482-0343
FX: (202)501-2548
E-mail: Jeff_Rohlmeier@ita.doc.gov
URL: http://www.ita.doc.gov/td/icp/ifac.html
Contact: Jeffrey M. Rohlmeier, Designated Fed.Off.

History: Committee was established August 17, 1999, by the Secretary of Commerce and the U.S. Trade Representative as a public advisory committee. It is a joint committee of the Department of Commerce and the Office of the U.S. Trade Representative and part of the Industry Consultations Program, established under the Trade Act of 1974, as amended by the Trade Agreements Act of 1979. The Program provides advice concerning trade agreements entered into and on other matters in connection with the administration of U.S. trade policy. Committee provides the Secretary of Commerce and the U.S. Trade Representative with information and advice with respect to negotiating objectives and bargaining positions before entering into a trade agreement concerned with electronic commerce. **Memberships:** Committee consists of 23 members who are industry experts in international trade and electronic commerce policy. **Meetings:** Committee meets approximately four times a year. Some meetings may be closed to the public for discussion of trade sensitive issues.

∎ 3128
INFORMATION INFRASTRUCTURE TASK FORCE

U.S. Department of Commerce
Office of the Secretary
14th St. and Constitution Ave. NW
Washington, DC 20230
PH: (202)482-2112
FX: (202)482-4576
Contact: William Daley, Ch.

History: Task Force was established by the President Clinton in January 1994 to implement the Administration's vision for the National Information Infrastructure (NII). It is an interagency task force operating under the aegis of the White House Office of Science and Technology and the National Economic Council. Task Force develops policies and initiatives to accelerate the deployment of the National Information Infrastructure, which is the integration of hardware, software, and skills that will make it easy and affordable to connect people with each other, with computers, and with a vast array of services and information resources. **Memberships:** Task Force consists of high-level representatives of the federal agencies that play a major role in the development and application of information and telecommunications technologies.

∎ 3129
THE INFORMATION INFRASTRUCTURE TASK FORCE (IITF)

1401 Constitution Ave., NW
Washington, DC 20230
PH: (202)482-7002
URL: http://www.iitf.nist.gov

Description: The Information Infrastructure Task Force was established to implement the Administration's vision for the National Information Infrastructure. The Task Force consists of high-level representatives of the Federal agencies that play a major role in the development and application of information technologies.

∎ 3130
INFORMATION TECHNOLOGY ASSOCIATION OF AMERICA (ITAA)

1401 Wilson Blvd., Ste. 1100
Arlington, VA 22209
PH: (703)522-5055
FX: (703)525-2279
URL: http://www.itaa.org
Contact: Harris Miller, President

Staff: 34. **Description:** The Information Technology Association of America (ITAA) web site provides information for the Information Technology industry, it's issues, association programs, publications, meetings and seminars

∎ 3131
INSTITUTE FOR TELECOMMUNICATION SCIENCES (ITS)

325 Broadway
Boulder, CO 80305
PH: (303)497-5216
E-mail: info@bldrdoc.gov
URL: http://www.its.bldrdoc.gov
Contact: Val M. O'Day, Executive Officer

Founded: 1967. **Staff:** 7. **Description:** The Institute for Telecommunication Sciences (ITS) is the research sector for the NTIA. ITS supports all telecommunication objectives of the NTIA such as, promotion of advanced telecommunications and information infrastructure development in the United States, enhancement of domestic competitiveness, improvement of foreign trade opportunities for U.S. telecommunication firms and to promote a more efficient and effective use of the radio spectrum

∎ 3132
THE NATIONAL COORDINATION OFFICE FOR INFORMATION TECHNOLOGY RESEARCH AND DEVELOPMENT (NCO/ITR&D)

4121 Wilson Blvd., Ste. II-405
Arlington, VA 22230
PH: (703)292-4873
E-mail: nco@itrd.gov
URL: http://www.hpcc.gov
Contact: Cita M. Furlani, Director

Staff: 19. **Description:** The National Coordination Office for Information Technology Research and Development coordinates planning, budget and assessment activities for the Federal Networking and IT Research and Development program.

∎ 3133
THE NATIONAL INFORMATION INFRASTRUCTURE ADVISORY COUNCIL (NIIAC)

1401 Constitution Ave. N.W.
Washington, DC 20230
PH: (202)482-7002
Contact: Delano E. Lewis, Co-Chairman

Founded: 1994. **Members:** 36. **Description:** The National Information Infrastructure Advisory Council helps to define the role of the public and private sector; maintains the balance of protection of intellectual rights of creators and copyright owners with the needs of users; generates national strategies for developing applications in electronic commerce, manufacturing, education, and lifelong learning, health care, government information and services, and public safety. The NIIAC also conceives approaches to maximize interconnections and interoperability of networks, and addresses the important issues of privacy and security.

∎ 3134
NATIONAL INFRASTRUCTURE PROTECTION CENTER (NIPC)

J. Edgar Hoover Bldg.
935 Pennsylvania Ave. NW
Washington, DC 20535
PH: (202)323-3205
TF: 888-585-9078

FX: (202)323-2079
E-mail: www.nipc.watch@fbi.gov
URL: http://www.nipc.gov
Contact: Mr. Ron Dick, Director

Founded: 1998. **Description:** National Infrastructure Protection Center (NIPC) serves as national infrastructure threat assessment, warning, vulnerability and law enforcement investigation and response entity, related to computer and information technologies.

∎ 3135
THE NATIONAL SCIENCE AND TECHNOLOGY COUNCIL (NSTC)

Office of Science and Technology Policy
Executive Office of the President
Washington, DC 20502
PH: (202)395-7347
E-mail: ostpinfo@ostp.eop.gov

Founded: 1993. **Description:** The National Science and Technology Council helps to establish clear national goals for Federal science and technology investments in areas ranging from information technologies and health research, to improving transportation systems and strengthening fundamental research. The NSTC prepares research and development strategies that are coordinated across agencies to form an investment package aimed at accomplishing many national goals.

∎ 3136
THE NATIONAL TELECOMMUNICATIONS AND INFORMATION AGENCY (NTIA)

US Department of Commerce
1401 Constitution Ave. NW
Washington, DC 20230
PH: (202)482-7002
URL: http://www.ntia.doc.gov
Contact: Mr. Michael D. Gallagher, Deputy Assistant Secretary

Founded: 1978. **Description:** The National Telecommunications and Information Advisory Committee (NTIA) works to spur innovation, encourage competition, help create jobs and provide consumer with more choices and better quality telecommunications products and services at lower prices.

∎ 3137
NETWORK RELIABILITY AND INTEROPERABILITY COUNCIL (NRIC)

600 Stinson Blvd., Rm. 1N
Minneapolis, MN 55413
PH: (763)531-6000
URL: http://www.nric.org
Contact: Pam Stegora-Axberg, Steering Committee Chair

Founded: 1996. Description: The purpose of The Network Reliability and Interoperability Council (NRIC) is to provide recommendations to the FCC and to the telecommunications industry that will assure optimal reliability and interoperability of public telecommunications networks.

∎ 3138
OFFICE OF INTERNATIONAL AFFAIRS (OIA)

National Telecommunications and Information Administration
U.S. Department of Commerce
1401 Constitution Ave. NW, Rm. 4701
Washington, DC 20230
PH: (202)482-1866
FX: (202)482-1865
E-mail: rlayton@ntia.doc.gov
URL: http://www.ntia.doc.gov/oiahome/oiahome.html
Contact: Robin R. Layton, Associate Administrator

Staff: 11. Description: The Office of International Affairs (OIA) promotes the need for competition and liberalization and telecommunications and information policies worldwide. OIA's goal is to provide policy analysis, technical guidance and representation, so as to advance the strategic interests and international competitiveness of the United States before an international audience.

∎ 3139
OFFICE OF POLICY ANALYSIS AND DEVELOPMENT (OPAD)

U.S. Department of Commerce, Rm.4725
Washington, DC 20230
PH: (202)482-1880
FX: (202)482-6173
E-mail: webopad@ntia.doc.gov
URL: http://www.ntia.doc.gov/opadhome/opadhome.html
Contact: Kelly Levy, Associate Administrator

Description: Office of Policy Analysis and Development (OPAD) supports NTIA's role as principal adviser to the President, Vice President and Secretary of Commerce on telecommunications and information policies. OPAD's goal is to enhance the public interest by generating, articulating and advocating creative and influential policies and programs in the telecommunications and information sectors.

∎ 3140
THE OFFICE OF SCIENCE AND TECHNOLOGY POLICY (OSTP)

Executive Office of the President
Washington, DC 20502
PH: (202)395-7347
E-mail: ostpinfo@ostp.eop.gov
URL: http://www.ostp.gov/html/OSTP_insideostp.html

Contact: John H. Marburger III, PhD

Founded: 1976. Description: The Office of Science and Technology Policy was created to provide the President with timely policy advice and to coordinate the science and technology investment. OSTP has had a prominent role in advancing fundamental science, educating and scientific literacy, investment in applied research, and international cooperation.

∎ 3141
OFFICE OF SPECTRUM MANAGEMENT (OSM)

U.S. Department of Commerce/NTIA
1401 Constitution Ave. NW
Washington, DC 20230
PH: (202)482-1850
E-mail: laronow@ntia.doc.gov
URL: http://www.ntia.doc.gov/osmhome/osmhome.html
Contact: Frederick Wentland, Director

Description: The Office of Spectrum Management (OSM) is responsible for managing the Federal Government's use of the radio frequency spectrum. OSM develops plans for wartime and peacetime use. OSM also prepares for, participates in and implements the results of international radio conferences, assigning frequencies, maintaining use databases for the spectrum, reviewing Federal Agency's new telecommunications system and certifying that spectrum will be available.

∎ 3142
OFFICE OF TELECOMMUNICATIONS AND INFORMATION APPLICATIONS (OTIA)

U.S. Department of Commerce
1401 Constitution Ave., NW
Washington, DC 20230
PH: (202)482-5802
FX: (202)501-5136
E-mail: bmcguire-rivera@ntia.doc.gov
URL: http://www.ntia.doc.gov/otiahome/otiahome.html
Contact: Dr. Bernadette McGuire-Rivera, Associate Administrator

Description: The Office of Telecommunications and Information Applications (OTIA) assists local and state governments, educational and health care entities, libraries, public service agencies, and other groups in effectively using telecommunications and information technologies to better provide public services and advance the national goals.

∎ 3143
THE PARTNERSHIP FOR CRITICAL INFRASTRUCTURE SECURITY (PCIS)

US Chamber of Commerce
Special Programs
1615 H St. NW

Washington, DC 20062
PH: (202)463-5517
FX: (202)463-5308
E-mail: robert.haines@ciao.gov
URL: http://www.pcis-forum.org

Founded: 1998. **Description:** Partnership for Critical Infrastructure Security (PCIS) was developed from initiatives outlined in the Presidential Decision Directive-63 published in 1998 to promote the protection and assurance of the nations critical infrastructures such as, energy, financial services, transportation, communications and information services and vital human services including health, safety and water

▌3144

PRESIDENT'S INFORMATION
TECHNOLOGY ADVISORY COMMITTEE

4201 Wilson Blvd., Ste. II-405
Arlington, VA 22230
PH: (703)292-4873
FX: (703)292-9097
E-mail: ac-comments@itrd.gov
URL: http://www.itrd.gov
Contact: Cita M. Furlani, Dir.

History: Committee was originally established by President Clinton by Executive Order 13035, dated February 11, 1997, and under the authority of P.L. 102-194, the High-Performance Computing Act of 1991, as the Presidential Advisory Committee on High-Performance Computing and Communications, Information Technology, and the Next Generation Internet; name changed in 1998. It is a presidential advisory committee that functions under the National Science and Technology Council (see separate entry), Office of Science and Technology Policy. PRG Committee provides advice and information to the President about high-performance computing and communications, information technology, and the Next Generation Internet. Committee also provides an independent assessment of: progress made in implementing the High-Performance Computing and Communications (HPCC) Program; progress in designing and implementing the Next Generation Internet initiative; the need to revise the HPCC Program; balance among components of the HPCC program; whether the research and development undertaken pursuant to the HPCC Program is helping to maintain United States leadership in advanced computing and communications technologies and their applications; and other issues as specified by the Director, Office of Science and Technology Policy. **Memberships:** Committee consists of no more than 30 nonfederal members appointed by the President, including representatives of the research, education, and library communities, network service providers, and representatives from critical industries. **Meetings:** Committee meets quarterly.

▌3145

THE PRESIDENT'S INFORMATION
TECHNOLOGY ADVISORY COMMITTEE
(PITAC)

The National Coordination Office for Information Technology
Research and Development

4201 Wilson Blvd., Ste. II-405
Arlington, VA 22230
PH: (703)292-4873
FX: (703)292-9097
E-mail: ac-comments@itrd.gov
URL: http://www.itrd.gov/ac
Contact: Eric Benhamou, Ph.D., Director

Founded: 1999. **Members:** 26. **Description:** The President's Information Technology Advisory Committee provides the President, Congress, and the Federal agencies involved in information technology research and development with expert, independent advice on keeping America's preeminence in advanced information technologies, including such critical elements of the national infrastructure as high performance computing, large scale networking, and high assurance and systems design software.

▌3146

TECHNOLOGICAL ADVISORY COUNCIL

Office of Engineering & Technology
Federal Communications Commission
445 12th St. SW
Washington, DC 20554
PH: (202)418-2046
FX: (202)418-1944
E-mail: snewman@fcc.gov
URL: http://www.fcc.gov/oet/tac/
Contact: David Farber, Staff Contact

History: Council was established December 11, 1998. It is a public advisory council of the Federal Communications Commission. Council advises the Federal Communications Commission on advances in technology that have resulted in innovations in how telecommunications services are provided to, and assessed by, users of those services. Many of these advances are increasing the rate of convergence among categories of services that have traditionally been viewed as distinct, such as cable television services, telephony, data services, and internet services. **Memberships:** Members represent the field of telecommunications, private sector companies, and technical executives. Council comprises thirty-two members. **Meetings:** Council meets two to three times a year.

▌3147

TECHNOLOGY OPPORTUNITIES
PROGRAM (TOP)
OFFICE OF THE TELECOMMUNICATIONS AND
INFORMATION APPLICATION

National Telecommunications and Information Administration
1401 Constitution Ave. NW, Rm. 4092
Washington, DC 20230
PH: (202)482-2048
FX: (202)501-5136
E-mail: top@ntia.doc.gov
URL: http://www.ntia.doc.gov/top/
Contact: Amy Borgstrom

Staff: 11. **Description:** Technology Opportunities Program is a merit-based program that brings digital network technologies to communities throughout the United States.

▌3148
U.S.-KOREA COMMITTEE ON BUSINESS COOPERATION

Off. of Korea and Southeast Asia
Deparment of Commerce
14th St. & Constitution Ave. NW, Rm. 3203
Washington, DC 20230
PH: (202)482-1695
FX: (202)482-4760
Contact: Susan M. Blackman, Staff Contact

History: Committee is a public advisory council under the International Trade Administration, Department of Commerce. Committee facilitates stronger commercial ties between U.S. and Korean private sector businesses. In doing so, Committee identifies commercial opportunities, impediments, and issues of concern to the respective business communities; improves the dissemination of appropriate commercial information on both markets; adopts sectoral or project-related approaches to expand business opportunities, addresses specific problems, and makes recommendations to decision-makers where appropriate; promotes trade/business development and promotion programs to assist the respective business communities in accessing each market, including trade missions, exhibits, seminars, and other events; and facilitate where appropriate technical cooperation. **Memberships:** Committee consists of an equal number of private sector representatives from the United States and Korea. Committee is chaired by the Secretary of Commerce and the Korean Minister of Commerce, Industry and Energy.

▌3149
UNITED STATES TELECOM ASSOCIATION (USTA)

1401 H St., Ste. 600
Washington, DC 20005
PH: (202)326-7300
FX: (202)326-7333
Contact: Walter B. McCormick, Jr., President

Founded: 1897. **Description:** The United Telecom Association provides a place where local telephone companies can come together to address the concerns of the telecommunications industry.

▌3150
THE VIRTUAL INSTITUTE OF INFORMATION (VII)

Uris Hall
3022 Broadway, Room 809
New York, NY 10027

PH: (212)854-4222
TF: (212)932-7816
URL: http://www.vii.org

Description: The VII is the global center for discussion and debate of telecommunications and mass media issues. The Institute's mission is to research and exhibit telecommunications and mass media information while fostering the continued understanding of these fields for the future economic and social development of society.

PUBLICATIONS

▌3151
101 WAYS TO BOOST YOUR WEB TRAFFIC : INTERNET PROMOTION MADE EASIER
INTESYNC

PO Box 950
Union City, CA 94587
PH: (510)429-7222
E-mail: 101ways@intesync.com
URL: http://www.intesync.com

Description: Book by Thomas Wong, retails for $24.95. Provides advice on how to selectively and effectively market your web site. Provides information on which web traffic increasing tools should be used and under what circumstances. Covers all types of web sites and services. 2nd edition, publication date 2002.

▌3152
ACCESS DENIED : THE COMPLETE GUIDE TO PROTECTING YOUR BUSINESS ONLINE
OSBORNE/MCGRAW-HILL

2600 10th St., 6th Fl.
Berkeley, CA 94710
TF: 800-227-0900
E-mail: pbg.ecommerce_custserv@mcgraw-hill.com
URL: http://www.osborne.com

Description: A practical guide to protecting an online business. Covers topics such as email, ecommerce, and desktop security. Title chapters include Establishing Safe Business Practices, Understanding Hackers and How they Attack and Evaluating Data Backup Systems. Written by Cathy Cronkhite and Jack McCullough, published 2001.

▌3153
ADVISING EBUSINESS
WEST GROUP

610 Opperman Dr.
Eagan, MN 55123
PH: (651)687-7000

URL: http://www.westgroup.com

Description: Monthly looseleaf or email publication covering the major legal and business issues in the online community. Written for the lay person by a well known lawyer in the field, Jonathan D Robbins, and includes legal, business and technical analysis. Topics covered include privacy, intellectual property, marketing, unfair competition, patents, online contracts, digital payment, taxation, and crime, among others.

▋ 3154

B TO B: THE MAGAZINE FOR MARKETING AND E-COMMERCE STRATEGISTS
CRAIN COMMUNICATIONS

965 E Jefferson Ave.
Detroit, MI 48207-3187
PH: (313)446-0450
FX: (313)446-6777
E-mail: subs@crain.com
URL: http://www.btobonline.com

Description: Focuses on ecommerce advertising and industrial marketing. Companion web site provides current industry news, and offers email alterts and newsletters. Subscriptions to the print magazine are available for $59/year. ISSN: 1530-2369

▋ 3155

B2B AND BEYOND : NEW BUSINESS MODELS BUILT ON TRUST
WILEY

111 River St.
Hoboken, NJ 07030
PH: (201)748-6000
FX: (201)748-6088
URL: http://www.wiley.com

Description: Focuses on the changing nature of business relationship models in an environment where competitors are often also customers, and the internet makes easy price comparisions available to all. Explores ways to provide quality, service and e-trust as a means to distinguish oneself and engender customer loyalty. Written by Harry B. Demaio, publication date 2001. Retails for $39.95. ISBN: 0471054666

▋ 3156

THE B2B E-COMMERCE HANDBOOK : HOW TO TRANSFORM YOUR BUSINESS-TO-BUSINESS GLOBAL MARKETING STRATEGY
KOGAN PAGE

120 Pentonville Rd.
London N19JN, United Kingdom
PH: 44 020 72780433
FX: 44 020 78376348
E-mail: kpinfo@kogan-page.co.uk

URL: http://www.kogan-page.co.uk

Description: Explores the emerging world of B2B e-marketing. Provides information on how online companies can incorportate B2B services to increase their market. Written by Matt Haig, publication date 2001. Retails for $32.50. ISBN: 0749435771.

▋ 3157

BACKBONE : THE STRENGTH OF EBUSINESS
PUBLIMEDIA COMMUNICATIONS INC.

200 - 1140 Homer St.
Vancouver, BC, Canada V6B2X6
PH: (604)609-9841
TF: 888-609-8809
FX: (604)609-9891
E-mail: info@backbonemag.com
URL: http://www.backbonemag.com

Description: Bi-monthly Canadian magazine focusing on e-business and e-commerce. Includes marketing, trend analysis, investing, new markets and technology.

▋ 3158

BEST PRACTICES FOR WEBSITE CONTENT MANAGEMENT
FAULKNER INFORMATION SERVICES

114 Cooper Ctr.
7905 Browning Rd.
Pennsauken, NJ 08109-4319
PH: (856)662-2070
TF: 800-843-0460
FX: (856)662-3380
E-mail: info@faulkner.com
URL: http://www.faulkner.com

Description: Explores the world of content management and ways to best keep web documents and materials up-to-date. There are many solutions to the problem depending on the size and complexity of the organization and site. Available only as a PDF ebook. Published 2001 and retails for $96. ISBN: B000066CXP.

▋ 3159

BIGWIG BRIEFS, ONLINE ADVERTISING : INDUSTRY EXPERTS REVEAL THE SECRETS TO SUCCESSFUL ONLINE ADVERTISING PROGRAMS
ASPATORE BOOKS

330 Washington St., Ste. 400
Boston, MA 02108
E-mail: info@aspatore.com
URL: http://www.aspatore.com

Description: Provides information on online advertising strategies from the executive ''bigwigs'' in the industry, including doubleclick and 24/7 Media. Chapter titles include

The Best Way to Spend Marketing Dollars, Key Trends in Internet Marketing and How to Calculate Marketing ROI. Published in 2001. Retails for $14.95. ISBN:1587620162

■ 3160

BUILDING AN INTELLIGENT E-BUSINESS
PREMIER PRESS

36 S. Pennsylvania St., Ste. 610
Indianapolis, IN 46204
TF: 800-428-7267
E-mail: customercare1@premierpressbooks.com
URL: http://www.premierpressbooks.com

Description: Covers all the basic components of successful e-businesses. Topics include corporate strategy, supply chain management, customer service, user interface design and data security. Includes companion CDROM with demos of software and web site editing and management tools. Written by David Ferris and Larry Whipple. Published in 2000 and retails for $49.99. ISBN: 076152763X

■ 3161

BUILDING ELECTRONIC COMMERCE WITH WEB DATABASE CONSTRUCTIONS
ADDISON-WESLEY

75 Arlington St., Ste. 300
Boston, MA 02116
PH: (617)848-6000
URL: http://www2.awl.com

Description: Provides both a theoretical and a practical view of how to build basic databases on the web. Assumes some knowledge of database theory, provides background, and then walks the reader through several of the current tools availabe for web database implementation, such as ASP, JSP and activeX. Accompanying CDROM and web site access allow users to try out tools as they learn about them. Written by Anne Nelson and William H. M. Nelson. Published in 2002 and retails for $71.00. ISBN: 020174130X

■ 3162

BUILDING EFFECTIVE WEB SITES
PRENTICE HALL

1 Lake St.
Upper Saddle River, NJ 07458
TF: 800-282-0693
FX: 800-835-5327
URL: http://www.prenhall.com

Description: Starts with the basic concepts of web site design, and follows the process through from planning to marketing. Emphasizes user interface principles and design. Includes tutorials on Dreamweaver, FrontPage and Photoshop. Targets new and beginner web site developers. Written by Raymond Frost and Judy Strauss. Published in 2002 and retails for $21. ISBN: 0130932884.

■ 3163

BUSINESS 2.0
BUSINESS 2.0 MEDIA INC.

Time Life Bldg.
Rockefeller Ctr.
New York, NY 10020
PH: (212)522-8263
TF: 800-317-9704
E-mail: subsvcs@business2.customersvc.com
URL: http://www.business2.com

Description: Website and print publication providing news on the internet marketplace. Website offers daily editorials and features, along with a free newsletter available by email. Print publication contains articles on technologies, best business practices, market reports and the people behind the machines. Print publication is monthly except combined issues in Jan./Feb. and Aug./Sept. ISSN: 1538-1730

■ 3164

BUSINESS PROCESS ORIENTATION : GAINING THE E-BUSINESS COMPETITIVE ADVANTAGE
ST. LUCIE PRESS

2000 NW Corporate Blvd.
Boca Raton, FL 33431
PH: (561)994-0555
TF: 800-272-7737
FX: 800-374-3401
URL: http://www.crcpress.com

Description: Explores the Business Process Orientation (BPO) in depth in order to build a horizontal, integrated business structure that can survive in the current marketplace. Covers topics such as customer relevance, internally consistent decisions making, and detailed planning. Chapter titles include BPO and Organizational Performance, Benchmarking Using the BPO Maturity Model and Implementing and Evaluating BPO Effectiveness. Includes case studies and assessment tools. Written by Kevin P. McCormack and William C. Johnson. Published in 2001 and retails for $39.95. ISBN: 1574442945.

■ 3165

BUSINESSFINANCEMAG.COM
PENTON TECHNOLOGY MEDIA

PO Box 3438
Loveland, CO 80539
PH: (970)203-2926
FX: (970)593-1050
E-mail: info@businessfinancemag.com
URL: http://www.businessfinancemag.com

Description: Online and print magazine written for finance and accounting professionals. Includes sections on e-business, how-to articles, and reviews of accounting software. Companion web site includes searchable archive back to 1995. Print subscriptions are free to qualifying professionals, or $115/yr.

■ **3166**

CASES IN ELECTRONIC COMMERCE

MCGRAW-HILL

1221 Avenue of the Americas
New York, NY 10020
PH: (212)512-2000
URL: http://www.mcgraw-hill.com

Description: Contains 25 case studies focusing on the implications of various ecommerce issues, such as product choices, ISPs and digital cash. Provides real world stories to assist others in learning the ins and outs of the ecommerce business. Written by business school professors Sidney Laurence Huff, Michael Wade, Scott L. Schneberger and Sid Huff, 2nd edition published in 2002. Retails for $64.65. ISBN: 0072457317.

■ **3167**

CASES ON WORLDWIDE E-COMMERCE : THEORY IN ACTION

IDEA GROUP PUBLISHING

701 E Chocolate Ave., Ste. 200
Hershey, PA 17033
TF: 800-345-4332
FX: (717)533-8661
E-mail: cust@idea-group.com
URL: http://www.idea-group.com

Description: Provides detailed case studies of issues and opportunities in global ecommerce. Chapter titles include: e-learning business models: framework and best practice examples, growth and consolidation in the spanish-speaking e-commerce market, and SAFECO: leveraging the web in a knowledge-based service industry. Edited by Mahesh Raisinghani and published in 2002. Retails for $74.95. ISBN: 1930708270.

■ **3168**

CASES IN E-COMMERCE

MCGRAW-HILL/IRWIN

1221 Avenue of the Americas
New York, NY 10020
PH: (212)512-2000
URL: http://www.mhhe.com/catalogs/irwin

Description: 37 case studies of top businesses. Focuses on decision making processes. This book is a companion to the textbook ''Introduction to e-Commerce'', by the same authors. Written by Jeffrey F. Rayport and Bernard J. Jaworski, and published in 2001. Retails for $108.65. ISBN: 0072500956.

■ **3169**

COMPILATION OF STATE AND FEDERAL PRIVACY LAWS

PRIVACY JOURNAL

Providence, RI
URL: http://townonline.com/privacyjournal

Description: Provides quick comparisons statutory laws on privacy, topic by topic, state by state. Written by Robert

Ellis Smith, published in 2002 and retails for $35.00. ISBN: 0930072170.

■ **3170**

COMPLETE INTERNET & WORLD WIDE WEB PROGRAMMING TRAINING COURSE

PRENTICE HALL

1 Lake St.
Upper Saddle River, NJ 07458
TF: 800-282-0693
FX: 800-835-5327
URL: http://www.prenhall.com

Description: Textbook style introduction to web programming, starting with HTML and moving on through to client and server scripting and programming languages such as javascript, ASP and VBScript, Perl/CGI, database connectivity with PHP and SQL, and XML among others topics. Includes end of chapter exercises and CDROM tutorials. 2nd edition published in 2001 and retails for $109.99. ISBN: 0130895504.

■ **3171**

COMPLETE E-COMMERCE BOOK : DESIGN, BUILD & MAINTAIN A SUCCESSFUL WEB-BASED BUSINESS

CMP BOOKS

6600 Silacci Way
Gilroy, CA 95020
PH: (408)848-3854
TF: 800-500-6875
FX: (408)848-5784
E-mail: cmp@rushorder.com
URL: http://www.cmpbooks.com

Description: Covers all aspects of building an e-business, step by step. Includes topics such as user interface design, server software, choosing and using consultants and customer satisfaction. Published in 2000 and written by Janice Reynolds and Roya Mofazali. Retails for $29.95. ISBN: 157820061X.

■ **3172**

COMPLETE IDIOT'S GUIDE TO INTERNET PRIVACY AND SECURITY

PEARSON/ALPHA BOOKS

201 W 103rd St.
Indianapolis, IN 46290
PH: (317)581-3500
TF: 800-428-5331
URL: http://www.idiotsguides.com

Description: Written for the consumer, provides information on protecting data and personal information while online. Reviews common threats and how to best defend against them, from email viruses and spam, to cookies and encryption methods. Written by Preston Gralla and published in 2002. Retails for $19.95 2002 ISBN: 0028643216.

▌3173

COMPUTER, INTERNET AND
ELECTRONIC COMMERCE TERMS :
JUDICIAL, LEGISLATIVE AND TECHNICAL
DEFINITIONS
CARSWELL (A THOMSON COMPANY)

1 Corporate Plz.
Toronto, ON, Canada M1T3V4
PH: (416)609-8000
TF: 800-387-5164
URL: http://www.carswell.com

Description: Comprehensive dictionary containing computer, internet technology and legal terms pertaining to the field of e-commerce. Includes Canadian and European terms and definitions. Published annually and priced at $92. Edited by Barry Sookman. ISBN: 0459261967

▌3174

CONTENT MANAGEMENT BIBLE
HUNGRY MINDS

111 River St.
Hoboken, NJ 07030
PH: (201)748-6000
FX: (201)748-6088
URL: http://www.wiley.com

Description: Written for those managing or intended to manage complex web sites with dynamic and frequently updated content. Provides an overview of the technologies and examples of content management systems and their pros and cons. Both a theoretical and practical work. Written by Bob Boiko and and published in 2002. Retails for $49.99. ISBN: 076454862X.

▌3175

CORPORATE COUNSEL'S E-COMMERCE
ADVISER
BUSINESS LAWS, INC.

11630 Chillicothe Rd.
Chesterland, OH 44026
PH: (440)729-7996
TF: 800-759-0929
FX: (440)729-0645
E-mail: inquiry@businesslaws.com
URL: http://www.businesslaws.com/ecommadv.htm

Description: Monthly newsletter focusing on the legal aspects of ecommerce, including jurisdiction, intellectual property and company profiles. Subscription rates are $195.00 per year. Sample issues are available via the web site.

▌3176

CREATE DYNAMIC WEB PAGES USING
PHP AND MYSQL
ADDISON-WESLEY

75 Arlington St., Ste. 300
Boston, MA 02116
PH: (617)848-6000
URL: http://www2.awl.com

Description: Written for the beginner covers the aspects of PHP most likely to be used in web page generation. Topics include data structures, form processing, session management and database applications such as shopping carts. Written by David Tansley and published in 2002. Retails for $39.99. ISBN: 0201734028.

▌3177

CREATING A WINNING E-BUSINESS
COURSE TECHNOLOGY

25 Thompson Pl.
Boston, MA 02210
PH: (617)757-7900
TF: 800-648-7450
E-mail: reply@course.com
URL: http://www.course.com

Description: Covers creating an e-business starting with idea generation and working all the way through to a running business. Includes both managerial and technical topics, and provides an in depth case study. Written by Albert Napier, Philip Judd, and Stuart Wagner and published in 2002. Retails for $51.95. ISBN: 061903386X.

▌3178

CUSTOMER CALL CENTER OUTBACK : A
FRONTLINE SUPERVISOR'S MAP TO
SUCCESS
PURDUE UNIVERSITY PRESS

30 Amberwood Pkwy.
PO Box 388
Ashland, OH 44805
TF: 800-247-6553
FX: (419)281-6883
URL: http://www.thepress.purdue.edu

Description: Focuses on supervision of a call center, including managerial issues such as customer relations, and human resources and supervision issues. Written by Michael D. Trotter and published in 2002. Retails for $29.95. ISBN: 1557532591.

▌3179

DEVELOPING E-COMMERCE SITES : AN
INTEGRATED APPROACH
ADDISON-WESLEY

75 Arlington St., Ste. 300
Boston, MA 02116
PH: (617)848-6000
URL: http://www2.awl.com

Description: Explores the programming languages used for web development of ecommerce sites by leading the reader through the develompent of a complex site. Topics covered include servlets, Jserv, JDBC, SQL, and XML among others.

Written by Vivek Sharma and Rajiv Sharma and published in 2000. Retails for $39.95. ISBN: 0201657643.

3180
DICTIONARY OF E-BUSINESS : A DEFINITIVE GUIDE TO TECHNOLOGY AND BUSINESS TERMS
WILEY PUBLISHING

111 River St.
Hoboken, NJ 07030
PH: (201)748-6000
FX: (201)748-6088
URL: http://www.wiley.com

Description: Book by Francis Botto, published in 2000. Contains dictionary style entries explaining common and uncommon vocabulary used in ecommerce. ISBN: 0471881457

3181
DIGITAL CAPITAL : HARNESSING THE POWER OF BUSINESS WEBS
HARVARD BUSINESS SCHOOL PRESS

60 Harvard Way
Boston, MA 02163
PH: (617)783-7500
TF: 800-988-0886
FX: (617)783-7555
URL: http://www.hbsp.harvard.edu

Description: Explores new business models required for success in the ecommerce world. Section titles include: new models of wealth creation, alliances, digital business models, the human and relationship elements of digital capital, and how do you weave a b-web. Written by Don Tapscott, David Ticoll, and Alex Lowy, published in 2000. Available in print, microsoft reader and pdf e-book format, and retails for $27.50. ISBN: 1578511933.

3182
DIGITAL LEXICON : NETWORKED BUSINESS AND TECHNOLOGY FROM A-Z
ADDISON-WESLEY

75 Arlington St.
Boston, MA 02116
PH: (617)848-6000
TF: 800-447-2226
URL: http://www.awl.com

Description: Dictionary covering vocabulary, terminology, acronyms and ideas in the e-commerce business and IT environments. Entries range from short definitions to in-depth discussions. Authors are Keith Haviland and Nigel Barnes. Published 2002, retail price $34.99. ISBN: 0-201-78473-4

3183
DIGITAL LEXICON : NETWORKED BUSINESS AND TECHNOLOGY FROM A-Z
ADDISON-WESLEY

75 Arlington St., Ste. 300
Boston, MA 02116
PH: (617)848-6000
URL: http://www2.awl.com

Description: A dictionary and encyclopedia of technology terms. Written for the lay person covers new and emerging technology words, topics and acronyms. Written by Nigel Barnes and Keith Haviland and published in 2002. Retails for $34.99. ISBN: 0201784734.

3184
DIRECTORY OF INTERNATIONAL DIRECT AND E-MARKETING
KOGAN PAGE

120 Pentonville Rd.
London N19JN, United Kingdom
PH: 44 020 72780433
FX: 44 020 78376348
E-mail: kpinfo@kogan-page.co.uk
URL: http://www.kogan-page.co.uk

Description: Country by country directory of e-marketing providers, complete with full contact information and list of services provided. Also includes topical essays on current issues with titles such as ''current legal issues in email marketing''. Includes a glossary of direct marketing terms. 6th edition published in 2002. ISBN: 0749437820.

3185
DOCUMENTING E-COMMERCE TRANSACTIONS
BUSINESS LAWS, INC.

11630 Chillicothe Rd.
Chesterland, OH 44026
PH: (440)729-7996
TF: 800-759-0929
FX: (440)729-0645
E-mail: inquiry@businesslaws.com
URL: http://www.businesslaws.com/toc213.htm

Description: Looseleaf publication covering the legal issues of ecommerce computer transactions. Chapter titles include: e-commerce legal survival kit, electronic signatures in global and national commerce act, trademarks on the internet and international privacy issues. Originally published in 2000 and kept current via periodic supplements. ISBN 1567890687.

3186
THE E-BUSINESS HANDBOOK
ST. LUCIE PRESS

2000 NW Corporate Blvd.
Boca Raton, FL 33431
PH: (561)994-0555

TF: 800-272-7737
FX: 800-374-3401
URL: http://www.crcpress.com

Description: Focusing on e-commerce, discusses technological, social and managerial issues. Topics include business strategy, web development, new technologies, telecommuting, international issues, intelligent agents, and customer service. Published in 2002, and retails for $99.95. Edited by Paul Benjamin Lowry, J. Owen Cherrington, Ronald R. Watson. ISBN: 1574443054.

∎ 3187

E-BUSINESS LEGAL HANDBOOK : 2002 EDITION
PANEL PUBLISHERS

1185 Avenue of the Americas
New York, NY 10036
PH: (212)597-0200
FX: (212)597-0338
URL: http://www.aspenpublishers.com

Description: Designed to help companies understand and anticipate the legal risks in e-business. Includes topics such as creating a corporate identity, email and internet usage policies, civil liabilty online, intellectual property issues, contacts, and employee training. Retails for $175. Written by Michael Rustad and Cyrus Daftary. 2002 edition. ISBN: 0735517266

∎ 3188

E-BUSINESS LEGAL HANDBOOK 2002
ASPEN LAW & BUSINESS

1185 Avenue of the Americas
New York, NY 10036
PH: (212)597-0200
FX: (212)597-0338
URL: http://www.aspenpublishers.com

Description: Written by law professors with the intention ''to help companies seeking a presence on the Internet anticipate risks and liabilities''. Chapter titles include: establishing and maintaining an identity on the internet, civil liability in cyberspace and e-mail and internet usage policies. Written by Cyrus Daftary and Michael L. Rustad and retails for $175.00. ISBN: 0735521883.

∎ 3189

E-BUSINESS ADVISOR
ADVISOR PUBLICATIONS

PO Box 429002
San Diego, CA 92142-9002
PH: (858)278-5600
TF: 800-336-6060
FX: (858)278-0300
URL: http://e-businessadvisor.com

Description: Covers all technical aspects of ebusiness. Topics include web servers, datbase management, programming,

marketing strategies, legal issues, wireless and mobile technologies, supply chain integration and more. Provides news, strategies, best practices, trend analysis and ''Advisor Tips'' from industry leaders.Published monthly, subscriptions are available for $39/year. ISSN: 1098-8912.

∎ 3190

E-BUSINESS FORMULA FOR SUCCESS : HOW TO SELECT THE RIGHT E-BUSINESS MODEL, WEB SITE DESIGN, AND ONLINE PROMOTION STRATEGY FOR YOUR BUSINESS
MAXIMUM PRESS

605 Silverthorn Rd.
Gulf Breeze, FL 32561
PH: (850)934-0819
TF: 800-989-6733
FX: (850)934-9981
E-mail: moreinfo@maxpress.com
URL: http://www.maxpress.com

Description: Guides the business owner towards creating a profitable online business by outlining business models and related technologies needed to accomplish them. Includes information on designing an effective website appropriate to the chosen business model, and how to market and drive traffic to that site. Written by Susan Sweeney and published in 2001. Retails for $34.95. ISBN: 1885068603.

∎ 3191

A PRACTICAL GUIDE TO PLANNING FOR E-BUSINESS SUCCESS : HOW TO E-ENABLE YOUR ENTERPRISE
ST. LUCIE PRESS

2000 NW Corporate Blvd.
Boca Raton, FL 33431
PH: (561)994-0555
TF: 800-272-7737
FX: 800-374-3401
URL: http://www.crcpress.com

Description: Written for new businesses, describes how to develop a sucessful e-business strategy, moving beyond a simple web presence. Provides templates, exaples, checklists and FAQs to guide one along the process. Written by Anita Cassidy and published in 2002. Retails for $49.95. ISBN: 1574443046.

∎ 3192

E-BUSINESS STRATEGIES
CORNHILL PUBLICATIONS LTD.

Kings Court
2-16 Goodge St.
London W1P1FF, United Kingdom
PH: 44 020 72401515
FX: 44 020 73797371
E-mail: info@cornhillpublications.com
URL: http://www.cornhillpublications.com/titles/ebs.html

673

Description: Written for executives and decision makers, contains in depth articles and analysis on the global marketplace and provides strategies for managing ebusiness in an era of rapid change. Includes detailed reports and analysis from successful European business and industry leaders.

▌3193

E-BUSINESS WORKFLOW

SODEN

20 Mead Rd.
Uxbridge UB81AU, United Kingdom
PH: 44 01895 233194
E-mail: info@sodan.co.uk
URL: http://www.sodan.co.uk

Description: First published in 1993 and dedicated to workflow management on the online business, this publication is only distributed electronically in PDF format. Coverage includes topics such as reviews of workflow product developments and software, industry professional opinions, and user case studies and profiles. Subscriptions are available for 250 pounds UK, and can be ordered online in pounds sterling, euros, US dollars or Japanese yen.

▌3194

E-BUSINESS WORLD

INTERNATIONAL DATA GROUP

1 Exeter Plaza
Boston, MA 02116-2851
FX: (650)524-5730
E-mail: questions@idg.com.
URL: http://www.e-businessworld.com

Description: Free online newsletter sponsered by IDG.net and funded by advertising. Covers ecommerce markets, best practices, and backend technology. Daily email newsletters on selected topics are also available.

▌3195

E-BUSINESS WORLD : BUSINESS & POLICY ISSUES IN ELECTRONIC TRADE AND COMMERCE

INTERNATIONAL CHAMBER OF COMMERCE

156 5th Ave., Ste. 417
New York, NY 10010
PH: (212)206-1150
FX: (212)633-6025
E-mail: info@iccpub.net
URL: http://www.iccbooks.com

Description: ICC's newsletter on electronic commerce. Covers international electronic business issues such as privacy protection, dutyfree and tax issues, domain names, data protection and cybercrime. Published every two months. e-BusinessWorld may ordered from ICC's Business Bookstore at www.iccboks.com or by contacting ICC Publishing.

▌3196

E-COMMERCE LOGISTICS AND FULFILLMENT : DELIVERING THE GOODS

PRENTICE HALL

1 Lake St.
Upper Saddle River, NJ 07458
TF: 800-282-0693
FX: 800-835-5327
URL: http://www.prenhall.com

Description: Examines in depth the processes that take place AFTER a user clicks the ''buy'' button. Section titles include: integrating inventory and fufillment, protecting a consumers privacy online, and e-business cost reduction potential. Written by Deborah L. Bayles and published in 2001. Retails for $44.99. ISBN: 0130303283.

▌3197

E-COMMERCE : FUNDAMENTALS AND APPLICATIONS

WILEY

111 River St.
Hoboken, NJ 07030
PH: (201)748-6000
FX: (201)748-6088
URL: http://www.wiley.com

Description: Covers all aspects of ecommerce, including web current technologies and how to integrate them into business applications. Edited by Henry Chan and published in 2001. Retails for $49.95. ISBN: 0471493031.

▌3198

E-COMMERCE LAW & STRATEGY

AMERICAN LAWYER MEDIA, INC.

105 Madison Ave.
New York, NY 10016
TF: 800-537-2128
E-mail: lawcatalog@amlaw.com
URL: http://www.lawcatalog.com

Description: Published monthly, focuses on the current legal issues in e-commerce. Covers topics such as privacy, contracts, tax law, and intelectual property. Includes sections on terminology, software patents, recent legal decisions and news in the field. ISSN: 1536-2698

▌3199

E-FINANCE

SWEET & MAXWELL

100 Avenue Rd.
London NW33PF, United Kingdom
PH: 44 020 73937000
FX: 44 020 73937010
URL: http://www.sweetandmaxwell.co.uk

Description: Covers the topic of e-commerce finances in the European Union. Presents the financial legal issues involved in online commerce with each of the member countries. By Quentin Bargate and Martin Shah. Publication date 2003. ISBN: 0421747900

▌3200
E-FINANCE
JOSSEY-BASS/CAPSTONE

989 Market St.
San Francisco, CA 94103-1741
PH: (415)433-1740
FX: (415)433-0499
URL: http://www.josseybass.com

Description: Explores the technologies and emerging trends in the world of e-finance. Coveres IT and management topics. Provides case studies along with examples from large institutions such as Citicorp and Charles Schwab. Includes a glossary of terms and concepts and a resource guide. Written by Andrew Fight and published in 2002. Available either in print or as a Microsoft Reader or PDF e-book. Retails for $14.00. ISBN: 1841123315.

▌3201
E-MARKETING
JOSSEY-BASS/CAPSTONE

989 Market St.
San Francisco, CA 94103-1741
PH: (415)433-1740
FX: (415)433-0499
URL: http://www.josseybass.com

Description: Provides information on successful techniques in e-marketing from some leading businesses such as Hotmail and Honda. Covers topics such as banner ads, e-mail alerts, and affiliating. Includes glossary and resource guide. Written by Steve Shipside and published in 2002. Availble in print or as a PDF e-book and retails for $16.50. ISBN: 1841121991.

▌3202
E-MERGING BUSINESS
MONTGOMERY RESEARCH INC.

300 Montgomery St., Ste. 1135
San Francisco, CA 94104
PH: (415)732-1220
E-mail: inquiries@ebmagz.biz
URL: http://www.ebmagz.com

Description: Written for small business, provides practical information on ''hands-on and how-to'' information on all facets for business from e-commerce and online services to management to global competion. Annual subscription are available for $6.99 plus $4.00 shipping. Current issue also available on website. ISSN: 1531-0612

▌3203
E-MMERCE
ARK GROUP LTD.

4th Fl., Zeeta House
200 Upper Richmond Rd.
London SW152SH, United Kingdom
PH: 44 020 87852700
FX: 44 020 87859373
URL: http://www.emmercemagazine.com

Description: Print and online magazine dedicated to B2B trade, exports and technology. Contains news, surveys, opinions, and covers such topics as legal and regulatory issues, security, and supply chain fulfilment. Subscriptions are availablle for $365/yr and include access to archives on website. ISSN: 1469-0462.

▌3204
E-PRIVACY IMPERATIVE : PROTECT YOUR CUSTOMERS' INTERNET PRIVACY AND ENSURE YOUR COMPANY'S SURVIVAL IN THE ELECTRONIC AGE
AMACOM

1601 Broadway
New York, NY 10019
PH: (212)586-8100
TF: 800-262-9699
FX: (212)586-8168
URL: http://www.amanet.org/books

Description: Written for site developers, managers and executives, provides information on protecting both consumer and corporate private data. Topics include consumer concerns, legal issues, policies, tools for enacting policies, P3P, and more. Written by Mark S. Merkow and James Breithaupt and published in 2002. Retails for $34.95. ISBN: 0814406289.

▌3205
E-SERVICE JOURNAL
INDIANA UNIVERSITY PRESS

601 N Morton St.
Bloomington, IN 47404
PH: (812)855-9449
TF: 800-842-6796
FX: (812)855-8507
E-mail: journals@indiana.edu
URL: http://muse.jhu.edu/journals/esj/

Description: Multidisciplinary journal devoted to to research on electronic services. Includes design, delivery, and social implications of the various technologies. Covers both public and private sectors, including e-businss and e-government. ISSN: 1528-8226

■ **3206**

E-SUPPLY CHAIN MANAGEMENT : FOUNDATIONS FOR MAXIMIZING TECHNOLOGY AND ACHIEVING BREAKTHROUGH PERFORMANCE

ST. LUCIE PRESS

2000 NW Corporate Blvd.
Boca Raton, FL 33431
PH: (561)994-0555
TF: 800-272-7737
FX: 800-374-3401
URL: http://www.crcpress.com

Description: Focuses on describing how supply chain management can be maximized in an e-commerce environment. Discusses software, processes, and services to increase time to market and performance. Written by David F. Ross and published in 2002. ISBN: 1574443240.

■ **3207**

E-SUPPLY CHAIN : USING THE INTERNET TO REVOLUTIONIZE YOUR BUSINESS

BERRETT-KOEHLER

235 Montgomery St., Ste. 650
San Francisco, CA 94104
PH: (415)288-0260
TF: 800-929-2929
FX: (415)362-2512
E-mail: bkpub@bkpub.com
URL: http://www.bkpub.com

Description: Focuses on how to develop effecive supply chains in an e-business. Offers case studies of models that do and don't work in an increasingly b2b world. Chapter titles include: the connection with business strategy, the impact of marketing, sales and customer service, and a guide to the future. Written by Charles C. Poirier and Michael J. Bauer and published in 2000. Retails for $39.95. ISBN: 1576751171.

■ **3208**

EAI JOURNAL

THOMAS COMMUNICATIONS, INC.

9550 Skillman St., Ste. 415
Dallas, TX 75243
PH: (214)340-2147
FX: (214)341-7081
E-mail: info@eaijournal.com
URL: http://www.eaijournal.com

Description: Magazine focusing on ebusiness, application integration and web services. Free subscriptions are available to those in the IT fields in the U.S. and Canada. Outside the U.S. or non-qualifying individuals may subscribe for $96/yr. Topics covered include ecommerce, b2b, data interchange, XML, process flow, middleware and web services.

■ **3209**

EBUSINESS ESSENTIALS : TECHNOLOGY AND NETWORK REQUIREMENTS FOR MOBILE AND ONLINE MARKETS

JOHN WILEY & SONS

111 River St.
Hoboken, NJ 07030
PH: (201)748-6000
FX: (201)748-6088
URL: http://www.wiley.com

Description: Up-to-date handbook on ebusiness focusing on technologies, especially mobile and wireless. Explains technologies and terminologies and where they may most successfully be applied. The intended audience for this book is planners, engineers, managers and developers. Covered topics include mBusiness technologies such as UMTS and WAP, security issues, payment, supply chain integration, and virtual mobile network operations. Written by Mark Norris and Steve West, published in 2001. List price $45. ISBN: 0471521833.

■ **3210**

EBUSINESS JOURNAL

PLESMAN COMMUNICATIONS LTD.

25 Sheppard Ave. W, Ste. 100
Toronto, ON, Canada M2N6S7
PH: (416)733-7600
FX: (416)227-8300
URL: http://www.plesman.com

Description: Monthly Canadian publication written for management and professionals and focusing on the digital marketplace. Covers economic, legal and technological issues. Includes news and analysis, issues and trends, business models and marketing techniques. Companion website includes daily global IT news and free email newsletters. Qualifying Canadians can receive a 1 year free subscription. US subscription rate is $115/yr.

■ **3211**

ECOMMERCE TIMES

TRIAD COMMERCE GROUP, LLC

15260 Ventura Blvd., Ste. 1420
Sherman Oaks, CA 91403
TF: 888-528-8280
URL: http://www.ecommercetimes.com

Description: Free website funded by advertising. Provides industry news, analysis and features. Sections include technology and trends, small business issues, imarketing, b2b issues, cybercrime and more. Includes product guides, newsmaker profiles, calendar of ecommerce events and a message board.

∎ 3212

EFFECTIVE PROMOTIONAL PLANNING FOR E-BUSINESS

BUTTERWORTH-HEINEMANN

200 Wheeler Rd., 6th Fl.
Burlington, MA 01803
PH: (781)221-2212
TF: 800-545-2522
FX: (781)221-1615
E-mail: custserv.bh@elsevier.com
URL: http://www.bh.com

Description: Provides an introductory text for marketing e-businesses. Provides international case studies, along with a resource web site including examples of campaigns. Topics covered include branding, building an effective web site, B2B and B2C communications. Section titles include: planning your marketing communications, public relations—more than just a goodwill exercise, and managing implementation. Written by Cathy Ace and published in 2002. Retails for $24.99 ISBN: 0750652683.

∎ 3213

EFFECTIVE E-MAIL MARKETING : THE COMPLETE GUIDE TO CREATING SUCCESSFUL CAMPAIGNS

AMACOM

1601 Broadway
New York, NY 10019
PH: (212)586-8100
TF: 800-262-9699
FX: (212)586-8168
URL: http://www.amanet.org/books

Description: Provides real world examples of email campaigns that succeed, and those that fail. Discusses topics such as what is considered spam and how to obtain targeted, quality email lists, along with tips on designing effective messages. Written by Herschell Gordon Lewis and retails for $24.95. Published in 2002. ISBN: 0814471471.

∎ 3214

ELECTRONIC COMMERCE 2002 : A MANAGERIAL PERSPECTIVE

PRENTICE HALL

1 Lake St.
Upper Saddle River, NJ 07458
TF: 800-282-0693
FX: 800-835-5327
URL: http://www.prenhall.com

Description: An in-depth introduction to all aspects of e-commerce. Includes management and technology topics, along with case studies. Divided into six sections which cover fundamentals and technology, marketing, B2B, systems, security and implementations. Edited by Efraim Turban and published in a second edition in 2002. Retails for $105.33. ISBN: 0130653012.

∎ 3215

ELECTRONIC COMMERCE & LAW REPORT (BNA)

BUREAU OF NATIONAL AFFAIRS, INC.

1231 25th St. NW
Washington, DC 20037
TF: 800-372-1033
E-mail: customercare@bna.com
URL: http://www.bna.com/products/ip/eplr.htm

Description: Weekly legal bulletin for lawyers and executives covering the national and international issues of concern in the e-commerce marketplace. Covers news, trends and opinions on the digital economy. ISSN: 1098-5190.

∎ 3216

ELECTRONIC COMMERCE NEWS

PBI MEDIA, LLC

1201 Seven Locks Rd., Ste. 300
Potomac, MD 20854
PH: (301)354-2000
TF: 800-777-5006
FX: (301)309-3847
E-mail: clientservices@pbimedia.com
URL: http://www.telecomweb.com/ebusiness/

Description: Covers communications industry e-business news, market research, and analysis. Global in scope, covers all facets of the industry, including wireless, broadband, satellite and fiber optics. Companion website, TelcomWeb E-Business, provides some free access, and access to archives for subscribers. Print subscritions the this bi-weekly magazine cost $897/yr.

∎ 3217

ELECTRONIC COMMERCE RESEARCH

KLUWER ACADEMIC PUBLISHERS

101 Philip Dr.
Assinippi Park
Norwell, MA 02061
PH: (781)681-0571
FX: (781)871-7507
URL: http://www.kluweronline.com/issn/1389-5753

Description: Dedicated to research on all aspects of ecommerce, including technological, social, political and economic. Topics covered include global economic impact, computer and communication technologies, security and privacy, EDI, marketing, collaborative work, middleware, and service creation, among many others. Published quarterly, subscriptions are availabe for $331/year. ISSN: 1389-5753

∎ 3218

EMARKETER

EMARKETER

821 Broadway, 3rd fl.
New York, NY 10003
PH: (212)677-6300

TF: 877-378-2871
FX: (212)777-1172
E-mail: sales@emarketer.com
URL: http://www.emarketer.com

Description: Free website and email newsletter. Culls research and industry development news from over 1000 sources and compiles a weekly newsletter covering all aspects of e-business, "from Advertising to Wireless". Also provides an eStat database containing internet and ebusiness statistics. Indepth industry reports are available on the web site for purchase.

▋ 3219

EMARKETING EXCELLENCE : THE HEART OF EBUSINESS
BUTTERWORTH-HEINEMANN

200 Wheeler Rd., 6th Fl.
Burlington, MA 01803
PH: (781)221-2212
TF: 800-545-2522
FX: (781)221-1615
E-mail: custserv.bh@elsevier.com
URL: http://www.bh.com

Description: Published in association with the Chartered Institute of Marketing, focuses on e-marketing strategies and techniques. Written by P. R. Smith and Dave Chaffey and published in 2002. Retails for $25.00. ISBN: 0750653353.

▋ 3220

ESSENTIAL GUIDE TO INTERNET BUSINESS TECHNOLOGY
PRENTICE HALL PTR

1 Lake St.
Upper Saddle River, NJ 07458
TF: 800-282-0693
FX: 800-835-5327
URL: http://www.prenhall.com

Description: Written for managers and executives, and a general audience, provides a primer on internet technologies to assist in informed decision making. Divided into four sections: technology basics, front end: presentation, nuts and bolts of internet business and back end: support. Topics include databases, e-commerce technologies, XML, SOAP.-Net, Linux and more. Written by Kipp Martin and Gail Honda and published in 2002. Retails for $34.99. ISBN: 0130428205.

▋ 3221

ESSENTIAL BUSINESS TACTICS FOR THE NET
WILEY

111 River St.
Hoboken, NJ 07030
PH: (201)748-6000
FX: (201)748-6088

URL: http://www.wiley.com

Description: Provides information on using the internet both internally to improve business practices and flow and externally for marketing and sales. Section titles include: cutting costs across your enterprise, http://007 spying on your competition and yourself, your brand image and the internet, and direct marketing and sales support. Written by Larry Chase and Eileen Shulock, 2nd edition published in 2001. Retails for $29.99. ISBN: 0471403970.

▋ 3222

EUROMONEY E-BUSINESS AND FINANCE HANDBOOK 2001/2
EUROMONEY INSTITUTIONAL INVESTOR PLC

2a Altons House Office Park
Gatehouse Way
Aylesbury HP103XU, United Kingdom
PH: 44 01494 771930
FX: 44 01494 778994
URL: http://www.biz-lib.com/ZEMB204.html

Description: Resource book for e-business strategies, focused on the European Union. Includes finance and trading. Published by Euromoney in 2001 and retails for $170. ISBN: 1-85564-867-9.

▋ 3223

EWEEK
ZIFF DAVIS MEDIA

28 E 28th St.
New York, NY 10016-7930
PH: (781)393-3700
E-mail: eweek@ziffdavis.com
URL: http://www.eweek.com

Description: Weekly trade publication covering internet, IT and ecommerce issues, written for IT professionals. Provides news and analysis, benchmarking and commentary on a wide variety of IT topics and technologies. Sections include security, wireless, storage, news and commentary. Free to qualifying individuals in the U.S. and Canada; otherwise subscriptions are availabe for $195/year. ISSN: 1530-6283

▋ 3224

EXECUTIVE'S GUIDE TO E-BUSINESS: FROM TACTICS TO STRATEGY
WILEY

111 River St.
Hoboken, NJ 07030
PH: (201)748-6000
FX: (201)748-6088
URL: http://www.wiley.com

Description: Written by Pricewaterhousecoopers professionals, presents ecommerce topics and strategies for use by executives. Chapter titles include: channel enhancement, value chain integration, industry transformation and managing risk in e-business. Published in 2000 and retails for $39.95. ISBN: 0471376396.

∎ 3225

FLASH AND XML : A DEVELOPER'S GUIDE
ADDISON-WESLEY

75 Arlington St., Ste. 300
Boston, MA 02116
PH: (617)848-6000
URL: http://www2.awl.com

Description: Tutorial for web developers on using Flash and XML to create content and media rich sites. Also covers other technologies such as PHP and MySQL. Includes sample projects. Written by Dov Jacobson and Jesse Jacobson and published in 2001. Retails for $34.99. ISBN: 0201729202.

∎ 3226

FROM BRICKS TO CLICKS : 5 STEPS TO CREATING A DURABLE ONLINE BRAND
MCGRAW-HILL

1221 Avenue of the Americas
New York, NY 10020
PH: (212)512-2000
URL: http://www.mcgraw-hill.com

Description: Written for managers and executives interested in moving offline brand recognition and loyalty to the online marketplace. Offers step by step strategy along with case studies and discussion of the technologies and cultures. Written by Serge Timacheff, Douglas E. Rand and Mark Eppley and published in 2001. Retails for $24.95. ISBN: 0071371893.

∎ 3227

GET-STARTED GUIDE TO E-COMMERCE
AMACOM

1601 Broadway
New York, NY 10019
PH: (212)586-8100
TF: 800-262-9699
FX: (212)586-8168
URL: http://www.amanet.org/books

Description: Provides information on starting an e-commerce web site for those new to the field. Divided into four major areas: getting online, creating successful web sites, order fulfillment and getting noticed. Chapter titles include: analyzing your internet potential, building the page and making it sell. Written by Danielle Zilliox and published in 2001. Retails for $19.95 ISBN: 081447117X.

∎ 3228

GLOBAL ELECTRONIC COMMERCE : A POLICY PRIMER
INSTITUTE FOR INTERNATIONAL ECONOMICS

1750 Massachusetts Ave. NW
Washington, DC 20036-1903
PH: (202)328-9000
FX: (202)659-3225
URL: http://www.iie.com

Description: A policy primer written for lawmakers, though useful for companies wishing to understand the issues and opportunites. Covers issues such as dealing with a more information rich and highly networked international marketplace and the social and legal implications thereof. Includes discussions and examples of issues in areas such as telecommunications, finance, trade, taxation, and distribution. Published in the year 2000 and written by Catherine Mann, Sue Eckert and Sarah Cleeland Knight. Retails for $20. ISBN: 0881322741

∎ 3229

GLOBAL E-COMMERCE : TEXT AND CASES
PRENTICE HALL

1 Lake St.
Upper Saddle River, NJ 07458
TF: 800-282-0693
FX: 800-835-5327
URL: http://www.prenhall.com

Description: Provides 16 case studies of companies operating in differnet countries, emphasizing the opportunities and changing nature of business online. Dividedinto four sections: building a new business ecosystem, cunducting business in the marketspace, building and managing e-relationships and transforming the enterprise. Written by Ali Farhoomand and Peter Lovelock and published in 2001. Retails for $88.05. ISBN: 0130612294.

∎ 3230

GLOBAL E-COMMERCE AND ONLINE MARKETING : WATCHING THE EVOLUTION
QUORUM BOOKS

88 Post Rd. W
Westport, CT 06881
PH: (203)226-3571
TF: 800-225-5800
URL: http://

Description: Explores the effects that the internet, globalization and rapid technological change are having on e-commerce and marketing. Provides context for managers and decision makers marketing in the global marketplace. Written by Nikhilesh Dholakia and published in 2002. Retails for $64.95. ISBN: 1567204074.

▌3231

HANDBOOK ON ELECTRONIC COMMERCE

SPRINGER VERLAG

175 5th Ave.
New York, NY 10010
PH: (212)460-1500
TF: 800-777-4643
FX: (212)473-6272
E-mail: service@springer-ny.com
URL: http://www.springer-ny.com

Description: Covers all aspects of electronic commerce. Includes online storefronts, b2b issues, interface design, online financial transactions, legal issues and business models and stategies. Edited by Michael Shaw, Robert Blanning and Troy Strader and published in the year 2000. ISBN: 354065822X.

▌3232

HANDBOOK OF ONLINE MARKETING RESEARCH: KNOWING YOUR CUSTOMER USING THE NET

MCGRAW-HILL

1221 Avenue of the Americas
New York, NY 10020
PH: (212)512-2000
URL: http://www.mcgraw-hill.com

Description: Provides tools and analysis to reach targeted markets online. Includes topics such as qualitative and quantitative research methods, questionnaire design, and assessing the competition. Written by Joshua Grossnickle and Oliver Raskin and published in 2000. Retails for $39.95. ISBN: 0071361146.

▌3233

THE DISTANCE MANAGER : A HANDS-ON GUIDE TO MANAGING OFF-SITE EMPLOYEES AND VIRTUAL TEAMS

MCGRAW-HILL

1221 Avenue of the Americas
New York, NY 10020
PH: (212)512-2000
URL: http://www.mcgraw-hill.com

Description: Written for managers whose businesses are more virtual than physical, and who have employees in more than one location. Topics include mastering people skills, virtual team building, and effective use of email, videoconferencing and videoconferencing. Written by Kimball Fisher and Mareen Duncan Fisher and published in 2001. Retails for $24.95. ISBN: 0071360654.

▌3234

HOW TO GET YOUR BUSINESS ON THE WEB : A LEGAL GUIDE TO E-COMMERCE.

NOLO

950 Parker St.
Berkeley, CA 94710-2524
TF: 800-728-3555
FX: 800-645-0895
E-mail: cs@nolo.com
URL: http://www.nolo.com

Description: Nuts and bolts information of putting a business online. Defines technical and legal jargon for the lay person. Topics include getting a domain name, hiring a designer and host, selling online legally and online credit card transactions. Written by Fred Steingold and published in 2002. Retails for $29.99. ISBN: 0873377532.

▌3235

INFORMATION SYSTEMS : FOUNDATION OF E-BUSINESS

PRENTICE HALL

1 Lake St.
Upper Saddle River, NJ 07458
TF: 800-282-0693
FX: 800-835-5327
URL: http://www.prenhall.com

Description: Written for managers and non-technical executives this book lays the foundations for understanding information system tehcnologies and how the effect e-business. Topics include types of information systems, business processes, e-commerce, ethical issues, networking and telecommunications and security. Written by Steven Alter and retails for $109.33. 4th edition published in 2002. ISBN: 0130617733.

▌3236

INFORMATION SYSTEMS AND E-BUSINESS MANAGEMENT

SPRINGER-VERLAG NEW YORK INC.

PO Box 2485
Secaucus, NJ 07096
FX: (201)348-4505
E-mail: orders@springer-ny.com
URL: http://www.springer.de/economics/journals/c_10257.html

Description: Research journal for IS and ebusiness professionals. Covers all aspects of IS and ebusiness integration including systems, human resources, economic, organizational and technological issues. Also covers business digitisation, e-commerce, enterprise strategy, and management.

∎ 3237
INTERNATIONAL HANDBOOK OF ELECTRONIC COMMERCE
FITZROY DEARBORN PUBLISHERS

919 N Michigan Ave., Ste. 760
Chicago, IL 60611
PH: (312)587-0131
TF: 800-850-8102
FX: (312)587-1049
E-mail: customer_service@fitzroydearborn.com
URL: http://www.fitzroydearborn.com

Description: Covers all aspects of ecommerce, including marketing and advertising, EDI, security, electronic banking, legal issues, taxation, websites and hosting services and intra and extranets. Written by Jae K Shim, an published in the year 2000. ISBN: 0814405800

∎ 3238
INTERNATIONAL JOURNAL OF E-BUSINESS STRATEGY MANAGEMENT
WINTHROP PUBLICATIONS

Brunel House
55-57 N Wharf Rd.
London W21LA, United Kingdom
PH: 44 020 79159634
FX: 44 020 79159636
E-mail: info@winpub.demon.co.uk
URL: http://www.winthrop-publications.co.uk/EBSMFrontpage.htm

Description: Devoted to providing best practices and practical ebusiness management information. Topics include security and privacy, Inter and Intra office communications and workflow, human resource issues and training, knowledge management and EDI, business risk and insurance issues, and integration with corporate strategy. Published quarterly subscriptions are available for $578. ISSN: 1467-0305

∎ 3239
INTERNET MARKETING : INTEGRATING ONLINE AND OFFLINE STRATEGIES
MCGRAW-HILL/IRWIN

1221 Avenue of the Americas
New York, NY 10020
PH: (212)512-2000
URL: http://www.mhhe.com/catalogs/irwin

Description: Provides in depth information on traditional and online marketing and how to make them blend for a sucessful business. Written by Mary Lou Roberts and published in 2002. ISBN: 0071124179.

∎ 3240
INTERNET AND ONLINE PRIVACY : A LEGAL AND BUSINESS GUIDE
ALM PUB.

345 Park Ave. S
New York, NY 10010
TF: 800-888-8300

URL: http://www.americanlawyermedia.com/books

Description: Written by lawyers in the field for managers and business leaders, covers both the historical trends and cases and the current laws and litigation in online privacy. Covers the United States, both as a whole and individual states, and its major trading partners. Written by Andrew Frackman, Claudia Ray, and Rebecca Martin. Published in 2002 and retails for $34.95. ISBN: 097059707X.

∎ 3241
INTERNET AND BUSINESS
MCGRAW-HILL/DUSHKIN

Sluice Dock
Guilford, CT 06437-3450
PH: (203)453-4351
TF: 800-243-6532
FX: (203)453-6000
E-mail: customer.service@mcgraw-hill.com
URL: http://www.dushkin.com

Description: Provides selected and compiled articles from Business Week over the ast year. Focuses on internet topics and provides an overview of the current trends and concerns. Edited by Robert W. Price and retails for $20.95. 2001 edition ISBN: 0072396245

∎ 3242
INTERNET COMMERCE AND SOFTWARE AGENTS : CASES, TECHNOLOGIES, AND OPPORTUNITIES
IDEA GROUP PUBLISHING

701 E Chocolate Ave., Ste. 200
Hershey, PA 17033
TF: 800-345-4332
FX: (717)533-8661
E-mail: cust@idea-group.com
URL: http://www.idea-group.com

Description: Covers the emerging technologies of agents and bots, and their relationship to e-commerce. Divided into five sections: introducing internet commerce and software agents; agents in e-commerce: introduction and impact; agents in e-commerce: frameworks, aplications and cases; human interface to software agents; payment systems, recommender systems and the future. Written by Syed Mahbubur Rahman, Robert J. Bignall and published in 2001. Retails for $84.95. ISBN: 1930708017.

∎ 3243
INTRODUCTION TO INFORMATION SYSTEMS : ESSENTIALS FOR THE INTERNETWORKED E-BUSINESS ENTERPRISE
MCGRAW-HILL/IRWIN

1221 Avenue of the Americas
New York, NY 10020
PH: (212)512-2000

URL: http://www.mhhe.com/catalogs/irwin

Description: Textbook covering business information systems for intra and internet. Written for those seeking to manage complex systems in a rapidly changing environment. Written by James A. O'Brien and published in 2001. Retails for $99.80. ISBN: 0072423242.

∎ 3244
INTRODUCTION TO E-COMMERCE
MCGRAW-HILL/IRWIN

1221 Avenue of the Americas
New York, NY 10020
PH: (212)512-2000
URL: http://www.mhhe.com/catalogs/irwin

Description: Introductory textbook on business and e-commerce. Covers network infrastucture, online business strategy, legal issues, marketing and more. Companion book titled ''Cases in E-commerce'' provides real world applications of topics discussed. Written by Jeffrey F. Rayport and Bernard J. Jaworski and published in 2001. Retails for $110.05. ISBN: 0072510242.

∎ 3245
JOURNAL OF ORGANIZATIONAL COMPUTING AND ELECTRONIC COMMERCE
LAWRENCE ERLBAUM ASSOCIATES, INC.

10 Industrial Ave.
Mahwah, NJ 07430-2262
PH: (201)258-2200
TF: 800-936-6579
FX: (201)236-0072
E-mail: orders@erlbaum.com
URL: http://www.erlbaum.com/Journals/journals/JOCE/joce.htm

Description: An official publication of the Association for Information Systems, this journal is written for professionals in the field of ecommerce including consultants, information scientists and managers. Topics include technologies, EDI, organizational development, electronic agents, digital security and more. Includes book and software reviews and meeting announcements. Subscription rates for individuals are $55/year.

∎ 3246
LAW FOR E-COMMERCE
WEST/THOMSON LEARNING

610 Opperman Dr.
Eagan, MN 55123
PH: (651)687-7000
URL: http://www.westgroup.com

Description: Textbook covering the legalities of e-commerce. In addtion to a broad overview of the topic, includes managment, marking, finance, human resources and other business areas as they relate to online business. Written by

Roger Leroy Miller and Gaylord A. Jentz and published in 2002. Retails for $83.95. ISBN: 0324122799.

∎ 3247
LINE56
B2B E-COMMERCE INTERNATIONAL

10940 Wilshire Blvd., Ste. 600
Los Angeles, CA 90024
PH: (310)443-4226
FX: (310)443-4230
E-mail: info@line56.com
URL: http://www.line56.com

Description: Covers all aspects of e-business technologies. Includes industry news and trends, case studies and benchmark research. Companion website offers news and free email newsletters. Published quarterly subscriptions are available for $199/year. ISSN: 1534-5408

∎ 3248
M-COMMERCE CRASH COURSE : THE TECHNOLOGY AND BUSINESS OF NEXT GENERATION INTERNET SERVICES
MCGRAW-HILL

1221 Avenue of the Americas
New York, NY 10020
PH: (212)512-2000
URL: http://www.mcgraw-hill.com

Description: Focuses on the technologies enabling the move to wireless communications and commerce. Covers wireless network technologies, services and economies. Chapter titles include: business models, network signaling: mobile and wired business space, and e-commerce and mobile e-commerce. Written by P. J. Louis and published in 2001. Retails for $34.95 and available in print or in Microsoft Reader or Adobe e-book format. ISBN: 0071369945

∎ 3249
MARKETING ON THE INTERNET : SEVEN STEPS TO BUILDING THE INTERNET INTO YOUR BUSINESS
MAXIMUM PRESS

605 Silverthorn Rd.
Gulf Breeze, FL 32561
PH: (850)934-0819
TF: 800-989-6733
FX: (850)934-9981
E-mail: moreinfo@maxpress.com
URL: http://www.maxpress.com

Description: Covers tricks and techniques of successful marketing online. Includes topics such as web site design and interface, using web statistics, online transactions, marketing, and customer service. Includes case studies. Written by Jan Zimmerman and Jerry Yang, 6th edition published in 2002. Retails for 34.95. ISBN: 1885068808.

∎ 3250

MARKETING PLAN HANDBOOK FOR
BUSINESS AND E-BUSINESS

PRENTICE HALL

1 Lake St.
Upper Saddle River, NJ 07458
TF: 800-282-0693
FX: 800-835-5327
URL: http://www.prenhall.com

Description: Provides instruction, guidance and examples
of creating marketing plans. Includes Marketing Plan Pro
software which allows for the creation of marketing plans
for all types of organizations. Written by Marian Burk Wood,
and published in 2002. Retails for $26.67. ISBN:
0130613177

∎ 3251

MAX-E-MARKETING IN THE NET
FUTURE : THE SEVEN IMPERATIVES FOR
OUTSMARTING THE COMPETITION

MCGRAW-HILL

1221 Avenue of the Americas
New York, NY 10020
PH: (212)512-2000
URL: http://www.mcgraw-hill.com

Description: Provides ideas, tips and tricks for marketing
online. Covers technological and managerial perspectives.
Chapter titles include: use what you know to drive what you
do, do as little as possible yourself, and make business
responsible for marketing and marketing responsible for
business. Written by Stan Rapp and Chuck Martin, and
published in 2001. Retails for $24.95. ISBN:

∎ 3252

MIDDLEWARE AND ENTERPRISE
APPLICATION INTEGRATION : THE
ARCHITECTURE OF E-BUSINESS
SOLUTIONS

SPRINGER VERLAG

175 5th Ave.
New York, NY 10010
PH: (212)460-1500
TF: 800-777-4643
FX: (212)473-6272
E-mail: service@springer-ny.com
URL: http://www.springer-ny.com

Description: Written for managers and consultants, this text
covers the technologies known as middleware that link web
sites with back office information systems. Technologies
covered include RPC, hub and spoke, COBRA and java,
and provides discussion of how the can be used to interate
processes and applications. Written by Daniel Serain. 2nd
edtion pubished in 2002 and retails for $64.95. ISBN:
185233570X.

∎ 3253

MUTUAL FUND MARKET NEWS

SECURITIES DATA PUBLISHING

11 Penn Plz., 17th Fl.
New York, NY 10001
PH: (212)631-9710
TF: 888-280-4820
FX: (212)631-9711
URL: http://www.mfmarketnews.com

Description: Weekly publication and exclusive daily online
news focusing on the financial services industry in the online
marketplace. Written for strategic planners, marketing executives, and webmasters alike. Carries news stories, case
studies and analysis, and technology reviews.

∎ 3254

NATIONAL TOLL-FREE & INTERNET
BUSINESS BUYER'S GUIDE 2001

VOLT DIRECTORY MARKETING

1 Sentry Pky.
Blue Bell, PA 19422
TF: 800-458-8658
E-mail: vdm2@earthlink.net
URL: http://www.voltdirectory.com

Description: Business to business directory providing listings of companies that offer products and/or services to
other business. Provides both toll-free numbers and web site
addresses. A useful directory of what companies are doing
business online. Compiled by Bob Epstein, Patricia Selden
and Robert Epstein, 2001 edition retails for $27.99 ISBN:
0925133698.

∎ 3255

NETNOMICS: ECONOMIC RESEARCH
AND ELECTRONIC NETWORKING

KLUWER ACADEMIC PUBLISHERS

101 Philip Dr.
Assinippi Park
Norwell, MA 02061
PH: (781)681-0571
FX: (781)871-7507
URL: http://www.kluweronline.com/issn/1385-9587

Description: Economic research on networks, internet, e-
business and e-commerce. Published 3 times a year. Subscription rates for either print or online access are $152/
year. ISSN: 1385-9587

∎ 3256

NEW YORK TIMES EBUSINESS SECTION

NEW YORK TIMES

229 W 43rd St.
New York, NY 10036
PH: (212)556-1234
TF: 800-698-4637
E-mail: help@nytimes.com

URL: http://www.nytimes.com/pages/technology/ebusiness/

Description: Part of the Technology section of the NY Times, the ebusiness section contains current in the fields of business and technology. Articles are accessible on the web site for one week after publication date. Access is free, though registration is required.

■ 3257

ONLINE PROMOTIONS : WINNING STRATEGIES AND TACTICS

WILEY

111 River St.
Hoboken, NJ 07030
PH: (201)748-6000
FX: (201)748-6088
URL: http://www.wiley.com

Description: Covers a wide variety of inexpensive online promotions to draw traffice to your site. Includes sweepstakes, coupons, rebate and loyalty programs. Chapter titles include: how to create a multibrand promotion, promoting the promotion and what to do after the promotion. Companion CDROM contains templates and sample promotional materials. Written by Bill Carmody and published in 2001. Retails for $34.99 ISBN: 0471403989.

■ 3258

ONLINE CONSUMER PRIVACY 2001: WHAT YOUR COMPANY NEEDS TO KNOW RIGHT NOW

BUSINESS FOR SOCIAL RESPONSIBILITY:
EDUCATION FUND

609 Mission St., 2nd Fl.
San Francisco, CA 94105
PH: (415)537-0890
FX: (415)537-0889
E-mail: info@bsr.org
URL: http://www.bsr.org/Meta/about/PressReleasesDetail.-cfm?DocumentID=547

Description: Published by Business for Social Responsibility, this guide is intended to guide companies in creating and implementing socially responsibly privacy policies. Includes emerging trends and issues in online privacy as well as legistlative issues, along with a glossary of terms. Published in 2001 and retails for $45, availalbe through the BSR online store at: http://www.bsr.org/store.

■ 3259

ONLINE NEWSLETTERS FROM THE E-BUSINESS COMMUNICATION ASSOCIATION

E-BUSINESS COMMUNICATION ASSOCIATION

462 Boston St.
Topsfield, MA 01983
URL: http://www.ebusinessca.org

Description: The e-Business Communication Association (eBCA) is a global membership association and an affiliate unit of International Data Group (IDG). Membership costs $295/year and, in addition to access to materials such as industry analysis, market research and online courses, includes subscriptions and access to the following online newsletters: E-Business Community, E-Commerce Best Practices, e-Marketing Best Practices, e-Publishing Best Practices, Web Development Best Practices, IT Management Best Practices and CRM Best Practices.

■ 3260

PLANNING YOUR INTERNET MARKETING STRATEGY : A DOCTOR EBIZ GUIDE

WILEY

111 River St.
Hoboken, NJ 07030
PH: (201)748-6000
FX: (201)748-6088
URL: http://www.wiley.com

Description: Provides information on how to create an effective strategy for marketing an e-business. Topics include clarifying goals, profiling customers, product differentiation and online marketing tips. Written by Ralph F. Wilson and published in 2001. Retails for $19.95. ISBN: 0471441090.

■ 3261

PLUNKETT'S E-COMMERCE & INTERNET BUSINESS ALMANAC

PLUNKETT RESEARCH LTD

PO Drawer 541737
Houston, TX 77254-1737
PH: (713)932-0000
FX: (713)932-7080
E-mail: Customersupport@plunkettresearch.com
URL: http://www.plunkettresearch.com

Description: Contains industry overviews, trends, statistics, technologies, strategies and analysis, along with in-depth company profiles of the top 400 ebusiness companies. Includes online retailers, software companies, service providers, manufactures and more. 2001/2002 volume retails for $249. ISBN for 2001/2002 volume: 1891775219

■ 3262

PROFITABLE E-MARKETING : SUCCESS STRATEGIES THAT PAY OFF

PRENTICE HALL

1 Lake St.
Upper Saddle River, NJ 07458
TF: 800-282-0693
FX: 800-835-5327
URL: http://www.prenhall.com

Description: Describes marketing tips and techniques to effectively take advantage of the online environment. Written by Al Bredenberg and published in 2002. Retails for $115.00. ISBN: 0735203105.

▌3263

SEARCH ENGINE POSITIONING

WORDWARE PUBLISHING

2320 Los Rios Blvd., Ste. 200
Plano, TX 75074
TF: 800-229-4949
E-mail: info@wordware.com
URL: http://www.wordware.com

Description: Describes how to increase a web sites search engine ranking, both with technical and strategic adjustments. Chapter titles include: understanding search referrals and traffic, choosing the right keywords in the right combinations, and submitting your site. Includes reference sheets for the top search engines. Written by Fredrick W. Marckini and published in 2001. Retails for $49.95. ISBN: 155622804X.

▌3264

SEARCH ENGINE REPORT

INT MEDIA GROUP, INC.

23 Old Kings Hwy. S
Darien, CT 06820
PH: (203)662-2800
FX: (203)655-4686
E-mail: info@internet.com
URL: http://searchenginewatch.com/sereport/

Description: Free monthly e-newsletter designed to keep web marketers and searches up to date with current trends in technologies in search engines. Covers topics such as pay per click services, ranking strategies, and linking opportunities. Companion web site, http://searchenginewatch.com, provides inside information on how search engines work and rank sites. Access is restricted to subsribers.

▌3265

SECRETS AND LIES: DIGITAL SECURITY IN A NETWORKED WORLD

WILEY

111 River St.
Hoboken, NJ 07030
PH: (201)748-6000
FX: (201)748-6088
URL: http://www.wiley.com

Description: Written by an expert in cryptography and electronic security, provides practical and realist views of digital security, and how to protect oneself before and after breakins. Divided into 3 sections: the landscape, technologies and strategies. Written by Bruce Schneier and published in 2000. Retails for $29.99. ISBN: 0471253111.

▌3266

THE ELECTRONIC MARKETPLACE : STRATEGIES FOR CONNECTING BUYERS & SELLERS.

SIMBA INFORMATION INC.

11 River Bend Dr. S
PO Box 4234
Stamford, CT 06907-0234

PH: (203)358-4100
TF: 800-307-2529
FX: (203)358-5824
E-mail: info@simbanet.com
URL: http://www.simbanet.com

Description: A yearly publication offering analysis of e-commerce trends and issues for the marketer. Includes forecasts, tips from the experts, company profiles, case studies and strategies. 5th edition, 2001, retails for $1995.00.

▌3267

SMART THINGS TO KNOW ABOUT E-BUSINESS

JOSSEY-BASS/CAPSTONE

989 Market St.
San Francisco, CA 94103-1741
PH: (415)433-1740
FX: (415)433-0499
URL: http://www.josseybass.com

Description: A beginners guide to e-business, gives an overview of most topics relevant to the field such as technologies, marketing, business strategy and customer care and emerging trends. Chapter titles include: e-commerce technologies that matter, building your own strategy and making it happen - doing e-commerce. Written by Michael J. Cunningham with revised edition published in 2002. Retails for $19.95. ISBN: 1841120405

▌3268

STARTING AN ONLINE BUSINESS FOR DUMMIES

IDG BOOKS WORLDWIDE

111 River St.
Hoboken, NJ 07030
PH: (201)748-6000
FX: (201)748-6088
URL: http://www.wiley.com

Description: Complete guide to starting a small online business. Covers writting a business plan and strategy, seeking funding, web site setup and technologies. Chapter titles include: your online business equipment list, choosing your web host and design tools, and marketing to a worldwide audience. Written by Greg Holden and with 2nd edition published in 2000. Retails for $24.99. ISBN: 0764506889

▌3269

STARTING AND RUNNING A BUSINESS ON THE INTERNET

TTL/NET.WORKS

PO Box 200
Harrogate HG12YR, United Kingdom
PH: 44 1423 507545
FX: 44 1423 526035
E-mail: sales@takethat.co.uk/networks.htm
URL: http://www.takethat.co.uk

Description: Written for the small or new business owner wishing to have a simple online presence. Covers all aspects of taking a small business online, from builing your website to online payment collection. Written by Alex Kiam and Tim Ireland and published in 2000. Retails for $11.95. ISBN: 1873668783.

▌3270
STRATEGIES FOR ECOMMERCE SUCCESS
IRM PRESS

701 E. Chocolate Ave., Ste. 200
Hershey, PA 17033
TF: 800-345-4332
FX: (717)533-8661
E-mail: cust@idea-group.com
URL: http://www.idea-group.com

Description: Covers key topics in e-commerce and provides discussion of their impact, including global e-commerce, economics, and technologies. Chapter titles include: social issues in electronic commerce: implications for policy makers, internet payment mechanisms: acceptance and control issues, and mobile agents, mobile computing and mobil users in the global e-commerce. Edited by Bijan Fazlollahi and published in 2002. Retails for $59.95. ISBN: 193177708X.

▌3271
STRATEGIES FOR E-BUSINESS SUCCESS
JOSSEY-BASS

989 Market St.
San Francisco, CA 94103-1741
PH: (415)433-1740
FX: (415)433-0499

Description: Compilation of artices written by experts in e-business. Offers insights into integrating e-business into the way of doing business, and doing it bettter. Section title include marketing, technology, strategy and implementation. Edited by Erik Brynjolfsson and Glen L. Urban and published in 2001. Retails for $19.00 ISBN: 0787958484

▌3272
STRATEGIES FOR WEB HOSTING AND MANAGED SERVICES
WILEY

111 River St.
Hoboken, NJ 07030
PH: (201)748-6000
FX: (201)748-6088
URL: http://www.wiley.com

Description: Describes the technologies and terminologies that one must understand in order to sucessfully choose a web hosting service or to build a successful server in-house. Covers topics such as shared and dedicated servers, colocation, managed service providers, service agreements, site monitoring, caching and security. Written by Doug Kaye and published in 2002. Retails for $39.99. ISBN: 0471085782.

▌3273
STREETWISE B2B.COM : HOW TO USE THE INTERNET TO BUY AND SELL YOUR WAY TO SUCCESS
ADAMS MEDIA CORP.

57 Littlefield St.
Avon, MA 02322
PH: (508)427-7100
FX: (508)427-6790
E-mail: webmaster@adamsmedia.com
URL: http://www.adamsmedia.com

Description: Covers marketing and business to other business and using the internet to strategic advantage in a b2b world. Written by Jon Zonderman and published in 2002. ISBN: 1580625673

▌3274
STREETWISE INTERNET BUSINESS PLAN : CREATE A COMPELLING PLAN FOR YOUR.COM BUSINESS THAT WILL GET IT FINANCED, AND LEAD IT TO SUCCESS
ADAMS MEDIA CORP.

57 Littlefield St.
Avon, MA 02322
PH: (508)427-7100
FX: (508)427-6790
E-mail: webmaster@adamsmedia.com
URL: http://www.adamsmedia.com

Description: Covers the essentials components of a business plan, from strategy to funding to implementation, focusing on e-business. Section titles include: just what is a business, build your business plan from the ground up, and presenting your idea. Includes sample business plans. Written by Robert Weinberg and published in 2001. Retails for $19.95. ISBN: 1580625029.

▌3275
SUPPLY CHAIN E-BUSINESS
KELLER INTERNATIONAL PUB.

150 Great Neck Rd.
Great Neck, NY 11021
PH: (516)829-9210
FX: (516)829-7265
E-mail: mmarotta@kellerpubs.com
URL: http://www.supplychainebusiness.com/mediakit/gls_media.htm1

Description: Written for managers involved in ebusiness, this magazine is devoted to online supply-chain applications. Provides feature articles on specific software and applications, market segments and forecasting, fufillment and customer relations, among others. Includes Web Briefs with industry news and developments, and Web Reviews of applications. ISSN: 1529-8167

▌3276
TECHNICIAN'S GUIDE TO DAY AND SWING TRADING
MCGRAW-HILL

1221 Avenue of the Americas
New York, NY 10020
PH: (212)512-2000
URL: http://www.mcgraw-hill.com

Description: Written for technical day and swing traders, covers topics such as understanding market dynamics, selecting securities, and timing entry and exit poits. Describes how technical and fundamental analysis can increase the profitability of day and swing trading. Written by Martin J. Pring and published in 2002. Retails for $49.95 ISBN: 0071384006.

▌3277
VIRTUAL BUSINESS MAGAZINE
ARKGROUP

4th Fl., Zeeta House
200 Upper Richmond Rd.
London SW152SH, United Kingdom
PH: 44 020 87852700
URL: http://www.vbmagazine.com/

Description: Magazine providing case studies for managers and professionals working with intra and extranets, and company portals. Includes news and reviews, technology updates, along with case studies. Subscription include full access to to archives on via the web site. Annual subscription including web site access is available for $460. Electronic subscription, including access to all issues of the magazine but no paper copies, are available for $275.

▌3278
WEAVING A WEBSITE : PROGRAMMING IN HTML, JAVASCRIPT, PERL AND JAVA
PRENTICE HALL

1 Lake St.
Upper Saddle River, NJ 07458
TF: 800-282-0693
FX: 800-835-5327
URL: http://www.prenhall.com

Description: Provides an introduction to programming web sites with 4 languages. Starts with basic HTML and moves progressively forward to JavaScript and programming concepts, Perl and pattern matching, and Java and applets. Includes 200 sample programs such as dictionaries and crosswords. Written by Susan Anderson-Freed and published in 2002. Retails for $60.00. ISBN: 0130282200.

▌3279
WEB SITES BUILT TO LAST
ADAMS MEDIA CORP.

57 Littlefield St.
Avon, MA 02322
PH: (508)427-7100
FX: (508)427-6790
E-mail: webmaster@adamsmedia.com
URL: http://www.adamsmedia.com

Description: Covers how to build a web site and sell online. Covers topics such as developing a business plan, building a site that fits your needs, effective marketing stategies, and using consultants. Written by Marc Kramer and published in 2002. Retails for $14.95.

▌3280
WEB CONTENT REPORT
RAGAN COMMUNICATIONS, INC.

316 N Michigan Ave., Ste. 300
Chicago, IL 60601
TF: 800-878-5331
FX: (312)960-4106
E-mail: cservice@ragan.com
URL: http://www2.ragan.com

Description: Written for web designers and content managers, provides current information and discussion of design and software issues. Includes marketing tips, monitoring, new technologies, evaluation and hot topics. Annual subscriptions to this monthly publication are available for $299.

▌3281
WEB INFORMANT ESSAYS
DAVID STROM

600 Community Dr.
Manhasset, NY 11030
PH: (516)562-7151
FX: (413)473-0515
E-mail: dstrom@cmp.com
URL: http://www.webinformant.com

Description: Free online mostly weekly newsletter, written by Senior Technology Editor for CMP's VAR Business magazine, David Strom. Each issue is devoted to one topic dealing with the current state of the internet. Titles from issues past include: federated identities create new security risks, separating ads from edit on search sites and billing your customers. ISSN: 1524-6353.

▌3282
WEB COMMERCE TODAY
WILSON INTERNET SERVICES

PO Box 308
Rocklin, CA 95677-0308
PH: (916)652-4659
URL: http://www.wilsonweb.com

Description: Bi-weekly email newsletter focusing on ecommerce. Covers topics such as shopping cart software, marketing tips and strategies, designing an effective web site and writting a business plan. Annual subscriptions are available for $49.95 and include access to archives back to 1997, topical e-books and full access to restricted areas of the website.

■ **3283**

WEB BUSINESS BOOT CAMP : HANDS-ON INTERNET LESSONS FOR MANAGERS, ENTREPRENEURS, AND PROFESSIONALS

WILEY

111 River St.
Hoboken, NJ 07030
PH: (201)748-6000
FX: (201)748-6088
URL: http://www.wiley.com

Description: Written for managers and professionals, provides information on how to effectively market your e-businss. Topics include identifying online opportunities, project management, and increasing web site traffic. Written by Richard Seltzer and published in 2002. Retails for $19.95. ISBN: 0471164194.

■ **3284**

WEB PROTOCOLS AND PRACTICE : HTTP/1.1, NETWORKING PROTOCOLS, CACHING, AND TRAFFIC MEASUREMENT

ADDISON-WESLEY

75 Arlington St., Ste. 300
Boston, MA 02116
PH: (617)848-6000
URL: http://www2.awl.com

Description: Written from an engineering perspective for technical readers interested in the underlying protocols of the internet and how the function. Covers http, and tcp/ip, along with web server design issues such as caching and proxying. Written by Balachander Krishnamurthy and Jennifer Rexford and published in 2001. Retails for $50.00. ISBN: 0201710889.

■ **3285**

WEB PRIVACY WITH P3P

O'REILLY & ASSOCIATES

1005 Gravenstein Hwy. N
Sebastopol, CA 95472
PH: (707)827-7000
TF: 800-998-9938
FX: (707)829-0104
E-mail: nuts@oreilly.com
URL: http://www.oreilly.com

Description: Learn more about the emerging privacy standard for use on business websites. Provides information on implementing P3P both from a provider and consumer standpoint. Written by Lorrie F. Cranor, publication date 2002. Retails for $34.95.

■ **3286**

WEB SECURITY, PRIVACY & COMMERCE, 2ND EDITION

O'REILLY & ASSOCIATES

1005 Gravenstein Hwy. N
Sebastopol, CA 95472
PH: (707)827-7000

TF: 800-998-9938
FX: (707)829-0104
E-mail: nuts@oreilly.com
URL: http://www.oreilly.com

Description: 2nd edition with updated information on the wide variety of security and privacy issues facing both consumers and businesses alike. Covers SSL, cryptography, digital signatures and certificates, P3P, intellectual property, cookies, log files and much more. Written by Simson Garfinkel and Gene Spafford, published in 2001. Retails for $44.94. ISBN: 0596000456.

■ **3287**

WEB SERVICES JOURNAL

SYS-CON MEDIA

135 Chestnut Ridge Rd.
Montvale, NJ 07645
PH: (201)802-3000
TF: 888-303-5282
FX: (201)782-9601
E-mail: info@sys-con.com
URL: http://www.sys-con.com

Description: Monthly magazine covering internet technologies. Covers new products and services, for example.Net, J2EE, Oracle9i and SOAP. Also provides essays on hot topics such as security and middleware, along with book reviews. Yearly subscriptions are available for $69.99. Free subscriptions to the archives are available via the website.

■ **3288**

WEBWORKS : E-COMMERCE

ROCKPORT PUBLISHERS INC.

33 Commercial St.
Gloucester, MA 01930
PH: (978)282-9590
FX: (978)283-2742
E-mail: questions@rockpub.com
URL: http://www.rockpub.com

Description: Written for those desiging ecommerce sites. Covers the melding of functionality and aesthetics. Includes topics such as branding, appropriate use of bandwidth, and integration with databases. Divided into sections covering realworld stores in the fields of retail, finance, b2b and others. Written by Katherine Tasheff Carlton and published in 2001. Retails for $40.00. ISBN: 1564966615.

■ **3289**

WIRELESS RULES : NEW MARKETING STRATEGIES FOR CUSTOMER RELATIONSHIP MANAGEMENT ANYTIME, ANYWHERE

MCGRAW-HILL

1221 Avenue of the Americas
New York, NY 10020
PH: (212)512-2000

URL: http://www.mcgraw-hill.com

Description: Written for marketers wanting to poise themselves for the wireless revolution. Covers both the technology and the customer relations aspects of wireless, and how to effectively use them for marketing. Written by Frederick Newell and Katherine Newell Lemon and published in 2001. Retails for $29.95. ISBN: 007137437X.

■ **3290**

WORLD E-COMMERCE & IP REPORT
BNA INTERNATIONAL INC.

Heron House
10 Dean Farrar St.
London SW10DX, United Kingdom
PH: 44 020 75594800
FX: 44 020 72220294
E-mail: customerservice@bnai.com
URL: http://www.bnai.com

Description: Monthly publication providing news and analysis of intellectual property issues in the e-commerce world. Global in scope, tracks cases and provides analysis of national and international news, cases, legislation and policy in the online intellectual property world.

■ **3291**

WORLD STOCK EXCHANGE FACT BOOK
MERIDIAN SECURITIES MARKETS LLC

2424 Hunters Run Dr.
Plano, TX 75025
PH: (972)727-7792
FX: (972)727-7619
E-mail: info@worldstockexchangefactbook.com
URL: http://www.worldstockexchangefactbook.com

Description: Annual publication provides current directory and statistics on stock exchanges around the world. Also contains historical data on stock exchanges. ISSN: 1087-500X

■ **3292**

WORLD WIDE WEB MARKETING : INTEGRATING THE WEB INTO YOUR MARKETING STRATEGY
WILEY

111 River St.
Hoboken, NJ 07030
PH: (201)748-6000
FX: (201)748-6088
URL: http://www.wiley.com

Description: Written for marketing and advertising professionals working in the online marketplace. Provides strategies for both designing and marketing sucessful ebusiness web sites. Topics include usability, e-metrics, feedback and value added marketing. Written by Jim Sterne and with 3rd edition published in 2001. Retails for $29.99. ISBN: 0471416215.

■ **3293**

3D DESIGN EXPO AND INDUSTRIAL DESIGN CONFERENCE.
ADVANSTAR COMMUNICATIONS INC.

545 Boylston St.
Boston, MA 02116
PH: (617)267-6500
E-mail: information@advanstar.de
URL: http://www.advanstar.com

Founded: 1994. **Description:** This seminar includes the latest industry developments in animation, computer graphics, media asset management, multimedia, special effects, video editing and web design.Understand the commercial and creative benefits of new technologies.

■ **3294**

802.11 PLANET CONFERENCE AND EXPO
INT MEDIA GROUP

23 Old Kings Hwy. S
Darien, CT 06820
PH: (203)662-2800
TF: (203)655-4686
E-mail: cobrienats@internet.com
URL: http://www.intmediaevents.com

Description: At 802.11 Planet Conference and Expo, 802.11 experts and business leaders will converge to develop successful strategies that put the power of 802.11 technology to work for their businesses. Conference highlights include: Multihop/Mesh Networks, 802.11 Security, building a Linux-box Access Point, inside testing tools, equipment and techniques for avoiding interference before setting up WLAN, and using Wi-Fi to enhance meetings.

■ **3295**

ACCESS VB SQL ADVISOR SUMMIT
ADVISOR MEDIA INC.

5675 Ruffin Rd.
San Diego, CA 92123-5675
PH: (858)278-5600
TF: 800-336-6060
E-mail: Events@Advisor.com
URL: http://www.advisor.com/www/AdvisorEvents

Description: The Advisor Summit is an event for developers on Microsoft Access, VB and SQL Server. The conference showcases how-to from top experts, proven methods and undocumented secrets, jumpstarts on new technology, codes to use immediately, new ideas and power tips, and free trial subscriptions to Access-VB-SQL Advisor Magazine and VB.NET Advisor Journal. This is where the experts show their IT colleagues the best ways to use key technology, the truth about what really works, and the know-how to implement ideas.

▮ 3296
ACHIEVING MAXIMUM R.O.I. THROUGH EFFECTIVE WEBSITE CONTENT MANAGEMENT
INTERNATIONAL QUALITY AND PRODUCTIVITY CENTER

PO Box 401
150 Clove Rd.
Little Falls, NJ 07424
PH: (973)256-0211
TF: 800-882-8684
E-mail: info@content-net.com
URL: http://www.iqpc.com
Contact: Todd Smith, Sales Manager, Sponsorship and Exhibits

Description: Discover and discuss how successful website content management can increase profits, brand awareness and improve information distribution. At this conference, the attendee will learn how to ensure financial, time and employee investment on a website, enhance customer relationship management through determining how to make content easy to navigate and the site easy to find, ease pressure on alternative customer service points by ensuring the website is a compelling point of contact, and improve the quality of the entire site by identifying and enhancing the most appealing web pages.

▮ 3297
ACT
AITEC UK LTD

15 High St.
Graveley PE196PL, United Kingdom
PH: 44 14 80831300
FX: 44 14 80831131
E-mail: admin@aitec-africa.com
URL: http://www.aitecafrica.com
Contact: Sean Moroney, AITEC Group Chairman

Description: The African Computing and Telecommunications Summit is a gathering of IT users, suppliers, service providers, policy-makers and innovators. Delegates should attend the Summit in order to gain access to the top-level education program, to the market information, and to the industry contacts that the Summit provides. The exhibition should also be attended by resellers, suppliers and manufacturers from South Africa, the rest of Africa and the international IT industry.

▮ 3298
AD:TECH
IMARK COMMUNICATIONS

1 Apple Hill Dr., Ste. 301
Natick, MA 01760
PH: (508)647-8600
TF: 800-955-1226
FX: (508)647-0241
E-mail: dkorse@imark-com.com
URL: http://www.imark-com.com
Contact: David Korse, President and CEO

Description: ad:tech is an event focusing on interactive advertising, marketing and Commerce. It will be a gathering of industry leaders who are driving the creative and technological advances.

▮ 3299
ADOBE PHOTOSHOP SEMINAR
KW COMPUTER TRAINING, INC.

333 Douglas Rd. E
Dunedin, FL 34698
PH: (813)433-5000
TF: 800-201-7323
FX: (813)433-5015
E-mail: info@photoshopseminars.com
URL: http://www.photoshopseminars.com

Description: Adobe Photoshop Seminar coverd techniques, the latest special effects, and real world tips and tricks of the pros. Featuring Photoshop User magazine editor Scott Kelby, the seminar coverd topics such as mastering layers, scanning/correcting, photo retouching, and designing web graphics.

▮ 3300
ADVANCED GUI DESIGN WORKSHOP: APPLYING NEW TECHNOLOGIES TO THE INTERFACE (DCI)
DIGITAL CONSULTING INSTITUTE

204 Andover St.
Andover, MA 01810
PH: (978)470-3880
URL: http://www.dci.com

Description: This two-day seminar is the natural next step to GUI training. This class is designed to teach even the most senior GUI developer tips, tricks, and helpful hints to ensure a more effective user interface. Upon completion of the seminar, attendees will be able to discuss advanced principles of GUI design, identify the components of an effective GUI, and apply solid GUI design principles for complex applications. In addition, attendees work on complex problems and apply Rapid Application Development (RAD) techniques. This seminar also addresses emerging technologies such as pen, multimedia and mobile applications and how they impact the effectiveness of the user interface.

▮ 3301
ADVANCED MARKETING RESEARCH
FROST AND SULLIVAN

7550 W I 10, Ste. 400
San Antonio, TX 78229
PH: (210)247-2461

E-mail: cfsales@frost.com
URL: http://www.frost.com/prod/conf.nsf/0/482FC2A3-
D94720AE88256A6C006ECBA8
Contact: Lisa Lee, Event Planner

Founded: 1998. **Description:** The Executive Summit brings together hundreds of marketing research practitioners from a broad range of industries (healthcare, IT, telecommunications, industrial high tech-companies, etc) for an immersion into state of the art marketing research methodologies. A virtual think-tank of new ideas and techniques that can be immediately used to take action and advance your marketing research initiatives.

∎ 3302
ADVISOR SUMMIT GROUPWISE
ADVISOR MEDIA INC.

5675 Ruffin Rd.
San Diego, CA 92123-5675
PH: (858)278-5600
TF: 800-336-6060
E-mail: Events@Advisor.com
URL: http://www.advisor.com/www/AdvisorEvents

Description: Features the original and only all-GroupWise technical conference. Provides three days of technical education, learning from the top experts, and collaborating with colleagues from around the world on Novell GroupWise.

∎ 3303
AFFILIATEFORCE
AFFILIATEFORCE.COM

777 Arthur Godfrey Rd., Ste. 200
Miami Beach, FL 33140
PH: (305)716-9237
FX: (305)716-9237
URL: http://www.affiliateforce2002.com

Description: AffiliateFORCE gathers affiliates, merchants, business owners, managers, consultants, webmasters and entrepreneurs from around the world. These groups gather for guidance on how to orchestrate a successful Internet commerce strategy, using affiliate programs and performance marketing.

∎ 3304
AGILITY
AGILE SOFTWARE CORPORATION

One Almaden Blvd.
San Jose, CA 95113-2253
PH: (408)975-3900
FX: (408)271-4862
E-mail: info@agilesoft.com
URL: http://www.agile.com

Description: Agility represents an opportunity available to network with thought leaders from every industry. These are the people who have broken down the walls internally and with suppliers and customers, resulting in improved product quality, 50% reductions in product introduction cycle times, 15% reductions in direct materials costs, and improved metrics across the board.

∎ 3305
AIIM CONFERENCE AND EXPOSITION
ADVANSTAR COMMUNICATIONS INC.

545 Boylston St.
Boston, MA 02116
PH: (617)267-6500
E-mail: information@advanstar.de
URL: http://www.advanstar.com
Contact: Doug Washburn

Description: Focus is on the technologies used to create, capture, customize, deliver and manage content together to strengthen strategies and solutions to make business processes more powerful and profitable. Exhibitors are software and application developers, manufacturers and solution providers of ECM technologies and services. Enterprise Content Management creates successful synergies between paper, document, and web content. At AIIM, attendees get the tools needed to build the best Enterprise Content Management Solution for their organization through 104 targeted Conference sessions specially geared toward their ECM interests.

∎ 3306
AITEC
AITEC UK LTD

15 High St.
Graveley PE196PL, United Kingdom
PH: 44 14 8083 1300
FX: 44 14 8083 1131
E-mail: admin@aitec-africa.com
URL: http://www.aitecafrica.com
Contact: Sean Moroney, AITEC Group Chairman

Founded: 1997. **Description:** The AITEC exhibition is a computing, telecommunications and broadcasting exhibition. It is a platform to reach out to high-quality corporate and government ICT users in West Africa and beyond.

∎ 3307
ANNUITY SYSTEMS WORKSHOP
LOMA

2300 Windy Ridge Pkwy., Ste. 600
Atlanta, GA 30339-8443
PH: (770)951-1770
TF: 800-275-5662
FX: (770)984-0441
E-mail: meetings@loma.org
URL: http://www.loma.org

Description: The Annuity Systems Workshop was created by the demand of LOMA members and other industry leaders. Topics discussed will be the functions and features of annuity systems. Attendees will have the opportunity to share views and hear ideas from peers.

▮ 3308

APPLICATION INTEGRATION AND WEB SERVICES

GARTNER INC.

56 Top Gallant Rd.
Stamford, CT 06904
PH: (203)316-1111
FX: (203)324-7901
URL: http://www.gartner.com

Founded: 2000. **Description:** At this Conference, attendees will learn how to make web services work better. Sessions will be given on how practices, procedures and operations can be made more efficient, more cost-effective and even more productive. Other areas to be covered will be: how to easily improve business agility, why smoother integration creates better processes, how integrated effectiveness supports enterprise agility, easier ways to provision web services for customers, how to sell services successfully over the web, and real-time monitoring of the right kind of business intelligence.

▮ 3309

APPLICATION PROTECTION

MARCUS EVANS LTD.

303 E Wacker Dr.
Chicago, IL 60601
PH: (312)540-3000
E-mail: marketing@marcusevans.com
URL: http://www.marcusevansconferences.com
Contact: Greta Molepske, Marketing Manager

Description: Demonstrated by leading international case studies this marcus evans conference offers the practical information to deliver a secure business environment that makes a company easier to do business with.

▮ 3310

APPLYING THE BUSINESS RULE APPROACH (DCI)

DIGITAL CONSULTING INSTITUTE

204 Andover St.
Andover, MA 01810
PH: (978)470-3880
URL: http://www.dci.com

Description: This seminar explains what business rules are and why they are crucial to a business. It shows attendees how to identify and specify business rules from the business perspective and to establish an approach to managing them that will enable faster change in business processes. There are practical hands-on techniques for harvesting, defining and organizing business rules. The focus is on knowing what a company's business rules are and establishing traceability for them within both the business and system contexts. Key concepts in the seminar are reinforced by numerous examples and workshop problems. It explores how business rules relate to knowledge management, revealing a new vision for the knowledge-conscious, customer-oriented company in the 21st century.

▮ 3311

ARCHIVING WEB PAGES: ENTERPRISES AT RISK

GARTNER INC.

56 Top Gallant Rd.
Stamford, CT 06904
PH: (203)316-1111
FX: (203)324-7901
URL: http://www.gartner.com

Description: Archiving Web Pages: Enterprises at Risk features three main topics to be answered. They are: what are best practices in Web archive management, what are other enterprises doing to save this valuable source of content, and what technologies are available to help. Millions of pages of Web content are created everyday, and millions of pages of content and Web transactions are being lost everyday. This conference will focus on how to save and archive these resources.

▮ 3312

ASIAN IT EXPO - ASIAN INFORMATION TECHNOLOGY EXHIBITION

ADSALE EXHIBITION SERVICES, LTD.

4/F Stanhope House
734 King's Rd.
Hong Kong, People's Republic of China
E-mail: exhibition@adsale.com.hk

Founded: 1990. **Frequency:** Annual. **Audience:** Corporate decision makers, trade professionals and general public. **Principle Exhibits:** Equipment, supplies, and services as it applies to the internet, telecommunictions, and world wide web; Business applications & solutions, E-commerce, networking securities, hardware, and peripherals.

▮ 3313

ASM CONFERENCE (APPLICATIONS OF SOFTWARE MEASUREMENT)

SOFTWARE QUALITY ENGINEERING

330 Corporate Way, Ste. 300
Orange Park, FL 32073
PH: (904)278-0707
TF: 800-423-8378
FX: (904)278-4380
E-mail: sqeinfo@sqe.com
URL: http://www.sqe.com

Description: The ASM (Applications of Software Measurement) Conference explores how accurate metrics can improve the development process and project success. Delegates learn measurement basics, acquire new techniques for specific projects, and keep abreast of metrics advances. The ASM conference is an annual event covering vital measurement activities to assess and improve results. The conference features international experts, in-depth tutorials, presentations, and the Management and Measurement EXPO. The side-by-side delivery of SM and ASM covers the breadth of software management along with the vital measurement activities to assess and improve results.

3314

ASSOCIATION OF BUSINESS SUPPORT SERVICES INTERNATIONAL ANNUAL CONVENTION

ASSOCIATION OF BUSINESS SUPPORT SERVICES INTERNATIONAL

5852 Oak Meadow Dr.
Yorba Linda, CA 92886-5930
E-mail: abssi4you@aol.com

Founded: 1981. **Frequency:** Annual. **Audience:** Independent business support service owners. **Principle Exhibits:** Exhibits relating to independent business support services offering a variety of secretarial and support services such as word processing, telephone answering, desktop publishing, editing, spreadsheets, executive suite and transcription.

3315

ASUG (ASUG)

AMERICAS' SAP USERS' GROUP

401 North Michigan Ave.
Chicago, IL 60611-4267
PH: (312)321-5142
FX: (312)245-1081
E-mail: itug@itug.org
URL: http://www.asug.com

Description: ASUG provides an opportunity for attendees to get answers to specific questions about SAP's e-Business solutions by meeting one-on-one with an expert team of platinum consultants. By attending the Annual Conference and Vendor Fair, Group and Chapter meetings or participating in the ASUG online discussion forums, members are provided with face-to face and interactive ways for talking, sharing and networking with other SAP users.

3316

AUDITING CLIENT/SERVER SYSTEMS (ISACA)

INFORMATION SYSTEMS AUDIT AND CONTROL ASSOCIATION

3701 Algonquin Rd., Ste.1010
Rolling Meadows, IL 60008
PH: (847)253-1545
FX: (847)253-1443
E-mail: conference@isaca.org
URL: http://www.isaca.org

Description: During this program, practical approaches and techniques for reviewing and evaluating client/server systems will be presented using the UNIX operating system and a TCP/IP network. Starting with an overview of how client/server systems function, representative examples of client/server processing are introduced, security and audit complexities discussed, typical control exposures are examined, and review procedures are explained.

3317

AUDITING ORACLE (ISACA)

INFORMATION SYSTEMS AUDIT AND CONTROL ASSOCIATION

3701 Algonquin Rd., Ste.1010
Rolling Meadows, IL 60008
PH: (847)253-1545
FX: (847)253-1443
E-mail: conference@isaca.org
URL: http://www.isaca.org

Description: During this seminar, attendees will be introduced to practical approaches and techniques for reviewing and evaluating the implementation of Oracle in client/server environments. Audit and security complexities will be discussed including workstation and application security, network security, server operating system security and the internal database security features of Oracle 7.

3318

AUTO-TECH

QAD INC.

6450 Via Real
Carpinteria, CA 93013
PH: (805)684-6614
E-mail: info@qad.com
URL: http://www.qad.com

Founded: 1989. **Description:** AUTO-TECH is a conference and exhibition that showcases the work of AIAG member volunteers, in the development of new technologies and the standards that govern their usage. This annual event provides the perfect forum for initiating proactive planning and improving trading partner relationships for the past several years. It brings OEMs and suppliers together to discuss and inform attendees of the current trends and standards in the supply chain. The conference agenda offers over 120 educational sessions ranging from informational sessions that provide overviews of technology, to implementation plans for suppliers, to discussions on supplier programs.

3319

AZCENTRAL.COM IT BUSINESS EXPO

AZCENTRAL.COM

3710 S Terrace
Tempe, AZ 85282
PH: (480)491-8373
E-mail: info@azinco.com
URL: http://www.azinco.com

Description: For six years, the goal of this Expo has been to assist Arizona business find technology that can improve their business productivity. With the support of azcentral.com, AZSOFT.net and the Greater Phoenix Chamber of Commerce, this event has become a must for business leaders and IT decision makers to attend. Besides over 100 exhibitors, the Expo features education seminars presented by industry leaders in two seminar areas all day long. There is no addition charge to attend the seminars.

▌3320

B2B APPLICATION INTEGRATION: APPROACHES, TECHNIQUES AND TECHNOLOGY TO EBUSINESS ENABLE YOUR ENTERPRISE (DCI)

DIGITAL CONSULTING INSTITUTE

204 Andover St.
Andover, MA 01810
PH: (978)470-3880
URL: http://www.dci.com

Description: The purpose of this seminar is to take B2B to the next level, providing the attendee with an understanding of enabling technology and standards, such as message brokers and XML, as well as the ability to apply the technology to a typical B2B problem domain. Case studies will be employed to drive the concepts home, as well as references to existing technology that the attendee can purchase on site.

▌3321

B2B FOCUS ON BUSINESS CONFERENCE AND EXPOSITION

DJM ASSOCIATES

PO Box 1242
Paramus, NJ 07653
PH: (201)646-6593
E-mail: info@djmassociates.com
URL: http://www.djmassociates.com

Description: Business-to-Business 2002 Conference and Exposition is a business conference integrated with a technology exhibition designated to provide small and medium-size company enterprises, women business owners, senior. Allows business owners to hear about challenges faced by innovative companies, meet leading technology providers, speak with corporate solutions experts, network with business professionals, exchange ideas, compare notes, and discuss critical issues in the business.

▌3322

B2E - COMMUNICATION STRATEGIES

MARCUS EVANS LTD.

303 E Wacker Dr.
Chicago, IL 60601
PH: (312)540-3000
E-mail: LisaR@marcusevansch.com
URL: http://www.brandslam-summit.com
Contact: Greta Molepske, Marketing Manager

Description: This two day conference will help Chief Information Officers and Heads of internal communications, employee communications, and human resources, develop people portals that deliver sense of employee ownership without information overload. The conference will feature key speakers covering the following topics: Analysing the benefits gained by implementing employee empowerment strategies; Examining the challenge of re-engineering B2E communication strategy; Strengthening the link between corporate identity and employee commitment; Measuring the success of internal communication strategy; Strategic benefits and challenges of deploying mobile B2E applications.

▌3323

BEA EWORLD

BEA SYSTEMS INC.

2315 N 1st St.
San Jose, CA 95131
PH: (408)570-8000
TF: 800-817-4232
FX: (408)570-8901
E-mail: info@bea-eworld.com
URL: http://www.bea.com

Founded: 1998. **Description:** BEA eWorld Europe is focused not just on the business side of the equation, nor on the development side, but on both. One question has been posed to the speakers, presenters and exhibitors: How can the needs of the business be most successfully translated into an appropriate and effective information technology strategy? This question on how both sides must work together is the topic for this conference.

▌3324

BEST PRACTICE CORPORATE COMMUNICATION MANAGEMENT

INTERNATIONAL QUALITY AND PRODUCTIVITY CENTER

PO Box 401
150 Clove Rd.
Little Falls, NJ 07424
PH: (973)256-0211
TF: 800-882-8684
E-mail: registration@iqpc.com.au
URL: http://www.iqpc.com
Contact: Todd Smith, Sales Manager, Sponsorship and Exhibits

Description: This conference features leading edge case studies and interactive discussions that relate directly to the success of long term KM strategy. Discover how to achieve greater ROI by sustaining a strong KM culture in the mentality of people, introduce localised knowledge sharing communities within a corporation that can deliver hard dollar results, use e-collaboration to bring the right people together at the right time and drive forward productivity, increase working efficiency by reducing time to competency, retain corporate memory during staff changes, mergers and acquisitions, structure internal and external access to the required security levels and knowledge needs, and measure the performance of KM strategy and translate the results into tangible statistics for senior management.

▌3325

BIOITWORLD CONFERENCE AND EXPO

IDG WORLD EXPO

3 Speen St.
Framingham, MA 01701
PH: (508)879-6700

E-mail: lauren_davis@idg.com
URL: http://www.bioitworldexpo.com
Contact: Charlie Greco, President and Chief Executive Officer

Description: BioITWorld Conference and Expo is an event for life science professionals to evaluate and understand advanced IT solutions and bioinformatics. This event is the first to exclusively showcase how information technologies are transforming the life sciences throughout the entire discovery and development processes. Leading visionaries from the pharmaceutical, biotechnology, academic and government markets come together to identify and learn the latest tools, services and training that speed, store, analyze and interpret the flood of information being produced by the life sciences industry.

∎ 3326

THE BOND MARKET ASSOCIATION -
FIXED INCOME SUMMIT EXPO ON E-
COMMERCE & TECHNOLOGY
FLAGG MANAGEMENT, INC.

353 Lexington Ave.
New York, NY 10016
E-mail: flaggmgmt@msn.com

Founded: 1990. **Frequency:** Annual. **Audience:** Bond Market Association members, government bond officers, fixed income brokers /dealers. **Principle Exhibits:** Online services, Internet systems, fixed-income trading and executions systems, real-time systems, Internet and other new products and solutions; online trading and execution systems; bond market services; online research and global markets information.

∎ 3327

BRAND SLAM SUMMIT
MARCUS EVANS LTD.

303 E Wacker Dr.
Chicago, IL 60601
PH: (312)540-3000
E-mail: LisaR@marcusevansch.com
URL: http://www.brandslam-summit.com
Contact: Greta Molepske, Marketing Manager

Description: The BrandSLAM Summit will offer assistance to senior-level marketing, branding, communications, promotions and merchandising executives looking for better day-to-day and long-term brand decisions. This summit provides a proactive series of keynote presentations, conference sessions, interactive think-tanks and one-on-one meetings with technology industry leaders.

∎ 3328

BUILDING AND MANAGING ENTERPRISE
SECURITY INFRASTRUCTURES (DCI)
DIGITAL CONSULTING INSTITUTE

204 Andover St.
Andover, MA 01810
PH: (978)470-3880

URL: http://www.dci.com

Description: This seminar will show how to analyze, design and maintain a baseline security infrastructure for an enterprise with Internet, intranet and extranet components. It will cover the fundamentals of security policy, the five cornerstones of Internet security, and infrastructure including cryptography, firewalls, certificates, Virtual Private Networks (VPNs), Public Key Infrastructure (PKI) and more. Attendees will examine and discuss intrusion detection models and intrusion detection, as well as preemptive deterrence countermeasures.

∎ 3329

BUILDING WEB FARMING SYSTEMS:
TOOLS AND TECHNIQUES AND
ENHANCED DATA WAREHOUSING FOR
YOUR ENTERPRISE (DCI)
DIGITAL CONSULTING INSTITUTE

204 Andover St.
Andover, MA 01810
PH: (978)470-3880
URL: http://www.dci.com

Description: The goal of this seminar is ''to organize outside data''. It is to move a company from an information refining process that is haphazard and intermittent to one that is systematic and continuous. By blending with existing warehousing systems, web farming can enable a company to adapt and even thrive upon the sudden changes happening in an industry. This seminar provides attendees with the practical skills for evaluating and implementing web farming systems for their company.

∎ 3330

BUSINESS INTELLIGENCE STRATEGY:
MAXIMISING ADVANTAGE IN
EUROPEAN BUSINESS
MARCUS EVANS LTD.

303 E Wacker Dr.
Chicago, IL 60601
PH: (312)540-3000
E-mail: LisaR@marcusevansch.com
URL: http://www.brandslam-summit.com
Contact: Greta Molepske, Marketing Manager

Description: The Pan-European Knowledge Strategy conference will address topics such as: Learning about laying strategic foundations and best practice frameworks for a knowledge management program according to Sasol; Discover how Zurich Financial Services ensure information has a positive impact on bottom-line business results; Listen to a company of the size and complexity of British Telecom outline five knowledge competencies for success; Find out how diverse global enterprises like Solvay build flexible Business Intelligence systems; Participate in an event where a multinational enterprise in the ICI Group discuss how to maximise the business value of their intellectual capital; Network with global leaders in Business Intelligence.

695

■ **3331**

BUSINESS INTELLIGENCE WORLD

TERRAPINN LTD.

100 Hatton Garden, Level 2, Ste. B
London EC1N8NX, United Kingdom
PH: 44 207 242 1548
FX: 44 207 242 1508
E-mail: james.smith@terrapinn.com
URL: http://www.terrapinn.com

Description: This event is for business decision makers and decision support engineers who use or structure information to aid the formulation of business strategy and optimize organizational effectiveness. Features a three day conference plus a choice of two workshops. Provides two international keynotes, 12 case studies from various industries, two panel discussions and one dedicated CRM track day. Offers workshops in KM Strategy and BI Strategy.

■ **3332**

BUSINESS PROCESS INTEGRATION (DCI)

DIGITAL CONSULTING INSTITUTE

204 Andover St.
Andover, MA 01810
PH: (978)470-3880
URL: http://www.dci.com

Description: At the Business Process Integration Conference, real-time visibility is provided into end-to-end processes that cross applications as well as organizations, which allows companies to leverage their existing IT resources, extend them to e-Business and manage it all in real-time as a single business process. DCI and ebizQ's Business Process Integration Conference is designed to provide companies with both a strategic and technical understanding of BPI. Attendees will leave this 3-day event knowing how to leverage their existing assets while implementing BPI to increase the value of their business and gain competitive advantage.

■ **3333**

BUSINESS RULES FORUM

BUSINESS RULES FORUM

3115 Foothill Blvd., Ste. M287
La Crescenta, CA 91214
PH: 877-604-8622
FX: (818)352-5107
URL: http://www.businessrulesforum.com

Founded: 1998. **Description:** The Business Rules Forum is an international conference dedicated to the advancement of the Business Rule Approach to managing enterprise-wide information and building business rules-based applications. It is co-chaired by two experts in business rule management and technologies: Ronald Ross, Business Rules Solutions, LLC and Terry Moriarty, Inastrol.

■ **3334**

BUSINESS SECURITY CONFERENCE

IDC

5 Speen St.
Framingham, MA 01701
PH: (508)872-8200
URL: http://www.idc.com

Description: IDC's Business Security Conference will address the main business issues of security across the enterprise. It will examine the problems that organizations can face and the responsibilities they hold, as well as the costs involved and the overall consideration that it is possible to show a return on investment when implementing security solutions. IDC's Business Security Conference is intended for executives responsible for addressing risk in the company, CIOs, CTOs, IT directors, security managers, and eCommerce/ebusiness managers.

■ **3335**

BUY SIDE STP

MARCUS EVANS LTD.

303 E Wacker Dr.
Chicago, IL 60601
PH: (312)540-3000
E-mail: marketing@marcusevans.com
URL: http://www.marcusevansconferences.com
Contact: Greta Molepske, Marketing Manager

Description: The objective of this conference is to bring the investment management community together in a forum with the other trading counter parties to discuss the most successful business and technology strategies that will drive efficiencies and profitability to a higher level, and push the entire financial industry forward in their effort to achieve global straight through processing.

■ **3336**

CALGARY INTERNET CONFERENCE & TRADE SHOW

SILVER SHOWS

333 4th Ave. SW
Calgary, AB, Canada T2P0H9

Principle Exhibits: Internet equipment, supplies, and services.

■ **3337**

CALIFORNIA ACCOUNTING & BUSINESS SHOW AND CONFERENCE

FLAGG MANAGEMENT, INC.

353 Lexington Ave.
New York, NY 10016
E-mail: flaggmgmt@msn.com

Founded: 1986. **Frequency:** Annual. **Audience:** CPAs, accounting professionals, business & client managers, tax preparers, business owners, IT managers of corporations. **Principle Exhibits:** Accounting and business systems and services, computer accounting systems, tax software, integrated accounting systems, Internet and e-accounting solutions, brokerage and investment advisory services, financial and business services, hardware, computer and business systems, and tax preparation, accounting, audit, and practice management software.

∎ 3338
CALL CENTER DEMO AND CONFERENCE
CMP MEDIA INC.

12 W 21st St.
New York, NY 10010
TF: 888-428-3976
FX: (917)305-3341
E-mail: info@cmpevents.com
URL: http://www.cmp.com
Contact: Julie Hogan, Conference Project Manager

Description: Call Center Demo and Conference will provide a mix of content-rich conferences and hands-on product demonstrations. With over 100 of the industry's best in the demo hall, attendees are encouraged to interact one-on-one with vendors and discuss today's innovations.

∎ 3339
CAPTURING BUSINESS RULES (DCI)
DIGITAL CONSULTING INSTITUTE

204 Andover St.
Andover, MA 01810
PH: (978)470-3880
URL: http://www.dci.com

Description: This seminar describes business rule techniques and methodology in full and details how its business-driven approach can dramatically improve business analysis, requirements development, and system design in a company. It offers practical hands-on techniques for using business rules to develop better business solutions, business process models, data models and use cases or procedures. The focus is on using business rules to sharpen an approach and ensure the right questions are answered in the right way, at the right times. It examines how business analysis and IT requirements specification can be coordinated for maximum business advantage. It also shows how to improve communication between the business and IT sides to ensure that designs truly reflect business thinking.

∎ 3340
CATALOGTECH
CATALOG SUCCESS

401 N Broad St., 5th Floor
Philadelphia, PA 19108
PH: (215)238-5300
URL: http://www.catalogtechexpo.com

Description: The CatalogTech conference and exhibition is sponsored by Catalog Success, Publishing and Production Executive, and Target Marketing. The conference addresses Internet retailing, database developments, digital photography, e-commerce solutions, the latest technologies, digital asset management, and more. Features a technology pavilion, roundtable discussions, keynote addresses, and more than 30 sessions.

∎ 3341
CFO SUMMIT
MARCUS EVANS LTD
MARCUS EVANS LTD.

303 E Wacker Dr.
Chicago, IL 60601
PH: (312)540-3000
E-mail: marketing@marcusevansbb.com
URL: http://www.cfosummits.com
Contact: Greta Molepske, Marketing Manager

Description: The CFO Summit caters to delegates representing all major industries who will learn the latest cash flow management techniques, regulatory compliance issues and balance sheet management skills. Allows leading solution providers represented by their executive decision-making officers to join delegates in high-level meetings and closed discussions.

∎ 3342
CHOOSING AND USING EAI TOOLS AND TECHNOLOGIES (DCI)
DIGITAL CONSULTING INSTITUTE

204 Andover St.
Andover, MA 01810
PH: (978)470-3880
URL: http://www.dci.com

Description: This seminar provides a detailed review of a variety of Middleware technologies and products, and shows how an enterprise can use them to develop and integrate directories, portals, web services, data warehouses, operational and other applications using software from IBM, Microsoft, Software AG, BEA Systems, Borland, and other vendors. Real-world case studies are used for illustration. The materials are supplemented by relevant articles and references to resources such as web-sites and books.

∎ 3343
CIO SUMMIT.NET
EVENT MANAGEMENT SERVICES

5200 SW Macadam Ave., Ste. 300
Portland, OR 97201
TF: 800-422-0251
FX: (503)234-4253
E-mail: sbaumann@techshows.com
URL: http://www.techshows.com
Contact: Stacey Baumann

Description: The CIO Summit is a forum for not only establishing strategic advantages through new alliances, but for networking with those who may already have solutions that can be applied with the knowledge they have been implementing successfully. It is designed for Chief Information Officers, Chief Technology Officers, Directors and Managers of Information Systems and those directing the technology for the corporate environment in the private sector and government organizations.

▌3344
CITY IT AND THE E.FORUM - FINANCIAL SERVICES
RICHMOND EVENTS LTD.

St. Leonards House, St. Leonards Rd.
London SW147LY, United Kingdom
PH: 44 20 8487 2200
FX: 44 20 8487 2300
URL: http://www.richmondevents.com

Description: The purpose of CITY IT is to create an environment where the top financial IT and e.commerce professionals can come together to learn, network with peers and identify new supplier companies. Speakers at the conference sessions will be experts in their own particular fields and will be addressing strategic IT issues, management and personal development.

▌3345
CLICK2LEARN USER CONFERENCE
VNU BUSINESS MEDIA.

50 S 9th St.
Minneapolis, MN 55402
PH: (612)333-0471
TF: 800-328-4329
FX: (612)340-4759
E-mail: conferences@vnulearning.com
URL: http://www.vnulearning.com

Founded: 1998. **Description:** The Click2learn User Conference is a conference-within-a-conference and allows attendees to explore all of Online Learning 2002's offerings with the added benefit of attending programs, sessions and hands-on labs that focus specifically on Click2learn's industry-leading enterprise e-learning solutions, including the Aspen Enterprise Learning Platform and ToolBook. These performance-enhancing technologies have been implemented in numerous Fortune 1000 companies. Click2learn User Conference presenters include some of the most seasoned learning professionals with dozens of years of experience, ensuring that clients realize successful return on their learning investment.

▌3346
CLICKZ E-MAIL STRATEGIES
INT MEDIA GROUP

23 Old Kings Hwy. S
Darien, CT 06820
PH: (203)662-2800
TF: (203)655-4686
E-mail: emailstrategies@internet.com
URL: http://www.intmediaevents.com/email/spring02/index.html

Contact: Rob Dougherty

Description: This is an event for e-mail marketing and production. Topics covered are how to write a great message that delivers and increases response, build a successful list, calculate the ROI of an e-mail campaign, nourish customer relationships, generate new leads, and understand program marketing and how to use it. Also offers the workshop ClickZ E-Mail Strategies to learn marketing and production insight needed to launch effective e-mail campaigns and the tools to measure success.

▌3347
COLLABORATIVE COMMERCE
GARTNER INC.

56 Top Gallant Rd.
Stamford, CT 06904
PH: (203)316-1111
FX: (203)324-7901
URL: http://www.gartner.com

Description: This conference provides a measurement framework that will help enterprises understand and manage entire value chain initiatives as well as relevant metrics for current and future operations. The collaborative aspects of supply chains are among the most important business processes because of their high visibility, high velocity and range of collaboration. The conference will focus on: managing the impact on relationships with customers, suppliers, partners and employees, how to maximize supply chain efficiency through the exchange of knowledge and information between sales, production, warehousing and distribution, how to use technology to turn supply chain relationships into demand chain partnerships, which vendors and applications offer the best solutions for an operation, how to accurately measure the performance of planning and forecasting initiatives, and how to assess the cost of collaboration vs. the cost of procrastination.

▌3348
COLLABORATIVE COMMERCE CONFERENCE AND EXPOSITION
ADVANSTAR COMMUNICATIONS INC.

545 Boylston St.
Boston, MA 02116
PH: (617)267-6500
E-mail: information@advanstar.de
URL: http://www.advanstar.com
Contact: Susan R. Schoonover, Marketing and Public Relations

Description: Through the event's multi-tiered program of seminars, industry forums and technology exhibits, this next generation of decision-makers can explore the entire spectrum of business, technology, legal and regulatory issues involved in starting, managing and operating collaborative trading networks, exchanges, private and industry-wide e-marketplaces. This is the first event to bring together business and technology decision makers from global 2000 companies, trading consortia, exchanges and marketplaces from specifically targeted industries to explore the entire spectrum of business, technology, legal and regulatory issues involved in starting, managing and operating collaborative trading networks, exchanges, private and industry-wide e-market-places.

∎ 3349
COLLABORATIVE COMMERCE AND INTEGRATION
IMARK COMMUNICATIONS

1 Apple Hill Dr., Ste. 301
Natick, MA 01760
PH: (508)647-8600
FX: (508)647-0241
E-mail: lkriebel@imark-com.com
URL: http://www.cciexpo.com
Contact: David Korse, President and Chief Executive Officer

Description: Collaborative Commerce and Integration Conference and Expo is an event that brings senior level end users together to discuss proven strategies from their experiences in implementing and integrating collaborative commerce into their organizations. Provides business and technology strategies that will reduce costs, create efficiencies, and improve profits within an organization.

∎ 3350
COLORADO SOFTWARE SUMMIT, JAVA AND XML PROGRAMMING CONFERENCE
KOVSKY CONFERENCE PRODUCTIONS INC.

PO Box 1461
Monument, CO 80132-1461
PH: (719)481-3389
TF: 800-481-3389
FX: (719)481-8069
E-mail: mail_list@softwaresummit.com
URL: http://www.softwaresummit.com/

Description: The Colorado Software Summit is an intensely technical conference, created by and for professional programmers who are working with Java and XML. Conference sessions emphasize real-world programming in Java, with practical examples and plenty of source code to illustrate concepts and techniques. Many of the tutorials are presented by the lead programmers, analysts, architects and designers of the tools they are teaching people to use, while the remainder are taught by people who are using those tools themselves to build comprehensive projects.

∎ 3351
COMDEX EXECUTIVE SYMPOSIUM
KEY3MEDIA GROUP

5700 Wilshire Blvd., Ste. 325
Los Angeles, CA 90036
PH: (323)954-6000
FX: (323)954-6010
E-mail: jeff.bockweg@key3media.com
URL: http://www.key3media.com
Contact: Jeff Bockweg, Conference Sales Manager

Description: The Executive Symposium was created to provide high level insights, advice and strategies to business and IT executives. Programs zero in on the most current technology-related issues today's executives are facing as they look to increase efficiency and productivity within their organizations.

∎ 3352
COMDEX TECHNOLOGY CONFERENCE
KEY3MEDIA GROUP

5700 Wilshire Blvd., Ste. 325
Los Angeles, CA 90036
PH: (323)954-6000
FX: (323)954-6010
E-mail: jeff.bockweg@key3media.com
URL: http://www.key3media.com
Contact: Jeff Bockweg, Conference Sales Manager

Description: COMDEX is the universal IT marketplace that unites technology buyers and sellers online and in person. While continuing global expansion and influence, COMDEX is steadily refining its customer-centric philosophy by segmenting and personalizing everything from the exhibit floor to conference content to encourage community development, making it easier for buyers and sellers to meet and make smarter purchasing decisions. Engaging conferences, potent keynotes, exciting special events, an exhibit floor with cutting-edge technology solutions, a comprehensive online presence and timely show publications are components of the community-driven COMDEX experience, creating more relevancy for the individual and facilitating valuable relationships between technology buyers from around the world.

∎ 3353
COMMUNICATIONS
CANADIAN WIRELESS TELECOMMUNICATIONS ASSOCIATION

500-275 Slater Street
Ottawa, ON, Canada K1P5H9

Founded: 1969. **Frequency:** Annual. **Audience:** Buyers of wireless telecommunication products and services. **Principle Exhibits:** Mobile communications, broadband wireless, elcetronic commerce, wireless internet, fibre optics of the future, switching systms, ADSL, and wirelss local loop.

∎ 3354
COMMVERGE CONFERENCE AND EXHIBITION
REED EXHIBITION CO.

383 Main Ave.
Norwalk, CT 06851
PH: (203)840-5662
FX: (203)840-9662
E-mail: inquiry@reedexpo.com
URL: http://www.reedexpo.com

Description: CommVerge is an event focused on the convergence of voice, video and data and the services that are enabled by them. CommVerge is a high-level event for the team responsible for developing innovative products for the convergence market. This includes senior engineers, business development managers, ''C-level'' executives, and network/IT professionals. All sessions are tightly market-focused, offering a balanced mix of technical data and strategic intelligence from internationally recognized experts and industry pioneers. Developed by leading research groups Cahners IN-STAT and MicroDesign Resources and the editors of CommVerge, EDN, and e-inSITE.

❚ 3355

COMNET CONFERENCE AND EXPO

IDG WORLD EXPO

3 Speen St.
Framingham, MA 01701
PH: (508)879-6700
E-mail: stephen_athan@idg.com
URL: http://www.comnetexpo.com
Contact: Charlie Greco, President and Chief Executive Officer

Description: COMNET Conference and Expo, produced by IDG World Expo, is the catalyst for buyers and sellers in the communication networking industry to connect with the newest technologies and meet the experts driving the industry. COMNET empowers network executives, service providers, carriers, suppliers/resellers and government agencies to make informed technology decisions for their network infrastructure at the beginning of each year. COMNET is an opportunity to learn from successful implementations of new technologies, with a special focus on security, web services, storage and wireless infrastructure.

❚ 3356

COMPETITIVE INTELLIGENCE EXECUTIVE SUMMIT

FROST AND SULLIVAN

7550 W I 10, Ste. 400
San Antonio, TX 78229
PH: (210)247-2461
E-mail: cfsales@frost.com
URL: http://www.frost.com/prod/conf.nsf/0/482FC2A3-D94720AE88256A6C006ECBA8
Contact: Lisa Lee, Event Planner

Description: Competitive Intelligence Executive Summit helps business professionals develop world-class business intelligence functions by sharpening skills and expanding their arsenal of sources and analytical tools. Allows professionals to network with BI professionals, as well as research and business development executives, to find out how the business intelligence function can and should influence corporate strategy.

❚ 3357

COMPUTER AUDIT CONTROL AND SECURITY (ISACA)

INFORMATION SYSTEMS AUDIT AND CONTROL ASSOCIATION

E-mail: conference@isaca.org
URL: http://www.isaca.org

Founded: 1973. **Description:** Information Systems Audit and Control Association (ISACA), a recognized global leader in IT governance, control and assurance, is dedicated to offering the most dynamic and inclusive conference on IS audit, control and security; where new technology and practical application converge. For more than thirty years ISACA's North America Conference on Computer Audit Control and Security (North America CACS) has been the choice of IS audit, control and security professionals seeking ways to meet their technical training needs. Each year, the conference delivers the interactive and pragmatic training IS professionals need to expand their personal knowledge while maintaining their competitive edge. Those attending North America CACS will: experience state-of-the-art practices and strategies, discuss the latest technologies, systems and approaches, hear from leading IS audit, control and security experts, network with an unmatched group of experienced peers, and witness the latest in IT products and services.

❚ 3358

COMPUTER FAIRE

REED EXHIBITION CO.

383 Main Ave.
Norwalk, CT 06851
PH: (203)840-5662
FX: (203)840-9662
E-mail: inquiry@reedexpo.com
URL: http://www.reedexpo.com

Description: Computer Faire is Africa's most comprehensive information, communicaion and office automation showcase hosting national and international vendors and distributors. It will feature sessions on: accessories, barcode systems, boards, adaptors and components,CAD, CAM, CAE, card technology, computer graphics, data collection, digital imaging, hardware, internet and online services, monitors and displays, networking and telecommunications, peripherals and printers, services, software, storage and training.

❚ 3359

COMPUTER FEST

SHOWFEST PRODUCTIONS INC.

130 Bridgeland Ave., Ste. 409
Toronto, ON, Canada M6A1A4
PH: (416)925-4533
FX: (416)925-7701
E-mail: rahmad@compfest.com
URL: http://www.compfest.com
Contact: Rhyan Ahmad, Sales Manager

Description: Computer Fest is an opportunity to get the best deals on computer product along with everything needed for a new or growing small business. Over $12,000,000 in new used, overstocked and closeout computer product will be available at blowout prices from the better than 100 exhibitors in Computer Fest.

▌3360

THE COMPUTER AND TECHNOLOGY SHOWCASE

EVENT MANAGEMENT SERVICES

5200 SW Macadam Ave., Ste. 300
Portland, OR 97201
PH: 800-422-0251
FX: (503)234-4253
E-mail: lbruce@techshows.com
URL: http://www.techshows.com
Contact: Chris Camnnard, President

Description: This annual event is the forum for the region's IT executives to evaluate the latest in technology. It is an excellent opportunity to view technology, explore services and ask the questions one needs answered to further a business technology plan. This event encompasses a variety of opportunities to put a company in front of 3,000 to 5,000 corporate decision makers on average per market.

▌3361

COMTEK

ITE GROUP PLC

105 Salusbury Rd.
London NW66RG, United Kingdom
PH: 44 20 7596 5000
FX: 44 20 7596 5111
E-mail: Info@technology-events.com
URL: http://www.technology-events.com
Contact: Stephen Warshaw, Chief Executive Officer

Founded: 1991. **Description:** The Business Section of Comtek Exhibition - Business-to-Business (B2B) includes the following vertical exhibitions: 1. Software Expo features business-oriented software programs. It will also include the traditional Comtek ExpoCAD section. 2. e-Business Expo is dedicated to e-Commerce and e-Business development in general. 3. Business System Expo showcases a broad range of products for office use: equipment, peripherals, consumables, etc. 4. Photo Publishing Expo presents publishing systems, digital photo technologies, offset and post-print equipment, consumables, etc.

▌3362

CONNECT

REED EXHIBITION CO.

383 Main Ave.
Norwalk, CT 06851
PH: (203)840-5662
FX: (203)840-9662
E-mail: inquiry@reedexpo.com
URL: http://www.reedexpo.com

Description: Connect is Sweden's most popular trade fair for the world's fastest growing sectors. Some products and services to be offered are: hardware, software, wireless and e-business solutions.

▌3363

CONNECT - IT

VNU EXPOSITIONS

14685 Avion Parkway
Ste. 400
Chantilly, VA 20151

Founded: 2000. **Frequency:** Annual. **Audience:** Apparel industry professionals who make purchasing decisions for their companies - CEOs, CIOs, CFOs, COOs, designers, plant managers. **Principle Exhibits:** Exhibitors are companies who design, develop and implement solutions for the IT needs of all segments of the apparel and softgoods industry, from porduct development to retail point-of-sale. E-commerce, design software, internet, data integration, pattern making.

▌3364

CONTENT MANAGEMENT FORUM

IDG JAPAN INC.

3-4-5 Hongo Bunkyo-ku
Tokyo 113-0033, Japan
PH: 03 5800 3111
E-mail: cmf@idg.co.jp
URL: http://www.idg.co.jp

Description: This event features topics such as intellectual property and information management which are critical for the development of content business.

▌3365

CORPORATE AND E-BUSINESS PORTALS CONFERENCE (DCI)

DIGITAL CONSULTING INSTITUTE

204 Andover St.
Andover, MA 01810
PH: (978)470-3880
URL: http://www.dci.com

Description: This event is a forum on implementing portals for both internal corporate and e-Business use. Pragmatic and solution-oriented, the conference gives the strategies and practical advice needed to be successful in a portal project. It takes an in-depth look at portal architectures and technologies, and presents a practical guide to implementing portal applications. Detailed case studies from leading corporations show how portal technology is used in both internal business applications and in e-Business systems. Attendees also come away from this conference able to understand, compare and contrast the different vendor portal offerings.

∎ 3366

CORPORATE PORTAL MANAGEMENT: PROFITING FROM GREATER ACCESS TO INFORMATION, APPLICATIONS AND INNOVATION

MARCUS EVANS LTD.

303 E Wacker Dr.
Chicago, IL 60601
PH: (312)540-3000
E-mail: LisaR@marcusevansch.com
URL: http://www.brandslam-summit.com
Contact: Greta Molepske, Marketing Manager

Description: The aim of this conference is to cover the commercial aspect of portals and their capacity to manage secure, end-user access to a business' network of applications and resources for commercial proficiency. Building the ''business driven - IS executed'' approach to effective portal management is a key area of focus. Portal technology is not just an interface to information and applications but should be exploited as a platform on which to build eBusiness strategies.

∎ 3367

CPFR INSTITUTE

MOONWATCH MEDIA INC.

77 Oak St., Ste. 201
Newton Upper Falls, MA 02464
PH: (617)527-4626
FX: (617)527-8102
E-mail: info@moonwatchmedia.com
URL: http://www.retailsystems.com

Description: The CPFR Institute will bring together program leaders from academic and industry backgrounds to discuss the issues critical to a successful CPFR initiative. The Institute will focus on how to implement CPFR. Collaborative commerce experts will provide information on constantly evolving standards and guidelines, as well as implementation techniques. The two-day program has been broken into two sections, based on the attendee's level of exposure to CPFR design and implementation. At the conclusion of this training, participants will receive a certificate of completion.

∎ 3368

CREATING THE REAL-TIME ENTERPRISE (DCI)

DIGITAL CONSULTING INSTITUTE

204 Andover St.
Andover, MA 01810
PH: (978)470-3880
URL: http://www.dci.com

Description: This event is designed to lead the charge in the real-time enterprise marketplace. The program is developed to provide in-depth details on why a real-time enterprise is so crucial to all organizations competing in today's tough market conditions. Through concrete examples of real-time implementations presented in end-user case studies, industry visionary keynote addresses and unbiased product and service value comparisons, this event will provide attendees with a solid strategy for streamlining business processes to better manage customer relationships, sustain productivity gains, decrease costs and generate long-term profitability.

∎ 3369

CRITICAL ISSUES IN ENTERPRISE ARCHITECTURE (DCI)

DIGITAL CONSULTING INSTITUTE

204 Andover St.
Andover, MA 01810
PH: (978)470-3880
URL: http://www.dci.com

Description: At Critical Issues In Enterprise Architecture, attendees will discover what must be done to begin, stabilize or expand an enterprise architecture function in an organization. In an intensive single-track format, attendees will learn from experts in the field through sessions designed to help discover the pieces needed to complete an enterprise architecture puzzle. This event will focus on the boundary between art and science that is enterprise architecture. When perceived as strictly a modeling exercise, EA efforts rarely succeed. When focused only at the project or technology level, EA efforts often fail to distinguish themselves. It is only through a thorough appreciation of ALL elements, including the enterprise level business vision, people issues, process integration, project realities and modeling rigor, that an EA effort will yield true enterprise results. The event's speakers will give valuable insights that can be used to initiate an enterprise architecture, restart stalled efforts or move on-going effort to a new level.

∎ 3370

CRM: AN EXECUTIVE OVERVIEW (DCI)

DIGITAL CONSULTING INSTITUTE

204 Andover St.
Andover, MA 01810
PH: (978)470-3880
URL: http://www.dci.com

Description: CRM: An Executive Overview offers a fast-paced look at sales automation and process improvement best practice essentials. This course covers the seven-step planning technique advocated by the Sales Automation Association. Content is presented in sufficient depth so that executives, senior level sponsors, and staff associated with the sales process improvement effort can speak a common language, set clear goals, and work effectively with members of the day-to-day working team to achieve concrete business results. The one-day format makes this program an ideal kickoff for planning meetings in support of first, second, or higher generation efforts.

∎ 3371

CRM EXECUSUMMIT

SWISSOTEL BOSTON

PH: (845)473-0199
FX: (253)541-2870

E-mail: rorbach@execusummit.com
URL: http://www.execusummit.com

Description: The CRM ExecuSummit is two days of high impact sessions filled with cutting edge info, case studies and networking opportunities. The Summit provides fresh knowledge regarding a variety of topics within the CRM industry and also provides new tools, cutting edge strategies and techniques to enhance CRM initiative.

■ **3372**

CRM SOLUTIONS
ADVANSTAR COMMUNICATIONS INC.

545 Boylston St.
Boston, MA 02116
PH: (617)267-6500
E-mail: information@advanstar.de
URL: http://www.advanstar.com

Description: Customer Relationship Management spending is on the rise and CRM software and strategies continue to be a major consideration for call center managers and corporate executives. Find out what is working at CRM Solutions. This one-of-a-kind case studies-driven conference program features high-impact sessions focused on quality management, channel integration, outsourcing, and expert analysis. CRM Solutions offers conference content, application showcase theatres, industry forums and industry-leading vendors, creating a wealth of educational opportunities and unveiling the latest trends and challenges of CRM initiatives in today's economy.

■ **3373**

CRM SUMMIT: BUILDING CUSTOMER LOYALTY THROUGH TECHNOLOGY
GARTNER INC.

56 Top Gallant Rd.
Stamford, CT 06904
PH: (203)316-1111
FX: (203)324-7901
URL: http://www.gartner.com

Description: Gartner's CRM Mexico Summit is an event offering unbiased analysis of CRM's value for Mexican businesses that are seeking to evaluate, reassess or implement CRM technologies and processes. Specifically, attendees will learn how to: balance strategy, tactics, processes and technology for ideal customer-centric solutions, understand what companies that are leading the pack in CRM are doing, what's working and what's not, identify potential pit falls, evaluate the requirements for a CRM architecture, and assess vendor alternatives for developing and integrating CRM applications and technologies.

■ **3374**

CRM TECHNOLOGY DECISIONS
TECHTARGET

117 Kendrick St., Ste. 800
Needham, MA 02494
PH: (781)657-1000

TF: 888-274-4111
FX: (781)657-1100
E-mail: info@techtarget.com
URL: http://www.techtarget.com
Contact: Ken Berquist, Vice President of Conferences

Description: CRM Technology Decisions will feature sessions on how to analyze specific CRM requirements to determine need and how to manage a CRM program to achieve the highest ROI. Attendess will benefit from real-world case studies of successful CRM programs, make the smartest CRM infrastructure/technology purchasing decisions, implement processes and people without breaking the bank, and the latest CRM integration tools.

■ **3375**

CSI ANNUAL COMPUTER SECURITY CONFERENCE AND EXHIBITON
COMPUTER SECURITY INSTITUTE

600 Harrison St.
San Francisco, CA 94107
PH: (415)947-6320
FX: (415)947-6023
E-mail: csi@cmp.com
URL: http://www.gocsi.com

Founded: 1974. **Description:** Setting the industry standard for 29 years, this event is the largest and most comprehensive in the industry. The program features over 130 sessions focusing on Internet/intranet/extranet security, VPNs, PKI/cryptography, NT security, WWW, network intrusions and Counter measures, distributed denial of service attacks, response teams, management and awareness issues and much more.The conference is designed for anyone with responsibility for or involvement or interest in information and network security, and has sessions for those new to security as well as for seasoned professionals. Over 3000 information security professionals from around the world are expected to attend.

■ **3376**

CUSTOMER 360
KEY3MEDIA GROUP

5700 Wilshire Blvd., Ste. 325
Los Angeles, CA 90036
PH: (323)954-6000
FX: (323)954-6010
E-mail: mike.moreno@key3media.com
URL: http://www.key3media.com
Contact: Mike Moreno, General Manager

Description: Customer 360 is a business-to-business industry event focused on ebusiness strategies and CRM, the customer-centric approach that leading-edge organizations use to identify, acquire, service and retain customers. Customer 360 is geared toward any and all business executives, managers and professionals whose role involves creating a better experience for their customer. Customer 360 helps organizations strengthen and enhance their business process technologies to more effectively service their customers.

▌3377

CUSTOMER CONTACT CENTER CONFERENCE AND EXPOSITION (DCI)
DIGITAL CONSULTING INSTITUTE

204 Andover St.
Andover, MA 01810
PH: (978)470-3880
URL: http://www.dci.com

Description: The CCC Conference and Exposition will equip attendees with the highest level of education to transform the Call Center into a true multi-channel, profit-generating Customer Contact Center. The instructors will teach how to integrate the Customer Contact Center into enterprise-wide CRM solution to give a company maximum competitive advantage.

▌3378

CUSTOMER CONTACT DAYS 3
BRUSSELS FAIRS AND EXHIBITIONS

Place de Belgique
B-1020 Brussels, Belgium
E-mail: delcofleur@bfe.be

Founded: 1998. **Frequency:** Annual. **Audience:** Top management, customer service managers, marketing managers, HR managers, callcenter managers, IT managers, and operation managers. **Principle Exhibits:** CRM solutions, e-service and e-support, knowledge-based solutions, consultancy, outsourcing, recruitment, training, call center solutions, e-commerce, IT solutions, direct marketing agencies, fulfillment/handling, data management, postal and telecom operators, furniture/workstations, development agencies.

▌3379

CUSTOMER CONTACT WORLD
TERRAPINN, LTD.

100 Hatton Garden, Level 2, Ste. B
London EC1N8NX, United Kingdom
PH: 44 207 2421548
FX: 44 207 2421508
E-mail: james.smith@terrapinn.com
URL: http://www.terrapinn.com

Description: Customer Contact World China 2002 addresses the need for a customer-centric strategy for businesses big or small. It is about managing customers in an ever-increasing competitive environment where price and product provides fewer differentiation features. It starts with the change in mind-set and attitude and leads to the systems and processes. The programme also addresses the importance of making a customer-centric strategy integral to overall corporate strategy.

▌3380

CUSTOMER INTEGRATION: THE LIFEBLOOD OF CRM
GARTNER INC.

56 Top Gallant Rd.
Stamford, CT 06904
PH: (203)316-1111
FX: (203)324-7901
URL: http://www.gartner.com

Description: Customer Integration: The Lifeblood of CRM focuses on the following key topics: overview of customer data quality considerations and CDI technologies, the nature of customer data and its role in effective CRM, the three basic data types and their interaction in a customer database, and important considerations regarding data channels and analysis for CRM.

▌3381

CUSTOMER RELATIONSHIP MANAGEMENT CONFERENCE AND EXPOSITION (DCI)
DIGITAL CONSULTING INSTITUTE

204 Andover St.
Andover, MA 01810
PH: (978)470-3880
URL: http://www.dci.com

Description: This advanced course is designed to go above and beyond the basic, beginner level eCRM courses, providing attendees with detailed information and strategies on eCRM implementation. This course is a perfect complement to eCRM University 101, taking the height of the educational content and strategy details provided to the next level.

▌3382

CUSTOMER RELATIONSHIP MANAGEMENT (CRM) ASIA SUMMIT
FROST AND SULLIVAN

7550 W I 10, Ste. 400
San Antonio, TX 78229
PH: (210)247-2461
E-mail: myfrostasia@frost.com
URL: http://www.frost.com/prod/conf.nsf/0/
C4C3542EE9D03CF086256B80000DBEDA
Contact: Lisa Lee, Event Planner

Description: The Customer Relationship Management (CRM) Asia Summit brings key speakers from around the world to discuss issues such as: Analytics, Wireless and Business Process Outsourcing (BPO). Provides the opportunity to pick the mind of the top gurus on critical matters in today's CRM environment.

▌3383

CUSTOMER SERVICE CONFERENCE
LOMA

2300 Windy Ridge Pky., Ste. 600
Atlanta, GA 30339-8443
PH: (770)951-1770

TF: 800-275-5662
FX: (770)984-0441
E-mail: meetings@loma.org
URL: http://www.loma.org

Description: At the LOMA Customer Service Conference, attendees will discover strategies to select and develop the best employees and service delivery methods, build strong customer relationships and retain the best customers. Learn the latest developments in customer service and gain perspectives on how one can achieve service excellence within an organization.

▌3384

DATA ANALYSIS AND LOGICAL DATA MODELING FOR THE DATA WAREHOUSE (DCI)

DIGITAL CONSULTING INSTITUTE

204 Andover St.
Andover, MA 01810
PH: (978)470-3880
URL: http://www.dci.com

Description: This seminar focuses on the key expectations from any data warehouse, namely to provide clean, consistent and integrated data to business users in support of their decision-making needs. This is not a database design issue. Instead, this is a data analysis, data cleansing and data transformation issue. This seminar teaches how to address these three issues by using two logical data modeling techniques. The technique of top-down data modeling teaches how to create an integrated logical data model, which is fully normalized and populated with key business attributes. The technique of bottom-up data modeling teaches how to validate and map source data into logical data model, as well as how to find dirty data in the source file and transform it using the formal Normalization rules.

▌3385

DATA CENTER CONFERENCE

GARTNER INC.

56 Top Gallant Rd.
Stamford, CT 06904
PH: (203)316-1111
FX: (203)324-7901
URL: http://www.gartner.com

Founded: 1982. **Description:** This conference focuses on the issues involved in managing complex heterogeneous platforms, servers, storage, and operating systems. The conference will explore in depth topics such as the growing maturity of Windows in the data center, delve into the future of the mainframe and Unix platforms, separate the hype from reality on topics such as Linux and autonomic computing, and investigate the ways to deal with the explosive growth in storage requirements.

▌3386

DATA MINING: EVALUATING METHODS AND TOOLS: AN INTENSIVE INTRODUCTION TO THE METHODS, APPLICATIONS, TOOLS, AND TECHNIQUES (DCI)

DIGITAL CONSULTING INSTITUTE

204 Andover St.
Andover, MA 01810
PH: (978)470-3880
URL: http://www.dci.com

Description: This seminar focuses on various approaches to real-world Data Mining techniques. The instructor has been involved with the development of Data Mining methods and the means of their use. Actual products will be used to illustrate tools and method evaluations, as will results drawn from real Data Mining applications. Attendees will depart with a binder full of slides, supporting text and a valuable index of Data Mining resource references.

▌3387

DATA MINING: LEVEL I: AN INTENSIVE INTRODUCTION TO METHODS, TOOLS AND RESOURCES (DCI)

DIGITAL CONSULTING INSTITUTE

204 Andover St.
Andover, MA 01810
PH: (978)470-3880
URL: http://www.dci.com

Description: This two-day course offers an introduction to data mining terminology, methods, resources and business issues. Attendees learn about various methods of data modeling, competitive advantages, and common pitfalls that cause data mining projects to fall short of their potential.

▌3388

DATA MINING LEVEL II: THE DATA MINING PROCESS, TECHNIQUES AND APPLICATIONS (DCI)

DIGITAL CONSULTING INSTITUTE

204 Andover St.
Andover, MA 01810
PH: (978)470-3880
URL: http://www.dci.com

Description: This second level offering presents a deeper examination of the data mining process at a functional level. Attendees observe and participate in demonstrations of computer-guided analytical techniques for extracting and interpreting complex business rules from data. It is designed to be a rapid and substantial boost in understanding of data mining concepts, tools, techniques and supporting methods.The intent of this seminar is to offer attendees a stronger grasp of data mining techniques, and a solid understanding of how various methods and tools apply to different kinds of data intensive problems.

▌3389

DATA WAREHOUSE AND CUSTOMER RELATIONSHIP MANAGEMENT EXPO AND CONFERENCE

REED EXHIBITIONS JAPAN LTD.

Shinjuku-Nomura Bldg. 18F
1-26-2 Nishishinjuku
Shinjuku-ku
Tokyo 163-0570, Japan
PH: 81 3 33498501
TF: 81 3 33498599
E-mail: goto@reedexpo.co.jp
URL: http://www.reedexpo.co.jp
Contact: Nana Goto

Description: Data Warehouse and Customer Relationship Management Expo and Conference in Tokyo 2002 had firmly established itself as one of Japan's most important data warehousing and CRM trade shows serving a market that has thousands of new and high quality and latest technologies.

▌3390

DATA WAREHOUSING CONFERENCE AND EXPOSITION (DCI)

DIGITAL CONSULTING INSTITUTE

204 Andover St.
Andover, MA 01810
PH: (978)470-3880
URL: http://www.dci.com

Description: This seminar is the first of two covering dimensional data warehouse design in detail. This seminar introduces dimensional data warehouse design by addressing the key issues involved in designing the physical database structures necessary to support both the anticipated and the unanticipated analytical requirements of the enterprise. Participants learn the basic techniques of dimensional data warehouse design, which will ensure that the data in their data warehouse will be accessible by the business community and still provide optimal performance.

▌3391

DCI'S CUSTOMER CONTACT CENTER CONFERENCE AND EXPOSITION (DCI)

DIGITAL CONSULTING INSTITUTE

204 Andover St.
Andover, MA 01810
PH: (978)470-3880
URL: http://www.dci.com

Description: Companies installing enterprise-wide CRM applications have recognized that the Customer Contact Center, a system integrating all customer contact channels (web, telephone, email, fax, Internet chat) to provide 24x7 availability is crucial for achieving the greatest success. The CCC Conference and Exposition will equip attendees with the highest level of education to transform the Call Center into a true multi-channel, profit-generating Customer Contact Center. The instructors will teach attendees how to integrate

the Customer Contact Center into an enterprise-wide CRM solution to give the company maximum competitive advantage.

▌3392

DCI'S CUSTOMER RELATIONSHIP MANAGEMENT CONFERENCE AND EXPOSITION

DCI

204 Andover St.
Andover, MA 01810
PH: (978)470-3870
FX: (978)470-1992
E-mail: nkwok@dci.com
URL: http://www.CRMevent.com
Contact: Dr. George Schussel, Founder, Chairman, & CEO

Description: DCI's CRM conference is a solution source for today's business and technology challenges. This event promises to be the program that will enable one to develop career-enhancing education and tools necessary to meet customers' evolving demands and keep ahead of the competition.

▌3393

DEVELOPING WEB ENTERPRISE APPLICATIONS (DCI)

DIGITAL CONSULTING INSTITUTE

204 Andover St.
Andover, MA 01810
PH: (978)470-3880
URL: http://www.dci.com

Description: This seminar shows how an enterprise can deploy the best emerging Web technology for competitive advantage, to reduce operating costs, and to improve productivity. It describes strengths, weaknesses, and best practices for available tools and technologies. This is not an overview - delegates will leave with a practical, not theoretical, understanding of Web development methodology, techniques, vendors, and technology for e-commerce, data warehouse, web services, and operational applications. The seminar employs a number of case studies, articles, web-sites, and other resources to supplement and support the course materials.

▌3394

DIGITAL INFORMATION FORUM

REED EXHIBITION CO.

383 Main Ave.
Norwalk, CT 06851
PH: (203)840-5662
FX: (203)840-9662
E-mail: inquiry@reedexpo.com
URL: http://www.reedexpo.com

Description: Digital Information Forum is Thailand's first software and networking exhibition and conference. Some topics discussed will be: Data warehousing, relational database and management systems.

▌3395

DIMENSIONAL DATA WAREHOUSE DESIGN: STRATEGIC DESIGN TECHNIQUES FOR AN EFFICIENT ENTERPRISE (DCI)

DIGITAL CONSULTING INSTITUTE

204 Andover St.
Andover, MA 01810
PH: (978)470-3880
URL: http://www.dci.com

Description: This seminar is the first of two covering dimensional data warehouse design in detail. This seminar introduces dimensional data warehouse design by addressing the key issues involved in designing the physical database structures necessary to support both the anticipated and the unanticipated analytical requirements of the enterprise. Participants learn the basic techniques of dimensional data warehouse design, which will ensure that the data in their data warehouse will be accessible by the business community and still provide optimal performance.

▌3396

DISTRIBUTION COMPUTER EXPO

C.S. REPORT, INC.

Box 696
Uwchland, PA 19480
E-mail: info@logistar.com

Founded: 1983. **Frequency:** Annual. **Audience:** Distribution, transportatio, logistics, and warehouse professionals. **Principle Exhibits:** Computer programs and computerized services for the logistics, distribution, transportation, and truck fleet operation & warehousing industries & supply chain management, e-commerce, B to B, and B to C.

▌3397

DISTRIBUTION TECHNOLOGY CONFERENCE

LOMA

2300 Windy Ridge Pkwy., Ste. 600
Atlanta, GA 30339-8443
PH: (770)951-1770
TF: 800-275-5662
FX: (770)984-0441
E-mail: meetings@loma.org
URL: http://www.loma.org

Description: The LOMA Distribution Technology Conference has the strategies and solutions that will help to revamp strategies, boost profits and come out on top.

▌3398

DMS - DESIGN ENGINEERING & MANUFACTURING SOLUTIONS EXPO & CONFERENCE

REED EXHIBITIONS (JAPAN)

18F Shinjuku-Nomura Bldg.
1-26-2 Nishi-Shinjuku
Shinjuku-ku
Tokyo 163-0570, Japan
E-mail: rej@reedexpo.co.jp

Founded: 1990. **Frequency:** Annual. **Audience:** CEOs, presidents, board members, design and production engineers, QA and information systems professional, R&D personnel. **Principle Exhibits:** CAD/CAM/CAE, virtual manufacturing, plotter/printer/scanner, PDM, ERP, e-commerce, system integration, processing and production management systems, SCM.

▌3399

DMS EXPO EUROPE

ADVANSTAR COMMUNICATIONS INC.

545 Boylston St.
Boston, MA 02116
PH: (617)267-6500
FX: (617)267-6900
E-mail: information@advanstar.de
URL: http://www.advanstar.com

Description: The strapline for DMS EXPO is Content meets Knowledge, which explains that the connection between information and knowledge will become more important in this global-oriented business market. Secure electronic archive systems are the basis for the integration of both current and historical information and documents in decision-making processes. With secure electronic information logistics and a digital signature, this information and knowledge is made available anywhere and any time, both company-wide and worldwide. DMS EXPO showcases all these solutions and much more.

▌3400

DOCUMATION

REED EXHIBITION CO.

383 Main Ave.
Norwalk, CT 06851
PH: (203)840-5662
FX: (203)840-9662
E-mail: inquiry@reedexpo.com
URL: http://www.reedexpo.com

Description: Documation is an European event on content and information management, Intranet and corporate portals.

▌3401

DOCUMATION ESPANA

REED EXHIBITION CO.

383 Main Ave.
Norwalk, CT 06851
PH: (203)840-5662

FX: (203)840-9662
E-mail: inquiry@reedexpo.com
URL: http://www.reedexpo.com

Description: This conference and exhibition show will offer a large spectrum of activities including an exhibition, educational conferences and tutorials and several product demonstration sessions offered by the exhibiting companies. More specifically, Documation Espana, will cover topics such as: content management, corporate portals, knowledge management, Intranet publishing, and XML applications and architectures.

∎ 3402

DS EXPO: DATA STORAGE EXPO AND CONFERENCE
REED EXHIBITION CO.

383 Main Ave.
Norwalk, CT 06851
PH: (203)840-5662
FX: (203)840-9662
E-mail: inquiry@reedexpo.com
URL: http://www.reedexpo.com

Description: Data Storage Expo and Conference in Tokyo (DS EXPO) offers 6 specialized zones. Specifically they are: Bluetooth Zone; Embedded Linux Zone; Embedded Java Zone; FPGA/PLD Zone; Board Computer Zone; Design Services and Consulting Zone.

∎ 3403

E-BUSINESS CHINA - CHINA INTERNATIONAL ELECTRONIC BUSINESS NETWORKING EQUIPMENT & AFFILIATED PRODUCTS EXHIBITION
WORLDWIDE CONVENTIONS & EXPOSITIONS, LTD

Ste. 611, 6/F, Telford House
16 Wang Hoi Rd.
Hong Kong, People's Republic of China
E-mail: info@ww-expo.com

Frequency: Annual. **Audience:** Trade and general public. **Principle Exhibits:** Internet, intranet, computer peripherals, information technology and equipment, security technology and systems, network solutions for electronic payment, electronic commerce software, multi-media technology and equipment.

∎ 3404

E - BUSINESS EXPO
REED EXHIBITION CO.

383 Main Ave.
Norwalk, CT 06851
PH: (203)840-5662
FX: (203)840-9662
E-mail: inquiry@reedexpo.com
URL: http://www.reedexpo.com

Description: e-Business Expo is an annual forum of excellence for executives and decision makers to find everything that is new in terms of technology, products and services as applied to the world of e-business. Some of the content that will be covered is: E commerce, telecomms, e business strategy, e-procurement, E leasing, CRM, web sites, supply chain, and e security.

∎ 3405

E-BUSINESS UNIVERSITY: A PROFESSIONAL CERTIFICATION PROGRAM (DCI)
DIGITAL CONSULTING INSTITUTE

204 Andover St.
Andover, MA 01810
PH: (978)470-3880
URL: http://www.dci.com

Description: In this accelerated "How To" workshop, attendees will learn proven Best Practice Methodologies that will enable them to successfully implement their own e-Business strategy. This hands-on workshop offers an opportunity to fulfill strategic objectives for e-Business while at the same time helping to avoid expensive and painful mistakes. Whether already in the middle of a project or getting ready to begin, these Best Practice Methodologies bring structure and standardization to project planning efforts. All aspects of e-Business implementation will be covered by a select group of industry leaders who will guide attendees through a series of practice activities designed to increase learning.

∎ 3406

E-COMMERCE
ON-LINE MARKETING GROUP

PO Box 6074
Ocean View, HI 96737
PH: (808)929-7377
FX: (808)929-9991
E-mail: kaubiz@hialoha.net
URL: http://www.e-comprofits.com

Founded: 2000. **Description:** E-COMMERCE-Strategies For Converting Net Surfers Into Sales is specifically created to teach how to maximize the potential of the internet, and the world-wide-web. The in's-and-out's of the insiders will be taught. Professionals explain how to use highly refined e-commerce skills to create rapid profits, improve customer service, lower operating costs, expand markets, shorten selling cycles, and dramatically boost revenues.

∎ 3407

E-COMMERCE EXPO
REED EXHIBITION COMPANIES (UK) LTD.

Oriel House
26 The Quadrant
Richmond, Surrey TW91DL, England
E-mail: info@reedexpo.co.uk

Founded: 1995. **Frequency:** Annual. **Audience:** Trade. **Principle Exhibits:** Products and services for conducting business electronically; messaging, internet, security, electronic banking, product coding, worlwide web commerce.

▌ 3408
E-FESTIVAL ASIA
REED EXHIBITION CO.

383 Main Ave.
Norwalk, CT 06851
PH: (203)840-5662
FX: (203)840-9662
E-mail: inquiry@reedexpo.com
URL: http://www.reedexpo.com

Description: e-Festival Asia showcases the latest interactive media and online technologies. It aims to provide an learning experience for visitors and create a buzz for the broadband multimedia industry. Some products and services offered are: e-transactions, e-entertainment, and e-learning.

▌ 3409
E-FULFILLMENT IMPLEMENTATION STRATEGIES (IQPC)
INTERNATIONAL QUALITY AND PRODUCTIVITY CENTER

PO Box 401
150 Clove Rd.
Little Falls, NJ 07424
PH: (973)256-0211
TF: 800-882-8684
E-mail: info@iqpc.com
URL: http://www.iqpc.com
Contact: Todd Smith, Sales Manager, Sponsorship and Exhibits

Description: e-fulfillment is one of the fastest growing interest areas for organizations engaging in e-commerce, requiring senior-level attention and resources to develop the strategies to create the much-needed capabilities. The success of a business relies on the ability to deliver the goods at the speed of ''e''. For this reason the Warehouse Advisory Council, a division of IQPC, has developed this seminar on e-fullfillment. Attendees will leave this seminar with the knowledge base and innovative strategies it takes to be a leader in order fulfillment and a leader in e-commerce.

▌ 3410
E-HR: TRANSFORMING THE HR FUNCTION
MARCUS EVANS LTD.

303 E Wacker Dr.
Chicago, IL 60601
PH: (312)540-3000
E-mail: LisaR@marcusevansch.com
URL: http://www.brandslam-summit.com
Contact: Greta Molepske, Marketing Manager

Description: Highlighting strategic, innovative and best-in-class presentations, The Pan European conference provides value to all HR professionals, in particular through eminent case studies such as, Nike Europe, Carrefour, British American Tobacco, Nokia, Cable and Wireless, BP, Siemens, Bertelsmann AG, Cisco Systems, and European Commission.

▌ 3411
E-LEARNING CONFERENCE
MARCUS EVANS LTD.

303 E Wacker Dr.
Chicago, IL 60601
PH: (312)540-3000
E-mail: LisaR@marcusevansch.com
URL: http://www.brandslam-summit.com
Contact: Greta Molepske, Marketing Manager

Description: The e-learning conference provides insight into how to effectively utilize e-learning as an additional training tool for ROI, where to implement e-learning within the business, which procedures/processes are best suited to online learning and training, and what are the key business benefits. This international event discusses and assesses the key drivers for improving the learning experience. The conference offers attendees the opportunity to hear and network with the global leaders in the pharmaceutical industry.

▌ 3412
E LEARNING EXPO AND CONFERENCE
ITE GROUP PLC

105 Salusbury Rd.
London NW66RG, United Kingdom
PH: 44 20 7596 5000
FX: 44 20 7596 5111
E-mail: info@technology-events.com
URL: http://www.technology-events.com
Contact: Stephen Warshaw, Chief Executive Officer

Founded: 2002. **Description:** E Learning Expo and Conference is targeted for organizations who identify the need to address the Eastern European, South German and Austrian eLearning market. It is also for organizations that have the need to focus an event specifically on the bigger and better consortiums now being formed between public sector education, distance learning bodies, business schools and corporations. The eLearnExpo conference will feature presentations, reports and live examples of latest collaborative initiatives involving universities, schools and corporations as well as consortiums providing large distance learning solutions for the general public and SME's.

▌ 3413
E-LEARNING SUPPLIER SUMMIT
VNU BUSINESS MEDIA.

50 S 9th St.
Minneapolis, MN 55402
PH: (612)333-0471
TF: 800-328-4329
FX: (612)340-4759

E-mail: conferences@vnulearning.com
URL: http://www.vnulearning.com

Founded: 2002. **Description:** The E-learning Supplier Summit is a forum for e-learning suppliers, analysts, venture capitalists and industry observers to meet and assess the current status and future prospects of industry. Co-located with Online Learning Conference and Expo and chaired by Online Learning Magazine Industry Watch Columnist Clark Aldrich, the E-learning Supplier Summit will explore issues and business opportunities that are of special interest to e-learning's key decision-makers and business leaders.

∎ 3414
E-MAIL NEWSLETTER STRATEGIES
INT MEDIA GROUP

23 Old Kings Hwy. S
Darien, CT 06820
PH: (203)662-2800
TF: (203)655-4686
E-mail: cobrienats@internet.com
URL: http://www.intmediaevents.com

Description: At E-mail Newsletter Strategies, profit and non-profit publishers, associations and organizations have the opportunity to learn best practices on how to use e-mail newsletters as a profit center, as a promotional tool to enhance brand awareness or to market services offered by their company or association. Additionally, companies that have successfully implemented e-mail newsletters as part of their business strategy will be on hand to share their knowledge and experience.

∎ 3415
E-PHARMA EXCHANGE
INTERNATIONAL QUALITY AND PRODUCTIVITY CENTER

PO Box 401
150 Clove Rd.
Little Falls, NJ 07424
PH: (973)256-0211
TF: 800-882-8684
E-mail: info@content-net.com
URL: http://www.iqpc.com
Contact: Todd Smith, Sales Manager, Sponsorship and Exhibits

Description: E-Pharma Exchange will bring together an audience of more than 100 E-Pharmaceutical professionals, including many companies who are only now embracing E-Business and investing in Internet Solutions. The Event Team is researching and interviewing delegates on a daily basis so as to pin-point the key issues and challenges in the Marketplace. Some of the topic areas that have been pinpointed for E-Pharma and will form the basis for some of the interactive workshop discussions include overview of E-Pharma, the future of E-Pharma, building the E- Pharma strategy into the overall Pharma Business Strategy, E Clinical Trials, E-CRM; Providing the human touch electronically, and E Sales and the use of E-Detailing.

∎ 3416
E-SECURITY CONFERENCE AND EXPOSITION
INT MEDIA GROUP

23 Old Kings Hwy. S
Darien, CT 06820
PH: (203)662-2800
TF: (203)655-4686
E-mail: jsigmann@internet.com
URL: http://www.esecurityevent.com

Description: This event, specifically designed for enterprise, government and corporate business and IT executives and managers, covers security from a management-level perspective, focusing on policy, procedure and ROI concerns while also covering key technology trends. In short, the eSecurity Conference puts security into terms technology decision-makers can understand. This power-packed conference, covering 5 comprehensive tracks, offers attendees the opportunity to learn from top eSecurity experts, meet with leading industry solution providers, and network with their peers.

∎ 3417
E-SUCCESS: AN EXECUTIVE BRIEFING (DCI)
DIGITAL CONSULTING INSTITUTE

204 Andover St.
Andover, MA 01810
PH: (978)470-3880
URL: http://www.dci.com

Description: This seminar is designed to make sense out of CRM and e-Business and is based on the book "e-Success: A Leadership/Alignment Model". The content provides a model for senior management and the entire team to better understand these technologies and the opportunities they represent. The briefing is appropriate for all organizations (for profit, not-for-profit, and governmental). It provides a clear path for moving the organization toward customer centricity by managing risk and investment in a logical and productive manner. All participants will receive a copy of "e-Success: A Leadership/Alignment Model" as well as the seminar notes.

∎ 3418
E SUPPORT CERTIFICATION (DCI)
DIGITAL CONSULTING INSTITUTE

204 Andover St.
Andover, MA 01810
PH: (978)470-3880
URL: http://www.dci.com

Description: The STI Knowledge eSupport Certification course is designed to decipher the eSupport riddle: What is it, and how can it help? This course provides the basic framework for eSupport and additional strategies and Best Practices for developing and implementing effective eSupport solutions. A wide range of topics will be discussed during the two-day course. During the class, eSupport will be defined and an in depth description of the basic framework for eSupport will be discussed.

∎ 3419

EBIZ - ASIAN INTERNATIONAL ELECTRONIC COMMERCE, INTERNET BUSINESS APPLICATIONS & SOLUTIONS EXHIBITION & CONFERENCE
SINGAPORE EXHIBITION SERVICES PTE. LTD.

47 Scotts Rd.
11th Floor Goldbell Towers
Singapore 228233, Singapore
E-mail: info@sesmontnet.com

Frequency: Annual. **Principle Exhibits:** Electronic commerce, internet business equipment, supplies, and services.

∎ 3420

EBIZ NETWORKS CONFERENCE
BUSINESS COMMUNICATIONS REVIEW

999 Oakmont Plz. Dr., Ste.100
Westmont, IL 60559-1381
PH: (630)986-1432
TF: 800-227-1234
FX: (630)323-5324
E-mail: info@bcr.com
URL: http://www.bcr.com
Contact: Jeff Bockweg, Conference Sales Manager

Description: The BCR eBiz Networks conference will focus on the enhancing and accelerating the 'Net for e-commerce, and on measuring the performance of applications and services. The program features a mix of plenary sessions, debates, tutorials and panels, with presentations from leading experts, vendors, analysts, service providers and e-commerce operators.

∎ 3421

EBUSINESS CONFERENCE
IDC

5 Speen St.
Framingham, MA 01701
PH: (508)872-8200
URL: http://www.idc.com

Description: eBusiness Conference is a conference focusing on eBusiness solutions and opportunities.

∎ 3422

EBUSINESS INTEGRATION CONFERENCE
BRAINSTORM GROUP INC.

386 W Main St.
Northboro, MA 01532
PH: (508)393-3266
FX: (508)393-8845
E-mail: info@brainstorm-group.com

URL: http://www.brainstorm-group.com
Contact: Dawn M. Eagan, Marketing Director

Description: The eBusiness Integration Conference Series is a forum specifically designed to provide business and IT leaders with solutions to the full spectrum of e-Business integration challenges. Featuring leading analysts, authors and end user case studies, this series details business driven strategies, the latest technological advancements, proven ''Best of Breed'' solutions and trends in e-Business integration.

∎ 3423

EBUSINESS RUSSIA CONFERENCE
ITE GROUP PLC

105 Salusbury Rd.
London NW66RG, United Kingdom
PH: 44 20 7596 5000
FX: 44 20 7596 5111
E-mail: info@technology-events.com
URL: http://www.technology-events.com
Contact: Stephen Warshaw, Chief Executive Officer

Founded: 2001. **Description:** The e-Business Russia Conference focuses on the implementation and use of Information Technologies in the Russian economy. The Conference brings together Russian and international companies representing such industries as banking and finance, automotive, metallurgy, machine building, oil and gas, commercial building and construction, transportation, food and food processing, telecommunications, and chemical and petrochemical. It will also feature representatives from areas such as: government officials from local and central offices, representatives of investment and financial institutions, specialists from major consulting companies, professional and trade publications, and recognized leaders of the IT industry.

∎ 3424

EC WORLD - ELECTRONIC COMMERCE WORLD
EC MEDIA GROUP

div. of Thomson Financial Publishing
2021 Coolidge St.
Hollywood, FL 33020-2400
E-mail: amy.fleming@tfn.com

Founded: 1996. **Frequency:** Annual. **Audience:** Mid to upper level management. **Principle Exhibits:** Equipment, supplies, and services for the electronic commerce industry.

∎ 3425

E.COM
MALMOMASSANI AB

(V. Varvsgatan 10)
20280 Malmo, Sweden
E-mail: tbernshed@malmomassan.se

Founded: 1997. Frequency: Annual. Audience: Trade proffessionals. Principle Exhibits: Exhibits the world of e-commerce.

∎ 3426

THE ECONOMICS OF IT - PROFITABILITY WITH THE RIGHT TECHNOLOGY CHOICES

GARTNER INC.

56 Top Gallant Rd.
Stamford, CT 06904
PH: (203)316-1111
FX: (203)324-7901
URL: http://www.gartner.com

Description: This conference will examine methods of lowering cost and minimizing risk while maximizing the benefits and rewards of the IT function. To help to optimize an organization's resources, this year's conference will include presentations on cost controls, measuring cost and fiscal management of the IT function. There will also be a session with an in-depth analysis of the new technologies on the near horizon with the greatest potential returns. Business and technology managers seeking direction in the high-stakes environment of today's IT industry should attend to hear the information, objective insights and actionable strategies presented at this conference.

∎ 3427

ECRM SOLUTION CONFERENCE AND EXPO

IDG JAPAN INC.

3-4-5 Hongo Bunkyo-ku
Tokyo 113-0033, Japan
PH: 03 5800 3111
E-mail: ctw@idg.co.jp
URL: http://www.idg.co.jp

Description: This CTI event enables visitors to experience the latest in CTI technology and solutions. The show also focuses on topics such as CRM and Internet Economy.

∎ 3428

ECRM UNIVERSITY 101: A PROFESSIONAL CERTIFICATION COURSE (DCI)

DIGITAL CONSULTING INSTITUTE

204 Andover St.
Andover, MA 01810
PH: (978)470-3880
URL: http://www.dci.com

Description: In this accelerated how to workshop, attendees will learn proven best practice methodologies that enable them to successfully develop a eCRM strategy and implement their own eCRM system. This hands-on workshop offers an opportunity to achieve strategic objectives for eCRM, while at the same time helping to avoid expensive and painful mistakes.

∎ 3429

ECRM UNIVERSITY 401: ADVANCED IMPLEMENTATION BEST PRACTICES (DCI)

DIGITAL CONSULTING INSTITUTE

204 Andover St.
Andover, MA 01810
PH: (978)470-3880
URL: http://www.dci.com

Description: This advanced course is designed to go above and beyond the basic, beginner level eCRM courses, providing attendees with detailed information and strategies on eCRM implementation. This course is a perfect complement to eCRM University 101, taking the educational content and strategy details provided to the next level. In this session attendees will learn to: optimize existing or planned eCRM system and tools, launch or re-launch eCRM to improve customer life-cycle management, personalize the experience that each customer has with an organization, put the ''customer'' into the eCRM strategy, define a relationship management process, leverage the latest trends in wireless eCRM, and intra-enterprise team selling with a channel.

∎ 3430

EEMA CONFERENCE (EEMA)

THE EUROPEAN FORUM FOR ELECTRONIC BUSINESS

Alexander House, High St.
Inkberrow WR74DT, United Kingdom
PH: 44 1386 793028
FX: 44 1386 793268
E-mail: info@EEMA.org
URL: http://www.eema.org

Description: EEMA is a three-day program packed with meetings, presentations, discussions, workshops and training sessions, all geared towards enhancing business. There are eight interest group meetings including Directories, e-Commerce, User, ECAF (security), Wireless, Legal, Change Management and e-Government and Public Sector - will meet during EEMA 2002. There will also be a meeting of the Global Directory Forum. In addition to three tracks that attendees can choose from Securing the Enterprise; Managing Identity Infrastructures; Supply Chain Collaboration and Integration.

∎ 3431

EENTERPRISE

IDG JAPAN INC.

3-4-5 Hongo Bunkyo-ku
Tokyo 113-0033, Japan
PH: 03 5800 3111
E-mail: gt@idg.co.jp
URL: http://www.idg.co.jp

Description: The event will provide attendees with the strategic knowledge necessary to succeed in a cost-effective investment in enterprise IT solutions.

∎ 3432

EFFECTIVELY MIGRATING APPLICATIONS TO THE WEB (DCI)

DIGITAL CONSULTING INSTITUTE

204 Andover St.
Andover, MA 01810
PH: (978)470-3880
URL: http://www.dci.com

Description: This seminar covers the fundamental and key principles of successfully migrating to Web Technology. Through this seminar, attendees will adopt the new Net-centric perspective and learn a practical understanding of Web Development and deployment technologies.

∎ 3433

EIPP

EBILLXCHANGE

420 Lexington Ave., Ste. 2533
New York, NY 10017
PH: (212)885-2732
E-mail: info@ebillx.com
URL: http://www.ebillx.com

Description: Focused on the issues facing the billing departments of B2B organizations, from Accounts Payable and Receivable to Credit and Collections to streamlining the entire billing process, this event will attract senior level executives responsible for implementing electronic invoicing and billing ventures, and for ensuring their continued success. The issues covered will be relevant to the complex B2B arena, such as customer adoption, business models and strategies for EIPP implementation, integration with existing systems, and automated dispute resolution and settlement, while relying on acclaimed industry analysts to provide an overall picture of where the industry is and what organizations need to be aware of in the quest to implement an EIPP program.

∎ 3434

ELECTRONIC COMMERCE WORLD

EC MEDIA GROUP

11 Penn Plz., 17th Fl.
New York, NY 10001
PH: (212)967-7000
FX: (212)967-7166
E-mail: amy.fleming@tfn.com
URL: http://www.ecmediagroup.com
Contact: Amy Fleming, Conference Sales

Founded: 1995. **Description:** Electronic Commerce World will help attendees answer critical business questions. Exhibitors will have an opportunity to interact with key purchase decision-makers who are actively determining their e-business technology and service needs. EC World is an annual event that draws senior executives, managers and directors of e-business operations. Attendees are highly knowledgeable and motivated professionals.

∎ 3435

EMBEDDED SYSTEMS CONFERENCE

EMBEDDED SYSTEMS PROGRAMMING

600 Harrison St.
San Francisco, CA 94107
PH: (415)947-6652
E-mail: esc@cmp.com
URL: http://www.esconline.com

Description: Embedded Systems Conference Boston is the East Coast's largest embedded exhibition, providing practical answers to embedded questions, and teaches skills and techniques to engineers, developers, and project managers. The technical conference focuses on sharing the knowledge and honing the skills necessary to make embedded designs better, faster, and more reliable. The show floor brings together leading companies exhibiting the hottest products in the embedded industry. The conference offers the latest technologies in 84 courses including 20 new classes.

∎ 3436

EMERGING TECHNOLOGY CONFERENCE

LOMA

2300 Windy Ridge Pky., Ste. 600
Atlanta, GA 30339-8443
PH: (770)951-1770
TF: 800-275-5662
FX: (770)984-0441
E-mail: meetings@loma.org
URL: http://www.loma.org

Description: The LOMA Emerging Technology Conference has speakers and topics relating to tech experts from financial services companies in the world sharing their latest projects and successes and keynotes who will speak about new technologies and ways to save on costs. It will feature sessions on the latest in e-business, IT security, product development, and technology savings strategies.

∎ 3437

EMPLOYEE RELATIONSHIP MANAGEMENT CONFERENCE AND EXPOSITION (DCI)

DIGITAL CONSULTING INSTITUTE

204 Andover St.
Andover, MA 01810
PH: (978)470-3880
URL: http://www.dci.com

Description: This event provides senior business and IT executives with strategies for improving managerial insight, accelerating communication of strategy and operating plans and improving productivity by empowering the workforce. Industry experts, analysts, consultants and visionaries will present the most crucial Employee Relationship Management issues through in-depth keynote addresses, real-world business case studies, informative breakout sessions, product cost and benefit comparisons and live demonstrations.

▌3438

EMPOWERING ENTERPRISE PORTALS

MARCUS EVANS LTD.

4 Cavendish Sq.
London W1G0BX, United Kingdom
PH: 44 20 74990900
FX: 44 20 76472313
E-mail: LisaR@marcusevansch.com
URL: http://www.brandslam-summit.com
Contact: Karine-Marie Benoist, Marketing Manager

Description: The Empowering Enterprise Portals Conference offers technical know-how and case study examples which will ensure that corporate heads are abreast of the latest intelligence in this increasingly dynamic and lucrative marketplace. The conference features key speakers covering the following topics: Integrating Enterprise Portals; Effective Content Management; Using XML to Integrate Enterprise Portals; Security and Scalability; Quantifying ROI.

▌3439

ENABLING ALL IP BASED MOBILE NETWORKS

MARCUS EVANS LTD.

303 E Wacker Dr.
Chicago, IL 60601
PH: (312)540-3000
E-mail: marketing@marcusevans.com
URL: http://www.marcusevansconferences.com
Contact: Greta Molepske, Marketing Manager

Description: Attendees to this event will be shown how to effectively plan, implement and profit from Mobile IP technology by early adopters and leading experts on Mobile IP. Host mobility is becoming increasingly important in this age of blossoming mobile workforces with laptop computers and the high desire to have continuous network connectivity to the corporate office anywhere the host happens to be.

▌3440

ENTERPRISE ANALYTICS AND DATA WAREHOUSING CONFERENCE AND EXPOSITION (DCI)

DIGITAL CONSULTING INSTITUTE

204 Andover St.
Andover, MA 01810
PH: (978)470-3880
URL: http://www.dci.com

Description: The conference will provide attendees with an understanding of enterprise analytics and how analytical applications, business intelligence and data warehousing technology are used to measure and monitor the business activities of an organization. By showcasing examples and the latest technology, attendees will learn how to maximize the benefits of their investment in this technology.

▌3441

ENTERPRISE APPLICATION INTEGRATION (IQPC)

INTERNATIONAL QUALITY AND PRODUCTIVITY CENTER

PO Box 401
150 Clove Rd.
Little Falls, NJ 07424
PH: (973)256-0211
TF: 800-882-8684
E-mail: info@iqpc-canada.com
URL: http://www.iqpc.com
Contact: Todd Smith, Sales Manager, Sponsorship and Exhibits

Description: Designed for and by practitioners, consultants and industry experts at this conference will address business cases and strategies for integration, using case studies that demonstrate both the return on investment for the initiative and the lessons learned by those companies that have already used the process. Some speakers and topics include a North American's author and thinker on integration, David Linthicum, Chief Technology Officer of Mercator Software, on getting the maximum return on an integration initiative, Hewlett-Packard on the evolution and impact of integrated applications, electronics giant Celestica on developing a business process strategy for integration, and RBC Financial Group on how they are integrating applications across all channels.

▌3442

ENTERPRISE ARCHITECTURE PLANNING: AN EXECUTIVE BRIEFING (DCI)

DIGITAL CONSULTING INSTITUTE

204 Andover St.
Andover, MA 01810
PH: (978)470-3880
URL: http://www.dci.com

Description: At this Executive Briefing, attendees will learn to gain commitment and keep it, how to align business objectives and architectures, how much time is needed to conduct EAP well, roles for leading, managing and participating, why phenomenal benefits outweigh cost constraints and risks, how the IT budget may be less than 20 percent of the true cost of IT, who has been successful with EAP and why, and how to coordinate EAP with other business initiatives.

▌3443

THE ENTERPRISE ARCHITECTURES CONFERENCE (DCI)

DIGITAL CONSULTING INSTITUTE

204 Andover St.
Andover, MA 01810
PH: (978)470-3880
URL: http://www.dci.com

Description: Join META Group and DCI at The Enterprise Architectures Conference and discover innovative ways to define enterprise architecture strategy. This event designed for Business Executives and IT Professionals is running for the sixth year and is the only event exclusively dedicated to enterprise architecture. At this conference, attendees will learn new ideas and techniques to align business and information technology through a portfolio view. Conference sessions are designed to provide people with the skills and knowledge to give the company the edge it needs.

▌3444

ENTERPRISE INTRANETS
INTERNATIONAL QUALITY AND PRODUCTIVITY CENTER

PO Box 401
150 Clove Rd.
Little Falls, NJ 07424
PH: (973)256-0211
TF: 800-882-8684
E-mail: update@iqpc.com
URL: http://www.iqpc.com
Contact: Todd Smith, Sales Manager, Sponsorship and Exhibits

Description: Born out of IQPC Canada's highly successful HR Intranets With Employee Self-Service, Corporate Desktop, and Internal Communication conferences, Enterprise Intranets has been researched and developed to help to address the business challenges employing an enterprise intranet can bring. Coupled with industry experts attendees will hear from leading organizations already benefiting from this type of initiative.

▌3445

ENTERPRISE IP STORAGE NETWORKS
MARCUS EVANS LTD.

303 E Wacker Dr.
Chicago, IL 60601
PH: (312)540-3000
E-mail: LisaR@marcusevansch.com
URL: http://www.brandslam-summit.com
Contact: Greta Molepske, Marketing Manager

Description: The Enterprise IP Storage Networks conference is tailored to small, medium and large enterprise executives who are interested in exploring the emerging market of IP Storage, and who are interested in adopting the technology for their companies needs. Potential partnership/business opportunities will be abundant at this event.

▌3446

ENTERPRISE LINUX FORUM CONFERENCE AND EXPO
INT MEDIA GROUP

23 Old Kings Hwy. S
Darien, CT 06820
PH: (203)662-2800
TF: (203)655-4686
E-mail: cobrienats@internet.com
URL: http://www.intmediaevents.com

Description: Enterprise Linux Forum Conference and Expo is an industry event that is dedicated to providing IT and business professionals with an understanding of all of the issues related to the application of Linux and Linux-based datacenter solutions in the large enterprise to cut costs, reduce risk, increase architectural flexibility and deliver real business value.

▌3447

ENTERPRISE PORTAL AND WEB SERVICES CONFERENCE
DELPHI GROUP

10 Post Office Sq., 10th Fl., S
Boston, MA 02109-4603
PH: (617)247-1511
TF: 800-335-7440
FX: (617)247-4957
E-mail: client.services@delphigroup.com
URL: http://www.delphigroup.com

Description: Attend this if interested in enterprise portals or Web services. Also featured are three mini-tracks that will provide attendees with take-aways to help create an enterprise taxonomy for portals, an ROI and Total Cost of Ownership analysis for portals, and an RFP for portal procurement or expansion. In these multipart sessions, Delphi advisors will lead attendees through the finer points of developing a Taxonomy, ROI, and RFP. Included will be templates and boilerplate materials. Attendees can schedule private 1-on-1 meetings with senior Delphi analysts as part of the conference "Ask Delphi" program.

▌3448

ENTERPRISE PORTAL AND WEB SERVICES SEMINAR SERIES
DELPHI GROUP

10 Post Office Sq., 10th Fl., S
Boston, MA 02109-4603
PH: (617)247-1511
TF: 800-335-7440
FX: (617)247-4957
E-mail: client.services@delphigroup.com
URL: http://www.delphigroup.com

Founded: 1999. **Description:** The Enterprise Portal and Web Services Seminar Series has become the benchmark of quality and content for anyone involved in or considering the use of Enterprise Portals. Attendees will learn not only about the technology behind the solutions but also about the business uses and cases for Portals and Web services. This seminar is intended to give a complete and balanced education. Speakers will deliver the details on how Portals and Web services work, including discussion about standards and the major platform players, such as IBM, Sun, and Microsoft and will also provide an insightful and radically new way to look at time-based business.

■ **3449**

ENTERPRISE SERVERVISION

IDC

5 Speen St.
Framingham, MA 01701
PH: (508)872-8200
URL: http://www.idc.com

Description: At the IDC Enterprise ServerVision conference, IDC's server team will delve into the realm of the Internet Infrastructure Hardware ecosystem. Industry executives will present information about this new era of computing and who they will trust to deliver on the promise of a better ebusiness Infrastructure.

■ **3450**

ENTERPRISE STORAGE STRATEGIES CONFERENCE AND EXPO

INT MEDIA GROUP

23 Old Kings Hwy. S
Darien, CT 06820
PH: (203)662-2800
TF: (203)655-4686
E-mail: cobrienats@internet.com
URL: http://www.intmediaevents.com

Description: INT Media Group's Enterprise Storage Strategies Conference and Expo is the industry's forum for IT executives, managers and decision makers responsible for developing and deploying enterprise-wide storage strategies. The conference is the first event to adopt a comprehensive view of enterprise storage management covering resources, data, networks and policy.The conference program has been developed in conjunction with the Enterprise Storage Group (ESG). Key industry executives, analysts, experts and end users will present around the issues associated with understanding, evaluating, selecting and implementing storage technologies for competitive advantage and business value.

■ **3451**

ENTERPRISE WEB AND CORPORATE PORTAL CONFERENCE AND EXPO

INT MEDIA GROUP

23 Old Kings Hwy. S
Darien, CT 06820
PH: (203)662-2800
TF: (203)655-4686
E-mail: cobrienats@internet.com
URL: http://www.intmediaevents.com

Description: Enterprise Web and Corporate Portal Conference and Expo is an executive level event that brings together key industry participants around the issues of enterprise web and corporate portal deployment and optimization. The conference focuses on the key role corporate portals can play as the nexus of content management and distribution, application and web services integration, and communication between corporations and their employees, customers and business partners.

■ **3452**

ENTERPRISE-WIDE SECURITY MANAGEMENT TOOLS (ISACA)

INFORMATION SYSTEMS AUDIT AND CONTROL ASSOCIATION

3701 Algonquin Rd., Ste.1010
Rolling Meadows, IL 60008
PH: (847)253-1545
FX: (847)253-1443
E-mail: conference@isaca.org
URL: http://www.isaca.org

Description: In this seminar attendees will learn the answers to important questions about enterprise-wide security and receive practical advice on how to identify, choose, and implement one of the available tools. Critical factors that highlight the need for an enterprise-wide solution will be highlighted and current methods for managing these problems will be discussed.

■ **3453**

ENTNET AT SUPERCOMM (IEC)

INTERNATIONAL ENGINEERING CONSORTIUM

549 W Randolph St., Ste. 600
Chicago, IL 60661-2208
PH: (312)559-4100
E-mail: info@iec.org
URL: http://www.iec.org

Founded: 2000. **Description:** The Enterprise Networking and Services Conference (EntNet) at SUPERCOMM presents an opportunity for enterprise networking and services professionals to examine key network technologies. They will also learn how these new technologies effect the introduction of new services and increase the efficiency and productivity of network operations.

■ **3454**

ENVIROTECH SUMMIT

MARCUS EVANS LTD.

303 E Wacker Dr.
Chicago, IL 60601
PH: (312)540-3000
E-mail: LisaR@marcusevansch.com
URL: http://www.envirotech-summit.com
Contact: Greta Molepske, Marketing Manager

Description: The EnviroTech Summit offers a proactive series of keynote presentations, conference sessions, interactive think-tanks and one-on-one meetings with industry solution leaders. The summit offers assistance to senior executives with purchasing authority, looking for better day-to-day and long-term environmental decisions.

■ **3455**

ERETAILING - FALL

VNU EXPOSITIONS

14685 Avion Parkway
Ste. 400
Chantilly, VA 20151

Founded: 1998. **Frequency:** Annual. **Principle Exhibits:** Premier solutions providers, including web services, internet communications, hardware, software and other products, services and tools for intenet retailers.

▌3456
ERETAILING - SPRING
VNU EXPOSITIONS

14685 Avion Parkway
Ste. 400
Chantilly, VA 20151

Founded: 1998. **Frequency:** Annual. **Principle Exhibits:** Primer solutions providers, including web services, internet communications, hardware, software and other products, services, and tools for internet retailers.

▌3457
E_SOLUTIONS: THE TRADE SHOW FOR EFFICIENT WORK PROCESSES AND NEW AREAS OF BUSINESS
REED EXHIBITION CO.

383 Main Ave.
Norwalk, CT 06851
PH: (203)840-5662
FX: (203)840-9662
E-mail: inquiry@reedexpo.com
URL: http://www.reedexpo.com

Description: At e_solutions The trade show for efficient work processes and new areas of business, the goal is to inform trade visitors on the latest and newest application solutions, specialized software and general programs and products. Market leaders like IBM and SAP will be represented by their regional partners. Some topics featured are: business solutions for management, marketing, organisation, logistic, production, finance, real estates, law and taxes.

▌3458
ESPWORLD
IDG WORLD EXPO

3 Speen St.
Framingham, MA 01701
PH: (508)879-6700
E-mail: stephen_athan@idg.com
URL: http://www.espworldexpo.com
Contact: Charlie Greco, President and Chief Executive Officer

Description: ESPWorld Conference and Expo is an enterprise end user event for end-to-end outsourcing solutions. ESPWorld offers a broad range of outsourcing products and services, and provides a conference program that informs about strategies and practices for the end user and their business to capitalize on this IT delivery model. This event showcases the entire range of outsourcing options from ASPs (Application Service Provider), ISPs (Internet Service Provider), NSPs (Network Service Provider), MSPs (Managed Service Provider), SSPs (Storage Service Provider), HSPs (Hosting Service Provider) and xSPs.

▌3459
ETAIL (WBR)
WORLDWIDE BUSINESS RESEARCH

420 Lexington Ave., Ste. 2533
New York, NY 10017
PH: (212)885-2720
FX: (212)885-2798
E-mail: adas@wbresearch.com
URL: http://www.wbresearch.com

Description: eTail is an online retailing show. eTail offers the chance to network with retailers who, having survived the shakeout, are now looking to build on their online presence, as well as integrate their off line efforts. This convention gives the benefit of over 20 case studies to learn from.

▌3460
EUROCHANNELS
SMITH, BUCKLIN AND ASSOCIATES, INC.

401 N Michigan Ave.
Chicago, IL 60611-4267
PH: (312)644-6610
FX: (312)644-0575
E-mail: info@smithbucklin.com
URL: http://www.sba.com

Founded: 1994. **Description:** EuroChannels is the first event to provide an executive level, Pan-European audience the opportunity to focus on both the strategic and day-to-day issues facing the businesses that create, integrate, deliver and service the IT products in the European market. EuroChannels, combined with EuroProduct ConneXion, brings together a combination of channel-specific content with product demonstrations in one place over three days. It will have two days of content and one day of enterprise and e-Business product presentations. EuroProduct ConneXion is designed to leverage the time of both the presenting companies, as well as VIP (channel partner) participants who are selected to participate by invitation only.

▌3461
EUROPEAN IT FORUM
IDC

5 Speen St.
Framingham, MA 01701
PH: (508)872-8200
URL: http://www.idc.com

Founded: 1991. **Description:** CEOs and top executives from European companies should attend the European IT Forum to gain an understanding of how they should lead themselves and their organizations through opportunities and challenges of the Internet economy.

▌3462

EVALUATION OF INTEGRATED DOCUMENT MANAGEMENT SOFTWARE PRODUCTS AND VENDORS

GARTNER INC.

56 Top Gallant Rd.
Stamford, CT 06904
PH: (203)316-1111
FX: (203)324-7901
URL: http://www.gartner.com

Description: Evaluation of Integrated Document Management Software Products and Vendors provides concrete recommendations regarding structure and evaluation criteria for the evaluation and implementation of document management applications. Topic areas will include a ''best practice'' approach to the evaluation, overview of market and technology trends, and key implementation considerations.

▌3463

EXPO COMM/INE-B MEXICO NORTE

E.J. KRAUSE DE MEXICO, S.A. DE C.V.

Av. Insurgentes Sur 664
piso 4
Col. del Valle
D.F.03100 Mexico City, Mexico
E-mail: mexinfo@ejkrause.com

Founded: 1998. **Frequency:** Annual. **Audience:** Technology, professionals, decision makers, CEOs, GMs, CFOs, Engineers. **Principle Exhibits:** Telecommunications, networking and e-commerce.

▌3464

EXTREME MARKUP LANGUAGES

IDEALLIANCE

100 Daingerfield Rd.
Alexandria, VA 22314
PH: (703)837-1070
FX: (703)837-1072
E-mail: info@idealliance.org
URL: http://www.xmlconference.org/xmlusa/

Description: Extreme Markup Languages is an intense 3.7-day conference preceded by two days of tutorials devoted to technical aspects of markup, markup languages, markup systems, and markup applications and everything touched by the question of how best to allow information to describe itself. Extreme Markup Languages software developers, markup theorists, philosophers of information, knowledge representers (and presenters!) devote the better part of a week to the unfettered pursuit of better understanding of problems of information management, knowledge systems, markup, formal languages, the search for a better parser interface, and the development of markup-related software.

▌3465

EYEFORCHEM USA

FIRST CONFERENCES LTD. BLACK LION HOUSE

45 Whitechapel Rd
Black Lion House, 3rd Fl.
London E11DU, United Kingdom
PH: 44 20 7375 7575
FX: 44 20 7375 7576
E-mail: moreinfo@eyeforchem.com
URL: http://www.eyeforchem.com
Contact: Nina Hattingh, Exhibition Manager

Description: The EyeforChem Exhibitions are the world's largest gathering of decision making professionals who are concerned with the impact of e-business on the Chemical and Plastics industry. It is for people that have an interest in securing excellent access and exposure to a concentration of strategic-level executives.

▌3466

FIELD SERVICE MANAGEMENT CONFERENCE AND EXPOSITION (DCI)

DIGITAL CONSULTING INSTITUTE

204 Andover St.
Andover, MA 01810
PH: (978)470-3880
URL: http://www.dci.com

Description: Field Service Management enables a company to schedule and communicate with field service personnel. It also allows the organization to monitor, report and measure field service activities. Recently, the role of field service management in an organization has changed focus from a cost center to a strategic line of business. A key challenge in today's business economy is the administration and coordination of field service management. The provision of full service to customers, adding value to both product sales and support, is an opportunity not be missed in today's tougher economy, thus becoming more service focused, rather than product centric.

▌3467

FIHT COMDEX: COMPUTER AND TELECOM SOLUTIONS

REED EXHIBITION CO.

383 Main Ave.
Norwalk, CT 06851
PH: (203)840-5662
FX: (203)840-9662
E-mail: inquiry@reedexpo.com
URL: http://www.reedexpo.com

Description: This conference presents the latest information on computer and information technology products and services.

▌3468

FILEMAKER DEVELOPER CONFERENCE

FILEMAKER INC.

5201 Patrick Henry Dr.
Santa Clara, CA 95052
PH: (408)987-7000
TF: 800-336-6060
E-mail: FileMakerDevCon@Advisor.com
URL: http://www.filemaker.com/devcon/

Description: Allows experts to learn from FileMaker employees and top independent developers in over 50 sessions, including pre-conference seminars and get one-on-one opportunities with expert speakers and FileMaker product development engineers. Offers special events that have product showcases that highlight the latest FileMaker-related products and services. Features tech support central and a hands-on lab, that give answers directly from FileMaker technical support personnel.

▌3469

FINANCE-IT

AITEC UK LTD

15 High St.
Graveley PE196PL, United Kingdom
PH: 44 14 8083 1300
FX: 44 14 8083 1131
E-mail: admin@aitec-africa.com
URL: http://www.aitecafrica.com
Contact: Sean Moroney, AITEC Group Chairman

Description: Finance-IT is a banking and finance technology forum catering to IT professionals and managers in financial institutions who need to be informed of latest technological and strategic developments.

▌3470

FINANCIAL TECHNOLOGY EXPO ASIA

CMP ASIA TRADE FAIRS PTE LTD

390 Havelock Rd., 05-00
King's Centre
Singapore 169662, Singapore
E-mail: cmpasia.com.sg

Founded: 1998. **Frequency:** Annual. **Audience:** Trade only. **Principle Exhibits:** Hardware, software and services for the finance industry. Electronic and home banking; imaging and check processing; intranet solutions; data mining and database marketing; ATM solutions; branch automation; f/x order processing; equity research and market data; internet trading; Windows and Java solutions.

▌3471

FLASH KIT

FLASHCORE

7095 Hollywood Blvd., No. 444
Hollywood, CA 90028
PH: (818)994-7199

E-mail: johntidwell@flashcore.com
URL: http://www.flashcore.com

Description: The Flash Kit Fall conference provides hands on knowledge through intense workshops, presentations from expert speakers, and allows developers an opportunity to be a part of the Flash movement around the world.

▌3472

FORUM ON FINANCIAL TECHNOLOGY

MARCUS EVANS LTD.

303 E Wacker Dr.
Chicago, IL 60601
PH: (312)540-3000
E-mail: marketing@marcusevans.com
URL: http://www.marcusevansconferences.com
Contact: Greta Molepske, Marketing Manager

Founded: 1999. **Description:** The Forum on Financial Technology has been carefully designed for an exclusive group of Chief Information Officers (CIOs), Chief Technology Officers (CTOs) and executive level Information Technology (IT) Officers from the financial services community. The Forum on Financial Technology will give each participant the opportunity to apply the latest industry solutions and advancements through several structured seminars, workshops, round-table discussions, think tanks, one-on-one meetings and informal networking sessions.

▌3473

FOSE'S INTERNET & GOVERNMENT ELECTRONIC COMMERCE CONFERENCE & EXHIBITION

CO. POST NEWSWEEK TECH MEDIA

10 G St. NE, Ste. 500
Washington, DC 20002
E-mail: fose.inquiry@postnewsweektech.com

Principle Exhibits: Internet and government electronic commerce exhibits.

▌3474

FRONTLINE SOLUTIONS EXPO AND CONFERENCE

ADVANSTAR COMMUNICATIONS INC.

545 Boylston St.
Boston, MA 02116
PH: (617)267-6500
E-mail: information@advanstar.de
URL: http://www.advanstar.com
Contact: Andrew Cary, Show Manager

Description: Exhibitors showcase new technologies to help companies extend their information systems into their manufacturing, warehousing, logistics, and field service environments.Frontline Solutions Expo and conference sessions help to understand and compare the latest generation of data collection and mobile computing technology so attendees

719

can automate systems for more accurate component traceability and coordination of multiple providers, integrate physical goods data into existing SCM, CRM, ERP and e-business systems, and accelerate sales and improve service by linking data from host systems to field service reps.

▌3475

FUNDAMENTALS OF INFORMATION SYSTEMS AUDITING (ISACA)
INFORMATION SYSTEMS AUDIT AND CONTROL ASSOCIATION

3701 Algonquin Rd., Ste.1010
Rolling Meadows, IL 60008
PH: (847)253-1545
FX: (847)253-1443
E-mail: conference@isaca.org
URL: http://www.isaca.org

Description: This cornerstone course applies modern audit principles and procedures to today's ever-changing technology. The result is an audit approach that can be used to perform information system (IS) environment reviews and application audits. Audit program features are presented and available Computer-Assisted Audit Techniques (CAATs) software is demonstrated. Participants will return to the job and begin using these skills immediately.

▌3476

FUTURE FORWARD
FUTURE FORWARD EVENTS LLC

354 Congress St., 2nd Fl.
Boston, MA 02210
PH: (617)423-0770
FX: (617)423-0460
E-mail: sgilbert@futureforward.com
URL: http://www.futureforward.com
Contact: Shayne Gilbert

Description: Future Forward will bring together 200 high level technology executives from around New England for debates with political leaders, seminars from top business leaders and analyses of the latest trends and issues.

▌3477

GARTNER PLANETSTORAGE
GARTNER INC.

56 Top Gallant Rd.
Stamford, CT 06904
PH: (203)316-1111
FX: (203)324-7901
URL: http://www.gartner.com

Description: Gartner PlanetStorage offers a complete view of storage markets and technologies from both end-user and vendor perspectives. End-users can learn more about new ways to implement customized storage solutions that truly meet specific performance and availability demands, while vendors have an opportunity to interact with end-users and more correctly gauge the competitive landscape. Attendees will explore traditional and future storage components and systems and analyze the alternative technologies and services that will help to fulfill the promise of scalable, compatible storage networks.

▌3478

GITEX 2002
GITEX

PO Box 9292
Dubai, United Arab Emirates
PH: 971 4 3086083
FX: 971 4 3314853
E-mail: janice.edgar@dwtc.com
URL: http://www.gitex.com/gitex2002.html
Contact: Janice Edgar, Public Relations Executive

Description: GITEX is the largest and most successful event of its kind in the Middle East. It has firmly established itself as the premier exhibition for computing and communication systems and applications dedicated to the IT industry and the entire business environment. The exhibition routinely features numerous IT product launches and major announcements about new developments in the Middle East's IT and communications markets.

▌3479

GLOBAL CRM AND MULTIMEDIA CONTACT CENTRE PROFESSIONAL USER FORUM
MARCUS EVANS LTD.

303 E Wacker Dr.
Chicago, IL 60601
PH: (312)540-3000
E-mail: LisaR@marcusevansch.com
URL: http://www.brandslam-summit.com
Contact: Greta Molepske, Marketing Manager

Description: Key topics at the Global CRM, and Multimedia Contact Centre Professional User Forum will be how to gain direct access to the tools, the framework, and the know-how leveraged by the world's best-practice, hear from Fortune 500 companies as they build rock solid CRM and DW and Call Centre strategies to deliver customers and profits, learn how to leverage people, processes, activities, information, and technologies to acquire new, more profitable customers, build long-term customer loyalty on a one-to-one basis, and drive powerful marketing opportunities and increase profits and shareholder value.

▌3480

GLOBAL E-PROCUREMENT
MARCUS EVANS LTD.

303 E Wacker Dr.
Chicago, IL 60601
PH: (312)540-3000
E-mail: marketing@marcusevans.com
URL: http://www.marcusevansconferences.com
Contact: Greta Molepske, Marketing Manager

Founded: 2000. **Description:** The Global e-Procurement conference will examine the opportunities for e-Procurement when exploring portals and B2B e-Marketplaces. The top-level speaker panel, including cutting edge case studies, will guide attendees through the full process from the drawing board, right through to creating value added services by utilizing portals and B2B e-Marketplaces.

▌3481

GLOBAL INTERNET PERFORMANNCE CONFERENCE

KEYNOTE SYSTEMS INC.

777 Mariners Island Blvd.
San Mateo, CA 94404
PH: (650)403-2400
FX: (650)403-5500
E-mail: phawkins@mosaicevents.com
URL: http://www.gipc2002.com
Contact: Pam Hawkins, Marketing Manager

Description: The GIPC is a performance conference offering track sessions, free training opportunities and technology. Topics inlude Keynote's new Application Performance Management (APM) strategy from CEO and industry visionary, Umang Gupta. Provides networking opportunities with notable industry analysts and Keynote customers. Offers exclusive discounts on five new Keynote services that will be launched at the show.

▌3482

GLOBAL RETAIL TECHNOLOGY FORUM

MOONWATCH MEDIA INC.

77 Oak St., Ste. 201
Newton Upper Falls, MA 02464
PH: (617)527-4626
FX: (617)527-8102
E-mail: info@moonwatchmedia.com
URL: http://www.retailsystems.com

Description: This annual conference brings together top IT decision-makers from major regional and global retailers from around the world to share ideas. This is the only retail IT forum that brings together executives from all sectors of retail, including apparel, hardgoods, grocery, department store, convenience and discount. They come to explore best technology practices, advance industry standards, and improve their businesses. In addition to learning from top level IT executives from the most innovative companies, attendees will have the opportunity to speak with peers from specific regions and other continents. Delegates come to the Global Retail Technology Forum because of its tradition of a fulfilling and open environment, where critical technology ideas are shared and analyzed.

▌3483

GOVERN-IT

AITEC UK LTD

15 High St.
Graveley PE196PL, United Kingdom
PH: 44 14 8083 1300

FX: 44 14 8083 1131
E-mail: admin@aitec-africa.com
URL: http://www.aitecafrica.com
Contact: Sean Moroney, AITEC Group Chairman

Description: Govern-IT is an eGovernance Forum.

▌3484

GOVERNANCE FOR EMUNICIPALITIES

INTERNATIONAL QUALITY AND PRODUCTIVITY CENTER

PO Box 401
150 Clove Rd.
Little Falls, NJ 07424
PH: (973)256-0211
TF: 800-882-8684
E-mail: info@iqpc-canada.com
URL: http://www.iqpc.com
Contact: Todd Smith, Sales Manager, Sponsorship and Exhibits

Description: This is an event that will help to identify future challenges with eMunicipality initiative and formulate strategies to combat them. Government Exchange and IQPC have brought together provincially, nationally, and internationally recognized eMunicipalities to share their past, present, and future challenges and strategies surrounding the issues of Governance for eMunicipalities.

▌3485

GOVERNMENT, BUSINESS AND EDUCATION TECHNOLOGY EXPO

IMARK COMMUNICATIONS

1 Apple Hill Dr., Ste. 301
Natick, MA 01760
PH: (508)647-8600
TF: 800-955-1226
FX: (508)647-0241
E-mail: dkorse@imark-com.com
URL: http://www.imark-com.com
Contact: David Korse, President and CEO

Description: The Government, Business and Education Technology Expo (GBET) brings together the information technology leaders of Southern California for three days of focused seminars and an exhibit floor. GBET brings together public and private sector partners in regular Vendor Forums.

▌3486

GOVERNMENT CIO SUMMIT

FCW MEDIA GROUP

3141 Fairview Park Dr., Ste. 777
Falls Church, VA 22042
PH: (703)876-5100
FX: (703)876-5126
E-mail: lucy_cooley@fcw.com
URL: http://www.fcw.com
Contact: Lucy Cooley, Events Director

Description: The GCIO Summit will tackle a challenge that has fast become a top priority for federal, state and local chief information officers: the need to acquire the executive skills necessary to help manage successful agencywide change, performance, and governance. Factors contributing to deepening the CIO's role in these areas include the demand to build a nationwide digital government architecture, and the increasingly essential role CIOs will play in helping integrate agencies and systems for homeland defense.

∎ 3487
GOVERNMENT IT MARKETING SUMMIT
FCW MEDIA GROUP

3141 Fairview Park Dr., Ste. 777
Falls Church, VA 22042
PH: (703)876-5100
FX: (703)876-5126
E-mail: lucy_cooley@fcw.com
URL: http://www.fcw.com
Contact: Lucy Cooley, Events Director

Founded: 1999. **Description:** FCW Media Group produces the Government IT Marketing Summit to help marketing professionals better understand the intricacies of the market by learning from some of the industry's most knowledgeable experts. This event is aimed at supporting marketing professionals who focus on reaching and influencing public sector IT buyers. A unique atmosphere is strived to be fostered that promotes learning through a program involving industry experts, lively panel discussions and networking opportunities. The IT Marketing Summit will cover such topics as maximizing investment in exhibitions, research and print advertising, the audit process, measuring ROI on marketing investment, and effectively working with the media.

∎ 3488
GUI DESIGN FOR WEB-BASED APPLICATIONS (DCI)
DIGITAL CONSULTING INSTITUTE

204 Andover St.
Andover, MA 01810
PH: (978)470-3880
URL: http://www.dci.com

Description: This two-day class for developers, end-users and managers explains how to apply concepts of graphical design to the new paradigm of Web-based development. Attendees will learn how to determine the best navigation for a Web site, proper use of Web-based GUI controls and how to convert existing client/server systems to the Web, many times using their existing client/server tool set.

∎ 3489
GUI DESIGN WORKSHOP: DESIGNING EFFECTIVE USER INTERFACES (DCI)
DIGITAL CONSULTING INSTITUTE

204 Andover St.
Andover, MA 01810
PH: (978)470-3880

URL: http://www.dci.com

Description: This seminar covers the fundamental and key principles of successful GUI design. Attendees will adopt the new GUI paradigm which includes: the event-driven mid-set, the user centric design, proper use and placement of GUI controls, and GUI architectural modeling. Attendees study examples of GUIs that differ based on the nature and type of application being designed. Hear how GUI design standards truly accelerate the development of consistent GUIs.

∎ 3490
HARD-CORE TECHNICAL EDUCATION
KEY3MEDIA GROUP

5700 Wilshire Blvd., Ste. 325
Los Angeles, CA 90036
PH: (323)954-6000
FX: (323)954-6010
E-mail: jeff.bockweg@key3media.com
URL: http://www.key3media.com
Contact: Jeff Bockweg, Conference Sales Manager

Description: The Extreme Knowledge Conference is designed for developers, network administrators, system administrators and all other technical professionals who want to enhance their technical skills in the latest hardware/software and design/development tools and applications. The conference includes an extensive Windows Technical Program featuring sessions on .NET server .NET development and XP technology. Other tracks focus on Web development and hot topics ranging from security to bandwidth and data integration.

∎ 3491
HONG KONG INFORMATION INFRASTRUCTURE EXPO & CONFERENCE
HONG KONG TRADE DEVELOPMENT COUNCIL

Services Promotion Department
38/F., Office Tower, Convention Plaza
1 Harbour Rd.
Hong Kong, People's Republic of China
E-mail: exhibitions@tdc.org.hk

Founded: 1998. **Frequency:** Annual. **Audience:** Trade and public. **Principle Exhibits:** Services & equipment provides in I.T., telecommunications, computer, internet, mobile services & interactive media.

∎ 3492
I2 PLANET
I2

11701 Luna Rd.
Dallas, TX 75234
PH: (469)357-3720
TF: 877-475-2638
FX: (469)357-3553
E-mail: planet@i2.com
URL: http://www.planet.i2.com

Description: i2 PLANET is a conference that helps attendess to understand what industry leading companies are doing to improve the quality of information, reduce complexity and accelerate improvements in their value chain in today's economy. Attendees can see how understanding trade offs, in near real-time, across the value chain is accomplished with decision support practices, evaluate technology and resources that have helped industry leaders transform information into action in hours,and hear the success stories of how industry leaders have used innovative strategies and tools to gather information from divisions and suppliers with disparate information sources.

∎ 3493

THE IASTED INTERNATIONAL CONFERENCE SOFTWARE ENGINEERING AND APPLICATIONS (IASTED)

INTERNATIONAL ASSOCIATION OF SCIENCE AND TECHNOLOGY FOR DEVELOPMENT

4500 16th Ave. NW, No. 80
Calgary, AB, Canada T3B0M6
PH: (403)288-1195
FX: (403)247-6851
E-mail: calgary@iasted.com
URL: http://www.iasted.org

Founded: 1997. **Description:** The IASTED International Conference on Software Engineering and Applications provides an opportunity for prominent specialists, researchers, and engineers throughout the world to share their latest research in software engineering and its applications in industry. The scope of SEA will include the following main areas: software design and development, software tools and techniques, software security, optimization and standardization, database and data mining, and software engineering applications.

∎ 3494

IEC COMMUNICATIONS FORUMS AT SUPERCOMM (IEC)

INTERNATIONAL ENGINEERING CONSORTIUM

549 W Randolph St., Ste. 600
Chicago, IL 60661-2208
PH: (312)559-4100
E-mail: info@iec.org
URL: http://www.iec.org

Description: IEC Communications Forums at SUPERCOMM offers workshops, seminars, and technical forums concerning the communication industry's newest technologies. This event targets anyone involved in telecommunications and data connection, including executives, directors, managers, planners, administrators, technical staff, and consultants.

∎ 3495

IEC EXECUTIVE FORUM AT SUPERCOMM (IEC)

INTERNATIONAL ENGINEERING CONSORTIUM

549 W Randolph St., Ste. 600
Chicago, IL 60661-2208
PH: (312)559-4100
E-mail: info@iec.org
URL: http://www.iec.org

Description: The IEC Executive Forum at SUPERCOMM is an event for senior-manager participants at SUPERCOMM. The Executive Forum helps executives refine their strategic plans according to the latest trends by offering a series of workshops and private receptions exclusive to forum participants. The IEC Executive Forum provides insights and networking opportunities with senior executives during private receptions and workshops exclusive to Executive Forum attendees.

∎ 3496

IEC - INTERNET & ELECTRONIC COMMERCE CONFERENCE AND EXPOSITION

ADVANSTAR COMMUNICATIONS INC.

One Phoenix Mill Ln., Ste. 401
Peterborough, NH 03458

Founded: 1996. **Frequency:** Annual. **Audience:** Technology decision makers including IT staff, systems integrators, operations, procurement, supplier relations, managers and consultants. **Principle Exhibits:** Electronic commerce and internet-related products, services, and solutions. Exhibitor categories include enterprise, application, integration, B2B integration, collaboration. Process management and workflow, computing hardware/servers, communications service providers, application and managed service providers, system integration and consulting.

∎ 3497

IEX - INTERNET EXPO

REED EXHIBITION CO.

383 Main Ave.
Norwalk, CT 06851
PH: (203)840-5662
FX: (203)840-9662
E-mail: inquiry@reedexpo.com
URL: http://www.reedexpo.com

Description: IEX is a forum where international companies can effectively demonstrate the features and benefits of their products thus shortening the sales cycle. It will feature sessions on E-Commerce solutions, E-Business, Intranets, Internet access services, VPN, VOIP, databases, web publishing tools, online media, portals, networking and more.

▌3498

IF@BO: INTERNATIONAL SPECIALIST TRADE FAIR FOR E-INTELLIGENCE, IT AND COMMUNICATIONS' SOLUTIONS
REED EXHIBITION CO.

383 Main Ave.
Norwalk, CT 06851
PH: (203)840-5662
FX: (203)840-9662
E-mail: inquiry@reedexpo.com
URL: http://www.reedexpo.com

Description: Ifabo is a clearly-focused structure that is a trade-only B2B event. With its strong focus on SMEs, Ifabo is one of Austria's most important IT and T platform for small and medium companies. It features increased involvement of the telecom industry, clear marketing and advertising strategy, and coverage of multimedia. The product groups that will be avaialable to choose from include: e-intelligence, task-specific software, industry-specific software, hardware, systems and content providers, networking, telecoms, and IT security.

▌3499

IFE - INTERNATIONAL FOOD AND DRINK EXHIBITION
MONTGOMERY EXHIBITIONS LTD.

11 Manchester Sq.
London W1M5AB, England
E-mail: exhibit@montnet.com

Founded: 1979. **Frequency:** Biennial. **Audience:** Trade only. **Principle Exhibits:** Food and drink, packaging and design, and e-business solutions.

▌3500

IITELMIT (ITE)
INTERNATIONAL TRADE EXHIBITIONS GROUP PLC

105 Salusbury Rd.
London NW66RG, United Kingdom
PH: 44 20 75965000
FX: 44 20 75965111
E-mail: info@iitelmit.com
URL: http://www.iitelmit.com/

Description: IITELMIT is Indonesia's largest annual exhibition of cutting edge info-communications technologies and services. Displaying the latest telecommunications and network infrastructure products, the newest IT solutions, and the best local and international content, IITELMIT 2002 continues to be the showcase of choice for multinational and domestic businesses operating in Indonesia.

▌3501

IMPACT: A TOTAL PRICE/COST APPROACH TO SUPPLY MANAGEMENT (ISM)
INSTITUTE FOR SUPPLY MANAGEMENT

PO Box 22160
Tempe, AZ 85285-2160
PH: (480)752-6276

TF: 800-888-6276
FX: (480)752-7890
URL: http://www.ism.ws

Description: Relying on actual business experience, this program presents new trends, fresh ideas, and practical solutions to directly impact an organization's success. Supply management touches all aspects of the organization including finance, production, development, even sales and marketing. ISM recognizes that effective supply management professionals have the responsibility to deliver value to all facets of the network and presents this conference in support of that model. Impact attempts to focus on lessons learned and success stories giving new perspectives and proven strategies to help give the organization a competitive edge.

▌3502

IN-IP WORLD FORUM (IEC)
INTERNATIONAL ENGINEERING CONSORTIUM

549 W Randolph St., Ste. 600
Chicago, IL 60661-2208
PH: (312)559-4100
FX: (312)559-4111
E-mail: info@iec.org
URL: http://www.iec.org

Description: The IN-IP World Forum is where incumbent service providers, CLECs, wireless operators, and other carriers from around the world discuss the reality of making enhanced services on the next-generation network a reality. It is where they examine new IP services and applications, discuss legacy infrastructure migration strategies, evaluate new business models, share deployment experiences, and collectively drive the future of the converging packet network. Attendees will come away from the event equipped with valuable information, a firmer grasp of current IN and IP issues and solutions, and a clearer view of their place in the next-generation world.

▌3503

INFORMATION ARCHITECTURE FOR ENTERPRISE WEB SITES (DCI)
DIGITAL CONSULTING INSTITUTE

204 Andover St.
Andover, MA 01810
PH: (978)470-3880
URL: http://www.dci.com

Description: At this seminar, participants will attend discussions on topics such as: step-by-step methodologies for developing and implementing a web site's information architecture, the role of the information architect in developing a web site, how to research a site's mission, vision, budget, timeline, audiences, content, and functionality, how to see a Web site from the perspective of a user's needs and expectations, and how to understand how people really search. Attendees should include: anyone who maintains a web site, intranet, or extranet where users get lost or have difficulty in finding the information they need, anyone who wants to create web sites that are can be browsed, searched, and navigated by customers, partners, and employees, anyone who needs to organize a large amount of complex content into a usable and useful web site or intranet, or Data Administrators and Database Administrators responsible for web data and content.

▌3504
THE INFORMATION SECURITY CONFERENCE (DCI)
DIGITAL CONSULTING INSTITUTE

204 Andover St.
Andover, MA 01810
PH: (978)470-3880
URL: http://www.dci.com

Description: At The Information Security Conference, the focus will be on security programs that work. META Group pioneered enterprise security program management in 1997 with the publication of Security in Enterprise Computing: A Practical Guide. The security approach first launched in that document has been revised to capture all of the knowledge acquired by the META Group security analyst team since then. The result is an advanced approach to enterprise information security available from any source today.

▌3505
INFORMATION SECURITY MANAGERS SYMPOSIUM
MIS TRAINING INSTITUTE

498 Concord St.
Framingham, MA 01702-2357
PH: (508)879-7999
FX: (508)872-1153
E-mail: mis@misti.com
URL: http://www.misti.com

Description: This seminar includes how to detect and react to system intrusions, minimize the impact of catastrophic security incidents, test the security of systems, and more.

▌3506
INFORMATION SECURITY SOLUTIONS EUROPE (EEMA)
THE EUROPEAN FORUM FOR ELECTRONIC BUSINESS

Alexander House, High St.
Inkberrow WR74DT, United Kingdom
PH: 44 0 1386793028
FX: 44 0 1386793268
E-mail: info@EEMA.org
URL: http://www.eema.org

Description: ISSE 2002 will look at the manifold aspects of security and trust in the Internet environment. Leading technologists, heads of industry, representatives from the political world and the legal professions will present you with the most recent information on the development of IT security.

▌3507
INFORMATION SECURITY WORLD
TERRAPINN, LTD.

100 Hatton Garden, Fl. 2, Ste. B
London EC1N8NX, United Kingdom
PH: 44 207 2421548
FX: 44 207 2421508
E-mail: chris.rodrigues@terrapinn.com
URL: http://www.terrapinn.com

Description: Information Security World Australasia is a large and dedicated IT security show. The conference and exhibition attract decision-makers from all the vertical markets, all wanting to access the latest in information security. The exhibition is a comprehensive technology showcase that demonstrates innovative solutions in technology, equipment, products and services. The industry meets to discuss strategies, develop alliances and more importantly do business. The annual conference brings together senior executives and decision-makers from across the region, making this event the one to be at.

▌3508
INFORMATIONWEEK CONFERENCE
CMP MEDIA INC.

12 W 21st St.
New York, NY 10010
TF: 888-428-3976
FX: (917)305-3341
E-mail: info@cmpevents.com
URL: http://www.cmp.com

Description: Join InformationWeek editors, industry luminaries, and Business Technology Executives to explore the new issues raised by the next step in leveraging Collaborative Business, experience real-world problems and solutions, and learn how to apply these lessons to an organization.

▌3509
INFOSECURITY EUROPE
REED EXHIBITIONS

Oriel House, 26 The Quadrant
Richmond TW91DL, United Kingdom
PH: 44 20 89107910
E-mail: inquiry@reedexpo.co.uk
URL: http://www.infosec.co.uk

Description: Only conference dedicated entirely to the IT security industry and to gather information and expand knowledge of all the existing and new products and services the exhibitors offer.

▌3510
INFOSECURITY SCANDINAVIA
IT SCANDINAVIA EXHIBITIONS

SE-20280 Malmo, Sweden
E-mail: info@itscandinavia.com

Founded: 2001. **Frequency:** Annual. **Audience:** IT directors, senior managers, consultants, and managers from industry sectors. **Principle Exhibits:** Network security, internet security, disaster recovery and physical computer security, mobile security, secure e-business, critical business information.

∎ 3511

INFOSYSTEM - INTERNATIONAL FAIR OF TELECOMMUNICATION, INFORMATION TECHNOLOGY AND ELECTRONICS
POZNAN INTERNATIONAL FAIR LTD.

Glogowska 14
PL-60-734 Poznan, Poland
E-mail: info@mtp.com.pl

Founded: 1987. **Frequency:** Annual. **Audience:** Trade and general public. **Principle Exhibits:** Telecommiunications, networks, internet, intelligent building (comprehensive system solutions,), intergrated information systems, specialized application software, hardware, audio-visual systems, electronics, automation, services, specialized publications.

∎ 3512

INSTANT MESSAGING PLANET CONFERENCE AND EXPO
INT MEDIA GROUP

23 Old Kings Hwy. S
Darien, CT 06820
PH: (203)662-2800
TF: (203)655-4686
E-mail: cobrienats@internet.com
URL: http://www.intmediaevents.com

Description: Instant Messaging Planet Asia Conference and Expo is designed for professionals interested in better understanding the business opportunities and effectiveness presented by enterprise Instant Messaging (IM). While IM is best known for its use by consumers, its vast untapped potential is in the enterprise business sector, where it has rapidly become a critical tool for business communications, Customer Relationship Management (CRM) and business process integration. Companies worldwide have discovered that Instant Messaging within their enterprises have saved them valuable time and money, and in crisis conditions has even proven to be more reliable and more effective than their email systems.

∎ 3513

INTEGRATED ENTERPRISE SUMMIT
DELPHI GROUP

10 Post Office Sq., 10th Fl., S
Boston, MA 02109-4603
PH: (617)247-1511
TF: 800-335-7440
FX: (617)247-4957
E-mail: client.services@delphigroup.com
URL: http://www.delphigroup.com

Description: Delphi's Integrated Enterprise Summit will explore the intersection of business and technology where web services, enterprise portals and BPM converge. Delphi's Integrated Enterprise Summit is dedicated to the challenge and opportunity organizations faces today: the integration of applications and processes. It's an event to bring together the critical areas of technology and business that are at the forefront of today's IT investments. In three days, the latest development in the application of web services, enterprise portals and BPM will be covered.

∎ 3514

INTEGRATED SOLUTIONS FOR RETAILERS
RETAIL EVENTS LTD.

Lupus House
11-13 Macklin St.
London WC2B5NH, United Kingdom
PH: 44 20 7430 0077
FX: 44 20 7430 0055
E-mail: info@retailevents.co.uk
URL: http://www.is4r.com

Description: With many businesses now offering multi channel customer facing routes to market, a best practice of retailing via these channels and platforms has begun to emerge. This conference will address these issues from a technology perspective; however, from the standpoint of technology being an enabler not the driver of successful multi channel retailing. Attendees and sponsors of this conference will be learning and sharing the lessons learned by major retailers in their quest to achieve efficient and profitable multi channel delivery to their customers.

∎ 3515

INTEGRATING KNOWLEDGE MANAGEMENT WITH DATA WAREHOUSING FOR THE 21ST CENTURY (DCI)
DIGITAL CONSULTING INSTITUTE

204 Andover St.
Andover, MA 01810
PH: (978)470-3880
URL: http://www.dci.com

Description: This seminar will provide an understanding of what Knowledge Management (KM) is and how it fits in with Data Warehousing (DW). Because KM is so new and so controversial, a framework for KM will be learned that provides a solid base for organizations moving into the 21st Century with a knowledge program.

∎ 3516

INTERACTIVE EGO CONFERENCE AND EXHIBITION
GLOBAL TRADE WINDS CORP.

115 Jaffrey St.
Weymouth, MA 02188
PH: (508)748-3091
FX: (508)748-3092

E-mail: info@interactiveego.com
URL: http://www.interactiveego.com

Description: Interactive Ego is a U.S. based E-Business and B2B showcase designed exclusively for an international clientele. The Interactive Ego Conference will be the only place in the USA where attendees can come for answers and solutions on what is happening with Internet technology globally. The conference program is designed to create networking opportunities, learn from the top international visionaries, explore new opportunities, and discuss the latest practices and technologies.

▌3517

INTERNAL WEB SITES FOR HUMAN RESOURCES
INTERNATIONAL QUALITY AND PRODUCTIVITY CENTER

TF: 800-882-8684
E-mail: update@iqpc.com
URL: http://www.iqpc.com

Description: At the conference for Internal Websites for Human Resources, some topics covered will be how to develop web-based solutions that enhance employee communication and knowledge, maintain security and privacy on a HR intranet, launch and manage a human resources web-site, implement self-service applications and portals for employees and managers, create a business case, cost justification and strategic plan for a HR intranet, and evaluate the latest online technology for HR.

▌3518

INTERNATIONAL CONFERENCE (ISACA)
INFORMATION SYSTEMS AUDIT AND CONTROL ASSOCIATION

E-mail: conference@isaca.org
URL: http://www.isaca.org

Founded: 1974. **Description:** Information Systems Audit and Control Association(ISACA) has long been recognized throughout the world for providing in-depth coverage of the leading-edge technical and managerial issues facing IT governance, control, security and assurance professionals. The International Conference will enhance ones ability to stay informed of the latest advances in information technology, witness and understand the latest innovations, strategies and techniques, discuss new ideas and tools to maintain a competitive advantage, and find creative solutions to IT audit, control and security challenges.

▌3519

INTERNATIONAL EPURCHASING SUMMIT (IQPC)

INTERNATIONAL QUALITY AND PRODUCTIVITY CENTER
PO Box 401
150 Clove Rd.
Little Falls, NJ 07424
PH: (973)256-0211
TF: 800-882-8684
E-mail: info@iqpc.com
URL: http://www.iqpc.com
Contact: Todd Smith, Sales Manager, Sponsorship and Exhibits

Description: The ePurchasing Summit will feature top corporate practitioners and thought leaders presenting case studies, hard facts and strategies for success. Several conference sessions are highly interactive roundtables with industry leaders, allowing for the opportunity to drive the content of the meeting and discuss tough ePurchasing challenges, such as secrets to strategic sourcing, contract and supplier management, and category management, recognizing and overcoming cultural and organizational barriers to forming healthy supplier/vendor relationships, finding raw materials, components and assemblies, surplus inventories, used equipment and MRO supplies using the Internet, and P-cards and the improvement purchasing efficiencies.

▌3520

INTERNATIONAL IT SERVICE MANAGEMENT SUMMIT
INT MEDIA GROUP
23 Old Kings Hwy. S
Darien, CT 06820
PH: (203)662-2800
TF: (203)655-4686
E-mail: cobrienats@internet.com
URL: http://www.intmediaevents.com

Description: The IT Service Management Forum's (ITSMF) International IT Service Management Summit is a vendor neutral conference dedicated to educating IT and business executives on how standardized processes and best practices can be systematically applied across the entire range of IT support and delivery functions, to deliver superior services, while reducing risks and effectively managing costs.

▌3521

INTERNATIONAL SUPPLY MANAGEMENT CONFERENCE AND EDUCATIONAL EXHIBIT (ISM)
INSTITUTE FOR SUPPLY MANAGEMENT
PO Box 22160
Tempe, AZ 85285-2160
PH: (480)752-6276
TF: 800-888-6276
FX: (480)752-7890
URL: http://www.ism.ws

Founded: 1916. **Description:** Join colleagues during the International Supply Management Conference and Educational Exhibit and learn proven methods to stay on track.

727

Discover how to lead the way within an organization and how to add value. The five distinct learning tracks can put people on the right path to success. Pick the track that's right or mix and match to get an overview of the entire supply arena. Track 1: Supply Management: A Strategic Approach, Track 2: Making the Most of Supplier Relationships, Track 3: Tools for the Effective Supply Manager, Track 4: Making Sense of the E-Commerce Revolution, and Track 5: Professional Growth: The Key to Your Future.

▌3522
INTERNET BUSINESS EXPO
KEITH REED MEDIA EVENTS

303 Vintage Park Dr.
Foster City, CA 94404
E-mail: mtrask@zdcf.com

Principle Exhibits: The only internet conference and exposition focused entirely on the importance of Java technology and cutting-edge internet, intranet and extranet products for IT professionals.

▌3523
INTERNET EXPO
DIGITAL CONSULTING INC.

204 Andover St.
Andover, MA 01810

Principle Exhibits: Internet expo.

▌3524
INTERNET EXPO ZURICH
REED EXHIBITION COMPANIES (ZURICH)

Hurstrasse 5
CH-8336 Zurich, Switzerland

Principle Exhibits: Internet/Intranet applications, e-commerce, and web media equipment, supplies, and services.

▌3525
INTERNET MARKETING STRATEGIES
FROST AND SULLIVAN

7550 W I 10, Ste. 400
San Antonio, TX 78229
PH: (210)247-2461
E-mail: ebrown@frost.com
URL: http://www.summits.frost.com/IMK
Contact: Lisa Lee, Event Planner

Description: The Internet Marketing Strategies Conference covers every major aspect of online marketing and advertising strategies. Features key speakers discussing how to effectively use the Internet to expand marketing communications, develop new markets, drive business to a site, and successfully sell, service, and build relationships with eCustomers. The conference will also cover key issues such as personalization and consumer privacy.

▌3526
THE INTERNET - SECURITY, AUDIT AND CONTROL CONCERNS (ISACA)
INFORMATION SYSTEMS AUDIT AND CONTROL ASSOCIATION

3701 Algonquin Rd., Ste.1010
Rolling Meadows, IL 60008
PH: (847)253-1545
FX: (847)253-1443
E-mail: conference@isaca.org
URL: http://www.isaca.org

Description: This program demonstrates the Internet architecture, where it fits into telecommunication networks, and discusses the information services. Controls are identified and a framework is introduced to minimize Internet risks. This framework includes information policies, security policies, procedures to assess risks associated with using the Internet, "firewall" minimum components, as well as specific application and management control development

▌3527
INTERNET TELEPHONY WORLD EXPO
IDG JAPAN INC.

3-4-5 Hongo Bunkyo-ku
Tokyo 113-0033, Japan
PH: 03 5800 3111
URL: http://www.idg.co.jp

Description: This conference and demonstration will focus on the current trend and future direction of IP telephony and related technology.

▌3528
INTERNET WORLD
PENTON TECHNOLOGY MEDIA

288-290 Worton Rd.
Isleworth TW76EL, United Kingdom
PH: 44 20 82321600
FX: 44 20 82321650
URL: http://www.internetworld.co.uk

Description: Internet World UK 2002 is an Internet event for every industry and every discipline. Combines an exhibition, a conference and a major networking opportunity, featuring best of breed vendors, massive education programme, and dozens of features, awards and parties.

▌3529
INTERNET WORLD ARGENTINA
MECKLERMEDIA CORP.

16 Thorndal Cir.
Darien, CT 06820-5421
E-mail: international@mecklermedia.com

Principle Exhibits: Internet related equipment, supplies, and services.

▌3530

INTERNET WORLD ASIA HONG KONG
REED EXHIBITIONS (HONG KONG)

11/F East Wing, Hennessy Center
500 Hennessy Road
Causeway Bay
Hong Kong, People's Republic of China
E-mail: ask@reedexpo.com.hk

Founded: 1999. **Frequency:** Annual. **Audience:** Trade visitors. **Principle Exhibits:** Internet event targeting buyers across the Asia Pacific region, featuring ISP/networking technologies, enterprise Internet applications, e-commerce, advertising and marketing products, website design and development.

▌3531

INTERNET WORLD ASIA@SINGAPORE
REED EXHIBITIONS PTE. LTD.

1 Temasek Ave.
17-01 Millenia Tower
Singapore 039192, Singapore
E-mail: ask@reedexpo.com.sg

Audience: Professionals and general public. **Principle Exhibits:** Internet solutions and technology.

▌3532

INTERNET WORLD BERLIN
MECKLERMEDIA CORP.

16 Thorndal Cir.
Darien, CT 06820-5421
E-mail: international@mecklermedia.com

Principle Exhibits: Internet related equipment, supplies, and services.

▌3533

INTERNET WORLD COLOMBIA
MECKLERMEDIA CORP.

16 Thorndal Cir.
Darien, CT 06820-5421
E-mail: international@mecklermedia.com

Principle Exhibits: Internet related equipment, supplies, and services.

▌3534

INTERNET WORLD EGYPT
MECKLERMEDIA CORP.

16 Thorndal Cir.
Darien, CT 06820-5421
E-mail: international@mecklermedia.com

Principle Exhibits: Internet related equipment, supplies, and services.

▌3535

INTERNET WORLD FRANCE
MECKLERMEDIA CORP.

16 Thorndal Cir.
Darien, CT 06820-5421
E-mail: international@mecklermedia.com

Principle Exhibits: Internet related equipment, supplies, and services.

▌3536

INTERNET WORLD INDIA
MECKLERMEDIA CORP.

16 Thorndal Cir.
Darien, CT 06820-5421
E-mail: international@mecklermedia.com

Principle Exhibits: Internet related equipment, supplies, and services.

▌3537

INTERNET WORLD IRELAND
MECKLERMEDIA CORP.

16 Thorndal Cir.
Darien, CT 06820-5421
E-mail: international@mecklermedia.com

Principle Exhibits: Internet related equipment, supplies, and services.

▌3538

INTERNET WORLD ISRAEL
MECKLERMEDIA CORP.

16 Thorndal Cir.
Darien, CT 06820-5421
E-mail: international@mecklermedia.com

Principle Exhibits: Internet related equipment, supplies, and services.

▌3539

INTERNET WORLD JAPAN
MECKLERMEDIA CORP.

16 Thorndal Cir.
Darien, CT 06820-5421
E-mail: international@mecklermedia.com

Principle Exhibits: Internet related equipment, supplies, and services.

▌3540

INTERNET WORLD MALAYSIA
MECKLERMEDIA CORP.

16 Thorndal Cir.
Darien, CT 06820-5421
E-mail: international@mecklermedia.com

Principle Exhibits: Internet related equipment, supplies, and services.

■ 3541

INTERNET WORLD MEXICO
MECKLERMEDIA CORP.

16 Thorndal Cir.
Darien, CT 06820-5421
E-mail: international@mecklermedia.com

Principle Exhibits: Internet related equipment, supplies, and services.

■ 3542

INTERNET WORLD MIDDLE EAST
MECKLERMEDIA CORP.

16 Thorndal Cir.
Darien, CT 06820-5421
E-mail: international@mecklermedia.com

Principle Exhibits: Internet related equipment, supplies, and services.

■ 3543

INTERNET WORLD NORWAY
MECKLERMEDIA CORP.

16 Thorndal Cir.
Darien, CT 06820-5421
E-mail: international@mecklermedia.com

Principle Exhibits: Internet related equipment, supplies, and services.

■ 3544

INTERNET WORLD PORTUGAL
MECKLERMEDIA CORP.

16 Thorndal Cir.
Darien, CT 06820-5421
E-mail: international@mecklermedia.com

Principle Exhibits: Internet related equipment, supplies, and services.

■ 3545

INTERNET WORLD PRAGUE
MECKLERMEDIA CORP.

16 Thorndal Cir.
Darien, CT 06820-5421
E-mail: international@mecklermedia.com

Principle Exhibits: Internet related equipment, supplies, and services.

■ 3546

INTERNET WORLD SPAIN
MECKLERMEDIA CORP.

16 Thorndal Cir.
Darien, CT 06820-5421
E-mail: international@mecklermedia.com

Principle Exhibits: Internet related equipment, supplies, and services.

■ 3547

INTERNET WORLD TURKEY
MECKLERMEDIA CORP.

16 Thorndal Cir.
Darien, CT 06820-5421
E-mail: international@mecklermedia.com

Principle Exhibits: Internet related equipment, supplies, and services.

■ 3548

INTERNET WORLD UK SPRING
LEARNED INFORMATION LTD.

Woodside
Hinkey Hill
Oxford OX15AU, England
E-mail: conferences@learned.co.uk

Founded: 1992. **Frequency:** Annual. **Audience:** General public. **Principle Exhibits:** Internet equipment, supplies, and services.

■ 3549

INTERNET WORLD VENEZUELA
MECKLERMEDIA CORP.

16 Thorndal Cir.
Darien, CT 06820-5421
E-mail: international@mecklermedia.com

Principle Exhibits: Internet related equipment, supplies, and services.

■ 3550

INTERNETBUSINESS - INTERNATIONAL SHOW FOR BUSINESS APPLICATIONS ON THE INTERNET
SINGAPORE EXHIBITION SERVICES PTE. LTD.

47 Scotts Rd.
11th Floor Goldbell Towers
Singapore 228233, Singapore
E-mail: info@sesmontnet.com

Frequency: Biennial. **Audience:** Trade professionals only. **Principle Exhibits:** Authoring/development tools and software, electronic commerce products and services, internet service providers, internet security, internet telephony, internet access, online services, web browsers/search tools and engines, web hosting, web servers, web server management.

∎ 3551

INTERNETWORKING EVENT - THE INFORMATION AND COMMUNICATION TECHNOLOGY EVENT

Founded: 1992. **Frequency:** Annual. **Audience:** General managers, finance managers, network consultants and managers, telecommunications managers, EDP managers, data and database managers and consultants. **Principle Exhibits:** Computer networks, internetworking, Internet, intranet, data communication, telecommunication, mobile communications. E-Commerce, security products, bridges, gateways, routers, isdn, asdl, atm, electronic mail.

∎ 3552

INTRANET CONTENT MANAGEMENT WEEK
INTERNATIONAL QUALITY AND PRODUCTIVITY CENTER

PO Box 401
150 Clove Rd.
Little Falls, NJ 07424
PH: (973)256-0211
TF: 800-882-8684
E-mail: update@iqpc.com.sg
URL: http://www.iqpc.com
Contact: Todd Smith, Sales Manager, Sponsorship and Exhibits

Description: Intranet Content Management Strategies is for true knowledge sharing. Learn from world class leaders and incorporated Intranet content management strategies. Some topics will cover how to formulate an Intranet content management plan to accelerate the deployment of content management solutions, build a secure Intranet culture that encourages the dissemination of intelligence whilst maintaining the necessary multi-security level collaborative environment, transforming the structure and process of an organization to drive knowledge management initiatives, creating a sustained dynamic content management culture to promote innovation and creativity, leverage content management for effective learning throughout the organization, and benchmark an Intranet content management systems against performance metrics.

∎ 3553

IS AUDIT AND CONTROL TRAINING WEEK
INFORMATION SYSTEMS AUDIT AND CONTROL ASSOCIATION

3701 Algonquin Rd., Ste. 1010
Rolling Meadows, IL 60008
PH: (847)253-1545
FX: (847)253-1443

E-mail: conference@isaca.org
URL: http://www.isaca.org/trainwk.htm
Contact: Sandy Arens, Conference Coordiinator

Description: IS Audit and Control Training Week, presented by the Information Systems Audit and Control Association, is specifically designed to help meet and defeat daily challenges. Whether an IS audit, control, security or accounting professional, this pragmatic, thought provoking and informative program will provide a person with the confidence and assurance needed to maintain or increase competitive advantage.

∎ 3554

ISM ANNUAL INTERNATIONAL SUPPLY MANAGEMENT CONFERENCE
INSTITUTE FOR SUPPLE MANAGEMENT

2055 E. Centennial Cir.
PO Box 22160
Tempe, AZ 85285-2160

Founded: 1915. **Frequency:** Annual. **Audience:** Purchasing professionals and general public. **Principle Exhibits:** Auctions, business service, capital equipment, computer hardware/software, consulting services, e-business services/software, logistics and transportation, MRO, office supply, procurement card services.

∎ 3555

ISPCON AUSTRALIA
MECKLERMEDIA CORP.

16 Thorndal Cir.
Darien, CT 06820-5421
E-mail: international@mecklermedia.com

Principle Exhibits: Internet service provider market exhibition.

∎ 3556

ISPCON FALL
MECKLERMEDIA CORP.

16 Thorndal Cir.
Darien, CT 06820-5421
E-mail: international@mecklermedia.com

Founded: 1997. **Frequency:** Annual. **Principle Exhibits:** Internet service provider market exhibition.

∎ 3557

ISPCON SPRING
MECKLERMEDIA CORP.

16 Thorndal Cir.
Darien, CT 06820-5421
E-mail: international@mecklermedia.com

Founded: 1997. **Frequency:** Annual. **Principle Exhibits:** Internet service provider market exhibition.

■ 3558

ISPCON UK

MECKLERMEDIA CORP.

16 Thorndal Cir.
Darien, CT 06820-5421
E-mail: international@mecklermedia.com

Principle Exhibits: Internet service provider market exhibition.

■ 3559

ISPE/CE2002 CONFERENCE AND
EXHIBITION

CETEAM INTERNATIONAL

2966 Penman St.
Tustin, CA 92782
PH: (714)389-2662
E-mail: roy@ceconf.com
URL: http://www.ceteam.com
Contact: Dr. Rajkumar Roy, Conference General Chair

Founded: 1994. **Description:** Topics addressed in this conference include e-Strategy, e-Work and e-Business, Agile Manufacturing and CE, Collaborative Decision-Making in CE, Internet-based Modeling in CE, Mobile Computing in Engineering, Digital Product Development and CE and many more.

■ 3560

THE IT DIRECTORS' FORUM

RICHMOND EVENTS LTD.

St Leonards House, St Leonards Rd.
London SW147LY, United Kingdom
PH: 44 20 8487 2200
FX: 44 20 8487 2300
URL: http://www.richmondevents.com

Founded: 1992. **Description:** The IT Directors' Forum is a well-established event where the aim is to create an environment where the top IT professionals can come together to learn, network and identify new IT supplier companies. It is targeted for senior executives from IT supplier companies. Speakers at the conference sessions will be experts in their own particular fields and will be addressing personal development, management and strategic IT issues.

■ 3561

IT LEADERSHIP

INTERNATIONAL QUALITY AND PRODUCTIVITY
CENTER

PO Box 401
150 Clove Rd.
Little Falls, NJ 07424

PH: (973)256-0211
TF: 800-882-8684
E-mail: info@iqpc-canada.com
URL: http://www.iqpc.com
Contact: Todd Smith, Sales Manager, Sponsorship and Exhibits

Description: Guide IT Leadership will address everything on the CIO's desk, including:business alignment and performance measurement, emerging technologies, security, risk and business continuity, and managing value in tough economic times.

■ 3562

IT TRADE: THAILAND'S AND
INDOCHINA'S INFORMATION
TECHNOLOGY TRADE EXPOSITION

REED EXHIBITION CO.

383 Main Ave.
Norwalk, CT 06851
PH: (203)840-5662
FX: (203)840-9662
E-mail: inquiry@reedexpo.com
URL: http://www.reedexpo.com

Description: An advanced open-end information technology exposition specifically designed to provide a strategic platform for international IT manufacturers to build partnerships and alliances with dealers, distributors, corporate and professional buyers in Thailand.

■ 3563

IT FOR WALLSTREET

KEY3MEDIA GROUP

5700 Wilshire Blvd., Ste. 325
Los Angeles, CA 90036
PH: (323)954-6000
FX: (323)954-6010
E-mail: mike.moreno@key3media.com
URL: http://www.key3media.com
Contact: Mike Moreno, General Manager

Description: The IT for Wall Street Summit provides securities industry executives with the critical information they need to transition their investments in functional legacy technology into newer and more robust infrastructures capable of meeting the demands of the 21st century. As the preeminent event to address both the strategic and technological challenges facing the financial services industry, The IT for Wall Street Summit program will be of significant interest to IT and business professionals from all sectors of the securities industry.

■ 3564

ITEC EVENTS

IMARK COMMUNICATIONS

1 Apple Hill Dr., Ste. 301
Natick, MA 01760
PH: (508)647-8600

FX: (508)647-0241
E-mail: doehl@imark-com.com
URL: http://www.goitec.com/home
Contact: David Korse, President and Chief Executive Officer

Description: ITEC is the nation's largest series of Information Technology events. With over 48 events, ITEC specializes in meeting the unique regional technology needs of business, government and academic organizations. ITEC events provide the latest in turn-key technologies that are ready to meet immediate needs in IT security, storage, wireless, eBusiness, IT training /consulting and more. Each ITEC event is built with a local advisory panel and is customized to the unique regional needs of the area's business community.

∎ 3565

ITUG/DECUS
ITUG

401 North Michigan Ave.
Chicago, IL 60611
PH: (312)321-6851
TF: 800-845-4884
FX: (312)245-1064
E-mail: itug@itug.org
URL: http://www.itug.org

Description: The ITUG/DECUS Joint European Conference is for Compaq enterprise computing users. It will concentrate on OpenVMS, Tru64 UNIX, and NonStop Himalaya tailored specifically to unique needs.

∎ 3566

JACKSON COMPUTER & TECHNOLOGY SHOWCASE
EVENT MANAGEMENT SERVICES

516 S.E. Morrison St., Lower Level
Portland, OR 97214
E-mail: rglanville@techshows.com

Founded: 1995. **Frequency:** Annual. **Audience:** Corporate purchasers and information technology professionals. **Principle Exhibits:** Products and services for computers, imaging, wireless communication, networking, application development, and e-commerce.

∎ 3567

JAVA FOR THE ENTERPRISE: SERVER SIDE JAVA (DCI)
DIGITAL CONSULTING INSTITUTE

204 Andover St.
Andover, MA 01810
PH: (978)470-3880
URL: http://www.dci.com

Description: This four-day class for developers, project managers and system architects explores the use of Java on the server. The key topics covered include an in depth study of the J2EE architecture - servlets, Java Server Pages and Enterprise Java Beans - where students gain hands-on exposure to the J2EE. Over the 4 days, students will develop several small applications in Java and learn how to incorporate the J2EE architecture. All applications are built using a text editor; no RAD tools, IDEs or proprietary APIs are used. This approach allows students to focus on the Java language itself as opposed to the features of a given tool.

∎ 3568

JAVA FUNDAMENTALS (DCI)
DIGITAL CONSULTING INSTITUTE

204 Andover St.
Andover, MA 01810
PH: (978)470-3880
URL: http://www.dci.com

Description: This four-day Java course focuses on the fundamentals of using the Java programming language to build business applications. Students will create a fully functional Java application and gain hands on exposure to Java by working with several classes in J2SE. To ensure the proper fundamentals are learned, no IDEs, RAD tools or proprietary APIs are used. This approach allows students to focus on the Java language itself as opposed to functionality or code that might be generated by a tool.

∎ 3569

THE JAVAONE CONFERENCE
KEY3MEDIA GROUP

5700 Wilshire Blvd., Ste. 325
Los Angeles, CA 90036
PH: (323)954-6000
FX: (323)954-6010
URL: http://www.key3media.com

Description: The JavaOne conference is an opportunity for Java(TM) technology developers to network with peers, and attend technical sessions that assist in future development solutions.

∎ 3570

JAVAPRO TRACK (FTP)
FAWCETTE TECHNICAL PUBLICATIONS, INC.

209 Hamilton Ave.
Palo Alto, CA 94301
PH: (650)833-7100
TF: 800-848-5523
E-mail: conferences@fawcette.com
URL: http://www.ftpconferences.com
Contact: James E. Fawcette, President

Founded: 1990. **Description:** JavaPro Magazine's Java track at the BorCon conference covers the latest features of Borland JBuilder in addition to JavaBeans, EJB, portability and efficiency issues, Java on Linux, Java 2 Enterprise Edition, Java 2 Micro Edition, and a host of other Java APIs and topics.

733

∎ 3571

LINUXWORLD CONFERENCE AND EXPO

IDG WORLD EXPO

3 Speen St.
Framingham, MA 01701
PH: (508)879-6700
E-mail: kathy_moran@idg.com
URL: http://www.linuxworldexpo.com
Contact: Charlie Greco, President and Chief Executive Officer

Description: LinuxWorld Conference and Expo is a comprehensive event focused exclusively on Linux and Open Source solutions. Features hundreds of leading hardware and software vendors on an interactive exhibit floor where they will be showcasing state of the art products, services and solutions needed to manage, scale and implement Linux into an infrastructure.

∎ 3572

LINUXWORLD EXPO

IDG JAPAN INC.

3-4-5 Hongo Bunkyo-ku
Tokyo 113-0033, Japan
PH: 03 5800 3111
E-mail: linux@idg.co.jp
URL: http://www.idg.co.jp

Description: The show is dedicated to Linux products. The show focuses on expanding usage of Linux products at enterprise in Japan and tries to introduce topics and business models of Linux products.

∎ 3573

LOGICON - THE PREMIER LOGISTICS AND SUPPLY CHAIN MANAGEMENT CONFERENCE (WBR)

WORLDWIDE BUSINESS RESEARCH

420 Lexington Ave., Ste. 2533
New York, NY 10017
PH: (212)885-2720
FX: (212)885-2798
E-mail: adas@wbresearch.com
URL: http://www.wbresearch.com

Description: Logicon is the supply chain management conference for Logistics, Supply Chain, and Customer Relationship Management professionals in food, beverage and consumer packaged goods manufacturing and related retail stores.

∎ 3574

THE LOGISTICS AND E-SUPPLY CHAIN FORUM

RICHMOND EVENTS INC.

48 W 38th St., 6th Fl.
New York, NY 10018
PH: (212)651-8700
TF: (212)651-8701
E-mail: syork@richmondevents.com
URL: http://www.logisticsforum.com/
Contact: Shane York, Conference Manager

Description: The Logistics and e-Supply Chain Forum brings together over 200 invited delegates, representing the top logistics and e-supply chain executives from major corporations for two days of pre-scheduled, meetings, conference sessions, think tanks and networking. Set onboard the renowned ocean liner QE2, it is the only event in the US to bring together supply chain and operating executives responsible for trillions of dollars in logistics, fulfillment, procurement and customer relationship management budgets. The Logistics Forum is held annually in the US and UK, and is the industry's foremost gathering of the world's key logistics and supply chain decision makers from the major manufacturing, retail, and service organizations.

∎ 3575

LOTUS ADVISOR DEVCON

ADVISOR MEDIA INC.

5675 Ruffin Rd.
San Diego, CA 92123-5675
PH: (858)278-5600
TF: 800-336-6060
E-mail: Events@Advisor.com
URL: http://www.advisor.com/www/AdvisorEvents

Description: TSW is a developer conference focusing on IBM Lotus software for web and collaboration solutions, featuring Domino, Notes, new Notes/Domino 6, Sametime, QuickPlace, iNotes Web Access, Discovery System, Mobile Notes and more.

∎ 3576

MAC EXPO

SHOWFEST PRODUCTIONS INC.

130 Bridgeland Ave., Ste. 409
Toronto, ON, Canada M6A1Z4
PH: (416)925-4533
FX: (416)925-7701
E-mail: rahmad@compfest.com
URL: http://www.compfest.com
Contact: Ryhan Ahmad, Sales Manager

Description: At the MacExpo, visitors can spend the whole day at the Macintosh Stage, taking in demonstrations by the leading companies, along with independent seminars by some of the city's best-known Mac authorities. The Mac Training Centre at the show offers an opportunity to get introductory sessions on all the leading Macintosh programs. Publishing and design programs will be well represented in the Mac Training Centre by PageMaker, Illustrator, Quark XPress, and PhotoShop.

▌3577

MACROMEDIA WEB WORLD (FTP)

FAWCETTE TECHNICAL PUBLICATIONS INC.

209 Hamilton Ave.
Palo Alto, CA 94301
PH: (650)833-7100
TF: 800-848-5523
E-mail: conferences@fawcette.com
URL: http://www.ftpconferences.com
Contact: James E. Fawcette, President

Founded: 1990. **Description:** Macromedia Web World is a conference that addresses the full spectrum of Macromedia Web tools and solutions. The conference covers Dreamweaver and Fireworks for high-impact web design and site management, Sitespring for Web-team collaboration and project management, Flash and Shockwave for next-generation animation and interactivity, and Dreamweaver UltraDev and ColdFusion UltraDev Studio for web application development and database publishing.

▌3578

MACWORLD CONFERENCE AND EXPO

IDG WORLD EXPO

3 Speen St.
Framingham, MA 01701
PH: (508)879-6700
E-mail: stephen_athan@idg.com
URL: http://www.macworldexpo.com
Contact: Charlie Greco, President and Chief Executive Officer

Description: Macworld Conference and Expo continues to be the an informative location for the Mac community to gather, network, socialize, and experience the excellence of Mac technology. In addition to up-to-date, targeted and in-depth Macintosh training offered by the show's world-renowned Conference programs, there are many show attractions to be taken advantage of and enjoyed.

▌3579

MANAGING ENTERPRISE ARCHITECTURE PLANNING: BLUEPRINTS FOR KNOWLEDGE MANAGEMENT (DCI)

DIGITAL CONSULTING INSTITUTE

204 Andover St.
Andover, MA 01810
PH: (978)470-3880
URL: http://www.dci.com

Description: The emphasis of this course is on managing every aspect of the enterprise architecture planning effort from the perspective of an expert who has guided dozens of such projects in virtually every industry. The common sense approach presented is completely flexible and adaptable to different corporate cultures. Examples of architectures, procedures, checklists and useful guidelines will be provided for each and every step. Sample reports and presentation outlines are included. Issues and experiences of attendees and their firms will be discussed. Attendees will leave

the seminar knowing what must be done to lead and direct a successful EAP project for their company.

▌3580

MANAGING AND OPTIMISING ENTERPRISE STORAGE TECHNOLOGIES

MARCUS EVANS LTD.

303 E Wacker Dr.
Chicago, IL 60601
PH: (312)540-3000
E-mail: LisaR@marcusevansch.com
URL: http://www.brandslam-summit.com
Contact: Greta Molepske, Marketing Manager

Description: This event features case-study based presentations and open, informal debate on the key enterprise storage issues from a diverse and international range of large corporate end-users and leading industry experts from vendors, service providers, associations and analysts. The conference also explores the data management and hosting offerings being made available from the telecommunications sector.

▌3581

MANUFACTURING AND SUPPLY CHAIN SUMMIT

GARTNER INC.

56 Top Gallant Rd.
Stamford, CT 06904
PH: (203)316-1111
FX: (203)324-7901
URL: http://www.gartner.com

Description: This event is designed to help to exploit Collaborative Commerce (or "C-Commerce") principles to drive significant improvements in corporate productivity and profitability. Attendees will learn how new technologies and business models can be used to optimize demand and production planning, how to maximize supply chain efficiency through the exchange of knowledge and information between sales, production, warehousing and distribution, how advances in collaborative design and engineering are being used to enhance product innovation, reduce time to market and minimize production costs, the state of private marketplaces and how they'll impact sourcing and procurement activities and which vendors and applications offer the best solutions for an operation. This event is targeted for manufacturing executives responsible for Product Design/Engineering, Supply Chain Management/Logistics, Plant/Manufacturing Operations, IT/IS, and others with PandL and/or process improvement responsibility.

▌3582

MAXIMISING BUSINESS PERFORMANCE THROUGH STRATEGIC INTRANET PLANNING

INTERNATIONAL QUALITY AND PRODUCTIVITY
CENTER
PO Box 401
150 Clove Rd.
Little Falls, NJ 07424
PH: (973)256-0211
TF: 800-882-8684
E-mail: enquire@iqpc.co.uk
URL: http://www.iqpc.com
Contact: Todd Smith, Sales Manager, Sponsorship and Exhibits

Description: This content-packed conference has 15 world-class intranet case studies to help learn how to align the intranet with corporate strategy to ensure it's used as an effective business tool, measure intranet communications and optimize ROI, ensuring intranet strategy is integrated into business objectives, evaluate critical success factors for the development of second and third generation B2E communication and successfully implement application and portal based intranet sites, implement effective governance processes to qualify and build logical up-to-date content in line with specific business strategy, and develop multilingual, community global portals to ensure effective knowledge sharing.

∎ 3583

MEASUREMENT PERFORMANCE FOR
INTRANET CONTENT
INTERNATIONAL QUALITY AND PRODUCTIVITY
CENTER

TF: 800-882-8684
E-mail: update@iqpc.com.sg
URL: http://www.iqpc.com

Description: Seminars explain how to maximize the profitability of a website both in ROI and in the attitude of employees. Subjects discussed include understanding what a portal is and how it fits into an organization, improving the functionality of an intranet, continuing to evolve intranet to keep pace with a company, employees and technology resources, developing a methodology for measuring an intranet, and building an ROI based on performance.

∎ 3584

MEDIACAST
REED EXHIBITIONS
Oriel House
26 The Quadrant
Richmond TW91DL, United Kingdom
PH: 44 20 89107910
E-mail: helpline@reedexpo.co.uk
URL: http://www.mediacast.co.uk/splash/splash.cfm

Description: MEDIACAST is Europe's largest springtime event for broadband media distribution technologies. The event is for network operators, services providers and content owners who are seeking technology partners to enable then to deliver new broadband services over any type of wireless

and wireline network - cable, satellite, broadcasting, telecoms and wireless. Visitors can see the latest in broadband access, high speed internet, iTV and t-commerce, VOD, DRM and streaming media.

∎ 3585

MEDIAVISION COLOGNE - TRADE FAIR
FOR MEDIA COMMUNICATIONS
COLOGNEMESSE
Messeplatz 1
D-50679 Cologne, Germany

Frequency: Annual. **Principle Exhibits:** E-commerce, multimedia, film and video broadcasting, intranet, internet, business television, digital print, telecommunications.

∎ 3586

METAMORPHOSIS PLUS! CONFERENCE
AND TECHNOLOGY SHOWCASE (DCI)
DIGITAL CONSULTING INSTITUTE
204 Andover St.
Andover, MA 01810
PH: (978)470-3880
URL: http://www.dci.com

Description: At METAmorphosis Plus! Conference and Technology Showcase, some topics to be covered are Business Value, Metrics, and Innovation, Human Capital Management and Organization, Operational Excellence, Infrastructure Development, Portals, Web Services, and Integration, Customer Relationship Management and Commerce Portfolios, and Security, Trust and Privacy.

∎ 3587

MID-OHIO INTERNET EXPO(COLUMBUS)
EXPO SOURCE INC.
8041 Hosbrook, Ste. 201
Cincinnati, OH 45236
E-mail: exposource@fuse.net

Frequency: Annual. **Audience:** Business owners, managers, CEOs, CFOs, purchasing agents, chief information officers, computer consultants, industrial companies. **Principle Exhibits:** Computer hardware, software, computer networking and integration, internet service providers, website design and hosting E-commerce, telecommunications services and equipment, telephone systems, service, cellular, digital, record storage.

∎ 3588

MIDDLEWARE: A DETAILED LOOK AT
THE DEVELOPMENT AND INTEGRATION
OF E-BUSINESS APPLICATIONS FROM
MIDDLEWARE 101 TO WEB SERVICES
(DCI)
DIGITAL CONSULTING INSTITUTE
204 Andover St.
Andover, MA 01810
PH: (978)470-3880

URL: http://www.dci.com

Description: This seminar provides an in-depth education on Middleware as enabling technologies for e-Business Application Development and Enterprise Application Integration (EAI). It covers the functionality that Middleware offers and provides attendees with the knowledge required to solve the major challenges that corporations are facing today. These challenges are: integration of existing applications within the enterprise (A2A), across enterprises (B2B) and development of new component-based applications. After attending this seminar, attendees will gain real and practical knowledge of "Middleware" and EAI technologies, including an in-depth look at a number of real-world EAI architectures that have been built for Fortune 500 companies and the products that have been used to achieve them.

▌**3589**

MOBILE BUSINESS AND TECHNOLOGY CONFERENCE

GARTNER INC.

56 Top Gallant Rd.
Stamford, CT 06904
PH: (203)316-1111
FX: (203)324-7901
URL: http://www.gartner.com

Description: At the Mobile Business and Technology Conference, attendees will learn how to exploit mobile technology safely, securely and profitably. They will hear about practical case studies of what works today, and strategic predictions for what will work in the future. Practical actionable advice will be provided on issues such as: which mobile applications will provide positive ROI and which ones won't, how one can make wireless applications and devices secure, which mobile devices, form factors and operating systems will dominate, which mobile technology vendors will survive and which will fail, which products and services will European consumers expect to deliver on mobile devices; and, critically, what they will pay for.

▌**3590**

MOBILE COMMERCE WORLD

TERRAPINN, LTD.

100 Hatton Garden, Lvl. 2, Ste. B
London EC1N8NX, United Kingdom
PH: 44 207 2421548
FX: 44 207 2421508
E-mail: james.smith@terrapinn.com
URL: http://www.terrapinn.com

Description: The Mobile Commerce World Australia conference allows experts to explore the enterprise opportunities of mobile business, commerce and content in a senior level, strategic environment with industry leaders. Provides the opportunity to develop an understanding of the global wireless economy and find out how successful case studies can impact on future business.

▌**3591**

MOBILE ENTERPRISE STRATEGIES SEMINAR SERIES

BRAINSTORM GROUP INC.

386 W Main St.
Northboro, MA 01532
PH: (508)393-3266
FX: (508)393-8845
E-mail: info@brainstorm-group.com
URL: http://www.brainstorm-group.com
Contact: Dawn M. Eagan, Marketing Director

Description: The Mobile Enterprise Strategies Seminar Series will serve IT and business executives seeking an unbiased source of education, insight and expertise in order to ensure the success of their mobile initiatives. This Series features a strategic management perspective presented by industry luminaries, independent analysts and experienced practitioners from world class organizations and will run concurrently with the eBusiness Integration Conference Series.

▌**3592**

MOBILE INTERNET SERVICES

MARCUS EVANS LTD.

303 E Wacker Dr.
Chicago, IL 60601
PH: (312)540-3000
E-mail: marketing@marcusevans.com
URL: http://www.marcusevansconferences.com
Contact: Greta Molepske, Marketing Manager

Description: Mobile Internet Services will explore fast moving new market, which is providing next generation services to the mobile user. By analyzing the whole value chain from infrastructure and application development through to content delivery, this forum will ensure that the latest services from the industry's leaders are assessed. Vital aspects such as generating revenue and key applications will be discussed in depth, providing a thorough and balanced view of the rapidly expanding Mobile Internet Services market. MIS aims to present a realistic, truthful and credible view of the emerging Mobile Internet Services opportunity and to provide a neutral global platform to translate and transform 3G technology and demand for new high-value services into expansive new revenue streams and customer satisfaction. MIS will bring together the leaders of the mobile Internet community to share new ideas and address the fundamental challenges to 3G Internet services deployment and new market creation at the highest level across Europe, Asia-Pacific and the US.

▌**3593**

MOBILE MESSAGING AND INTERNET APPLICATIONS

ADVANCED COMMUNICATION TECHNOLOGIES CONFERENCES

PO Box 14421
Springfield, MO 65814-0421
TF: 888-274-7720

737

E-mail: info@actconferences.com
URL: http://www.actconferences.com

Description: The Mobile Messaging and Internet Applications conference focuses on the latest mobile messaging technologies and internet applications on the market. The conference is targeted towards: Manufacturers (devices and infrastructure); Service Providers (paging/messaging, ISPs, telecom, etc.); Financial Services; Content and Applications Providers; E-Business Services; Consulting Firms; Government Organizations; Press/Media.

∎ 3594
MOBILE OFFICE
MEDIA SALON

6 bis, Rue des Cendriers
75020 Paris, France

Founded: 2001. **Frequency:** Annual. **Audience:** Enterprise end users, CEO and managers (sales, logistics, maintenance services,etc.). **Principle Exhibits:** Mobile services, such as information systems, computer engineering and maintenance companies, and Internet and telecommunications companies; mobile applications, such as software editors; and mobile tools, such as telephone telecommunications equipment manufacturers.

∎ 3595
MOBILE SCENE, MOBILE INTERNET EXHIBITION WITH SEMINARS
DOCUMENTA LOGISTICS CVBA/SCRL

Bld A Reyerslaan 80
B-1030 Brussels, Belgium
E-mail: info@tmab.be

Founded: 2001. **Frequency:** Annual. **Principle Exhibits:** Mobile internet exhibition. WAP, ASP, mobile auctions, SMS, mobile banking, content providers, WASP, mobile platforms, mobile protals, WXML, UMTS, and mobile media.

∎ 3596
MODERNER STAAT
REED EXHIBITION CO.

383 Main Ave.
Norwalk, CT 06851
PH: (203)840-5662
FX: (203)840-9662
E-mail: inquiry@reedexpo.com
URL: http://www.reedexpo.com

Description: MODERNER STAAT is a German event calling for more efficiency in public administration. The exhibition and the conference highlight the current innovations for public management. Some products and services offered are: e-Government solutions, IT-products, data warehousing, software, hardware and consultancy.

∎ 3597
NATIONAL INDUSTRIAL ENTERPRISE IT SHOW AND CONFERENCE
REED EXHIBITION CO.

383 Main Ave.
Norwalk, CT 06851
PH: (203)840-5662
FX: (203)840-9662
E-mail: inquiry@reedexpo.com
URL: http://www.reedexpo.com

Description: The National Industrial Enterprise IT Show is a fast growing show in National Manufacturing Week. It is a comprehensive annual forum for the display of industrial technology innovations and solutions for manufacturers in North America. The National Industrial Enterprise IT show is targetted for manufacturers looking to move to the next level of competitiveness.

∎ 3598
NETEXPO WASHINGTON
LINDSAY COMMUNICATIONS GROUP, INC.

2032 Virginia Ave.
McLean, VA 22101-4940
E-mail: Lindsay@Multicomexpo.com

Founded: 1997. **Frequency:** Annual. **Audience:** Buyers of e-business services. **Principle Exhibits:** Companies offering e-business products and services for the B2B marketplace.

∎ 3599
NET.FIN@NCE (WBR)
WORLDWIDE BUSINESS RESEARCH

420 Lexington Ave., Ste. 2533
New York, NY 10017
PH: (212)885-2720
FX: (212)885-2798
E-mail: adas@wbresearch.com
URL: http://www.wbresearch.com

Description: In a rapidly changing retail financial services market, where there are significant developments in multichannel distribution strategies, from multi-media messaging tools, to digital TV, alliances with portals, aggregation and e-mail dialogues, Net.Fin@nce will give the clarification needed. Although there are many undisputed success stories, not all CRM, integration and distributions strategies go to plan. Net.Fin@nce will provide hard facts and proven case studies from over 30 world-class financial institutions, helping to avoid the pitfalls that have damaged others and plot the path to success.

∎ 3600
NETSEC NETWORK SECURITY CONFERENCE
COMPUTER SECURITY INSTITUTE

600 Harrison St.
San Francisco, CA 94107
PH: (415)947-6320

FX: (415)947-6023
E-mail: csi@cmp.com
URL: http://www.gocsi.com

Description: The CSI NetSec network security conference is an event devoted exclusively to network security. NetSec will offer over 85 sessions on Internet/intranet, secure electronic commerce, VPNs, computer crime, denial of service attacks, forensic investigation, response teams, cryptography/PKI, intrusion detection, NT, privacy, policies, awareness, remote access and much more. The Exhibition will feature over 70 exhibitors of network security products. The conference is designed for information security managers, directors and staff, analysts, engineers, network and system adminstrators, CIOs, webmasters, and anyone involved in network security in their organization. Over 1500 network security professionals are expected to attend from around the world.

▌3601
NETSTORAGE AND SOLUTIONS CONFERENCE AND EXPO
INFOEX-WORLD SERVICES LTD.

202 GITIC Ctr.
28 Queens Rd. E
Hong Kong
PH: 852 2865 1118
FX: 852 2865 1129
E-mail: info@infoexws.com
URL: http://www.infoexevents.com
Contact: Peter Lee, Conference Manager

Description: NetStorage and Solutions Conference and Expo targets IT directors at leading banks, financial institutions, telecom operators, broadcasters, data centers, service providers, government departments, and enterprises who are seeking optimal ways to design, develop and enhance their storage network infrastructures. The conference, supported by an exposition, enables audiences to gain valuable knowledge and get ahead of the learning curve of networked technology through educational sessions and product demos.

▌3602
NETWORK PENETRATION PREVENTION TOOLS AND TECHNIQUES (ISACA)
INFORMATION SYSTEMS AUDIT AND CONTROL ASSOCIATION

3701 Algonquin Rd., Ste.1010
Rolling Meadows, IL 60008
PH: (847)253-1545
FX: (847)253-1443
E-mail: conference@isaca.org
URL: http://www.isaca.org

Description: This technical program is designed to demonstrate penetration tools and techniques currently available to discover security exposures found within networks such as those based on Novell NetWare, Windows NT and Windows 95. Areas covered include network entry, physical access to cable, password "grabbers" and trojan horses,

Ethernet packet capture and analysis and remote workstation operations.

▌3603
NETWORK SECURITY CONFERENCE (ISACA)
INFORMATION SYSTEMS AUDIT AND CONTROL ASSOCIATION

E-mail: conference@isaca.org
URL: http://www.isaca.org

Founded: 2000. **Description:** Information Systems Audit and Control Association (ISACA) Network Security Conference includes hard-hitting technical problems, their solutions and approaches to assess and mitigate risk. Whether it is learning about Internet attacks or how to respond to an incident, ISACA's Network Security Conference will address the issues with the time it takes to understand the topics. Network Security Conference is designed for experienced IS Security professionals to keep pace with the increasingly complex network environments; for experienced IS Audit professionals to gain detailed knowledge and competencies; and for IS Control professionals to participate in the debate and discussions on how to guard the organization's most valuable assets. Each conference session is presented initially at an intermediate level. The presenters will tailor the level of instruction to meet the needs of the attendees.

▌3604
NETWORKING DECISIONS
TECHTARGET

117 Kendrick St., Ste. 800
Needham, MA 02494
PH: (781)657-1000
TF: 888-274-4111
FX: (781)657-1100
E-mail: info@techtarget.com
URL: http://www.techtarget.com
Contact: Ken Berquist, Vice President of Conferences

Description: Networking Decisions is designed to not only tackle the most critical concerns with networking, it delivers a unique conference model. Promoters extensively surveyed hundreds of top networking professionals to deliver the exact solutions to the most important networking-specific challenges faced right now.

▌3605
NETWORKS TELECOMDENMARK
REED EXHIBITION CO.

383 Main Ave.
Norwalk, CT 06851
PH: (203)840-5662
FX: (203)840-9662
E-mail: inquiry@reedexpo.com
URL: http://www.reedexpo.com

Description: This conference is focused on computer networking, data, telecommunications, Internet and Intranet.

∎ 3606

NETWORKS THAI TELECOM - INDOCHINA'S ONLY ENTERPRISE NETWORKING TELECOM EVENT

CMP MEDIA (THAILAND) CO. LTD.

41 Lertpanya Bldg., Ste. 801
8th Fl., Soi Lertpanya
Kwaeng Thanon Phyathai
Khet Rajathewee
Bangkok 10400, Thailand
E-mail: info@cmpthailand.com

Founded: 1999. **Frequency:** Annual. **Audience:** Trade professionals and general public. **Principle Exhibits:** High speed networking, infrastructure, integration, Internet, network management, network software & services, support, multimedia & support, and WAN products & services.

∎ 3607

NETWORLDINTEROP

KEY3MEDIA GROUP

5700 Wilshire Blvd., Ste. 325
Los Angeles, CA 90036
PH: (323)954-6000
FX: (323)954-6010
E-mail: scott.dominguez@key3media.com
URL: http://www.key3media.com
Contact: Scott Dominguez, Show Manager

Description: The NetWorldInterop conference, exposition and industry event delivers educational forum and interactive business-to-business solutions for today's enterprise and Internet communities. It is a comprehensive gathering of networking, Internet, and telecommunications professionals from around the world.

∎ 3608

NEW JERSEY BUSINESS & TECHNOLOGY SHOW

FLAGG MANAGEMENT, INC.

353 Lexington Ave.
New York, NY 10016
E-mail: flaggmgmt@msn.com

Frequency: Annual. **Principle Exhibits:** Accounting and business systems and services, computer accounting systems, tax software, integrated accounting systems, Internet and e-accounting solutions, brokerage and investment advisory services, financial and business services, hardware, computer and business systems, and tax preparation, accounting, audit, and practice management software.

∎ 3609

NEW MEDIA MARKETING

REED EXHIBITION COMPANIES (UK) LTD.

Oriel House
26 The Quadrant
Richmond, Surrey TW91DL, England
E-mail: info@reedexpo.co.uk

Founded: 2000. **Frequency:** Annual. **Audience:** Marketers who use new media in their campaigns. **Principle Exhibits:** Marketing technologies, data, digital TV, e-business solutions, interactive design and development, biosks, internet, on-line marketing, rich media, search engine promotion, viral marketing, WAP, web design and development.

∎ 3610

NEW YORK CPA, BUSINESS & TECHNOLOGY SHOW & CONFERENCE

FLAGG MANAGEMENT, INC.

353 Lexington Ave.
New York, NY 10016
E-mail: flaggmgmt@msn.com
URL: http://www.wallstreet-tng.com

Founded: 1974. **Frequency:** Annual. **Audience:** CPAs, accounting professionals, corporation financial executives, tax preparers, financial planners & advisors, CPAs in industry, business & financial execs. **Principle Exhibits:** Accounting and business systems and services, computer accounting systems, tax software, integrated accounting systems, Internet and e-accounting solutions, brokerage and investment advisory services, financial and business services, hardware, computer and business systems, and tax preparation, accounting, audit, and practice management software.

∎ 3611

NEXT GENERATION TELECOMMUNICATIONS EXECUTIVE SUMMIT

FROST AND SULLIVAN

7550 W I 10, Ste. 400
San Antonio, TX 78229
PH: (210)247-2461
E-mail: cfsales@frost.com
URL: http://www.summits.frost.com
Contact: Lisa Lee, Event Planner

Description: This conference has become the definitive networking and information forum for ISPs, infrastructure providers, telecom companies, cable companies and end users with an interest in the next generation Internet. Panel sessions offer timely updates on the convergence of voice, video and data over the Internet. Tomorrow's business models, partnerships and technologies are discussed in detail. The industry's most influential CEOs will discuss the opportunities and threats, as well as proactive strategies, for integrating this market information into planning.

▌3612

NGN VENTURES
BUSINESS COMMUNICATIONS REVIEW

999 Oakmont Plz. Dr., Ste.100
Westmont, IL 60559-1381
PH: (630)986-1432
TF: 800-227-1234
FX: (630)323-5324
E-mail: info@bcr.com
URL: http://www.bcr.com
Contact: Jeff Bockweg, Conference Sales Manager

Description: NGN Ventures features areas for new network ventures, with penetrating sector analysis from co-chairmen Dr. John M. McQuillan and Dave Passmore, CEO presentations from more than 40 top networking startups, board level perspectives on each hot market from leading venture capitalists and industry experts, and a premier showcase of the most exciting new networking companies and products. This will all help an understanding of the future of networking, explain how venture investing is affecting the industry and which venture-backed startups are most likely to win.

▌3613

NORTH AMERICAN RESEARCH / TEACHING SYMPOSIUM ON PURCHASING AND SUPPLY CHAIN MANAGEMENT (ISM)
INSTITUTE FOR SUPPLY MANAGEMENT

PO Box 22160
Tempe, AZ 85285-2160
PH: (480)752-6276
TF: 800-888-6276
FX: (480)752-7890
URL: http://www.ism.ws

Founded: 1989. **Description:** North American Research/ Teaching Symposium on Purchasing and Supply Chain Management provides an innovative program focused on research and teaching innovations in the fields of purchasing, supply chain management, logistics, and materials management. Join distinguished colleagues from academia, research, and business in a stimulating program to explore current research findings, ongoing research, future trends, research methodologies, future research needs, innovative pedagogy, instructional techniques, and classroom material.

▌3614

NORTH EAST EBUSINESS IT AND TELECOMS SHOW
AMERICAN FACILITIES MANAGEMENT LTD

The Johnston House, Fairgreen Rd.
Markethill BT601PW, Ireland
PH: 44 28 3755 1920
FX: 44 28 3755 2539
E-mail: info@americanfm.co.uk
URL: http://www.americanfm.co.uk

Description: The Business IT and Telecomms Show with conference and seminar opportunities is a business to business event targeting IT professionals, business managers and directors of companies wishing to improve and develop their ICT systems or to gain knowledge on the latest industry products and services.

▌3615

NOVELL NETWARE: SECURITY, AUDIT AND CONTROL (ISACA)
INFORMATION SYSTEMS AUDIT AND CONTROL ASSOCIATION

3701 Algonquin Rd., Ste.1010
Rolling Meadows, IL 60008
PH: (847)253-1545
FX: (847)253-1443
E-mail: conference@isaca.org
URL: http://www.isaca.org

Description: This program reviews and evaluates controls in Local Area Network (LAN) security and internetworking environments through the comparison of basic NetWare 3.1X security control structures, specific implementation experiences and cautions with NetWare 4.0. Key control features are identified and critiqued through a demonstration of a working Novell NetWare system. Business risk is discussed and an audit program is developed to evaluate the productivity benefits and integrity of networked systems connected to a LAN.

▌3616

ONLINE LEARNING CONFERENCE AND EXPO
VNU BUSINESS MEDIA.

50 S 9th St.
Minneapolis, MN 55402
PH: (612)333-0471
TF: 800-328-4329
FX: (612)340-4759
E-mail: conferences@vnulearning.com
URL: http://www.vnulearning.com

Description: At the Online Learning Conference and Expo, resources are brought together with expertise and opportunities to accelerate the online learning curve. From the Expo hall and our Hands-on Learning Labs to in-depth breakout sessions and case studies, everything can be found to create, deliver and manage online learning in an organization.

▌3617

OPEN FOR BUSINESS
AITEC UK LTD

15 High St.
Graveley PE196PL, United Kingdom
PH: 44 14 8083 1300
FX: 44 14 8083 1131
E-mail: admin@aitec-africa.com
URL: http://www.aitecafrica.com

Contact: Sean Moroney, AITEC Group Chairman

Description: Open for Business is a computing, communications and office equipment exhibition.

■ **3618**

OPT-IN E-MAIL MARKETING STRATEGIES
WORLD RESEARCH GROUP

16 E 40th St., 5th Fl.
New York, NY 10016
PH: (212)869-7231
TF: 800-647-7600
FX: 800-717-3237
E-mail: info@worldrg.com
URL: http://www.worldrg.com

Description: Sponsored by TargitMail.com and @Brint.com, this event brings together a team of email marketing pioneers to provide attendees with strategies to either help launch or improve their existing email marketing programs. The event offers three workshops and case studies from more than 15 companies. Topics to be addressed include the evolution of email marketing, the impact that current privacy mandates are having on email marketers, security, and more.

■ **3619**

OPTICON
BUSINESS COMMUNICATIONS REVIEW

999 Oakmont Plz. Dr., Ste.100
Westmont, IL 60559-1381
PH: (630)986-1432
TF: 800-227-1234
FX: (630)323-5324
E-mail: info@bcr.com
URL: http://www.bcr.com
Contact: Jeff Bockweg, Conference Sales Manager

Description: Opticon is a leading event on intelligent optical networking. The conference program puts a heavy emphasis on informed and independent opinions from leading market analysts in order to put vendor perspectives into context. There is also emphasis on service provider case studies focusing on successful implementations of optical networking systems.

■ **3620**

OPTIMIZING DIMENSIONAL DATA WAREHOUSE DESIGN (DCI)
DIGITAL CONSULTING INSTITUTE

204 Andover St.
Andover, MA 01810
PH: (978)470-3880
URL: http://www.dci.com

Description: This seminar is the second of two covering dimensional data warehouse design in detail. This seminar addresses advanced issues involved in designing and implementing a dimensional data warehouse. Participants learn advanced dimensional data warehouse design techniques to handle the more difficult design problems. Attendees leave with the understanding of how different design choices affect both the usability and performance of their database design. The last day of the class focuses on the ETL processes necessary to support their designs.

■ **3621**

PARCEL LOGISTICS EXPO
ADVANSTAR COMMUNICATIONS INC.

One Phoenix Mill Ln., Ste. 401
Peterborough, NH 03458

Founded: 1997. **Frequency:** Annual. **Audience:** Trade only. **Principle Exhibits:** Shipping information and equipment for companies managing e-commerce web sites, fulfillment and delivery services.

■ **3622**

PCIA GLOBALXCHANGE
PERSONAL COMMUNICATIONS INDUSTRY ASSOCIATION

500 Montgomery St., Ste. 700
Alexandria, VA 22314-1561

Founded: 1949. **Frequency:** Annual. **Audience:** Wireless communications industry professionals. **Principle Exhibits:** Wireless internet, enhanced voice, wireless portals, wireless e-commerce, advanced data, third generation content.

■ **3623**

PENETRATING WINDOWS NT SERVER 4.0 (ISACA)
INFORMATION SYSTEMS AUDIT AND CONTROL ASSOCIATION

3701 Algonquin Rd., Ste.1010
Rolling Meadows, IL 60008
PH: (847)253-1545
FX: (847)253-1443
E-mail: conference@isaca.org
URL: http://www.isaca.org

Description: This one-day seminar provides an understanding of a number of methods that can be used to penetrate NT Server. The seminar will describe methods for obtaining user accounts lists, performing denial of service attacks and cracking NT passwords. Attendees will learn how to penetrate Windows desktop controls as well as NT Server, and gain access to NT from either source. Lastly, they will learn what can be done to prevent it (where possible).

■ **3624**

PHOTOSHOP CONFERENCE (FTP)
FAWCETTE TECHNICAL PUBLICATIONS, INC.

209 Hamilton Ave.
Palo Alto, CA 94301
PH: (650)833-7100

TF: 800-848-5523
E-mail: conferences@fawcette.com
URL: http://www.ftpconferences.com
Contact: James E. Fawcette, President

Founded: 1990. **Description:** The Photoshop Convention gives an inside look at how to maximize the features in the new version of Photoshop 7.0, and probe the depths of many of the long-time standard features. Features presenters that have been working with the latest version for several months. The convention is three days filled with workshops to teach new tool and palette controls, completely reworked brush engine, the pattern maker filter, enhanced web production tools, and accessing/manipulating files with File Browser.

∎ 3625
POCKET PC SUMMIT
MULTIMETEOR, INC.

7095 Hollywood Blvd., No.444
Hollywood, CA 90028
PH: (323)436-0169
TF: (818)994-7199
E-mail: inquiries@multimeteor.com
URL: http://www.pocketpcsummit.com
Contact: John Tidwell, CEO and Co-Founder

Founded: 2000. **Description:** The Pocket PC Summit provides users with real-world solutions for effectively deploying Pocket PC technology in any enterprise, network with the top entrepreneurs, visionaries, and trend-setters in the Pocket PC community, and return home armed with the tools and applications needed to start deploying learned solutions immediately. The conference is geared for the Pocket PC industry and community professionals and all those who wish to network with and target the Pocket PC community such as hardware manufacturers, software publishers, service providers, integrators, analysts and journalists.

∎ 3626
PROCURECON 2002 (WBR)
WORLDWIDE BUSINESS RESEARCH

420 Lexington Ave., Ste. 2533
New York, NY 10017
PH: (212)885-2720
FX: (212)885-2798
E-mail: adas@wbresearch.com
URL: http://www.wbresearch.com

Description: At PROCURECON speakers will cover 3 main areas in depth including strategic procurement challenges, supplier relationship management and collaboration, and e-procurement implementation. Some of the topics include financial benefits of a strategic sourcing function, challenges in developing a regional or global sourcing function, risks and investments in driving forward the e-transformation of regional procurement strategy, benchmarking supplier performance and much more.

∎ 3627
PROJECT LEADERSHIP CONFERENCE
IMARK COMMUNICATIONS

1 Apple Hill Dr., Ste. 301
Natick, MA 01760
PH: (508)647-8600
TF: 800-955-1226
FX: (508)647-0241
E-mail: dkorse@imark-com.com
URL: http://www.imark-com.com
Contact: David Korse, President and CEO

Description: The Project Leadership Conference (PLC) is the only independent summit dedicated to the IT executive who works in a project management based environment. The PLC will provide a unique opportunity for IT professionals to fully understand and utilize the principles, applications, and solutions of project management in an IT world, as well as create an innovative networking forum. IT Professionals will walk away from this event with the knowledge and know-how to establish an efficient project environment while producing better returns for their organization.

∎ 3628
PROVING GROUND FOR TAXONOMY AND INFORMATION ARCHITECTURE
DELPHI GROUP

10 Post Office Sq., 10th Fl., S
Boston, MA 02109-4603
PH: (617)247-1511
TF: 800-335-7440
FX: (617)247-4957
E-mail: client.services@delphigroup.com
URL: http://www.delphigroup.com

Description: This two day event puts business information strategists and their supporting teams on a fast track to the creation of a comprehensive information architecture. The workshop takes take a unique approach to developing the skills and support needed to design an information architecture and deploy a taxonomy in the most demanding environments. There will be sessions about Information Architecture and Taxonomy Design in an interactive fashion, from a faculty of advisors with experience in taxonomy development, strategic IT architecture deployments and pragmatic solutions. This workshop will be attended by a select group of teams intent on developing innovative solutions for classic information organization and access challenges.

∎ 3629
RETAIL SYSTEMS CONFERENCE AND EXPOSITION
MOONWATCH MEDIA INC.

77 Oak St., Ste. 201
Newton Upper Falls, MA 02464
PH: (617)527-4626
FX: (617)527-8102
E-mail: info@moonwatchmedia.com
URL: http://www.retailsystems.com

Founded: 1990. **Description:** The Retail Systems Conference and Exposition will feature topics that discuss how to: upgrade an entire enterprise, leverage key Web and networking tools, enhance trading with CPFR processes, and improve product demand forecasting.

■ **3630**

RETAIL TECHNOLOGY SUMMIT

MOONWATCH MEDIA INC.

77 Oak St., Ste. 201
Newton Upper Falls, MA 02464
PH: (617)527-4626
FX: (617)527-8102
E-mail: info@moonwatchmedia.com
URL: http://www.retailsystems.com

Description: The Retail Technology Summit is designed to introduce the industry executives the most up to date information on such topics as: approaches to the advanced distribution system of both domestic and foreign markets, intercorporate collaborative vision, and standardization of advanced technology, in the form of lectures by the celebrated opinion leaders and specialists.The latest device / systems through demonstrations by IT-related companines will be demonstrated.

■ **3631**

RICHMOND COMPUTER AND TECHNOLOGY SHOWCASE/INTERNET EXPO

EVENT MANAGEMENT SERVICES

5200 SW Macadam Ave., Ste. 300
Portland, OR 97201
TF: 800-422-0251
FX: (503)234-4253
URL: http://www.techshows.com

Description: The Computer and Technology Showcase acts as a forum for the IT industry in over 18 cities nationwide. This event encompasses a variety of opportunities to put a company in front of 3,000 to 5,000 corporate decision makers on average per market. It also hosts the CIO Summit, which gathers key individuals together in one place at one time. Numerous associations and groups are involved in the Computer and Technology Showcase.

■ **3632**

SAPPHIRE

SAP AMERICA INC.

3999 W Chester Pike
Newtown Square, PA 19073
PH: (610)661-3200
FX: (610)661-4020
URL: http://www.sap.com

Founded: 1972. **Staff:** 27800. **Description:** Each year SAP offers several key opportunities for current and future customers, as well as partners, consultants, and users, to learn about SAP solutions. SAPPHIRE is the flagship SAP event

for customers and partners provides a showcase for the latest e-business strategies and information about new SAP solutions. SAPPHIRE focuses on the needs of decision makers from companies of all sizes. The event is held in Europe, Asia, and the Americas.

■ **3633**

SAUDI INTERNET WORLD

RIYADH EXHIBITIONS CO. LTD.

PO Box 56010
Riyadh 11554, Saudi Arabia
E-mail: Info@recexpo.com

Founded: 2001. **Frequency:** Annual. **Principle Exhibits:** International internet products and internet service providers exhibition.

■ **3634**

SEARCH ENGINE STRATEGIES 2002

INT MEDIA GROUP

23 Old Kings Hwy. S
Darien, CT 06820
PH: (203)662-2800
TF: (203)655-4686
E-mail: cobrienats@internet.com
URL: http://www.intmediaevents.com

Description: Search Engine Strategies 2002 features two days of presentations and panel discussions that cover all aspects of search engine-related promotion. Teaches business professionals how search engines interact with their Web site and ways to improve listings.

■ **3635**

THE SEARCHSAP.COM CONFERENCE

TECHTARGET

117 Kendrick St., Ste. 800
Needham, MA 02494
PH: (781)657-1000
TF: 888-274-4111
FX: (781)657-1100
E-mail: info@techtarget.com
URL: http://www.techtarget.com
Contact: Ken Berquist, Vice President of Conferences

Description: The SearchSAP.com Conference is designed for administrators and managers who tackle SAP's toughest implementation and customization challenges. Attendee sessions focus on decision-making and strategic planning, as well as implementing and managing large-scale SAP installations. Topics covered include security, Workflow, application development, CRM, business intelligence, application integration, BAPI's, management, strategy decisions, mobility and more.

▌3636

SECURE E-BIZ EXECUTIVE SUMMIT (ICH)
INTEROPERABILITY CLEARINGHOUSE

904 Clifton Dr.
Alexandria, VA 22308
PH: (703)768-0400
E-mail: cameron@ichnet.org
URL: http://www.ichnet.org

Description: Architectures and Infrastructures for Secure E-Biz is a summit for IT leaders, CEO's, CIO's and CTO's from industry and government. It features over 25 interlocking sessions that addresses the critical success factors for assuring implementation success. Three parallel tracks will be targeted as a mission for the summit: CIO Strategies for Information Defense, Advances in Enterprise Architectures, and Secure E-Business Workshops.

▌3637

SECURING YOUR ENTERPRISE'S E-COMMERCE AND M-COMMERCE (DCI)
DIGITAL CONSULTING INSTITUTE

204 Andover St.
Andover, MA 01810
PH: (978)470-3880
URL: http://www.dci.com

Description: The perfect complement to Building and Managing Enterprise Security Infrastructures, this seminar focuses on securing an enterprise's e-Commerce-related operations. Over the two-day course, attendees will analyze a number of typical e-Commerce application architectures and learn how to augment security infrastructure by securing all application architecture components. These components include clients, Web, application and data servers and the channels connecting them, as well as the transactions carried out over them. This seminar will focus a great deal on m-Commerce as well as e-Commerce, including security challenges and solutions for location-based wireless Internet services.

▌3638

SECURITY DECISIONS
TECHTARGET

117 Kendrick St., Ste. 800
Needham, MA 02494
PH: (781)657-1000
TF: 888-274-4111
FX: (781)657-1100
E-mail: info@techtarget.com
URL: http://www.techtarget.com
Contact: Ken Berquist, Vice President of Conferences

Description: This conference is designed for high-level IT managers who need to keep critical data secure and protected from disaster or malice. Conference topics include security best practices, policy development and implementation, infrastructure strategies, virus maneuvers and education, disaster recovery, incident response, safeguarding e-commerce, and more.

▌3639

SECURITY FORUM - IT SECURITY FOR THE ENTERPRISE
TECHNOLOGY MANAGERS FORUM

160 Riverside Dr., Ste. 4E
New York, NY 10024
PH: (212)787-1122
FX: (212)580-1976
E-mail: info@techforum.com
URL: http://www.techforum.com

Description: Security Forum speakers will feature IT managers from companies such as Prudential, JP Morgan Chase, Citigroup, Morgan Stanley, Pfizer, United Parcel Service, and other Fortune 1000 companies. Security managers and industry insiders will provide an in-depth look at security metrics and present examples and case studies to show how corporations are valuing data and measuring the effectiveness of their security practices; explore how organizations are developing a secure infrastructure for e-business transactions; and discuss how business managers, data architects, developers, infrastructure people and data center groups are collaborating to create effective IT security for their companies.

▌3640

SECURITY TECH UPDATE
IDG JAPAN INC.

3-4-5 Hongo Bunkyo-ku
Tokyo 113-0033, Japan
PH: 03 5800 3111
URL: http://www.idg.co.jp

Description: Security Tech Update has topics that relate to E-Commerce, Network Security, Firewalls, Virus Protection, and Digital Certificates.

▌3641

SELECTING THE BEST ENTERPRISE RESOURCE PLANNING APPLICATION
GARTNER INC.

56 Top Gallant Rd.
Stamford, CT 06904
PH: (203)316-1111
FX: (203)324-7901
URL: http://www.gartner.com

Description: Selecting the Best Enterprise Resource Planning (ERP) Application focuses on these main questions: How should project teams structure their ERP selection methodology, and ensure that their organization's mandatory strategic as well as tactical requirements are met, and how should users' functional and technical requirements be defined and expressed in an evaluation.

▌3642

SEMI-ANNUAL CONFERENCE AND EXHIBITION (ASCENT)

745

THE ASSOCIATION OF COMMUNICATIONS
ENTERPRISES

1401 K St. NW, Ste. 600
Washington, DC 20005
PH: (202)835-9898
FX: (202)835-9893
E-mail: Conferences@ascent.org
URL: http://www.ascent.org

Founded: 1997. **Description:** ASCENT conferences are
known throughout the industry as the place where business
gets done and new partnerships are formed. Learn from
communications experts about ways to improve a business
plan. Explore new revenue opportunities. Discover innovative technologies from more than 100 exhibitors.

▌ 3643

SEYBOLD SEMINARS

KEY3MEDIA GROUP

5700 Wilshire Blvd., Ste. 325
Los Angeles, CA 90036
PH: (323)954-6000
FX: (323)954-6010
E-mail: jeff.bockweg@key3media.com
URL: http://www.key3media.com
Contact: Jeff Bockweg, Conference Sales Manager

Description: The Conference Sales Manager is an information and education provider for the Web/Internet and print
publishing marketplace. They help publishing professionals
make the right strategic and tactical publishing technology
purchase decisions.

▌ 3644

SM CONFERENCE (SOFTWARE
MANAGEMENT)

SOFTWARE QUALITY ENGINEERING

330 Corporate Way, Ste. 300
Orange Park, FL 32073
PH: (904)278-0707
TF: 800-423-8378
FX: (904)278-4380
E-mail: sqeinfo@sqe.com
URL: http://www.sqe.com

Description: The SM (Software Management) Conference
is the first software conference to bring together all of the
management components that drive successful software development, delivery, and support. The SM Conference provides concrete management techniques and practices for
each area of software management. The SM conference is
an annual event covering the breadth of software management and features international experts, in-depth tutorials,
presentations, and the Management EXPO. SM Conference
topics include: Configuration Management Techniques, Policies and Standards, Improving Team Productivity, Requirements Management, Building Effective Teams, Risk Analysis and Management, Test Management, Managing Software
Quality, and Managing Outsourcing.

▌ 3645

SODEC:SOFTWARE DEVELOPMENT EXPO
AND CONFERENCE

REED EXHIBITION CO.

383 Main Ave.
Norwalk, CT 06851
PH: (203)840-5662
FX: (203)840-9662
E-mail: inquiry@reedexpo.com
URL: http://www.reedexpo.com

Description: Software Development Expo and Conference
in Tokyo (SODEC) offers 3 specialized zones. Specifically
they are: Outsourcing and Consulting Zone; Form Designing
Tools and Electrical Form System Zone; Project Management Tools Zone. SODEC is designed for professionals
that are System engineers, system development engineers,
manufacturing engineers, advanced programmers, and managers of information systems and business development/
planning section.

▌ 3646

SOFTWARE DEVELOPMENT CONFERENCE
AND EXPO

CMP MEDIA INC.

12 W 21st St.
New York, NY 10010
TF: 888-428-3976
FX: (917)305-3341
E-mail: info@cmpevents.com
URL: http://www.cmp.com

Founded: 1988. **Description:** The Software Development
Conference and Expo provides the place where the best and
brightest gather to learn about the next big thing. Whether
it is C, OOP, Java, COM, UML, XML or Web Services, SD
has been there providing professional software development
teams high quality content, delivered by the industry's leading experts. SD brings together all the major players in the
software development community in support of language
neutral, platform neutral, adaptive applications delivered
over a programmable, transactional web. The curriculum
combines the best of the traditional and next-generation
development. All of the educational tracks expected from
SD including C, JAVA, COM, XML, C, Web Services and
Project/Process management will be discussed.

▌ 3647

SOFTWARE TEST AUTOMATION
CONFERENCE

SOFTWARE QUALITY ENGINEERING

330 Corporate Way, Ste. 300
Orange Park, FL 32073
PH: (904)278-0707
TF: 800-423-8378
FX: (904)278-4380
E-mail: sqeinfo@sqe.com
URL: http://www.sqe.com

Description: The Software Test Automation Conference will address issues and needs concerning testing and provides viable and practical solutions for the most critical software test automation problems. The Software Test Automation Conference features best practices in Web testing, how to ensure reliability on the Internet, the latest in testing tools and support, outsourcing test automation implementation projects and ongoing automated test activities, and methods and processes that work best in Web time.

∎ 3648

SOFTWORLD ACCOUNTING AND FINANCE

IMARK COMMUNICATIONS

1 Apple Hill Dr., Ste. 301
Natick, MA 01760
PH: (508)647-8600
FX: (508)647-0241
E-mail: sdombrosky@imark-com.com
URL: http://www.softworld.com
Contact: David Korse, President and Chief Executive Officer

Description: Features leading accounting and finance software vendors all under one roof in one day. Offers educational sessions, free consulting, networking, and product demonstrations. Provides the opportunitio to buy or just gather information, helping to condense months of research into a single day.

∎ 3649

SOFTWORLD EVOLVING SUPPLY CHAIR SOLUTIONS

SOFTWORLD/IMARK COMMUNICATIONS

One Apple Hill Dt., Ste. 301
Natick, MA 01760

Founded: 1991. **Frequency:** Annual. **Audience:** Executives, financial managers and IT professionals with involvement in the purchase of software and or application solutions in large companies. **Principle Exhibits:** Logistics and distribution; warehouse management; internet applications for eCommerce; MRPII/ERP; supply chain management; advance planning and scheduling; manufacturing execution systems; sales force automation; electronic data interchange. Procurement, fulfillment scm.

∎ 3650

SOURCING APPLICATIONS: THE SHIFTING SHAPE OF APPLICATION DEVELOPMENT

GARTNER INC.

56 Top Gallant Rd.
Stamford, CT 06904
PH: (203)316-1111
FX: (203)324-7901
URL: http://www.gartner.com

Description: The Shifting Shape of Application Development (AD) focuses on the following key topics: How can AD organizations that are relying on hosted services be sure to meet their enterprise responsibilities, how can enterprises effectively use application service providers, and how can AD organizations use Web resource exchanges and knowledge communities for staff augmentation, training and information.

∎ 3651

SOUTH CHINA INFORMATION AND NETWORK SECURITY CONFERENCE

INFOEX-WORLD SERVICES LTD.

202 GITIC Ctr.
28 Queens Rd. E
Hong Kong
PH: 852 2865 1118
FX: 852 2865 1129
E-mail: info@infoexws.com
URL: http://www.infoexevents.com
Contact: Peter Lee, Conference Manager

Description: The South China Information and Network Security Conference (IT SECURITY) brings together domestic and global industry, research and government experts in information systems security and technology. Facilitates debate, dialogue, and action on the latest major information systems security issues. Provides a rich educational experience and business networking opportunity to IT and IT security communities on major information systems security issues and solutions. Promotes demand for and investment in information systems security products, solutions, and research. Challenges the IT community to provide solutions, research, and applied technology that are usable, interoperable, scalable, and affordable.

∎ 3652

THE SPECTRUM 2002 CONFERENCE: USING TECHNOLOGY TO BETTER YOUR BOTTOM LINE

IDEALLIANCE

100 Daingerfield Rd.
Alexandria, VA 22314
PH: (703)837-1070
FX: (703)837-1072
E-mail: info@idealliance.org
URL: http://www.xmlconference.org/xmlusa/

Description: The annual five-day SPECTRUM Conference provides a forum for the spectrum of segments in the graphic arts community-advertising, creative, prepress, printing, publishing and manufacturing-to improve workflow, production and management. The purpose of this conference is to position a viewpoint to improve the through-line-of-action across all the participants. Over its 25-year history, Spectrum has become an agenda-setting meeting for the industry in print production, process control, color management, digital printing, electronic data interchange and e-commerce. Participants in this hard-hitting program receive the latest and evolving information and trends on changing business practices, methods to apply new technologies to day-to-day operations, and processes to improve production and communications.

■ 3653

SQL SERVER MAGAZINE LIVE

TECH CONFERENCES, INC.

731 Main St., Ste. D-3
Monroe, CT 06468
PH: (203)268-3204
TF: 800-438-6720
FX: (203)261-3884
E-mail: devcon@devconnections.com
URL: http://www.devconnections.com

Description: SQL Server Magazine LIVE is a conference where there'll be real-world experts speaking on data warehousing and business intelligence, development, administration, and a variety of other topics. Relevant information will be given that can be put to use immediately when at home. There will be sessions by Microsoft and leading third-party developers and gurus.

■ 3654

SQL2THEMAX (FTP)

FAWCETTE TECHNICAL PUBLICATIONS, INC.

209 Hamilton Ave.
Palo Alto, CA 94301
PH: (650)833-7100
TF: 800-848-5523
E-mail: conferences@fawcette.com
URL: http://www.ftpconferences.com
Contact: James E. Fawcette, President

Founded: 1990. **Description:** SQL2TheMax is an event empowering developers, systems analysts, and IT managers working with enterprise-level, intranet-enabled applications. From performance tuning to XML and e-commerce, from ASP to hardware architectures for delivering 24x7 high-capacity service, SQL2TheMax provides the information to help build current and future solutions.

■ 3655

SSPA HORIZONS WORLD CONFERENCE

SERVICE AND SUPPORT PROFESSIONALS
ASSOCIATION

11031 Via Frontera, Ste. A
San Diego, CA 92127
PH: (858)674-5491
FX: (858)674-6794
E-mail: info@supportgate.com
URL: http://www.supportgate.com
Contact: Ron Johnson

Description: SSPA Horizons World Conference is specifically designed as a forum where industry executives can explore and discuss the critical issues facing support services into the 21st century. SSPA's Horizons World Conference

will provide attendees with the information needed to both anticipate and prepare for the future of customer service. The conference is set in a relaxed, casual environment with presentations, discussion sessions, leisure activity, and dinner featuring the SSPA STAR Award winners.

■ 3656

STAR (SOFTWARE TESTING ANALYSIS AND REVIEW) CONFERENCE

SOFTWARE QUALITY ENGINEERING

330 Corporate Way, Ste. 300
Orange Park, FL 32073
PH: (904)278-0707
TF: 800-423-8378
FX: (904)278-4380
E-mail: sqeinfo@sqe.com
URL: http://www.sqe.com

Description: STAR is a gathering place for software testers, developers, and managers to interact and learn how to improve software-testing practices. STAR's approach delivers the latest testing advances and strategies being used by leading software organizations. STAR conferences feature international testing experts in featured sessions, concurrent sessions on testing related topics, in-depth tutorials, and the Testing EXPO with the latest testing tools and services.

■ 3657

STORAGE DECISIONS

TECHTARGET

117 Kendrick St., Ste. 800
Needham, MA 02494
PH: (781)657-1000
TF: 888-274-4111
FX: (781)657-1100
E-mail: info@techtarget.com
URL: http://www.techtarget.com
Contact: Ken Berquist, Vice President of Conferences

Description: Storage Management is the only storage event that is produced by a major information provider that is exclusively focused on storage management. This invitation-only event brings top storage professionals together with experts, analysts and vendors who can help make sense of the information overload dominating the space right now. Attendee sessions focus on the day-to-day storage management challenges blended with strategic planning, as well as implementing, managing and maintaining large-scale storage installations.

■ 3658

STORAGE NETWORKING DETAIL/TOKYO

IDG JAPAN INC.

3-4-5 Hongo Bunkyo-ku
Tokyo 113-0033, Japan
PH: 03 5800 3111
URL: http://www.idg.co.jp

Description: This conference and expo will tackle key issues and feature case studies on such topics as the latest storage networking technologies and its future, storage outsourcing, SAN interoperability, managing storage and server assets, the role of storage systems within the Internet infrastructure and integrating diverse environments, and storage network implementation.

▌3659

STRATEGIC INTRANET PLANNING DEVELOPMENT

INTERNATIONAL QUALITY AND PRODUCTIVITY CENTER

PO Box 401
150 Clove Rd.
Little Falls, NJ 07424
PH: (973)256-0211
TF: 800-882-8684
E-mail: registration@iqpc.com.au
URL: http://www.iqpc.com
Contact: Todd Smith, Sales Manager, Sponsorship and Exhibits

Description: Hear what the key players in corporate communications, HR, information and knowledge management are doing to transform their enterprise intranets into a powerful communication tool. By benchmarking intranet strategy against 15 of the best the attendee will learn how to gain maximum business benefit from the intranet by identifying cost savings and increasing efficiencies, plan strategically to rein in diverse intranets and information from a group and corporate perspective, structure and organzie the intranet to foster collaboration and enhance knowledge sharing, successfully manage intranet development and processes, enhance content to keep the intranet alive, active and relevant, and explore the value of the intranet from the perspectives of HR, communications and knowledge management.

▌3660

STRATEGIC PLANNING FOR KNOWLEDGE MANAGEMENT

INTERNATIONAL QUALITY AND PRODUCTIVITY CENTER

PO Box 401
150 Clove Rd.
Little Falls, NJ 07424
PH: (973)256-0211
TF: 800-882-8684
E-mail: info@iqpc-canada.com
URL: http://www.iqpc.com
Contact: Todd Smith, Sales Manager, Sponsorship and Exhibits

Description: IQPC includes some of knowledge management's best experts to share their experiences in harnessing people's knowledge to gain competitive advantage and drive their bottom line. This conference is not about knowledge management theory, it's about practice. This four-day conference agenda reflects practical, in-the-trenches examples from knowledge management experts.

▌3661

STRATEGIES AND TOOLS FOR SUCCESSFUL DATA WAREHOUSES (DCI)

DIGITAL CONSULTING INSTITUTE

204 Andover St.
Andover, MA 01810
PH: (978)470-3880
URL: http://www.dci.com

Description: The seminar is designed to provide attendees with the objective information, practical demonstrations, exercises, and advice needed to build a data warehouse for an organization. It explains the different strategies, architectures, and tools that are available, and shows how to select a mix of products to meet specific data warehousing requirements.

▌3662

STREAMING MEDIA

IDG JAPAN INC.

3-4-5 Hongo Bunkyo-ku
Tokyo 113-0033, Japan
PH: 03 5800 3111
E-mail: mokamoto@idg.co.jp
URL: http://www.idg.co.jp

Description: This Internet audio and video event is a broadband content marketplace among broadband content providers, users, creators and distributors. The event also provides a place for participants to meet and discuss strategies, develop alliances and exchange ideas.

▌3663

THE SUMMIT ON STORAGE MANAGEMENT (DCI)

DIGITAL CONSULTING INSTITUTE

204 Andover St.
Andover, MA 01810
PH: (978)470-3880
URL: http://www.dci.com

Description: Storage management is the management of storage assets with an eye towards maximizing applications availability, service level, speed and flexibility. Data storage is increasingly being recognized as the key to effectively and efficiently supporting enterprise IT applications. Driven by the growth of e-Commerce, globalization and users' expectation of zero latency, the need to intelligently manage access to, and storage of, data is becoming mission-critical. At the same time, sound storage and back-up strategies are essential to a business continuity plan.

▌3664

SUMMIT ON WEB SERVICES (DCI)

DIGITAL CONSULTING INSTITUTE

204 Andover St.
Andover, MA 01810
PH: (978)470-3880

URL: http://www.dci.com

Description: The Summit on Web Services will provide IT executives with a broad range of unbiased and practical information, enabling them to leverage this technology for a competitive advantage. These decision-makers will have the opportunity to visit the solution providers and key platform vendors rolling out Web services architectures. In addition, attendees absolutely value the unique and valuable access they have to META experts on-site.

▌ 3665

SUMMIT ON WIRELESS COMPUTING
(DCI)
DIGITAL CONSULTING INSTITUTE
204 Andover St.
Andover, MA 01810
PH: (978)470-3880
URL: http://www.dci.com

Description: The program will be designed to give step-by-step techniques, supported by case studies, for implementing and integrating mobile applications in your organization. Topics covered are choosing an infrastructure platform, data integrity and synchronization solutions, developing mobile applications: tools, servers and databases, integrating mobile applications and processes with existing systems, choosing and managing portable devices, and securing data.

▌ 3666

THE SUPER SHOW
COMMUNICATIONS AND SHOW MANAGEMENT, INC.
1450 NE 123rd St.
North Miami, FL 33161
E-mail: Supershow@aol.com

Founded: 1986. **Frequency:** Annual. **Audience:** Retailers, distributors, wholesalers, importers/exporters and other buyers of sports related products. **Principle Exhibits:** Sports equipment, apparel, footwear, accessories, and e-commerce products and services.

▌ 3667

SUPERCOMM
TELECOMMUNICATIONS INDUSTRY ASSOCIATION
2500 Wilson Blvd., Ste. 300
Arlington, VA 22201
PH: (703)907-7700
FX: (703)907-7727
E-mail: tia@tia.eia.org
URL: http://www.tiaonline.org

Founded: 1988. **Description:** SUPERCOMM features more than 800 exhibitors, nearly 200 educational sessions and thousands of communications professionals from around the world. SUPERCOMM curriculum provides a concentrated dose of information on key topics and industry segments,

helping experts understand the current issues and anticipate future trends in business.

▌ 3668

SUPPLIER RELATIONSHIP MANAGEMENT
MARCUS EVANS LTD.
303 E Wacker Dr.
Chicago, IL 60601
PH: (312)540-3000
E-mail: LisaR@marcusevansch.com
URL: http://www.brandslam-summit.com
Contact: Greta Molepske, Marketing Manager

Description: This international flagship event will examine the very latest trends within Supplier Relationship Management by presenting the best success stories in the industry of today.

▌ 3669

SUPPLY CHAIN AND LOGISTICS CONFERENCE AND EXHIBITION
PENTON MEDIA, INC.
1300 E 9th St.
Cleveland, OH 44114-1503
FX: (216)696-1267
URL: http://www.penton.com
Contact: Joe Jackson

Description: SCL hosts a high-level conference that will give ideas and information on how to create a smooth flow of products, services and data throughout the supply chain, from suppliers, through the organization, and ultimately to customers. This event gives knowledge, network and solutions you needed. This conference will feature approximately 30 sessions and will feature speakers and break-out sessions in a variety of formats conducted by both users and vendors. Conference topics include e-Commerce Strategies, e-Procurement, Transportation Management Systems, Customer Relationship Management, Warehouse Management Systems, and much more.

▌ 3670

SUPPLY NETWORK CONFERENCE (ISM)
INSTITUTE FOR SUPPLY MANAGEMENT
PO Box 22160
Tempe, AZ 85285-2160
PH: (480)752-6276
TF: 800-888-6276
FX: (480)752-7890
URL: http://www.ism.ws

Founded: 2002. **Description:** Today's economy is putting tremendous pressure on companies to better manage their supply networks. In turn, companies are placing a heavier burden on managers to help launch supply network initiatives that focus on the global customer, take advantage of new opportunities, bolster the bottom line, and improve cost efficiencies in existing operations. These efforts require solid strategies, clear prioritization, the understanding and buy-in from internal business units as well as strategic partners, and the right infrastructure and resources in place to support it all. Executives in procurement, supply chain, manufacturing, operations, and engineering management roles need to create an environment and fashion the partnerships and processes to make this happen. The Supply Network Conference is the premier conference addressing all of these issues. Gain powerful insights from trusted people: peers at leading companies in the electronics industry, financial and market research community, and academia.

▌3671

SUPPORT SERVICES CONFERENCE AND EXPO

KEY3MEDIA GROUP

5700 Wilshire Blvd., Ste. 325
Los Angeles, CA 90036
PH: (323)954-6000
FX: (323)954-6010
E-mail: mike.moreno@key3media.com
URL: http://www.key3media.com
Contact: Mike Moreno, General Manager

Description: The Support Services Conference features the industry's leading presenters and thinkers, covering issues and challenges from e-support to benchmarking to the newest technologies. In addition to valuable conference sessions, there are a dozen full-day workshops to choose from, as well as Help Desk Certification courses, provocative keynotes and a State of the Industry panel.

▌3672

SYBASE TECHWAVE USER TRAINING AND SOLUTIONS CONFERENCE

SYBASE

5000 Hacienda Dr.
Dublin, CA 94568
PH: (925)236-5000
TF: 800-879-2274
URL: http://www.sybase.com
Contact: Ric Rogers

Description: At the Sybase TechWave User Training and Solutions Conference, get product training and network with others facing the same challenges. In an intense four days, Sybase Tec Wave will deliver a technical learning experience including: accelerated Sybase Education training courses, technical sessions, on-site free technical support, attendee-only product discounts and trial software offers, on-site Professional Certification testing, and networking opportunities and contact with Sybase executives and technical staff.

▌3673

SYMPOSIUM/ITXPO

GARTNER INC.

56 Top Gallant Rd.
Stamford, CT 06904
PH: (203)316-1111
FX: (203)324-7901

URL: http://www.gartner.com

Description: Symposium/Itxpo is an opportunity to tap the vein of intelligence and advice. Calibrated for senior IT executives, Symposium/ITxpo is rich in content - both analyst-led strategy sessions focus on the most pressing issues. Itxpo is an interactive exhibit floor loaded with the latest technology solutions. Backed by Gartner research, over 180 sessions cover highly pertinent categories including revenue preservation, security and privacy, Web services, wireless infrastructure, CRM, strategic sourcing, and more.

▌3674

SYSTEMS FORUM

LOMA

2300 Windy Ridge Pky., Ste. 600
Atlanta, GA 30339-8443
PH: (770)951-1770
TF: 800-275-5662
FX: (770)984-0441
E-mail: meetings@loma.org
URL: http://www.loma.org

Description: At the Systems Forum, important tech topics will be covered such as security, e-business, project management, software solutions, and much more.

▌3675

TECHED

SAP AMERICA INC.

3999 W Chester Pike
Newtown Square, PA 19073
PH: (610)661-3200
FX: (610)661-4020
URL: http://www.sap.com

Founded: 1972. **Staff:** 27800. **Description:** SAP TechEd is a highly regarded technical conference. This concentrated learning experience gives the full story on the power and flexibility of the mySAP.com e-business platform. SAP TechEd is an opportunity for to gain useful, practical knowledge about the technology behind SAP's solutions. From installation and configuration to open integration and security. From new software releases and system optimization to XML-based messaging. SAP TechEd delivers valuable information that users can really use on the job.

▌3676

TECHNOFED

KEY3MEDIA GROUP

5700 Wilshire Blvd., Ste. 325
Los Angeles, CA 90036
PH: (323)954-6000
FX: (323)954-6010
E-mail: jeff.bockweg@key3media.com
URL: http://www.key3media.com
Contact: Jeff Bockweg, Conference Sales Manager

Description: This is a one day event that was developed in partnership with Quebec Regional Council and the organizers of Technology in Government Week to recognize and celebrate the special challenges and achievements of federal public service employees in implementing IT enables service delivery projects in the Quebec Region.

■ **3677**

TECHNOLOGY IN GOVERNMENT WEEK

KEY3MEDIA GROUP

5700 Wilshire Blvd., Ste. 325
Los Angeles, CA 90036
PH: (323)954-6000
FX: (323)954-6010
E-mail: jeff.bockweg@key3media.com
URL: http://www.key3media.com
Contact: Jeff Bockweg, Conference Sales Manager

Description: Technology in Government Week is a forum focused on managing information and technology to improve government programs and operations.

■ **3678**

TECHVIBES VANCOUVER

TECHVIBES MEDIA INC.

1008 Cambie, Ste. 300
Vancouver, BC, Canada V6B6J7
PH: (604)562-5667
E-mail: info@techvibes.com
URL: http://www.techvibes.com/
Contact: Lindsay Smith, Chief Executive Officer

Description: Monthly networking event for Vancouver tech-professionals. Features digital presentations, elevator pitch contests, prizes, tech-toys and more.

■ **3679**

TECHXNY / PC EXPO

CMP MEDIA INC.

12 W 21st St.
New York, NY 10010
TF: 888-428-3976
FX: (917)305-3341
E-mail: info@cmpevents.com
URL: http://www.cmp.com
Contact: Christina Condos, Show Director

Founded: 1982. **Description:** At the TECHXNY / PC EXPO attendees will get a full week of business and technology expositions, conferences, seminars, and tutorials. PC EXPO is a full-service trade show where IT professionals from small and medium-sized businesses and large enterprises experience the technologies that drive growth and efficiency. TECHXNY emphasizes education whether in its guided show-floor tours, keynotes, or rich conference programs.

■ **3680**

TELECOM CITY

DOCUMENTA LOGISTICS CVBA/SCRL

Bld A Reyerslaan 80
B-1030 Brussels, Belgium
E-mail: info@tmab.be

Founded: 1982. **Frequency:** Annual. **Principle Exhibits:** Telecom and Internet equipment, supplies, and services.

■ **3681**

TOTALSUPPLYCHAINONLINE CONFERENCE AND EXPO

PENTON MEDIA, INC.

1300 E 9th St.
Cleveland, OH 44114-1503
FX: (216)696-1267
E-mail: dturbide@penton.com
URL: http://www.penton.com
Contact: Debby Turbide, Director of Business Development

Description: The TOTALsupplychainONLINE Conference and Expo provides Internet-based professional development opportunities. The quarterly Internet event consists of a program of regularly scheduled, one-hour online presentations combined with valuable resource information found in TSC EXPO, the exclusive exhibitor section of TOTALsupplychainSOURCE, Penton's Supply Chain Online Buyers Guide. All that is needed is a computer, an Internet connection and a telephone. The sessions will make use of Internet video and conferencing technology, combined with teleconferencing, to create a strong visual presentation with audio, polling, messaging, chats, etc. The TOTALsupplychainONLINE Conferences will provide a diverse collection of information on five vital areas of the supply chain.

■ **3682**

TRADETECH (WBR)

WORLDWIDE BUSINESS RESEARCH

420 Lexington Ave., Ste. 2533
New York, NY 10017
PH: (212)885-2720
FX: (212)885-2798
E-mail: adas@wbresearch.com
URL: http://www.wbresearch.com

Description: TradeTech is an event which explores the dynamic world of electronic trading and connectivity, and exits the other end with a fresh, focused and dynamic approach to the automated trading challenge. TradeTech2002 provides an unrivalled platform for learning with a speaker faculty delivering over 25 up-to-the-minute, need to know case studies.

■ **3683**

TRAINING INSTITUTE

DELPHI GROUP

10 Post Office Sq., 10th Fl., S
Boston, MA 02109-4603
PH: (617)247-1511

TF: 800-335-7440
FX: (617)247-4957
E-mail: client.services@delphigroup.com
URL: http://www.delphigroup.com

Description: The Training Institute provides attendees with the definitive education on Knowledge Management. Attendees will learn how to leverage Knowledge Management to establish a new level of competitive advantage in an era marked by increased global competition, increased product commoditization, free agents, high turnover and heightened communication. This seminar will explore the cultural infrastructures, procedural rules, business models, technology tools, and techniques that leading-edge companies are using to create adaptive, knowledge-based organizations. Some topics to be discussed are the technologies and links of Document Management, Workflow, and Portals as building blocks for effective Knowledge Management. Included each day is a comprehensive Case Study showcasing each class of technology.

∎ 3684

TRANSFORMING YOUR BUSINESS USING CRM AND PRM

FROST AND SULLIVAN

7550 W I 10, Ste. 400
San Antonio, TX 78229
PH: (210)247-2461
E-mail: cfsales@frost.com
URL: http://www.frost.com/prod/conf.nsf/0/
1F7F6A8814385C2D86256AF7007E1B90
Contact: Lisa Lee, Event Planner

Description: The Summit is a roadmap to proactively developing, implementing and refining CRM initiatives. Offers tangible ways to use customer information and metrics to drive business strategies. Features key speakers relating CRM business success stories, thereby accelerating the learning curve by benefiting from the implementation lessons learned by CRM peers.

∎ 3685

UK STORAGE CONFERENCE

IDC

5 Speen St.
Framingham, MA 01701
PH: (508)872-8200
URL: http://www.idc.com

Description: The focus of this IDC conference is on how to get the best business value out of storage. Through presentations on the latest innovation and product developments, attendees will not only learn about issues such as virtualization, storage over IP and the state of SAN and NAS, but also about how this can translate into real value for enterprises.

∎ 3686

USER INTERFACE 7 EAST

USER INTERFACE ENGINEERING

242 Neck Rd.
Bradford, MA 01835
PH: 800-588-9855
FX: (978)374-9175
E-mail: jspool@uie.com
URL: http://www.uiconf.com

Description: The User Interface 7 East Conference provides a full day of learning from top design and usability experts.

∎ 3687

VBITS - VISUAL BASIC INSIDERS' TECHNICAL SUMMIT (FTP)

FAWCETTE TECHNICAL PUBLICATIONS, INC.

209 Hamilton Ave.
Palo Alto, CA 94301
PH: (650)833-7100
TF: 800-848-5523
E-mail: conferences@fawcette.com
URL: http://www.ftpconferences.com
Contact: James E. Fawcette, President

Founded: 1990. **Description:** This conference and exposition for strategic business application developers brings the latest in-depth information on Visual Basic, Windows 2000, XML, COM, database techniques, BizTalk, SOAP, and more, from experts in the trenches, the Microsoft Visual Basic development team and top-notch trainers from around the globe.

∎ 3688

VCDC - VISUAL C DEVELOPERS CONFERENCE (FTP)

FAWCETTE TECHNICAL PUBLICATIONS, INC.

209 Hamilton Ave.
Palo Alto, CA 94301
PH: (650)833-7100
TF: 800-848-5523
E-mail: conferences@fawcette.com
URL: http://www.ftpconferences.com
Contact: James E. Fawcette, President

Founded: 1990. **Description:** The premier C specific event brings the hard-core development information on Windows 2000, COM, ATL, database technology and more. Industry leaders and the Microsoft Visual C development team bring real-world solutions for using MFC, Web development strategies, core C programming, as well as tools and techniques.

∎ 3689

VIETNAM TELECOMP - INTERNATIONAL EXHIBITION IN VIETNAM ON TELECOMMUNICATIONS, ELECTRONICS AND INFORMATICS

ADSALE EXHIBITION SERVICES, LTD.

4/F Stanhope House
734 King's Rd.
Hong Kong, People's Republic of China

E-mail: exhibition@adsale.com.hk

Founded: 1992. **Frequency:** Biennial. **Audience:** Trade. **Principle Exhibits:** Broadcasting equipment, computer hardware & systems, e-commerce, education & training, electronics products, components, internet, mobile communucation, networking solutions & equipment, office automation systems, security systems, satelite communications and software solutions. Telecommunication and information technology; office equipment and computers.

▌3690

VISUAL FOXPRO DEVCON
ADVISOR MEDIA INC.

5675 Ruffin Rd.
San Diego, CA 92123-5675
PH: (858)278-5600
TF: 800-336-6060
E-mail: Events@Advisor.com
URL: http://www.advisor.com/www/AdvisorEvents

Description: VISUAL FOXPRO DEVCON is an annual conference, offering technical education for serious FoxPro developers. DEVCON puts developers face-to-face with the leading FoxPro experts, members of the Microsoft Visual FoxPro product team, and FoxPro professionals from around the world.

▌3691

VOICECON
BUSINESS COMMUNICATIONS REVIEW

999 Oakmont Plz. Dr., Ste.100
Westmont, IL 60559-1381
PH: (630)986-1432
TF: 800-227-1234
FX: (630)323-5324
E-mail: info@bcr.com
URL: http://www.bcr.com
Contact: Jeff Bockweg, Conference Sales Manager

Founded: 1991. **Description:** A conference for enterprise voice networking professionals to get the latest information on new systems and on enhancing existing systems to meet new requirements. VoiceCon arms enterprise voice professionals with the knowledge and perspective to make wise choices for enterprise voice networks in the months ahead.

▌3692

VON - VOICE ON THE NET
KEY3MEDIA GROUP

5700 Wilshire Blvd., Ste. 325
Los Angeles, CA 90036
PH: (323)954-6000
FX: (323)954-6010
E-mail: jeff.bockweg@key3media.com
URL: http://www.key3media.com
Contact: Jeff Bockweg, Conference Sales Manager

Description: Voice on the Net (VON) is the place where the industry gets together to conduct business. At VON, a person has the opportunity to meet with the CEOs of the leading companies within the industry. This VON conference will be focusing on the businesses, technologies and issues facing the VON industry today.

▌3693

VSLIVE! (FTP)
FAWCETTE TECHNICAL PUBLICATIONS, INC.

209 Hamilton Ave.
Palo Alto, CA 94301
PH: (650)833-7100
TF: 800-848-5523
E-mail: conferences@fawcette.com
URL: http://www.ftpconferences.com
Contact: James E. Fawcette, President

Founded: 1990. **Description:** VBITS, Visual C Developers Conference and SQL2TheMax have co-located to create the ultimate Visual Studio mega event. VSLive! encompasses the full content and quality of the conferences users come to rely on for Windows development learning.

▌3694

VS.NET CONNECTIONS
TECH CONFERENCES, INC.

731 Main St., Ste. D-3
Monroe, CT 06468
PH: (203)268-3204
TF: 800-438-6720
FX: (203)261-3884
E-mail: devcon@devconnections.com
URL: http://www.devconnections.com

Description: VS.NET Connections will feature cutting-edge sessions by Microsoft and leading third-party developers and gurus. There will be access to the latest information on Visual Basic.NET, C.NET, and C.NET.

▌3695

WEB BUILDER (FTP)
FAWCETTE TECHNICAL PUBLICATIONS, INC.

209 Hamilton Ave.
Palo Alto, CA 94301
PH: (650)833-7100
TF: 800-848-5523
E-mail: conferences@fawcette.com
URL: http://www.ftpconferences.com
Contact: James E. Fawcette, President

Founded: 1990. **Description:** VSLive! is the leading event for developers who work with the Visual Studio.NET tool suite. Features solid technical content to help solve development challenges faced today and build the next generation applications of tomorrow.

▌3696

WEB DESIGN WORLD (FTP)

FAWCETTE TECHNICAL PUBLICATIONS, INC.

209 Hamilton Ave.
Palo Alto, CA 94301
PH: (650)833-7100
TF: 800-848-5523
E-mail: conferences@fawcette.com
URL: http://www.ftpconferences.com
Contact: James E. Fawcette, President

Founded: 1990. **Description:** Thunder Lizard's Web Design World offers web design tips, tricks and techniques. The seminar teaches professionals how to build expert-quality web sites using Dreamweaver Mxpert Track, Photoshop, Advanced Web Graphics, and Flash MX.

▌3697

WEB-ENABLED INSURANCE SERVICES (IQPC)

INTERNATIONAL QUALITY AND PRODUCTIVITY CENTER

PO Box 401
150 Clove Rd.
Little Falls, NJ 07424
PH: (973)256-0211
TF: 800-882-8684
E-mail: info@iqpc.com
URL: http://www.iqpc.com
Contact: Todd Smith, Sales Manager, Sponsorship and Exhibits

Description: IQPC's two-day conference, Web-Enabled Insurance Services, provides strategic solutions to the biggest e-commerce challenges. This is an opportunity to meet and strategize with insurance industry leaders and Internet commerce experts. Attendees will hear critical case studies and best practice presentations from on-line innovators. Attendees will receive valuable, expert advice from experienced practitioners, analysts and consultants.

▌3698

WEB ENABLEMENT STRATEGIES FOR ENTERPRISE APPLICATIONS: BUILDING WEB APPLICATIONS - FROM 101 TO JAVA APPLICATION SERVERS (DCI)

DIGITAL CONSULTING INSTITUTE

204 Andover St.
Andover, MA 01810
PH: (978)470-3880
URL: http://www.dci.com

Description: This seminar presents a comprehensive overview of existing and emerging Internet, Intranet, and Extranet technologies for corporate deployment of Web applications. It reveals enough detail for IS professionals to understand the technology and to make strategic decisions. The seminar provides an in-depth review of requirements for building, deploying and integrating enterprise Web applications.

▌3699

WEB INFORMATION ARCHITECTURE FOR THE ENTERPRISE (DCI)

DIGITAL CONSULTING INSTITUTE

204 Andover St.
Andover, MA 01810
PH: (978)470-3880
URL: http://www.dci.com

Description: This seminar is a step-by-step course in creating the information architecture for a web site, including a review of currently available tools and technologies and a Case Study. It prepares information architects and those responsible for the enterprise web to clarify the mission and vision of a side, balance the needs of the enterprise and its web visitors, and determine the content and function of the site. Next, delegates will learn how to help user find information on the site by defining its organization, navigation, labeling, and searching systems. Because web sites are dynamic, this seminar focuses on the ability of a site to accommodate change and growth.

▌3700

WEB PORTALS EXPO

CP EXHIBITION - BRANCH OF CHINA PROMOTION LTD.

Tung Wai Commercial Bldg., Rm. 1703
109 Gloucester Rd.
Hong Kong, People's Republic of China
E-mail: cp@cpexhibition.com

Principle Exhibits: People and organizations engaging in the supply or utilization of internet related services.

▌3701

WEB SERVICES CONFERENCE

IDG JAPAN INC.

3-4-5 Hongo Bunkyo-ku
Tokyo 113-0033, Japan
PH: 03 5800 3111
URL: http://www.idg.co.jp

Description: This conference and demonstration is a place to examine the newest trend in web technology from the technical and business point of view.

▌3702

WEB SERVICES SEMINAR: THE NEW WAY TO INTEGRATE

BRAINSTORM GROUP INC.

386 W Main St.
Northboro, MA 01532
PH: (508)393-3266
FX: (508)393-8845
E-mail: info@brainstorm-group.com
URL: http://www.brainstorm-group.com
Contact: Dawn M. Eagan, Marketing Director

755

Description: This seminar will discuss why leading enterprises such as Boeing, Credit Suisse, and Nordstrom are looking beyond traditional EAI and B2B solutions to Web services to achieve profound, revenue-generating business results. For IONA, Web services integration is driven by two ideas. First, any application, whether firmly entrenched or newly developed, should be able to interact with any other relevant application, no matter where it resides or how it was developed. Second, application development and application integration should not be treated as separate processes. In a fully connected world, they must be part of the same process.

▌ 3703

WEBSEC
MIS TRAINING INSTITUTE

498 Concord St.
Framingham, MA 01702-2357
PH: (508)879-7999
FX: (508)872-1153
E-mail: mis@misti.com
URL: http://www.misti.com

Founded: 1996. **Description:** This technical conference features industry experts and delivers real-world solutions to the most pressing e-security challenges including, securing Web browsers, Internet connections, wireless devices, and more, and how to protect systems from war dialing, malicious code, and hacker attacks.

▌ 3704

WEBSITE CONTENT MANAGEMENT FOR GOVERNMENT (IQPC)
INTERNATIONAL QUALITY AND PRODUCTIVITY CENTER

PO Box 401
150 Clove Rd.
Little Falls, NJ 07424
PH: (973)256-0211
TF: 800-882-8684
E-mail: info@iqpc-canada.com
URL: http://www.iqpc.com
Contact: Todd Smith, Sales Manager, Sponsorship and Exhibits

Founded: 2000. **Description:** In the previous Website Content Management for Government events, the focus was to develop and define content management issues and strategies. Now it is time to evaluate its success and to move forward in delivering those essential services to the public effectively. Some topics will include Developing a Comprehensive Strategy for Managing Website Content, Understanding how to Link a Website to a Database, Organizing the Fundamental Structure to Maintain Dynamic and User-Centric Websites, Learning How to Effectively Market a Website, and Interactive Focus Sessions Discussing Website Content Management Technology and Gaining Buy-In from Senior Management.

▌ 3705

WEBSPHERE ADVISOR DEVCON
ADVISOR MEDIA INC.

5675 Ruffin Rd.
San Diego, CA 92123-5675
PH: (858)278-5600
TF: 800-336-6060
E-mail: Events@Advisor.com
URL: http://www.advisor.com/www/AdvisorEvents

Description: WebSphere Advisor DevCon is a conference on IBM WebSphere software for e-business, featuring Java, J2EE, web services, XML, integration, portals, administration, and more. Teaches developers how to integrate existing technologies and resources into e-business, how to build an e-commerce system in WebSphere, how to tune WebSphere for optimal performance, tips and trick to compete in the e-business world, and strategies to use WebSphere technology as the core of their business.

▌ 3706

WINDOWS DECISIONS
TECHTARGET

117 Kendrick St., Ste. 800
Needham, MA 02494
PH: (781)657-1000
TF: 888-274-4111
FX: (781)657-1100
E-mail: info@techtarget.com
URL: http://www.techtarget.com
Contact: Ken Berquist, Vice President of Conferences

Description: The Windows Decisions conference is designed for administrators and managers who want to tackle today's toughest Windows decisions, implementation challenges and prepare for the onslaught of new hardware and software solutions.

▌ 3707

WINDOWS NT: SECURITY, AUDIT AND CONTROL (ISACA)
INFORMATION SYSTEMS AUDIT AND CONTROL ASSOCIATION

3701 Algonquin Rd., Ste.1010
Rolling Meadows, IL 60008
PH: (847)253-1545
FX: (847)253-1443
E-mail: conference@isaca.org
URL: http://www.isaca.org

Description: This new course provides practical approaches and techniques for auditing and reviewing the security features and functionality of Windows NT. Detailed audit approaches are provided that cover physical and operational security and control, as well as administration and maintenance assessment tools.

■ 3708

WIRELESS INTERNET (UCLA)

UNIVERSITY OF CALIFORNIA LOS ANGELES

School of Engineering and Applied Science
46121 Engineering 4
Mailbox 159710
Los Angeles, CA 90095
PH: (310)794-4082
FX: (310)206-4830
E-mail: wireless@seas.ucla.edu
URL: http://www.wireless.ucla.edu
Contact: Dr. Pavel Ikonomov

Description: UCLA's Wireless Internet conference covers topics and technologies essential for the development of business models and platforms in the wireless sector. The event includes over 80 lectures and 11 keynotes by experts in wireless technology from industry, academia and research establishments. The technical program spans key areas from physical layer to network layer to applications.

■ 3709

WIRELESS LANS FOR PUBLIC ACCESS

MARCUS EVANS LTD.

303 E Wacker Dr.
Chicago, IL 60601
PH: (312)540-3000
E-mail: marketing@marcusevans.com
URL: http://www.marcusevansconferences.com
Contact: Greta Molepske, Marketing Manager

Description: This conference examines the business proposition behind Wireless LANs and investigates how services should be implemented in order to maximise revenue. Players from both traditional telecom and new backgrounds, including independent WISPs, mobile network operators, infrastructure providers and equipment manufacturers are joining the fight for WLAN coverage, users and revenues.

■ 3710

XML AND ASP WEB DEVELOPMENT (DCI)

DIGITAL CONSULTING INSTITUTE

204 Andover St.
Andover, MA 01810
PH: (978)470-3880
URL: http://www.dci.com

Description: This 3-day seminar will teach students how to build Client/Server web applications using XML. This seminar provides a starting point for web developers new to XML, and who want to know more about what XML is and what its potential applications are. It also teaches developers how to build a Web application that connects to and retrieves data from a database, displays the data by using XML, and saves updates from the client back to the database.

■ 3711

XML CONFERENCE AND EXPOSITION

IDEALLIANCE

100 Daingerfield Rd.
Alexandria, VA 22314
PH: (703)837-1070
FX: (703)837-1072
E-mail: info@idealliance.org
URL: http://www.xmlconference.org/xmlusa/

Description: XML is an event dedicated to XML and related technologies. XML features a comprehensive lineup of up-to-the-minute tutorials and special interest day programs preceding the conference, intensive, multi-level conference tracks, plenary sessions, important keynotes and an exhibition area featuring the leading vendors of XML products and services. It is developed and managed by the Graphic Communications Association (GCA).

■ 3712

XML MAGAZINE'S TECH SUMMIT (FTP)

FAWCETTE TECHNICAL PUBLICATIONS, INC.

209 Hamilton Ave.
Palo Alto, CA 94301
PH: (650)833-7100
TF: 800-848-5523
E-mail: conferences@fawcette.com
URL: http://www.ftpconferences.com
Contact: James E. Fawcette, President

Founded: 1990. **Description:** XML Tech Summit gives developers the skills needed to build the next generation of distributed applications. Provides users with cutting-edge information not given anywhere else. Teaches hard-core, pragmatic information from architects of the XML revolution and developers in the trenches already using XML to build the next wave of enterprise web technologies.

■ 3713

XML AND WEB SERVICES CONNECTIONS

TECH CONFERENCES, INC.

731 Main St., Ste. D-3
Monroe, CT 06468
PH: (203)268-3204
TF: 800-438-6720
FX: (203)261-3884
E-mail: devcon@devconnections.com
URL: http://www.devconnections.com

Description: XML and Web Services Connections explores these technologies and provides cutting-edge sessions by leading XML and Web Services gurus. This conference will focus on the newest XML technologies.

■ 3714

XML AND WEB SERVICES FOR THE ENTERPRISE (DCI)

DIGITAL CONSULTING INSTITUTE

204 Andover St.
Andover, MA 01810
PH: (978)470-3880

URL: http://www.dci.com

Description: This seminar addresses the roles, benefits, and implementation of XML and Web Services, including application development, deployment, key technologies, vendors, products, standards, best practices, and data exchange. Attendees will receive a resource kit of relevant articles and references to books, web sites, magazines, and other information.

■ **3715**
XML WEB SERVICES ONE
SIGS/101 CONFERENCES
9121 Oakdale Ave., Ste.101
Chatsworth, CA 91311
TF: 800-871-7447
FX: (818)734-1529
URL: http://www.xmlconference.com

Description: Professionals from a wide variety of disciplines join programmers and developers to learn to create and implement winning strategies with XML and Web services. This event will address the issues most relevant to a company's software and Web services development and helps them learn to extend the capabilities of the services. Attendees will learn how to implement both to personalize architecture, create secure transactions, use intelligent agents, and utilize wireless features.

■ **3716**
XPLOR
XPLOR INTERNATIONAL
24238 Hawthorne Blvd.
Torrance, CA 90505-6505
PH: (310)791-9521
TF: 800-669-7567
FX: (310)375-4240
E-mail: info@xplor.org
URL: http://www.xplor.org

Description: At Xplor(R), information concerning best practices and the latest products and services for business communications will be featured. Attendees will be able to network and exchange ideas with industry professionals from more than 40 countries around the globe, and uncover new ways to leverage documents within the organization. There will be over 100 education-packed conference sessions and over 200 presenters, document technology experts and users to address some of their most complex technology challenges.

WEBSITE DESIGNERS

■ **3717**
1EZ CONSULTING

2 Mareblu, Ste. 106
Aliso Viejo, CA 92656
PH: (949)360-3669

FX: (949)360-3674
E-mail: info@1ezconsulting.com
URL: http://www.1ezconsulting.com

Description: 1EZ Consulting is an interactive design firm that offers services including web site design and hosting, programming, multimedia, branding, copy writing, branding, and search engine placement. 1EZ Consulting uses the latest technologies to build e-commerce and transaction based development, serving clients worldwide.

■ **3718**
2 CAN DESIGN

2730 Attala Rd. 3120
West, MS 39192
PH: (662)290-6978
FX: (662)290-0124
E-mail: info@2candesign.com
URL: http://www.2candesign.com

Description: 2 Can Design is a full service Internet solutions provider. 2 Can Design offers custom web site design, content management, database development, as well as a variety of graphic design services. In addition, 2 Can Design offers multimedia, including interactive catalogs, Flash and streaming media production.

■ **3719**
2ADVANCED STUDIOS

65 Enterprise
Aliso Viejo, CA 92656
PH: (949)330-7580
FX: (949)330-7581
E-mail: info@2advanced.com
URL: http://www.2advanced.com

Description: Focusing on creativity to transform client's messages into an intuitive expression of the subject matter, 2Advanced Studios offers a range of services including web design and development, multimedia, and corporate identity for its clients.

■ **3720**
2ND LOOK DESIGN

1321 Wakarusa Dr., Ste. 2102
Lawrence, KS 66049
PH: (785)550-0162
E-mail: contact@2ndlookdesign.com
URL: http://www.2ndlookdesign.com

Description: 2nd Look Design focuses on creating a distinctive look for each of its clients. 2nd Look is a full service design firm offering services including individual web site design and maintenance, web site hosting and domain registration, marketing, print design, and advertising.

∎ 3721
3 MEDIA WEB SOLUTIONS

420 Boston Post Rd.
Shrewsbury, MA 01545
PH: (508)845-8900
TF: 877-325-1131
E-mail: admin@3mediaweb.com
URL: http://www.3mediaweb.com

Description: 3 Media Web Solutions offers strong design using technology to allow emerging-growth companies to develop an effective Internet presence. Services provided by 3 Media Web Solutions include custom web development, site management, web hosting, and network installation.

∎ 3722
3 TUNA PRODUCTIONS

431 E 20th St., Ste. 3A
New York, NY 10010
PH: (917)-689-1813
E-mail: joes@3tuna.com
URL: http://www.3tuna.com
Contact: Joe Santoro, Kingfish

Description: 3 Tuna Productions is a small design firm specializing in graphic design and web site design and development. 3 Tuna has a clearly defined strategy for helping clients succeed, which includes needs analysis, planning, creative development, production and testing, and documentation and maintenance.

∎ 3723
3STONE

2921 Canton
Dallas, TX 75226
PH: (214)653-1120
FX: (214)741-1775
E-mail: info@3stone.com
URL: http://www.3stone.com

Description: Founded in 1994, 3Stone has developed network-based solutions for clients in many industries, including telecommunications, media, publishing, bioinformatics, internet services, retail and healthcare. 3Stone can concept, engineer, and build successful eBusiness applications including online media planning, brand positioning, communications strategies, and collateral support.

∎ 3724
3W DESIGN GROUP, INC.

340 Meadow Ln.
PO BOX 191
Sister Bay, WI 54234-0191
PH: (920)854-9459
TF: (866)854-9459
FX: (920)854-5327
E-mail: ideas@3wdesign.com
URL: http://www.3wdesign.com

Description: 3W Design Group is a design firm specializing in customized technology solutions for its business clients. 3W Design Group offers services including custom web site services, fully functional e-commerce web sites, print design, integrated media design, search engine registration, web site hosting, and CD-ROM presentations.

∎ 3725
3W PLANET

1070 E Dominguez St., Unit K
Carson, CA 90746
PH: (310)763-1225
FX: (310)764-1762
E-mail: info@3wplanet.com
URL: http://www.3wplanet.com

Description: 3W Planet studios is a multi-disciplinary design team that can provide its clients with web site design and development, implementation of Internet strategies, intranets, and web based applications. 3W Planet also offers multimedia corporate presentations, and print media production. 3W Planet creates graphics, architecture, and HTML for its clients' web sites, and can integrate web site information with its print media.

∎ 3726
3W-PRESENCE

PO Box 304
Wyckoff, NJ 07481
PH: (201)652-8151
FX: (201)652-0362
E-mail: scanlan@3w-presence.com
URL: http://www.3w-presence.com

Description: 3W-Presence is a web design and development company that creates custom web sites that are easy to navigate. Other services provided by 3W-Presence include domain name registration, graphics, web hosting and maintenance, and e-commerce sites.

∎ 3727
3W STUDIOS

2074 Centre Point Blvd.
Tallahassee, FL 32308
PH: (850)878-6663
TF: 800-232-4017
FX: (850)878-3858
E-mail: info@3wstudios.com
URL: http://www.3wstudios.com

Description: 3W Studios is an interactive design firm specializing in e-business systems integration and e-marketing. Services offered by 3W Studios include strategic online planning, graphic design and production, Internet marketing, and web site management.

▌3728
13PT

Box 2013
New York, NY 10013
PH: (212)966-2312
E-mail: info@13pt.com
URL: http://www.13pt.com

Description: 13pt is a design firm that specializes in web site design and custom font development. 13pt creates precision design and engineering both for the web and for fonts.

▌3729
20TWENTY WEB SERVICES

PO Box 4290
Penrith, NSW 2750, Australia
PH: 61 414 312 372
FX: 61 2 8572 5252
E-mail: info@20twenty.ws
URL: http://www.20twenty.ws/

Description: 20Twenty Web Services is a company that provides services including web site design for both small and large firms, site maintenance, and web site redevelopment. 20Twenty is committed to providing its clients with an online presence that will get noticed, whether it is a simple web page or a flash animation.

▌3730
32 STUDIOS, LLC

PO Box 832
Brusly, LA 70719
PH: (225)749-2795
E-mail: info@32studios.com
URL: http://www.32studios.com

Description: 32 Studios creates interactive web sites for the community of West Baton Rouge, including high-end multimedia, 3D stereo sound, and real time active content. 32 Studios also offers its clients graphic design, database connectivity and consulting services.

▌3731
101 INTERNET SERVICES

910 W San Marcos Blvd.
San Marcos, CA 92069
PH: (760)736-3700

TF: 888-398-4703
URL: http://www.101web-design.com

Description: 101 Internet Services provides web site design and hosting. Web sites are designed from templates, or custom designed to fit the needs of each client. 101 Internet services offers complete e-commerce package web design, including shopping cart.

▌3732
877 WEB TEAM

4220 Rye Glen
Arlington, TX 76017
PH: (817)572-7180
TF: 877-932-8326
FX: (817)483-9329
E-mail: design@877webteam.com
URL: http://www.877webteam.com

Founded: 1996. **Description:** 877 Web Team specializes in web site development, site redesign, web site hosting and maintenance, and Internet consulting. 877 Web Team designs an online presence unique to each client's goals, and works to assure their successful Internet presence.

▌3733
1650 DIGITAL DESIGN

1301 Eureka Ave.
Davis, CA 95616
PH: (530)756-9542
E-mail: info@1650digitaldesign
URL: http://www.1650design.com

Description: 1650 Digital Design is a small firm that specializes in custom web site design, graphics design, web site hosting, Internet marketing and redesign of existing web pages. 1650 Digital Design is dedicated to customer satisfaction and offers reasonable prices for their work.

▌3734
30|20, INC.

3660 N Lake Shore Dr., Ste. 2509
Chicago, IL 60613
PH: 888-327-3020
E-mail: info@3020.com
URL: http://www.3020.com

Description: 30|20, Inc. offers Internet services including custom web site design and implementation, e-commerce solutions, interactive media, online marketing, online database development, data mining, and enterprise reporting.

■ 3735

AANAVRIN.COM

123 N Centennial Way, Ste. 210
Mesa, AZ 85201-6747
PH: (480)968-3312
TF: 888-560-3312
E-mail: info@ aanavrin.com
URL: http://www.aanavrin.com

Description: Aanavrin.com is a web design and development company that is focused on offering Internet solutions to small and medium sized businesses. Services provided by Aanavrin include dynamic and reliable web site design, web hosting, e-commerce solutions, content management, search engine positioning, print and other media. Aanavrin also offers financing programs to its clients.

■ 3736

AARON-DAVIS INTERNET TECHNOLOGIES

11717 Bernardo Plaza Ct., Ste. 102-101
San Diego, CA 92128
PH: (760)630-3180
FX: (760)726-8408
E-mail: info@aaron-davis.com
URL: http://www.aaron-davis.com

Description: Aaron-Davis Internet Technologies is an award winning design firm that creates Internet projects for Fortune 500 companies as well as smaller organizations. Aaron-Davis provides complete e-commerce web sites, custom designed small business web sites, and redesigns and updates existing web sites.

■ 3737

AASOFTECH, INC.

1909 Baton Dr.
Vienna, VA 22182
PH: (703)938-4608
E-mail: design@aasoftech.com
URL: http://www.aasoftech.com

Description: AASoftech provides web site design and development as well as consulting services. AASoftech specializes in e-commerce Internet solutions, and also offers online database management and state of the art multimedia. AASoftech strives to make technology transparent, focusing on the clients' products and services.

■ 3738

ABLE DESIGN

3769 Mica View Ct. SE
Salem, OR 97302
PH: (503)370-9969

E-mail: dan@abledesign.com
URL: http://www.abledesign.com

Description: Able Design provides a full spectrum of web design and development options. Services offered include an initial free consultation, web design, graphic design, copy writing, site maintenance and hosting, domain name registration and web site promotion.

■ 3739

ABSINTHE CREATIONS

84 The Fenway, Ste. 14
Boston, MA 02115
PH: (617)794-5895
E-mail: info@absinthecreations.com
URL: http://www.absinthecreations.com

Description: Absinthe Creations provides clients with many services to market their company or product. Services offered include web site design, print media creation, banner ads, company logos, corporate identity, video and audio production.

■ 3740

ABSOLUTE MOTION WEB TECHNOLOGIES

PO Box 39911
Phoenix, AZ 85069
PH: (602)336-0333
TF: 800-958-5559
FX: (602)778-9333
E-mail: amsales@absolutemotion.com
URL: http://www.absolutemotion.com

Description: Absolute Motion has the objective of making the Internet profitable for its clients. Services provided by Absolute Motion include e-commerce web sites with customized storefronts, web sites that reflect client companies' vision, and a full range of web hosting services.

■ 3741

ABSTRACTIONS WEB DESIGN

2116 W Wilden Ave.
Goshen, IN 46526
PH: (574)537-0253
FX: (574)534-2730
E-mail: webmaster@abstractionswebdesign.com
URL: http://www.abstractionswd.com

Description: Abstractions Web Design provides a variety of web services including web site design and development, web hosting, web-based application development, and secure e-commerce solutions.

■ **3742**

ACADIAN WEB DESIGN

4745 East Ridge Rd.
Cornville, ME 04976
PH: (207)474-8212
E-mail: info@acadianwebdesign.com
URL: http://www.acadianwebdesign.com

Description: Acadian Web Design creates unique web sites designed to promote each client's products or services, with search engine optimization built into the structure of the web site. Services offered by Acadian Web Design include market research, web design, content development, secure merchant services, strategic links, and search engine and directory submission.

■ **3743**

ACCENT INTERACTIVE

156 Westbury Rd.
Lutherville, MD 21093
PH: (410)321-9327
FX: (410)825-2468
E-mail: creativity@accentinteractive.net
URL: http://www.accentinteractive.net

Description: Accent Interactive is a firm focused on creativity and business, bringing the best of technology to small and mid-sized companies. Services offered by Accent Interactive include unique and effective web site design, web site hosting, graphic design, video production and music composition.

■ **3744**

ACCESS 2001

21300 San Simeon Way, R-10
Miami, FL 33179
PH: (305)653-2069
FX: (305)999-9867
E-mail: customer@access2001.com
URL: http://www.access2001.com

Description: Access 2001 provides a variety of Internet access solutions, including web site design, hosting and e-commerce sites. Access 2001 offers custom web site design for companies of any size, and follows a process of market research, strategy, distribution, and follow-up and improvement to ensure the success of its customers' web sites.

■ **3745**

ACCESSZONE DESIGN

921 NW Oakridge Dr.
Blue Springs, MO 64015
PH: (816)228-3814
TF: 888-872-4420

FX: (775)254-6161
E-mail: bradmiller@accesszone.com
URL: http://www.accesszonedesign.com

Description: Accesszone Design is a web design and hosting company that emphasizes customer service and use of the best technology. Services offered by Accesszone Design include several web design packages, including an e-commerce and shopping cart system, domain registration, and web site hosting.

■ **3746**

ACCUFIND INTERNET SERVICES, INC

196 West Moorestown Rd.
Wind Gap, PA 18091
PH: (610)759-5456
TF: 888-932-3371
FX: (610)759-7607
URL: http://www.accufind.com

Description: AccuFind Internet Services provides a variety of services including web site design and development, web hosting, and e-commerce development. AccuFind also offers automated e-commerce and database administration, as well as email marketing.

■ **3747**

ACCUVIS

200 E 5th Ave., Ste. 128
Naperville, IL 60563
PH: (630)717-8283
FX: (630)717-8465
URL: http://www.accuvis.com

Description: AccuVis is a web design consulting firm that uses its creativity, and expertise in marketing and technology, to achieve its clients' business goals. AccuVis provides web design and implementation, web site promotion, intranet and extranet strategies, as well as web site management and hosting.

■ **3748**

ACD DESIGN

208 E 84, No. 5B
New York, NY 10028
PH: (212)452-4847
E-mail: aaron@acddesign.com
URL: http://www.acddesign.com

Description: ACD Design offers custom web design and Internet marketing for small and medium sized businesses, political campaigns, and associations. ACD Design provides complete web services from basic informational web pages to full e-commerce sites. Animation, multimedia, graphic design and web hosting are some of the other services offered by ACD Design.

▌3749
ACEWEBHOST

PO Box 1087
Branford, CT 06405-8087
PH: (203)488-4262
FX: (203)488-4262
E-mail: aceweb@acewebhost.com
URL: http://www.acewebhost.com

Description: AceWebHost offers web site design and hosting services to businesses of all sizes. Services provided by AceWebHost include basic web sites designed from hosting software, custom web site design, graphic design, database development, and site hosting.

▌3750
ACHOATE INFORMATION SERVICES

Box 49153
Austin, TX 78765-9153
PH: (512)371-1055
FX: (512)453-1686
E-mail: info@achoate.com
URL: http://www.achoate.com

Description: Achoate Information Services provides a full range of Internet services including web site design and maintenance. Other professional work offered by Achoate includes graphics design, database programming, e-commerce programming or set-up, multimedia production, technical writing, and training and troubleshooting.

▌3751
ADDIS GROUP, INC.

2515 9th St.
Berkeley, CA 94710
PH: (510)704-7500
FX: (510)704-7501
E-mail: newbiz@addis.com
URL: http://www.addis.com

Description: The Addis Group is an independent design firm specializing in brand strategy and web design. The Addis Group philosophy of web design is one of integration with while maintaining brand authenticity, fostering a shared experience of the brand.

▌3752
ADVANCED WEB SITE PUBLISHING

PO Box 891167
Houston, 77289-1167
PH: (713)724-7483
E-mail: info@awsp.com
URL: http://www.awsp.com

Description: Advanced Web Site Publishing creates unique web sites designed to fit the business needs of the client. An assessment is done before the web site is designed to ensure that client goals are met. Other services provided by Advanced Web Site Design include custom art and text, client logos, easy navigation, and compatibility with major browsers.

▌3753
ADVANCES.COM

7810 NW 4th St.
Ft. Lauderdale, FL 33324
PH: (954)452-8466
TF: 800-593-HOST
FX: (954)452-1139
E-mail: info@advances.com
URL: http://www.advances.com

Description: Advances.com specializes in web design and hosting. Custom web-based software applications and multimedia services are also provided. Advances.com furnishes creative logos, animation, banner ads, and other graphic design services as well as software development and systems integration.

▌3754
ADVANTAGE INFORMATION SYSTEMS

16498 Howard Dr.
Macomb, MI 48042
PH: (810)781-6342
TF: 800-203-0546
FX: (810)781-6443
E-mail: webmaster@advantageinfosys.com
URL: http://www.advantageinfosys.com

Description: Advantage Information Systems provides website design and development created to enhance clients business. Advantage Information Systems offers complete design, creation, copywriting, and photography services, as well as site add-ons such as calendars and ads.

▌3755
ADVENSA.COM

PO Box 3623
Carmel, IN 46032
PH: (317)815-0449
FX: (317)815-0449
E-mail: info@advensa.com
URL: http://www.advensa.com

Description: Advensa.com is a new media design firm specializing in graphic design, corporate identity, logo design and website design and development. Advensa.com assists clients in building business websites that will create new customers and provide customer satisfaction.

763

▌3756

AEROMEDIA, INC.

PO Box 27740
Las Vegas, NV 89126
PH: (702)257-2236
FX: 877-560-7351
E-mail: info@aeromedia.com
URL: http://www.aeromedia.com

Description: Aeromedia is an Internet services and consulting firm that specializes in designing web sites for the aviation industry. Services offered by Aeromedia include web site design, consulting, and production; web site hosting, registration and advertising, and web site maintenance and updates.

▌3757

AFFINITY INTERNET GROUP

P O Box 2179
Ocean City, MD 21843-2179
PH: (410)250-6000
TF: 800-519-3404
FX: (410)250-8695
E-mail: webinfo@aigweb.com
URL: http://www.aigweb.com

Description: Affinity Internet Group offers web site design, consulting, advertising, and hosting for business clients. Services provided on Affinity Internet Group's web sites include financial calculators for Real Estate, online Real Estate listings, e-commerce merchant services, auto-responders to mail files, and online web cameras.

▌3758

AGENCY.COM

20 Exchange Pl., 15th Fl.
New York, NY 10005
PH: (212)358-2600
URL: http://www.agency.com

Description: Agency.com is a company that specializes in offering its clients the best of interactive technology. Agency.com focuses on the client's needs, and provides ways to acquire and retain customers, and improve sales and marketing efficiency. Services offered include web site design, technical and information systems architecture, and systems integration for e-commerce platforms.

▌3759

ALAN ENTERPRISES

Box 336
Ambridge, PA 15003
PH: (724)266-5230
FX: (724)266-5230

URL: http://www.alanent.com

Description: Alan Enterprises provides web site design and development, e-commerce solutions, web site marketing, and e-commerce consulting services. Alan Enterprises offers secure and complete e-commerce web sites, and well as web sites designed with successful search engine positioning in mind.

▌3760

ALEX REISNER WEB SITE DESIGN

120 Lindy Ln.
Lincroft, NJ 07738-1815
PH: (732)933-1291
E-mail: design@alexreisner.com
URL: http://www.alexreisner.com

Description: Alex Reisner Web Site Design is a small firm that specializes in web sites that have great content and are fast and easy to use. Alex Reisner Web Site Design has an emphasis on customer service and offers strategy consultation, content creation, graphic and interaction design, as well as web site hosting and maintenance.

▌3761

ALLISON ROYCE AND ASS.

85 NE Loop 410, Ste. 418
San Antonio, TX 78232
PH: (210)564-7000
E-mail: sales@allisonroyce.com
URL: http://www.allisonroyce.com

Description: Allison Royce and Associates is a company which focuses on professional e-commerce web site design. Additional services include search engine placement, mail server and corporate domain hosting, mailing list services, and experienced technical support.

▌3762

ALLSOLDOUT, INC.

1901 N Moore St., Ste. 1100
Arlington, VA 22209
PH: (703)387-4000
FX: (703)387-4001
E-mail: info@allsoldout.net
URL: http://www.allsoldout.net

Description: AllSoldOut is a full service Internet solutions company that serves both large and small clients worldwide. AllSoldOut provides complete e-commerce web design, strategic planning, corporate web site design and redesign, database development, site hosting, and marketing services.

∎ 3763
ALLSTAR CREATIVE

PO Box 13310
San Luis Obispo, CA 93406-3310
PH: (805)781-8717
TF: 877-255-8959
FX: (805)781-8718
E-mail: info@allstarcreative.com
URL: http://www.allstarcreative.com

Description: AllStar Creative provides both web site design and development and digital media services, including DVD production. AllStar Creative also offers banner ad creation, motion graphics, logo design, CD cover design, and complete e-commerce web site design.

∎ 3764
ALPHAPLEX, INC.

5265 N Academy, Ste. 1200
Colorado Springs, CO 80918
PH: (719)599-3449
TF: (866)599-3449
E-mail: info@alphaplex.net
URL: http://www.alphaplex.net

Founded: 1997. **Description:** Alphaplex provides Internet solutions for businesses of varying sizes. Services that Alphaplex offers include web site design and development, multimedia web sites, wireless web, intranets, and marketing and local promotion. Alphaplex focuses on Internet projects that create benefits for their clients.

∎ 3765
ALTUS ONLINE, INC.

116 N Tennessee St.
McKinney, TX 75069-4320
PH: (972)569-8934
E-mail: info@altusonlineinc.com
URL: http://www.altusonlineinc.com

Description: Altus Online, Inc. specializes in e-commerce web site design, development and hosting for small to medium sized businesses. Some features of Altus Online's e-commerce web sites include Flash introduction, multiple email accounts, search engine submission, and online and toll-free technical support.

∎ 3766
AMERICAN EAGLE.COM

1550 N Northwest Hwy., Ste. 402
Park Ridge, IL 60068
PH: (847)699-0300
FX: (847)699-4207
E-mail: info@americaneagle.com
URL: http://www.americaneagle.com

Description: American Eagle.com builds and hosts high quality web sites for businesses and associations ranging in size from a few employees to Fortune 500 companies. American Eagle.com offers services such as strategy and consulting to determine needs; web site design and development, including e-commerce; and full service hosting and maintenance.

∎ 3767
ANDYS PLAYGROUND

PO Box 655
Fort Collins, CO 80522
PH: (866)867-5309
FX: (240)414-2269
E-mail: help@andysplayground.com
URL: http://www.andysplayground.com

Description: Andys Playground is a small firm offering web design and graphic design services. Andys Playground provides comprehensive web site design, and specializes in creating an effective web presence for professional services organizations. Andys Playground web sites are usable, maintainable, and optimized for fast download.

∎ 3768
APKE WEB SERVICES

29156 Mira Vista
Laguna Niguel, CA 92677-4325
PH: (949)364-9094
FX: (949)364-9094
E-mail: info@apke.com
URL: http://www.apke.com

Description: Apke Web Services provides complete web site design. Services include domain name registration, analysis of competitor's sites, preparing photos and logos for use on the web site, creation of a shopping cart system, setting up web pages for approval, registration of web sites on major search engines, and access to an online report with statistics about web site visitors.

∎ 3769
ART FUSION, LTD.

31 Dublin St. Ln. N
Edinburgh, Lothian EH36NT, United Kingdom
PH: 011 44 131 558 8870
FX: 810963-4148
E-mail: info@artfusion.com
URL: http://www.artfusion.com
Contact: Kirsten Guthrie, Managing Director

Description: Art Fusion provides Internet development and management services. Services offered include web site development, for customer service or sales; e-commerce or auction web sites, such as online stores; and online marketing and advertising campaigns.

∎ 3770
ARTISTIC INTERNET SERVICES

95 Calle Vadito NW
Albuquerque, NM 87120
PH: (505)836-7665
FX: (505)839-0190
E-mail: info@artisticinternet.com
URL: http://www.artisticinternet.com

Founded: 1995. **Description:** Artistic Internet Services specializes in web site design, development, and hosting for small to medium sized businesses. Web sites are custom designed for each business, and range from simple one page sites to searchable online catalogs with shopping carts and interactive databases.

∎ 3771
ARTROPOLIS, INC.

8401 Wayzata Blvd., Ste. 310
Golden Valley, MN 55426
PH: (952)545-8488
FX: (952)545-8516
E-mail: info@artropolis.com
URL: http://www.atsartropolis.com

Description: Artropolis is a company that provides its clients with creative concepts and online interactive development. Services offered by Artropolis include online storefronts with e-commerce capabilities, graphic design, user-centered interface design, custom database applications, and online marketing strategies.

∎ 3772
AURAGEN COMMUNICATIONS, INC.

620 Park Ave., Ste. 177
Rochester, NY 14607
PH: (716)242-8759
TF: 877-AUR-AGEN
FX: (716)242-0417
E-mail: info@auragen.com
URL: http://www.auragen.com

Description: Auragen Communications provides its clients with web site design, as well as design for intranets, handhelds, and interactive television. Auragen has a clear methodology for assessing client needs and developing their Internet presence.

∎ 3773
AUTOMATED DESIGN CORP.

21 Benway Ct., Ste. 204
Baltimore, MD 21228
PH: (410)526-5471
TF: (866)362-8937
FX: (419)781-4340
E-mail: sales@adcglobal.com
URL: http://www.adcglobal.com

Description: Automated Design Corporation is an IT solutions provider that offers a variety of services including web site design; web based applications, and software design and development. Automated Design Corporation provides e-commerce web sites, order entry, online reservation and online database integration.

∎ 3774
B N S WEB CREATIONS

18 Brown Ave.
Grapeville, PA 15634
PH: (724)522-1609
E-mail: info@b-n-s.com
URL: http://www.b-n-s.com

Description: B n S Web Creations is a full service web design and development firm. Services offered by B n S Web Creations include domain name registration, graphics development, multimedia production, marketing, search engine submission, and technical support.

∎ 3775
BACK 40 DESIGN, INC.

PO Box 2
Prague, OK 74864
PH: (405)567-4800
FX: (405)567-1521
E-mail: dave@back40design.com
URL: http://www.back40design.com

Description: Back 40 Design is a family owned web development business that specializes in designing and hosting web sites, and creating content for web sites. Working with both PC and Mac platforms, Back 40 Design focuses on creating value for the client in each unique web site they create.

∎ 3776
BACKSLASH.COM, INC.

60 Orland Sq. Dr., Ste. 201
Orland Park, IL 60462
PH: (708)403-4884
FX: (708)403-4896
E-mail: sales@bslash.com

URL: http://www.bslash.com

Description: Backslash.com is a full service web design firm that is a subsidiary of Worldwide Translation Technologies, Inc. Back slash.com specializes in creating content-rich web sites for small to medium sized companies, as well as specializing in the internationalization of web sites and international marketing.

▌3777

BAD DOG DESIGN, INC.

Box 2119
Sechelt, BC, Canada V0N3A0
PH: (604)885-5913
FX: (604)885-5978
E-mail: wag@baddogdesign.com
URL: http://www.baddogdesign.com

Description: Bad Dog Design provides its customers with web site design and development, e-business consulting and development, and e-marketing strategy. Bad Dog Design also offers community web site development plans for tourism and other community organizations. Bad Dog Design is committed to increasing the effectiveness of its clients' online presence.

▌3778

BALLAS WEB DESIGN

PO Box 52
Parker, CO 80134
PH: (303)807-4561
FX: (720)294-9975
E-mail: info@ballaswebdesign.com
URL: http://www.ballaswebdesign.com

Description: Ballas Web Design is a full-service Internet solutions company that provides creative custom design tailored to its client's needs. Services offered by Ballas Web Design include e-commerce, web design and development, intranet development, and integrated online marketing.

▌3779

BALLISTIC WEB DESIGN, INC.

615 S Broadway
Tyler, TX 75701
PH: (903)533-0088
FX: (903)533-8667
E-mail: web@ballisticwebdesign.com
URL: http://www.ballisticwebdesign.com

Description: Ballistic Web Design offers services in all aspects of web design, development, marketing, and planning. Ballistic Web Design also provides copy writing services, graphic design and marketing strategy to ensure the success of customer's web sites.

▌3780

BANNERVIEW.COM

3859 S Valley View Blvd., No. 4
Las Vegas, NV 89103
PH: (702)312-9444
FX: (702)312-9477
E-mail: info@bannerview.com
URL: http://www.bannerview.com

Description: Bannerview.com is an e-business solutions provider that is developing web-enabled platforms. Bannerview.com offers a variety of services, including several e-commerce web site design packages and custom solutions, as well as programming, copy writing and various graphic design services at an hourly or per-piece rate.

▌3781

BDR WEB SERVICES

PO Box 671145
Flushing, NY 11367-9998
PH: (718)969-2824
E-mail: info@bdrweb.com
URL: http://www.bdrweb.com

Description: BDR Web Services is a web design and e-business consulting agency that specializes in developing a strong Internet presence for its clients. Services offered by BDR Web Services include web construction, maintenance, hosting and search engine registration.

▌3782

BELSTAR MEDIA

1735 Brighton Beach Rd.
Menasha, WI 54952
PH: (920)731-6939
FX: 888-844-4856
E-mail: information@belstarmedia.com
URL: http://www.belstarmedia.com

Description: Belstar Media has a mission of providing quality web sites and personalized service at a reasonable cost to its customers. Belstar offers e-commerce services, web design and redesign, a variety of programming services, multimedia, site promotion and hosting, and remote administration of customers' web sites.

▌3783

BIZ FULFILLMENT.COM

2103 Brentwood St.
High Point, NC 27263
PH: (336)887-3700
TF: 800-221-0262
FX: (336)887-3773
E-mail: bizfulfillment@graphikdimensions.com

URL: http://www.bizfulfillment.com
Contact: Rodney Suggs

Description: Biz Fulfillment.com offers solutions to e-business needs through complete web site design and development to order processing and fulfillment. Biz Fulfillment.com focuses on web sites that generate profits, and draw and retain customers, creating sites that fit the needs of each individual client.

■ 3784

BLUETRUCK.NET

826 Bellvue Ave.
Reading, PA 19605
PH: (610)929-4281
FX: (610)929-4283
E-mail: sales@bluetruck.net
URL: http://www.bluetruck.net

Description: Bluetruck.net builds clean looking web sites designed for every browser. Services that Bluetruck.net provides include database design and development, custom scripts, e-commerce solutions, shopping carts, graphic design, and animation.

■ 3785

BRAIN RIDE

116 Sumner Meadows Ln
Hendersonville, TN 37075
PH: (615)826-7567
FX: (615)826-7568
E-mail: info@brainride.com
URL: http://www.brainride.com

Description: Brain Ride specializes in comprehensive web and software development using leading edge technologies. Brain Ride offers web site design and redesign, content development, site promotion, and software design document generation.

■ 3786

BRYSON WEB PRODUCTION, INC.

RR 1 Box 1323
Spout Spring, VA 24593
PH: (434)352-3308
FX: (434)352-3328
E-mail: info@brysonweb.com
URL: http://www.brysonweb.com

Description: Bryson Web Production, Inc. is an Internet service company specializing in the design and development of online applications and web sites. Clients are offered a range of web services and custom-built web packages that can establish their Internet presence in an efficient and cost-effective manner. Bryson Web Production staff members

have been involved in web projects since 1993, with online experience dating back to 1983.

■ 3787

BUSINESS INFORMATION MANAGEMENT, INC.

121 NE 52 St., Ste. 201
Oklahoma City, OK 73105-1803
PH: (405)524-4246
FX: (405)524-4925
E-mail: info@businfo-online.com
URL: http://www.businfo-online.com

Description: Business Information Management, Inc. offers a range of information management services including web site design, creation, and hosting services; custom programming and consulting and systems analysis.

■ 3788

BUSINESS OL

11260 Roger Bacon Dr., Ste. 300
Reston, VA 20190
PH: (858)866-0619
TF: (866)333-1BOL
FX: (703)471-0168
E-mail: info@businessol.com
URL: http://www.businessol.com

Description: Business OL (On Line) is a company offering e-commerce and e-business solutions for its clients. BOL works to ensure that the web sites it designs do their job, making a good first impression and contributing to the bottom line. Business OL uses its RIPCORD platform and administrative tools, making it easy to make changes and updates in web sites.

■ 3789

BUYER ZONE.COM, INC.

125 Walnut St.
Watertown, MA 02472
PH: (617)868-5757
TF: 888-393-5000
FX: (617)868-6161
URL: http://www.buyerzone.com

Founded: 1992. **Description:** Buyer Zone.com is a provider of purchasing tools and advice for small to mid-sized businesses. Buyer Zone functions as a clearinghouse to bring web site designers and purchasers together. Businesses needing a web site designed, maintained or upgraded can fill out an online form to receive quotes on their project from Buyer Zone's web site designers.

3790

C. A. WEB DESIGN, INC.

PO Box 1062
Los Alamitos, CA 90720
PH: 888-223-3744
FX: (562)598-4487
E-mail: info@cawebdesign.com
URL: http://www.cawebdesign.com

Description: C. A. Web Design offers a range of Internet services including web design, hosting, marketing, and e-commerce solutions. Web design can include original logos, animation, web counter, and sound files. C. A. Web Design's e-commerce solutions include what clients need to fully operate and maintain a successful Internet presence.

3791

CAMPBELL COMMUNICATIONS

20241 Westview, Ste. 210
Northville, MI 48167
PH: (248)348-4246
FX: (248)344-1260
E-mail: pegcampbell@mediaone.net
URL: http://www.campbellcommunications.net

Description: Campbell Communications provides its clients with a complete promotional package, including web site design, updating, and maintenance. Other services offered by Campbell Communications include marketing and public relations.

3792

THE CANTON GROUP

2929 O'Donnell St.
Baltimore, MD 21224
PH: (410)675-5708
FX: (410)675-5111
E-mail: sales@cantongroup.com
URL: http://www.cantongroup.com

Description: The Canton Group offers Internet and new media development solutions to companies, governmental agencies, and educational entities. Services provided by the Canton Group include web design and development, e-commerce applications, web marketing, and interactive applications such as kiosks and CD-ROMs.

3793

CAPEMAYWEB.COM, INC.

PO Box 411
Cape May, NJ 08204
PH: (609)889-1117
E-mail: info@capemayweb.com
URL: http://www.capemayweb.com

Description: CapeMayWeb.com offers its clients many Internet services including web site design and hosting, e-commerce solutions, development of an online catalog, search engine submissions, and a web based control panel to set up and update mailing lists.

3794

CAPERNAUM, INC.

6320 St. Augustine Rd., Ste. 3
Jacksonville, FL 32217
PH: 888-333-2046
E-mail: info@capernaum.com
URL: http://www.capernaum.com

Description: Capernaum offers services including web design and computer telephony. Internet solutions include corporate web site design, e-commerce, strategic planning, intranet and extranet, interactive presentations, information architecture, and database development.

3795

CAPRIS LIMITED

215 Traders Blvd.E, Unit 4
Mississauga, ON, Canada L4Z3K5
PH: (905)507-8151
TF: 888-748-9636
FX: (905)507-8683
E-mail: info@capris.com
URL: http://www.capris.com

Description: Capris Limited is a company focused on delivering e-business solutions. Capris has developed a plan called Deploy by Logic, that lays out a framework for its clients. Elements of Deploy by Logic include plan, attract, engage, deliver, transact, and transform.

3796

CARA HASKEY DESIGN

2607 2nd Ave., Ste. B
Seattle, WA 98121
PH: (206)956-8557
FX: (206)956-8559
E-mail: info@ckhdesign.com
URL: http://www.ckhdesign.com

Description: Cara Haskey Design is a full service design and communications company. Services offered by Cara Haskey Design include web site design, graphic design, software and systems development, multimedia development, copy writing, and data integration and warehousing.

▌3797

CARBONHOUSE

3204 N Davidson St.
Charlotte, NC 28205
PH: (704)333-5800
FX: (704)333-5808
E-mail: sales@carbonhouse.com
URL: http://www.carbonhouse.com

Description: Carbonhouse is a webcentric branding and communications firm that fuses creativity, strategy, design and technology to enable client companies to communicate effectively. Services offered by Carbonhouse include Internet and intranet, application development, and multimedia production; as well as integrated marketing, brand identiy and strategy.

▌3798

CARDBOARDGALAXY.COM

PO Box 688
Mount Desert, ME 04660
PH: (207)288-8996
URL: http://www.cardboardgalaxy.com

Description: Cardboard Galaxy.com is a web design and hosting company that serves small and mid-sized businesses in Maine. Cardboard Galaxy offers secure web site hosting and web site development services, including e-commerce solutions.

▌3799

CAROLINA ADVANCED DIGITAL

PO Box 318
125 Siler Crossing
Siler City, NC 27344
PH: (919)663-2211
TF: 800-435-2212
FX: (919)742-2279
E-mail: cad@cadinc.com
URL: http://www.cadincweb.com

Description: Carolina Advanced Digital is a company that offers a variety of Internet solutions, including web site design, e-commerce and web site hosting. Focusing on small businesses, Carolina Advanced Digital provides informational web site design, Flash animation, and full service e-commerce sites.

▌3800

CARVE MEDIA, INC.

14 Renz Rd.
Mill Valley, CA 94941
PH: (415)389-9981
FX: (415)389-9961

E-mail: info@carve.com
URL: http://www.carve.com

Description: Carve Media offers a full range of web design and development services for all sizes of companies. Carve media provides consulting services, web design services including Flash, Shockwave, and online branding and identity; information architecture and other web development services.

▌3801

CAST SHADOW DESIGN

2730 Adrian St.
San Diego, CA 92110
PH: (619)222-1447
FX: (619)255-3076
E-mail: gensd@castshadow.com
URL: http://www.castshadow.com

Description: Cast Shadow Design focuses on web site design, development and maintenance. Services offered by Cast Shadow Design include web site planning, design, redesign, graphics, programming, maintenance, hosting, and e-commerce using several applications to build customers' storefronts.

▌3802

CATALYST INTERNET, INC.

1021 Egypt Rd.
Phoenixville, PA 19460
PH: (610)246-9672
FX: (215)893-3973
E-mail: contact@catalystinternet.com
URL: http://www.catalystinternet.com

Description: Catalyst Internet, Inc. provides a variety of services created to meet the needs of each client. Services offered include web site design and development, hosting, web site management, e-business, and consulting.

▌3803

CATEGORY 4 DESIGN

300 W Main St., Ste. 201
Charlottesville, VA 22903
PH: (434)296-9963
TF: (866)296-9963
FX: (434)296-4453
E-mail: jhoyt@category4.com
URL: http://www.category4.com

Description: Category 4 Design is a company that offers web design and development services, specializing in e-commerce. Category 4 Design provides both custom web design, including information design, content development, graphics, and interaction design; and ready-made e-commerce solutions including their product Ecomm4.

▌3804
CAUGHT WEB SERVICES

2506 Ashmore Cir., Ste. 24
Thousand Oaks, CA 91362
PH: (866)236-1303
E-mail: caught@caughtweb.net
URL: http://www.caughtweb.net

Description: Caught Web Services offers web site design, hosting and maintenance. Web site design services include new site design, existing site redesign, creation of original graphics, custom JavaScripting, and conversion of sound and video to web format.

▌3805
CAVIAN TECHNOLOGY

12755 Brookhurst St., Ste. 202
Garden Grove, CA 92840
PH: (714)638-9990
FX: (714)638-9997
E-mail: support@cavian.com
URL: http://www.cavian.com

Description: Cavian Technology is a company that designs and develops web sites, information technology, and software. Services offered by Cavian Technology include custom web site development and architecture, database mining, integration, and Cavian Technology's e-commerce web package, WebFront Commerce.

▌3806
CAZARIN WEB GROUP

15250 Wayzata Blvd., Ste. 105
Wayzata, MN 55391
PH: (952)404-1222
FX: (952)404-1219
E-mail: info@cazarin.com
URL: http://www.cazarin.com

Description: Cazarin Web Group is a web site development company. Cazarin Web Group offers web site design and development, marketing services, graphic design, programming, multimedia, and Internet marketing strategy.

▌3807
CCS INTERACTIVE

1655 North Mountain Ave., Ste. 144
Upland, CA 91784
PH: (909)981-6331
FX: (909)982-2254
URL: http://www.ccsinteractive.com

Description: CCS Interactive is the Internet division of California Computer Schools, and provides custom web development and hosting. Services offered by CCS Interactive include web design and development, graphic design, multimedia, custom software, multimedia, and marketing strategy.

▌3808
CCS WEB MARKETING

PO Box 691746
Charlotte, NC 28227-7030
PH: (704)545-6699
FX: (704)573-3777
E-mail: email@ccswebmarketing.com
URL: http://www.ccswebmarketing.com

Description: CCS Web Marketing specializes in creating custom designed web sites. CCS Web Marketing services include, web site design and development, site marketing, management, and hosting, Flash design, search engine registration, and e-commerce storefronts as well as PayPal.

▌3809
C.DALTON INC

1402 JFK Cswy.
PMB 126
North Bay Village, FL 33141
PH: (305)751-4871
FX: (425)940-7405
URL: http://www.cdalton.com

Description: C. Dalton, Inc. offers its customers web site design and hosting services. These include domain name registration, e-commerce enabled shopping cart, web server co-location, and search engine submission.

▌3810
CEE NETWORK SERVICES

PO Box 530398
Livonia, MI 48153
PH: (734)261-5571
E-mail: info@ceenet.com
URL: http://www.ceenet.com

Description: CEE Network Services is a multimedia service provider. CEE Network Services provides web site design and development, electronic brochures, banner ad design, CD-ROMs, and intranet, as well as web site hosting and maintenance.

▌3811
CEEME.COM

12600 Kavanaugh Ln.
Bowie, MD 20715
PH: (301)805-0784

771

E-mail: info@ceeme.com
URL: http://www.ceeme.com

Description: CeeMe.com designs, develops and hosts web sites that showcase marketing and customer services. CeeMe.com specializes in web sites for non-profit organizations, small and home based businesses. Services offered include web site design and development, hosting, domain name registration, bulk emails, and WebCards, CeeMe.com's product.

▌3812
CENTRAL MAINE WEB

PO Box 318
Waterville, ME 04903
PH: (207)872-2368
E-mail: designer@centralmaineweb.com
URL: http://www.centralmaineweb.com

Description: Central Maine Web focuses on quality, workable web sites. Services provided by Central Maine Web include personal web sites, non-profit web sites, full-service e-commerce web sites, and small business web sites.

▌3813
CENTRIC WEB, INC.

407 Ashbury Dr.
Hinsdale, IL 60521
PH: (630)734-0741
TF: 888-920-2120
FX: (630)734-1923
E-mail: info@centricweb.com
URL: http://www.centricweb.com

Description: Centric Web, Inc. is a customer-oriented Internet service company that offers services including web design and creation, web hosting, shopping cart, credit card processing and security, Internet marketing, solutions for B2B or B2C, domain name registration, search engine placements and maintenance.

▌3814
CEO DESIGN INC.

313 Main St.
St. Joseph, MI 49085
PH: (616)983-7233
FX: (616)983-7238
E-mail: info@ceodesign.com
URL: http://www.ceodesign.com

Description: CEO Design, Inc. offers a variety of services in both digital and traditional media. Professional work includes web site design, graphic design, site architecture, audio and video, branding and stationery, marketing strategy, banner ads, search engine submission, online and email marketing, and e-commerce shopping carts and secure transactions.

▌3815
CERES COMMUNICATIONS

7221 Prairie Rd. NE
Albuquerque, NM 87109
PH: 877-560-1343
E-mail: info@ceres-communications.com
URL: http://www.ceres-communications.com

Description: Ceres Communications focuses on offering affordable web services specializing in small and home-based businesses. Those services include web site design and development, hosting, site maintenance, search engine submission, and customized online marketing plan.

▌3816
CFR WEB PRODUCTIONS

2341 Ellis Ave.
St. Paul, MN 55114
PH: (651)644-3879
E-mail: design@cfrcomm.com
URL: http://www.cfrcomm.com

Description: CFR Web Productions provides complete custom web page design and development. CFR Web Productions uses state of the art web design tools and makes web sites with high production values, strong content, and that are easy to navigate.

▌3817
CFX WEB DESIGN

4152 Meridian Street, Ste. 105-219
Bellingham, WA 98226
PH: (514)493-3601
TF: 877-682-2914
FX: (514)493-3572
URL: http://www.cfxwebdesign.com

Description: CFX Web Design is a design firm offering a variety of services in both digital and print media. Services provided by CFX Web Design include award winning web site design, web site hosting and analysis, web site redesign, graphic design and print advertising, e-commerce sites with secure transaction processing, as well as marketing, public relations, and consulting.

▌3818
CGK TECHNOLOGIES GROUP, INC.

172 Dunlop St. W, Loft A
Barrie, ON, Canada L4N1B3
PH: (705)733-9099

FX: (705)733-8859
E-mail: info@cgkgroup.com
URL: http://www.cgkgroup.com

Description: CGK Technologies Group, Inc. specializes in e-commerce web solutions. CGK Technologies Group offers Hot Banana, an e-business web content management system, as well as complete e-commerce web design and hosting services, streaming media, web statistics, web based applications, and other e-commerce marketing consultation services.

▎3819
CHAMERLIK COMPULOGIC

7840 N Lincoln Ave., Ste. 210
Skokie, IL 60077
PH: (847)679-5030
TF: 877-932-8478
FX: (847)933-9413
E-mail: info@designtech1.com
URL: http://www.designtech1.com

Description: Chamerlik Compulogic provides turnkey e-commerce solutions to its clients, including web site design and development, hosting, and web-based software. Chamerlik Compulogic also offers intranet and extranet design, web site content management, and e-marketing consulting.

▎3820
CHANNEL 88 MEDIA GROUP

1-2456 W 5th Ave.
Vancouver, BC, Canada V6K1S8
PH: (604)737-7534
FX: (604)737-7503
E-mail: info@channel88.com
URL: http://www.channel88.com

Description: Channel 88 Media Group provides web design and development services, and specializes in webcasting. Services offered include web strategy and architecture, custom programming, Flash, e-commerce web sites, streaming audio and video, and video production for webcasts.

▎3821
CHARLOTTE'S WEB STUDIOS, L.L.C.

3517 Prosperity Ave.
Fairfax, VA 22031-3322
PH: (703)876-0185
TF: (866)242-7568
FX: (703)876-0679
E-mail: solutions@charlotteswebstudios.com
URL: http://www.charlotteswebstudios.com

Description: Charlotte's Web Studios is a full service multimedia design studio that handles projects of various sizes and budgets. Services provided by Charlotte's Web Studios

include web design and development, CD-Rom production, video, Power Point presentations, displays, logos, and traditional print design.

▎3822
A CHEAP WEBSITE

Two Mid America Plz., Ste. 800
PMB 80027
Oakbrook Terrace, IL 60181
PH: 888-458-1201
E-mail: info@a-cheap-website.com
URL: http://www.acheapwebsite.com

Description: A Cheap Website is a company that specializes in low cost set-up and hosting for commercial web sites. Services provided include a 5 page web site, graphics, hosting, search engine site registration, customized web addresses, and free email accounts.

▎3823
CHERRYLAND ONLINE SERVICES

5930 US 31 S
Grawn, MI 49637
PH: (231)486-9278
FX: (231)943-8204
E-mail: sales@cosdesign.com
URL: http://www.cosdesign.com

Description: Cherryland Online Services specializes in interactive business web sites. Services provided by Cherryland Online Services include web site design and development, branded Internet access, Human Resources management, Real Estate web sites, graphic and logo design, and marketing packages.

▎3824
CHILLA COMPUTER AND INTERNET SERVICES

200 Cherokee Ln.
Jacksboro, TN 37757
PH: (423)566-1484
FX: (801)912-5161
E-mail: info@chilla.net
URL: http://www.chilla.net

Description: Chilla Computer and Internet Services offers both design and technology services to their customers. Web site design, e-commerce solutions, multimedia presentations, custom graphic design, and intranet development are some of the services that Chilla Computer and Internet Services provide.

773

▌3825
CHOPPING BLOCK

216 W 18th St., Ste. 1204
New York, NY 10011
PH: (212)463-7574
FX: (212)242-9886
E-mail: info@choppingblock.com
URL: http://www.choppingblock.com
Contact: Keith Pizer

Founded: 1996. **Description:** The Chopping Block is a design firm which believes that good design spans all mediums. Chopping Block helps Internet start-ups establish their web presence, as well as creating or expanding web sites for large corporate clients. Chopping Block prides itself on flexibility and the ability to blend technology and good design.

▌3826
CHRYSALIS LLC

2484 Warwick Ave., PMB 215
Warwick, RI 02889
PH: (401)737-0224
E-mail: info@chrysalisllc.cc
URL: http://www.chrysalisllc.cc

Description: Chrysalis LLC specializes in creative web sites and 360 degree virtual web site tours. Services include new web site design, existing site redesign, as well as photography and web site hosting.

▌3827
CIM PLICITY TECHNICAL SERVICES

5825 Sandstone Dr.
Oxford, MI 48371
PH: (248)628-2402
FX: (248)628-6957
E-mail: cimtech@cimplicitytech.com
URL: http://www.cimplicitytech.com

Description: Cim Plicity Technical Services specializes in building custom web sites. Cim Plicity's services include web site design and development, e-commerce web sites, streaming content, search recognition, site promotion, programming, and web site maintenance.

▌3828
CINCY WEB DESIGN

7719 Five Mile Rd.
Cincinnati, OH 45230
PH: (513)232-9200
FX: (513)474-8998
E-mail: info@cincywebdesign.com
URL: http://www.cincywebdesign.com

Description: Cincy Web Design offers professionally designed business web sites. Cincy Web Design provides custom graphics and logos, web design and development, site promotion, hosting and customer support.

▌3829
CIRCLE R DESIGNS

PO BOX 72375
Davis, CA 95617
PH: (530)669-6634
FX: (815)461-3450
E-mail: rodney@globie.com
URL: http://www.circlerdesigns.com

Description: Circle R Designs specializes in building fast loading, easy to use web sites. Web sites can include online order and feedback forms, counters, JavaScript, and secure servers, and are web promotion ready.

▌3830
CIRE NETWORKING, LLC

803 S Sheridan St.
Philadelphia, PA 19147-2920
PH: (215)413-2699
E-mail: inquiry@cirenet.com
URL: http://www.cirenet.com

Description: Cire Networking, LLC provides a wide variety of Internet and information technology service to its clients. Services include web site design and development, graphic design, database design and management, marketing strategies, networking, and training.

▌3831
CIRITH CONCEPTS

8727 FM 1960 E, Ste. B
Humble, TX 77346
PH: (281)852-6167
TF: (866)689-1985
FX: (281)852-6177
E-mail: sales@cirith.com
URL: http://www.cirith.com

Description: Cirith Concepts offers a range of web design and development services including streaming audio and video, database interactivity, web-enabled applications, security, supply chain management, Internet meetings, commercial transactions, and paid advertising.

▌3832
CISCO SYSTEMS INC.

170 W Tasman Dr.
San Jose, CA 95134
PH: (408)526-7208

TF: 800-553-6387
E-mail: info@cisco.com
URL: http://business.cisco.com
Contact: Sue Bostrom, Sr. Vice President

Description: One of the worldwide leaders in Internet networks, Cisco systems provides full service design and website management. Standardized and flexible architecture, well-managed content, and advanced user management systems that help rather than hinder business processes are key components of a successful Web strategy. A strategically designed website will be built around the company's long-term goals, rather than the short-term goals of individual business units, and will be built with a view toward flexibility. This type of design can unify the company's technology systems and facilitate the introduction of new business initiatives.

■ 3833
CITITECH SOLUTIONS, INC.

9101 Greenwood Ave., Ste. 303
Niles, IL 60714
PH: (847)803-8371
TF: 800-311-3888
FX: (847)257-0627
E-mail: info@cititech.net
URL: http://www.cititech.ne

Description: Cititech Solutions, Inc. is an Internet development company that provides a range of digital services. Cititech Solutions services include web site design and development, web site maintenance, e-commerce solutions, web application development, Flash animation, marketing and web site promotion, and training.

■ 3834
CITRACOM

13833-E4 Wellington Trace, Ste. 214
Wellington, FL 33414
PH: (561)792-9855
FX: (509)463-6311
E-mail: designs@citracom.com
URL: http://www.citracom.com

Description: CitraCom is a Web Development Trust, specializing in complete upscale web design and development services for web based companies. Services provided by CitraCom include web and multimedia design, web site development and maintenance, hosting, and advertising and marketing.

■ 3835
CITY DIRECT

250 Altamonte Commerce Blvd.
Altamonte Springs, FL 32714
PH: (407)682-0359

FX: (407)682-0986
E-mail: info@citydirect.com
URL: http://www.citydirect.com

Description: City Direct is a provider of Internet and technology services. City Direct offers web site design, web site hosting, ASP services, network design, custom graphic design, and e-commerce interfacing.

■ 3836
CKFS WEB PAGE DESIGN

246 Scott Dr.
Lancaster, OH 43130
PH: (740)653-7018
FX: (740)653-7018
E-mail: ckfs@greenapple.com
URL: http://www.ckfswebpagedesign.com

Description: CKFS Web Page Design is a full service, custom design web design firm. Services provided by CKFS Web Page Design include web site design, development and maintenance, small business e-commerce solutions, web page rescue and restoration, graphic design, animation, original music, and advertising and marketing.

■ 3837
CLASSY LINKS

707568 County Road 21
R.R. No. 2
Lisle, ON, Canada L0M1M0
PH: (705)466-5999
TF: 877-687-7488
E-mail: sales@classylinks.on.ca
URL: http://www.classylinks.ca/

Description: Classy Links is a company that offers web design, hosting, and programming to its customers. Services provided by Classy Links include corporate multi-leveled web site design with animated scripts and images, domain name registration, web site statistics, and secure web site hosting.

■ 3838
CLEAR CONCEPTS BUSINESS SOLUTIONS INC

264 Portage Ave.
Winnipeg, MB, Canada R3C0B6
PH: (204)943-4777
TF: (866)943-4777
E-mail: info@clearconcepts.ca
URL: http://www.clearconcepts.ca

Description: Clear Concepts Business Solutions offers its customer s a variety of Internet services. Clear Concepts provides web site design, custom, modular and starter web

775

sites, as well as offering hosting services, logo design, network consulting, and search engine strategies.

∎ 3839
CLEAR PAGES.COM

2600 N Broadway
St. Louis, MO 63102
PH: (314)621-5300
FX: (314)621-3412
E-mail: info@clearpages.com
URL: http://www.clearpages.com

Description: Clear Pages.com is a web site design firm specializing in e-commerce. Clear Pages.com analyzes the needs of its customers, then designs their web site to meet their objectives. Services offered by Clear Pages.com include HTML and Flash web development, e-commerce applications, database architecture, motion graphics, marketing, and print media.

∎ 3840
CLEARDAZE.COM

c/o Kevin Griffin
2333 Kapiolani Blvd. No.1609
Honolulu, HI 96826-4433
PH: (808)943-9238
E-mail: information@cleardaze.com
URL: http://
Contact: Kevin Griffin

Description: Clear Daze.com offers a lineup of Internet services designed to fill the needs of each client. Service include web site authoring, web site hosting, web management and scripting services, graphics design, site promotion, and community advocacy.

∎ 3841
CLEARMARK, INC.

6493 Ridings Rd.
Syracuse, NY 13206
PH: (315)432-5545
E-mail: jphelps@clearmark.com
URL: http://www.clearmark.com

Description: Clear Mark is a company that offers business, technical and design services to its clients. Clear Mark works as part of the client's team to ensure the best results for each project. Services provided include web site design and implementation, web enabled commerce, data base design and integration, custom applications, and documentation and training.

∎ 3842
CLICK.COM

4521 Sharon Rd., Ste. 410
Charlotte, NC 28211
PH: (704)365-9970
FX: (704)365-8770
E-mail: sales@click.com
URL: http://www.clickcom.com

Description: Click.com provides a range of Internet services, including web site design, w-commerce sites with shopping cart, interactive sites, web site hosting, web site add-ons for those who already have a web site, specialty search engine submission, domain registration, and distribution of customers web sites in hard copy form.

∎ 3843
CLICKERHEAD INTERACTIVE, LLC

PO Box 37
Wolfeboro, NH 03894
PH: (603)569-6441
FX: (603)569-8280
E-mail: info@clickerhead.com
URL: http://www.clickerhead.com

Description: Clickerhead Interactive, LLC is a company focused on producing turnkey web solutions that are functional and have visual impact. Services provided by Clickerhead Interactive include web site consultation and design, hosting set-up, e-commerce sites, custom graphics, photography, interactive forms, and marketing and promotion.

∎ 3844
CLIFTON DESIGN GROUP

6278 N Federal Hwy., Ste. 258
Ft. Lauderdale, FL 33308
PH: (954)782-9887
FX: (954)782-5674
URL: http://www.clifton.com

Description: Clifton Design Group is a multi-faceted design firm that produces design and advertising on the Internet and in print. Services offered by Clifton Design Group include web design, custom animations, collages, Quicktime VR and video, e-commerce web sites, hosting, and I-marketing.

∎ 3845
CLINE COMMUNICATIONS, CORP.

PO Box 3078
Richland, WA 99352-1500
PH: (509)-943-3699
E-mail: info@clinecom.net
URL: http://www.clinecommunications.net

Description: Cline Communications offers web site hosting, web site design and development for businesses, government, nonprofit organizations and personal use. Graphic design and marketing services are also provided by Cline Communications.

▌3846
CLOSERLOOK, INC.

212 W Superior St.
Chicago, IL 60610
PH: (312)640-3700
FX: (312)640-3750
E-mail: dormesher@closerlook.com
URL: http://www.closerlook.com
Contact: Dave Ormesher, CEO

Founded: 1987. **Description:** Closerlook is a company that is dedicated to helping clients connect with their customers. Closerlook provides a strategic analysis, then develops each project for its customers, including web site design, development of intranets, marketing plans and brand management, both online and offline.

▌3847
CLOUDSPACE

10244 E Colonial Dr., Ste. 106
Orlando, FL 32817
PH: (407)823-8808
FX: (407)823-8112
E-mail: info@cloudspace.com
URL: http://www.cloudspace.com

Description: Cloudspace is an Internet service company focused on web site design and development. Other services offered by Cloudspace include online software development, multimedia, digital design and content management systems for the entertainment and professional services industry.

▌3848
CLUE, INC.

81 Washington St., No. 3C
Brooklyn, NY 11201
PH: (718)254-0999
E-mail: kimberly@clueinc.net
URL: http://www.clueinc.net

Description: Clue, Inc. is a company that specializes in custom design web site and software development, as well as technical guidance for new Internet ventures. Services offered by Clue, Inc. include web site and graphic design, network architecture and deployment, technical consultation and Internet-oriented marketing advice.

▌3849
CMAIS.COM

PO Box 1602
New York, NY 10101
PH: (516)539-2310
E-mail: info@cmais.com
URL: http://www.cmais.com

Description: CMais.com offers web site design and development and web site hosting. Services provided by CMais.com include a pre-design consultation, graphic design, web site testing, search engine submission, and other marketing strategies.

▌3850
COASTAL INTERACTIVE

1116 8th St., Ste. 244
Manhattan Beach, CA 90266
PH: (310)374-5406
TF: 888-452-6278
FX: (310)376-3476
E-mail: sales@cinteract.com
URL: http://www.cinteract.com

Description: Coastal Interactive is a firm that provides both technical and creative services to businesses who would like an Internet presence. Services offered by Coastal Interactive include web site design and development, strategic consulting, e-commerce integration, site hosting and maintenance, database and networking services.

▌3851
COASTLINE WEB DESIGN

1104 S Missouri Ave., No. 206
Clearwater, FL 33756
PH: (727)446-9950
E-mail: info@coastlineinternet.com
URL: http://www.coastlinewebdesign.com

Description: CoastLine Web Design specializes in custom web site design for small and medium sized businesses. Services offered by CoastLine Web Design include web site design and redesign, customized and fully functional e-commerce sites, hosting, database solutions, and intranet design.

▌3852
COCO DESIGN ASS., INC.

1216 E Lee St.
Pensacola, FL 32503-5621
PH: (850)434-COCO
TF: 800-640-7197
URL: http://www.cocodesign.com

Description: Coco Design Associates, Inc. is a corporate communications provider that offers a variety of Internet services. Coco Design Associates provides web design, Flash animation, Internet marketing, web site maintenance and consulting, web site hosting and application development.

▌ 3853

COLLABNET, INC.

8000 Marina Blvd., Ste. 600
Brisbane, CA 94005-1865
PH: (650)228-2500
FX: (650)228-2501
URL: http://www.collab.net

Founded: 1999. **Description:** CollabNet offers its clients collaborative development of web-based software applications and a variety of consulting services, including web site design and development. CollabNet can help its clients get to market faster and reduce overall development costs.

▌ 3854

COLONY ONE ONLINE, INC.

101 SE 2nd Pl., Ste. 203
Gainesville, FL 32601
PH: (352)335-5100
TF: (866)276-6397
FX: (352)377-3452
E-mail: sales@colony1.net
URL: http://www.colony1.net

Description: Colony One Online offers many services focused on doing business on the Internet. Services provided by Colony One Online include web site design, graphic design, search engine optimization, web site modification and updates, hosting services, and marketing campaigns.

▌ 3855

COLORADO IDEA NET, INC.

1602 S Parker Rd., Ste. 107
Denver, CO 80231
PH: (303)695-4282
FX: (303)695-8320
E-mail: info@idea-net.com
URL: http://www.idea-net.com

Description: Colorado Idea Net is a full service web development firm. Services provided by Colorado Idea Net include web design and development, from story board layout to site development, e-commerce packages, web site hosting, database design, software development, and secure site services.

▌ 3856

COMDUIT, INC.

233 Wellington Rd.
Wilmington, DE 19803
PH: (302)425-4800
FX: 877-484-6248
E-mail: info@comduit.com
URL: http://www.comduit.com

Description: Comduit, Inc. is a full service web design agency, specializing in creativity and innovation. Services provided by Comduit include web design, development, and hosting, web site promotion, user interface design, and photography.

▌ 3857

COMET MEDIA

307A 23rd St.
Brooklyn, NY 11215
PH: (718)768-2572
E-mail: sales@cometmedia.com
URL: http://www.cometmedia.com

Description: Comet Media is a design studio specializing in web graphics. Services provided by Comet Media include web site design and development, graphic design, content management, animation, and web site maintenance.

▌ 3858

COMITNOW

P.O. Box 446
Clay, AL 35048-0446
PH: 877-266-8913
FX: (205)853-1779
E-mail: sales@comitnow.com
URL: http://www.comitnow.com

Description: Comitnow offers web design and hosting services, including complete layout and design. Comitnow also offers graphic design, Flash design, CGI programming, and marketing services.

▌ 3859

COMMARK

330 3rd St. NE
Mayville, ND 58257
PH: (701)786-4670
FX: (701)786-4671
E-mail: marketservices@commark.com
URL: http://www.commark.com

Description: ComMark provides communications and marketing tools for businesses and other organizations. ComMark offers services including complete web site design, database-driven web based information system design, web site hosting, business process analysis and solution design and development, marketing, and training.

∎ 3860
COMMERCIAL-RESOURCES.COM

5331 S Meade
Chicago, IL 60638
PH: (773)735-5144
E-mail: sales@commercial-resources.com
URL: http://www.commercial-resources.com

Description: Commercial-Resources.com is a studio that offers web site design and hosting. Services provided by Commercial-Resources.com include custom web design, do-it-yourself web design packages, e-commerce and merchant accounts, shopping carts, web site maintenance, and online marketing.

∎ 3861
COMMOTION INTERACTIVE

2515 McKinney Ave., Ste. 1585
Dallas, TX 75201
PH: (214)303-1320
FX: (214)303-1285
E-mail: questions@commotioninteractive.com
URL: http://www.commotioninteractive.com

Description: ComMotion serves businesses from new start-ups to Global 100 companies, offering complete web site design and development specializing in animation and motion graphics, as well as web site hosting, and strategic marketing consultation services.

∎ 3862
COMMPACT DIGITAL ARTS, INC.

2760 Tech Dr., No. 102
Bettendorf, IA 52722
PH: (319)332-1401
E-mail: info@commpact.com
URL: http://www.commpact.com

Description: CommPact Digital Arts, Inc. provides businesses with Internet and multimedia programming. CommPact Digital Arts designs web site, creates interactive multimedia CD-ROMs, and offers web site hosting services.

∎ 3863
COMPANYV.COM CORP.

1007 Montana Ave., No.102
Santa Monica, CA 90403
PH: (310)395-7456
FX: (310)395-9176

URL: http://www.companyV.com

Description: CompanyV offers a range of Internet services including web site design and development. CompanyV specializes in web sites that work, and also provides web site hosting, strategy design, marketing, and public relations services.

∎ 3864
COMPLEXERO, INC.

851 Miles Ave., No. 26
Winter Park, FL 32789
PH: (321)287-4718
FX: (240)597-5807
E-mail: info@complexero.com
URL: http://www.complexero.com

Description: CompleXero, Inc. specializes in small business web design and excellent customer service. Professional work provided by CompleXero includes affordable web site design and hosting, e-commerce, Flash, graphic design, banner ads, web site promotion and web site redesign.

∎ 3865
COMPROTEX WEB DEVELOPMENT

1805 Brazoria Dr.
Mesquite, TX 75150
PH: (972)681-4104
TF: 888-334-9573
E-mail: sales@comprotex.com
URL: http://www.comprotex.com

Description: Comprotex Web Development is a full service web design and development firm offering a turnkey approach to web development projects. Services offered include complete web design and development, Flash presentation, animation, database design and development, hosting, marketing consultation, and web site promotion.

∎ 3866
COMPSAVER COMPUTERS

72 Outwater Rd.
Bennington, VT 05201
PH: (802)442-9427
E-mail: sales@compsaver2000.com
URL: http://www.compsaver2000.com

Description: Compsaver Computers specializes in inexpensive and professional web sites. Services offered by Compsaver Computers include custom web site design, web site hosting, and web site promotion.

■ 3867

COMPUDOC

PO Box 934
Hanover, PA 17331
PH: (717)630-8868
E-mail: info@compudocinc.com
URL: http://www.comp-doc.com

Description: Compudoc provides its clients with e-commerce solutions, web site design and development, hosting, domain name registration, autoresponders, web site statistics, and email accounts.

■ 3868

COMPUNERDZ WEB CREATIONS

500 N Congress Ave., No. C212
Delray Beach, FL 33445
PH: (561)330-7501
TF: 888-558-6928
FX: (419)818-0438
E-mail: info@compunerdz.com
URL: http://www.compunerdz.com

Description: CompuNerdz Web Development offers complete web design and development, as well as web hosting. Services provided include special development for Bed and Breakfast companies, as well as e-commerce sites, database integration, graphic design, and web site promotion.

■ 3869

COMPUTER BUSINESS SOLUTIONS, INC

85 Sheer Plz.
Plainview, NY 11803
PH: (516)746-1950
FX: (516)746-1951
E-mail: info@cbsits.com
URL: http://www.cbsits.com

Description: Computer Business Solutions, Inc. is a firm that offers a variety of computer and Internet solutions. Services provided by Computer Business Solutions include web site design, e-commerce web sites that can be maintained by the client, web site marketing, and web site maintenance.

■ 3870

COMPUTER EVOLUTIONS, INC.

1455 Rosedale Ave.
Middletown, PA 17057
PH: (717)939-6905
FX: (717)986-9155
E-mail: info@ceidesign.com
URL: http://www.computer-evolutions.com

Description: Computer Evolutions is an Internet solutions company that provides a variety of services. Computer Evolutions offers web site design, including site redesign, e-commerce solutions, web site marketing, advanced applications, and web site hosting.

■ 3871

COMPUTER GRAPHICS UNLIMITED, INC.

2051 Acushnet Ave.
New Bedford, MA 02745
PH: (508)985-0051
TF: (866)GOT-AWEB
FX: (617)687-8387
E-mail: sales@cguweb.com
URL: http://www.cguweb.com

Description: Computer Graphics Unlimited, Inc. is a web design firm that offers complete custom web design projects. Services provided include corporate web sites, e-commerce sites, web site hosting, site support and maintenance, and web site promotion.

■ 3872

COMPUTER TECHNIQUES, INC.

980 Sunrise Hwy.
Babylon, NY 11704
PH: (631)422-0531
E-mail: cathy@loyal.net
URL: http://www.computertechniques.net

Description: Computer Techniques, Inc. offers creative and affordable web site design. Services provided include interactive forms, custom graphics, Flash, Java, HTML coding, e-commerce web sites, and web site maintenance and promotion.

■ 3873

COMPUTING MAGIC

PO Box 1052
Melbourne, FL 32902-1052
PH: (866)243-7114
E-mail: webmaster@computingmagic.net
URL: http://www.computingmagic.net

Description: Computing Magic offers a several Internet services, including web design and development. Services provided by Computing Magic include web site design, graphics, Flash, video and sound, database design, domain name services, and web site hosting.

■ 3874

COMPUTR WEB DESIGN

461 Lawnview Cir.
Morgantown, WV 26505
PH: (304)599-6465

E-mail: webdesigns@computr.net
URL: http://www.computr.net

Description: CompuTR Web Design specializes in designing web sites. Services offered by CompuTR Web Designs include e-commerce web sites, web site design and maintenance, JavaScripting, and site search functionality.

∎ 3875
COMSITE WEB SERVICE

321 Clark St.
Auburn, NY 13021
PH: (315)258-8330
TF: 800-863-8330
E-mail: info@com-site.com
URL: http://www.com-site.com

Description: ComSite Web Service specializes in web site design for businesses and nonprofit organizations. Services provided include web site design, graphic design, e-commerce, secure shopping, email forms, web site hosting and promotion.

∎ 3876
CONCEPT DEVELOPERS, LLC

PO Box 1685
College Park, MD 20741-1685
PH: (240)381-3888
FX: (503)213-6445
E-mail: info@conceptdevelopers.com
URL: http://www.conceptdevelopers.com

Description: Concept Developers, LLC offers professional web site development focused on the client's needs. Concept Developers offers web site planning, web site design and redesign, logo development, Flash, banner ads, search engine placement, marketing strategy, and web site hosting.

∎ 3877
CONCEPT FACTORY

116 E Greenway, Ste. 100
Mesa, AZ 85203
PH: (480)649-3400
E-mail: webmaster@concept-factory.com
URL: http://www.concept-factory.com

Description: Concept Factory offers web site design and development focused on client objectives. Services provided by Concept Factory include e-commerce development, web site planning, design, and development, graphic design, corporate identity, database development, and web site hosting and maintenance.

∎ 3878
CONCEPTURE SOLUTIONS

PO Box 414
Molineort, IL 61266
PH: (309)764-2022
TF: (866)402-4678
FX: (309)764-4490
E-mail: info@concepture.net
URL: http://www.concepture.net

Description: Concepture Solutions offers a variety of e-business solutions. Services provided by Concepture Solutions include web design and development, e-commerce, graphic design, databases, intranets, secure hosting, domain names, and web site statistics.

∎ 3879
CONNECTEC COMMUNICATIONS, INC.

210 Interstate N Pkwy., Ste. 700
Atlanta, GA 30339
PH: (770)618-0862
FX: (770)517-2975
E-mail: info@connectec.com
URL: http://www.connectec.com

Description: ConnecTec Communications, Inc. focuses on helping clients develop a presence on the Internet. Services offered by ConnecTec Communications include web site design and hosting, interactive applications, suggestions on site promotion, email hosting, and touchscreen kiosks.

∎ 3880
CONNELLY DESIGN

3113 Frazer Ave. NW
Canton, OH 44709
PH: (330)492-4757
E-mail: tellmemore@connelly-design.com
URL: http://www.connelly-design.com

Description: Connelly Design provides web site design services to all sizes of business. Connelly Design offers web site design, Flash animation, e-commerce, and database integration.

∎ 3881
CONOR COMMUNICATIONS

1501 Little Gloucester Rd., No.F29
Blackwood, NJ 08012
PH: (206)309-6626
FX: (856)374-5875
E-mail: webmaster@conorcomms.com
URL: http://www.conorcomms.com

Description: Conor Communications offers full service web site design and hosting, focusing on e-commerce sites. Conor Communications provides web page building tools so that business professionals can build their own sites, as well as providing site design and maintenance services.

▌3882
CONQUER THE WEB

904 Pompton Ave.
Cedar Grove, NJ 07009
PH: (973)857-6551
TF: 877-843-0932
URL: http://www.conquertheweb.com

Description: Conquer The Web offers a range of web site design and hosting services, focusing on e-commerce. Services provided include web site design, shockwave, site redesign, promotion, and hosting.

▌3883
CONTACT DESIGNS

8960 E Raintree Dr., Ste. 400
Scottsdale, AZ 85260
PH: (480)921-1732
FX: 800-863-7359
E-mail: info@contactdesigns.com
URL: http://www.contactdesigns.com

Description: Contact Designs is a full service Internet solutions and design firm, offering its products and services to a variety of industries. Contact Designs provides web site design, database integration, e-commerce, application development, hosting, and online marketing.

▌3884
CONTROL V INTERACTIVE

19016 E 34th Ter.
Independence, MO 64057
PH: 800-383-5266
E-mail: sales@supplyanddemand.com
URL: http://www.controlv.com

Description: Control V Interactive is a full service new media company. Control V specializes in e-commerce web site design and development, and offers services including interface design, shockwave-interactive presentations, audio and video editing, catalogs, package design, web community integration, graphics and streaming multimedia.

▌3885
CONTROLTEC

330 S Main St.
Fallbrook, CA 92028
PH: (760)723-2104

FX: (760)723-5255
E-mail: info@controltec.com
URL: http://www.controltec.com

Description: Controltec is a company that offers a variety of Internet services, including e-business web design and application development. Controltec provides services including, web site design and hosting, secure payment systems, customer personalization, database management and analysis, as well as KinderProducts software.

▌3886
CONVEX MEDIA

24 S Main St.
Oconomowoc, WI 53066
PH: (262)244-0005
TF: 888-433-2689
FX: (262)244-0008
E-mail: info@convexmedia.com
URL: http://www.convexmedia.com

Description: Convex Media is an information technology outsourcing company that provides web site design and development, informational and e-commerce sites, hosting, web site maintenance, and Internet consulting services.

▌3887
CONWAYCO

114 N Charlotte St.
Lancaster, PA 17603-3402
PH: (717)295-0009
URL: http://www.conwayco.net

Description: ConwayCo is a firm that serves its clients through multimedia, design and marketing services in a variety of media. ConwayCo offers web site design and development, functional e-commerce site design, streaming media, banner ads, interactive multimedia, database management, and software development; as well as providing advertising and marketing in both traditional and new media.

▌3888
COOL WEB DESIGN

PO Box 22
Rome, OH 44085
PH: (216)373-1525
FX: (216)373-1535
E-mail: webms@cool-webdesign.com
URL: http://www.cool-webdesign.com

Description: Cool Web Design offers its clients a variety of web design options. Services provided by Cool Web Design include web design and development, streaming video, e-commerce web sites, dynamic databases, interactive multimedia, and web site hosting.

▌3889
CORAZON DEL ORO COMMUNICATIONS, LLC

PO Box 914
Cortaro, AZ 85652-0914
PH: (520)572-0145
TF: (866)398-4228
E-mail: corazondeloro@corazondeloro.com
URL: http://www.corazondeloro.com

Description: Corazon del Oro Communications, LLC specializes in providing Internet services to socially conscious businesses and organizations, including clients such as educational and scientific institutions, charities and non-profits. Services offered include web site design and development, e-commerce hosting, site promotion and web site maintenance.

▌3890
CORP IMAGES.NET

131 11th. St., SE, Ste. B
Washington, DC 20003
PH: (202)546-4424
TF: 877-472-7997
FX: (801)516-3854
E-mail: sales@corpimages.net
URL: http://www.corpimages.net

Description: Corp Images.net offers its web site design and development services in English, Spanish, and Italian. Services provided by Corp Images include web site design, domain name registration, web site hosting, web site programming, and Internet marketing consultations.

▌3891
CORPORATE TECHNOLOGY, INC.

38 W 32nd St.
New York, NY 10001
PH: (212)239-3900
FX: (212)239-8270
E-mail: info@corptechusa.com
URL: http://www.corptechusa.com

Founded: 1984. **Description:** Corporate Technology, Inc. serves a mix of clients from small businesses and nonprofit organizations, to large corporations. Services provided by Corporate Technology include e-commerce enabled web sites designed to generate revenue, search engine optimization, and database design.

▌3892
CORPORATE WEB SERVICES, INC. (CWS)

829 3rd Ave. SE, Ste. 225
Rochester, MN 55904
PH: (507)289-2229
TF: 888-426-7793
FX: (507)289-0349
E-mail: sales@cws.net
URL: http://www.cws.net

Description: Corporate Web Services designs business web sites with the client's purpose in mind. Services offered by Corporate Web Services include e-commerce site design, HTML, graphics design, web site hosting, and search engine registration.

▌3893
CORTECH

7257 Beverly Blvd., Ste. 108
Los Angeles, CA 90036
PH: (323)634-7557
E-mail: sales@cortech.com
URL: http://www.cortech.com

Description: CorTech offers a variety of technical services to its customers, including web site design and development. CorTech provides both informational and e-commerce web site development, animation, graphic design, application development, and enterprise network sales.

▌3894
COSMOPOLITAN WEB DESIGNS

P.O. Box 1487
Dearborn, MI 48121
PH: (248)399-5338
E-mail: webmaster@cosmopolitanwebdesigns.com
URL: http://www.cosmopolitanwebdesigns.com

Description: Cosmopolitan Web Designs offers web site design and development. Specializing in cross cultural and politically correct designs, Cosmopolitan Web Designs also provides services including multi-lingual web sites, e-commerce, secure sites, Internet advertising and marketing, and connections to major search engines.

▌3895
COSMOS DESIGNS

5434 Sherwood Dr.
Shawnee Mission, KS 66205-2235
PH: (913)677-4437
E-mail: designpro@cosmosdesigns.com
URL: http://www.cosmosdesigns.com

Description: Cosmos Designs specializes in designing commercial and corporate web sites, and focuses on personal service. Cosmos Designs offers web site design and development, e-commerce sites, site promotion, banner ads, and web site maintenance and hosting.

▌3896
CPROS, INC.

1094 Clayton Rd.
Powhatan, VA 23139
PH: (804)492-4777
FX: (804)492-3524
E-mail: info@cprosvcs.com
URL: http://www.cprosvcs.com

Description: CProS, Inc. is a company that offers web site design and development, and hosting services. CProS provides custom web site design in line with current client advertising, as well as general consulting on Internet business issues.

▌3897
CRAFTIX TECHNICAL SOLUTIONS

833 Hilltop Rd.
Baltimore, MD 21228-5310
PH: (410)788-5651
FX: (410)788-5651
E-mail: info@craftix.com
URL: http://www.craftix.com

Description: Craftix Technical Solutions specializes in web site design and development at affordable prices. Services offered by Craftix Technical Solutions include custom web site design, hosting, web site statistics, interactive forms, search engine registration, e-commerce sites, and web-enabled database solutions.

▌3898
CREATE-A-WEBSITE

PO Box 846
2341 Boston Rd.
Wilbraham, MA 01095
PH: (413)596-4321
TF: 877-596-4321
FX: (413)596-9807
E-mail: info@createawebsite.net
URL: http://www.createawebsite.net

Description: Create-A-Website is a full service Internet presence provider, offering services including web site design, development, and hosting, as well as e-commerce web sites, and database solutions.

▌3899
CREATING GENIUS, INC.

244-39 88th Rd.
Bellerose, NY 11426
PH: (718)831-9313
TF: (866)224-3648
FX: (718)962-0137

E-mail: rkirkwood@creatinggenius.com
URL: http://www.creatinggenius.com

Description: Creating Genius, Inc. specializes in web site design, development and hosting. Services offered by Creating Genius include graphic design, programming, site authoring, multimedia, applications and databases, e-commerce and B2B web sites, and site promotion.

▌3900
CREATIVE COMMUNICATIONS

2 The Court, The Green
Stoke Gifford
Bristol BS348PD, United Kingdom
PH: 44 0 117 979 3223
FX: 44 0 117 979 3495
E-mail: mail@creativecomm.co.uk
URL: http://www.creativecomm.co.uk

Description: Creative Communications provides web site design as well as other services including public relations, copywriting, media liason, brochures, and corporate identities. Creative Communications offers creative web site design, tailored to meet the clients needs.

▌3901
CREATIVE COMPUTER TECHNOLOGIES

4578 N 1st St., No. 199
Fresno, CA 93726
PH: (559)346-1035
TF: (866)346-1035
FX: (559)485-4422
E-mail: info@cctechnologies.net
URL: http://www.cctechnologies.net

Description: Creative Computer Technologies provides web design and development services to businesses in the central California area. Services offered by Creative Computer Technologies include custom web site development, hosting, e-commerce sites, web database development, intranet and extranet, auctions, and Real Estate web sites and databases.

▌3902
CREATIVE DATA DECISIONS, INC.

72 Hope Rd., Ste. 101
Holland, PA 18966
PH: (215)364-4079
E-mail: mail@creativedd.com
URL: http://www.creativedd.com

Description: Creative Data Decisions, Inc. specializes in the development of e-commerce web sites and software, including encryption services. Creative Data Decisions also provides systems integration services and specialty software application development.

∎ 3903
CREATIVE DESIGN ASSOCIATES

PO Box 7261
Rochester, MN 55903-7261
PH: 877-208-8975
E-mail: wayne@creativedesignassociates.com
URL: http://www.creativedesignassociates.com
Contact: Wayne Cichanski, CEO

Description: Creative Design Associates is an interactive media development firm that offers its clients web site design, CD-ROM and multimedia development, and marketing and business development. Creative Design Associates designs and implements web sites and e-commerce sites for companies of any size.

∎ 3904
CREATIVE FUSION DESIGN

2141 E Broadway Rd., Ste. 214
Tempe, AZ 85282
PH: (480)703-8475
E-mail: info@creativefusiondesign.com
URL: http://www.creativefusiondesign.com

Founded: 1994. **Description:** Creative Fusion Design is a full service web design company focused on web site design, virtual reality, e-commerce, and database development. Other services offered by Creative Fusion Design include graphic design, photography and print media.

∎ 3905
CREATIVE INTENTIONS

3740 N Romero Rd., No. 166
Tucson, AZ 85705
PH: (520)405-0942
FX: (520)888-0024
E-mail: CreativeIntentions@angelfire.com
URL: http://www.creativeintentions.com

Description: Creative Intentions specializes in do-it-yourself web site designs, and also provides custom web site design services. Creative Intentions also offers web site hosting, and guaranteed search engine ranking.

∎ 3906
CREATIVE MEDIA GROUP

245 Main St.
Chester, NJ 07930
PH: (908)879-9565
FX: (908)879-9638
E-mail: ralph@cmg.net
URL: http://www.cmg.net

Description: Creative Media Group specializes in e-commerce solutions, working with both large corporations and smaller businesses. Services provided by Creative Media Group include multi-lingual web sites, web site development, maintenance and hosting, corporate intranets, online support services, and training.

∎ 3907
CREATIVE MOONLIGHTER.COM

5001 Baum Blvd., Ste. 696
Pittsburgh, PA 15213
PH: (412)687-1316
FX: (412)687-4466
URL: http://www.creativemoonlighter.com

Description: Creative Moonlighter.com is a provider of design resources for businesses. Companies needing temporary or part-time creative expertise and moonlighters wanting to make an extra income or expand their client base, are brought together at Creative Moonlighter.com. Designers are available to assist clients in web site design and other graphic arts needs.

∎ 3908
CREATIVE PLANNING FOR PROFESSIONALS

78-44 80TH St., 2nd Fl.
Glendale, NY 11385
PH: (718)456-7648
E-mail: info@creativeplanning.org
URL: http://www.creativeplanning.org

Description: Creative Planning specializes in providing web site design and hosting for small businesses. Other services offered by Creative Planning include animation, graphics, banner ads, and planning.

∎ 3909
CREATIVE SYSTEMS SOLUTIONS

1945 Camino Vida Roble, Ste. L
Carlsbad, CA 92008
PH: (760)438-1200
FX: (760)438-1265
E-mail: info@creative-sys.com
URL: http://www.creative-sys.com

Founded: 1990. **Description:** Creative Systems Solutions offers a full spectrum of web services, as well as other information technology solutions. Services provided by Creative Systems Solutions include web design, development and support, and marketing consultation.

■ 3910
CREED COMMUNICATIONS

PO Box 705
Lebanon, IN 46052
PH: (317)535-9350
FX: (928)563-8853
E-mail: info@creedcomm.com
URL: http://www.creedcomm.com

Description: Creed Communications specializes in designing web sites for small businesses. Services offered by Creed Communications include web site design and redesign, graphics, search engine submission, web site hosting, and customer support services.

■ 3911
CREOLE WEB DESIGN

1405 N Turnbull Dr.
Metairie, LA 70001
PH: (504)606-3201
E-mail: sales@creolewebdesign.com
URL: http://www.creolewebdesign.com

Description: Creole Web Design focuses on creating web sites for small businesses. Creole Web Design also offers web site hosting, site maintenance, networking, graphics, and web site statistics.

■ 3912
CRIBELLUM

PO Box 963
Novi, MI 48376-0963
PH: (248)596-1901
FX: (248)596-1899
URL: http://www.cribellum.com

Description: Cribellum offers web site design, development, and hosting services for both personal and business web sites. Services include HTML page design, programming, graphic design, and database connection.

■ 3913
CROSS WEB DESIGN AND HOSTING

6405 Sefton Ave.
Baltimore, MD 21214
PH: (410)254-1802
TF: 877-CROSS-WEB
FX: (240)536-0065
E-mail: sales@cross-web.com
URL: http://www.cross-web.com

Description: Cross Web Design and Hosting offers custom designed and user-friendly web sites for small to medium sized businesses. Services provided include web site design, search engine optimization, image enhancement, browser design, and web site hosting.

■ 3914
CRYSTALINK, INC.

332 W Broadway, Ste. 1620
Louisville, KY 40202
PH: (502)583-9907
FX: (502)583-9757
E-mail: info@crystalink.net
URL: http://www.crystalink.net

Description: CrystaLink provides web site design and development, custom designed e-commerce sites, pre-packaged e-commerce sites, web hosting, and intranet development.

■ 3915
CSR SOLUTIONS,INC.

14 Piedmont Dr.
Old Bridge, NJ 08857
PH: (732)607-6499
FX: (732)607-6474
E-mail: info@csr-solutions.com
URL: http://www.csr-solutions.com

Description: CSR Solutions,Inc. provides a variety of web services to businesses. CSR Solutions offers web site design, Flash animations, graphics, custom forms, web site hosting, site promotion, and web site back-up services.

■ 3916
CUESTA TECHNOLOGIES, LLC

1791 Broadway, Suite 203
Redwood City, CA 94063
PH: 888-932-9004
E-mail: info@cuesta.com
URL: http://www.cuesta.com

Description: Cuesta Technologies, LLC is a full service web engineering company that builds web pages, and offers web site hosting. Cuesta Technologies also provides a remote web publishing tool, and creates online catalogs complete with security and transaction processing.

■ 3917
CUSTOM WEB DESIGN AND HOSTING

3 Aylesford Ln.
Bella Vista, AR 72715
PH: (501)855-2991
E-mail: info@customwebdesignandhosting.com
URL: http://www.customwebdesignandhosting.com

Description: Custom Web Design and Hosting specializes in web site design and hosting for small and home-based businesses. Services provided by Custom Web Design and Hosting include custom web site design, hosting, e-commerce sites, web site maintenance, and site promotion.

∎ 3918
CUSTOM WEB PAGES

4016 E Riverside Dr.
PO Box 15992
Evansville, IN 47716-0992
PH: (812)474-9754
E-mail: allen@customwebpages.com
URL: http://www.customwebpages.com

Description: Custom Web Pages focuses on creating web pages for small businesses, entrepreneurs, and nonprofit organizations. Custom Web Pages provides web page design, e-commerce site design, Flash, site re-design and updating, web site hosting, and search engine submission.

∎ 3919
CWEB COMMUNICATIONS

207 W Main
Denison, TX 75020
PH: (903)463-6958
FX: (903)463-5838
E-mail: webdesign@cwebcomm.com
URL: http://www.cwebcomm.com

Description: Cweb Communications is a full service web design firm. Cweb Communications offers web site design, domain registration, hosting, e-commerce development, logo design, search engine submission, and advertising planning and consulting.

∎ 3920
CYBAIM

c/o Customer Service, HalfPrice Domain
615 N Wolfe St., No. 84
Baltimore, MD 21205
PH: 800-204-9904
FX: 888-240-9250
URL: http://www.cybaim.com

Description: Cybaim offers fully outsourced web development solutions for its clients. Cybaim provides web design and development, interactive web sites, e-commerce solutions for small to medium sized businesses, and a variety of programming services.

∎ 3921
CYBER ARTISANS WEB DEVELOPERS

53 Charlotte Rd.
Newton, MA 02459
PH: (617)965-4110
FX: (617)332-7270
E-mail: info@cyberartisans.com
URL: http://www.cyberartisans.com

Description: Cyber Artisans Web Developers is a company which designs and maintains web sites. Cyber Artisans also revamps existing web sites and provides web site hosting services. With experienced staff members, Cyber Artisans offers consulting in the areas of marketing and communications.

∎ 3922
CYBER COMMUNICATIONS INTERNET MARKETING

1169 SW Fox Den Way
Palm City, FL 34990
PH: (561)223-6313
FX: (561)223-1044
E-mail: sales@cyberchoice.com
URL: http://www.cyberchoice.com
Contact: Craig Cuthrell

Description: Cyber Communications Internet Marketing focuses on offering Internet solutions for small businesses. Web site design and hosting, shopping cart set up, submission to major search engines, and Internet access plans are some of the services Cyber Communications offers to the small business professional. One on one attention to each customer is a consideration of Cyber Communications.

∎ 3923
CYBER DIMMENSIONS

218 S Fordham Ave.
Aurora, IL 60506
PH: (630)859-2828
E-mail: sales@cyberdimmensions.com
URL: http://www.cyberdimmensions.com

Description: Cyber Dimmensions provides web site design and hosting services. Professional work offered by Cyber Dimmensions includes programming, graphic design, database integration for e-commerce, intranets, and search engine optimization.

∎ 3924
CYBER VILLAGE NETWORKERS

7773 Blueberry Hill
Ellicott City, MD 21043-7911
PH: (410)579-1993

FX: (410)579-1773
E-mail: connie@cybernetworkers.com
URL: http://www.cybernetworkers.com
Contact: Connie S. Mazur, President and Marketing Director

Founded: 1996. **Description:** Cyber Village Networkers provides its clients with services including web site design and development, web site hosting and maintenance, Flash and video production and streaming, banner ad design, domain name registration, e-commerce purchasing and tracking, CD multimedia, and secure members only sites.

▌3925
CYBERHOSTINGBD.NET

PO Box 181
Delware Water Gap, PA 18327
PH: (570)341-5669
FX: (570)341-5669
E-mail: info@cyberhostingbd.net
URL: http://www.cyberhostingbd.net

Description: Cyberhostingbd.net offers web site design, including consultation, sound, animation, or video, e-commerce web sites, as well as hosting, site maintenance and a variety of promotion options.

▌3926
CYBERNOESIS

Attn: Stephen Johnson
2701 Beech Way
Longmont, CO 80503
PH: (303)678- 5389
FX: (303)678 - 5389
E-mail: sjohnson@cybernoesis.com
URL: http://www.cybernoesis.com

Description: Cybernoesis creates custom database driven web sites and web applications. Services provided by Cybernoesis include business and organization web sites, game web sites, online surveys, and online tracking systems.

▌3927
CYBERONIC INTERNET COMMUNICATIONS, INC.

10 Mechanic St.
Worcester, MA 01608
PH: (508)753-4545
TF: 888-929-2372
FX: (508)831-7325
E-mail: info@cyberonic.com
URL: http://www.cyberonic.com

Description: Cyberonic Internet Communications offers a several complete web site design packages, as well as Internet hosting and software development. The web site design packages are created for businesses with a need to simply publish their company's information, and for those businesses that need interactive sessions with web site visitors.

▌3928
DAGAN DESIGNS

2-198 Bell St. N
Ottawa, ON, Canada K1R7E5
PH: (613)563-0223
E-mail: richard@dagandesigns.com
URL: http://www.dagandesigns.com

Description: Dagan Designs specializes in web site design for small businesses, nonprofit organizations, and individuals who would like to establish an Internet presence. Services provided include an initial consultation, web site design, graphics creation, hosting, and search engine registration.

▌3929
DAKIS AND ASSOCIATES

153 Dufferin St., Ste. 100
Toronto, ON, Canada M6K1Y9
PH: (416)516-7335
FX: (416)516-9733
URL: http://www.dakisdna.com

Description: Dakis and Associates is a design communications firm that offers a variety of services including web site design, interactivity, corporate identity, and branding.

▌3930
DAKOTA GROUP

5754 Pacific Center Blvd., Suite 202
San Diego, CA 92121
PH: (858)777-7000
FX: (858)777-7001
E-mail: sglidden@dakotagroup.com
URL: http://www.dakotagroup.com

Description: The Dakota Group offers a wide variety of communications services, including web site design. Other services provided by the Dakota Group include Flash animation, content management, e-commerce architecture, streaming video, CD-ROM production, web site hosting, and secure servers.

▌3931
DALTIN DESIGNS

PO Box 941134
Plano, TX 75094
PH: (214)282-8539

E-mail: info@daltindesigns.com
URL: http://www.daltindesigns.com

Description: Daltin Designs offers professional web design services. Daltin Designs provides web site design and layout, site hosting and set-up, graphics, and domain registration.

▌3932
DANA POINT COMMUNICATIONS

24681 La Plaza
Dana Point, CA 92629
PH: (949)443-4172
FX: (949)443-9516
E-mail: sales@beach.net
URL: http://www.beach.net

Description: Dana Point Communications specializes in e-commerce web sites and client/server software development. Other services provided by **Dana Point Communications** include web-enabled e-commerce solutions, e-commerce consulting, B2B, transaction processing, and database design and integration.

▌3933
D'ANCONIA DESIGN

4711 W 33rd Ave.
Denver, CO 80212
PH: (303)909-3180
E-mail: support@danconiadesign.com
URL: http://www.danconiadesign.com

Description: D'Anconia Design creates complete web site solutions, specializing in high-end web site design and implementation such as Flash animation, database design and implementation. Other services offered include HTML and graphic design.

▌3934
DANSO

7460 NW 4th St., Ste. 204
Plantation, FL 33317
PH: (954)683-7970
E-mail: sales@danso.com
URL: http://www.danso.com

Description: Danso offers Internet services including web site design and development, including e-commerce sites, wireless web applications, web site maintenance and web site marketing.

▌3935
DAPPER TECHNOLOGIES

358 N. La Cumbre Rd.
Santa Barbara, CA 93110
PH: (805)451-5745

E-mail: info@dapperdesign.com
URL: http://www.dapperdesign.com

Description: Dapper Technologies focuses on e-business applications and services. Dapper Technologies provides web site design, redesign, web application development, web strategy consulting, e-commerce development, intranet and extranet design, and Flash development.

▌3936
DARK HORSE DESIGN

148 Brandon Ct.
Neshanic Station, NJ 08853
PH: (732)235-1110
E-mail: webmaster@dhdesign.com
URL: http://www.dhdesign.com

Description: Dark Horse Design designs and develops web sites for all sizes of business. Services offered by Dark Horse Design include basic web site design, custom web sites, original graphics and logo design, hosting, and promotion services.

▌3937
DARKSTAR DESIGN, INC.

PO Box 8261
Nashville, TN 37076
PH: (615)883-3399
FX: (615)885-0120
E-mail: info@darkstardesign.com
URL: http://www.darkstardesign.com

Description: Darkstar Design offers Internet solutions including web site design and development services, e-commerce site development, Internet marketing, graphic design, interactive multimedia, and web site hosting.

▌3938
THE DARN BARN

PO Box 48
Stanhope, NJ 07874
PH: (973)426-9294
E-mail: info@thedarnbarn.com
URL: http://www.thedarnbarn.com

Description: The Darn Barn is a design firm that builds custom web sites for its clients. Other services offered by The Darn Barn include web site redesign, Flash, shopping cart systems for e-commerce sites, web site hosting and maintenance, and streaming video production.

▌3939
DAR'S BY DESIGN

825 Blaine St.
Steilacoom, WA 98388
PH: (253)582-5048
TF: 800-839-3625
E-mail: design@darsbydesign.com
URL: http://www.darsbydesign.com

Description: Dar's By Design provides an international team of web site designers and developers to serve their clients. Services offered by Dar's By Design include web site design, redesign and maintenance, graphic design, database development, Flash animation, logos, and web site hosting.

▌3940
DARWYN WEB STUDIOS

4921 Douglas Ave., Ste. 5
Des Moines, IA 50310
PH: (515)331-1658
FX: (515)331-0885
E-mail: info@darwyn.com
URL: http://www.darwyn.com

Description: Darwyn Web Studios begins each web design project with a rigorous planning process to define client objectives. Services provided by Darwyn Web Studios include web site design and maintenance, database driven web sites, marketing, and branding strategies.

▌3941
DAS SOFTWARE

690 Innovation Dr.
Kingston, ON, Canada K7K7E7
PH: (613)549-3131
E-mail: admin@das.ca
URL: http://www.das.ca

Description: DAS Software is a full service web development company that specializes in the creation of dynamic database driven web sites. Services offered include e-commerce site development, supply chain integration, database web applications, multimedia development, and Internet presence development.

▌3942
DAS STUDIO

209 N Grove Ave., Ste. 3
Chicago, IL 60302
PH: (312)933-4988
E-mail: info@dasstudio.com
URL: http://www.dasStudio.com

Description: Das Studio is a full service web production company offering a variety of Internet solutions. Das Studio provides web site design and architecture, database integration, e-commerce solutions, site auditing, site marketing, banner ads, and industry research.

▌3943
DASHAVER GRAPHICS AND WEB DESIGN

PO Office Box 594
Galesburg, IL 61402-0594
PH: (309)337-7732
FX: (309)343-0027
E-mail: info@dashaver.com
URL: http://www.dashaver.com

Description: DaShaver Graphics and Web Design specializes in Internet solutions for small businesses. DaShaver Graphics and Web Design offers domain name registration, web site design and development, graphics, hosting, and search engine registration.

▌3944
DASLWEB INC

995 Wellington, Ste. 203
Montreal, PQ, Canada H3C1V3
PH: (514)874-9809
FX: (514)874-0660
E-mail: info@daslweb.com
URL: http://www.daslweb.com

Description: DaslWeb, Inc. is a design firm that integrates print and advertising identity into an Internet presence. Dasl-Web provides web site design and development, domain name registration, web site hosting, marketing services, web site maintenance, and programming services.

▌3945
DATA COM TECHNOLOGY SERVICES

2503 S Padre Island Dr.
Corpus Christi, TX 78415
PH: (361)906-2061
E-mail: info@datacom-services.net
URL: http://www.datacom-services.net

Description: Data Com Technology Services offers a range of Internet services including web design and development. Data Com Technology Services also provides e-commerce enabled web sites with shopping cart, search engine strategy, content management, hosting services, web site marketing, web site statistics, custom web applications, and other information technology services.

■ 3946
DATA DESIGN GROUP, LTD.

1275 Harlem Rd.
Buffalo, NY 14206
PH: (716)891-8635
E-mail: creative@datadesigngroup.com
URL: http://www.datadesigngroup.com

Description: Data Design Group, Ltd. is a full service web design group creating both personal and business web sites. Services offered by Data Design Group include customized web site design, graphic design, logo design, custom multimedia and Flash, and creative web marketing.

■ 3947
DATA MINE CORP.

601 Franklin St., Ste. 206
Michigan City, IN 46360
PH: (219)861-2345
TF: 877-328-2646
FX: (219)861-2344
E-mail: info@datamine.net
URL: http://www.datamine.net

Description: Data Mine Corp. focuses on the needs of businesses to design and develop web sites. Services provided by Data Mine include a variety of informational and e-commerce web sites, graphic design, Flash, multimedia, corporate identity, web promotion and hosting.

■ 3948
DATA SAVERS

4402 S. Newberry Rd.
Tempe, AZ 85282
PH: (480)363-9786
E-mail: krlst@uswest.net
URL: http://www.data-savers.com

Description: Data Savers specializes in the design and development of web sites for small to medium sized businesses in the Tempe, Arizona area. Services offered by Data Savers include web design, graphics, search engine submissions, e-commerce web sites, and web site hosting.

■ 3949
DATABOSS, INC.

518 - 5 Ave. S
Lethbridge, AB, Canada T1J0T8
PH: (403)327-6200
FX: (403)394-1212
E-mail: terry@theboss.net
URL: http://www.theboss.net

Description: DataBoss, Inc. provides a variety of information technology services, including web site design and development. DataBoss offers web site design, e-commerce site design, custom programming in a range of languages, search engine submission and site linking, graphics design, hosting, and database design.

■ 3950
DATAGLYPHICS, INC.

449 Central Ave.
St. Petersburg, FL 33701
PH: (727)827-3939
FX: (727)827-3940
URL: http://www.datag.com

Description: DataGlyphics, Inc. offers turnkey Internet solutions to its clients. DataGlyphics provides e-commerce solutions, web site design and development, multimedia production, e-marketing strategies, database integration, site management, and web site hosting services.

■ 3951
DATAPEER, INC.

2115 Linwood Ave.
Fort Lee, NJ 07024
PH: (201)228-1000
TF: (866)432-8273
E-mail: info@datapeer.com
URL: http://www.datapeer.com

Description: While founded as a data storage company, DataPeer now provides its clients with a variety of services including web hosting services, virtual web hosting and e-commerce solutions.

■ 3952
DATATECH DESIGNS, INC.

1873 Maple St.
Bethlehem, NH 03574
PH: (603)869-5777
TF: 888-311-5777
FX: (603)869-5411
E-mail: datatech@datatechdesigns.com
URL: http://www.datatechdesigns.com

Description: DataTech Designs, Inc. is a full service web design and marketing firm. Services offered by DataTech Designs include e-commerce web sites, web graphics, web site maintenance and support, copy writing and technical writing, web site promotion, site hosting, and print media services.

∎ 3953
DATATRONICS INFORMATION SYSTEMS

62 Elmwood Dr.
Tonawanda, NY 14150
PH: (716)876-5320
E-mail: services@datatronics.net
URL: http://www.datatronics.net

Founded: 1996. **Description:** Datatronics Information Systems provides web site design services for personal and business use. Datatronics Information Systems offers e-commerce web site development, site promotion and updates, custom scripting and programming, graphics, and web site hosting.

∎ 3954
DAVINCI INTERACTIVE

PO Box 50
Alton Bay, NH 03810
PH: (603)875-3045
TF: 888-346-5973
FX: (603)875-1733
E-mail: sales@davinciia.com
URL: http://www.davinciia.com

Description: daVinci Interactive focuses on creating a web presence for its customers. Services provided by daVinci Interactive include web design, custom web programming, site maintenance, marketing, consultation, hosting, and information to help people design their own web sites.

∎ 3955
DAYSPRING TECHNOLOGIES

58 2nd St., 3rd Fl.
San Francisco, CA 94105
PH: (415)247-9420
FX: (415)247-9425
E-mail: info@dayspring-tech.com
URL: http://www.dayspring-tech.com

Description: Dayspring Technologies provides complete web development services for businesses and nonprofit organizations. Dayspring Technologies offers an initial consultation, software and graphic design, web site development, and site support and maintenance.

∎ 3956
DAYSTREAM ENTERPRISES

1441 Deerwood Dr.
Decatur, GA 30030
PH: (404)373-8848
FX: (419)735-2263
E-mail: info@daystream.com
URL: http://www.daystream.com

Description: Daystream Enterprises works with businesses of different sizes, offering web site design and development. Daystream Enterprises provides e-commerce site development, multimedia, and web site hosting.

∎ 3957
D'BUGZ COMPUTER SOLUTIONS

195 Wynford Dr., Ste. 901
Don Mills, ON, Canada M3C3P3
PH: (416)822-4482
E-mail: support@dbugz.com
URL: http://www.dbugz.com

Description: D'Bugz Computer Solutions offers web site design, custom programming, site hosting, email addresses, and support services.

∎ 3958
DC WEB SITE DESIGN

10 Lyngate Ct.
Hamilton, ON, Canada L8J2K1
PH: (905)573-3116
URL: http://www.dcwebsitedesign.com

Description: DC Web Site Design offers both personal and business web site design. Services provided by DC Web Site Design include personal resume sites, e-commerce web sites, search engine submission, graphic design, and site hosting.

∎ 3959
DCAS SOFTWARE SOLUTIONS, INC.

5720 LBJ Fwy.
PO Box 800883
Dallas, TX 75380
PH: (972)239-2327
E-mail: edisales@dcas.net
URL: http://www.dcas.net

Description: DCAS Software Solutions, Inc. specializes in business-to-business solutions using EDI standards. DCAS software Solutions offers secure business web sites designed to view the status of EDI transactions.

∎ 3960
DCS NETLINK

1830A S Main
Rice Lake, WI 54868
PH: (715)236-7424
FX: (715)236-7423
E-mail: sales@dcsnetlink.com
URL: http://www.dcsnetlink.com

Description: DCS Netlink offers a range of Internet solutions including web site design and development. Other services provided by DCS Netlink include e-commerce web sites, site hosting, and network services.

▌3961
DEAD HERO CREATIONS

309 Meadowview Ln.
Eden, NC 27288
PH: (336)623-1585
FX: (336)623-4307
E-mail: info@deadherocreations.com
URL: http://www.deadherocreations.com

Description: Dead Hero Creations specializes in custom web site creation. Services provided by Dead Hero Creations include web site design, web site hosting, logos, corporate identity, and print media design.

▌3962
DEEP HARBOR

1068 Judy Ln.
Stanley, VA 22851
PH: (540)778-2444
FX: (540)778-1193
E-mail: info@deepharbor.net
URL: http://www.deepharbor.net

Description: Deep Harbor offers web design and development services. Deep Harbor provides e-commerce web sites, shopping cart sites, application integration and administration, and web site hosting.

▌3963
DEEP INTERACTIVE

120 N Green St.
Chicago, IL 60607
PH: (312)226-8339
FX: (312)226-3760
E-mail: info@deepinteractive.com
URL: http://www.deepinteractive.com

Description: Deep Interactive believes that good design starts with information architecture, an important part of the process of web design and development. Deep Interactive offers web site design, development and implementation, including e-commerce.

▌3964
THE DEFINITIVE WEB

P.O. Box 876
Richboro, PA 18954
PH: (215)364-3984

FX: (215)364-0722
E-mail: Linda@thedefinitiveweb.com
URL: http://www.thedefinitiveweb.com

Description: The Definitive Web provides original web site design by a graphic artist. The Definitive Web offers services including web site design, video, intranets, search engine submission, Internet marketing strategies, graphics, and web site maintenance.

▌3965
DENKEN DESIGN

1040 Abernathy Ln., No. 100
Apopka, FL 32703
PH: (407)682-1686
E-mail: sales@denken.com
URL: http://www.denken.com

Description: DenKen Design focuses on providing affordable web design and hosting services to small businesses primarily in the Central Florida area. DenKen Design offers web site design, graphic design, e-commerce, and web site hosting services.

▌3966
DENWEB WEB DESIGN

PO Box 1942
Joshua Tree, CA 92252
PH: (760)362-0234
E-mail: webmaster@denwebdsn.com
URL: http://www.denwebdsn.com

Description: DenWeb Web Design is a small web design firm offering advanced technical services at affordable prices. DenWeb Web Design provides HTML, server side scripting, image creation, e-commerce services, database interface, security, and web site hosting.

▌3967
DESEDGE, INC.

353 W 45th St.
New York, NY 10036
PH: (212)956-0794
E-mail: info@desedge.com
URL: http://www.desedge.com

Description: Desedge, Inc. offers custom design and programming for online businesses. Services provided by Desedge include web site design and programming, concept and strategy, B2B and B2C solutions, including e-commerce, intranets, multimedia, and database design and integration.

∎ 3968
DESERT BLOOM PRODUCTIONS

PO Box 15108
Greenville, SC 29610
PH: (864)609-0636
FX: (864)609-0637
E-mail: info@desertbloom.com
URL: http://www.desertbloom.com

Description: Desert Bloom Productions focuses on providing Internet solutions to small and medium sized businesses. Services offered by Desert Bloom include web site design and hosting, e-commerce web site design, databases, private networks, and consulting.

∎ 3969
DESERT WEB DESIGN

PO Box 1252
Rancho Mirage, CA 92270
PH: (760)328-2380
FX: (760)328-7222
E-mail: info@desertwebdesign.com
URL: http://www.desertwebdesign.com

Description: Desert Web Design offers web page design and development, graphic design and animation, Flash, e-commerce services, database integration, Internet marketing, and audio/video services.

∎ 3970
DESIGN 2010

8863 Greenback Ln. PMB 233
Orangevale, CA 95662
PH: (916)967-5414
FX: (916)967-0443
E-mail: info@design2010.com
URL: http://www.design2010.com

Description: Design 2010 offers its clients a variety of design and hosting options, including e-commerce site development. Other services provided by Design 2010 include web site design, logo design, web site maintenance, and web site hosting.

∎ 3971
DESIGN BY AZECHE

1006 Diamond Ave., Ste. 1
Evansville, IN 47711
PH: (812)424-9817
FX: (812)491-3630
E-mail: moffice@azeche.com
URL: http://www.azeche.com

Description: Design by Azeche specializes in e-commerce web site design and development for small businesses. Design by Azeche provides services including e-commerce site design, including shopping cart, web site design, redesign, and maintenance, graphic design, and web site marketing.

∎ 3972
DESIGN CORE, INC.

385 Sylvan Ave., 2nd Fl.
Englewood Cliffs, NJ 07632
PH: (201)871-0070
FX: (201)871-8778
E-mail: info@dcimedia.com
URL: http://www.dcimedia.com

Founded: 1994. **Description:** Design Core, Inc. is a full-service advertising agency specializing in Internet, print media, and public relations. Design Core offers web site design and development, user interfaces for web applications, interactive services, and e-business solutions.

∎ 3973
THE DESIGN PEOPLE

12 Washington Blvd., 2nd Fl.
Marina del Rey, CA 90292-5124
PH: (310)577-9111
TF: 800-850-7707
FX: (310)577-9444
E-mail: info@thedesignpeople.com
URL: http://www.thedesignpeople.com

Description: The Design People is a web consulting and design firm dedicated to collaboration, communication, and client service at every step of the design process. The Design People specializes in website design and hosting, animation, online branding, and Internet marketing.

∎ 3974
DESIGN AND TRAFFIC

2604B El Camino Real, Ste. 210,
Carlsbad, CA 92008
PH: (760)730-7300
E-mail: sales@designandtraffic.com
URL: http://www.designandtraffic.com

Founded: 1999. **Description:** Design and Traffic provides web site design and development to businesses in many industries. Services offered by Design and Traffic include e-commerce site design, interactive web design, domain registration, web marketing, and web programming.

■ **3975**

DESIGNETT

38692 State Hwy. 38
Deer River, MN 56636
PH: (218)326-4177
FX: (218)326-3301
E-mail: sales@designett.com
URL: http://www.designett.com
Contact: Peggy Halverson

Description: Designett specializes in creating web sites for small businesses, including crafters; as well as e-commerce, personal, and family tree sites. Services provided by Designett include logos, HTML hand scripted, animation, e-commerce, guest book, interactive tools and domain name registry.

■ **3976**

DGSWIFT DESIGN GROUP

14603 Condon Ave.
Lawndale, CA 90260
PH: (310)355-0170
E-mail: webdzign@yahoo.com
URL: http://www.dgswift.com

Description: DGSwift Design Group is a design firm specializing in interactive and identity design in various media. DGSwift Design Group offers services that include web site design and redesign, logo and brand design, animation, and print design.

■ **3977**

DIGI XP

7730 Larson Rd.
Prince George, BC, Canada V2N6S1
PH: (250)964-1456
TF: 877-536-5557
E-mail: sales@digixp.com
URL: http://www.digixp.com

Description: Digi XP is a company that specializes in designing web sites for small to medium sized companies that provide a true presentation of their client's business. Digi XP takes time to assess the needs of its clients and then uses the latest technology of the web to custom design a site that meets those needs.

■ **3978**

DIGITAL ARCHITECTURES, INC.

3803 Half Turn Rd., Ste. 311
Colorado Springs, CO 80917
PH: (719)213-6262
E-mail: info@digitalarchitectures.com
URL: http://www.digitalarchitectures.com

Description: Digital Architectures, Inc. is an international web design, multimedia and database development company. Backgrounds of members include federal, military and corporate surroundings. Digital Architectures' designs are simple and elegant, focused on communicating the clients' message.

■ **3979**

DIGITAL BEACON COMPUTER SERVICES, INC.

3850 Wake Robin Way
Cumming, GA 30040
PH: (770)205-5961
FX: (770)844-6605
E-mail: sales@dbcswebservices.com
URL: http://www.dbcswebservices.com

Description: Digital Beacon Computer Services, Inc. offers web site hosting and web site design, custom web site design, site maintenance, web site promotion, graphics, interactive forms, and database integration.

■ **3980**

DIGITAL MINDS, INC.

39010 Ruann Ct.
Zephyrhills, FL 33540
PH: (813)779-0959
TF: 877-399-5378
FX: (813)779-3909
E-mail: info@digitalmindsinc.com
URL: http://www.digitalmindsinc.com

Description: Digital Minds, Inc. are business experts that create an Internet presence for its clients. Services provided by Digital Minds include custom web site design and development, web site and database hosting, e-commerce solutions, graphic design, and application development.

■ **3981**

DIGITAL SYSTEMS SUPPORT, INC.

1334 Sumter St.
Columbia, SC 29201
PH: (803)233-0826
FX: (803)233-0532
E-mail: Girish@dssit.com
URL: http://www.dssit.com

Description: Digital Systems Support, Inc. is an information technology firm that offers a wide range of services. Digital Systems Support, Inc. provides web site design, development and support, email and Internet solutions, hosting, and wireless applications.

▌3982
DOUBLE DIAMOND DESIGN, INC.

303 Church St., Ste. 100
Nashville, TN 37201
PH: (615)463-0620
FX: (615)463-0619
E-mail: us@dddinc.com
URL: http://www.dddinc.com

Description: Double Diamond Design is multi-disciplinary full-service design firm specializing in new media as well as providing advertising and design in other media. Services offered by Double Diamond Design include web site design, development and updating, multi-media press releases, email correspondence, and e-marketing.

▌3983
DOWNEAST.NET

P.O. Box 5093
Ellsworth, ME 04605
PH: (207)667-7414
E-mail: merlin@downeast.net
URL: http://www.downeast.net

Founded: 1995. **Description:** Downeast.net offers complete web site design and maintenance. Services provided by Downeast.net include tiered design rates, contact and email information included, statistical information, secure e-commerce web sites, and virtual domain hosting.

▌3984
DUNIYA

164 Andrew Dr., Ste. 400
Stockbridge, GA 30281
PH: (770)898-3735
TF: 800-779-4655
FX: (770)898-6422
URL: http://www.duniya.net

Description: Duniya is an agency that specializes in web products and services for both commercial and nonprofit organizations. Services offered by Duniya (duniya is a word that means earth or world) include web site design and development, creative services, motion graphics, web based applications and hosting.

▌3985
E-COM OUTLET, INC.

PO Box 2428
Philadelphia, PA 19147
PH: (215)334-5119
E-mail: fpassiojr@e-comoutlet.com
URL: http://www.e-comoutlet.com
Contact: Frank Passio, Jr.

Description: E-com Outlet, Inc. is a small business Internet development company. E-com Outlet offers web site design, e-commerce site design, database development, interactive web sites, and hosting services.

▌3986
E-COMMERCE SOLUTIONS CONSULTANTS, LLC

3688 Clearview Ave., Ste. 101
Atlanta, GA 30340
PH: (770)455-1288
E-mail: info@ecsc.net
URL: http://www.ecsc.net

Description: E-Commerce Solutions Consultants, LLC offers web site design, including e-commerce, Flash, multimedia, database design, site hosting, search engine placement, and ''Instant Websites'' an affordable solution for businesses with a smaller budget.

▌3987
E-COMMERCESAFE

5082 E Hampden Ave., Ste. 289
Denver, CO 80222
PH: (303)369-3644
FX: (303)745-6103
E-mail: info@ecommercesafe.com
URL: http://www.eCommerceSafe.com

Description: E-CommerceSafe specializes in creative interactive e-commerce web services including web site design and development, online catalogs, web site marketing and search engine submission, and web site hosting.

▌3988
E-VISUAL SOLUTIONS, LLC

2812 Preistcliff Dr.
Smyrna, GA 30080
PH: (404)285-1146
E-mail: info@evisualsolutions.com
URL: http://www.evisualsolutions.com

Description: E-Visual Solutions, LLC is a multi-disciplinary Internet design firm. E-Visual Solutions offers services including web site design, development, maintenance and hosting, content management, multimedia presentations, e-commerce solutions, database driven web sites, online promotions, streaming audio and video, and graphic design and production.

▌3989
EARNEST AND ALLEN INTERNET SOLUTIONS

3220 S. Higuera St., Ste. 309
San Luis Obispo, CA 93401
PH: 800-560-8819
FX: (805)781-0725
E-mail: sales@eainternet.com
URL: http://www.eainternet.com

Description: Earnest and Allen Internet Solutions is a firm which designs e-business applications for its clients. Services provided by Earnest and Allen include web development and marketing, wireless networking, XML custom forms applications, network and web security, and e-business applications.

▌3990
EASE WEB DEVELOPMENT (EWD)

1011 East Touhy Ave.
Des Plaines, IL 60018
PH: (847)824-6200
E-mail: info@ewd.cc
URL: http://www.easewebdevelopment.com

Description: Ease Web Development offers many services including web site design, site promotion and database integrated shopping carts. Features of Ease Web Development's web designs include custom design for each client, fast downloads, easy navigation, site statistics, submission to major search engines, web access to email, interactive forms, shopping carts, and Flash introductions.

▌3991
EBIZ BUILDERS, LLC.

801 Deer Hollow Ct.
Wake Forest, NC 27587
PH: 877-471-0356
E-mail: info@ebizbuilders.com
URL: http://www.ebizbuilders.com

Description: eBiz Builders serves small to medium size businesses by providing services including web application development: Perl, Java, Cold Fusion; web hosting, and e-commerce consulting.

▌3992
EC BRIDGE

147 S River St.
PO Box 8405
Santa Cruz, CA 95061-8405
PH: (831)460-1621
TF: 800-696-6620
E-mail: webmaster@ecbridge.com

URL: http://www.ecbridge.com

Description: EC Bridge specializes in promoting e-commerce for small to medium sized businesses. Services offered by EC Bridge include web site design, production and maintenance, strategic consulting, complex Internet commerce solutions, marketing and communications, and database programming.

▌3993
EC-ONESOURCE.COM

315 Market St., Ste. 23
Sunbury, PA 17801
PH: (570)847-8772
FX: (570)286-7159
E-mail: service@ec-onesource.com
URL: http://www.ec-onesource.com

Description: EC-Onesource.com is a full service web development company specializing in advance web site design. EC-Onesource also provides e-commerce site design, database system development, web site design and development, Internet marketing in a variety of media, web site hosting and site maintenance.

▌3994
ECLECTIC DESIGNS

1511 Texas Ave. S, PMB 325
College Station, TX 77840-3328
PH: (979)691-8422
FX: (240)250-5638
E-mail: info@eclectic-designs.com
URL: http://www.eclectic-designs.com

Description: Eclectic Designs focuses on offering the best design at affordable prices. Eclectic Designs provides web site design, web application design, database design and development, graphics and Flash, hosting services and domain registration.

▌3995
ECLIPSE MULTIMEDIA

6630 Huntsbay Rd. NW
Calgary, AB, Canada T2K4R3
PH: (403)815-2145
E-mail: info@eclipsemultimedia.net
URL: http://www.eclipsemultimedia.net

Description: Eclipse Multimedia is an interactive marketing services firm. Eclipse Multimedia offers web site design and production, e-commerce web site creation, site hosting, stand alone kiosks, CD-ROM production, animation, corporate identity, and print media services.

■ **3996**

ECLIPSE WEB SOLUTIONS, INC.

281 Wren Rd.
Piedmont, SC 29673
PH: (864)845-7049
E-mail: sales@eclipsewebs.com
URL: http://www.eclipsewebs.com

Description: eClipse Web Solutions, Inc. focuses on building user-friendly web sites. Services offered by eClipse Web Solutions include web site design, e-commerce, intranet and extranet design, graphic design, Flash animation, and logo design.

■ **3997**

ECLIPSE WEB TECHNOLOGIES

60 Middle Rd.
Lake George, NY 12845
PH: (518)668-9318
FX: (518)668-9318
E-mail: webwork01@aol.com
URL: http://www.eclipsewebtechnologies.com

Description: Eclipse Web Technologies is a small business providing an array of design services. Eclipse Web Technologies offers web site design and development, Flash animation, Internet graphics, original logo and graphic design, promotion, and print media development.

■ **3998**

E | COASTSTUDIOS

2 Attenborough Dr., Ste. 301
Baltimore, MD 21237
PH: (410)933-1875
FX: (503)218-1396
E-mail: sales@ecoastdesign.com
URL: http://www.ecoastdesign.com

Description: e|CoastStudios focuses on e-commerce web design and development. In addition, e|CoastStudios offers web development, e-commerce integration and engineering, intranet development, interactive design, graphic design, database applications, and web storage.

■ **3999**

ECODESTREAM ENTERPRISE SOLUTIONS

517 S San Julian St., Ste. 436
Los Angeles, CA 90013
PH: (213)300-3406
E-mail: info@e-codestream.com
URL: http://www.e-codestream.com

Description: eCodestream Enterprise Solutions provides web application development and enterprise application integration. Other areas of expertise include secure e-commerce solutions, content creation and management, multimedia, graphic design, web site hosting and management, and web site promotion.

■ **4000**

ECOMBUFFET.COM, LLC

16417 Lazare Ln.
Huntington Beach, CA 92649
PH: (562)592-5347
E-mail: sales@ecombuffet.com
URL: http://www.ecombuffet.com

Description: EcomBuffet.com, LLC offers a variety of business Internet solutions. Services provided by EcomBuffet.com include web site design, e-commerce and merchant accounts, graphic design, programming, copy writing, hosting and international business solutions.

■ **4001**

ECOMNETS

2 Pidgeon Hill Dr., Ste. 340
Sterling, VA 20165
PH: (703)723-5585
FX: (703)995-0836
E-mail: info@ecomnets.com
URL: http://www.ecomnets.com

Description: Ecomnets offers multi-platform business solutions for information-intensive service companies. Ecomnets provides custom services designed to fit the needs of each client. Ecomnets' staff helps client businesses with the design and implementation of large-scale e-business solutions.

■ **4002**

ECOR

9 E 45th St., 5th Fl.
New York, NY 10165
PH: (212)599-0722
FX: (212)599-0724
E-mail: info@ecorweb.com
URL: http://www.ecorweb.com

Description: Ecor offers an array of Internet and information technology solutions to companies of all sizes. Services provided by Ecor include custom web site conception, design and production, programming, systems integration, e-business, database implementation, as well as various design services.

∎ 4003
EDATAWEB, INC.

11020 Audelia Rd., Ste. B215
Dallas, TX 75240
PH: (214)221-8838
E-mail: info@edataweb.com
URL: http://www.edataweb.com

Description: eDataWeb, Inc. offers a variety of custom Internet solutions. Services provided include web site design, development and maintenance, e-commerce systems, systems integration, database and dynamic programming, B2B systems, as well as intranet and Internet training and consulting.

∎ 4004
EDC COMPUTERS, INC.

716-11th St S
Benson, MN 56215
PH: (320)843-3930
TF: 877-939-2400
E-mail: al@edccs.com
URL: http://www.edccs.com

Description: EDC Computers, Inc. offers web site design and development that fit the needs of a specific business. Services provided include a variety of web site packages, custom designed web sites, e-commerce sites, and custom programming options.

∎ 4005
EDEN HOSTING, INC.

1820 E Garry Ave., Ste. No. 112
Santa Ana, CA 92705
PH: 800-603-2796
FX: (949)863-1435
E-mail: info@edenhosting.net
URL: http://www.edenhosting.net

Description: Eden Hosting, Inc. offers a range of Internet services including site hosting and design. Eden Hosting provides web site design and development, graphic design, multimedia, database design, custom programming, web applications, site optimization, and web site hosting.

∎ 4006
EDEN MARKETING

157 Morris Ave.
Athens, OH 45701
PH: (740)592-5617
E-mail: info@edenmarketing.com
URL: http://www.edenmarketing.com

Description: Eden Marketing offers a variety of business services including web site design, e-commerce sites, web site maintenance and redesign, graphics and ad design, and marketing.

∎ 4007
EDEN PRODUCTION

4155 Sheppard Ave. E, Ste. 206
Toronto, ON, Canada M1S1T4
PH: (416)916-2231
FX: (416)916-2252
E-mail: sales@edenproduction.com
URL: http://www.edenproduction.com

Description: Eden Production is a web development company specializing in designing for e-commerce. Services offered by Eden Production include web site design and consulting, database development, automated web, web site hosting, and remote access.

∎ 4008
EDEZIGNHAUS

3315 E Russell Rd., No. 1080
Las Vegas, NV 89120
TF: 888-411-0592
FX: (603)649-5849
E-mail: webguru@edezignhaus.com
URL: http://www.edezignhaus.com

Description: Edezignhaus produces interactive solutions for individuals, small businesses, and corporate clients. Services offered by Edezignhaus include web site design and development, e-commerce, interactive media, digital sound and video, information architecture, online marketing, and print media production.

∎ 4009
EDIGITAL GROUP

1319 Woodbridge Station Way
Edgewood, MD 21040
PH: (410)671-7104
FX: (410)676-2304
E-mail: info@edigitalgroup.com
URL: http://www.edigitalgroup.com

Description: eDigital Group offers information technology services to government and business clients. EDigital Group provides e-business web site development and hosting, strategy development, multimedia, CD-Rom products, and Flash animation.

▌4010
EDISTRICT, INC.

550 Saint Charles Dr., Ste. 208
Thousand Oaks, CA 91360
PH: (805)557-9992
FX: (805)435-1433
E-mail: info@edistrict.com
URL: http://www.edistrict.com

Description: eDistrict, Inc. focuses on creating e-business and Internet solutions. Services offered by eDistrict include web site design and development, e-commerce web sites, custom online catalogs, intranets and extranets, web marketing systems, site management and hosting, and identity and branding services.

▌4011
EDOMINANT STUDIOS

10 Walnut St.
Rehoboth, MA 02769
PH: (508)226-8071
E-mail: info@edominantstudios.com
URL: http://www.edominantstudios.com

Description: eDominant Studios focuses on web site design and development. eDominant Studios offers custom web site design, small business solutions, Flash, interactive web sites, and web site hosting.

▌4012
EDS DIGITAL ENABLEMENT

5400 Legacy Dr.
Plano, TX 75024
PH: (866)337-2584
URL: http://www.bluesphere.eds.com

Description: EDS Digital Enablement is an interactive agency offering a wide variety of web solutions. Services provided by EDS Digital Enablement include web site design and implementation, content management consulting, visual design, net marketing, web portal development, and site hosting.

▌4013
E.E. S. DIGITAL DESIGNS

4827 Jean-Brillant
Montreal, PQ, Canada H3W1T5
PH: (514)735-9685
FX: (514)737-0106
E-mail: info@eesdesigns.ca
URL: http://www.eesdesigns.ca

Description: E.E. S. Digital Designs offers web site design and development, Flash animations, interactive CD-ROMs, graphic design, and animated design and 3D modeling.

▌4014
EFFECTIVE-E

1820 Lancaster St., Ste. 200
Baltimore, MD 21231
PH: (410)534-4800
FX: (410)534-4810
E-mail: solutions@effective-e.com
URL: http://www.effective-e.com

Description: Effective-E offers client focused web solutions. Effective-E provides strategic planning, web site design, solution development, e-commerce, web-enabled applications, multimedia, portal development, intranet and extranet development, and web site hosting.

▌4015
EFFUSION

1800 Glenarm Pl., Ste. 800
Denver, CO 80202
PH: (303)692-0202
E-mail: sales@ef-fusion.com
URL: http://www.ef-fusion.com

Description: Effusion provides its clients with individualized web site design and development. Services offered include strategy consulting, e-commerce sites, and CRM.

▌4016
EFINITY TECHNOLOGIES

PO Box 71
Monroe, WA 98272
PH: (360)805-8483
E-mail: sales@efinitytech.com
URL: http://www.efinitytech.com

Description: Efinity Technologies offers its clients web site design and development, web application development, e-commerce sites, and web hosting services.

▌4017
EFX GRAPHICS

19935 Upland Creek Dr.
Katy, TX 77449
PH: (281)856-9784
E-mail: info@efxgraphics.com
URL: http://www.efxgraphics.com

Description: EFX Graphics offers a variety of services including web site and graphic design, corporate branding,

Flash, programming, sound effects, logo design, and promotion.

▌ 4018
EGM WEB SERVICES

1819 Clarkson Rd., Ste. 301
Chesterfield, MO 63017
PH: (636)530-1967
FX: (636)530-7777
E-mail: sales@egoupmanager.com
URL: http://www.egmwebservices.com

Description: eGM Web Services is a complete web solutions company. Services offered by eGM Web Services include web site design and redesign, Flash design, web programming, e-commerce, enterprise portals, Internet marketing, and site hosting.

▌ 4019
EGOTAG

1900 Preston Rd., Ste. 267-PMB 90
Plano, TX 75093
PH: (214)495-0150
FX: (214)495-0384
E-mail: emily@egotag.com
URL: http://www.egotag.com

Description: EgoTag specializes in affordable Internet solutions. EgoTag offers web site design and consulting, e-commerce applications, database integration, web site redesign, interactive services, and Internet marketing.

▌ 4020
ELANCE: WEB DEVELOPMENT SERVICE

820A Kifer Rd.
Sunnyvale, CA 94086
PH: (408)524-7600
FX: (408)524-4814
E-mail: service@elance.com
URL: http://www.elance.com

Description: Elance Web Development Services is an online marketplace where business can post their web site design needs and receive quotes from professional web site designers and consultants.

▌ 4021
ELECTRA DIGITAL DESIGN STUDIOS, INC.

101 Park Ave., Ste. 670
Oklahoma City, OK 73102
PH: (405)235-4343
TF: (866)227-4345
FX: (405)415-5467
E-mail: info@electradigital.com
URL: http://www.electradigital.com

Description: Electra Digital Design Studios, Inc. offers a variety of services including e-commerce web site development, Internet strategy, graphic design, multimedia CD-Roms, Internet marketing, intranet development, and systems integration.

▌ 4022
ELECTRIC COWBOY

PO Box 3207
Coppell, TX 75019
PH: (972)459-1885
URL: http://www.ElectricCowboy.com

Description: Electric Cowboy provides its clients with a range of web design services. Electric Cowboy offers custom web site design, site redesign, e-commerce, domain name registration, databases, Flash development, audio/video support, and wireless access.

▌ 4023
ELECTRIC CRAYONS

678 13th St., Ste. 103
Oakland, CA 94110
PH: (510)452-4186
FX: (510)452-4228
E-mail: info@ecrayons.com
URL: http://www.ecrayons.com

Description: Electric Crayons offers web site design and redesign. Services provided by Electric Crayons include information architecture, user interface design, online marketing including banner ads and email campaigns, strategic planning, and technical specification.

▌ 4024
ELECTRIC SPEED

66 Daughtrey Ave., No. 111
Waco, TX 76706
PH: (254)753-2545
E-mail: info@electricspeed.com
URL: http://www.electricspeed.com

Description: Electric Speed works with companies developing small to medium sized web sites and offers Internet application development services as well as Internet consulting.

▌4025
ELECTRONIC INK, INC.

One S Broad St., 19th Fl.
Philadelphia, PA 19107
PH: (215)922-3800
FX: (215)922-3880
E-mail: info@electronicink.com
URL: http://www.electronicink.com

Description: Electronic Ink, Inc. web site design and development services, as well as systems integration, enterprise solution integration, database administration, usability and branding.

▌4026
ELECTRONICART DESIGN

302 Purcell Ave.
Cincinnati, OH 45205
PH: (513)471-8990
E-mail: info@electronicart.com
URL: http://www.electronicart.com

Description: ElectronicArt Design is a multimedia design firm offering services including web site design and maintenance, web application development, Flash animation, e-commerce with secure shopping carts, content development, and print media design and production.

▌4027
ELEPHANTS AND ANTS

1414 Dexter Ave. N, Ste. 150
Seattle, WA 98109
PH: (206)256-0769
TF: 877-727-9528
FX: (206)282-3312
E-mail: info@elephantsandants.com
URL: http://www.elephantsandants.com

Description: Elephants and Ants provides e-business web site design and development, interactive site design, corporate identity, streaming media, Flash, marketing, and print design services.

▌4028
ELEV8

1140 Castro St.
San Francisco, CA 94114
PH: (415)828-2690
FX: (509)479-4304
E-mail: jeff@elev8.net
URL: http://www.elev8.net

Description: Elev8 offers a range of design and Internet services including complete web site design and development, site architecture, web site hosting, branding, and print collateral materials.

▌4029
ELEVEL, INC.

2745 N Dallas Pky., Ste. 200
Plano, TX 75093
PH: (972)980-7660
TF: 877-353-8351
FX: (972)980-7671
E-mail: info@elevel.com
URL: http://www.elevel.com

Description: eLevel, Inc. is a design firm focusing on electronic media. Services offered by eLevel include web site design, a variety of e-commerce solutions, 2D and 3D graphics, streaming video, animation, systems integration, and marketing and consulting.

▌4030
ELEVEN

PO Box 17123
Charlotte, NC 28227
PH: (704)577-1633
E-mail: eric@designeleven.com
URL: http://www.designeleven.com

Description: Eleven is a web site design company that offers services including graphic design, web site design and redesign, streaming video, Flash animation, programming, and web site maintenance.

▌4031
ELLIOTTSWEB.COM

618 Executive Dr.
Willowbrook, IL 60527
PH: (630)325-5400
FX: (630)325-5444
URL: http://www.elliottsweb.com

Description: Elliottsweb.com offers web site design and development services, as well as e-commerce solutions with shopping cart, Internet marketing services, search engine submissions, and web site hosting.

▌4032
ELMEKIA WEB DESIGN SERVICES

340 E 2nd St., Ste. 306
Los Angeles, CA 90012
PH: (213)613-0621
URL: http://www.elmekia.com

Description: Elmekia Web Design Services focuses on web site design and development for businesses of any size. Elmekia Web Design Services begins with consultations to determine objectives for the web site, then develops content, information architecture, and the user interface. A variety of graphic design services are also offered by Elmekia Web Design Services.

▌4033
ELMWOOD MEDIA

1243 Skytop Mountain Rd., Ste. 2
Port Matilda, PA 16870
PH: (814)238-6680
FX: (814)238-6012
E-mail: info@elmwoodmedia.com
URL: http://www.elmwoodmedia.com

Description: Elmwood Media provides a variety of Internet services, including web site design and application development, digital graphic design, technology evaluation and consulting, and network design, installation, and upgrades.

▌4034
ELOQUENT DESIGN, LLC

11619-11 B Vantage Hill Rd.
Reston, VA 20190
PH: (703)787-5714
FX: (703)787-9837
E-mail: info@eloquentdesign.com
URL: http://www.eloquentdesign.com
Contact: Diane Black, Owner and Senior Designer

Description: Eloquent Design, LLC is a small firm specializing in design and marketing services for businesses. Eloquent Design offers services including web site design and development, graphic design, e-commerce solutions, custom programming, content development, and marketing.

▌4035
ELRO CORP.

244 Madison Ave, No. 357
New York, NY 10016
PH: 800-305-3576
FX: (212)202-3766
E-mail: info@elro.com
URL: http://www.elro.com

Description: Elro Corp. focuses on making easy to use web sites with unique charisma that fit the needs of the client. Services offered by Elro include web site design, fully integrated e-commerce solutions, web site hosting, content management, and colocation.

▌4036
ELTING WEB DESIGN

11514 Turnstone Ct.
Charlotte, NC 28226
PH: (704)607-4182
FX: (704)544-7559
E-mail: edie@eltingweb.com
URL: http://www.eltingweb.com

Description: Elting Web Design provides web site design and development services. Elting offers domain name registration, web site design, graphics, Flash animation, content organization, search engine optimization, site redesign, maintenance, and hosting, as well as digital publishing services.

▌4037
ELUTRIS.COM

1161-C Wainiha St.
Honolulu, HI 96825-2657
PH: (808)395-5360
FX: (808)396-5360
E-mail: info@elutris.com
URL: http://www.elutris.com

Description: Elutris.com is a full service business web site development company. Services offered by Elutris.com include web site design and construction, usability testing, databases, and programming.

▌4038
EMANON COMMUNICATIONS

6347 Blvd. Couture
St. Leonard, PQ, Canada H1P3J5
PH: (514)327-7222
TF: 877-920-7222
E-mail: info@emanoncommunications.com
URL: http://www.emanoncommunications.com

Description: Emanon Communications offers its clients web site design and development, Flash animation, streaming video, search engine ranking, CD-ROM production, graphic design, pre-press processing, networking solutions, and a variety of other IT solutions.

▌4039
EMANTRAS, INC.

2130 Trade Zone Blvd.
San Jose, CA 95131
PH: (408)957-8885
URL: http://www.emantras.com

Description: Emantras, Inc. offers a variety of Internet and information technology services including multilingual web sites, e-commerce web sites, online catalogs, multimedia presentations, Flash animation, enterprise information portals, and back office integration.

∎ 4040
EMERON

1701 Shallcross Ave., Ste. B
Wilmington, DE 19806
PH: (302)654-9735
TF: (866)EME-RON1
FX: (302)654-9737
URL: http://www.emeron.com

Description: Emeron is an Internet development, hosting, and consulting company. Emeron focuses on developing an Internet presence that is a part of its clients' business strategy. Emeron designs web sites based on clients needs, and develops web sites using the latest Internet technology.

∎ 4041
EMPTY STREET PRODUCTIONS

22287 Mulholland Hwy., Ste. 343
Calabasas, CA 91302
PH: (818)887-4940
E-mail: info@emptystreet.com
URL: http://www.emptystreet.com

Founded: 1994. **Description:** Empty Street Productions is a full service web design studio, and one of the 12 original web companies in the world. Empty Street Productions offers its services to mid-sized to large businesses, including startups and motion picture studios. Web site design and development, web application development, e-commerce, and web-enabled CD-ROMs are some of the services provided by Empty Street Productions.

∎ 4042
END POINT CORP.

210 E 68th St.
New York, NY 10021
PH: 888-351-3239
FX: (212)879-6923
URL: http://www.endpoint.com

Description: End Point Corp. is a full service web development firm. Services offered by End Point include web site design and development, secured e-commerce, information architecture, database scripting, user interface design, web site hosting, and interactive marketing.

∎ 4043
ENVISION COMMUNICATIONS, INC.

Two Fenview, Ste. 100
Oakwood Hills, IL 60013-1067
PH: (847)462-9637
FX: (847)462-0537
E-mail: mpost@envisioncom.com
URL: http://www.envisioncom.com
Contact: Marcialynn Post, President and CEO

Description: Envision Communications is a marketing communications firm providing web site design, technical writing, and other communications services. Envision Communications focuses on offering strategic marketing plans and web sites with regularly changing content. Envision benchmarks clients' sites against competitors and helps evaluate the web site's success.

∎ 4044
EONS

3201 Gold Tree Ct.
Louisville, KY 40220
PH: (502)298-9670
E-mail: info@eons.com
URL: http://eons.com

Description: EONS is an Internet company that specializes in design, development and management of web sites and e-commerce solutions for small businesses. EONS develops new web sites and re-designs existing web sites to better achieve their clients goals. EONS offers technical, marketing and strategic expertise to create websites that will be successful for their clients.

∎ 4045
ETI

Suite 105 Centennial Ctr.
Cross Keys Rd.
Berlin, NJ 08009
PH: 888-429-8638
FX: (856)753-9838
E-mail: access@eticomm.net
URL: http://www.eticomm.net

Description: ETI offers a variety of e-business services to its customers. Web hosting, web site development, applications, and e-commerce web site development are some of the services ETI provides. ETI focuses on translating a brick and mortar business to an Internet presence.

∎ 4046
EVOLUTION WEB DEVELOPMENT, LLC

945 Old Las Vegas Hwy.
Santa Fe, NM 87505
PH: (505)466-8292
TF: (866)466-8292
E-mail: ray@evolutionwebdev.com
URL: http://www.evolutionwebdev.com
Contact: Ray Gulick, Partner

Description: Evolution Web Development is a partnership focused on implementing e-business web site solutions. Evolution Web Development provides expertise in marketing, information architecture, and visual design allowing them to offer services integrating both online and print messages.

∎ 4047
THE FACTORY INTERACTIVE, INC.

5838 SW 144 Circle Pl.
Miami, FL 33183-1069
PH: (305)752-9400
FX: (305)644-7883
E-mail: info@thefactoryi.com
URL: http://www.thefactoryi.com

Description: The Factory Interactive, Inc. is a full service interactive media company that develops solutions for companies of all sizes. Services offered by The Factory Interactive include interactive web site design and development, e-commerce solutions, intranet/extranet development, brand development, data mining, marketing and other digital media creation.

∎ 4048
FAST WEB DESIGN

3115 Foothill Blvd., Ste. M-293
La Crescenta, CA 91214
PH: 877-576-6076
E-mail: contact@fastwebdesign.com
URL: http://www.fastwebdesign.com

Description: Fast Web Design offers a variety of Internet services including web design, graphics, e-commerce solutions, logo design, Flash, and web site hosting.

∎ 4049
FAUVE CREATIONS

12762 Archwood St.
North Hollywood, CA 91606
PH: (818)755-0000
E-mail: fauve@fauvecreations.com
URL: http://www.fauvecreations.com
Contact: Ramiro Fauve

Description: Creators of some of the mega-murals in Los Angeles, Fauve Creations is a web site design company providing custom web site design, Flash and animated graphics, logo design, CD design, collateral print media design, and illustration and photography.

∎ 4050
FERITUR'S DESIGNS

4550 NW 9th St., Ste. 314
Miami, FL 33126
PH: (305)773-2603

E-mail: info@feritur.com
URL: http://www.feritur.com

Description: Feritur's Designs offers custom web site design services in both English and Spanish. Services provided by Feritur's Designs include web site layout and design, e-commerce solutions, web site promotion and marketing, graphic design, Flash and Shockwave production, and custom programming.

∎ 4051
FILLERUP.NET

685 Spring St., No. 2250
Friday Harbor, WA 98250-8058
PH: (360)317-5794
E-mail: mel@fillerup.net
URL: http://www.fillerup.net

Description: Fillerup.net is a web site design and development firm. Services offered by Fillerup.net include web site design and information architecture, site development, marketing, web site redesign, e-commerce, and search engine and keyword registration.

∎ 4052
FILNET, INC.

1690 Old Bridge Rd., Ste. 200
Lake Ridge, VA 22192-2448
PH: (703)492-4420
TF: 877-730-8600
FX: (703)492-4405
E-mail: info@filnetinc.com
URL: http://www.gofilnet.com

Description: Filnet, Inc. provides a variety of web development services, focusing on clients in the public sector. Filnet offers content management and portal development, as well as web site design and development.

∎ 4053
FINE BRAND MEDIA, INC.

502 Missouri St.
San Francisco, CA 94107
PH: (415)970-0171
FX: (415)642-8558
E-mail: info@finebrand.com
URL: http://www.finebrand.com

Description: Fine Brand Media, Inc. offers an array of Internet services including web site design and maintenance, web application development, Flash design, graphic design, e-commerce, streaming media, online marketing, search engine placement, and intranet/extranet development.

▌4054
FINE WINE WEB DESIGN

1330 Maureen Ave.
Madison Heights, MI 48071
TF: 877-877-4878
FX: (413)832-7692
E-mail: info@webmaster-designs.com
URL: http://www.michiganwebdesignservices.com

Description: Fine Wine Web Design provides web site design for businesses and individuals. Services offered by Fine Wine Web Design include web site design, maintenance and hosting, copy writing and content development, Flash animation, graphics and desktop publishing.

▌4055
FIREFLY COMMUNICATIONS

1738 Elton Rd., Ste. 140
Silver Spring, MD 20903
PH: (301)408-4080
TF: 800-FIR-EFLY
FX: (301)431-0077
E-mail: staff@glow.com
URL: http://www.glow.com

Description: Firefly Communications is an Internet presence provider. Services offered by Firefly Communications include online enterprises, web site design and development, interactive brochures, and virtual branch offices.

▌4056
FIREWIRE, INC.

1607 Independence Rd.
Fort Collins, CO 80526
PH: (970)222-8260
E-mail: tpr@firewiregraphics.com
URL: http://www.firewiregraphics.com

Description: Firewire, Inc. offers a variety of services including web site design, e-commerce solutions, Internet marketing, databases, Flash animation, streaming video and audio, as well as photography.

▌4057
FIRST TIME SOLUTIONS, LLC

328-B W Morgan St.
Raleigh, NC 27613
PH: (919)838-5007
E-mail: info@1timesolutions.com
URL: http://www.1timesolutions.com

Description: First Time Solutions is a company that works with small and medium sized businesses to help them create an Internet presence. First Time Solutions offers custom web site design, graphic design, web hosting, and market strategies consulting.

▌4058
FIRSTBORN MULTIMEDIA

630 9th Ave., Ste. 605
New York, NY 10036
PH: (212)581-1100
E-mail: info@firstbornmultimedia.com
URL: http://www.firstbornmultimedia.com

Description: Firstborn is a design firm specializing in interactive digital design, created to be seen on computers, including websites, CD-ROMs, and intranet sites. Their design philosophy focuses on keeping things simple, sophisticated, and uncluttered.

▌4059
FIRSTTEL.COM

123 W Hanley Ave.
Coeur D Alene, ID 83814
PH: (208)676-1455
TF: 888-333-7778
FX: (208)676-9255
E-mail: info@firsttel.com
URL: http://www.firsttel.com

Description: FirstTel.com provides regional and national customers with comprehensive web site development and e-commerce solutions. Services offered by FirstTel.com include web site design, graphic design, multimedia development, database integration, Internet marketing, and web site hosting.

▌4060
FISHHEAD DESIGNZ

4620 Eastwind Dr.
Plant City, FL 33566
PH: (813)928-3907
FX: (813)659-4445
E-mail: info@fishheaddesignz.com
URL: http://www.fishheaddesignz.com

Description: Fishhead Designz focuses on one stop creative services. Fishhead Designz offers web site design, interactive CD design, graphic design, marketing, branding, copy writing, media placement, as well as other design services.

▌4061
FIXMYPAGES.COM

P O Box 2581
Hemet, CA 92546
PH: (909)658-3526

E-mail: info@fixmypages.com
URL: http://www.fixmypages.com
Contact: Jan Meyer

Description: FixMyPages.com focuses on repairing broken web pages and redesigning mismatched or slow loading web pages. Other service offered by FixMyPages.com include web site design, site updates, and e-commerce solutions.

■ **4062**
FMP COMPUTER SERVICES

PO Box 126
Leander, TX 78646
PH: (512)259-1190
FX: (512)259-5631
E-mail: fmouse@fmp.com
URL: http://www.fmp.com

Description: FMP Computer Services is a family owned business that provides custom web site design, development and hosting for small businesses. Services offered by FMP Computer Services include web site design unique to each client, with time taken to understand each client's products, business goals and Internet needs. Many of FMP's customers are artists, or are involved with businesses that serve the arts.

■ **4063**
FORMIDABLE SOLUTIONS, LLC

960 Grand St.
Morgantown, WV 26501
PH: (304)216-3001
E-mail: richardc@formidablesolutions.com
URL: http://www.formidablesolutions.com

Description: Formidable Solutions, LLC offers web page design, graphic design, networking, consultation services, site hosting, and server and game server colocation.

■ **4064**
FREELANCE GRAPHIC DESIGN

7 4TH Ave., No.101
Oswego, NY 13126
PH: (315)342-3364
FX: (425)675-4952
E-mail: info@fgdesign.com
URL: http://www.fgdesigner.com

Description: Freelance Graphic Design offers web site design, free consulting, and custom design packages for each client. Services from Freelance Graphic Design include web page creation, logos and photos, testing and links, as well as logo creation, banner ads, and design of printed material.

■ **4065**
FROG DESIGN, INC.

1327 Chesapeake Ter.
Sunnyvale, CA 94089
PH: (408)734-5800
FX: (408)734-5801
E-mail: info@frogdesign.com
URL: http://www.frogdesign.com

Description: Frog Design is a provider of integrated design and brand solutions. With five offices in the USA and one in Germany, Frog Design offers multidisciplinary innovations serving each client's needs. Frog Design creates high quality logos, web sites and total branding packages for large companies.

■ **4066**
FROGNET.COM, INC.

120 East Ave.
Norwalk, CT 06851
PH: (203)851-5600
E-mail: info@frognet.com
URL: http://www.frognet.com

Description: Frognet.com, Inc. delivers both online and offline communications. Services offered by Frognet.com include web site design, hosting and maintenance, e-commerce solutions, information architecture, Flash animation, multimedia production, e-marketing, and traditional media production.

■ **4067**
THE FRONT PAGE, INC.

4532 W Kennedy Blvd., Ste. 335
Tampa, FL 33609
PH: (813)874-7425
FX: (813)871-5626
E-mail: pagemkr@thefrontpage.com
URL: http://www.thefrontpage.com

Description: The Front Page offers its customers full service web design and hosting services on the Web. The Front Page does all of the design and programming for its clients, enabling them to have an Internet presence.

■ **4068**
FUTURE TECHNOLOGY SOLUTIONS, INC.

850 E Higgins, Ste. 121
Schaumburg, IL 60173
PH: (847)781-9363
TF: 877-781-9363
FX: (847)781-9463
E-mail: sales@4fts.com
URL: http://www.4fts.com

Description: Future Technology Solutions, Inc. offers a range of Internet services including web site design, maintenance, and hosting, e-commerce solutions, business-to-business, graphic design, database programming, and marketing.

∎ 4069
G WIZ DIGITAL DESIGN, INC.

4456 Hidden Shadow Dr.
Tampa, FL 33614
PH: (813)243-5351
TF: 888-749-9327
E-mail: contact@gwizwebs.com
URL: http://www.gwizwebs.com

Description: G Wiz Digital Design, Inc. offers web site design, web mastering, site hosting, Internet marketing, multimedia creation, publishing, and trademark/copyright services.

∎ 4070
GAEANET DESIGN, INC.

1320 Kemper Meadow Dr., Ste. 100
Forest Park, OH 45240
PH: (513)851-1100
FX: (513)851-8041
E-mail: sales@gaeanet.com
URL: http://www.gaeanet.com

Description: Gaeanet Design, Inc. focuses on web site design that is user friendly and technologically current. Services include web site design, redesign, and updating, e-commerce web site development, graphic design, application development, and Internet marketing.

∎ 4071
GAGE DESIGN

80 S Jackson St., Ste. 307
Seattle, WA 98104
PH: (206)622-0905
FX: (206)622-8824
URL: http://www.gagedesign.com

Description: Gage Design looks at the visual message businesses send to their clients, and focuses on its dynamic communication. Gage Design offers web site design, development and hosting services, e-commerce development, multimedia creation, and graphics production.

∎ 4072
GAINS-WEB.COM

1075-B Pookela Rd.
Makawao, HI 96768
PH: (808)268-1397

E-mail: info@gains-web.com
URL: http://www.gains-web.com

Description: Gains-Web.com offers affordable web services to both individuals and businesses. Gains-Web.com provides web site design, e-commerce development, domain registration, site hosting, search engineering, and professional photography.

∎ 4073
GALATIA WEB SERVICES, INC.

1153 Bordeaux Dr., Ste. 202
Sunnyvale, CA 94089
PH: (408)743-9000
FX: (408)743-9009
E-mail: info@galatia.com
URL: http://www.galatia.com

Description: Galatia Web Services, Inc. specializes in building custom designed interactive databases for businesses. Other services provided by Galatia Web Services include web site design and redesign, web application development, and customer support.

∎ 4074
GALAXY INTERNET

PO Box 12163
Costa Mesa, CA 92627
PH: (949)722-0727
TF: 800-588-5537
E-mail: webmaster@kjr.net
URL: http://www.kjr.net

Description: Galaxy Internet offers a variety of Internet services including web site design and hosting, e-commerce site development with custom shopping cart, database applications, file management, and custom programming.

∎ 4075
GALLANT TECHNOLOGIES, INC.

3705 Arctic Blvd.
Anchorage, AK 99515
PH: (907)264-6749
E-mail: sales@gallanttech.com
URL: http://www.gallanttech.com

Description: Gallant Technologies, Inc. offers an array of information technology services. Gallant Technologies provides web site design and development, e-commerce development, dynamic portal creation, graphics, database integration, site hosting, and software and network services.

■ 4076
GASLIGHT MEDIA

120 E Lake St.
Petoskey, MI 49770
PH: (231)487-0692
TF: 877-427-5444
FX: (231)487-0313
E-mail: info@gaslightmedia.com
URL: http://www.gaslightmedia.com

Description: Gaslight Media is a full service web application, Internet, and database application development firm. Services offered by Gaslight media include web site design and development, graphic design, multimedia production, search engine registration, custom e-commerce applications, database development, and web site hosting.

■ 4077
GATEWAY MARKETING.COM

40335 Winchester Rd., Ste. E, 315
Temecula, CA 92591
PH: (909)821-0087
FX: (253)484-1959
E-mail: info@gatewaymarketing.com
URL: http://www.gatewaymarketing.com

Description: Gateway Marketing.com offers a range of Internet services including web site design for individuals and businesses, creative naming, search engine registration, online brand identity, domain registration, shopping carts, and web site hosting.

■ 4078
GEARBOX WEB DESIGN

PO BOX 952
Woodstock, IL 60098
PH: (815)338-8256
E-mail: info@gearboxwebdesign.com
URL: http://www.gearboxwebdesign.com

Description: Gearbox Web Design offers web site design, Flash animation, graphic design, logo design, e-commerce web sites, and web site hosting services.

■ 4079
GECKO MEDIA

7825 N Dale Mabry, Ste. 104
Tampa, FL 33614
PH: (813)936-8919
FX: (813)932-9314
E-mail: sales@geckomedia.com
URL: http://www.geckomedia.com

Description: Gecko Media offers a variety of creative and technological design services. Gecko Media provides interactive web site design, e-commerce site design, CD business cards, custom programming, corporate identity, graphics, print media, and advertising and promotion.

■ 4080
GEORAPID INC.

One Resource Sq.
10925 David Taylor Dr., Ste. 100
Charlotte, NC 28262
PH: (704)944-5564
FX: (240)757-4037
E-mail: info@georapid.com
URL: http://www.georapid.com

Description: GeoRapid Inc. is a worldwide provider of information technology solutions. Services offered by GeoRapid include web design and hosting, e-commerce development, content management, business solutions, and IT consulting.

■ 4081
GEOSTORM GLOBAL

13220 S 48th St., Ste. 2058
Phoenix, AZ 85044
PH: (480)821-7002
E-mail: sales@geostormglobal.com
URL: http://www.geostormglobal.com

Description: Geostorm Global provides Internet services to individuals and businesses. Geostorm Global offers web site design and hosting, advertising, promotion, search engine listing, e-commerce web site design, graphics, interactive design, and animation.

■ 4082
GET AESTHETICS

PO Box 510912
Salt Lake City, UT 84151
PH: (801)328-1490
FX: (801)328-1485
E-mail: sales@aestheticswebdesign.com
URL: http://www.getaesthetics.com

Description: Get Aesthetics offers web site design and redesign, e-commerce site design with shopping cart, multimedia, Flash animation, and web site hosting services.

■ 4083
GET CUSTOMER TRAFFIC.COM, LLC

18 W State St., Ste. 208-212
Doylestown, PA 18901
PH: (215)230-4691

E-mail: info@getcustomertraffic.com
URL: http://www.getcustomertraffic.com

Description: Get Customer Traffic.com is a web advertising and marketing agency for Fortune 500 companies that also offers e-commerce consultation. Get Customer Traffic.com provides web site design and online marketing expertise. Search engine optimization and search engine positioning are also services provided by Get Customer Traffic.com.

∎ 4084
GET NOTICED, INC.

7600 Hwy. 107 N, Ste. C
Sherwood, AR 72120
PH: (501)227-6557
TF: 877-203-9459
E-mail: info@getnoticed.cc
URL: http://www.getnoticed.cc

Description: Get Noticed, Inc. is a full service Internet solutions provider. Get Noticed offers web site design and development, graphic design, animation, e-business site development, database development, web master services, site hosting, and Internet marketing strategies.

∎ 4085
GFX DESIGN

714 Virginia Ave.
Norfolk, VA 23508
PH: (757)623-1655
FX: (425)675-3094
E-mail: sales@gfx-design.com
URL: http://www.gfx-design.com

Description: gfx Design offers web site design and hosting services, as well as ''Instant Websites,'' easy to use web site templates.

∎ 4086
GIO CORP.

170 Broad St., 1st Fl.
Washington, NJ 07882-1802
PH: (908)689-3593
TF: (866)RIN-GGIO
FX: (908)547-6925
E-mail: info@giocorp.com
URL: http://www.giocorp.com

Description: Gio Corporation provides a range of Internet services including web site development, graphic design, custom programming, database programming, marketing, and web site hosting.

∎ 4087
THE GIVING WEB

286 Engle St., 2nd Fl.
Englewood, NJ 07631
TF: (866)448-3932
FX: (603)947-0991
E-mail: info@thegivingweb.com
URL: http://www.thegivingweb.com

Description: The Giving Web provides a range of services to meet the needs of its clients. Services offered by The Giving Web include web site design and development, concept development, programming, animation, secure e-commerce capabilities, and copy writing.

∎ 4088
GK CUSTOM WEB DESIGN

PO Box 48505
Spokane, WA 99228
PH: (509)328-3841
E-mail: ask@customwebdesign.info
URL: http://www.customwebdesign.info

Description: GK Custom Web Design offers web site design and development to businesses, organizations, groups and clubs. Services provided by GK Custom Web Design include web site design, graphics, online marketing, search engine submission, and web site hosting.

∎ 4089
GLOBAL BUSINESS INTEGRATION TECHNOLOGIES

PO Box 52358
Shreveport, LA 71135-2358
PH: (318)797-4492
FX: (318)797-5894
E-mail: info@gbitech.com
URL: http://www.gbitech.com

Description: Global Business Integration Technologies is a multi-disciplinary team that offers customized web site design and development services, as well as graphic design, e-commerce solutions, web site marketing, search engine submissions, and site hosting services.

∎ 4090
GLOBAL FOCUS DIGITAL MEDIA

132 E Broadway, Ste. 423
Eugene, OR 97401
PH: (541)342-5717
E-mail: info@globalfocusdm.com
URL: http://www.globalfocusdm.com

Description: Global Focus Digital Media specializes in offering customized web site design and maintenance to small businesses and individuals. Global Focus Digital Media focuses on high quality web site development from a design perspective.

∎ 4091
GLOBAL FORUM

1124 3rd Ave.
Salt Lake City, UT 84103
PH: (801)596-2760
E-mail: steve@globalforum.net
URL: http://www.globalforum.net

Description: Global Forum specializes in high quality e-business solutions for companies of all sizes. Services offered by Global Forum include corporate web pages, e-commerce development, custom programming, and web site hosting.

∎ 4092
GLOBAL INTERNET MANAGEMENT

11 Bala Ave., Ste. 6
Bala Cynwyd, PA 19004
PH: (610)617-4515
FX: (610)667-9165
E-mail: info@gim.net
URL: http://www.gim.net

Description: Global Internet Management specializes in full service e-business solutions for business, government and nonprofit organizations. Services offered by Global Internet Management include web site design and development, marketing, application development, consulting, and integration.

∎ 4093
GLOBAL LYNX, INC.

PO Box 3256
Omaha, NE 68103-0256
PH: (402)342-3005
FX: (402)827-1525
E-mail: info@glx.net
URL: http://www.glx.net

Description: Global Lynx, Inc. provides a range of Internet services including web site design, graphics and multimedia design, e-commerce solutions, secure transactions, video and audio streaming, web site hosting, and cyber marketing and advertising.

∎ 4094
GLOBAL MANAGEMENT SOLUTIONS, INC.

340 SW 10th Ave., Ste. 4
Miami, FL 33130
PH: (305)324-6888
FX: (305)324-0615
E-mail: info@globalinstinct.com
URL: http://www.globalinstinct.com

Description: Global Management Solutions, Inc. offers Internet services including custom web site design, graphics, animation, interactive forms, 3D graphics, multimedia production, web site marketing, and web site hosting and maintenance.

∎ 4095
GLOBAL NETWORK ACCESS (GNA.NET)

2505 N Mayfair Rd., Ste. 222
Wauwatosa, WI 53226
PH: (414)290-4622
TF: 800-236-7116
FX: (414)290-4629
E-mail: sales@gna.net
URL: http://www.gna.net

Description: Global Network Access (GNA.net) provides its customers with a variety of Internet services, including web site design and development. GNA offers custom programming, database applications, web site design, e-commerce services and consulting.

∎ 4096
GLOBAL STUDIO

9590 Prototype Ct., Ste. 100
Reno, NV 89511
PH: (775)853-8333
TF: 800-932-2787
FX: (775)853-0200
E-mail: info@globalstudio.com
URL: http://www.globalstudio.com

Description: Global Studio is an interactive agency. Global Studio offers services including web site design and development, graphic design, multimedia creation, Flash animation, and marketing.

∎ 4097
GLOBAL WEB, INC.

11814 S Election Rd.
Draper, UT 84020
PH: (801)523-1003
E-mail: csr@g-web.net
URL: http://www.g-web.net

Description: Global Web is a provider of Internet based services, including web design and e-business solutions. Global Web offers software and consulting services that allow companies to create, maintain, and edit a web site themselves.

▌ 4098
GLOBAL WEB SOLUTIONS

1354 Hancock St., Ste. 203
Quincy, MA 02169
PH: (617)773-4033
TF: (866)932-5255
FX: (617)786-0273
E-mail: services@globalwebsolutions.com
URL: http://www.globalwebsolutions.com

Description: With offices in Canada, Italy and the US, Global Web Solutions specializes in developing e-business web sites for small to mid sized companies. Services offered by global Web Solutions include web site design and development, e-commerce solutions: B2C and B2B, graphic design, marketing, multimedia, intranet and extranet development, and web site hosting.

▌ 4099
GLOBAL-WEBB

PO Box 541
Pittsburg, CA 94565
PH: (925)432-9322
TF: 800-973-0777
FX: (925)432-9325
E-mail: info@global-webbusa.com
URL: http://www.global-webbusa.com

Description: Global-Webb focuses on web site design and development. Services offered by Global-Webb include web site creation, search engine positioning, copy writing, and content management.

▌ 4100
GMI DESIGN

190 Hartford Dr.
Newport Beach, CA 92660
PH: (949)417-1290
FX: 888-588-7446
URL: http://www.gmidesign.com

Description: GMI Design is a full service design and digital media marketing communications company. Services offered by GMI Design include web site design and development, e-commerce enabled web sites, Flash animation, programming and database integration, graphic design, site hosting, online marketing and promotion, and commercial photography.

▌ 4101
GOFREDO.COM INTERNET SERVICES

PO Box 7433
Arlington, TX 76005-7433
PH: (817)466-4269
E-mail: info@gofredo.com
URL: http://www.gofredo.com

Description: Gofredo.com Internet Services is a full service web site design and hosting company. Services offered by Gofredo.com include web site design in English or German that are optimized for fast loading times, domain registration, site hosting, and web design packages.

▌ 4102
GOOD DOG DESIGN

114 Ryan Ave.
Mill Valley, CA 94941
PH: (415)383-3099
FX: (415)383-3274
E-mail: info_us@gooddogdesign.com
URL: http://www.gooddogdesign.com

Description: Good Dog Design is a small design firm with offices in the US and Australia. Services offered by Good Dog Design include complete web site design, from concept to digital development, animation, Flash and Shockwave, CD-ROMs production and game design.

▌ 4103
GOOSEDOWN GRAPHICS

4153 Queens Grant Rd.
Jamestown, NC 27282-8732
PH: (336)883-7145
FX: (413)403-9821
E-mail: info@goosedown.com
URL: http://www.goosedown.com

Description: Goosedown Graphics offers a range of Internet and design services including custom web site design and development, site redesign, e-marketing, search engine optimization and submission, database integration, and web site hosting.

▌ 4104
GORILLA DESIGN WORKS

517 Twin Oaks Dr.
Havertown, PA 19083
PH: (610)834-1211
E-mail: info@gorilladesignworks.com
URL: http://www.gorilladesignworks.com

Description: Gorilla Design Works is a full service multimedia design agency that focuses on communications solutions.

Gorilla Design Works offers services including web site design, interactive multimedia, corporate identity, advertising, and print media production.

▌4105
GORILLA POLYMEDIA

1015 W Lake St.
Chicago, IL 60607
PH: (312)243-8777
E-mail: info@gorillapolymedia.com
URL: http://www.gorillapolymedia.com

Description: Gorilla Polymedia is a full service web solutions provider. Gorilla Polymedia offers web site design, architecture and programming, as well as e-commerce applications to serve sales and revenue objectives. Gorilla Polymedia also provides web marketing strategy to ensure web site's visibility.

▌4106
GRA INTERACTIVE

802 W Bannock St., Ste. 404
Boise, ID 83702
PH: (208)345-4143
E-mail: tguy@guyrome.com
URL: http://www.grainteractive.com

Description: GRA Interactive is a comprehensive interactive design company. GRA Interactive offers web site design and development, site hosting and maintenance, online advertising, strategic planning and consulting, CD-ROM production, and kiosk design.

▌4107
GRAND-I-DESIGN

3402 Baseline Rd.
Grand Island, NY 14072
PH: (716)773-8779
E-mail: sales@grand-i-design.com
URL: http://www.grand-i-design.com

Description: Grand-I-Design serves its western New York state clients with web site design and programming services. Grand-I-Design offers web site design packages including e-commerce solutions, multimedia design, database development, custom graphics, and search engine submission.

▌4108
GRAND JUNCTION DESIGN

433 Ethan Allen Ave.
Takoma Park, MD 20912
PH: (301)270-3825
E-mail: margaux@grandjunctiondesign.com

URL: http://www.grandjunctiondesign.com

Description: Grand Junction Design specializes in affordable web site design for small businesses, nonprofit organizations, community groups, and individuals. Services offered by Grand Junction Design include web site design and maintenance, conversion of printed materials for the web, multimedia and Flash development, copyediting, and web site hosting.

▌4109
GRANITE WEB DESIGN, INC.

8 Angela Ln.
Lake Grove, NY 11755
PH: (631)580-1632
FX: (631)580-5612
URL: http://www.granitewebdesign.com

Description: Granite Web Design, Inc. focuses on providing a variety of Internet solutions for small to mid-sized businesses. Services offered by Granite Web Design include web site design and development, complete e-commerce solutions, Internet access, marketing and promotion, and web site hosting.

▌4110
GRAPHIC EDGE

158 Latonka Dr.
Mercer, PA 16137
PH: (724)475-3890
E-mail: sales@graphicedge.net
URL: http://www.graphic-edge.net

Description: Graphic Edge is a design firm that focuses on the creation of web sites and their components. Graphic Edge offers custom web site design and development, database integration, interactivity, custom online auctions, e-commerce shopping carts and applications, as well as other web applications.

▌4111
GRAPHIC WEB DESIGN

5384 Okaloosa Dr.
Las Vegas, NV 89120
PH: (702)433-6815
E-mail: webmaster@graphicwebdesign.net
URL: http://www.graphicwebdesign.net

Description: Graphic Web Design offers web design services, Internet marketing and consulting, graphics design, e-commerce solutions, multimedia design, streaming video and audio, and web site hosting.

∎ 4112
GRATR GRAPHICS AND DESIGN

6016A Hwy. 84
Waynesboro, MS 39367
PH: (601)735-3749
E-mail: staff@gratrgraphics.com
URL: http://www.gratrgraphics.com

Description: Gratr Graphics and Design is a web design and production company focusing on web sites for businesses and organizations. Services offered by Gratr Graphics and Design include web site design packages, graphic design, and multimedia.

∎ 4113
GREATWORKS WEB DESIGN

PO Box 210023
Anchorage, AK 99521
PH: (907)332-0134
E-mail: mail@greatworks.net
URL: http://www.greatworks.net

Description: GreatWorks Web Design focuses on building business web sites for companies in the Anchorage, Alaska area. Services provided by GreatWorks Web Design include custom web site design, web site redesign and maintenance, domain name registration, Flash animation, web graphics, photography, and web site hosting.

∎ 4114
GREEN BRIDGE STATION TECHNOLOGIES

4 Crozerville Rd.
Aston, PA 19014
PH: (610)358-9800
TF: 888-363-6111
FX: (610)358-9896
E-mail: info@gbs.com
URL: http://www.gbs.com

Description: Green Bridge Station Technologies is an Internet services provider specializing in web sites. Services offered by Green Bridge Station Technologies include web site design, Internet connectivity, custom programming, CD-Rom production, e-commerce consulting, and customer support services.

∎ 4115
GREENLEAF MEDIA

2501 University Ave.
Madison, WI 53705
PH: (608)233-1737
FX: (608)233-1770
E-mail: greenleaf@jvlnet.com
URL: http://www.grnleaf.net

Description: GreenLeaf Media is a full service design firm offering professional work that includes web site design and development, programming, logo creation, e-commerce solutions, search engine registration, and advertising and print design services.

∎ 4116
GROUP 22

200 W Grand Ave.
El Segundo, CA 90245
PH: (310)322-2210
FX: (310)322-0617
E-mail: studio@group22.com
URL: http://www.group22.com

Description: Group 22 is a visual communications company that offers services including interactive web site design. Group 22 creates intuitive user interfaces and sophisticated design, for corporate web sites and full e-commerce web sites that harmonize with clients' visual strategy.

∎ 4117
GROWING DESIGN, INC.

28 Vernon Rd., Ste. 525
Brattleboro, VT 05301
PH: (802)254-8468
TF: (802)254-5265
E-mail: info@growingdesign.com
URL: http://www.growingdesign.com

Description: Growing Design, Inc. offers a range of Internet services including web site design and development, e-commerce solutions, application development, and consulting services.

∎ 4118
HALL MARKETING

PO Box 6877
Scarborough, ME 04070-6877
PH: (207)885-0694
FX: (801)659-2818
E-mail: info@hallme.com
URL: http://www.hallme.com

Description: Hall Marketing focuses on providing Internet services to small and medium sized businesses. Hall Marketing offers web site design and development, graphic creation, site promotion, search engine listing, and web site maintenance and hosting services.

∎ 4119
HARBOUR LIGHT PRODUCTIONS

172 Hanover St.
Portsmouth, NH 03801
PH: (603)427-2821

FX: (603)427-0938
E-mail: info@harbourlight.com
URL: http://www.harbourlight.com

Description: Harbour Light Productions is a full service design studio. Professional work provided by Harbour Light Productions includes web site design and creation, content management, database integration, web applications, site hosting, brand identity, custom multimedia production, and print media services.

▌4120
HARLAND COMMUNICATIONS

PO Box 213
Bedford, MA 01730
PH: (978)362-1950
FX: (978)362-1960
E-mail: inquiry@harlandwebs.com
URL: http://www.harlandwebs.com

Description: Harland Communications offers a wide range of communications services. Harland Communications provides web site design and development, graphics design, copy writing, search engine registration, marketing communications, and public relations services.

▌4121
HARRIS MEDIA

20 W 20th St., 2nd Fl.
New York, NY 10011
PH: (212)822-8840
TF: 800-466-4262
FX: (212)208-4607
E-mail: info@harrismedia.com
URL: http://www.harrismedia.com

Description: Harris Media specializes in web site design and hosting for small businesses. Services offered by Harris Media include web site design and implementation, e-commerce web site design, searchable databases, graphic design, video and audio file conversion, and web site hosting and maintenance.

▌4122
HARVEST MOON STUDIO

3534-A Larga Ave.
Los Angeles, CA 90039
PH: (323)668-2000
FX: (323)668-2011
E-mail: info@harvestmoonstudio.com
URL: http://www.harvestmoonstudio.com

Description: Harvest Moon Studio offers a variety of Internet design services including web site design and development. Other services provided by Harvest Moon Studio include XML based e-commerce solutions, streaming media, database development, site maintenance, kiosk development, CD-ROM production, and interactive exhibit development.

▌4123
HC STUDIOS

750 Van Buren Dr. NW
Salem, OR 97304
PH: (503)399-4774
TF: (866)816-3929
E-mail: info@hcstudios.com
URL: http://www.hcstudios.com

Description: HC Studios is a web design and development boutique. Services offered by HC Studios include web site design and maintenance, Flash animation, banner ads, logos and branding graphics, search engine marketing and promotion projects.

▌4124
HEADQUARTERS.COM, INC.

14640 W Greenfield Ave.
Brookfield, WI 53005
PH: (262)789-2179
TF: 800-788-1298
FX: (262)789-2172
E-mail: sales@headquarters.com
URL: http://www.headquarters.com

Description: Headquarters.Com, Inc. offers a variety of web solutions to businesses. Services provided by Headquarters.Com include web site planning, design, and implementation, custom web development, e-commerce and database applications, Internet marketing and promotion, and web site hosting.

▌4125
HELIUS.NET

3213 Duke St. No. 163
Alexandria, VA 22314
PH: (703)622-4292
FX: (413)410-1122
E-mail: info@helius.net
URL: http://www.helius.net

Description: Helius.net is a web design and consulting firm that works with both large and small companies, providing high quality web design and graphics. Services offered by Helius.net include web site design, building, and applications, intranets, extranets, and e-commerce applications for business-to-business and business-to-customer.

▌4126
HILLMANCURTIS, INC.

57 E 11th St., 9th Fl.
New York, NY 10003
PH: (917)612-6814
FX: (646)365-2108
E-mail: contact@hillmancurtis.com
URL: http://www.hillmancurtis.com

Description: Hillmancurtis, Inc. is a design company that applies a simple approach to help their clients achieve their purpose and vision. Hillmancurtis works to create an ideal theme to support their client's message throughout the web site or in other media.

▌4127
HIWAAY INTERNET SERVICES

PO Box 86
Huntsville, AL 35804
PH: (256)533-4296
TF: 888-244-9229
FX: (256)533-5686
E-mail: sales@hiwaay.net
URL: http://www.hiwaay.net

Description: Hiwaay Internet Services offers a variety of services to both residential and business customers. Web site design and hosting, e-commerce solutions, are some of the services provided by Hiwaay Internet Services. Customers can use Hiwaay's professional designers to create a basic web site or complete e-commerce presence.

▌4128
HOT WAX MEDIA

200 Clock Tower Pl., Ste. E-200
Carmel, CA 93923
PH: (831)626-5757
TF: (831)626-5759
E-mail: info@hotwaxmedia.com
URL: http://www.hotwaxmedia.com

Description: Hot Wax Media provides comprehensive web design and development services, including e-commerce web sites, secure web sites, intranet and extranet development, database design and implementation, online promotion, graphic design and print media production.

▌4129
HUGE, INC.

55 Washington St., 8th Fl.
Brooklyn, NY 11201
PH: (718)625-4843
FX: (718)625-5157
E-mail: info@hugeinc.com

URL: http://www.hugeinc.com

Description: Huge offers its clients excellence in website design, e-commerce strategy and online branding. Huge works with clients to provide high design, content, usability and the best of emerging technologies to fulfill their website design needs.

▌4130
I 2 INTEGRATION

3410 Lansing Rd.
Lansing, MI 48917
PH: (517)371-3931
FX: (517)371-2217
E-mail: info@i2integration.com
URL: http://www.i2integration.com

Description: I 2 Integration provides complete web development packages to its clients. Services offered by I 2 Integration include web site design, development and hosting, multimedia design, e-commerce solutions, content management systems, database integration, graphics, intranet and extranet development, and strategy planning.

▌4131
I-NET DESIGNS

2375 Wesley Chapel Rd., Ste. No. 3-1277
Decatur, GA 30035
PH: (770)322-6848
FX: (770)322-9915
E-mail: webmaster@i-netdesigns.com
URL: http://www.i-netdesigns.com

Description: I-Net Designs is a web design company dedicated to offering reasonable rates to create a dynamic presence on the Web for its clients. I-Net Design provides marketing and strategic planning expertise as well as web design. I-Net Designs also offers website maintenance services, to keep clients' web sites current.

▌4132
IARCHITECTS

1500 Park Ave., Ste. 128
Emeryville, CA 94608
PH: (510)588-5100
FX: (510)655-8912
E-mail: info@iarchitects.com
URL: http://www.iarchitects.com

Description: iArchitects specializes in providing its clients with web-based business strategies. Services offered by iArchitects include web site design and implementation, programming, web marketing, graphic and multimedia design, database technologies, and web site hosting and colocation.

4133
ICABOB DESIGN, INC.

26103 I-45 N, Ste. 204
The Woodlands, TX 77380
PH: (281)681-3121
FX: (281)292-6690
E-mail: info@icabobdesign.com
URL: http://www.icabob.com

Description: Icabob Design, Inc. provides a range of Internet services including web site design and development, intranet development, various consulting services, database management, and web site hosting.

4134
ICG LINK, INC.

7003 Chadwick Dr., Ste. 111
Brentwood, TN 37027
PH: (615)370-1530
FX: (615)370-9997
E-mail: info@icglink.com
URL: http://www.icglink.com

Description: ICG Link, Inc. offers web site design and hosting. Services provided by ICG Link include affordable web site design, site statistics, web site promotion, and web site maintenance and hosting.

4135
ILLUMINE STUDIOS

10624 S Eastern, Ste. A-409
Henderson, NV 89052
PH: (702)897-7755
E-mail: info@IllumineStudios.com
URL: http://www.illuminestudios.com

Description: Illumine Studios offers web site production, graphics design, Flash animation, audio and video production, and database development.

4136
IMAGE SOURCE CREATIVE

1401 Brook Dr.
Downers Grove, IL 60515
PH: (630)932-1200
FX: (630)932-1220
E-mail: mailbox@iscreative.com
URL: http://www.iscreative.com

Description: Image Source Creative offers fully interactive web site development designed to meet clients' goals. In addition to web site development, Image Source Creative also offers multimedia design, Flash, CD-ROM production,

video and Powerpoint presentations, print media services, and courtroom visuals.

4137
IMAGES AND WORDS, INC.

240-56 68th Ave.
Douglaston, NY 11362
PH: (718)224-9010
E-mail: info@imagesandwords.net
URL: http://www.imagesandwords.net

Description: Images and Words, Inc. provides business web site design services. Images and Words also offers web site promotion, online storefronts, marketing, and web site hosting services.

4138
IMAGESMITH

PO Box 1724
Santa Cruz, CA 95061
PH: (831)460-9155
E-mail: info@imagesmith.com
URL: http://www.imagesmith.com
Contact: Greg Paulson, CEO

Description: Imagesmith focuses on advancing customers' goals with their web site development. Services offered by Imagesmith include web site design, content management, multimedia development, and web application development.

4139
IMAGEWORKS, LLC

27 Valley View Ln.
PO Box 3184
Vernon, CT 06066
PH: (860)870-7555
FX: (860)871-0258
E-mail: info@imagesites.com
URL: http://www.imagesites.com

Description: ImageWorks, LLC offers a variety of web site design and hosting packages to serve their clients. ImageWorks provides custom web site design, e-business web sites, database integration, web site maintenance, and marketing.

4140
IMAGINE THAT

550 Warrenville Rd., Ste. 101
Lisle, IL 60532
PH: (630)960-9361
FX: (630)960-0840
URL: http://www.imaginethat.com

Description: Imagine That offers a variety of services including web site design, micro sites, Flash applications, interface design, multimedia, online ads, and marketing services.

■ **4141**
IMAGINET STUDIO

2003 Archer Dr.
Fayetteville, AR 72701
PH: (501)444-0845
E-mail: kevin@imaginetstudio.com
URL: http://www.imaginetstudio.com

Description: Imaginet Studio is a full service web site publisher. Services offered by Imaginet Studio include web site design, Flash animation, e-commerce shopping carts, database creation, audio and video, and Internet marketing solutions.

■ **4142**
IMAGO WEB DESIGN

PO Box 92022
Santa Barbara, CA 93190
PH: (805)962-8999
FX: (805)899-2604
E-mail: info@imagowebdesign.com
URL: http://www.imagowebdesign.com

Description: Imago Web Design develops online presence and e-commerce web sites. Additional services offered by Imago Web Design include web site design, redesign and maintenance, graphic design, multimedia production, interactive sites, database development, Flash animation, and web site promotion.

■ **4143**
IMC DIGITAL UNIVERSE

PO Box 7249
Endicott, NY 13761
PH: (607)748-5056
FX: (607)748-1677
E-mail: contact@imcuniverse.com
URL: http://www.imcuniverse.com

Description: IMC Digital Universe focuses on effective and gorgeous web site design. IMC Digital Universe offers e-commerce web site design, simple and easy to use interfaces, site promotion, and consulting services including topics such as e-commerce strategy and planning.

■ **4144**
IMPACT WEB MEDIA, LLC

PO Box 26622
Overland Park, KS 66225
PH: (913)402-8569

FX: (913)981-2221
E-mail: info@impactwebmedia.com
URL: http://www.impactwebmedia.com

Description: Impact Web Media, LLC specializes in web site design, marketing and maintenance. Services offered by Impact Web Media include web site design and layout, e-commerce web sites, database development, online marketing, consulting, and web site hosting.

■ **4145**
IMPEND TECHNOLOGIES

1213 State St., Ste. L
Santa Barbara, CA 93101
PH: (805)966-2649
FX: (805)966-2849
E-mail: info@impend.com
URL: http://www.impend.com

Description: Impend Technologies focuses on Internet web site design, development and marketing. Services offered by Impend Technologies include contemporary web site design, intranet and extranet development, graphic design, and search engine placement.

■ **4146**
IMPRESSION WEB

625 Brademas Ct.
Simi Valley, CA 93065
PH: (805)494-5524
FX: (805)581-3602
E-mail: sales@impressionweb.net
URL: http://www.impressionweb.net

Description: Impression Web provides affordable web site design for businesses and individuals. Impression Web offers web template design, custom design, and web site hosting services.

■ **4147**
INDEPENDENT MEDIA SOLUTIONS

101 W Mississippi Dr., Ste. MO1
Muscatine, IA 52761
PH: (319)621-7696
FX: 877-465-8481
E-mail: info@imediasolutions.net
URL: http://www.imediasolutions.net

Description: Independent Media Solutions offers its clients web site design, database integration, live streaming web cams, e-commerce shopping carts, Flash and Shockwave programming, custom applications, and web site hosting and maintenance.

▮ 4148
INETCIS.COM

3600 SW 135th Ave.
Miami, FL 33183
PH: (305)752-8580
E-mail: questions@inetcis.com
URL: http://www.inetcis.com

Description: Inetcis.com offers web site hosting and design services, as well as e-commerce systems, custom application development, and consulting and project planning.

▮ 4149
INFINITE CONCEPTS

2131 Hacienda Blvd.
Hacienda Heights, CA 91745
PH: (626)934-8918
TF: 877-WEB-DSGN
E-mail: contact@infiniteconcepts.com
URL: http://www.infinite-concepts.com

Description: Infinite Concepts is a full service web development company that focuses on creativity. Infinite Concepts offers services including web site design, development and maintenance, Flash presentations, e-commerce solutions, multimedia and graphic design, database development, and print design.

▮ 4150
INFOTECH SOLUTIONS, LLC

4887 Twin Branches Way
Atlanta, GA 30038
PH: (770)393-0595
FX: (770)393-0171
E-mail: info@it-sol.com
URL: http://www.it-sol.com

Description: InfoTech Solutions, LLC offers web solutions for clients ranging from Fortune 100 companies to new start-up ventures. Services provided by Info Tech Solutions include dynamic web site design and development, e-commerce solutions, design and development of interactive business applications, systems integration, search engine optimization, and print and CD-ROM production.

▮ 4151
INFRONTWEB.COM

49 Quinnipiac Ave., Ste. D
North Haven, CT 06473
PH: (203)865-5500
FX: (203)865-5514
E-mail: sales@infrontweb.com
URL: http://www.infrontweb.com

Description: InfrontWeb.com creates custom Internet solutions for small to medium sized businesses. Services offered by InFrontWeb.com include web site design and development, e-commerce applications, secure payment processing, web application development, copy writing, content management, and multimedia production.

▮ 4152
INKSPOT MEDIA, INC.

4201 Wilson Blvd., Ste. 110-432
Arlington, VA 22203-1859
PH: (703)302-5445
FX: (703)997-8692
E-mail: info@inkspotmedia.com
URL: http://www.inkspotmedia.com

Description: InkSpot Media, Inc. focuses on producing graphically creative and functional web sites. InkSpot Media offers services including web site design and development, online application development, interactive Flash design and production, and web promotion campaigns.

▮ 4153
INNERACTIVE.NET

465 Court St.
Reno, NV 89501
PH: (775)323-4500
FX: (775)323-5572
E-mail: info@inneractive.net
URL: http://www.inneractive.net

Description: Inneractive.net is a new media firm specializing in building web sites. Services offered by Inneractive.net include custom web site design and development, as well as Flash and Shockwave animation production.

▮ 4154
INNERVISIONS INTERNET SERVICES, INC.

107 South St., Ste. BA
Boston, MA 02111
PH: (617)312-2610
E-mail: info@innervisionsinternet.com
URL: http://www.innervisionsinternet.com

Description: InnerVisions Internet Services, Inc. is a web development company that offers services including web strategy and planning, web site design and development, e-commerce strategy and applications, multimedia design, and database design and integration.

▮ 4155
INSITE COMMUNICATIONS

300 N Washington St., Box 1956
Gettysburg, PA 17325
PH: (540)580-1161

E-mail: info@insitecomm.net
URL: http://www.insitecomm.net

Description: InSite Communications provides its clients with a variety of new media services. InSite Communications offers professional work including web site design and construction, electronic brochures, custom graphic design, and banner ad creation.

▊ 4156
INTEG ENTERPRISE CONSULTING

38 E Park St.
Newark, NJ 07102
PH: (973)642-2420
FX: (973)642-2677
E-mail: questions@integec.com
URL: http://www.integec.com

Description: Integ Enterprise Consulting helps companies take advantage of the Internet to meet their business goals. Services offered include web site design and implementation and complete Java-based e-business application development.

▊ 4157
INTELART INC.

No. 10, 1535 - 12th Ave. SW
Calgary, AB, Canada T3C0R1
PH: (403)228-2842
E-mail: contact@intelart.com
URL: http://www.intelart.com

Description: IntelArt Inc. is a full service web design firm that specializes in developing both personal and business web sites. Services provided by IntelArt include e-business consultation and web site design, web site design and development, graphics, animation, copy writing, marketing, and web site hosting and maintenance.

▊ 4158
INTELETEK TECHNOLOGIES

3750 W Main, 7 Park
Norman, OK 73072
PH: (405)364-5473
TF: 800-353-3696
FX: (405)364-0910
URL: http://www.intelek-tech.com

Description: Inteletek Technologies provides an array of Internet and programming services to its clients. Services offered by Inteletek Technologies include e-commerce web site design and development, informational web site creation, web-based applications, graphic design, intranet and extranet development, and web site hosting.

▊ 4159
INTELLIGENTWEBSITES.COM

PO BOX 370520
Las Vegas, NV 89137
PH: (702)562-4932
TF: 800-786-1201
FX: (702)562-4932
E-mail: services@intelligentwebsites.com
URL: http://www.intelligentwebsites.com

Description: Intelligentwebsites.com offers a variety of web site design packages, including features like multimedia and interactivity. Intelligentwebsites.com also provides e-commerce enabled web sites, web site promotion and web site hosting services.

▊ 4160
INTELOQUENCE, INC.

227 W State St.
Geneva, IL 60134
PH: (630)262-9282
FX: (630)262-9284
E-mail: info@inteloquence.com
URL: http://www.inteloquence.com

Description: Inteloquence, Inc. offers a variety of communications and marketing services including web site design and development. Other services provided by Inteloquence include e-commerce site design, graphic design, media strategy, brand development, and video and photography.

▊ 4161
INTERACT! MULTIMEDIA CORP.

Historic 100 Ctr., Ste. 20
100 N Center St.
Mishawaka, IN 46544
PH: (574)255-7000
FX: (574)255-6091
E-mail: info@interactmultimedia.com
URL: http://www.interactmultimedia.com

Description: Interact! Multimedia Corp. specializes in creating interactive web sites, DVDs, and CD-ROMs for Fortune 100 companies. Services offered by Interact! Multimedia include business-to-business e-commerce web sites, CD-ROM based e-catalogs, e-marketing, and 3D animation.

▊ 4162
INTERACTIVE PALETTE

120 Gaslight Dr., No. 12 S
Weymouth, MA 02190
PH: (781)682-9960
FX: (413)431-5814
E-mail: web@interactivepalette.com

URL: http://www.interactivepalette.com

Description: Interactive Palette is a web design company specializing in web development for small to mid-sized companies worldwide. Interactive Palette offers services including web site design and development, Flash design and development, search engine submissions, and web site hosting and maintenance.

■ **4163**
INTERBIT GROUP

18375 Ventura Blvd., No. 501
Tarzana, CA 91356
PH: (818)375-5027
FX: (818)909-2500
E-mail: info@interbit.net
URL: http://www.interbit.net

Description: Interbit Group offers a variety of services including, web site design and development, Internet advertising, web marketing, custom programming, multimedia production, and voice over IP.

■ **4164**
INTERFUEL INTERACTIVE DESIGN GROUP

3445 Telegraph Rd., Ste. 230
Ventura, CA 93003
PH: (805)642-2200
FX: (805)642-2836
URL: http://www.interfuel.com

Description: InterFUEL Interactive Design Group offers a wide variety of new media design. Services provided by InterFUEL include web site design, Flash design, e-commerce solutions, intranet and extranet development, search engine registration, Internet advertising, and web site hosting and maintenance.

■ **4165**
INTERNATIONAL WEB DESIGN

P.O. Box 40204
Nashville, TN 37204
PH: (615)315-0908
E-mail: iwd@intlwebdesign.com
URL: http://www.intlwebdesign.com

Description: International Web Design is a company that specializes in quick and attractive web site design. International Web Design offers web site design and web site hosting services.

■ **4166**
INTERNATIONALWEBWORKS.COM

4 South Wahsatch Ave.
Colorado Springs, CO 80903
PH: (719)886-0389
FX: (719)886-0388
E-mail: info@iwwc.net
URL: http://www.internationalwebworks.com

Description: InternationalWebworks.com offers both custom web site design and Build your own web site services. InternationalWebworks.com also offers search engine optimization consultation, and web site hosting.

■ **4167**
INTERNET ADVERTISING SOLUTIONS

4736 Agape Dr.
Lexington, KY 40514-1475
PH: (859)219-0389
FX: (859)219-0169
URL: http://www.iasweb.com

Description: Internet Advertising Solutions provides its clients with web site design, e-commerce site design, database programming, web site hosting, and web site promotion services.

■ **4168**
INTERNET BUSINESS SOLUTIONS

2746 Kenwood Dr.,
Duluth, GA 30096
PH: (770)418-1592
E-mail: info@ibizsol.com
URL: http://www.ibizsol.com

Description: Internet Business Solutions focuses on commercial web site design and development. Services provided by Internet Business Solutions include web site design, redesign and hosting, e-commerce solutions, interactive forms, web site analysis, and web site marketing.

■ **4169**
INTERNET CONCEPTS, INC.

6426 Covecreek Pl.
Dallas, TX 75240-5452
PH: (972)788-2364
TF: 888-588-4926
FX: (972)788-5049
E-mail: info@inetconcepts.net
URL: http://www.inetconcepts.net

Description: Internet Concepts, Inc. specializes in Internet services, including web site design. Other services offered by Internet Concepts include web site hosting, site promotion, and domain registration.

▮ 4170
INTERNET DESIGNS

PO Box 1412
Evergreen, CO 80437
PH: (303)670-8658
FX: (303)670-9265
E-mail: info@internetdesigns.tv
URL: http://www.internetdesigns.tv

Description: Internet Designs offers customized web site design, e-commerce site design, Internet access, web site hosting, and web site promotion services.

▮ 4171
INTERNET GROUP OF COLORADO, INC. (IGOCO)

1624 S Lemay Ave., Ste. 10-147
Fort Collins, CO 80525
PH: (970)377-0191
E-mail: pfardal@igoco.net
URL: http://www.igoco.net

Description: Internet Group of Colorado, Inc. (IGOCO) offers web site design and development, fully enabled e-commerce sites, interactivity, animation, search engine submission, marketing, database integration, and web site hosting services.

▮ 4172
INTERNET STUDIO, INC.

4262 Old Grand, Ste. 103
Gurnee, IL 60031
PH: (847)623-8777
TF: 800-268-6458
FX: (847)623-8778
E-mail: contact@theistudio.com
URL: http://www.theistudio.com

Description: Internet Studio, Inc. offers a range of Internet services including web site design, complete e-commerce programs, search engine optimization, custom scripting and solutions, and marketing tools and products.

▮ 4173
INTERNET WEB FACTORY

2330 California St., No. 9
Mountain View, CA 94040
PH: (650)520-4052
E-mail: info@internetwebfactory.com

URL: http://www.InternetWebFactory.com
Contact: Philip Chin

Description: Internet Web Factory provides web site design and development services, enterprise web sites, custom programming, and training services.

▮ 4174
INTERON TECHNOLOGY GROUP, LTD.

3322 Hillcrest Ave.
Cleveland, OH 44109-4921
PH: (216)398-4838
FX: (216)398-9718
URL: http://www.interontech.com

Description: Interon Technology Group, Ltd offers web site design, graphics design, e-commerce web site production, search engine submission, and print media services.

▮ 4175
INTERRATECH

PO Box 42
Mount Ephraim, NJ 08059
PH: (856)614-5400
TF: 888-589-4889
FX: (856)614-5495
E-mail: infobiz@interratech.com
URL: http://www.interratech.com

Description: InterraTech focuses on easy to use e-commerce solutions. Services offered by InterraTech include e-commerce web sites, EDI on the web, system integration, and customer support.

▮ 4176
INTERWEBCREATIONS.NET

PO Box 174
Wake Forest, NC 27588
PH: (919)556-7467
E-mail: info@interwebcreations.net
URL: http://www.interwebcreations.net

Description: InterWebCreations.net offers its clients information technology solutions. Services provided by InterWebCreations.net include web site design and hosting, digital images, professional scanning, graphics, and computer and Internet consulting.

▮ 4177
INTREPID WEB SITE DEVELOPMENT

167 Gates Pond Rd.
Berlin, MA 01503
PH: (978)239-4731

E-mail: info@intrepidwsd.com
URL: http://www.intrepidwsd.com

Description: Intrepid Web Site Development specializes in custom web sit design and development for small to medium sized businesses. Services offered by Intrepid Web Site Development include custom web site design, graphics, animation, interactive forms, multimedia production, web site promotion, and site hosting.

▮ 4178
INTROSCOPE MARKETING

1312 Splice Cir.
Okemos, MI 48864
PH: (517)944-0886
FX: (530)686-5041
E-mail: sales@cyberhostit.com
URL: http://www.cyberhostit.com

Description: Introscope Marketing offers web site design and hosting packages designed for e-commerce, and business. In addition, Introscope Marketing also offers custom web site design and programming and domain name service.

▮ 4179
INVISIBLE INK CORP.

1400 Old Country Rd.
Westbury, NY 11590
PH: (516)338-5283
FX: (516)876-8032
E-mail: info@inink.com
URL: http://www.inink.com

Description: Invisible Ink Corp. offers web site design, information architecture, custom programming, data mining, database marketing, media planning, and public relations services.

▮ 4180
ION MEDIA

15397 117th Ave.
Edmonton, AB, Canada T5M3X4
PH: (780)486-2238
FX: (780)443-6539
E-mail: info@ionmedia.ca
URL: http://www.ionmedia.ca

Description: Ion Media offers its clients a range of design and communications services. Ion Media provides web site design packages for individuals and businesses, graphics, custom programming, web site maintenance and hosting, print media and promotion services.

▮ 4181
IORESEARCH

63 Presidio Ave., Studio C
Mill Valley, CA 94941
PH: (415)381-4008
E-mail: info@ioresearch.com
URL: http://www.ioresearch.com
Contact: Kris Griffith

Description: ioReasearch is a company that specializes in interactive design and installations. IoResearch creates web sites, digital installations, and digital stories and documentaries.

▮ 4182
IOWEB PUBLISHING

5001 SW 9th St., Ste. B4
Des Moines, IA 50315
PH: (515)285-4833
TF: 800-357-7795
FX: (515)287-6424
E-mail: info@ioweb.com
URL: http://www.ioweb.com

Description: IoWeb Publishing focuses on web site design. Services offered by IoWeb Publishing include web site design and development, custom programming, and web site hosting.

▮ 4183
IP STRATEGY, INC.

5353 Mission Center Rd., Ste. 212
San Diego, CA 92108
PH: (619)308-0180
FX: (619)839-3652
E-mail: info@ipstrategy.com
URL: http://www.ipstrategy.com

Description: IP Strategy, Inc. offers an array of Internet and information technology services. Professional work provided by IP Strategy includes web site design and development, Flash development, e-commerce solutions, strategy consulting, intranet and extranet development, custom application design, site hosting and maintenance, search engine ranking, and print media services.

▮ 4184
ISFREE.COM

275 W 231st St., Ste. 2020
Riverdale, NY 10463
PH: (718)549-6775
FX: (413)235-9836
E-mail: info@isfree.com
URL: http://www.isfree.com

Description: IsFree offers a variety of Internet services, including a build-it-yourself e-commerce web site package. The e-commerce site package includes the web site, shopping cart, credit card processing, secure transactions, virtual terminal and merchant accounts.

∎ 4185
ISITE SERVICES, INC.

2405 Forest Ave., Ste. 200
San Jose, CA 95128-1505
PH: (408)554-6740
FX: (408)554-6741
E-mail: info@isite.net
URL: http://www.isite.net

Description: ISite Services, Inc. specializes in e-business applications. Services offered by ISite Services include e-commerce solutions, managed security services, web site hosting, and Internet consulting.

∎ 4186
ITEAM GRAPHICS, INC.

7017 Dove Dr.
Schererville, IN 46375
PH: (219)756-6227
TF: 877-478-2440
FX: (219)756-6227
E-mail: webmaster@iteams.com
URL: http://www.iteams.com

Description: Iteam Graphics, Inc. offers its clients a variety of web site design and hosting packages. Iteam Graphics provides e-commerce sites including shopping carts, animation, databases, custom web site design and programming, site hosting and promotion.

∎ 4187
IWEBMINDS.COM

7428 Hillock Ln.
Reading, PA 19606-9725
PH: (610)370-2904
E-mail: iwebminds@iwebminds.com
URL: http://www.iwebminds.com

Description: iwebminds.com focuses on helping small to medium sized businesses develop an Internet presence. Services offered by iwebminds.com include web site design and development, web site evaluations, multimedia presentations, and logo and graphic design.

∎ 4188
J D FUSIONS

919 Garnet Ave., Ste. 19
San Diego, CA 92109
PH: (858)274-5233

FX: (858)274-6545
E-mail: Sales@JDFusions.com
URL: http://www.jdfusions.com

Description: J D Fusions offers a wide range of online services including web site design, e-commerce solutions, online database creation, CD-ROM presentations, online marketing, web site hosting, and consultation services.

∎ 4189
J AND J IT CONSULTING SERVICES

PO Box 355
Harriman, NY 10926-0355
PH: (845)782-7016
FX: (845)774-1178
E-mail: customerservice@ jnjitconsulting.com
URL: http://www.jnjitconsulting.com

Description: J and J IT Consulting is a small information technology consulting firm affiliated with larger firms that offers web site design, graphics, web site hosting and other IT services.

∎ 4190
J AND M NETWORK, INC.

1605 Martin St. S, Ste. 5
Pell City, AL 35128
PH: (205)884-3410
FX: (205)338-1845
E-mail: webmaster@pell.net
URL: http://www.pell.net

Description: J and M Network provides Internet services, including web site design and hosting to the Pell City, Alabama area.

∎ 4191
JACQUARD WEB SITE DESIGN

3165 Link Ct. S
Salem, OR 97302-9509
PH: (503)363-1914
E-mail: info@jwsd.com
URL: http://www.jwsd.com

Description: Jacquard Web Site Design offers services including custom web site design and layout, site maintenance, domain name registration, Flash design, search engine submission, and digital photography services.

∎ 4192
JADE INTERNET SOLUTIONS

604 38th Ave.
Greeley, CO 80634
PH: (970)351-6794

FX: (970)356-2348
E-mail: webmaster@jadeinternetsolutions.com
URL: http://www.jadeinternetsolutions.com

Description: JaDe Internet Solutions offers different Internet solutions packages to meet client needs. Services provided by JaDe Internet Solutions include web site design and development, site hosting and maintenance, secure pages and catalogs, and search engine registration.

∎ 4193
JASNIK SERVICES, LLC

21830 Greenfield Rd., Ste. 205
Oak Park, MI 48237
PH: (248)967-4700
TF: (866)GOT-WEB7
FX: (248)967-5892
E-mail: info@jasnik.net
URL: http://www.jasnik.net

Description: Jasnik Services, LLC focuses on web site design for small to medium sized businesses. Jasnik Services offers web site design, graphics, Flash design, database integration, web site hosting, and Internet marketing strategies.

∎ 4194
JCA UNLIMITED, LLC

7413 N Heathcliff Ave.
Tucson, AZ 85741
PH: (520)744-0506
FX: (520)744-6923
E-mail: sales@jcau.com
URL: http://www.jcau.com

Description: JCA Unlimited, LLC offers web site design and hosting services to businesses. In addition, JCA Unlimited provides several types of marketing and promotion services, domain registration, and support services.

∎ 4195
JESPERSDESIGNS.COM

570 Beale St., Ste. 120
San Francisco, CA 94105
PH: (415)546-7274
TF: 877-376-7217
E-mail: info@jespersdesigns.com
URL: http://www.jespersdesigns.com

Description: JespersDesigns.com is a graphic design and multimedia firm specializing in online business solutions for small to mid-sized businesses and personal web sites. Services offered by JespersDesigns.com include web design and development, database programming, e-commerce solutions, and graphic arts production.

∎ 4196
JEWEL DESIGNS

PO Box 36166
Grosse Pointe, MI 48236
PH: (313)864-1781
TF: 888-745-8771
E-mail: sales@jeweldesigns.net
URL: http://www.jeweldesigns.net

Description: Jewel Designs offers web site design and development services including Flash and Shockwave design, e-commerce site design, custom programming, graphic design, search engine submission, and site hosting and maintenance.

∎ 4197
JK3 PRODUCTIONS, INC.

5102 Conway St.
Cincinnati, OH 45227
PH: (513)623-1850
E-mail: info@jk3.com
URL: http://www.jk3.com

Description: JK3 Productions, Inc. specializes in web site design and hosting for small to medium sized businesses. Services offered by JK3 Productions include web site design, logo and graphic design, and site hosting.

∎ 4198
JLT INTERACTIVE

13 Cornell Rd.
Latham, NY 12110
PH: (518)782-3000
TF: 800-366-7315
URL: http://www.jltinteractive.com

Description: JLT InterActive designs, develops and implements customized Internet solutions. Services offered by JLT InterActive include web site design and development, creating online sales channels, integrating business processes, and enterprise portal creation.

∎ 4199
JOBSOFT DESIGN AND DEVELOPMENT, INC.

100 E Vine St., Ste. 401
Murfreesboro, TN 37130
PH: (615)904-9559
FX: (615)890-8941
E-mail: info@jobsoft.com
URL: http://www.jobsoft.com

Description: Jobsoft Design and Development, Inc. provides its clients with web site design and implementation,

825

web application development, custom programming, database development, and software development.

▌4200
JOE WEEKS GRAPHICS, INC.

14309 Thornwood Trl.
Hudson, FL 34669
PH: (727)919-6684
FX: (813)996-1572
E-mail: Semper_Fi@joeweeksgraphics.com
URL: http://www.joeweeksgraphics.com

Description: Joe Weeks Graphics, Inc. is a full service web development firm that focuses on we sites for small businesses, organizations and individuals. Services offered by Joe Weeks Graphics include web site design, layout and construction, and site hosting and maintenance.

▌4201
JOHN NICHOLSON WEB DESIGNS

2451 Cumberland Pkwy., Ste. 3175
Atlanta, GA 30339-6157
PH: (678)945-9163
E-mail: jn@jnwd.com
URL: http://www.JNWD.com

Description: John Nicholson Web Designs provides web site design solutions for a variety of clients. Services offered include e-commerce and informational site design, Flash animation, and a range of web site special effects.

▌4202
JOMARTECH.COM, INC.

4201 Church Rd., Ste. 208
Mount Laurel, NJ 08054
PH: (856)273-8808
FX: (856)273-8803
E-mail: webmaster@jomartech.com
URL: http://www.jomartech.com

Description: JomarTech.com, Inc. is a customer service oriented web design company. Services provided by JomarTech.com include web site design and construction, database integration, e-commerce solutions, Internet marketing, and advertising.

▌4203
JPW SOLUTIONS

25 Greentree Ln., Ste. No. 22
Weymouth, MA 02190
PH: (781)331-4408
E-mail: info@jpwsolutions.com
URL: http://www.jpwsolutions.com

Description: JPW Solutions is an Internet services firm. Services offered by JPW Solutions include web site design, development and maintenance, Internet presence strategy consulting, w-commerce design and installation, intranet and extranet development, and presentations on Internet technology.

▌4204
JRH WEB DESIGN AND HOSTING

141 High St., Ste. 13
Geneva, NY 14456
PH: (315)781-8480
FX: (315)781-9277
E-mail: support@jrhwebdesign.com
URL: http://www.jrhwebdesign.com

Description: JRH Web Design and Hosting specializes in e-commerce applications, and offers web site design and hosting services to businesses and individuals. Other professional work provided by JRH Web Design and Hosting includes graphic design, Flash animation, web site promotion and web site maintenance.

▌4205
JUSTCALL, INC.

3666 Flora Pl.
St. Louis, MO 63110
PH: (314)865-1778
TF: 888-707-3581
FX: (314)771-1760
E-mail: bob@justcallinc.com
URL: http://www.justcallinc.com

Description: JustCall, Inc. is a provider of Internet business services. JustCall offers web site design, e-commerce applications, database design, web-based applications, and site promotion and hosting services.

▌4206
JUXT INTERACTIVE

858 Production Pl.
Newport Beach, CA 92663
PH: (949)752-5898
FX: (949)573-5921
E-mail: info@juxtinteractive.com
URL: http://www.juxtinteractive.com

Description: Juxt Interactive is a company that works to juxtapose technology and design to create a seamless website experience. Juxt combines content with image, sound, and animation for use on the web to achieve their client's business objectives. Juxt has been cited for excellence and won awards for website design.

▌4207
K AND K DESIGN

51 Ramapo Dr.
Basking Ridge, NJ 07920
PH: (908)963-7352
E-mail: info@kk-design.com
URL: http://www.kk-design.com

Description: K and K Design specializes in web site and graphic design. Services offered by K and K Design include web site design and development, custom graphics, search engine registration, and site maintenance and hosting.

▌4208
KALISTII LABS

295 Greenwich St. No. 526
New York, NY 10007
PH: (866)KAL-ISTI
E-mail: info@kalistii.com
URL: http://www.kalistii.com

Description: Kalistii Labs is a full service Internet development firm, focusing on serving small to medium sized companies. Services offered by Kalistii Labs include web site design and development, multimedia design, domain name registration, e-commerce solutions, Internet marketing, and web site hosting.

▌4209
KAPLAN COMMUNICATIONS, INC.

2635 Century Pky., Ste. 900
Atlanta, GA 30345
PH: (404)633-8535
FX: (404)633-0063
URL: http://www.kapcom.com

Description: Kaplan Communications, Inc. offers a range of services to its clients including web development, e-commerce solutions, Internet programming, and database applications.

▌4210
THE KARCHER GROUP

4450 Belden Village St., Ste. 502
Canton, OH 44718
PH: (330)493-6141
FX: (330)493-5756
URL: http://www.thekarchergroup.com

Description: The Karcher Group specializes in e-commerce, and offers services including web site design, e-commerce solutions, custom programming, Flash animation, web promotion, web site hosting, and print media production.

▌4211
KATALYZE

Unit F Ashleigh Mews
Woodland Grove
Blackpool FY39HD, United Kingdom
PH: 01253 393255
E-mail: reaction@katalyze.co.uk
URL: http://www.katalyze.co.uk

Description: Katalyze offers web site design, e-commerce solutions, interactivity, 2D and 3D animation, search engine positioning, and programming services.

▌4212
KATTARE INTERNET SERVICES

867 SE Bethel Pl.
Corvallis, OR 97333
PH: (541)753-1079
TF: 888-599-5877
E-mail: support@kattare.com
URL: http://www.kattare.com

Description: Kattare Internet Services offers a variety of Internet services including web site design and development, graphic design, customized programming, e-commerce solutions, web site hosting, and Internet access.

▌4213
KAVATECH CORP.

PO Box 480755
Charlotte, NC 28269-5306
PH: (704)599-0865
TF: 888-476-8200
URL: http://www.kavatech.com

Description: Kavatech Corp. offers custom web site design and programming services, as well as web site hosting, site promotion, Flash and Shockwave design, and e-commerce support.

▌4214
KAWIN INTERACTIVE, INC.

1201A Windham Pky.
Romeoville, IL 60446
PH: (630)679-1134
TF: 800-599-1667
FX: (630)679-1142
E-mail: info@kawininteractive.com
URL: http://www.kawininteractive.com

Description: Kawin Interactive, Inc. focuses on providing web site design and development for business clients. Services offered by Kawin Interactive include site design and construction, information architecture, multimedia production, e-commerce solutions and web site promotion and hosting.

▌ 4215
KDG INTERACTIVE

Yankee Square Office III
3460 Washington Dr., Ste. 101
Eagan, MN 55122
PH: (651)687-0228
FX: (651)687-0263
E-mail: info@kdg.com
URL: http://www.kdg.com

Description: KDG Interactive specializes in developing turnkey custom e-products for their clients. Services offered by KDG Interactive include e-commerce strategy, content development, technology development, CD-ROM production, kiosks, and marketing and business development.

▌ 4216
KEATOH.COM

PO Box 54-3860
Chicago, IL 60654-0860
PH: (312)391-8888
FX: (603)251-6467
E-mail: info@keatoh.com
URL: http://www.keatoh.com

Description: Keatoh.com provides innovative Internet solutions. Services offered by Keatoh.com include web site design and development, graphic design, e-commerce solutions, interactive and Flash development, database development, strategic consulting and identity design.

▌ 4217
KELKORP

3539 Blvd. St. Charles, Ste. 147
Kirkland, PQ, Canada H9H3C4
PH: (514)697-4683
E-mail: kel@kelkorp.com
URL: http://www.kelkorp.com

Description: KelKorp designs and develops high quality web sites emphasizing design, structure and content. KelKorp offers e-commerce web site development, Flash web site creation, site hosting and maintenance, marketing, graphic design, and multimedia development.

▌ 4218
KELLY ROAD, INC.

3521 E Kelly Rd.
Falmouth, MI 49632
PH: (231)826-3412

FX: (231)826-4174
E-mail: info@kellyroad.com
URL: http://www.kellyroad.com

Description: Kelly Road, Inc. offers web site design, custom programming, graphics, photography, and web site hosting services.

▌ 4219
KENIKA DESIGN LLC

364 Sudden Valley
Bellingham, WA 98226
PH: (360)220-4000
E-mail: info@kenikadesign.com
URL: http://www.kenikadesign.com

Description: Kenika Design LLC offers personalized web site design and hosting services. Kenika Design provides e-commerce solutions, web site development, web site hosting, and a free single ''starter page'' while customers' web sites are being designed.

▌ 4220
KEY GRAPHICS

PO Box 1902
Framingham, MA 01701
PH: (508)504-0020
FX: (508)877-1555
E-mail: info@keygraphics.com
URL: http://www.keygraphics.com

Description: Key Graphics provides its clients with professional and affordable web sites. Services offered by Key Graphics include web site design and development, graphic design, Flash animation, digital photography, e-commerce site development, and web site hosting and maintenance.

▌ 4221
KEYCOMM

408 Sherman Ave. Ste. 304
Coeur D Alene, ID 83814
PH: (208)769-7511
TF: 800-975-0880
FX: (208)664-8033
E-mail: info@keycommunications.com
URL: http://www.keycommunications.com

Description: KeyComm specializes in web development and new media production. KeyComm offers services including web site design and development, e-commerce solutions, custom web applications, multimedia, and web site promotion.

▮ 4222
KEYS WEB DESIGN

3781 41st St.
Marathon, FL 33050
PH: (305)743-0067
E-mail: info@keys-web-design.net
URL: http://www.keys-web-design.net

Description: Keys Web Design focuses on offering web site design and development to individuals and small to medium sized businesses. Services provided by Keys Web Design include web site design, domain registration and web site hosting.

▮ 4223
KEYSTROKE STUDIOS

16 Oliver St.
Watertown, MA 02472
PH: (617)926-2579
FX: (617)926-2579
E-mail: info@KeystrokeStudios.com
URL: http://bonney.org/keystrokestudios
Contact: William H. Bonney, Principal

Founded: 1996. **Description:** Keystroke Studios focuses on building web sites for small to medium sized businesses and start-up companies in the New England region. Services offered by Keystroke Studios include web site design and development, web site hosting and maintenance, search engine optimization and site promotion, e-commerce site development, multimedia design and collateral materials.

▮ 4224
KICKING HORSE TECHNOLOGIES, INC.

1609 14th St. SW
Calgary, AB, Canada T3C1E4
PH: (403)271-9146
TF: 877-271-9140
FX: (403)225-9422
E-mail: info@kickinghorsetech.com
URL: http://www.kickinghorsetech.com

Description: Kicking Horse Technologies, Inc. offers a full range of web site design and development services including interactive web sites, e-business solutions, database development, graphic and multimedia design, search engine optimization, web site hosting, and e-business planning.

▮ 4225
KIDOIMAGES LLC

67 Seventh St.
Norwich, CT 06360
PH: (860)204-9861
URL: http://www.kidoimages.com

Description: KidoImages LLC offers services including web site design, redesign, and development, Flash web site creation, database development, graphics, and web site hosting.

▮ 4226
KWOM COMMUNICATIONS, INC.

P.O. Box 57117
Chicago, IL 60657-7117
PH: (630)942-5940
E-mail: sales@kwom.com
URL: http://www.kwom.com

Description: KWOM Communications offers a range of Internet services including web site design and hosting. Other services provided are domain name registration and search engine submission. KWOM also offers gift certificates for their services.

▮ 4227
L2R CREATIVE

225 W 35th St., Ste. 800, 8th Fl.
New York, NY 10001
PH: (212)924-3400
TF: 800-865-1262
FX: (917)351-1723
E-mail: info@l2rcreative.com
URL: http://www.l2rcreative.com

Description: L2R Creative offers an array of business design services. L2R Creative provides e-commerce solutions, information architecture, intranet and extranet development, customer relationship management, interactive design, and brand development.

▮ 4228
LA WEB BUILDERS

PO Box 371025
Reseda, CA 91337
PH: (818)342-5171
E-mail: info@lawebbuilders.com
URL: http://www.lawebbuilders.com

Description: LA Web Builders offers web site design, domain name registration, custom graphics and programming, e-commerce solutions, search engine optimization, and web site hosting services.

▮ 4229
LABWERKS

3618 Penn Ave.
Pittsburgh, PA 15201
PH: (412)621-9375

FX: (412)621-6082
E-mail: info@labwerks.com
URL: http://www.labwerks.com

Description: Labwerks provides creative services in a variety of media, focusing on new media. Labwerks offers web site design and development, information architecture, e-commerce solutions, streaming media, intranet and extranet development, branding, multimedia, and print media production.

▌ 4230
LADUE DESIGN

239 Ulster Ave.
Saugerties, NY 12477
PH: (845)246-5552
FX: (845)246-5553
E-mail: info@laduedesign.com
URL: http://www.laduedesign.com

Description: LaDue Design focuses on Internet and graphic design. Services offered by LaDue Design include web development, e-commerce solutions, content management, security solutions, web site hosting, online auctions, graphic design, print design, and web marketing.

▌ 4231
LAKESIDE WEB PRODUCTIONS, LLC

4 Pine Trl.
East Hampton, CT 06424
PH: (860)267-1419
E-mail: info@lakesidewebproductions.com
URL: http://www.lakesidewebproductions.com

Description: Lakeside Web Productions, LLC provides web site design and hosting, e-commerce solutions, Flash animation, CD business cards, graphics design, programming and web site promotion.

▌ 4232
LANTECK, INC.

75 Maiden Ln.
New York, NY 10038
PH: (212)402-4230
FX: (212)402-4238
E-mail: worldwide@lanteck.net
URL: http://www.lanteck.net

Description: Lanteck, Inc. offers web site design, a full range of e-commerce services, Flash and Shockwave animations, web videos, custom database development, web language translation in 10 languages, business plan development, marketing, and web site hosting services.

▌ 4233
LARKIN WEB SOLUTIONS

4416 N 136th, Ste. 200
Omaha, NE 68134
PH: (402)431-0476
E-mail: tjlarkin@tconl.com
URL: http://www.tjlarkin.com

Description: Larkin Web Solutions builds and designs web sites. Services offered include web site design, redesign and development, e-commerce capable web sites, graphic design, search engine strategies, Flash development, web site testing, and web site statistics.

▌ 4234
LARSEN DESIGN INTERACTIVE

7101 York Ave. S
Minneapolis, MN 55435
PH: (952)835-2271
TF: 888-590-4405
FX: (952)921-3368
E-mail: info@larsen.com
URL: http://www.larsen.com

Description: Larsen Design Interactive offers a wide array of creative services. Larsen Design Interactive provides web site and e-commerce site design, motion graphics, intranet and extranet development, interactive kiosk design, 3D animation, online marketing, branding strategies, and print media services.

▌ 4235
LATEST WAVE, LLC

3145 Prairie SW
Grandville, MI 49418
PH: (616)532-8283
E-mail: webmaster@latestwave.com
URL: http://www.latestwave.com

Description: Latest Wave, LLC offers a range of Internet solutions. Services provided by Latest Wave include web site design and development, e-commerce enabled web sites, Flash animation, and web site hosting.

▌ 4236
LATITUDE 360

RWD Applied Technology Laboratory
5521 Research Park Dr.
Baltimore, MD 21228
PH: (410)869-1000
TF: 877-9LA-T360
FX: (410)869-3002
E-mail: webmaster@latitude360.com
URL: http://www.latitude360.com

Description: Latitude 360 is a division of RWD Technologies focused on e-business development. Services offered by Latitude 360 include the delivery of web-enabled business solutions, information technology development, creative design, systems integration, e-business strategy development, and customer relationship management.

■ 4237
LAUNCH 3, LLC

167 Cowpens Dr.
Orangeburg, NY 10962
TF: 800-341-7868
FX: (253)484-7807
E-mail: sales@launch3.com
URL: http://www.launch3.com

Description: Launch 3, LLC offers Internet services including web site design and development, online advertising, web site hosting, custom programming, shopping cart services, and banner ad design.

■ 4238
LEELANAU COMMUNICATIONS INC.

113 N Main
PO Box 562
Leland, MI 49654
PH: (231)256-2829
E-mail: lci@leelanau.com
URL: http://www.leelanau.com

Description: Leelanau Communications Inc. offers web site design and programming services, including logos, custom artwork, site redesign, search engine services, Internet applications, and web site hosting.

■ 4239
LEOPARD DESIGN, INC.

PO Box 280695
San Francisco, CA 94128-0695
PH: (650)259-8080
TF: 888-458-9020
FX: (650)259-8092
E-mail: sales@leopardesign.com
URL: http://www.leopardesign.com

Description: Leopard Design, Inc. offers its clients a range of design services including web site design and development, graphic design, multimedia production, e-commerce development, database integration, logo and corporate identity, and web site hosting and maintenance.

■ 4240
LEXICOM LTD.

No. 200, 305 - 10 Ave. SE
Calgary, AB, Canada T2G0W2
PH: (403)262-6610
TF: 877-426-6277
FX: (403)234-0119
E-mail: solutions@lexi.net
URL: http://www.lexi.net

Description: Lexicom Ltd. provides design, hosting, and Internet solutions. Services offered by Lexicom include web site design and hosting, graphic design, e-commerce solutions, database development, search engine placement, and site statistics and analysis.

■ 4241
LIBERTY HOSTING

172 Boston St.
Coventry, RI 02816
PH: (401)823-5252
FX: (401)828-7057
E-mail: webmaster@libertyhosting.net
URL: http://www.libertyhosting.net

Description: Liberty Hosting offers web site design and hosting services. Professional work provided by Liberty Hosting includes web site design, hosting and maintenance, logo and graphic design, programming, copy writing, and search engine optimization.

■ 4242
LIGHTMIX DESIGN STUDIO, LLC

P.O. Box 160
Vienna, VA 22183
PH: (703)963-3690
FX: (703)242-7947
E-mail: design@lightmix.com
URL: http://www.lightmix.com

Description: LightMix Design Studio, LLC provides complete web site design, development and deployment for businesses. Services offered by LightMix Design Studio include web site redesign, e-commerce solutions, custom user interface design, graphics and multimedia design, web and media advertising, and custom software development.

■ 4243
LIGHTSKY DESIGN STUDIO

1100 Chicago Ave. No. 14
Goshen, IN 46528
PH: (574)534-6654
TF: 888-477-7591
FX: (574)534-7574

E-mail: sales@lightsky.com
URL: http://www.lightsky.com

Description: LightSky Design Studio offers web development and interactive media production to businesses and organizations. Services provided by LightSky Design Studio include e-commerce solutions, interactive design, application development, and marketing.

▌ 4244
LIGHTSPEED DATALINKS

7270 North Lake Dr.
Columbus, GA 31909
PH: (706)327-1188
E-mail: support@ldl.net
URL: http://www.ldl.net

Description: Lightspeed was founded to Internet solutions to both business and residential customers. Among the services that Lightspeed provides are web site design and hosting. Lightspeed offers a complete e-commerce package, as well as domain registration, virtual e-mail, web site design and development.

▌ 4245
LINEANGLE

152 Huckleberry Pl.
Port Townsend, WA 98368
PH: (360)385-5304
TF: 877-576-9031
FX: (360)344-3987
E-mail: sales@lineangle.com
URL: http://www.lineangle.com

Description: LineAngle specializes in web site design and development. Other services offered by LineAngle include graphic design, database design, web site hosting, and CCTV camera security.

▌ 4246
LINK2CITY.COM

13727 SW 152 St., No. 339
Miami, FL 33177
PH: (305)259-7776
TF: 877-298-2104
E-mail: sales@link2city.com
URL: http://www.link2city.com

Description: Link2City.com offers web site design, hosting and maintenance, e-commerce solutions, domain name registration, web site marketing, graphics design, custom programming, and banner advertising.

▌ 4247
LIQUESPHERE WEB DESIGN

6 Church St., No. 3
Warren, RI 02885
PH: (401)965-8559
TF: 877-815-9891
FX: 877-815-9891
E-mail: info@liquesphere.com
URL: http://www.liquesphere.com

Description: Liquesphere Web Design offers streamlined and affordable web sites. Services provided by Liquesphere Web Design include web site design and development, site redesign, e-commerce and shopping carts, multimedia design, web site maintenance and hosting, domain name registration, and search engine submission.

▌ 4248
LIVE DIGITAL TECHNOLOGIES

595 Forest Ave., Ste. 11A
Plymouth, MI 48170
PH: (734)354-1840
TF: 800-660-1225
FX: (734)354-0397
E-mail: contact@livedigitech.com
URL: http://www.livedigitech.com

Description: Live Digital Technologies focuses on Internet technology solutions for businesses. Services offered by Live Digital Technologies include web site design and hosting, digital media production, database integration, and web marketing.

▌ 4249
LIVEWIRE COMMUNICATIONS

PO Box 140370
Gainesville, FL 32614
PH: (352)373-7090
FX: (352)373-7707
E-mail: info@lw.net
URL: http://www.lw.net

Description: Livewire Communications is a full service interactive media company. Services offered by Livewire Communications include web site design and development, e-commerce solutions, web site redesign, web-based application and online database programming, interactive marketing, and web site hosting.

▌ 4250
LOADED MEDIA, INC.

150 S Main Rd.
Vineland, NJ 08360-7828
PH: (856)825-2400

TF: 888-355-3200
FX: (856)794-8862
E-mail: info@loadedmedia.com
URL: http://www.loadedmedia.com

Description: Loaded Media, Inc. offers professional work in web site design tailored for small to medium sized businesses. Loaded Media also provides web site hosting, multimedia development, programming, and targeted web marketing.

∎ 4251
LOCUST CREEK GRAPHICS

154 Boudro Rd.
Randolph Center, VT 05061
PH: (802)728-3818
FX: (802)728-3731
E-mail: webmaster@locustcreek.com
URL: http://www.locustcreek.com

Description: Locust Creek Graphics is a complete Internet services provider. Locust Creek Graphics offers web site design and development, Internet strategy consulting, graphic design, application and database programming, and web site maintenance and hosting services.

∎ 4252
LONE STAR WEB DESIGNS

PO Box 501148
Dallas, TX 75250-1148
PH: (214)762-9815
E-mail: kim@lonestardesigns.net
URL: http://www.lonestardesigns.net

Description: Lone Star Web Designs offers a variety of Internet services including web site design, e-commerce solutions, graphics and forms development, search engine positioning, and web site hosting.

∎ 4253
LOOKNOMORE

99 Hawthorne Ave., Ste. 302
Valley Stream, NY 11580
PH: (516)256-2311
FX: (516)908-4164
E-mail: info@looknomore.com
URL: http://www.looknomore.com

Description: LookNomore provides everything needed to develop, design, and maintain a company's Internet presence. LookNomore designs and develops fully capable e-commerce web sites as well as informational web sites and transactional database applications.

∎ 4254
LOOSE LEAF COMMUNICATIONS

PO Box 45498
Madison, WI 53711
PH: (608)833-1629
E-mail: info@lleaf.com
URL: http://www.lleaf.com

Description: Loose Leaf Communications provides a variety of design services including web site design and development, database integration, Flash media, custom graphics, web site hosting, photography, multimedia design, and print media production.

∎ 4255
LOTHLORIEN STUDIOS, LLC

4030 Gregg Ct.
Fairfax, VA 22033
PH: (703)909-9027
FX: (413)521-2297
E-mail: thad@lothlorienstudios.com
URL: http://www.lothlorienstudios.com
Contact: Thad Pinney

Description: Lothlorien Studios, LLC specializes in web site design for small to mid-sized businesses, nonprofit organizations and associations. Lothlorien Studios offers services including web site design and development, e-commerce solutions, content management, database integration, event management, and donation systems.

∎ 4256
LOUDOFFICE.COM

61 Coburn St.
Lynn, MA 01902
PH: (617)596-8224
E-mail: info@loudoffice.com
URL: http://www.loudoffice.com

Description: LoudOffice.com offers a range of Internet services including web site design packages, site promotion and hosting, e-commerce solutions, interactive features and forms processing, multimedia development, and Internet marketing.

∎ 4257
LOUNGE LIZARD WORLDWIDE, INC.

3500 Sunrise Hwy., Ste. D214
Great River, NY 11739
PH: (631)581-1000
FX: (631)581-2170
E-mail: sales@loungelizard.com
URL: http://www.loungelizard.com

Description: Lounge Lizard Worldwide, Inc. is a full service communications agency. Offering services in both traditional media and interactive media, Lounge Lizard specializes in developing marketing and advertising solutions to fit any budget. Lounge Lizard develops web sites, e-commerce sites, multimedia and rich media, ads, brand identities and logos.

■ 4258
THE LOWCOUNTRY COMMUNITY ONLINE, LLC

745 B Johnnie Dodds Blvd.
Mount Pleasant, SC 29464
PH: (843)884-7275
FX: (843)884-0716
E-mail: info@tlco.com
URL: http://www2.tlco.com

Description: The Lowcountry Community Online, LLC offers web site design, graphic design, custom programming, e-commerce solutions with shopping carts, and online data management applications.

■ 4259
THE LUMIERE GROUP

PO Box 2156
Madison, WI 53701
PH: (608)213-6229
TF: (866)213-6229
FX: (608)827-7868
E-mail: info@thelumieregroup.com
URL: http://www.thelumieregroup.com

Description: The Lumiere Group specializes in web site design and development. Services offered by The Lumiere Group include e-commerce solutions, custom web applications, portal design, intranet and extranet development, 3D animation, interactive presentations, advertising, and illustration design.

■ 4260
LUMINAT TECHNOLOGIES

PO Box 1119
Midlothian, VA 23113
PH: (804)897-7555
E-mail: info@luminat.com
URL: http://www.luminat.com

Description: Luminat Technologies specializes in creating dynamic, functional web sites. Services offered by Luminat Technologies include web site development, database design, and intranet development.

■ 4261
LUNAR MEDIA INC.

621 S Plymouth Ct. Loft 301
Chicago, IL 60605
PH: (312)913-0856
TF: 800-252-8221
FX: (603)251-0726
E-mail: info@lunarmedia.net
URL: http://www.lunargraphics.net

Description: Lunar Media Inc. offers a variety of design services including web site design and redesign. Lunar Media also provides e-commerce solutions, Flash animation, logo and letterhead design.

■ 4262
M DESIGN STUDIOS

305 Crayford Pl.
Valrico, FL 33594
PH: (813)662-3990
E-mail: biz@mdesignstudios.com
URL: http://

Description: M Design Studios offers business web site design, web application development, web site hosting, logo design, branding, and print media production.

■ 4263
MACH 7

2565 Campus Dr., Ste. 7
Irvine, CA 92612
PH: (949)261-6690
FX: (949)261-5590
E-mail: sales@mach7.com
URL: http://www.mach7.com

Description: Mach 7 offers a variety of Internet and computer solutions. Services provided by Mach 7 include web site design and production, e-commerce solutions, custom programming, online database development, intranet development, and web site hosting.

■ 4264
MACH 10 DESIGN, INC.

7200 W 132nd St., Ste. 380
Overland Park, KS 66213
PH: (913)897-5301
E-mail: info@mach10design.com
URL: http://www.mach10design.com

Description: Mach 10 Design, Inc. offers both basic web design and custom web design services. Mach 10 Design also provides web site hosting and web consulting.

▌4265
MACROPIXEL SOLUTIONS

PO Box 550
Closter, NJ 07624-0550
PH: (201)784-9707
FX: (201)784-9717
E-mail: sales@macropixel.com
URL: http://www.macropixel.com

Description: Macropixel Solutions provides its customers with web site development and hosting, e-commerce solutions, streaming media, graphic and logo design, marketing and ad design, as well as custom printing production.

▌4266
MADDEN MEDIA

1650 E Ft. Lowell Rd., Ste. 100
Tucson, AZ 85719
PH: (520)319-6058
FX: (520)319-6059
E-mail: info@maddenmedia.com
URL: http://www.maddenmedia.com

Description: Madden Media offers a wide range of creative services, focusing on large and mid-sized businesses. Professional work provided by Madden Media includes web site design and development, application development, copy writing, content editing, marketing strategy, and sound and video production.

▌4267
MAGNUS SOFTWARE

410 Byron
Howell, MI 48843
PH: 800-700-0918
FX: (248)692-0307
E-mail: info@magnusoft.com
URL: http://www.magnusoft.com

Description: Magnus Software offers web site design and development, graphics design, database integration, web-based application development, multimedia creation, corporate identity, video production, and project management services.

▌4268
MAKFINITY.COM

2 Thornfield Ln.
Hawthorn Woods, IL 60047
PH: (847)550-9873
FX: (208)567-7049
E-mail: info@makfinity.com
URL: http://www.makfinity.com

Description: Makfinity.com specializes in web development services for small to medium sized businesses in the Chicago area. Makfinity.com offers e-commerce solutions, web site design and development, web site hosting, domain registration, and office applications.

▌4269
MAMMOTH SITES

PO Box 241
Mercer Island, WA 98040-0241
PH: (206)230-9096
E-mail: site@mmth.com
URL: http://www.mmth.com

Description: Mammoth Sites offers a range of web site development services. Mammoth Sites provides web site design and hypertext publishing, graphic and logo design, software engineering, and web site promotion and marketing.

▌4270
MANGO GRAPHICS

718 - 333 Brooksbank Ave., Ste. No. 142
North Vancouver, BC, Canada V7J3V8
PH: (604)980-5966
E-mail: info@mango-graphics.com
URL: http://www.mango-graphics.com

Description: Mango Graphics provides services including web site design and development, e-commerce solutions, database design, graphic design, illustrations, technical writing, and search engine submissions.

▌4271
MARATHON DIGITAL PUBLISHING

280 Elm St., Ste. 17
Marlborough, MA 01752-4536
PH: (508)460-6172
E-mail: consult@mdigital.com
URL: http://www.mdigital.com

Description: Marathon Digital Publishing specializes in database driven web site design and development and management, as well as CD-ROM and web-linked CD-ROM content design and production.

▌4272
MARKETNET, INC.

15443 Knoll Trail Dr., Ste. 200
Dallas, TX 75248
PH: (972)739-1900
FX: (972)774-1354
E-mail: info@marketnet.com

URL: http://www.marketnet.com

Description: MarketNet, Inc. provides expertise in secure e-commerce development, customer tracking, content management and online application building. MarketNet also offers services including intranet design, programming, logo and brand development, online catalogs, and marketing strategy.

∎ 4273
MAUS HAUS

525 Brannan St., Ste. 304
San Francisco, CA 94107
PH: (415)543-5997
FX: (415)543-1773
E-mail: mail@maushaus.com
URL: http://www.maushaus.com

Description: Maus Haus is a new media design firm. Services offered by Maus Haus include web site design and development, e-commerce applications, content development, information architecture, database integration, motion graphics, video, and marketing strategy.

∎ 4274
MAXIMUM DESIGN AND ADVERTISING, INC.

7032 Wrightsville Ave.
Wilmington, NC 28403
PH: (910)256-2310
FX: (910)256-5171
E-mail: sales@mxmdesign.com
URL: http://www.mxmdesign.com

Description: Maximum Design and Advertising, Inc. offers a variety of web services including web site design, domain registration, forms, web statistics, custom CGI scripts, site hosting, marketing, and print media and graphic design.

∎ 4275
MAYWORKS

7104 Radbourne Rd.
Upper Darby, PA 19082
PH: (610)626-5391
FX: (610)626-5646
E-mail: info@mayworks.com
URL: http://www.mayworks.com

Description: Mayworks specializes in business web site design and development. Services offered by Mayworks include e-commerce solutions, web site hosting, custom programming, Flash animation, custom graphics, business plan and marketing strategy.

∎ 4276
MEANDAUR INTERNET

1111 E Touhy, Ste. 160
Des Plaines, IL 60018
PH: 888-632-6328
URL: http://www.meandaur.com

Description: Meandaur Internet focuses on interactive business solutions. Services provided by Meandaur Internet include web site and database design, web site promotion and hosting, Flash development, CD-ROM production, application service provider, and web-enabled e-mail marketing.

∎ 4277
MEDIA DESIGN

133 W German St.
PO Box 1886
Shepherdstown, WV 25443
PH: (304)676-8990
FX: (304)876-3725
E-mail: webcontact@mediadesign.com
URL: http://www.mediadesign.com

Description: Media Design offers complete interactive web site creation for business clients. Services provided by Media Design include web design and development, database development, site updates, search engine listing management, and extranet development.

∎ 4278
MEDIA GRAPHICS, INC.

PO Box 25188
Raleigh, NC 27611-5188
PH: (919)838-8030
TF: 800-951-4005
FX: (919)838-0600
E-mail: sales@mediagraphics.com
URL: http://www.mediagraphics.com

Description: Media Graphics, Inc. offers web site design, graphics creation, e-commerce web sites development, site hosting, multimedia and print design services.

∎ 4279
MEDIAPOLIS

307 7th Ave., 11th Fl.
New York, NY 10001
PH: (212)377-3333
FX: (212)377-3334
E-mail: info@mediaopolis.com
URL: http://www.mediapolis.com

Founded: 1994. **Description:** Mediapolis is an interactive media company that specializes in high quality web sites that are easy to maintain. Mediapolis custom designs and develops web sites for large companies, with a design focus on efficiency and profitability.

▌4280
MEDIAPULSE

704 S Illinois Ave., Ste. C-201
Oak Ridge, TN 37830
PH: (865)482-4455
TF: 800-380-4514
FX: (865)482-4465
URL: http://www.mediapulse.com

Founded: 1995. **Description:** Mediapulse is a full service Internet services provider specializing in custom application development. Services offered by Mediapulse include web site design and development, Flash design, dynamic HTML development, database integration, custom programming, wireless development, and e-business consulting.

▌4281
MEDIARAVE STUDIOS, INC.

11 Ramon Blvd.
Freehold, NJ 07728-1434
PH: (508)831-6421
FX: (508)519-0725
E-mail: info@mediarave.net
URL: http://www.mediarave.net

Description: Mediarave Studios, Inc. offers web site design and development, including e-commerce solutions, graphic design, online databases and digital marketing. Mediarave Studios also provides an all-inclusive package that gives complete web services to small businesses.

▌4282
MEDIAZEN

17826 Canterbury Rd.
Cleveland, OH 44119
PH: (216)481-7500
FX: (216)481-7558
E-mail: start@mediazen.com
URL: http://www.mediazen.com
Contact: Terry Ross

Description: MediaZen provides web design and brand design to businesses. Services offered by MediaZen include web site design and development, e-commerce site development, branding, and web site hosting.

▌4283
MEGAPATH NETWORKS

6691 Owens Dr.
Pleasanton, CA 94588
PH: 877-634-2728

E-mail: info@megapath.net
URL: http://www.megapath.net

Description: Megapath Networks offers broadband services and web site design and hosting services to small and medium sized businesses as well as home offices and telecommuters. Megapath provides industry-specific templates allowing people to easily create and manage their own web sites, including e-commerce web sites with transaction capabilities.

▌4284
MERITAGE TECHNOLOGIES

18th St. Atrium Bldg.
1621 18th St., Ste. 150
Denver, CO 80202
PH: (303)295-2951
TF: (866)479-7500
URL: http://www.castlepoint.com

Description: Formerly known as Castlepoint Systems, Inc., Meritage Technologies offers a variety of Internet business solutions. Services provided by Meritage Technologies focus on e-commerce and include solution identification, architecture and design, development and integration, support, and project and quality management.

▌4285
MIDITECH.COM

26 - 911 Wonderland Rd S
London, ON, Canada
PH: (519)474-0224
E-mail: designer@miditech.com
URL: http://www.ontariobiz.on.ca/miditech

Description: Miditech.com offers custom web site design services. Miditech works closely with clients at each stage of the design process to ensure that business objectives are met. Miditech offers fast loading and eye-catching graphics to make a positive online impression, and to stay consistent with other communications media.

▌4286
MINDSHARE INTERNET CAMPAIGNS, LLC

1025 Vermont Ave. NW, Ste. 1200
Washington, DC 20005
PH: (202)654-0800
FX: (202)654-0839
E-mail: info@mindshare.net
URL: http://dev.mindshare.net

Founded: 1997. **Description:** Mindshare Internet Campaigns, LLC develops and implements online public affairs campaigns. Mindshare's professionals have won many awards including PR Week's best New Media Site of the Year. Mindshare's team will evaluate the client's needs, work to design the best website possible, then do usability testing, and integrate the new website into exiting intranets and extranets.

▌4287
MOUNTAIN MEDIA

28 Clinton St., Ste. 1
Saratoga Springs, NY 12866
PH: (518)583-0300
TF: 877-583-0300
E-mail: info@mountainmedia.com
URL: http://www.mountainmedia.com

Description: Mountain Media creates both informational online brochures and fully functional e-commerce storefronts. Services offered by Mountain Media include web site design and development, database programming, graphic design, search engine placement, and web and database hosting.

▌4288
MUNK AND PHYBER, INC

110b 2nd St. NE
Charlottesville, VA 22902
PH: (434)979-2980
E-mail: waldoandmax@munkandphyber.com
URL: http://www.munkandphyber.com

Description: Munk and Phyber, Inc specializes in building web sites. Services offered include custom programming and customized web site development for businesses, nonprofit organizations and associations, web application development, and client consulting.

▌4289
N2 DYNAMICS

PO Box 1436
Lake Forest, CA 92609
PH: (949)766-9575
FX: (949)766-5915
E-mail: info@n2dynamics.com
URL: http://www.n2dynamics.com

Description: N2 Dynamics focuses on web site design and development for businesses. Services offered by N2 Dynamics include concept design, interactive web site creation, graphic design, site promotion, and customer support.

▌4290
NATIONS DESIGN GROUP

90 Blue Ravine Rd.
Folsom, CA 95630
PH: (916)355-1865

FX: (916)985-4922
E-mail: sales@nationsdesigngroup.com
URL: http://www.nationsdesigngroup.com

Description: Nations Design Group offers a range of Internet services including web site design, e-commerce site design, Flash animation, web marketing, web business management, and site hosting.

▌4291
NATOLI DESIGN GROUP

3620 Falls Rd.
Baltimore, MD 21211
PH: (410)662-8373
FX: (410)662-9289
E-mail: info@natolidesign.com
URL: http://www.natolidesign.com

Description: Natoli Design Group provides its clients with an array of design services in various media. Services offered by Natoli Design Group include web site design, application interface design, motion graphics and television production, brand strategy and print media design.

▌4292
NDK STUDIO, INC.

PO Box 517
Point Pleasant, NJ 08742
PH: (732)892-2813
E-mail: info@ndkstudio.com
URL: http://www.ndkstudio.com

Description: NDK Studio offers multimedia services including web design, web site re-design, web site maintenance, search engine optimization, programming, and services in other types of multimedia. NDK focuses on customer input and personal attention as part of the design process.

▌4293
NEBULARIS INC.

900 Greenbank Rd., Ste. 374
Ottawa, ON, Canada K2J4P6
PH: (613)226-7665
TF: (866)632-8524
FX: (613)825-5960
E-mail: info @nebularis.com
URL: http://www.nebularis.com

Description: Nebularis Inc. offers web site design, creative consultation, technical and copy writing, e-commerce solutions, database development, and web site hosting.

▌ 4294
NEIGHBORNET ONLINE, INC.

4550 Post Oak Pl., Ste. 241
Houston, TX 77027
PH: (713)629-0030
FX: (713)629-0040
E-mail: neighbornet@neighbornet.net
URL: http://www.neighbornet.net

Description: NeighborNet Online, Inc. offers web site design, web site templates, domain name registration, search engine submission, intranet and extranet development, consulting services, and web site hosting.

▌ 4295
NEOWEB STUDIOS

1015-M S Taft Hill Rd., Ste. 143
Fort Collins, CO 80521
PH: (970)988-0033
FX: (970)221-2062
E-mail: info@neowebstudios.com
URL: http://www.neowebstudios.com

Description: NeoWeb Studios specializes in web site design and development for businesses and individuals. Services provided by NeoWeb Studios include web site creation, image and graphics optimization, Flash animation, custom programming, and password protected areas.

▌ 4296
NET-ARCHITECH, INC.

1205 E King St.
Lancaster, PA 17602-3235
PH: (717)293-3180
FX: (717)293-0231
E-mail: webmasters@net-architech.net
URL: http://www.net-architech.net

Description: Net-Architech, Inc. offers a range of information technology services including web site design and implementation. Net-Architech also provides web site maintenance, site promotion, e-commerce solutions, graphics and multimedia design.

▌ 4297
NET CIRQUE

7802 Mistic View Ct.
Derwood, MD 20877
PH: (301)947-3820
FX: (301)947-3820
E-mail: sales@netcirque.com
URL: http://www.netcirque.com

Description: Net Cirque provides a range of new media services including web site design and implementation, secure e-commerce solutions, database development, content management, graphics, Flash and Shockwave animation, intranet and extranet development, and e-publishing.

▌ 4298
NET DOCTORS

PO Box 2158
Seneca, SC 29679
PH: (864)882-1650
FX: (864)886-9903
E-mail: webmaster@netmds.com
URL: http://www.netmds.com

Description: Net Doctors offers Internet services including web site design and implementation, secure e-commerce sites, database development, web site hosting, and Internet access.

▌ 4299
NET2BUSINESS, LLC

9349 Santa Fe Dr.
Overland Park, KS 66212
PH: (913)385-1551
TF: 888-638-2249
FX: (913)895-9226
E-mail: images@net2business.com
URL: http://www.net2business.com

Description: Net2Business, LLC provides an variety of services including e-commerce web site design, Internet marketing, corporate and informational web site design, custom software development, and technical and network services.

▌ 4300
NETGALACTIC

7906 Sleepy Brooke Ct.
Springfield, VA 22153
PH: (703)813-8107
E-mail: infonetworkgalactic.com
URL: http://www.netgalactic.com

Description: Netgalactic is a full service information technology provider, offering complete turnkey programs as well as quality work on small projects. Netgalactic provides flexible solutions to web design and e-commerce needs.

▌ 4301
NETSTORM INTERNET SERVICES

26 Water St.
Frederick, MD 21701
PH: (301)631-6600

TF: 888-500-6277
FX: (301)631-2291
E-mail: sales@netstorm.net
URL: http://www.netstorm.net

Description: NetStorm Internet Services offers Internet access as well as web site design and hosting, including functional e-commerce sites. NetStorm provides domain registration, form mail and hit counters, email, design and copywriting services to its clients.

∎ 4302
NEW ANGLE MEDIA

750 W Baseline Rd., Ste. 1034
Tempe, AZ 85283
PH: (520)990-5292
E-mail: jf83@newanglemedia.com
URL: http://www.newanglemedia.com

Description: New Angle Media specializes in creating small to large web sites using Flash design. Other services offered by New Angle Media include HTML web design, graphic design, web content development, e-commerce solutions, digital business cards, and music and sound.

∎ 4303
NEW ENGLAND IT GROUP

7 Hawkins St., Ste. 2A
Danielson, CT 06239
PH: (860)774-7014
E-mail: infonewsletterenglanditgroup.com
URL: http://www.newenglanditgroup.com

Description: New England IT Group offers web design created especially for each client. Services provided by New England IT Group include web design and development, interactive web sites, Flash animation, graphic design, database integration, and digital photography.

∎ 4304
NEW HAMPSHIRE BUSINESS WEB, LLC

51 Pleasant St.
Hooksett, NH 03106-1453
PH: (603)485-7516
FX: (603)485-8570
E-mail: sales@nhbweb.com
URL: http://www.nhbweb.com

Description: New Hampshire Business Web, LLC offers its business clients a range of services including web site design, online business web sites, domain name registration, web site hosting, and software consulting.

∎ 4305
NEW MEDIA HEADQUARTERS

100 E Main St., Ste. 240
Norfolk, VA 23510
PH: (757)622-9693
FX: 877-461-7042
E-mail: info@newmediaheadquarters.com
URL: http://www.newmediaheadquarters.com

Description: New Media Headquarters is an interactive agency offering services including web site design, redesign, and development, web site promotion, graphic and logo design, animation, and web site hosting.

∎ 4306
NEW MEDIA PRODUCTIONS

5360 S Airport Rd.
Richmond, BC, Canada V7B1B4
PH: (604)273-1669
E-mail: james@verticaleclipse.com
URL: http://www.nmpros.com

Description: New Media Productions are electronic media specialists. Services offered by New Media Productions include HTML web site design, e-commerce solutions, databases, Flash animation, graphic design, web marketing, and audio and video production.

∎ 4307
NEW MILLENNIUM DESIGNS

101 Doubloon Dr.
Slidell, LA 70461
PH: (985)781-4471
TF: 888-NEW-WEB3
FX: (985)781-4434
E-mail: jazz@nmdesigns.com
URL: http://www.nmdesigns.com

Description: New Millennium Designs offers services including web site design with Flash animation and HTML, database design, e-commerce solutions, CD-ROM creation, corporate identity, and public relations and marketing.

∎ 4308
NEW ORLEANS WEB MASTERS

4201 Teuton St., Ste. 17
Metairie, LA 70006
PH: (504)251-2806
E-mail: webmaster@neworleanswebmasters.net
URL: http://www.neworleanswebmasters.net

Description: New Orleans Web Masters specializes in focused, fast loading web site design. New Orleans Web Masters also provides e-commerce services including shopping carts, online catalogs, and real time transactions.

∎ 4309
NEW TARGET INTERNET DESIGN AND DEVELOPMENT

228 S Washington St., Ste. 340
Alexandria, VA 22314
PH: (703)548-3433
FX: (703)548-5032
E-mail: web@newtarget.com
URL: http://www.newtarget.com

Description: New Target Internet Design and Development offers web site design and development, e-commerce solutions, database development, graphic design, application development, Internet marketing, and web site hosting services.

∎ 4310
NEW YORK DIGITAL DESIGN (NYD2)

220 Davidson Ave.
Somerset, NJ 08873
PH: (732)805-9297
FX: (732)805-0637
E-mail: info@nyd2.com
URL: http://www.nyd2.com

Description: New York Digital Design (NYD2) offers integrated communications management. Services provided by NYD2 include web site design and development, CD-ROM production, e-business solutions, and communications consulting services.

∎ 4311
NEWATLANTICWEB, INC.

370 Norfolk St.
Holliston, MA 01746
PH: (617)592-8515
E-mail: info@newatlanticweb.com
URL: http://www.newatlanticweb.com

Description: NewAtlanticWeb, Inc. offers web site design, e-commerce solutions, consulting, programming, database design, search engine listing, web/data integration, and marketing services.

∎ 4312
NEWFANGLED WEB FACTORY

177 N Main St.
Providence, RI 02903
PH: (401)861-3300
FX: (401)861-8883
E-mail: info@newfangled.com
URL: http://www.newfangled.com

Founded: 1995. **Description:** Newfangled Web Factory provides web site design and development services, as well as content management.

∎ 4313
NEXUS MEDIA GROUP

24 Main St.
Warwick, NY 10990
PH: (845)988-5002
TF: (866)639-8764
FX: (845)988-5005
E-mail: info@nexusmediagroup.com
URL: http://www.nexusmediagroup.com

Founded: 1997. **Description:** Nexus Media Group offers its clients design, technology and service. Nexus Media Group provides web design and new media design, in addition to services in print media. Nexus is committed to facilitating communications in all media, and furnishing successful design for its clients.

∎ 4314
NINTH DEGREE

16620 Aston St.
Irvine, CA 92606
PH: 888-453-5216
E-mail: contact@ninthdegree.com
URL: http://www.ninthdegree.com

Description: Ninth Degree offers its clients services including web site design and development, Flash animation, multimedia development, web programming, e-commerce solutions, promotion, and site hosting and server management.

∎ 4315
NOVAGIANT MEDIA, LLC

PO Box 277
Olive Branch, MS 38654
PH: 877-869-1450
E-mail: service@novagiant.com
URL: http://www.novagiant.com

Description: Novagiant Media, LLC offers its clients web site design and development services, as well as web site hosting, search engine submission, and domain name registration.

∎ 4316
NU-DESIGNS WEB DEVELOPMENT & HOSTING

1269 N Dutton Ave., Ste. 135
Santa Rosa, CA 95401
PH: (707)575-5373

TF: 800-575-1236
FX: (707)581-1811
E-mail: service@nu-designs.com
URL: http://www.nu-designs.com

Description: Nu-Designs Web Development & Hosting offers complete web site design and development services, including e-commerce solutions. Nu-Designs also provides Flash and multimedia design, web site promotion, web-based applications, streaming media, and site maintenance and hosting.

∎ 4317
NO. 1 WEB SITE DESIGN FLASH ANIMATION PAGE DESIGNER

113 Gail Dr.
Selton, CA 95018
PH: 800-514-8055
E-mail: questions@1-web-site-design-flash-animation-page-designer.com
URL: http://www.1-web-site-design-flash-animation-page-designer.com

Founded: 1998. **Description:** No. 1 Web Site Design Flash Animation Page Designer is a firm which specializes in Flash Animation web pages. This company can do the entire project, including design, copywriting, database design, and video, and offers fast turnaround on projects to its clients.

∎ 4318
NUMEDIA GROUP, LLP

PO Box 551627
Dallas, TX 75355
PH: (972)378-4108
FX: (972)473-2198
E-mail: info@numedia.com
URL: http://www.numedia.com

Description: Numedia Group, LLP provides comprehensive Internet solutions including web site design and development, strategic planning, application development, interactive marketing and branding, multimedia design, and web site hosting services.

∎ 4319
NUMINOUS DESIGN

1906 SE 35th Ave.
Portland, OR 97214
PH: (503)234-5771
E-mail: mike@numinous-design.com
URL: http://www.numinous-design.com
Contact: Michael Berkley

Description: Numinous Design specializes in creating dynamic, interactive web sites and applications. Services provided by Numinous Design include web site design and development, database development, e-commerce solutions, and multimedia creation.

∎ 4320
NURUN, INC.

1260 Lebourgneuf Blvd., Ste. 250
Montreal, PQ, Canada G2K2G2
PH: (514)627-2001
TF: 877-696-1292
FX: (514)627-2023
E-mail: lesley.cox@nurun.com
URL: http://www.nurun.com
Contact: Lesley Cox

Description: Nurun provides interactive business solutions including developing a company's complete Internet presence. Strategy, marketing, creativity, and technology are the focus of solutions offered to each customer. Nurun offers services including web site design, e-commerce sites, content management, customer relationship management, and e-marketing expertise.

∎ 4321
NYLON DESIGNS

6 W 14th St., 4th Fl.
New York, NY 10011
PH: (212)691-1134
FX: (212)691-3477
URL: http://www.nylondesigns.com

Description: Nylon Designs is the design division of Nylon Technology, a new media design and technology agency. Nylon Designs offers services including web site design and development, Flash and multimedia animation, e-commerce systems, database architecture, CD-ROM development, and web site hosting and maintenance.

∎ 4322
OCTET CORP.

133 Fifth Ave., 8th Fl.
New York, NY 10003
PH: (212)475-6393
FX: (212)475-1814
E-mail: info@octet.com
URL: http://www.octet.com

Description: Octet Corporation provides state of the art corporate web sites including custom graphic design and integration of existing corporate logos and designs, as well as custom designed web applications and online software systems for the financial industry.

▌4323
OHIO WEB DESIGN

PO BOX 6229
Chillicothe, OH 45601
PH: (530)706-8896
FX: (603)688-5830
E-mail: info@ohiowebdesign.com
URL: http://www.ohiowebdesign.com

Description: Ohio Web Design specializes in graphics, web design, copy writing, marketing, and promotion. Ohio Web Design gathers information from the client and works to create an effective, visually interesting and cost effective web presence.

▌4324
OLADAP, INC.

PO Box 3911
Peabody, MA 01960
PH: (978)538-7138
FX: (781)266-2176
URL: http://www.oladap.com

Description: Oladap is an Internet company dedicated to using cutting edge technology to create a strong Internet presence for its clients. Services Oladap provides include online stores, information management, customer databases, multimedia creations, search engine placement, and custom web applications.

▌4325
OLIVE, LLC

305 2nd Ave., Ste. 522
New York, NY 10003
PH: (212)254-9155
E-mail: info@olivemedia.com
URL: http://www.olivemedia.com

Description: Olive Media offers a variety of design and communications services, focused on clarity and making the message effective. Services provided include web design, e-commerce, branding, database development, games, and consulting in strategy and other areas.

▌4326
ON-LINE ON-TIME, INC.

5701 Kentucky Ave., No. 205
Minneapolis, MN 55428
PH: (763)537-1000
TF: 888-537-9070
FX: (763)535-5422
E-mail: sales@online-ontime.com
URL: http://www.online-ontime.com

Description: On-Line On-Time, Inc. offers web site design and development services, graphic design, programming in a variety of languages, Flash animation, e-commerce solutions, database integration, web site hosting, Internet access, and other information technology services.

▌4327
ON THE VERGE

8544 Sunset Blvd.
Los Angeles, CA 90069
PH: 877-999-8374
FX: (310)652-3854
E-mail: sales@ontheverge.com
URL: http://www.ontheverge.com

Description: On The Verge is an Internet solutions provider that offers services including web site design, logo design, animation, search engine optimization, marketing, e-commerce solutions, and web site hosting.

▌4328
ONE WEB SOURCE, LLC

109 Danbury Rd., Ste. 8B
Ridgefield, CT 06877
PH: (203)431-0920
E-mail: info@onewebsource.com
URL: http://www.onewebsource.com

Description: One Web Source, LLC offers web site design services, including e-commerce solutions. One Web Source also provides web site marketing, and web site maintenance.

▌4329
ONE9INE

54 W 21st St., No. 607
New York, NY 10010
PH: (212)929-7828
FX: (212)645-3409
E-mail: info@one9ine.com
URL: http://www.one9ine.com

Description: One9ine is a design company that creates and develops websites, does brand identity development, and offers creative direction in other areas of visual communication. One9ine is focused on using a fresh approach in creative work that engages the audience, client and designer.

▌4330
ONLINE DESIGN, INC.

1 W Campbell Ave., Ste. B24
Campbell, CA 95008
PH: (408)866-1800
FX: (408)866-1807

843

E-mail: sales@onlinedesigninc.com
URL: http://www.onlinedesigninc.com

Description: Online Design, Inc. offers web site design and development services, including e-comerce and database solutions. Online Design also provides Flash animation, streaming media, programming, logo design, brand identity creation, graphic design and web site hosting.

▌4331
ONLINE DEVELOPMENT AND MARKETING, INC.

138 W 25th St., 12th Fl.
New York, NY 10001
PH: (212)741-8057
FX: (212)741-8589
E-mail: info@odminc.com
URL: http://www.odminc.com

Description: Online Development and Marketing is an Internet development and consulting company that designs customized web sites and web based applications. Online Development and Marketing also offers desktop publishing, multimedia, marketing, content creation, and branding services.

▌4332
ONLINE RESOURCE GROUP, INC.

636 Squires Rd.
Lexington, KY 40515
PH: (859)271-6170
FX: (859)271-9490
E-mail: marla@onlinerg.com
URL: http://www.onlinerg.com

Description: Online Resource Group, Inc. offers services in web design, web marketing and multimedia design. Online Resource Group also provides e-commerce solutions, animation, interactive polls and contests, and web site hosting.

▌4333
OPENROAD COMMUNICATIONS, LTD.

220-353 Water St.
Vancouver, BC, Canada V6B1B8
PH: (604)694-0554
FX: (604)694-0558
E-mail: info@openroad.ca
URL: http://www.openroad.ca

Founded: 1994. **Description:** Openroad Communications solves business problems through user-centric design and rapid application development. Openroad Communications provides web site design and custom web applications to support clients' business objectives. Consulting services and system integration services are also available from Openroad Communications.

▌4334
OPTIC HOST CORP.

PO BOX 1259
Palm City, FL 34991-1259
PH: (561)221-8645
TF: 877-463-5264
FX: (561)221-9147
E-mail: info@optichost.net
URL: http://www.optichost.com

Description: Optic Host offers web site design and hosting, e-commerce solutions, and marketing services to small businesses, merchants, and developers. Optic Host's staff works with clients to get the client's message across, whether it is a small informational web site or a large database-driven e-commerce site.

▌4335
OPTION4 INTERACTIVE SOLUTIONS, INC.

520 Brickell Key Dr., Ste. O-206
Miami, FL 33132
PH: (305)379-7131
FX: (305)468-6100
E-mail: info@option4.com
URL: http://www.option4.com

Description: Option4 Interactive Solutions, Inc. is a web design and development firm offering services including e-commerce site development, web site design, programming, graphics, Flash animation, and web site promotion.

▌4336
ORAJEN GROUP, INC.

1412 Howard St.
Omaha, NE 68102
PH: (402)827-7500
FX: (402)827-7501
E-mail: info@orajen.com
URL: http://www.orajen.com

Description: Orajen Group, Inc. is a full service design firm offering web site design, construction and content development, database integration, custom web applications, e-commerce solutions and shopping cart systems, business card sites, and web site hosting.

▌4337
ORANGE GRAPHICS

PO Box 554
East Greenwich, RI 02818
PH: (401)345-7333
FX: (413)502-2711
E-mail: info@orangegraphics.com
URL: http://www.orangegraphics.com

Description: Orange Graphics offers a range of design services including web site design emphasizing multimedia. Orange Graphics also provides interactive CD-ROM production, kiosk design, marketing, corporate branding, and print media design.

▌4338
ORBIS INNOVATIONS

5500 N Elcarol Ct.
Wilmington, NC 28409
PH: (910)791-7296
FX: (910)791-1101
E-mail: generalinfo@orbisinnovations.com
URL: http://www.orbisinnovations.com

Description: Orbis Innovations is focused on offering customers Internet solutions that will help their businesses succeed. Services provided by Orbis Innovations include custom web site design tailored to each client, web hosting, e-commerce, Internet marketing, and online scheduling.

▌4339
ORDERGUARD

PO Box 1669
Glendale, CA 91204
PH: (818)345-7304
FX: (208)361-1906
E-mail: charlsea@pacbell.net
URL: http://www.orderguard.com

Description: OrderGuard offers web site design and development services, as well as full service web site hosting, and graphic design.

▌4340
ORGANIC

601 Townsend St.
San Francisco, CA 94103
PH: (415)581-5300
FX: (415)581-5400
E-mail: bizdev@organic.com
URL: http://www.organic.com

Founded: 1993. **Description:** Organic is a company offering digital business solutions. Organic has created websites that were first in their industry category and designed Yahoo!'s logo and user interface. Organic works with clients to provide multi-platform user interface and marketing, as well as online media buying and management.

▌4341
ORLANDO WEB SOLUTIONS

4185 W Lake Mary Blvd.
Lake Mary, FL 32746
PH: (407)324-3700
TF: (866)827-4944
FX: (407)328-0048
E-mail: info@orlandowebsolutions.com
URL: http://www.orlandowebsolutions.com

Description: Orlando Web Solutions offers a range of Internet services, including web site design and hosting, and wireless Internet. Orlando Web Solutions web site designers work with a variety of programming languages and can also create embedded streaming video/audio, as well as functional e-commerce sites.

▌4342
OSO GRANDE TECHNOLOGIES, INC.

5921 Jefferson St. NE
Albuquerque, NM 87109
PH: (505)345-6555
FX: (505)345-6559
E-mail: info@osogrande.com
URL: http://www.osogrande.com

Description: Oso Grande Technologies offers Internet services such as web site design and hosting as well as Internet access. High quality, fast loading web site design that effectively communicates the customer's message is a goal of Oso Grande Technologies.

▌4343
OSPREY NETWORK TECHNOLOGIES, INC.

1109 Commercial
Emporia, KS 66801
PH: (620)342-9297
TF: 888-677-7391
FX: (620)342-4836
E-mail: webmaster@osprey.net
URL: http://www.osprey.net

Description: Osprey Network Technologies, Inc. specializes in e-commerce services. Osprey Network Technologies provides online secure servers, web site design and hosting, searchable online databases, set-up and support of business networks, and online advertising.

▌4344
THE OTHER WEBSITE COMPANY, LLC

5717 Arapahoe Ave., Ste. 204
Boulder, CO 80303
PH: (303)786-9688
FX: (720)564-9903
E-mail: questions@towc.com
URL: http://www.towc.com

Description: The Other Website Company, LLC provides an array of web services including web site design and development. Professional work offered by The Other Website Company includes e-commerce system development, database design and development, Flash and 3D animation, graphic design, CD-ROM production, web site hosting, and print media design.

▌4345
OUTDOOR MIND, LLC

194 W Main St., Ste. 203
Woodland, CA 95695
PH: (530)662-1889
TF: 800-276-0770
FX: (530)668-4320
URL: http://www.outdoormind.net

Description: Outdoor Mind, LLC offers a variety of technical, design and marketing services to its clients. Outdoor Mind provides web site design and development, multimedia production, domain name registration, web site updates and maintenance, web site hosting and targeted advertising.

▌4346
THE OUTER EDGE CORP.

2209 Garden Oaks Dr.
Irving, TX 75061
PH: (972)513-0251
E-mail: info@t-oe.com
URL: http://www.t-oe.com

Description: With offices in the Netherlands and the US, The Outer Edge Corp. is a full service web development and multimedia firm providing a variety of services. The Outer Edge offers interactive Flash web sites, HTML web site design, 3D designs, logo design and e-branding services.

▌4347
OUTTA SITE, INC.

613 Steeplechase Dr.
Hurricane, WV 25526
PH: (304)562-7650
FX: (304)722-9209
E-mail: anyone@outtasiteinc.com
URL: http://www.outtasiteinc.com

Description: Outta Site, Inc. offers complete business Internet solutions including web site design and development, copy writing, custom programming, e-commerce implementation, database integration, graphic design services, promotional service, web site hosting, and other Internet support services.

▌4348
OVER THE NET

PO Box 1499
Camarillo, CA 93011-1499
PH: (805)384-1144

FX: (805)384-9111
E-mail: sales@otn.com
URL: http://www.overthenet.com

Description: Over The Net builds cost-effective custom web sites. Other services provided by Over The Net include custom programming, shopping cart development and e-commerce systems, graphic design, site hosting and maintenance, and web site marketing.

▌4349
OXFORD NETWORKS

511 Congress St.
Portland, ME 04101
PH: 800-520-9911
E-mail: contactus@oxfordnetworks.com
URL: http://www.oxfordnetworks.com

Description: Oxford Networks offers a range of Internet services including web site design, database development, web site maintenance and hosting, and streaming media development. ◦

▌4350
OZANET

793 Golf Ln.
Bensenville, IL 60106-1563
PH: (630)860-2800
FX: (630)860-1122
E-mail: info@ozanet.com
URL: http://www.ozanet.com

Description: OzaNet offers a range of web and traditional design services including web site design and development, e-commerce systems, web site marketing, and web hosting.

▌4351
OZONE RANCH

PO Box 1068
Sandpoint, ID 83864
PH: (208)266-1668
E-mail: webster@ozoneranch.com
URL: http://www.ozoneranch.com

Description: Ozone Ranch provides its clients with a wide range of Internet services including web site design and redesign, e-commerce systems, database applications, graphic design and multimedia content production, web site maintenance and marketing, and site hosting.

▌4352
P HARDY TECHNOLOGIES, INC.

PO Box 1024
Bay Shore, NY 11706
PH: (516)318-8334

URL: http://www.phardy.com

Description: P Hardy Technologies, Inc. provides Internet services to clients ranging in size from small businesses to Fortune 500 companies. P Hardy Technologies offers web site design, development and maintenance, application development, information security, and web site marketing.

▌ 4353
PACIFIC EXPRESS NETWORKS

5710 W Manchester Blvd., Ste. 209
Los Angeles, CA 90045
PH: (310)645-8828
E-mail: info@pacex.net
URL: http://www.pacex.net

Description: Pacific Express Networks offers Internet access and web site design and hosting services. Pacific Express Networks provides web site design, custom animation, e-commerce solutions, programming, and site hosting.

▌ 4354
PADDOCK AND COMPANY

PO Box 1722
Waterbury, CT 06721
PH: (203)596-8100
TF: 888-846-9198
FX: (203)596-8252
E-mail: info@paddock.net
URL: http://www.paddockandcompany.com

Description: Paddock and Company is an Internet marketing and design firm. Services offered by Paddock and Company include e-commerce solutions, Flash animation and multimedia design, graphic design, database development and integration, web site promotion, and consulting.

▌ 4355
PAGE BY PAGE DESIGNS

6835 St. Andrews Dr.
Mukilteo, WA 98275-4849
PH: (425)349-3672
TF: 877-548-9018
FX: (509)351-0427
E-mail: gail@pagebypagedesigns.com
URL: http://www.pagebypagedesigns.com

Description: Page by Page Designs offers web site design and development, e-commerce site creation, graphic and logo design, Flash animation, search engine submittals, and web site hosting services.

▌ 4356
PAGESKILLS.COM

2678 Gravel Dr.
Fort Worth, TX 76011
PH: (817)284-1288
FX: (817)284-1115
E-mail: info@pageskills.com
URL: http://www.pageskills.com

Description: PageSkills.com specializes in business web site creation. Services offered by PageSkills.com include web site design and development, Flash development, e-commerce systems, domain name registration, and search engine submissions.

▌ 4357
PAINT MY WAGON, LLC

24 Professional Pky. Ctr., Ste. 240
San Rafael, CA 94903
PH: (510)528-2023
E-mail: info@paintmywagon.com
URL: http://www.paintmywagon.com

Description: Paint My Wagon, LLC offers a range of computer and web services including web site design and development, custom graphics, e-commerce systems, database development, multimedia and CD creation, and site hosting and maintenance.

▌ 4358
PALLASART WEB DESIGN

101 Laurel Ln.
Austin, TX 78705
PH: (512)469-7454
TF: 888-426-9100
FX: (512)320-0391
E-mail: boba@pallasweb.com
URL: http://www.pallasweb.com

Description: Pallasart Web Design is a full service Internet design firm, specializing in e-commerce web sites. Pallasart offers a variety of design packages, from an e-commerce starter plan with basic services, to a large multi-page e-commerce site with many helpful tools to expand market penetration.

▌ 4359
PANORAMA POINT

3600 Cerrillos Rd., Ste. 724B
Santa Fe, NM 87507
PH: (505)424-4800
TF: 800-804-5844
FX: (505)424-4700
E-mail: inquiries@panoramapoint.com

URL: http://www.panoramapoint.com

Description: Panorama Point focuses on web site development for business clients. Services offered by Panorama Point include web site design, information architecture, programming, web site marketing, and site maintenance and hosting.

▌4360
THE PAPER MILL ELECTRONIC

468 E River Rd.
PO Box 191
Riverton, CT 06065
PH: (860)379-0276
FX: (860)738-1450
E-mail: twlack@tppm.com
URL: http://www.tppm.com

Description: The Paper Mill Electronic offers web site design services, graphic art and logo design, domain name registration, e-mail forms, and web site hosting services.

▌4361
PAPER STREET WEB DESIGN

16113 Kingsmoor Way
Miami Lakes, FL 33014
PH: (305)804-2218
E-mail: peteboyd@paperst.com
URL: http://www.paperstreetwebdesign.com

Description: Paper Street Web Design offers professional web site design for businesses, attorneys and law firms. Services offered by Paper Street Web Design include custom web design, content writing, Internet marketing, search engine optimization, and web site hosting.

▌4362
PARADIGM PIONEERS, INC.

PO Box 5115
Phillipsburg, NJ 08865
TF: 800-774-0905
FX: (908)325-0029
E-mail: info@ppihx.com
URL: http://www.ppihx.com

Description: Paradigm Pioneers, Inc. specializes in serving small businesses with its Internet solutions. Services offered by Paradigm Pioneers include web site design, custom applications and programs, and web site hosting.

▌4363
PARADIGM WEB DESIGN

2500 E Devon Ave., 3rd Fl.
Des Plaines, IL 60018
PH: (847)768-0018

TF: 888-737-0018
FX: (847)768-0017
E-mail: sales@paradigm-il.com
URL: http://www.paradigmwebdesign.com

Description: Paradigm Web Design is a full service design firm offering a variety of digital solutions. Services provided by Paradigm Web Design include web site design and development, Shockwave, dynamic HTML, and CGI programming, illustration and graphic design, CD-ROM production, and web marketing.

▌4364
PARADIGM WEB SOURCE

1214 Wallace Rd. NW, No. 195
Salem, OR 97304
PH: (503)375-2853
FX: (503)375-2853
E-mail: design@paradigm-web.net
URL: http://www.paradigm-web.net

Description: Paradigm Web Source offers complete, turnkey Internet solutions including complete e-commerce systems, web site design and development, graphic design, web marketing and search engine optimization, Flash animation, and web site hosting services.

▌4365
PARKBENCH PRODUCTIONS

10503 Grayslake Ct.
Tampa, FL 33626-2560
PH: (813)334-4382
FX: (813)854-6455
E-mail: info@parkbenchproductions.com
URL: http://www.parkbenchproductions.com

Description: ParkBench Productions offers design services in both traditional and digital media. ParkBench provides web site design and implementation, CD-ROM production, interactive kiosk design, logo and graphic design, and print media services.

▌4366
PASSTEK GROUP, INC.

417 E Manchester Rd.
Syracuse, NY 13219
PH: (315)345-3420
E-mail: info@passtek.com
URL: http://www.passtek.com

Description: PassTek Group, Inc. offers web site design, focusing on fast loading and easy to navigate pages. PassTek also provides custom e-business solutions for its clients.

▌4367
PATHFYNDER SYSTEMS

117 Spring St.
Three Rivers, MI 49093
PH: (616)273-5177
FX: (616)279-9561
URL: http://www.pathfynder.com

Description: Pathfynder Systems creates custom web sites for businesses. Services offered by Pathfynder Systems include content production, graphic design, database connectivity, e-commerce solutions, logo design, and web site hosting.

▌4368
PAUL KAUFMAN WEB DESIGN

700 Valley Dr.
Durham, NC 27704
PH: (919)620-5752
E-mail: info@pkwd.net
URL: http://www.pkwd.net

Description: Paul Kaufman Web Design is a small firm offering web site design and development. Services provided by Paul Kaufman Web Design include HTML site programming, graphic design, Flash development, copy writing, application development, search engine promotion, and site maintenance and hosting.

▌4369
PAWLIK CORP.

1626 SE 28th St.
Cape Coral, FL 33904
PH: (941)458-9232
E-mail: info@pawlikcorp.com
URL: http://www.pawlikcorp.com

Description: Pawlik Corp. offers web site design in English and German, web site marketing, firewall and Internet security solutions, web consulting, and web site hosting services.

▌4370
PAWSITRONIC.COM

PO Box 13619
Sissonville, WV 25360-0619
PH: (304)984-9804
FX: (304)766-5174
E-mail: webmaster@pawsitronic.com
URL: http://www.pawsitronic.com

Founded: 1996. **Description:** Pawsitronic.com is a full service web site design and development company offering a full line of web site design services, e-commerce-enabled web sites, targeted web marketing, and web site hosting.

▌4371
PAYSON LLC

PO Box 440
East Haddam, CT 06423
PH: (860)873-3399
FX: (860)873-1866
E-mail: stephen@paysonllc.com
URL: http://www.paysonllc.com

Description: Payson LLC specializes in Internet solutions for small businesses and nonprofit organizations. Services offered by Payson LLC include basic web site development, e-commerce systems, Flash animation, Java scripts, order forms, logo design, and site hosting.

▌4372
PC DUDES.COM

816 N 2nd St.
Mankato, MN 56001
PH: (507)345-1282
FX: (507)345-7689
E-mail: pcdudes@pcdudes.com
URL: http://www.pcdudes.com

Description: PC Dudes.com offers a variety of web services including web site design and development, multimedia production, e-commerce solutions, animation, interactive CDs, advertising, scripting, and web site hosting.

▌4373
PD WARNER PRODUCTIONS

PO Box 41
Scituate, MA 02066
PH: (781)545-5526
E-mail: ringmaster@pdwarner.com
URL: http://www.pdwarner.com

Description: PD Warner Productions is a full service design and production firm offering services which include web site design and development, corporate identity, graphic design and print media production.

▌4374
PEAKS MEDIA

18-2160 Sun Peaks Rd.
Sun Peaks, BC, Canada V0E1Z1
PH: (250)578-0207
FX: (250)578-0287
E-mail: cathy@peaksmedia.com
URL: http://www.peaksmedia.com

Description: Peaks Media offers web site design, development, maintenance and hosting services. In addition, Peaks Media also provides multimedia presentation production, web advertising, search engine submissions, and print and broadcasting media production.

■ 4375
PEBBLEHAVEN COMPANY

PO Box 216
Westwood, MA 02090
PH: (781)407-9957
TF: 877-777-9957
FX: (781)658-2066
E-mail: info@pebblehaven.com
URL: http://www.pebblehaven.com

Description: Pebblehaven Company provides complete web solutions. Services offered by Pebblehaven Company include web site design, implementation and hosting, Flash and multimedia development, e-commerce solutions, shopping carts, search engine registration and marketing consultation.

■ 4376
PECKMAN WEB TECHNOLOGIES

PO Box 1334
Randolph, MA 02368
PH: (781)986-1717
TF: (866)732-5932
FX: 800-538-5434
URL: http://www.peckweb.com

Description: Peckman Web Technologies offers web site design and redesign, e-commerce site design including shopping cart, secure transactions, graphic design, search engine submission, web site maintenance and site hosting services.

■ 4377
PEN PUBLISHING INTERACTIVE

PO Box 782302
Wichita, KS 67278-2302
PH: (316)651-0551
FX: (316)651-5868
E-mail: sales@penpublishing.com
URL: http://www.penpublishing.com

Description: Pen Publishing Interactive offers a variety of Internet services including web site design, complete e-commerce solutions, domain registration, dedicated servers, and web site hosting for small or large businesses.

■ 4378
PENNINGTON TECHNICAL ARTS

14002 Shire Oak
San Antonio, TX 78247
PH: (210)496-5095
FX: (210)491-3497

E-mail: pennington@penningtontechnicalarts.com
URL: http://www.penningtontechnicalarts.com

Description: Pennington Technical Arts specializes in adding programming and database capabilities to web sites, allowing clients to convert a web page into a software application. Pennington Technical Arts also provides e-commerce web site design, database design, and application development services.

■ 4379
PERCEPTIONS

101 Uptown Rd.,No. 25
Ithaca, NY 14850
PH: (607)257-1537
FX: (607)257-1537
E-mail: ed@perceptions-web-designers.com
URL: http://www.perceptions-web-designers.com
Contact: Ed Schulman

Description: Perceptions provides its clients with a variety of design services including web site design, e-commerce site design, web site promotion, animation, graphic design, digital photography, banner ads, print media design, and product models.

■ 4380
PERIWINKLE COMMUNICATIONS

PO Box 16722
West Haven, CT 06516
PH: (203)937-5406
FX: (203)931-9229
E-mail: periwinkle@toto.com
URL: http://www.toto.com

Description: Periwinkle Communications offers web site design, web application and database development, CGI programming, graphic design, database integration, search engine promotion, e-commerce solutions, and web site hosting services.

■ 4381
PERRYWORKS INTERACTIVE

1000 N Doheney Dr., Ste. 204
West Hollywood, CA 90069
PH: (310)274-1024
FX: (310)271-7808
E-mail: info@perryworks.com
URL: http://www.perryworks.com
Contact: Joe Perry

Description: PerryWorks Interactive is a web and interactive design studio specializing in quick delivery of web sites and e-commerce enabled web sites. PerryWorks Interactive also offers services including online stores, interactive presentations, CD, DVD and video production, graphic design and web site promotion.

▌ 4382
PIKES PEAK SOLUTIONS

1221 Lake Plaza Dr.
Colorado Springs, CO 80906
PH: (719)228-0133
FX: (719)228-0135
URL: http://www.pikespeaksolutions.com

Description: Pikes Peak Solutions specializes in business web site design and development. Services offered by Pikes Peak Solutions include web and print design, Flash animation, illustration, content development, web applications development, portal creation, and database management.

▌ 4383
POLAR DESIGN

809 Turnpike St., Ste. 201/203
North Andover, MA 01845
PH: (978)682-4211
FX: (978)682-4331
E-mail: contact@polardesign.com
URL: http://www.polardesign.com

Description: Polar Design combines art and technology to create and deliver multimedia business solutions for its clients. Services provided by Polar Design include e-business, web site design and development, content management, Internet marketing, application hosting, and customized software solutions.

▌ 4384
PREFERENCES

7 Rue Taylor
75010 Paris, France
PH: 33 1 48 03 05 44
FX: 33 1 48 03 45 04
E-mail: contact@preferences.fr
URL: http://www.preferences.fr

Description: Preferences is an interactive design firm based in Paris, France that offers advertising and promotional services in various media. Preferences specializes in the design of interactive CD ROMs and web sites.

▌ 4385
PUGET SOUND SYSTEMS

14023 NE 80 St.
Redmond, WA 98052
PH: (425)885-7014

FX: (206)289-3029
E-mail: info@pugetsystems.com
URL: http://www.pugetsystems.com/webdesign

Description: Puget Sound Systems is a company that provides custom built computer systems and custom web site design. Puget Sound Systems provides a complex administration system making it easy to update and edit information on websites. In addition to website design, Puget Sound Systems offers a complete e-commerce solution, including credit card processing.

▌ 4386
PULSITY, INC.

111 W Jackson Blvd., Ste. 1320
Chicago, IL 60604
PH: (312)341-1977
TF: (866)PUL-SITY
FX: (312)341-1571
E-mail: info@pulsity.com
URL: http://www.pulsity.com

Description: Pulsity, Inc. is an Internet solutions firm offering services including web site design and development, intranet and extranet development, e-commerce solutions, custom applications, and Internet marketing.

▌ 4387
Q4-2, INC. DIGITAL ARCHITECTS

9250 Amber Wood Dr.
Kirtland, OH 44094
PH: (440)256-3870
FX: (440)256-3878
E-mail: info@Q4-2.com
URL: http://www.q4-2.com

Description: Q4-2, Inc. Digital Architects provides a wide range of services focusing on building e-commerce solutions. Q4-2 Digital Architects offer complete web site design and implementation, branding and marketing strategies, user interface concepts, copy writing, custom web and applications development, business consultation, and secure hosting services.

▌ 4388
QUADRANT TECHNOLOGY, INC.

11655 Central Pky., Ste. 305
Jacksonville, FL 32224
PH: (904)998-1918
FX: (904)998-1941
E-mail: info@quadranttechnology.com
URL: http://www.quadranttechnology.com

Description: Quadrant Technology, Inc. offers a variety of Internet business solutions. Services provided by Quadrant

Technology include web site design and development, e-commerce solutions, e-marketing, database development, applications programming, multimedia production, and web site hosting.

∎ 4389
QUADSIMIA, LLC

587 Main St., Ste. 200
New York Mills, NY 13417-1463
PH: (315)768-4974
TF: 888-499-4440
FX: (315)768-7353
E-mail: info@quadsimia.com
URL: http://www.quadsimia.com

Description: Quadsimia, LLC offers a range of Internet services including web site design, implementation and maintenance, e-commerce web site design, graphic design, multimedia, streaming media, web site promotion, Internet access, customized software, and web site hosting.

∎ 4390
QUANTUM REDHEAD

1300 Adams Ave., Ste. 6A
Costa Mesa, CA 92626
PH: (714)437-9303
E-mail: info@quantumredhead.com
URL: http://www.quantumredhead.com

Description: Quantum Redhead is a full service Internet development firm offering professional work that includes web site design and information architecture, graphic design, branding, animation, intranet and extranet development, databases, digital illustration, and marketing services.

∎ 4391
QUINN INTERACTIVE, INC.

1050 Stanyan St., Ste. 5
San Francisco, CA 94117
PH: (415)566-1840
E-mail: info@quinn.com
URL: http://www.quinn.com

Description: Quinn Interactive, Inc. is a design firm that specializes in interactive design, information architecture, and visual communications. Quinn Interactive offers services including web site design, print media creation, e-commerce solutions, and corporate identity.

∎ 4392
QUINTESSENTIAL PROGRAMMING, INC.

45 Swift St., Ste. 9
South Burlington, VT 05403
PH: (802)863-5812
FX: (802)652-1597
E-mail: info@quintessentialprogramming.com
URL: http://www.quintessentialprogramming.com

Description: Quintessential Programming, Inc. specializes in web design, business software, and networking. Services offered by Quintessential Programming include informational and e-commerce web site design, database driven web sites, site updates and redesign, and web site hosting.

∎ 4393
R/GA

350 W 39th St.
New York, NY 10018
PH: (212)946-4000
FX: (212)946-4010
E-mail: web@rga.com
URL: http://www.rga.com

Description: R/GA is a design company with offices in New York and Los Angeles, dedicated to providing creative solutions with innovative technology. R/GA works with many large companies and offers services including digital brand marketing, e-commerce, kiosks and broadband, multi-channel and systematic design. R/GA was chosen interactive agency of the year 2001 by Adweek magazine.

∎ 4394
R7 MEDIA

1091 J St.
San Diego, CA 92101
PH: (619)255-9130
E-mail: info@r7media.com
URL: http://www.r7media.com

Description: R7 Media offers an array of Internet services including web site design and development, Flash animation, multimedia development, enterprise resource planning, programming, Internet marketing, search engine placement, and site hosting.

∎ 4395
RADICAL FRINGE

380 Lafayette St., Rm. 203
New York, NY 10003
PH: (917)412-9293
FX: (212)979-6876
E-mail: info@radicalfringe.com
URL: http://www.radicalfringe.com

Description: Radical Fringe specializes in custom developed e-business solutions, and also offers custom shopping cart applications, web-enabled database applications, intranet solutions, web site design, Java applications, and custom graphics.

▌ 4396
RANDOM ACCESS

1314 E Las Olas Blvd., No. 902
Fort Lauderdale, FL 33301
PH: (954)462-1107
FX: (954)462-1150
E-mail: team@rxs.com
URL: http://www.randomaccess.com

Description: Random Access creates custom web sites and provides information architecture development, Flash and Shockwave design, e-commerce solutions, custom programming, web site marketing, and public relations and consulting services.

▌ 4397
RARE EARTH INTERACTIVE DESIGN, INC.

105 Fargo Ave.
Buffalo, NY 14201
PH: (716)883-1601
TF: 877-883-1601
FX: (716)886-9725
E-mail: info@rareearthdesign.com
URL: http://www.rareearthdesign.com

Description: Rare Earth Interactive Design, Inc. offers a variety of Internet services including complete e-commerce solutions, database integration, EDI consulting, graphic design, sound and animation, web and mail hosting.

▌ 4398
RASPBERRY MEDIA

874 Gravenstein Hwy., S Ste. 14
Sebastopol, CA 95472
PH: (707)824-8235
FX: (707)824-4469
E-mail: info@raspberrymedia.com
URL: http://www.raspberrymedia.com

Description: Raspberry Media specializes in corporate marketing web sites and e-commerce sites. Services offered by Raspberry Media include creating user-friendly web sites, HTML authoring and database engineering, graphic design, marketing, streaming media and Flash animation, as well as usability testing and web site maintenance.

▌ 4399
RAVEN DIGITAL

3201 Tollview Dr.
Rolling Meadows, IL 60008
PH: (847)590-3000
TF: 800-373-4884
FX: (847)590-0912
E-mail: info@ravendigital.com
URL: http://www.ravendigital.com

Description: Raven Digital offers web site design, e-commerce design and development, Flash animation, logo design, audio/video multimedia, Internet marketing, and web site hosting services.

▌ 4400
RAZORFISH, INC.

32 Mercer St.
New York, NY 10013
PH: (212)966-5960
FX: (212)966-6915
URL: http://www.razorfish.com

Description: Razorfish offers digital solutions to help clients leverage the power of technology. Razorfish has several offices worldwide, and provides website design and user-centered solutions customized for the needs of each organization.

▌ 4401
RDVO, INC.

249 Elm St.
Somerville, MA 02144
PH: (617)629-9990
FX: (617)629-9793
E-mail: info@rdvo.com
URL: http://www.rdvo.com

Description: RDVO is a full service interactive agency offering professional work that includes web site design and development, digital marketing platforms, Flash and multimedia development, interactive application development, and strategy and planning.

▌ 4402
READY POINT CLICK

1810 N Maple Grove
Boise, ID 83704
PH: (208)713-6261
E-mail: info@readypointclick.com
URL: http://www.readypointclick.com

Description: Ready Point Click provides its clients with a range of Internet services including web site design, redesign, and development, e-commerce solutions, e-business strategy, application engineering, multimedia and Flash design, site promotion and advertising, and web site hosting.

▌ 4403
REAL INTERACTIVE

25 Business Park Dr.
Branford, CT 06405
PH: (203)488-8447

853

FX: (203)488-8660
E-mail: info@realinteractive.com
URL: http://www.realinteractive.com

Description: Real Interactive offers a variety of Internet development services. Professional work provided by Real Interactive includes web site design, lay out and content management services, graphic design, site programming, database integration and secure transactions for e-commerce, site promotion, media placement, and web site hosting.

▌ 4404
RED HOT DIGITAL OF FLORIDA, INC.

The Concord Bldg., Ste. 103
7 E Silver Springs Blvd.
Ocala, FL 34470
PH: (352)732-2170
E-mail: info@redhotdigital.com
URL: http://www.redhotdigital.com

Description: Red Hot Digital of Florida, Inc. provides a range of web development services including informational and e-commerce web site design. Red Hot Digital of Florida also offers interactive database development, secure credit card processing, custom programming, graphic design, on-line marketing, and web site hosting services.

▌ 4405
RED LINE GROUP

Box 25616
Tempe, AZ 85285
PH: (480)833-0196
E-mail: info@redlinegroup.com
URL: http://www.redlinegroup.com

Description: Red Line Group provides its clients with web site design and development, web application development, e-commerce solutions, graphic design, and web site mainte-nance and hosting services.

▌ 4406
RED LION WEB DESIGN, INC.

17 Craymor Ct.
Commack, NY 11725-1105
PH: (631)864-1031
E-mail: webmaster@redlionwebdesign.com
URL: http://www.redlionwebdesign.com

Founded: 1999. **Description:** Red Lion Web Design, Inc. is a small web design company specializing in business web sites. Red Lion Web Design provides web site design, implementation, site redesign and maintenance, search en-gine placement, and domain name registration.

▌ 4407
REFLEXIONS DESIGN, LLC

213 E Main St.
Mount Kisco, NY 10549
PH: (914)244-3711
E-mail: info@reflexionsdesign.com
URL: http://www.reflexions.net

Description: Reflexions Design, LLC is a full service soft-ware development and IT firm specializing in database-driven web applications. Services offered by Reflexions De-sign include applications and database development, web site design and development, e-commerce enabled web site development, and information technology consulting.

▌ 4408
RG2 SOLUTIONS

PO Box 18332
Oklahoma City, OK 73154
PH: (405)858-8632
FX: (405)858-8641
E-mail: roger@rg2solutions.com
URL: http://www.rg2solutions.com
Contact: Roger Grant

Description: RG2 Solutions specializes in technology and Internet solutions for the credit union industry. Services provided by RG2 Solutions include custom programming, web site design and development, intranet development, and database solutions.

▌ 4409
RIDGESTAR

12515 Willows Rd. NE, Ste. 205
Kirkland, WA 98034-8795
PH: (425)814-9000
FX: (425)823-9636
E-mail: info@ridgestar.com
URL: http://www.ridgestar.com

Description: RidgeStar specializes in meeting the Internet needs of small to medium businesses. Services offered by RidgeStar include e-commerce solutions, web site design and development, database technologies, graphic design, web site security, intranet development, site promotion, and hosting.

▌ 4410
RISE INTERACTIVE

7562 Ellis Ave., No. F-9
Huntington Beach, CA 92648
PH: (714)842-0888
E-mail: info@riseinteractive.com
URL: http://www.riseinteractive.com

Description: Rise Interactive provides design services including web site design, database integration, motion graphics for web sites and video, Flash design and development, interactive CD-ROM production, corporate identity, and marketing and advertising.

▌4411
RIVENDELL DESIGN

4806 Ave. F
Austin, TX 78751
PH: (512)797-6049
E-mail: info@rivendelldesign.com
URL: http://www.rivendelldesign.com

Description: Rivendell Design is an Internet technology and design firm specializing in graphic and multimedia design. Rivendell Design also offers services including full web site development, server-side scripting and database management, interactive Flash web site design with audio and video, secure e-commerce and dynamic programming.

▌4412
RIVERGY, INC.

501 Knights Run Ave.
Tampa, FL 33602
PH: (813)221-9539
TF: 877-932-5300
E-mail: info@rivergy.com
URL: http://www.Rivergy.com

Description: Rivergy, Inc. provides a variety of Internet services including web site design, Flash development, e-commerce solutions with shopping carts, custom applications, and Internet marketing and web site registration.

▌4413
RIVET DESIGN

9251 E Windrose Dr.
Scottsdale, AZ 85260
PH: (480)947-0470
FX: (602)330-9299
E-mail: info@rivetdesign.com
URL: http://www.rivetdesign.com

Description: Rivet Design is a small graphic and web design firm that offers services including web site design and programming, e-commerce solutions, Flash and Shockwave development, multimedia design, logo design, advertising and print media production.

▌4414
ROBUST TECHNOLOGY

12178 Fahrpark Ln.
St. Louis, MO 63146
PH: (314)991-5380

FX: (314)692-2735
E-mail: info@robusttech.com
URL: http://www.robusttech.com

Description: Robust Technology is an information technology outsourcing firm offering services that include web site design and development, Flash design, e-commerce development, database design and integration, Internet marketing and search engine optimization, custom applications, and web site hosting.

▌4415
ROLEN GRAPHIX WEB DESIGNS

PO Box 16461
Chattanooga, TN 37416
PH: (706)858-1303
URL: http://www.rolengraphix.com

Description: Rolen Graphix Web Designs offers a range of web-related services including web site design and implementation, e-commerce solutions, custom graphics, animation, databases and programming, and music encoding.

▌4416
ROSS BROWN DIGITAL

407 S Dearborn, Ste. 1401
Chicago, IL 60605
PH: (312)692-0986
FX: (312)692-0987
URL: http://www.rbimc.com

Description: Ross Brown Digital offers web site development, digital branding, e-business solutions, online marketing, e-catalogs, CD-ROMs, multimedia presentations, and integration and automation services.

▌4417
ROUNDTABLE TECHNOLOGY SOLUTIONS

7732 Goodwood Blvd., Ste. Z
Baton Rouge, LA 70806
PH: (225)205-5873
FX: (702)993-6003
E-mail: dknight@roundtableusa.com
URL: http://www.roundtableusa.com

Description: Roundtable Technology Solutions offers a range of information technology solutions including web site design and development. Roundtable Technology Solutions also provides database development, e-business site development, and software development and implementation.

855

▮ 4418
ROYAL TECHNOLOGY GROUP

Communications Wing
Scranton, PA 18510-4639
PH: (570)941-4123
FX: (570)941-7611
E-mail: constance.wisdo@scranton.edu
URL: http://www.scrantonrtg.com

Description: Formerly known as the Electronic Commerce Resource Center, and operated by the University of Scranton, the Royal Technology Group offers website design and assessment as well as marketing plan development. An analysis of a company's electronic capabilities as a whole is also performed to help re-engineer business processes to meet the requirements of e-business.

▮ 4419
RP DESIGN WEB SERVICES

1187 Highland Ave., 2nd Fl.
Cheshire, CT 06410
PH: (203)271-7991
E-mail: sales@rpdesign.com
URL: http://www.rpdesign.com

Description: RP Design Web Services specializes in web site design, redesign, e-commerce solutions, programming, promotion, as well as site maintenance and hosting services.

▮ 4420
RS CREATIONS

538 Oakwood
Grayslake, IL 60030
PH: (847)223-7569
FX: (847)543-1662
E-mail: info@rscreations.com
URL: http://www.rscreations.com

Description: RS Creations specializes in creating effective web sites for business-to-business and business-to-consumer. Services offered by RS Creations include web site design, redesign, development and maintenance, search engine optimization, e-commerce solutions, multimedia production, and web site hosting.

▮ 4421
RUSTYBRICK.COM

30 Briarcliff Dr.
Monsey, NY 10952-2503
PH: (845)352-3707
FX: (845)352-3525
E-mail: info@rustybrick.com
URL: http://www.rustybrick.com

Description: RustyBrick.com provides its clients with a range of design and Internet services. Professional work offered by RustyBrick.com includes web site design and development, e-commerce solutions, intranet and extranet development, Flash presentations, logo creation, online marketing, and web strategy consulting.

▮ 4422
RZ CONCEPTS, INC.

63 Midway St.
Babylon, NY 11702
PH: (631)321-6909
FX: (360)285-5068
URL: http://www.rzconcepts.com

Description: RZ Concepts, Inc. offers services including web site design, programming, content development, application development, Internet marketing, search engine promotion, and web site hosting.

▮ 4423
SAILBAY STUDIO

7770 Regents Rd., No. 113
San Diego, CA 92126
PH: (858)212-4837
FX: (858)212-4838
E-mail: info@sailbaystudio.com
URL: http://www.sailbaystudio.com

Description: SailBay Studio provides web site design and development services, as well as programming, content management, online marketing, strategic consulting, strategic web site maintenance, and interactive product design.

▮ 4424
SALINE SOLUTIONS

1050 Carmona Ave.
Los Angeles, CA 90019
PH: (310)428-1481
E-mail: info@salinesolutions.com
URL: http://www.salinesolutions.com

Description: Saline Solutions is a full service Internet development firm. Services offered by Saline Solutions include interactive design, e-business solutions, customized programming and databases, Internet marketing services, corporate identity and marketing collateral services, and web site hosting.

▮ 4425
SALTMINE, INC.

413 Pine St., 3rd Fl.
Seattle, WA 98101
PH: (206)284-7511

FX: (206)284-7875
E-mail: info@saltmine.com
URL: http://www.saltmine.com

Description: Saltmine, Inc. is a full service business solutions company that offers services including web site design and implementation, multimedia development, market research, application development, systems integration, and print media design and production.

∎ 4426
SCARLET'S WEB

3330 Saxonburg Blvd.
Pittsburgh, PA 15116
PH: (412)767-5268
FX: (419)793-9887
E-mail: info@scarletsweb.com
URL: http://www.scarletsweb.com

Description: Scarlet's Web offers web site design and construction, programming, database integration, e-commerce solutions, graphic design, site promotion and maintenance, and web site hosting services.

∎ 4427
SCION COMMUNICATIONS

111 Water St., Ste. 100
Vancouver, BC, Canada V6B1A7
PH: (604)718-7408
FX: (604)718-7404
E-mail: info@scioncommunications.com
URL: http://www.scioncommunications.com

Description: Scion Communications specializes in wireless and web applications. Scion communications offers mobile e-commerce solutions, content management, streaming video and audio, database connectivity, and maintenance and support services.

∎ 4428
SCOOTER DESIGNS

5204 S Sand Cherry Cir.
Sioux Falls, SD 57108
PH: (605)339-4529
E-mail: scooter@scooterdesigns.com
URL: http://www.scooterdesigns.com

Description: Scooter Designs provides web site design, redesign and development, custom graphics and logo design, database driven web sites, and database integration services.

∎ 4429
SCORE INTERACTIVE

130 S Bemiston
St. Louis, MO 63105
PH: (314)721-1835
FX: (314)862-1616
E-mail: solutions@scoreinteractive.com
URL: http://www.scoreinteractive.com

Description: Score Interactive provides its clients with a range of Internet services. Professional work includes web site development, graphics and animation, e-commerce solutions, custom programming, marketing and promotion, multimedia development, and site hosting.

∎ 4430
SCOUT PRODUCTIONS, LLC

7 Seir Hill Rd., Unit 38
Norwalk, CT 06850
PH: (203)849-3383
FX: (203)286-1035
E-mail: info@scoutproductions.com
URL: http://www.scoutproductions.com

Description: Scout Productions, LLC specializes in web development. Services offered by Scout Productions include web site design and development, e-commerce solutions, programming, streaming media production, site testing, and web site maintenance.

∎ 4431
SCRATCHPAD MEDIA

3047 Randleman Ct.
Oviedo, FL 32765
PH: (407)341-6516
E-mail: info@scratchpadmedia.com
URL: http://www.scratchpadmedia.com

Description: ScratchPad Media focuses on Internet-based design and marketing projects. Services offered include web site development, Flash and multimedia design, information architecture, application development, content strategy, online marketing, and corporate branding.

∎ 4432
SENAREIDER

340 Pine St., Ste. 503
San Francisco, CA 94104
PH: (415)288-0620
TF: 877-788-7362
FX: (415)288-0621
E-mail: john.reider@senareider.com
URL: http://www.senareider.com
Contact: John Reider, Creative Director

Description: SenaReider specializes in delivering e-commerce solutions with a strong marketing focus. Services offered by SenaReider include web site design and development, interactive site development, content creation, management and delivery, multimedia production, intranet development, and branding solutions.

■ **4433**

SEO OHIO WEB DESIGN

92 Lincoln Ave.
Cuyahoga Falls, OH 44221-2359
PH: (330)923-5843
E-mail: info@seo-ohio-web-design.com
URL: http://www.seo-ohio-web-design.com

Description: SEO Ohio Web Design specializes in web design and search engine optimization for small businesses and service industry businesses. Services provided by SEO Ohio Web Design include web site design and development, domain name registration, hosting, and search engine submission and optimization.

■ **4434**

SEVENET.COM LLC

6230 Wilshire Blvd., No. 1254
Los Angeles, CA 90048
PH: (310)621-6239
E-mail: info@sevenet.com
URL: http://www.sevenet.com
Contact: Troy Aldrich, Production Director

Description: Sevenet.com LLC focuses on visual design and functional performance in all the web sites they create. Sevenet.com offers web site design and development, information architecture, database devlelopment, and print media services.

■ **4435**

SEXTON IMAGE

166 5th Ave., 5th Fl.
New York, NY 10010
PH: (212)352-9975
TF: 877-330-8686
FX: (212)633-2220
E-mail: info@sextonimage.com
URL: http://www.sextonimage.com

Description: Sexton Image is a media and design company that creates a balance between results-driven tactics and creative ideas. Sexton Image views its clients as partners, working together to make contact with customers. Sexton Image designs web sites, CD-ROMs, and projects in print media.

■ **4436**

SG DESIGN GROUP

440 Viola Rd., Ste. 1
Spring Valley, NY 10977
PH: (845)371-7233
FX: (845)371-8978
E-mail: info@1sgdesign.com
URL: http://www.1sgdesign.com

Description: SG Design Group offers web site design and development, graphic design and package design. SG Design also provides e-commerce solutions, search engine optimization, streaming media and Flash development.

■ **4437**

SHARP DESIGNS

88 Waverley St.
Arlington, MA 02476
PH: (781)643-2806
TF: 800-811-3374
FX: 877-515-6693
E-mail: info@sharpdesigns.com
URL: http://www.sharpdesigns.com

Description: Sharp Designs focuses on custom web site design. Services offered by Sharp Designs include e-commerce site design, personal and corporate web sites, database-driven web sites, intranet and extranet development, and web site hosting.

■ **4438**

SHOWOFF! WEB SOLUTIONS

2217 Virginia Ave.
Everett, WA 98201
PH: (425)317-0644
URL: http://www.showoff.net

Description: ShowOff! Web Solutions offers its clients web site design, e-commerce enabled web sites, database development, interactive programming, custom graphics, and web site maintenance and hosting.

■ **4439**

SILVERSCAPE TECHNOLOGIES, INC.

602 S Main St.
Gainesville, FL 32601
PH: (352)374-9657
TF: 800-343-1312
FX: (352)374-6965
E-mail: info@silverscape.net
URL: http://www.silverscape.net

Description: Silverscape Technologies, Inc. provides services in both interactive media and integrated marketing.

Silverscape Technologies offers web site design, application development, Flash presentations, interactive CD-ROM production, web site hosting, web marketing, branding, and public relations services.

▌4440
SITE 9

116 W Illinois, Ste. 5W
Chicago, IL 60610
PH: (312)670-8469
FX: (312)670-2650
E-mail: info@site9.net
URL: http://www.site9.net

Description: Site 9 is an Internet solutions provider, following the principle that form follows function. Services offered by Site 9 include web site design and hosting, multimedia, and e-commerce. Site 9 helps clients design and build new sites or improve existing sites, blending design and programming skills to create an effective Internet presence.

▌4441
STREAMLINE INTERACTIVE COMMUNICATIONS

1495B Yarmouth Ave.
Boulder, CO 80304
PH: (303)444-6484
TF: 877-277-4424
FX: (720)294-8377
E-mail: info@streamlineIc.com
URL: http://www.streamlineic.com

Description: Streamline Interactive Communications offers services including web site design and development, multimedia and interactive design, database driven web sites, programming, site marketing and promotion, search engine optimization, and web site hosting services.

▌4442
TALLIN DEVELOPMENT CORP.

3212 Woodridge Ln.
Waukesha, WI 53188
PH: 877-499-9311
FX: (262)513-2838
E-mail: rebrod@tallin.com
URL: http://www.tallin.com

Description: Tallin Development Corp. offers a range of Internet services including custom web site design and development, e-commerce solutions, custom application development, online database production, site management and content, advertising and promotion, and web site hosting.

▌4443
TARGET WEB SERVICES, INC.

4710 Beidler Rd.
Willoughby, OH 44094
PH: (440)942-6543
FX: (440)349-9081
E-mail: sales@targetweb.net
URL: http://www.targetweb.net

Description: Target Web Services, Inc. specializes in web site design. Services provided by Target Web Services include secure e-commerce solutions, business informational web sites, storefront sites, Internet marketing, Internet access and web site hosting.

▌4444
TBL MEDIA

2331 Belleair Rd.
Clearwater, FL 33758
PH: (727)531-4848
TF: (866)825-5556
FX: (727)531-4994
E-mail: info@tblmedia.com
URL: http://www.tblmedia.com

Description: TBL Media has offices in the USA and Vietnam, and specializes in web-based business applications. TBL Media offers services that include web site design and development, e-commerce sites, content management, and specialized solutions for various industries.

▌4445
TEAM CREATIONS

PO Box 1052
O Fallon, IL 62269
PH: (618)624-1722
E-mail: info@teamcreations.com
URL: http://www.teamcreations.com
Contact: Ron Ferranti

Description: Team Creations has offices in Germany as well as the US and offers a variety of web design services. Team Creations provides web site design and development, e-commerce solutions with shopping carts, graphic design, logo creation, programming, promotion, and site hosting and maintenance services.

▌4446
TECHNOINTERACTIVE

608 Silver Spur Rd., Ste. 380
Rolling Hills Estates, CA 90274
PH: (310)265-5565
FX: (310)265-5564
E-mail: info@technointeractive.com

URL: http://www.technointeractive.com

Description: TechnoInteractive focuses on e-business solutions. Services offered by TechnoInteractive include complete e-business solutions with custom applications, strategy, branding, multimedia, and web site hosting.

▌4447
TECHNOVATION

6100 S Maple Ave., Ste. 101
Tempe, AZ 85283
PH: (480)897-1102
FX: (480)897-1130
E-mail: webmaster@technov.com
URL: http://www.technov.comwww.technov.com

Description: Technovation offers a variety of interactive business solutions including web site design and development. Other services provided by Technovation include graphic design, custom multimedia production, web marketing and hosting, application development, and interactive media development.

▌4448
THECITI.COM

398 Adelaide St. W, Ste. 200
Toronto, ON, Canada M5V1S7
PH: (416)760-9100
FX: (416)760-7924
E-mail: info@theciti.com
URL: http://www.theciti.com

Description: TheCiti.com provides its clients with a range of services including web site development, e-commerce site development, intranet and extranet design, content management, database applications, and wireless applications.

▌4449
THELIX INTERNET

29 South Pleasant St.
PO Box 221
Amherst, MA 01004-0221
PH: (413)253-7700
TF: 888-762-2283
FX: (702)442-4926
E-mail: infotheatrelix.net
URL: http://www.thelix.net

Description: Thelix Internet provides web site design and hosting services, as well as secure e-commerce solutions, search engine submissions, content management support systems, and programming.

▌4450
THEVSP.COM, INC.

PO Box 1983
Huntersville, NC 28070-1983
PH: 877-599-7764
E-mail: sales@thevsp.com
URL: http://www.thevsp.com

Description: The VSP.com offers web site design, hosting and marketing solutions for any size business. In addition to providing web design templates, The VSP.com also provides custom web site design based upon each client's unique needs. The VSP.com can redesign or update existing web sites to ensure an effective Internet presence.

▌4451
THINKWELLS

6715-A Fairview Rd.
Charlotte, NC 28210-3355
PH: (704)366-3394
FX: (704)366-3319
E-mail: jwells@thinkwells.com
URL: http://www.thinkwells.com
Contact: Jenny G. Wells, President

Description: ThinkWells offers an array of Internet and information technology solutions. Services provided by ThinkWells include web site design, e-commerce solutions, web site promotion, domain registration, data warehousing, graphic design, and database development.

▌4452
THOUGHTWARE, INC.

5156 Helen Hwy.
Sautee, GA 30571
PH: (706)865-9688
TF: 800-511-9902
FX: (706)219-3938
E-mail: support@thoughtwareinc.com
URL: http://www.thoughtwareinc.com

Description: ThoughtWare, Inc. is a full service web design firm that specializes in custom application development and e-commerce solutions. Other services offered by ThoughtWare include web site design and development, and web site hosting.

▌4453
TIM KENNEY MARKETING PARTNERS

3 Bethesda Metro Ctr., Ste. 630
Bethesda, MD 20814
PH: (301)718-9100
E-mail: info@tkm2.com
URL: http://www.tkenneydesign.com

Description: Tim Kenney Marketing Partners is a full service design firm offering clients web site design, interactive and multimedia design, print design, corporate identity, advertising and integrated marketing.

▌4454
TIMESTREAM

151 Searsmont Rd.
Appleton, ME 04862
PH: (207)785-5511
FX: (207)785-5533
E-mail: info@timestream.com
URL: http://www.timestream.com

Description: Timestream is a full service multimedia development firm that offers services including web site design, graphic design, CD-ROM production, programming, video production, and music composition.

▌4455
TMG MEDIA.NET

8601 Smoke Rise Ln., Ste. 2,
Chattanooga, TN 37421-2821
PH: (423)499-0706
FX: (423)499-0706
E-mail: admin@tmgmedia.net
URL: http://www.tmgmedia.net

Description: TMG Media.net provides web site design and implementation, graphic design, animation, copy writing, photography, videography, custom database development, and web site hosting services.

▌4456
TORNADO DESIGN

6628 E Beryl Ave.
Scottsdale, AZ 85253
PH: (480)609-0148
FX: (480)483-6697
E-mail: info@tornadodesign.com
URL: http://www.tornadodesign.com

Description: Tornado Design specializes in creative online design. Services offered by Tornado Design include web site design and development, e-commerce site development, brand strategy, and marketing strategy.

▌4457
TOTALNET SOLUTIONS

3651 Craigmillar Ave.
Victoria, BC, Canada V8P3H2
PH: (250)380-7099
FX: (250)380-7599

E-mail: info@totalnetsolutions.com
URL: http://www.totalnetsolutions.com

Description: Totalnet Solutions offers web site design, e-commerce solutions, domain registration, web site marketing and promotion, and site maintenance and hosting services.

▌4458
TOUCHWOOD, INC.

308 N 21st St.
St. Louis, MO 63103
PH: (314)421-9878
FX: (314)421-6276
E-mail: info@touchwood.net
URL: http://www.touchwood.net

Description: Touchwood, Inc. specializes in turnkey design projects in various media. Services offered by Touchwood include web site design and development, programming, scripting, graphic design, Flash animation, database integration, interactive multimedia production, web site hosting, as well as print media and video production.

▌4459
TRANSMISSIONS

3503 Pheasant Run Cir., No. 7
Ann Arbor, MI 48108
PH: (734)395-3296
E-mail: info@onlinetransmissions.com
URL: http://www.onlinetransmissions.com

Description: Transmissions focuses on creating a workable Internet presence for businesses. Services offered by Transmissions include web site development, logo and graphic design, web site software engineering, intranet development, branding, copy writing, web site hosting, and consulting.

▌4460
TRIPLECODE

370 South Doheny Dr., Ste. 204
Beverly Hills, CA 90211
PH: (310)278-2533
FX: (310)278-2535
E-mail: info@triplecode.com
URL: http://www.triplecode.com

Description: Triplecode is an interactive media design studio which creates websites, cd-roms, and environmental multi-media. Triplecode's professionals have backgrounds that include the MIT Media Lab and Art Center College of Design. Interaction, information, and motion work to give users access to a wide variety of content in Triplecode's designs.

■ **4461**

TRIRIBA WEB DESIGN AND CONSULTING, LLC

9901 Trailwood Dr.,Ste. 2062
Las Vegas, NV 89134
PH: (702)869-9381
FX: (702)233-3259
E-mail: info@tririba.com
URL: http://www.tririba.com

Description: Tririba Web Design and Consulting, LLC focuses on Internet solutions for businesses of any size. Services offered by Tririba Web Design and Consulting include web site design and creation, graphics design, animation, site marketing, maintenance and hosting, and consulting.

■ **4462**

THE TURING STUDIO, INC.

Saul Zaentz Film Center
2600 10th St.
Berkeley, CA 94710
PH: (510)666-0074
FX: (510)666-0093
E-mail: info@turingstudio.com
URL: http://www.turingstudio.com

Description: The Turing Studio, Inc. specializes in building secure database driven web applications. Services provided by The Turing Studio include e-commerce web sites, intranet and extranet development, and complex hosting installations.

■ **4463**

TYPOGRAPHIC

351 S Cochran Ave.
Los Angeles, CA 90036
PH: (323)935-3375
E-mail: info@typographic.com
URL: http://www.typographic.com

Description: Typographic is a company specializing in website design, motion graphics, and interactive design. Typographic's design is focused around a highly creative group of people creating innovative, effective designs to fulfill their client's business goals.

■ **4464**

ULTIMATE BUSINESS SOLUTIONS, INC.

12717 W Sunrise Blvd., No. 253
Sunrise, FL 33323
PH: 888-842-8785
FX: (954)845-9122
E-mail: info@ubsusa.com
URL: http://www.ubsusa.com

Description: Ultimate Business Solutions, Inc. provides services including web site design and construction, e-commerce solutions, domain name registration, search engine placement, and web site hosting.

■ **4465**

ULTRAWARP WEB DESIGN

43 Lynnwood Rd.
Lansdale, PA 19446
PH: (215)782-1751
E-mail: info@ultrawarp.com
URL: http://www.ultrawarp.com

Description: UltraWarp Web Design offers web site design, redesign and development services, as well as domain name registration, intranet development, and marketing strategy.

■ **4466**

UNITED TECHNOLOGY SERVICES

3265 Mayfield Hwy.
PO Box 229
Benton, KY 42025
PH: (270)527-5329
FX: (270)527-5322
E-mail: questions@unitedtechsolutions.com
URL: http://www.unitedtechsolutions.com

Description: United Technology Services specializes in corporate web site development. Solutions provided by United Technology Services include custom web site design, e-commerce development, intranet design, and web site maintenance and hosting.

■ **4467**

UNIVERSAL NET

901 Dover, Ste. 231
Newport Beach, CA 92660
PH: (949)650-3182
TF: 877-302-6335
FX: (949)650-2556
E-mail: info@unteam.com
URL: http://www.unteam.com

Description: Universal Netfocuses on designing web sites that are usable and functional. Services offered by Universal Net include web site design, maintenance and hosting, e-commerece solutions, web marketing, branding, and strategy development.

■ **4468**

UNIVERSAL WEB DESIGN STUDIO

1233 Prospect Ave.
Brooklyn, NY 11218
PH: 877-208-2712

FX: (718)504-3528
E-mail: info@universalwebdesigns.com
URL: http://www.universalwebdesigns.com

Description: Universal Web Design Studio is a web development and advertising firm that provides a variety of design solutions. Services offered by Universal Web Design include custom web site design, e-commerce site development, and web site hosting.

■ **4469**
VANDELAY ENTERPRISES

2156 Madden Blvd.
Oakville, ON, Canada L6H3M2
PH: (905)510-8845
E-mail: sales@vandelayenterprises.com
URL: http://www.vandelayenterprises.com

Description: Vandelay Enterprises focuses on Internet solutions, offering services that include web site design and implementation, database development, e-commerce solutions, graphic design, e-marketing, and web site hosting.

■ **4470**
VANTAGE ARCHITECTURE

15835 Cotswold Ct.
Davie, FL 33331
PH: (954)252-8406
E-mail: info@vantagearc.com
URL: http://www.vantagearc.com

Description: Vantage Architecture specializes in web design and development, and offers a range of services including programming, graphic design, Flash animation, Quicktime video, site hosting and maintenance, and search engine submission.

■ **4471**
VELOCITY 7

232 Broad St., Ste. C
Nevada City, CA 95959
PH: (530)470-9292
FX: (530)470-9293
E-mail: info@velocity7.com
URL: http://www.velocity7.com

Description: Velocity 7 offers web site design and development, graphic design, print design, business strategy, and software development.

■ **4472**
VERDI PRODUCTIONS

95 Susan Dr.
Jackson, NJ 08527
PH: (732)619-6127

E-mail: info@verdiproductions.com
URL: http://www.verdiproductions.com

Description: Verdi Productions provides web and graphic design for companies of any size. Services offered by Verdi Productions include web site design and development, e-commerce solutions, graphic design, multimedia production, Flash animation, Internet streaming video, and web site hosting.

■ **4473**
VERISIGN

487 E Middlefield Rd.
Mountain View, CA 94043
PH: (703)742-0914
TF: 888-642-9675
E-mail: advertising@verisign.com
URL: http://www.netsol.com

Description: Verisign offers a fast and simple way to build a website using one of over one hundred web sites. Verisign's service includes a web site editing tool, matching email address, your own domain name, and online support.

■ **4474**
VERITECH CORP.

37 Prospect St.
East Longmeadow, MA 01028
PH: 800-525-5912
FX: (413)525-7449
E-mail: info@veritechmedia.com
URL: http://www.veritechmedia.com

Description: Veritech Corp. specializes in multimedia production, and provides services including web site design, development and hosting, animation, e-business site development, and video, CD, and DVD production.

■ **4475**
VERSATILITY DATA MANAGEMENT

384 Jackson St., Ste. 16
Hayward, CA 94544
PH: (510)889-5995
URL: http://www.datajammin.com

Description: Versatility Data Management offers a variety of professional web services including web site design and hosting, e-commerce site design, Flash presentations, site maintenance and support, content management and development, copy writing and graphic design services.

■ 4476
VERTICAL 360

PO Box 6931
Katy, TX 77491
PH: (281)646-8191
FX: (281)966-1724
E-mail: infovermonttical360.com
URL: http://www.vertical360.com
Contact: Barry Ochsner, Creative Director

Description: Vertical 360 offers a variety of business and multimedia solutions. Services provided by Vertical 360 include template-based web site design, e-brochures, web hosting, and multimedia production.

■ 4477
VIANT CORP.

89 South St.
Boston, MA 02111
PH: (617)531-3700
E-mail: mskoletsky@viant.com
URL: http://www.viant.com

Description: Viant Corporation uses integrated multidisciplinary teams to enable clients to improve business performance. Services Viant offers include customer experience and content architecture to present content in an effective and usable way; and integrated technology solutions.

■ 4478
VIRTUAL DESIGN NETWORK

218 N Elm St.
Greensboro, NC 27401
PH: (336)389-0045
E-mail: sales@vdninc.com
URL: http://www.vdninc.com

Description: Virtual Design Network is a web design company that focuses on Internet marketing. Services provided by Virtual Design Network include web site design, database creation, intranet development, and e-commerce solutions.

■ 4479
VIRTUOSO WEB DESIGN SERVICES

10311 Riverside Dr., Ste. 107
Toluca Lake, CA 91602
PH: (818)692-6266
E-mail: info@vwds.com
URL: http://www.virtuosowebdesign.com

Description: Virtuoso Web Design Services is a full service web design company. Professional work provided by Virtuoso Web Design Services includes web site and graphic design, Flash programming, e-commerce solutions, database

driven web sites, Internet marketing, and search engine submissions and optimization.

■ 4480
VISINET

715 Middle Ground Blvd.
Newport News, VA 23606
PH: (757)873-4500
TF: 888-323-4500
E-mail: sales@visi.net
URL: http://www.visi.net

Description: Visinet designs custom web sites as well as full-service e-commerce project solutions. Other related services provided by Visinet include on-site digital photography, copy writing, logo creation and on-line site marketing and promotion.

■ 4481
VJ STUDIO

197 Route 18, Ste. 3000
East Brunswick, NJ 08816
PH: (732)698-9995
TF: 888-840-1849
E-mail: info@vjstudio.com
URL: http://www.vjstudio.com

Description: VJ Studio provides digital solutions and specializes in web design, custom web application development, and e-business strategy. Services offered by VJ Studio include visual design, web site management, corporate identity, wireless web, intranet and extranet, and integrated e-commerce solutions.

■ 4482
VOLARIS ONLINE

1101 Greenwood Blvd., Ste. 200
Lake Mary, FL 32746
PH: (407)708-1700
TF: (866)865-2747
E-mail: sales@vol.com
URL: http://www.vol.com

Description: Volaris Online offers a variety of products and services including web hosting, design and secure e-commerce solutions. Volaris provides an e-commerce browser based storefront management system, which includes shopping cart, cataloging, category maintenance, order and credit card processing.

■ 4483
W. P. CORCORAN AND ASS., INC.

1416 Providence Hwy., Ste. 222
Norwood, MA 02062
PH: (781)487-2223

FX: (781)487-7938
E-mail: sales@wpcorcoran.com
URL: http://www.corcoranweb.com

Description: W. P. Corcoran and Associates is a company focused on custom application design for the web. Corcoran uses the best technology to provide initial assessment, design and development, quality assurance and user testing, all with the client's business objectives in mind.

▌4484
WARREN WEBWORKS

PMB No. 233
2040 Spring Creek Pky., Ste. 141
Plano, TX 75023
PH: (972)423-2597
FX: (972)422-4697
E-mail: info@warrenwebworks.com
URL: http://www.warrenwebworks.com
Contact: Brooke B. Warren, Owner/Webmaster

Description: Warren WebWorks specializes in web site design for small businesses. Services offered by Warren WebWorks include web site design, development and implementation, e-commerce solutions, site maintenance, search engine submission, and marketing.

▌4485
WAVE DESIGN

46 Windsor Rd., Ste. B
New Britain, CT 06052
PH: (860)402-8081
E-mail: info@wavedesign.com
URL: http://www.wavedesign.com

Description: Wave Design offers web site design and development, graphic design, multimedia production, database design and integration, applications development, marketing, branding, and traditional media design.

▌4486
WCZ.COM

1115 Butterworth Rd.
Kingston Springs, TN 37082
PH: (615)441-5709
E-mail: webmaster@wcz.com
URL: http://www.wcz.com

Description: WCZ.com offers e-commerce web site design, informational or corporate web site design, graphics, search engine submission, and web site hosting and maintenance.

▌4487
WDDG-NEW YORK CITY

174 Hudson St., 3rd Fl.
New York, NY 10013
PH: (646)221-8556
E-mail: nyc_contact@wddg.com
URL: http://www.wddg.com

Description: WDDG is a company which offers interactive design services for websites, motion graphics, microsites, and full Internet presences. WDDG has experience in many types of design including games, user interfaces, content, graphics, and video. Solutions are provided in a timely and efficient manner based on client needs.

▌4488
WE CONCEPTS, INC.

38 Camino Barranca
Placitas, NM 87043
PH: (505)867-8606
TF: 877-932-9383
E-mail: info@weconcepts.com
URL: http://www.weconcepts.com

Description: WE Concepts, Inc. provides its clients with a range of web design and development services. WE Concepts offers graphics and interface design, e-commerce site development, logo design, Internet marketing, search engine optimization, and web site hosting and maintenance.

▌4489
WEB 2 MARKET, INC.

11900 Southwest Hwy., Ste. 203
Palos Park, IL 60464
PH: (708)361-9068
TF: 877-326-2167
FX: (708)361-9069
E-mail: info@web2market.com
URL: http://www.web2market.com

Description: Web 2 Market, Inc. provides complete turnkey e-commerce services for small to medium sized businesses. Web 2 Market offers web site design and development, graphic design, programming, and web site promotion.

▌4490
WEB AXIS, INC.

47 Royal Crest Dr., Unit 12
North Andover, MA 02433
PH: (978)689-2090
E-mail: info@webaxis.net
URL: http://www.webaxis.net

Description: Web Axis, Inc. offers a variety of web site design and hosting packages, as well as e-commerce site design, auction web sites, content development, marketing services, and web site hosting.

∎ 4491
WEB CREATORS, INC.

3002 Dow Ave., Ste. 414
Tustin, CA 92780
PH: (949)417-3838
FX: (949)417-3848
E-mail: info@webcreators.com
URL: http://www.1clickwebmasters.com

Description: Web Creators, Inc. designs professional, easy to use web sites for small and medium sized businesses. Web Creators uses industry-specific templates for fast, easy and affordable web site creation, and also creates custom web sites to serve the needs of its clients.

∎ 4492
WEB DESIGN CAROLINAS

6120 Narrow Way Ln.
Winston-Salem, NC 27105
PH: (336)744-2642
FX: (336)744-2656
E-mail: info@webdesigncarolinas.com
URL: http://www.webdesigncarolinas.com

Description: Web Design Carolinas provides a range of web development and marketing solutions for businesses of all sizes. Services offered include web site design, redesign, and maintenance, content development, custom e-business solutions, programming, animation and graphic design, and web site hosting.

∎ 4493
WEB DESIGN BY COOKIE

21 Frederick St., Ste. 303
Hartford, CT 06105-3234
PH: (860)424-4491
FX: (860)570-0696
E-mail: sales@wdbc.com
URL: http://www.webdesignbycookie.com

Description: Web Design by Cookie offers a variety of services ranging from web site templates for fast and inexpensive web solutions, to custom designed web sites. Other services provided include graphic design, planning, programming, search engine submission, and web site hosting and maintenance.

∎ 4494
WEB DESIGN PLACE

1150 S. Lake St., Ste. 09
Los Angeles, CA 90006
PH: (213)380-7655
E-mail: webdesignplace@cs.com
URL: http://www.webdesignplace.com

Description: Web Design Place specializes in web site design for small businesses. Services offered by Web Design Place include web site design, graphic design, e-commerce development, search engine submissions, site promotion, and marketing.

∎ 4495
WEB IDEA BANK TECHNOLOGIES

PO Box 4482
Rock Hill, SC 29732
PH: (803)417-3418
E-mail: info@webideabank.com
URL: http://www.webideabank.com

Description: Web Idea Bank Technologies is a small web development and computer services firm. Web Idea Bank Technologies offers services including web site design and development, custom web programming, web marketing, web site hosting, and CD-ROM creation for catalogs and business cards.

∎ 4496
WEB IMPACT, INC.

145 King St. W, Ste. 1000
Toronto, ON, Canada M5H1J8
PH: (416)815-2000
TF: (866)319-1573
FX: (416)815-2001
E-mail: info@webimpact.com
URL: http://www.webimpact.com

Description: Web Impact, Inc. provides web custom site design and devlopment, custom web applications, web site hosting, software, and information technology consulting services.

∎ 4497
WEB JUGGLER INTERNET COMMUNICATIONS

PO Box 346
Highland, MI 48357
PH: (248)887-4253
E-mail: info@webjuggler.com
URL: http://www.webjuggler.com

Description: Web Juggler Internet Communications offers a range of Internet solutions. Services provided by Web Juggler Internet Communications include e-commerce solutions, web site develement, maintenance, and hosting, web site redesign, graphics, database integration, interactive forms, and web advertising.

∎ 4498
WEB MARKETING TECHNOLOGIES

10674 SW 127th Ct.
Tigard, OR 97223
PH: (503)590-4451
FX: (503)524-2230
E-mail: info@webmtech.com
URL: http://www.webmtech.com

Description: Web Marketing Technologies provides complete web solutions, including web site design and development, graphic design, animation, programming, site redesign and maintenance, search engine submission, site marketing and promotion, and web site hosting.

∎ 4499
WEB PROS NOW

2919 Bellows Ct.
Davis, CA 95616
PH: (530)297-7845
TF: 877-570-0294
FX: (530)297-7845
E-mail: info@webprosnow.com
URL: http://www.webprosnow.com

Description: Web Pros Now is a company founded to fill a need in getting clients and qualified web designers together. This service is free to buyers who need a web site designed. Buyers submit a request for proposal describing the project that they need, and Web Pros Now puts the buyer and vendor together.

∎ 4500
A WEB SITE DESIGN COMPANY, INC.

19401 E 37th Pl.
Tulsa, OK 74014
PH: (918)355-0647
TF: (866)355-0600
E-mail: websales@awebsitedesigncompany.com
URL: http://www.webdesignelite.com

Description: A Web Site Design Company, Inc. specializes in web site design for small and home based businesses, as well as corporate clients. Services offered include web site design and development, custom programming, database development, and web site hosting.

∎ 4501
WEB SPECIALISTS, INC.

4606 FM 1960 W, Ste. 400
Houston, TX 77069
PH: (281)655-9486
FX: (281)257-1914
E-mail: sales@web-specialists.com
URL: http://www.wspecialists.com

Description: Web Specialists, Inc. provides Internet solutions for clients' business needs. Services offered by Web Specialists include e-commerce site development, web site design, graphic design, Flash animation, multimedia, marketing and promotion, as well as site hosting and maintenance.

∎ 4502
WEB WE CAN INTERNET SERVICES

PO Box 660186
Sacramento, CA 95866
PH: (916)971-0375
TF: (866)932-9322
FX: (978)389-4663
E-mail: info@webwecan.net
URL: http://www.webwecan.net

Description: Web We Can Internet Services provides a variety of Internet services including web site design, e-commerce solutions, logo creation, banner ads, search engine placement, marketing, web site hosting, and Internet access.

∎ 4503
WEBATIVE

1790 S Winchester Blvd., Ste. 3
Campbell, CA 95008
PH: (408)871-2800
FX: (408)871-6868
E-mail: info@webative.com
URL: http://www.webative.com

Description: Webative offers a range of services including web site design and development, e-commerce solutions, multimedia design, marketing, web site statistics, web site maintenance and archive creation.

∎ 4504
WEBBARREL.COM

4425 Jamboree Rd., Ste. 135
Newport Beach, CA 92660
PH: (949)724-3055
FX: (949)851-0450
E-mail: sales@webbarrel.com
URL: http://www.webbarrel.com

Description: WebBarrel.com offers an array of web services including custom web site design and development, e-commerce solutions, database-driven web site design, extranet design, web marketing, site maintenance and hosting.

▌4505
WEBCOMIT

539 Lookout Ridge Dr.
Lebanon, OH 45036
PH: (513)934-2686
E-mail: gordon@go-concepts.com
URL: http://webcomit.webhostme.com
Contact: Gordon Hammerle, Web Developer

Description: WebComit provides services including basic HTML web site design and construction, database-driven web sites, and database design.

▌4506
WEBCOMPOSER

21422 Evalyn Ave.
Torrance, CA 90503
PH: (310)792-1142
FX: (310)543-1844
E-mail: info@webcomposer.com
URL: http://www.webcomposer.com

Description: WebComposer offers services including brochure web site design, standard web site design and development, e-commerce site design, web site maintenance, promotion, and hosting.

▌4507
WEBCRAYON

PO Box 203396
Austin, TX 78720
PH: (512)917-8165
E-mail: webmaster@webcrayon.com
URL: http://www.webcrayon.com

Description: Webcrayon is a professional web development company offering services including web site design, multimedia, programming, secure transactions, graphic design, database development, enterprise solutions, multimedia design, and web site hosting.

▌4508
WEBCREATORS INTERNET SERVICES

3002 Dow Ave., Ste. 414
Tustin, CA 92780
PH: (949)417-3838
FX: (949)417-3848
E-mail: cliff@webcreators.com

URL: http://www.onlinestorebuilders.com
Contact: Cliff Balentine

Description: WebCreators Internet Services provides a range of web services, specializing in database driven e-commerce web solutions. WebCreators Internet Services also offers Flash animation, custom portal design, graphic design, database design, web hosting and secure hosting services.

▌4509
WEBDANCERS

18711 Tiffeni Dr., Ste. 17
Twain Harte, CA 95383
PH: (209)928-1486
FX: (209)928-4199
E-mail: info@webdancers.com
URL: http://www.webdancers.com

Description: Webdancers focuses on web site design and offers services including information design, graphics and animation, copy writing, database design and maintenance, programming, and web site maintenance.

▌4510
WEBDESIGNERNETWORK.COM

C/O Escapia Development Inc
7154 N University Dr., No.113
Tamarac, FL 33321
PH: 877-879-6707
FX: 877-879-6707
E-mail: info@webdesignernetwork.com
URL: http://www.webdesignernetwork.com

Description: Web Designer Network.com is a resource for small and medium sized businesses to find pre-screened full-service web site designers. Clients fill out a detailed request for proposal form which is then accessed by Web Designer Network's web design firms. The client is then contacted with quotes for their project.

▌4511
WEBENERTIA

940 Saratoga Ave., Ste. 230
San Jose, CA 95129
PH: (408)246-0000
FX: (408)246-1400
URL: http://www.webenertia.com

Description: WebEnertia is a full service web design and development company. Services offered by WebEnertia include complete web site design and construction, web site hosting, online marketing, and Internet consulting.

▌4512
WEBMASTER TECHNOLOGIES LLC

17160 Catherine Ct.
Livonia, MI 48152
PH: (734)422-0419
FX: (734)422-6168
E-mail: info@webmaster-technologies.com
URL: http://www.webmaster-technologies.com

Description: Webmaster Technologies LLC provides a full range of web design solutions. Webmaster Technologies offers services including web site design, graphic design, multimedia design, e-commerce solutions, programming, marketing and promotion, and web site hosting.

▌4513
WEBNAVIX

7341 Rockville Rd.
Indianapolis, IN 46214
PH: (317)243-0000
FX: (317)241-4868
E-mail: info@atssamedayweb.com
URL: http://www.samedayweb.com

Description: Webnavix offers a variety of web site design, development and hosting services. Webnavix provides web site design, e-commerce solutions, graphic design, Flash development, strategic planning, shopping carts, Internet-enabled databases, and search engine promotion.

▌4514
THE WEBSITE CONSTRUCTION COMPANY

3562 Stonecreek Dr., Exec. Ste. B
Cincinnati, OH 45209
PH: (513)631-9271
TF: 800-325-3745
E-mail: info@websitecc.com
URL: http://www.websitecc.com

Description: The Website Construction Company provides complete web site design and implementation solutions. Services offered include web site design, e-commerce solutions, Internet marketing, search engine submissions, and Internet consulting.

▌4515
WEBSITE WORLD

4516 Lynnmont Rd., Ste. 3C
Knoxville, TN 37921
PH: (865)379-7171
TF: 888-208-6616
FX: (865)584-1167
E-mail: sales@websiteworld.com
URL: http://www.websiteworld.com

Description: Website World provides its clients with web site design, domain name registration, business web sites, auction, realtor, and medical web sites, streaming video, and web site hosting services.

▌4516
WEBSTREET101

449A Boston Post Rd. E, No. 10
Marlboro, MA 01752
PH: (508)486-9232
FX: (208)439-2959
E-mail: sales@webstreet101.com
URL: http://www.webstreet101.com

Description: WebStreet101 offers an array of services including web site design and development, programming, interactive pages, animation, e-commerce solutions, web site promotion, search engine submission, and site hosting.

▌4517
XAO, INC.

221 E Walnut St., Ste. 102
Pasadena, CA 91101
PH: (626)584-9335
TF: 877-796-7437
FX: (626)584-9364
E-mail: sales@xao.com
URL: http://www.xao.com

Description: XAO, Inc. offers professional services focused on web site development and design based on Apache servers, complete e-commerce solutions, application integration, and XML databases.

▌4518
XCALIBUR INTERNET

26 Harvester Ave.
Batavia, NY 14020
PH: (716)344-1114
E-mail: webmaster@iinc.com
URL: http://www.iinc.com

Description: Xcalibur Internet offers a range of Internet services including web site design and construction, e-commerce solutions, interactive features, email accounts, domain name registration, web site hosting, and Internet access.

▌4519
XPLORENET, INC.

4610 S Ulster St., Ste. 150
Denver, CO 80237
PH: (303)741-3449

869

TF: 888-857-6749
FX: (303)741-3293
E-mail: info@xplorenet.com
URL: http://www.xplorenet.com

Description: XploreNet, Inc. serves clients from small businesses to Fortune 100 companies. Services offered by XploreNet include complete web site development, Flash animation, content development, online marketing, e-commerce implementation, customer relationship management, and database development.

▌4520
YELLOWDAWG WEB DESIGN

No. 210 - 27 Songhees Rd.
Victoria, BC, Canada V9A7M6
PH: (250)380-1151
TF: (866)380-1151
FX: (250)380-7168
E-mail: information@yellowdawg.com
URL: http://www.yellowdawg.com

Description: YellowDawg Web Design focuses on creating web sites that work. Services offered by YellowDawg Web Design include web site design and development, programming, secure forms, e-commerce enabled site development, graphic design, copy writing, and web site hosting and promotion.

▌4521
YETI ARTS, INC.

PO Box 75147
Seattle, WA 98125-0147
PH: (206)229-7947
FX: (206)364-2267
E-mail: info@yetiarts.com
URL: http://www.yetiarts.com

Description: Yeti Arts, Inc. is a full service web design and development firm offering an array of services including web site design, custom graphics, animation, e-commerce solutions, streaming media, photography, site maintenance and search engine listing.

▌4522
YOUR WEB OPTION

305 E Elm Haskell
Benton, AR 72015
PH: (501)778-7214
TF: (866)778-7214
E-mail: info@yourweboption.com
URL: http://www.yourweboption.com

Description: Your Web Option offers services including web site design, e-commerce solutions, search engine submissions, web site ranking reports, site compression, and web site hosting.

▌4523
ZAAZ

1924 1st Ave.
Seattle, WA 98101
PH: (206)341-9885
FX: (206)749-9868
E-mail: info@zaaz.com
URL: http://www.zaaz.com

Description: Zaaz specializes in web site design and development. Services offered by Zaaz include web site and graphic design, programming, relational database solutions, web management, and strategy consultation.

▌4524
ZANT DEVELOPMENT GROUP, INC.

PO Box 221
Glen Ellyn, IL 60138-0221
PH: (630)942-9440
E-mail: contact@zant.com
URL: http://www.zant.com

Description: Zant Development Group, Inc. focuses on technology solutions for small and mid-sized businesses. Services offered by Zant Development Group include web site design and development, e-commerce solutions, site marketing, web site management and hosting.

▌4525
ZAP5.COM

PO Box 683
Susanville, CA 96130
PH: (530)260-1474
E-mail: getasite@zap5.com
URL: http://www.zap5.com

Description: Zap5.com offers services including custom web site design, animation, sound effects, Flash introductions, multimedia, graphic design, online forms, brochures and training.

▌4526
ZERO ENTROPY

1332 Rubenstein Ave.
Cardiff, CA 92007
PH: (760)753-0072
FX: (760)753-5521
E-mail: info@zeroentropy.com
URL: http://www.zeroentropy.com

Description: Zero Entropy offers a range of creative services including web site design and development, programming, information architecture, e-commerce solutions, Flash design, web strategy and web site hosting.

WEBSITE HOSTING COMPANIES

▌4527
2 THE TOP

341 Fieldcrest Drive
Nashville, TN 37211
PH: (615)390-0407
URL: http://www.2thetop-website-design.com

Description: Web site design, promotion and hosting company. Web design services include promotion and search engine optimization. Custom designed web hosting plans can accomodate ecommerce sites.

▌4528
86HOST.COM

4757 E. Greenway Rd., Ste. 107B PMB105
Phoenix, AZ 85032
PH: (602)448-9785
TF: 877-798-1869
E-mail: customerservice@86host.com
URL: http://www.86host.com/

Description: Arizona based ISP and web hosting company providing dial-up and DSL access, and web hosting services. Unix based Hosting packages are availabe starting at $24.95 and include a basic shopping cart program, MySql database access, Front Page extensions and live chat. All hosting packages come with a guarentee of 99.9% uptime, with a partial refund available for any additional downtime.

▌4529
ACTIVE WEB HOSTING

1469 Flintrock Rd.
Henderson, NV 89014
PH: (702)434-4400
TF: 800-946-7764
E-mail: sales@activewebhosting.com
URL: http://www.activewebhosting.com

Description: No frills hosting company focusing on low cost. Offers a basic package for $10/month which includes unlimited web space, no bandwith charges, and database connectivity with MySQL. Secure server (SSL) not available.

▌4530
ADVANCED WEB SITE PUBLISHING

P.O. Box 891167
Houston, TX 77289-1167
PH: (713)724-7483

FX: (281)461-0186
E-mail: info@awsp.com
URL: http://www.awsp.com

Description: Texas based web site design and hosting company. Offers custom web design services with ecommerce options, or use their site builder tool to build a site for $199 plus hosting fees. Search engine marketing and application programming services are also available. Virtual shared web hosting packages are provided on Unix and Windows NT/2000 platforms and range from $19.95-$99/month.

▌4531
ALTERED IMAGES

300 N. Ash, Ste. 2
Casper, WY 82601
PH: (307)577-5908
FX: (307)234-4477
E-mail: altered@alteredimgs.com
URL: http://www.alteredimgs.com

Description: Wyoming based web hosting, design, ecommerce and internet marketing company. Ecommerce design packages range from $995-$7995 and include secure certificate, shopping cart software and web search engine submission. Ecommerce shared virtual hosting is available for $95/month and includes shopping cart and secure server (SSL).

▌4532
ANET.NET

Los Angeles, CA
PH: (310)360-7620
TF: 800-395-0692
FX: (310)652-7114
E-mail: info@anet.net
URL: http://www.anet.net/

Description: Los Angeles based internet access and web hosting company. Provides dialup and dedicated (ISDN, DSL) internet connectivity, and web hosting and ecommerce packages. Hosting is available on Sun, Mac, Cobalt or NT platforms. Ecommerce hosting packages include SSL (secure servers), online credit card authorization,and the MIVA shopping cart. Servers are monitored 24x7 and all packages include a 30 day money back guarentee. Hosting packages range from $24.95-$90/month. Collocation services are also avaiable.

▌4533
ARKANSASHOSTING.COM

114-A S. Rockingchair Rd.
Paragould, AR 72450
TF: 877-284-8451
E-mail: sales@ArkansasHosting.com
URL: http://www.arkansashosting.com/

871

Description: ArkansasHosting.com is part of TheComputer-Folks.com, and Arkansas based computer store for home and business. NT or Unix based plans are available and range form $7.95-$54.95/month. Ecommerce hosting includes a secure server, MySql database support and the Alacart shopping cart, which includes customizable tax tables. Real-time credit card processing is available with some packages. All servers are montiored 24x7.

▌4534
ATLAS-SOLUTIONS.NET

P.O. Box 666
Clemson, SC 29633
PH: (864)653-6155
E-mail: hosting@atlas-solutions.net
URL: http://hosting.atlas-solutions.net

Description: Web hosting, design and programming company. Design services can include ecommerce funtionality. Virtual shared hosting is provided on RedHat Linux serves and use MySQL and PHP for database connectivity. Hosting plans range from $12.95-$39.95/month. All plans include at least 1 MySQL database and MicroSoft Front Page Extensions.

▌4535
BIZMONTANA

PO Box 17262
Missoula, MT 59808
PH: (406)541-0044
TF: (866)406-0044
FX: (208)279-9850
E-mail: sales@bizmontana.com
URL: http://www.bizmontana.com

Description: Business web site development company offering design, evaluation, promotion and hosting. Design services can include multimedia and ecommerce options. Ecommerce package is available which includes 10 page custom design web site, shared hosting with secure server (SSL) and shopping cart, and promotion for $126.58/month. Basic ecommerce shared hosting is available for $34.95/month.

▌4536
BIZNET INTERNET SERVICES, INC.

2900 Hungary Rd.
Richmond, VA 23228
PH: (804)755-4885
E-mail: sales@biznet.net
URL: http://www.biznet.net

Description: Virginia based web site design, hosting and ecommerce company. Web design services can include multimedia, database programming and ecommerce functionality. Shopping cart services can be provided using their own

softare, Shopping Cart 3.0. Virtual shared hosting on NT or Unix platforms is available for $50/month and include secure server (SSL).

▌4537
BLUETRUCK.NET

826 Bellvue Ave.
Reading, PA 19605
PH: (610)929-4281
FX: (610)929-4283
E-mail: sales@bluetruck.net
URL: http://www.bluetruck.net

Description: Pennsylvania based ISP and web services company. Internet access options include dial-up, DSL, ISDN, high speed wireless, satellite and fractional T1s. Web design services can include database programming and ecommerce options. Ecommerce web hosting is available for $34.95/month and includes secure server (SSL) and MySQL database connectivity. Front Page Extensions are available for an additional $10/month.

▌4538
BUSINESSONLINE.COM

1720 Route 34
PO Box 1347
Wall, NJ 07719
PH: (518)724-5000
TF: (866)837-2638
E-mail: info@thebiz.net
URL: http://www.biznessonline.com/

Description: Providing a full range of internet services for businesses. Products include high speed dedicated internet access, including DSL and Frame Relay, web design and custom programming, and web hosting services with ecommerce packages. Hosting is available on both windows and unix platforms, and includes secure servers (SSL), database connectivity and 24x7 monitoring. Ecommerce services include credit card processing and tax calculation. Collocation services are also available.

▌4539
BYDESIGN

66 West St.
Leominster, MA 01453
PH: (978)840-3344
TF: 888-840-3344
E-mail: info@bydzyn.com
URL: http://www.bydzyn.com

Description: Graphic, web design and hosting company. Can design simple to complex web sites for businesses large and small. Shared virtual hosting packages range from $15-$40/month and can include a secure server (SSL) and the

AlaCart shopping cart program with secure credit card transactions. All packages include a web based maintenance tool.

■ 4540
CAROLINA ONLINE

4243 Seven Lakes Plz.
Seven Lakes, NC 27376
PH: (910)673-3868
FX: (910)673-1087
E-mail: sales@carolina.net
URL: http://http://www.carolina.net/

Description: North Carolina based internet service company providing access and web hosting. Internet access services include dial-up, DSL, leased lines and satellite. Basic virtual shared web hosting is availabe on Linux or Windows 2000 platform starting at $9.95. Secure server (SSL), including certificate, and the ecommerce programs StoreFront and BackOffice are available as add-ons for a one time fee of $99.95. Dedicated servers are available starting at $249.95/month. Collocation services are available for $500/month.

■ 4541
CATALOG.COM

6404 International Parkway, Ste. 2200
Plano, TX 75093
TF: 888-932-4376
FX: (972)380-0911
URL: http://www.catalog.com

Description: Billing itself as "The Home of Free Web Hosting Forever", catalog.com offers a variety of web hosting services. Their basic package of "free hosting with domain registration" includes a small web site space and technical support for 30 days. Up from there they offer shared, dedicated and managed hosting services on both Linux and Windows platforms. They offer standard database programs on both platforms (e.g. Access and MySQL), along with SSL for ecommerce transactions. Packages range from $25-$400/month.

■ 4542
CENTRAL MAINE BUSINESS

E-mail: info@centralmainebusiness.com
URL: http://www.centralmainebusiness.com

Description: Offers web site development, hosting and ecommerce solutions in the Central Maine area. Design services can include ongoing maintenance. Ecommerce hosting packages range from $55/month for a small site not requiring credit card transactions to $300/month for large sites. Packages can include Mercantec SoftCart for shopping cart functionality, browser based editing, online secure credit card processing and Msql or MySQL database connectivity. All packages include a 99.9% uptime guarentee.

■ 4543
CHOOSE2SAVE.COM

20 South Honey Dr.
Nampa, ID 83687
PH: (208)442-7158
FX: (208)442-7159
E-mail: info@choose2save.com
URL: http://www.choose2save.com

Description: Provides dial-up internet connectivity services and web hosting. Hosting is on Windows 2000 with IIS servers. Shopper and Corporate hosting plans ($65 and $150/month) include secure server (SSL) and basic shopping cart system. Domain registrations are available for $15.

■ 4544
CIRELLE ENTERPRISES INC.

25 Indian Rock Rd 421
Windham, NH 03087
PH: (603)425-2221
FX: (603)434-2865
E-mail: sales@cirelle.com
URL: http://cirelle.com

Description: Web design and hosting company specializing in data publishing and interactive data driven web sites for organizations of all sizes. Web site design can include multimedia, database and ecommerce options. Hosting services are provided by cedata.com. Ecommerce shared virtual hosting starts at $44.95 and includes secure server (SSL), shopping cart and database connectivity. Can also provide remote database access to plug into exsisting sites.

■ 4545
CNET NETWORKS, INC.

235 2nd St.
San Francisco, CA 94105
E-mail: Rebecca.Viksnins@cnet.com
URL: http://webservices.cnet.com
Contact: Rebecca Viksnins, Associate Editor, ISPs, browsers

Description: CNET, known for it's technology news, reviews and consumer information, provides a special section of their website for locating ISPs and hosting services. While searching by criteria is not available, hosting services are broken down into categories such as Managed Hosting, Collocation and E-commerce hosting. Within each catagory users may select hosts and click the "compare" button to get a side-by-side comparison of various hosts. Also provided are essays on how to pick a web host and picking ISP options and a glossary. **Major Partners:** ZDNet.

■ **4546**

CNWEB.COM

1126 N. Briggs Ave
Hastings, NE 68901
E-mail: aharpham@cnweb.com
URL: http://www.cnweb.com
Contact: Allen Harpham

Description: Web design, hosting and marketing company. Hosting services include FrontPage extensions and MySQL database connectivity. Ecommerce shared hosting is availabe for $35/month with secure server (SSL) and uses Cambist Merchant Solutions for credit card processing. Dedicated servers and collocation services also available.

■ **4547**

COMMAND TECHNOLOGY SOLUTIONS INC.

Big Rock Executive Center
47W210 Rt. 30
Big Rock, IL 60511
PH: (630)556-3731
E-mail: contact@commandt.net
URL: http://www.clandhosting.com/

Description: Provides web site design, development and hosting, offering both shared and virtual private server hosting. Ecommerce plans are hosted on FreeBSD unix platforms, and include secure server (SSL), database applications and Miva Merchant for credit card, shopping cart and inventory funtions. Business plans can include the Mercantec SoftCart software. Packages range from $65-$330/month.

■ **4548**

COMMSPEED

7411 E. Addis Ave.
Prescott Valley, AZ 86314
PH: (928)772-1111
TF: 888-772-1137
FX: (928)775-2809
E-mail: info@commspeed.net
URL: http://home.commspeed.net/

Description: Arizona based ISP providing internet services for residential and business customers. Services include dialup access, dedicated highspeed connections, wireless, local area networks and web site design and hosting. Hosting is available on either Unix or NT servers, and is supported 24x7. Hosting packages are avaiable starting at $24.95/month.

■ **4549**

COMPAREWEBHOSTS.COM

2740 E. Oakland Park Blvd, Ste. 300
Fort Lauderdale, FL 33306
PH: (954)630-3737

FX: (954)567-2659
E-mail: feedback@comparewebhosts.com
URL: http://www.comparewebhosts.com/

Description: Although rife with blinking banner ads, the power search to this directory of web hosting services provides a high degree of selectivity of hosting features. One may search by operating system, features such as PHP and Cold Fusion support, site management tools and access to log files. Provides detailed listings of companies, along with press releases, and user reviews if available. Also includes a brief tutorial on how to choose a host, and a directory of web designers.

■ **4550**

COMPUTER SOLUTIONS CONSULTING

12112 Frank Cordova Cir.
El Paso, TX 79936-4488
PH: (915)203-0193
TF: 888-855-9321
URL: http://http://www.cscweb.net/

Description: Offers web hosting and design services, along with on-site consulting, training, and installation of hardware. Design services can include custom databases and ecommerce solutions. Shared virtual hosting is provided on a Linux platform and includes secure server (SSL), MySQL for database connectivity and Microsoft Front Page Extensions. Hosting packages range from $19.95-$34.95/month.

■ **4551**

CORPORATE TECHNOLOGIES USA, INC.

1700 42nd Street SW
Fargo, ND 58103
PH: (701)281-5400
FX: (701)277-0012
E-mail: info@ctusa.net
URL: http://www.ctusa.net

Description: ISP, ASP and web hosting company offering dial-up connections, direct high-speed connections with dedicated lines, DSL, and secure server hosting products. Corporate web hosting services range from $24.95-$100/month. Corporate packages include secure server (SSL) and DNS hosting.

■ **4552**

CSLA.COM

E-mail: info@csla.com
URL: http://www.csla.com/

Description: Web site development, hosting and ecommerce solution company. Basic web sites built for $400, more advanced sites can include multimedia and database programming. Virtual hosting is provided on Linux OS with

Apache servers. Packages range from $18.95-$99.95 and can include secure server (SSL), MySQL database connectivity and shopping cart options.

▌4553
CYBERCONNECTICS

30240 SW Pkwy. 10
Wilsonville, OR 97070
TF: 888-292-2661
E-mail: support@cybcon.com
URL: http://www.cybcon.com

Description: Oregon based ISP, web design and web hosting company. Internet access services include dial-up and DSL. Web design services can include custom database programming and ecommerce funtions, and are billed at $60/hr. Basic ecommerce hosting starts at $49.95/month and includes Miva Merchant shopping cart and secure server (SSL). All hosting packages come with 99.99% uptime guarentee.

▌4554
CYBERGATE WEB HOSTING

Tacoma, WA
E-mail: contact@cgwebhosting.com
URL: http://www.cgwebhosting.com

Description: Provides virtual shared and dedicated hosting packages on Redhat Linux for individuals, businesses and resellers. Virtual shared hosting with secure server (SSL), Microsoft Front Page Extensions, and MySQL and PHP for database connectivity is available for $18/month. Dedicated servers range from $250-$750/month. An automated site mirroring and monitoring service to provide redundancy in case the current host site fails is available for $49/month.

▌4555
DAKOTASERVERS.NET

406 NE 8th Ave.
Aberdeen, SD 57401
PH: (605)622-7811
E-mail: sales@dakotaservers.net
URL: http://http://www.dakotaservers.com/

Description: Provides web hosting, domain hosting, dedicated servers and Instant Store services. Instant Store service includes design of ecommerce enabled web site for $500-%1500 plus $36.99/month hosting fee. Virtual shared hosting includes GeniusCart Pro and secure server (SSL). Dedicated and managed Cobalt Raq servers are also available. All hosting comes with a 99.99% network uptime guarentee.

▌4556
DATA SYNTHESIS INTERNET SERVICES

P.O. Box 20538
Wichita, KS 67208
PH: (316)683-7868
E-mail: webmaster@ictks.com
URL: http://www.ictks.com

Description: Web site design, marketing and hosting company focusing on the needs of small businesses and organizations. Offers basic web sites for under $1000, along with training to enable customer to perform maintenance. Virtual shared web hosting plans range from $12.95-$74.95 and can include secure server (SSL), Cart32 shopping cart, and SQL Server 2000. Site maintenance and site marketing packages are also available.

▌4557
DAYO, INC.

4555 Heritage Oak Dr.
Orlando, FL 32808
PH: (386)753-1400
FX: (386)753-1401
E-mail: sales@dayo.net
URL: http://www.dayo.net/

Description: Florida based web design, hosting and collocation company. Collocation services start at $99/month. Web design services are available and can include ongoing maintenance. Ecommerce packages use StoreFront and FrontPage. Secure server (SSL) and credit card processing are also available. Web hosting starts at $14.95/month, and are available Windows or Linux servers.

▌4558
DELAWARE.NET, INC.

28 Old Rudnick Ln., Ste. 200
Dover, DE 19901
PH: (302)736-5515
TF: 888-432-7965
FX: (302)736-5945
URL: http://www.delaware.net/

Description: Delaware based web services company. Provides dialup and dedicated acces, web design, virtual web hosting, dedicated servers and collocation services. Hosting service are availabe on Cobalt, Linux or NT, and include free SSL security certificate. Prices range from $4.95 - $129.95/month. Dedicated servers start at $100/month. Web site design can include graphic arts, database programming and ecommerce transaction services.

▌4559
DELLHOST

PH: 888-900-3355
E-mail: sales@dellhost.com

URL: http://www.dellhost.com

Description: Dellhost, a nationwide web hosting service, offers a wide variety of hosting options, all on Dell hardware. They can provide dedicated, E-commerce or shared hosting options. The also offer services in web design, e-commerce sites and site promotion. They offer 24x7 support and a guarentee of 99.9% uptime. A wizard guides you through selecting the appropriate service level. A glossary and FAQ are also provided. Plans range from $18 - $12,000, depending on the services required.

▌4560
DENNISTON ENTERPRISES

P.O. Box 177
Mt. Sterling, KY 40353-0177
PH: (859)498-4729
TF: 800-295-3476
E-mail: Contact@DennistonInc.com
URL: http://www.realtor.dennistoninc.com

Description: Internet design, consulting and hosting firm based Kentucky. Offers design and programming services including multimedia and database programming. Virtual hosting packages are available on both NT and Unix platforms. Ecommerce packages can include secure server (SSL) and a variety of shopping cart options such as Miva Merchant, Hassan or LinkPoint shopping cart. Plans range from $29.59 to $100/month. A 3 month minimum contract is required.

▌4561
DEV X STUDIOS

416 Beech St.
Connersville, IN 47331
E-mail: info@devxstudios.net
URL: http://www.devxstudios.net

Description: Internet services company providing web design and development, web hosting, computer service and repair, networking, and print and multimedia publications on CD. They can provide small business web sites, complex ecommerce sites and inter office networking. Web hosting packages are available on both windows and Unix platforms. Packages can include SQL Server, mySQL, secure server (SSL) and shopping cart software such as Cart32. Consulting and training services are also available.

▌4562
DISCOVERNET, INC

402 Graham Ave., Ste. 320
Eau Claire, WI 54701
TF: 888-284-4531
E-mail: sales@discover-net.net
URL: http://www.discover-net.net

Description: Wisconsin based ISP offering internet connectivity, web design, hosting and marketing services. Connectivity services include dial-up, ISDN, T1 and high speed wireless. Design services include an ecommerce package with includes design, hosting and secure storefront for $1649.95 plus $99.95/month. Virtual shared web hosting packages include basic dial-up connectivity and range from $39.95-$99.95/month.

▌4563
E-COM HAWAII

355 Hukilike St. 212
Kahului, HI 96732
PH: (808)244-0880
FX: (808)877-0611
E-mail: info@ecomhawaii.com
URL: http://www.ecomhawaii.com/

Description: Hawaii based web design and hosting company. Basic hosting packages begin at $12.95 and include secure server (SSL) and SQL database capabilities. Ecommerce packages include real-time credit card processing and tax calculation. Also includes flexible management interface with export capabilites. Startup packages include design and hosting and start at $165.

▌4564
EAGLE WEB DEVELOPMENT LLC

Rt 2 Box 406
Colonial Gateway Office Park
Clarksburg, WV 26301
PH: (304)622-5676
E-mail: info@eaglewd.com
URL: http://www.eaglewd.com

Description: Web developement and hosting company. Development services can include custom database programming, ecommerce functionality, multimedia, and web site maintenance. Shared virtual hosting services are available on Windows platform for $16.67-$200/month. Web site promotion and search engine submission services are available from $30-$2000.

▌4565
EAGLESERVER

Po Box 1617
Auburn, WA
PH: (253)896-0270
TF: 800-481-3245
E-mail: sales@eagleserver.com
URL: http://www.eagleserver.com

Description: Washington based ISP and web hosting and design company offering services to individuals and businesses. Access services include dial-up, ISDN, IDSL, DSL and dedicated lines. Custom website design is available at

$65/hour. Database and multimedia design is available for $125/hour. Virtual shared web hosting with secure server (SSL), shopping cart and database support is available for $129.95/month plus one-time setup fee of $500.

∎ 4566
EARTHLINK

1375 Peachtree St., Level A
Atlanta, GA 30309
PH: (404)815-0770
TF: 800-955-0186
E-mail: sales@corp.earthlink.net
URL: http://www.earthlink.com

Description: While best known for its national network of dialup internet connections, Earthlink also offers basic web hosting services. They offer packaged hosting bundles, which can include shopping cart services. All e-commerce packages are unix based and offer cgi and pop email. While not highly configurable, these packages may be right for small businesses on a budget, as they range in price from $30-$100 /mo. It is also worth considering Earthlink as a dialin internet service provider if your employees travel often in the United States and need intenet access.

∎ 4567
FRONT RANGE INTERNET, INC.

213 Linden St., Ste. 200
Fort Collins, CO 80524
E-mail: info@frii.com
URL: http://www.frii.com/

Description: Colorado based internet company providing internet acccess and web hosting services. They offer all types of access from dial-up, to dedicated ISDN, T1 or Gigabit Ethernet. They also over server collocation in their own facilities. Web design, construction, maintenance and custom program are available as separate services. Hosting is provided on their fully redundant web farm. Commerical hosting starts at $40/month and includes MySQL database access.

∎ 4568
FRONTPAGES WEB HOSTING NETWORK

1650 Des Peres Rd, Ste. 125
St. Louis, MO 63131
PH: (314)822-3901
TF: (866)780-4678
FX: (314)821-2464
E-mail: info@frontpages-web-hosting.net
URL: http://www.frontpages-web-hosting.net

Description: Web hosting company focused on microsoft platform and products. Shared hosting is available starting at $17.95 and can include secure server (SSL), Miva Merchant or StoreFront for shopping cart functionality. All plans

support FrontPage and Active Server Pages. Dedicated hosting is available starting at $295/month. Collocation services are also available.

∎ 4569
GLOBAL HOSTING NETWORK

Minneapolis, MN 55401
TF: (866)467-8692
E-mail: info@reactivehost.com
URL: http://www.reactivehost.com

Description: Web hosting company offering both virtual shared and dedicated hosting plans. Shared hosting ranges from $14.95-$34.95. Dediated hosting is on Linux platform using the Apache server and range from $299-$495/month depending on configuration. 24x7 technical and customer support is provided. Web design and application development services are also available. **Major Partners:** Part Of The Global Hosting Network.

∎ 4570
GSINET

PO Box 87
Weare, NH 03281-0087
PH: (603)529-9916
TF: 888-394-4772
E-mail: info@gsinet.net
URL: http://www2.gsinet.net

Description: New Hampshire based ISP and web hosting and development company. Internet access provided via dial-ip or ISDN. Virtual shared web hosting for ecommerce sites is available for $60/month and can include secure server (SSL) and Cyber Cash for credit card processing. Will design a basic one-page site for $300, and a seven-page site for $1,325.

∎ 4571
HACOM

c/o A1 Internet Services, Inc.
15825 Shady Grove Rd, Ste 50
Rockville, MD 20850
PH: (678)467-9415
TF: 877-210-4112
E-mail: info@hacom.net
URL: http://www.hacom.net/

Description: Maryland based ISP and web hosting company. Virtual Hosting services are on Linux platform with Apache servers. All packages include secure server (SSL) and Front Page extensions. Packages start at $29.95/month. Hacom also overs web design services, and ecommerce services such as shopping cart packages and credit card processing.

▌ 4572

HIWAAY INTERNET SERVICES

P.O. Box 86
Huntsville, AL 35804
PH: (256)533-4296
TF: 888-244-9229
E-mail: sales@hiwaay.net
URL: http://www.hiwaay.net

Description: Alabama based ISP and internet hosting service. Provides services for residential and small businesses ranging from dialip internet service to dedicated highspeed internet access. Also offers web site design and web hosting with ecommerce options. Will provide a complete web ''store front'' starting at $49/month. Also provides a variety of linux based hosting services, including managed servers and collocation services.

▌ 4573

HOOSIER ISP, INC.

310 N Michigan St., Ste. 101
Plymouth, IN 46563-1753
PH: (574)935-5597
TF: (866)564-6366
FX: (574)935-9376
URL: http://www.hoosierisp.com

Description: Indiana based ISP providing connectivity and hosting solutions. Provides dedicated internet service to businesses including ISDN, Frame Relay and T1 lines. Business site web hosting plans start at $129/month and includes secure server (SSL) and MS SQL Server. Plans can include the ShopSite shopping cart software.

▌ 4574

HOSTER.COM

Valley Brook Ave.
TF: 888-999-7722
FX: (201)460-4442
E-mail: sales@hoster.com
URL: http://www.hoster.com

Description: Web hosting company offering shared, dedicated, ecommerce and reseller hosting services. Ecommerce solutions use eVendo software to create and maintain online store fronts. Shared virtual hosting which includes a shopping cart system, Cyber Cash support, secure server (SSL) and mSQL database starts at $49.95. Dedicated Linux or Windows 2000 servers are available starting at $295/month. Web site development, consultation and database design and programming services are also available.

▌ 4575

HOSTINGVERMONT

70 South Winooski Ave., 193
Burlington, VT 05401
PH: (802)864-4100

FX: 888-283-0058
E-mail: sales@hostingvermont.com
URL: http://www.hostingvermont.com

Description: Vermont based web hosting company offering virtual shared hosting on Linux platform with Apache web server. Hosting packages with secure server (SSL), and SoftCart shopping cart range from $9.95-$29.95/month. Database connectivity is provided via MySQL and PHP. Microsoft Front Page Extensions are enabled on all packages.

▌ 4576

HOSTREVIEW.COM

E-mail: webmaster@hostreview.com
URL: http://www.hostreview.com

Description: Hosted by Cedent.com, a web hosting company, this directory provides a searchable direcory of over 1600 hosts. Searches may be limited by price, operating system, data transfer and various service options. Users may comment on web hosts and comments are included on results pages. Includes guides such as ''Are you Ready for a Dedicated Server'' and ''Free vs. Paid Web Hosting.'' Also includes links to web development resources such as HTML tutorials, clip art, and security sites.

▌ 4577

HOSTWAY CORP.

1 N State St., Ste. 1200
Chicago, IL 60602
TF: (866)467-8929
URL: http://www.hostway.com

Description: A large national hosting company, hostway can provide all types of hosting services, from as low as $9/month for small no frills site with one email address. The provide both windows and unix servers, and can provide secure shopping cart services. The provide most database and scripting language programs, and multimedia programs. They offer 24x7 support and daily data backup. They also offer managed servers from $197/month.

▌ 4578

IMPACT BUSINESS SOLUTIONS LLC

301 North Charles St., Ste. 403
Baltimore, MD 21201
PH: (410)256-4999
TF: 800-536-1573
FX: (410)256-0154
E-mail: support@impactbusiness.com
URL: http://www.impactbusiness.com/

Description: Maryland based ISP, web design and hosting company. Internet connectivity options range from dial-up to dedicated high speed ISDN, DSL or T1 lines. Can provide business office network setup. Web design services can include multimedia and database programming. Web hosting plans range from $20/month for basic shared hosting to $250/month for a dedicated server. Collocation services are available for $150/month. Live network support is available 24x7. Internet marketing and consultation services are available.

∎ 4579
INTELLIGENT HOSTING

PO Box 370520
Las Vegas, NV 89137
E-mail: sales@intelligenthosting.com
URL: http://www.intelligenthosting.com

Description: Web hosting company focused on the needs of the small business. Shared virtual hosting is available from $11.95-$34.95/month. Packages can include secure server(SSL) and database connectivity with MySQL. Offers basic "easy ecommerce" secure form for small merchants not needing the functionality of a shopping cart system. 99.95% uptime guaranteed

∎ 4580
INTERNET ALASKA, INC.

3900 Denali St.
Anchorage, AK 99503
URL: http://home.alaska.net/

Description: Fairbanks Alaska based ISP offering dialup and dedicated highspeed internet access. Also provides business network services including internet access, web site design and hosting, ecommerce sites, advertising and training. Basic web hosting business packages are available starting at $37.50/month. Ecommerce packages which include shopping cart options begin at $50/month.

∎ 4581
INTERNET DOORWAY INC

PO Box 22488
Jackson, MS 39225
PH: (601)969-1434
TF: 800-952-1570
E-mail: info@netdoor.com
URL: http://www.netdoor.com/

Description: Mississippi based ISP and web hosting company. Provides both home and business internet access products ranging from dial-up services to dedicated highspeed connections such as tiered T3 service. Can provide networking for large and small offices. Web development services include consulting, design, hosting and maintenance. Virtual shared hosting plans on Linux platform range from $50-$125/month. Collocation and dedicated servers also available.

∎ 4582
INTERNET NEBRASKA

P.O. Box 5301
Lincoln, NE 68505-5301
PH: (402)434-8680
TF: 888-293-3426
FX: (402)436-2660
E-mail: info@inebraska.com
URL: http://www.inebraska.com

Description: Nebraska based ISP and web hosting company. Offers dial-up, ISDN, ADSL, and dedicated line internet access. Web page design is available for $50/hour, database programming at $75/hour. Web hosting is available on Unix or Windows/NT platforms. Shared virtual hosting included secure server (SSL) is available for $35/month.

∎ 4583
INTERSTATE 29 WEB DESIGN

4977 Klitzke Dr.
Horace, ND 58047-9726
PH: (701)588-4541
URL: http://http://www.i29webdesign.com/

Description: North Dakota based web design and hosting company. Web design services for a small business with 5 information pages is availble for $210. Ecommerce sites including shopping cart range from $300-$550. Hosting services with shopping cart range from $9.95-$69.95/month, with the higher end packages including real-time credit card processing. Secure certificates for secure server (SSL) are available for $150/yr.

∎ 4584
IOWA E-BUSINESS, INC.

3114 Cumming Rd
Cumming, IA 50061
PH: (515)981-4026
E-mail: sales@iowaebusiness.com
URL: http://www.iowaebusiness.com

Description: Internet service and consulting company focusing primarily on web hosting and ecommerce for small businesses. Hosting packages start at $25/month and include database connectivity, shopping cart and management software. Will build basic web sites for $500-$800.

∎ 4585
IOWA WEB DESIGN

E-mail: info@iowawebdesign.com
URL: http://iowawebdesign.com/

Description: Iowa based web site design and hosting company. Design services includ multimedia sites and custom database programming. Shared ecommerce hosting starts at $55.95/month and includes MS SQL database connectivity, CyberCash and secure server (SSL). Dedicated hosting is available on Linux servers.

▌ 4586

ISP CHECK, LLC

PO Box 34560
Washington, DC 20043-4560
PH: (202)216-4390
FX: (202)216-4391
E-mail: sales@ispcheck.com
URL: http://www.ispcheck.com/
Contact: Misha Zilberter

Description: ISP Check provides extensive lists of webhosting and ISP services, diveded into categories such as operating system, hosting services (e.g. maganed, collocation, dedicated), and connectivity type (broadband, dsl, etc.) Within categories listings may be limited to maximum cost. Some of the listings on this site are paid advertisements, and placement at the top of a list is based on the bid the ISP or hosting service is willing to pay. Entries are not evaluated for quality, though many well known and reputable services are listed.

▌ 4587

KAINAW, INC.

2222 Ashley River Rd, 3E
Charleston, SC 29414
PH: (843)763-8500
E-mail: info@kainaw.com
URL: http://www.kainaw.com

Description: Internet and business services company offering custom programming, employee training, web design and web hosting. Web design services are offered at $80 without hosting, or $40 if the site is also hosted by Kainaw, and can include custom database programming and multimedia applications. Shared virtual web hosting services are offered at $20/month and include secure server (SSL). Miva Mercant shopping cart is available for an additional $10/month.

▌ 4588

KANSASNET

531 Ft. Riley Blvd.
Manhattan, KS 66502
PH: (785)776-1452
E-mail: webmaster@kansas.net
URL: http://www2.kansas.net

Description: ISP offering dedicated and dial-up access, ISDN, DSL, wireless, virtual private networks, computer and networking sales and service and web hosting services. Web hosting is offered on both Windows NT/2000 or Linux platforms. Shared hosting is availabe for $30/month and

includes unlimited data transfer and FrontPage and ASP support. Few built-in ecommerce options are available.

▌ 4589

KLAMATH FALLS INTERNET

132 W. Main St., Ste. 101
Medford, OR 97501
TF: 800-419-4804
FX: (541)773-9667
E-mail: help@kfalls.net
URL: http://www.kfalls.net

Description: ISP offering internet access and web hosting services. Access options include dial-up, ADSL, SDSL and Frame Relay. Web hosting is available for $25/month, with an additional $5/month for secure server (SSL) without certificate. Hosting includes one year free domain name registration.

▌ 4590

KONAWEBSITES.COM

P.O. Box 2837
Kailua Kona, HI 96745
PH: (808)327-1458
FX: (808)327-1458
E-mail: info@konawebsites.com
URL: http://www.konawebsites.com

Description: Website design, hosting and management company. Basic hosting packages begin at $30/month. Ecommerce Accounts includes a secure online store with shopping cart and credit card processing. Total website packages include hosting, weekly or monthly updates, marketing and ongoing site testing. Total packages start at $150/month.

▌ 4591

LIBERTY COMPUTER SOLUTIONS

172 Boston St.
Coventry, RI 02816
PH: (401)823-5252
FX: (401)828-7057
E-mail: webmaster@libertyhosting.net
URL: http://libertyhosting.net

Description: Rhode Island based web design and hosting company focusing on the needs of small business. Web design services can include custom programming and ecommerce options. Virtual shared web hosting is provided on RedHat Linux platform with the Apache server. Database connectivity is with MySQL and PHP. Microsoft Front Page Extensions are also available. Hosting packages including shared secure server (SSL) start at $12.95. Packages starting at $24.95 can support individual SSL certificates. All packages come with a free shopping cart.

▌4592

LONETREE.COM

211 West 19th St., Ste. 120
Cheyenne, WY 82001
PH: (307)632-0088
TF: 800-318-1370
FX: (307)632-0077
E-mail: info@lonetree.com
URL: http://www.lonetree.com

Description: ISP and web hosting company offering DSL, SDSL, Frame Relay, and wireless connectivity. Basic virtual shared hosting services are available for $20-$60/month and include SQL server access. Custom hosting packages including secure server (SSL) and other ecommerce options are available upon request. Database programming services are available. Collocation services are offered at $150/month.

▌4593

MAGPAGE INTERNET SERVICES, INC.

2892 Creek Rd., Ste. B2
P.O. Box 236
Yorklyn, DE 19736
TF: 800-250-2990
E-mail: info@magpage.com
URL: http://www.magpage.com/

Description: Delaware based ISP provides dialup Internet access throughout the nation, along with DSL and ADSL for their business customers. Web hosting is available on both Linux and Windows platforms, and includes secure servers (SSL), 24x7 network monitoring, online credit card authorization and a 99.9% uptime guarentee. They will build and mount a basic storefront starting at $495. Dedicated servers and collocation services are also available.

▌4594

MAINEHOST.COM

122 Front St.
Bath, ME 04530
PH: (207)442-9006
TF: 888-200-8008
E-mail: sales@mainehost.com
URL: http://mainehost.com

Description: Maine based web design, promotion and hosting company. Design services can accomodate small to large business and ecommerce sites, including database and multimedia production. Hosting plans are provided on Red Hat Linux platform with Apache web servers. Plans range from $15.95-$49.95. Ecommerce packages can include AlaCart or Miva Merchant shopping carts and store fronts. Secure server (SSL) and security certificates are included. Web site promotion plans guarentees top 3 placement in major search engines for $165/month.

▌4595

MARYLANDWEBDESIGNERS.COM

E-mail: contactmarylandylandwebdesigners.com
URL: http://www.marylandwebdesigners.com/

Description: Web design, hosting, marketing and maintenance company. Hosting plans range from $100 - $300/month, with only the most expensive including ecommerce options such as a shopping cart program. All plans include MySQL database connectivity. Marketing and maintence services include search engine placemnet, banner ads and flashmercials.

▌4596

MASTERS INFORMATION SYSTEMS

P.O. Box 519
Rehoboth, MA 02769
PH: (508)252-4772
E-mail: Josh@MastersInformation.com
URL: http://www.mastersinformation.com

Description: Small web hosting, web development, database development and networking comapany. Can provide intra office networking services for the small business. Ecommerce hosting plan availabe for $59.99/month, which includes as secure server (SSL). Database programming, maintenance and conversion services are available.

▌4597

MINNESOTASHOPPER.COM

P.O. Box 703
Grand Rapids, MN 55744
PH: (218)327-0795
E-mail: info@minnesotashopper.com
URL: http://MinnesotaShopper.com

Description: Web hosting company offering basic shared virtual hosting starting at $9.95/month. Hosting plans include basic shopping cart and secure server (SSL).Provides free web design based on available templates for up to 7 pages, with additional charges for editing after the first month. 99.5% uptime guarenteed.

▌4598

MIS

P.O. Box 130737
Ann Arbor, MI 48113-0737
PH: (734)997-7000
FX: (734)997-7010
E-mail: info@mintsol.com
URL: http://www.mintsol.com/

Description: Web site design, hosting, marketing and security company. Services include web design with multimedia and database integration, office networking and network security, intranet and internet web sites, and web site positioning. Virtual shared hosting packages range from $15/month for basic hosting to $60/month for ecommerce hosting. Ecommerce packages include secure server (SSL), shopoing cart and realtime transaction processing.

■ **4599**
MM2K

PO Box 644
New Monmouth, NJ 07748
TF: 877-688-5132
E-mail: customerservice@mm2k.net
URL: http://www.mm2k.net

Description: Internet company offering access, web hosting and web design. Access options include dial-up, ISDN and DSL. Virtual shared web hosting is available on Windows NT servers. Ecommerce plans start at $39.95/month and include secures server (SSL), Cyber Cash compatible and a 99.9% uptime guarentee. Web design and consulting services are also available.

■ **4600**
MOUNTAINNET

2816 Cranberry Square
Morgantown, WV 26508
PH: (304)594-9075
TF: 877-877-1136
FX: (304)594-9088
E-mail: info@mountain.net
URL: http://www.mountain.net

Description: West Virginia based ISP offering internet connectivity, networking, off site data storage, web design and web hosting services. Connectivity services include dial-up, ISDN and dedicated high speed lines. Web design services can include database integration. Virtual shared web hosting package including secure server (SSL) and search engine registration is available for $39.95/month.

■ **4601**
MOUSEWORKS

142 George Allen Rd.
Glocester, RI 02814-1775
PH: (401)568-4016
FX: (401)568-9089
E-mail: info@mouseworks.net
URL: http://www.mouseworks.net

Description: Web hosting company focused on the needs of small buisness and organizations. Web design services are offered at $35/hour and can include ecommerce options. Web site maintenace can be purchased at the same rate.

Hosting services are outsourced but handled through mouseworks. Basic packages are available fo r$219/yr. Ecommerce hosting options are available.

■ **4602**
MS WORLDNET INC.

4595 County Rd. J
Stevens Point, WI 54481
PH: (715)345-2391
FX: (715)592-4738
E-mail: info@msworldnet.com
URL: http://www.msworldnet.com

Description: ISP offering internet connectivity and web hosting services. Connectivity services include dial-up, DSL, ISDN, and T1 lines. Virtual shared hosting is available from $9.95-$49.95/month. All hosting packages include Microsoft Front Page Extensions and ASP scripting support. Optional add-ons include Microsoft Access and FoxPro ODBC connections and SQL server for database connectivity. Server collocation services are also available.

■ **4603**
MYSTIBLUE COMPUTING

2011 Oregon Ave.
Caldwell, ID 83605
PH: (208)484-0808
TF: 877-666-0879
E-mail: info@mystiblue.com
URL: http://www.mystiblue.com

Description: Idaho based web design and hosting company, providing custom design for web sites including ecommerce solutions. Website design services include multimedia and database options. Shared ecommerce hosting packages start at $24.95 and include secure server (SSL) and MySQL database access. Shopping cart software is also avaiable. Site maintenance services are also available.

■ **4604**
NATIONAL DATA TRANSPORT CO.

155 Northpoint Ave., Bldg. 203
High Point, NC 27265
PH: (336)841-5156
FX: (336)841-1126
E-mail: admin@nationaldatatransport.com
URL: http://www.nationaldatatransport.com

Description: ISP, ASP and web hosting company focusing on the needs of business. Internet access services included dedicated T1 lines and Virtual Private Networks. Application Services include accounting and finance and online catalog programs. Business class web hosting includes support for ecommerce technology.

▌4605
NETMONGER

2471 Merrick Rd.
Bellmore, NY
PH: (516)221-6664
FX: (516)221-9294
E-mail: info@netmonger.net
URL: http://www.netmonger.net

Description: Small ISP and web hosting company providing residential and small business solutions. Offers dial-up and ISDN internet access for $34.95/month. Basic shared virtual hosting is available for $40/month. Ecommerce hosting with secure server (SSL) is available for $110/month.

▌4606
NEW TECHNOLOGY WAY

1 Penn Plaza, Ste. 2200
New York, NY 10119
TF: 800-490-3033
FX: (212)290-2590
E-mail: sales@newtechnologyway.com
URL: http://www.newtechnologyway.com

Description: New York based web development, graphics and hosting company. Web development services include custom database programming for ecommerce, and 3-D graphic modeling. Linux platform hosting services are provided by usahostme.com. Hosting packages range from $14.95-$34.95. All packages include secure server (SSL) and ThatsAnOrder shopping cart. Database connectivity is available via MySQL.

▌4607
NTT/VERIO INC.

8005 S. Chester St., Ste. 200
Englewood, CO 80112
TF: 800-438-8374
URL: http://www.verio.com/products/hosting/web/

Description: NTT/Verio, an international company, offers dedicated, managed, virtual and e-commerce web hosting plans, along with collocation services. They also offer dedicated Internet Access service, through the NTT/VERIO Global Tier One Network. They offer T1, DS3, OC3 and OC12 lines and virtual private networks. They can provide services for the smallest of companies wishing only basic web page hosting to complex multi-site hosting with e-commerce databases and packages, with global internet connections. They offer linux and windows enviroments with configurable software and hardware components as needed by your company. Packages start from under $1000.

▌4608
OHIO WEB HOSTING

P.O. Box 228
Casstown, OH 45312-0228
PH: (937)440-8863
TF: (866)472-5715
E-mail: sales@ohiowebhosting.com
URL: http://www.ohiowebhosting.com

Description: Basic virtual shared web hosting company offering packages ranging from $8.95-$29.95. All packages include secured environment. Front Page extensions available for an additional $30.

▌4609
OKLAHOMAWEBDESIGN.COM

P.O. Box 890535
Oklahoma City, OK 73189-0535
PH: (405)688-7093
FX: (405)682-4019
URL: http://www.oklahomawebdesign.com

Description: Oklahoma based company providing web site design, web site hosting, domain registration, domain transfers, internet marketing, graphic design, and contact management services. Hosting services guarentee 99.9% uptime and support Microsoft Front Page Extensions. Design services include web traffic analysis and search engine submission.

▌4610
PENNSYLVANIA ONLINE

PO Box 6501
Harrisburg, 17112
PH: (717)657-0000
FX: (717)657-0132
E-mail: info@paweb.net
URL: http://www.paweb.net

Description: Web hosting services and design company. Hosting is offered at $24.95/month and includes domain name registration, secure server (SSL) and Microsoft Front Page Extensions. Offers a core web site design package for $450 plus hosting fees.

▌4611
PERLNET

1040 Crown Pointe Pkwy., Ste. 545
Atlanta, GA 30338
PH: (770)352-0111
FX: (770)351-0737
E-mail: info@pearlnet.com
URL: http://http://www.pearlnet.com/

Description: Georgia based ISP and web hosting company. Provides a full range of internet services from dialup and ISDN to application and web hosting. Shared web hosting ecommerce packages start at $225/month and include secure server and database driven site with a content management system. Dedicated hosting starts at $875, and managed servers are from $750/month. All packages provide a 99.9% guarenteed uptime.

■ **4612**

PLANETGUIDE.COM

4501 N. I-10 Service Rd. W.
Metairie, LA 70006
PH: (504)888-5384
TF: 888-878-4932
URL: http://www.planetguide.com

Description: Web design, programming and hosting company. Design services can include multimedia, database and ecommerce features. Shared web hosting is available for $49.95/month, dedicated servers start at $249/month. Ecommerce packages offer secure server (SSL) and credit card processing. Ecommerce options can be integrated into exsisting sites with "Buy Now" buttons, or can be tied to database queries. Collocation services are availble starting at $249.

■ **4613**

POC INCORPORATED

125 N. Water Street
Marine City, MI 48039
PH: (810)765-0068
FX: (810)765-0068
E-mail: inquiries@pinnacle-club.com
URL: http://www.pinnacle-club.com/

Description: Web site design and hosting company, also offering ecommerce solutions. Template based sites available for $35/page. Multimedia and database services available. Shared virtual hosting is available on both Linux and Windows2000 servers and range from $25-$95 a month. Ecommerce options such as secure server (SSL) and realtime credit card transactions are available via their PageSecure product (http://www.page-secure.com/) Page secure offers a low cost secure transactions by accessing a remotely hosted shopping cart. Provides an easy solution for small businesses. Sites need not be hosted on their servers to use PageSecure.

■ **4614**

PTI NET

P.O. Box 72215
Fairbanks, AL 99707
TF: 800-784-6384
FX: (907)459-6242
E-mail: service@ptialaska.net
URL: http://www.ptialaska.net/

Description: Alaskan-owned and operated ISP providing statewide dialup and dedicated internet access. Business services include dedicated connections, web hosting and messaging. Includes 30 day money-back guarentee. More information availble by contacting solutions@ptialaska.net.

■ **4615**

QX.NET

333 West Vine St., Ste. 210
Lexington, KY 40507
PH: (859)255-1928
FX: (859)255-1798
E-mail: info@qx.net
URL: http://www.qx.net

Description: Kentuky based ISP and web hosting company. Business internet connectivity options include ISDN, DSL and Frame Relay. Web hosting plans range from $24.95 - $94.95/month and can include a variety of options. Server collocation is available starting at $200 and includes emergency maintenance. Connectivity consulting services are also available.

■ **4616**

RECOL

Long Wharf Maritime Center
555 Long Wharf Drive, 12th Fl.
New Haven, CT 06511
PH: (203)776-4874
FX: (203)776-4943
E-mail: solutions@recol.com
URL: http://www.recol.net/

Description: Connecticut based web hosting and internet service provider. They offer dialup, ISDN, ADSL, and dedicated lines to residential and business customers for highspeed dedicated internet access. Web services include collocation services and dedicated Windows, FreeBSD and Linux Dell servers with 24x7 network monitoring. Web hosting services range from shared virtual hosting for $85/month to dedicated servers with custom programming starting at $395/month. They can provide secure online transactions and remote management and catalog updating tools. Web design and database development services are also available.

■ **4617**

REDMAGNET, INC.

499 Gloster Creek Village, Ste. I-5
Tupelo, MS 38801
PH: (662)840-2992
FX: (662)840-3839
E-mail: info@redmagnet.com
URL: http://http://www.redmagnet.com/
Contact: Richard Kuebler, Sales & Marketing

Description: IT company providing computer networking and repair, training, software development, interactive media and web access and hosting. Hosting plans range from $25 for a basic plan to $175 for ecommerce sites. Ecommerce plans include secure server (SSL). Web design services include multimedia and database connectivity.

∎ 4618
REESER'S WEB DESIGN AND WEBSITE HOSTING

Norman, OK 73071
PH: (405)447-6951
URL: http://www.reesers.com

Description: Web design and hosting company offering design, ecommerce, and search engine submissions. Hosting is provided on RedHat Linux and Windows2000 servers. They offer three ecommerce packages on Linux that include the Miva Merchant shopping cart and range from $44.95-$69.95. Database connectivity if provided with MySQL. Windows2000 hosting plans, which include secure server (SSL) range from $39.95-$119.95/month and provide database connectivity with Access.

∎ 4619
RRACKSPACE MANAGED HOSTING

112 E. Pecan, Ste. 600
San Antonio, TX 78205
TF: 800-961-2888
URL: http://www.rackspace.com

Description: Rackspace is well known for its high quality managed hosting services. They focus mainly on providing dedicated servers to companies who prefer not to maintain their own hardware, but prefer to maintain their own operating systems and software. Additionally they offer monitoring, security, database and backup services as additional products. Their web site offeres assistance in selecting an appropriate level of service, as well as providing live chat with a sales representative to answer questions. They offer %99.999 uptimeand what they term "fanatical" 24x7x365 live technical support.

∎ 4620
RT66 INTERNET

133 Wyatt Dr., Ste. 11
Las Cruces, NM 88005
PH: (505)348-5082
TF: (866)667-8639
E-mail: office@rt66.com
URL: http://www.rt66.com

Description: New Mexico based ISP and web hosting company offering dial-up, dedicated dial-up, ISDN, Web hosting and design, WAN, LAN and Intranet consulting and design. Ecommerce services using Miva Merchant are available for

$50/month. Shared virtual hosting packages on Sun servers range from $20-$60/month.

∎ 4621
SACWEB, INC.

1409 R St.
Sacramento, CA 95814
PH: (916)446-7457
TF: 888-772-2932
FX: (916)448-2702
E-mail: info@sacweb.com
URL: http://www.sacweb.com

Description: SacWeb offers a full range of web hosting and collocation services, including web site and multimedia design, NT or Unix hosting and internet marketing. Their ecommerce services can include realtime credit card authorization, and a large number of payment processors from which to choose. They also provide their own GoCart shopping cart software. Server leasing and management are availble from their "alliance" partners. More information is availabe by emailing info@sacweb.com

∎ 4622
SANTEL INTERNET

308 S. Dumont Ave.
P.O. Box 67
Woonsocket, SD 57385-0067
PH: (605)796-4411
TF: 888-796-4411
FX: (605)796-4419
E-mail: info@santel.net
URL: http://www.santel.net

Description: South Dakota based communitcations company offering internet access, cable tv, long distance services and web hosting. Internet access options include dial-up and high speed wireless for both residential and small business customers. Web design services are offered at $30/hr. A basic storefront can be created for $150 plus $40/month hosting fee. Commercial irtual shared web hosting including secure server(SSL) and Miva script start at $15/month with $100 one time setup fee.

∎ 4623
SOUTHLAND TECHNOLOGIES COMPANY, LLC

3331 Rainbow Dr., Ste. E - 119
Rainbow City, AL 35906-6264
PH: (256)413-1948
TF: 888-806-9795
E-mail: sales@southlandtech.net
URL: http://www.southlandtech.net

Description: An Alabama based ISP providing dialup services and web hosting. Hosting is on Sun servers and offer

24x7 tech support and network monitoring. Basic hosting packages start at \$9.95/month. Packages including secure servers and database access start at \$19.95/month. A 30 Day Satisfaction Guarantee is provided on all hosting packages.

▮ 4624
SPRINT

TF: (866)730-7943
URL: http://www.sprintbiz.com

Description: This telecommunications giant offers everything from highspeed secure internet connections between your global offices, to managed hosting for the small to mid-sized business. They offer a wide array of software, hardware, and support services for managed hosting or collocation services. They can also provide E-commerce, messaging, content management systems. Online live chat with salesand ordering services are availabe from their web site.

▮ 4625
SUCCESSFULHOSTING.COM

3006 Ave. M
Brooklyn, NY 11210
TF: 800-834-8438
FX: (718)258-3419
E-mail: Sales@SuccessfulHosting.com
URL: http://www.successfulhosting.com

Description: SuccessfulHosting provides shared and dedicated hosting on linux servers, with support for FrontPage and active server pages. Their ecommerce package includes SSL, shopping carts, and chat rooms. Databases are MySql. They offer 24x7 tech support and monitoring services. Shared hosting packages range from \$7-\$21/month while dedicated servers range from \$375-\$575/month.

▮ 4626
SUPERB INTERNET

700 W Pender St., 14th Fl.
Vancouver, BC, Canada V6C1G8
PH: (604)638-2525
TF: 888-354-6128
E-mail: GlobalSales@Superb.Net
URL: http://www.superb.net

Description: A national hosting company Superb Internet offers virtual hosting, dedicated hosting, exchange hosting, e-commerce hosting and collocation services. They also over virtual private servers, and reseller programs for those who in turn wish to run a hosting company on their servers. They offer most unix and windows operating systems and a wide variety of current internet software and database options. They boast multiple DS-3 direct connections to internet backbones, allowing for fast connections from most locations. Hosting plans range from \$16 - \$500 monthly. Their

web site provides a large collection of support documentation, along with access to their 24x7 helpdesk.

▮ 4627
TAOSNET

201 Camino de la Merced
Taos, NM
PH: (505)758-7598
E-mail: info@newmex.com,
URL: http://http://www.newmex.com/InternetCenter/Web-Hosting.html

Description: ISP and web hosting company offering services in the Taos area. Internet access services include dial-ip, ISDN, DSL and dedicated T1 wireless connections. Virtual shared web hosting is available from \$10-\$90/month. Ecommerce options using ShopSite are avaialble from \$30-\$250/month depending on services requires. Secure server (SSL) is available for an additional \$15/month. Collocation services are also available starting at \$250/month.

▮ 4628
TGR SOLUTION, INC.

2070 Overland Ave., Ste. 103
Billings, MT 59102
PH: (406)294-6000
TF: (866)484-7638
E-mail: tgrsales@tgrsolution.net
URL: http://https://secure.theglobalroad.com/

Description: Web services company offering access, web design and web hosting. Access services include dial-up, DSL and dedicated T1. Basic hared virtual hosting ranges from \$14.95-\$59.95/month. Ecommerce options are available for an additional cost. Web site design and consulting services also available.

▮ 4629
TOPHOSTS.COM

111 Peter St., Ste. 700
Toronto, ON, Canada M5V2H1
PH: (416)341-8950
FX: (416)341-8959
E-mail: corporate@tophosts.com
URL: http://www.tophosts.com

Description: Tophosts.com is a current directory of web hosting companies. Listings include over 10,000 web hosting companies. Their FastFind database allows users to search by criteria such as hosting platform, disk space requirements and price. Tophosts.com also list what it believes to be the top 25 hosts each month based on production testing and user feedback. Includes listsing for Virtual Private Servers and Collocation services.

▌4630
VIRGINIA.COM

1 Newbury Dr.
Stafford, VA 22554
PH: (540)658-9091
E-mail: sales@virginia.com
URL: http://host.virginia.com/

Description: Provides virtual shared hosting on Windows 2000 platform for individuals, businesses and resellers. Business hosting packages range from $19.95-$49.95/month and include secure server (SSL). Database connectivity using MS Access or SQL server and LaGarde StoreFront 5.0 Shopping Cart are available for an additional fee. All packages come with a 30 day money back guarentee.

▌4631
VIRTUAL HOST PROFESSIONALS

1250 S. Lincoln Ave., Bldg I, Ste. 3
Steamboat Springs, CO 80487
PH: (970)870-0495
TF: (866)727-3261
FX: (970)870-0642
E-mail: info@vhostpro.com
URL: http://

Description: Colorado based web hosting company offering virtual shared web hosting, dedicated servers and collocation services. Shared hosting plans range from $6.95-$24.95/month, and can optionally include SSL (sercure server) and Mysql database for an additional $10 each. Dedicated RedHat Linux or Windows 2000 servers are available for $520-$1200/month, depending on configuration. Dedicated servers can be managed by the user using Webmin or Plesk control panels. Support is available via phone or online trouble tracking system.

▌4632
VOLARIS ONLINE

1101 Greenwood Blvd., Ste. 200
Lake Mary, FL 32746
PH: (407)708-1700
TF: (866)865-2747
E-mail: customerservice@VOL.com
URL: http://www.volaris.com/

Description: Provider of internet connectivity and services. They provide dedicated highspeed lines such as from ISDN and DSL to dedicated T-1 lines. Also provide virtual private networks. Collocation services are available in their own facility starting at $199. Hosting services are provided on Windows 2000 and Solaris 8 platforms on Compaq and Sun hardware. Ecommerce packages include Miva Merchant, database connectivity and credit card processing.

▌4633
VTWEB.COM

PO Box 307
Pawlet, VT 05761
PH: (802)325-6262
FX: (802)325-6263
E-mail: webmaster@vtweb.com
URL: http://www.vtweb.com

Description: Web hosting, design and consulting company. Virtual shared hosting is available on Linux and Windows 2000 platforms. Hosting packages range from $30-$50/month depending on site traffic. Secure server is available for a one-time fee of $75. Shopping cart funtionality is provided by BuyWired.com and is available for a monthly fee. Collocation services are available for $50/month. Also provide web design, programming, consulting and maintenance services.

▌4634
WEB HOST DIRECTORY LTD.

Matrix House
Wick Lane
Christchurch
Dorset BH231HT, United Kingdom
PH: 44 1202 588960
FX: 44 1202 588969
URL: http://www.webhostdir.com/

Description: The Web Host Directory includes both paid advertising and free listings of thousands of web hosting companies. Their database allows searching by multiple criteria to locate hosts that match the needs of a company. E.g. one may limit searches to hosting companies that offer shell access and java servlets. Users may enter comments about their experiences with web hosting companies, and these comments are available to others to read. **Major Partners:** HostCompare.com ; HostingCatalog.com ; HostRecord.com

▌4635
WEB HOST INDUSTRY REVIEW, INC.

552 Church St., Ste. 89
Toronto, ON, Canada M4Y2E3
PH: (416)925-7264
FX: (416)925-9421
E-mail: info@thewhir.net
URL: http://thewhir.com

Description: Web Host Industry Review provides the WHIR web site for web host industry news for both web host sellers and consumers. Along with this news and industry oriented information is a directory of web hosts. The directory, while not very large, provides listings of major web hosting companies, arranged by services and by country. The ''Request a Quote'' service lets users enter the type of hosting in which they are interested and receive a list of quotes within 24 hours. Also provided is a weekly newletter for consumers with tips and advice on web hosting services.

887

▌4636
WEB HOSTING LIVE

1650 Des Peres Rd., Ste. 125
St. Louis, MO 63131
PH: (314)822-3901
TF: (866)808-5483
E-mail: info@whlive.com
URL: http://www.web-hosting-live.com/

Description: Missouri based hosting company offering a wide varity of hosting plans for site large and small. Ecommerce shared hosting plans start at $17.95/month and include SSL (secure server) and StoreFrontNow shopping cart. Miva Merchant is available as an additional product. Dedicated hosting is available starting at $295/month. Collocation services are also available.

▌4637
WEB HOSTING RATINGS

E-mail: webmaster@webhostingratings.com
URL: http://www.webhostingratings.com

Description: While smaller than some other web hosting directories Web Hosting Ratings is free of advertising and does not accept paid inclusions. Currently the database has over 1100 listings, and allows for searching by multiple criteria such as platform and database connectivity options. Included in this directory are several informative essays on topics such as domain names and 'gotchas'. Also includes a useful glossary.

▌4638
WEB HOSTING SOLUTIONS

1311 Darcann Dr.
Columbus, OH 43220
TF: 888-522-3738
E-mail: sales@webhostingsolutions.com
URL: http://www.webhostingsolutions.com

Description: Web hosting company offering shared and virtual private hosting services on unix platform. Small business shared hosting with secure server (SSL) is avaialbe from $34.95/month. Ecommerce hosting using ShopSite is available from $54.95/month. Virtual Private Servers are available on Solaris or FreeBSD platforms from $95-$375/month and include secure server (SSL).

▌4639
WEB PAGE CREATIONS, INC.

4636 Lebanon Pike 144
Hermitage, TN
PH: (615)883-6260
URL: http://http://www.webpagecreation.com/

Description: Web page design company offering design, maintenance and hosting services. Design services can include ecommerce and custom web applications. Virtual shared hosting packages include secure server (SSL). Web site maintenance packages are also available.

▌4640
WEBFOOT DESIGNS, INC

Manteno, IL
PH: (815)468-1524
FX: (815)468-1537
URL: http://www.webfoot-designs.com

Description: Illinois based web site design, development and hosting company. Design packages can include ecommerce options and custom database programming, along with maintenance packages. Virtual hosting plans begin at $19.95, and can include MySQL, Access, MS SQL database access, secure server (SSL) and shopping cart software. Hosting is available on both Windows and Solaris platforms. All packages come with a 99.7% guarenteed uptime.

▌4641
WEBHOSTERS.COM

E-mail: info@webhosters.com
URL: http://www.webhosters.com/

Founded: 1998. **Description:** Webhosters.com is a directory of web hosting companies. Their database is searchable by multiple criteria such as type of service, packages offered, support services, and age of company. Detailed listings and contact info of companies is provided along with customer reviews, which are perhaps the most valuable part of this directory. Advertising is accepted, but limited to banner and sidebar ads, and featured purchase promotions.

▌4642
WEBSERVERINDEX.COM

E-mail: webmaster@webserverindex.com
URL: http://www.webserverindex.com/

Description: WebServerIndex is a directory dedicated to collocated and dedicated server hosting companies. Searching is availble by criteria such as cost, max bandwidth and operating system. Also includes articles on topics such as "choosing a dedicated server" and "the difference between collocation and dedicated hosting."

▌4643
WEBWORKS WEB SOLUTIONS

150 Peter Creek Pass
Tumbling Shoals, AR 72581
E-mail: info@webworks1.net

URL: http://webworks1.net/

Description: Arkansa based web design and hosting company. Offers complete web site design and maintenance icluding digital photography or hosting services only. Also offers web search engine positioning services.

▌ 4644
WESTHOST, INC.

P.O. Box 6246
Logan, UT 84341-6246
PH: 800-222-2165
E-mail: Info@WestHost.com
URL: http://www.westhost.com

Description: Utah based web hosting company providing shared virtual hosting on RedHat Linux platform with the Apache server. Basic hosting packages range from $8.95-$29.95/month and include secure server (SSL). Ecommerce packages with Miva Merchant are available for $34.95/month.

▌ 4645
WIWORKS WEB DESIGN & WEB HOSTING

9710 S. 700 E., Ste. 205
Sandy, UT 84070
PH: (801)501-7500
TF: 800-727-1485

FX: (801)501-7556
E-mail: sales@wiworks.com
URL: http://www.wiworks.com

Description: Web design and hosting company offering hosting on linux servers. Web design services offer an ecommerce package including up to 15 pages, 3 months of web hosting, shopping cart and credit card transactions for $1150. Ecommerce virtual shared hosting package includes secure credit card processing and 2 years of domain registration. The Dansie Shopping Cart is available for $249. Search engine marketing and placement services also available.

▌ 4646
WWW.SPEEDYWEB.COM

TF: 888-416-4678
E-mail: sales@speedyweb.com
URL: http://www.speedyweb.com

Description: Speedyweb provides shared hosting, dedicated servers, virtual dedicated servers, ecommerce and ebusiness packages on both windows and linux platforms. They included popular standard database packages and shopping cart services, along with email, cgi and secure server options. All packages are guaranteed at 99.9% uptime, 24x7 technical support, and offer a 30 day money back guarantee. Basic ecommerce sites with shopping cart services on a shared server range from $20-$50/month. Virtual dedicated servers range from $70-$200/month. Dedicated servers range from $600-$1300/month depending on hardware and other services required, such as bandwidth requirements and secure servers.

Directory of Leading E-Commerce Companies

This section lists the leading e-commerce companies worldwide. Listings are arranged alphabetically with complete contact information and description. Revenue is in US$ millions.

▌1

1-800-FLOWERS.COM INC.

1600 Stewart Ave.
Westbury, NY 11590
PH: (516)237-6000
URL: http://www.1800flowers.com
Contact: Ken Young, Media/PR Officer

Founded: 1976. **Annual Revenue:** US$497. **Employees:** 2400. **Description:** Retail: Flowers and gifts sold through toll free number and internet.

▌2

3COM CORP.

5400 Bayfront Plz.
Santa Clara, CA 95052-8145
PH: (408)326-5000
E-mail: investor_relations@3com.com
URL: http://www.3com.com

Founded: 1979. **Annual Revenue:** US$1,478. **Employees:** 4615. **Description:** Manufacturing: Electronic switches, adapters and network components, data communications and networking business software.

▌3

24/7 REAL MEDIA INC.

1250 Broadway
New York, NY 10001
PH: (212)231-7100
URL: http://www.247media.com

Founded: 1997. **Annual Revenue:** US$52. **Employees:** 308. **Description:** Services: Global internet media and multi-platform technology company, marketing and advertising.

▌4

AFFINITY INTERNET INC.

101 Continental Blvd., 3rd Fl.
El Segundo, CA 90245
PH: (310)524-3000
URL: http://www.affinity.com
Contact: Pat Donohoe, Director of Product Management

Founded: 1999. **Description:** Services: Provider of domain name registration, web hosting, eCommerce, dedicated servers and advanced hosting services for small- and medium-sized business customers, resellers and private-label partners.

▌5

AGENCY.COM LTD.

20 Exchange Pl., 15th Fl.
New York, NY 10005
PH: (212)358-2600
E-mail: info@agency.com
URL: http://www.agency.com

Founded: 1995. **Annual Revenue:** US$202. **Employees:** 1500. **Description:** Services: Marketing and technology agency.

▌6

AIR PRODUCTS AND CHEMICALS INC.

7201 Hamilton Blvd.
Allentown, PA 18195-1501
PH: (610)481-4911
E-mail: info@apci.com
URL: http://www.airproducts.com

Founded: 1940. **Annual Revenue:** US$5,717. **Employees:** 17800. **Description:** Manufacturing: Industrial gases including oxygen, nitrogen, argon, hydrogen, carbon monoxide, carbon dioxide and helium and industrial organic and inorganic chemicals and equipment for cryogenic air separation, gas processing, natural gas liquefaction and hydrogen purification.

▌7

AKAMAI TECHNOLOGIES INC.

500 Technology Sq.
Cambridge, MA 02139
PH: (617)250-3000
E-mail: info@akamai.com
URL: http://www.akamai.com

Founded: 1998. **Annual Revenue:** US$163. **Employees:** 841. **Description:** Services: Provider of e-business systems infrastructure, distributed application, content delivery services and related software products.

■ **8**

ALASKA AIRLINES INC.

PO Box 68947
Seattle, WA 98168
PH: (206)431-7079
URL: http://www.alaska-air.com

Founded: 1932. **Annual Revenue:** US$1,751. **Employees:** 11025. **Description:** Transportation: Provider of scheduled air services.

■ **9**

ALLTEL COMMUNICATIONS CO.

PO Box 400
Cornelia, GA 30531
PH: (706)778-2201
URL: http://www.alltel.com

Founded: 1904. **Annual Revenue:** US$3,150. **Employees:** 300. **Description:** Communications: Telephone communications.

■ **10**

ALTICOR INC.

7575 Fulton St. E
Ada, MI 49355
FX: (616)682-4000
E-mail: mediainfo@alticor.com
URL: http://www.alticor.com

Founded: 2000. **Annual Revenue:** US$4,100. **Employees:** 10000. **Description:** Finance: Holding company for direct sales companies.

■ **11**

AMAZON.COM INC.

PO Box 81226
Seattle, WA 98108-8126
PH: (206)266-1000
E-mail: info@amazon.com
URL: http://www.amazon.com
Contact: Bill Curry, Public Relations Department

Founded: 1995. **Annual Revenue:** US$3,122. **Employees:** 7800. **Description:** Retail: Virtual online retailer selling items including books, music, DVDs, videos, electronics, software, video games and home improvement products. Services: information database.

■ **12**

AMERITRADE INC.

PO Box 2760
Omaha, NE 68103-2760
PH: (402)970-5805
URL: http://www.ameritrade.com

Founded: 1975. **Annual Revenue:** US$655. **Employees:** 2573. **Description:** Finance: Provider of online brokerage services. Services: Developer of prepackaged stock broker financial software.

■ **13**

AOL TIME WARNER INC.

75 Rockefeller Plz.
New York, NY 10019
PH: (212)484-8000
URL: http://www.aoltimewarner.com
Contact: Edward I. Adler, Senior Vice President, Corporate Communications

Founded: 1985. **Annual Revenue:** US$38,234. **Employees:** 88500. **Description:** Services: Provider of online services including electronic mail, Internet access, news, magazines, sports, weather, stock quotes, mutual fund transactions, software files, computing support and online classes. Movie, video, music production and distribution. Publishing: Periodical publisher. Communications: Cable television programming. Finance: Holding company.

■ **14**

APPLE COMPUTER INC.

1 Infinite Loop
Cupertino, CA 95014
PH: (408)996-1010
URL: http://www.apple.com

Founded: 1977. **Annual Revenue:** US$5,363. **Employees:** 11434. **Description:** Manufacturing: Develops, manufactures and licenses computer products and technology for business, education, consumer, science, engineering and government. Services: Developer of computer software.

■ **15**

APTIMUS INC.

95 S Jackson St., Ste. 300
Seattle, WA 98104
PH: (206)441-9100
URL: http://www.aptimus.com
Contact: John Wade, CFO

Founded: 1994. **Annual Revenue:** US$2. **Employees:** 28. **Description:** Services: Direct marketer via internet. Offers promotional items from over 400 various clients.

∎ 16
ARROW ELECTRONICS INC.
25 Hub Dr.
Melville, NY 11747-3509
PH: (516)391-1300
URL: http://www.arrow.com
Contact: Robert E. Klatell, Executive Vice President

Founded: 1946. **Annual Revenue:** US$10,128. **Employees:** 12200. **Description:** Wholesale: Electronic components, systems and computer products for industrial and commercial customers.

∎ 17
ASHFORD.COM INC.
3800 Buffalo Speedway, Ste. 400
Houston, TX 77098
PH: (713)369-1300
E-mail: sales@ashford.com
URL: http://www.ashford.com

Annual Revenue: US$67. **Employees:** 234. **Description:** Retail: Web-based retailer focused exclusively on luxury and premium products like watches, fine writing instruments, fragrances, sunglasses and other luxury goods.

∎ 18
ASHLAND INC.
PO Box 391
Covington, KY 41012-0391
PH: (859)815-3333
E-mail: ashland@ashland.com
URL: http://www.ashland.com
Contact: Robert C. Hughes, Investor Relations

Founded: 1936. **Annual Revenue:** US$7,719. **Employees:** 25100. **Description:** Manufacturing: Petroleum refining, distribution, specialty chemicals, oil and car care products. Services: Research and development laboratory. Mining: Coal. Construction: Highways.

∎ 19
ASK JEEVES INC.
5858 Horton St., Ste. 350
Emeryville, CA 94608
PH: (510)985-7400
E-mail: jeeves@askjeeves.com
URL: http://www.ask.com
Contact: Michele Mehl, Sr. Manager, Communications Strategy and Development

Founded: 1996. **Annual Revenue:** US$67. **Employees:** 416. **Description:** Services: Provides a Web-based question and answer service.

∎ 20
AURORA CASKET COMPANY INC.
10944 Marsh Rd.
Aurora, IN 47001
PH: (812)926-1111
URL: http://www.auroracasket.com

Founded: 1890. **Description:** Manufacturing: Manufactures caskets; metal stampings, cutting and shearing services

∎ 21
AUTOWEB.COM INC.
3270 Jay St.
Santa Clara, CA 95054
PH: (408)970-9100
URL: http://www.autoweb.com

Founded: 1995. **Annual Revenue:** US$52. **Employees:** 152. **Description:** Retail: New and used automobiles on the Internet.

∎ 22
AVENUE A INC.
506 Second Ave., 9th Fl.
Seattle, WA 98104
PH: (206)521-8800
E-mail: info@avenuea.com
URL: http://www.avenuea.com
Contact: Angela Gamba, Public Relations Manager

Founded: 1997. **Annual Revenue:** US$90. **Employees:** 230. **Description:** Services: Internet advertising services.

∎ 23
BACKWEB TECHNOLOGIES LTD.
PO Box 3581
52136 Ramat Gan, Israel
PH: 972 3 6118800
E-mail: info@backweb.com
URL: http://www.backweb.com

Founded: 1995. **Annual Revenue:** US$21. **Employees:** 180. **Description:** Services: Provider of personalized information delivered through channels over the Internet, developer of enterprise push software.

∎ 24
BARNES AND NOBLE INC.
122 5th Ave.
New York, NY 10011
PH: (212)633-3300
URL: http://www.barnesandnobleinc.com
Contact: Mary Ellen Keating, Senior Vice President, Corporate Communications & Public Affairs

Founded: 1873. **Annual Revenue:** US$4,870. **Employees:** 45000. **Description:** Retail: Book store chains and direct marketer of books. Finance: Holding company.

▌ 25

BE FREE INC.

154 Crane Meadow Rd., Ste. 100
Marlborough, MA 01752
E-mail: help@befree.com
URL: http://www.befree.com
Contact: Jennifer Roy, Director of Public Relations

Founded: 1996. **Annual Revenue:** US$23. **Employees:** 165. **Description:** Services: Provides targeted marketing technology through license and service agreemtns and providing high traffic Internets sites with syndicated content.

▌ 26

BELLSOUTH CORP.

1155 Peachtree St. NE
Atlanta, GA 30309-3610
PH: (404)249-2000
URL: http://www.bellsouthcorp.com
Contact: Jeff Battcher, BellSouth Media Relations

Annual Revenue: US$29,589. **Employees:** 87875. **Description:** Communications: Directory publishing and digital wireless communication systems. Finance: holding company.

▌ 27

BERTELSMANN INC.

1540 Broadway Fl. 24
New York, NY 10036
PH: (212)782-1000
URL: http://www.bertelsmann.com

Founded: 1975. **Annual Revenue:** US$12. **Employees:** 50. **Description:** Manufacturing: Book publishing

▌ 28

BEYOND.COM CORP.

3200 Patrick Henry Dr.
Santa Clara, CA 95054
FX: (408)327-6400
URL: http://www.beyond.com

Founded: 1998. **Annual Revenue:** US$120. **Employees:** 169. **Description:** Services: Developer of software for website design, construction, transaction processing, electronic ordering, marketing and merchandising and government systems.

▌ 29

BINGO.COM INC.

1166 Alberni St., Ste. 1405
Vancouver, Canada V6E3Z3
PH: (604)694-0300
URL: http://www.bingo.com

Founded: 1987. **Annual Revenue:** US$2. **Employees:** 6. **Description:** Services: Computer bingo services.

▌ 30

BLOCKBUSTER INC.

1201 Elm St.
Dallas, TX 75270
PH: (214)854-3000
URL: http://www.blockbuster.com

Founded: 1982. **Annual Revenue:** US$4,960. **Employees:** 89700. **Description:** Services: Video rental store chain. Finance: Franchiser of video rental store chain. Retail: Music store chain.

▌ 31

BLUEFLY INC.

42 W 39th St., 9th Fl.
New York, NY 10018
PH: (212)944-8000
E-mail: flyrep@bluefly.com
URL: http://www.bluefly.com

Founded: 1991. **Annual Revenue:** US$23. **Employees:** 66. **Description:** Retail: Internet retailer of designer fashions at outlet store prices.

▌ 32

BOISE CASCADE CORP.

PO Box 50
Boise, ID 83728-0001
PH: (208)384-6161
E-mail: bcweb@bc.com
URL: http://www.bc.com

Founded: 1957. **Annual Revenue:** US$7,422. **Employees:** 24168. **Description:** Manufacturing: Pulp and paper products, plywood and lumber specialty products, beams, engineered wood products, particle board and oriental strand board.

▌ 33

BURLINGTON NORTHERN SANTA FE CORP.

PO Box 961057
Fort Worth, TX 76161-0057
PH: (817)333-2000
E-mail: steven.forsberg@bnsf.com
URL: http://www.bnsf.com

Founded: 1995. **Annual Revenue:** US$9,208. **Employees:** 39000. **Description:** Transportation: Line-haul freight railroad. Finance: Holding company.

▌34
BUY.COM INC.

21 Brookline
Aliso Viejo, CA 92656
PH: (949)389-2000
URL: http://www.buy.com

Founded: 1996. **Annual Revenue:** US$788. **Employees:** 258. **Description:** Retail: Computers, software, books, vidoes, and games at low cost through a web based service.

▌35
CDW COMPUTER CENTERS INC.

200 N Milwaukee Ave.
Vernon Hills, IL 60061
PH: (847)465-6000
E-mail: Sales@web.cdw.com
URL: http://www.cdw.com

Founded: 1982. **Annual Revenue:** US$3,962. **Employees:** 2700. **Description:** Retail: Direct marketer of microcomputer products, including including hardware and peripherals, software, networking/communication products and accessories.

▌36
CENDANT CORP.

9 W 57th St.
New York, NY 10019
PH: (212)413-1800
URL: http://www.cendant.com
Contact: Sam Levinson, Senior Vice President Inveator Relations

Annual Revenue: US$8,950. **Employees:** 53000. **Description:** Finance: Franchisor of real estate offices, hotels and holding company. Services: Car rental, fleet management and tax preparation.

▌37
CFSB BANCORP INC.

112 E Allegan St.
Lansing, MI 48933
PH: (517)371-2911
Contact: Robert H. Becker, CEO/President

Founded: 1989. **Annual Revenue:** US$880. **Employees:** 279. **Description:** Finance: Bank holding company for state-chartered savings bank.

▌38
CHARLES SCHWAB AND CO. INC.

101 Montgomery St.
San Francisco, CA 94104
PH: (415)627-7000
E-mail: help@schwab.com
URL: http://www.schwab.com

Founded: 1971. **Annual Revenue:** US$2,839. **Employees:** 12000. **Description:** Finance: Securities brokerage, trading, investment advice, investment and financial products.

▌39
CHINADOTCOM CORP.

20/F Citicorp Ctr., 18 Whitfield Rd.
Causeway Bay, Hong Kong
PH: 852 2893 8200
E-mail: contact@hk.china.com
URL: http://www.corp.china.com

Founded: 1999. **Annual Revenue:** US$76. **Description:** Services: Provider of online services and gateway to the Internet.

▌40
CIENA CORP.

1201 Winterson Rd.
Linthicum, MD 21090-2205
PH: (410)694-5700
URL: http://www.ciena.com
Contact: Denny Bilter

Founded: 1996. **Annual Revenue:** US$1,603. **Employees:** 3778. **Description:** Manufacturing: Fiber optic communications equipment, including dense wave division multiplexers for communications service providers.

▌41
CISCO SYSTEMS INC.

170 W Tasman Dr.
San Jose, CA 95134-1706
PH: (408)526-4000
E-mail: rojenkins@cisco.com
URL: http://www.cisco.com
Contact: Claudia Ceniceros, PR director

Founded: 1984. **Annual Revenue:** US$18,915. **Employees:** 38000. **Description:** Manufacturing: Manufactures, develops and supports high performance, multi protocol Internetworking systems that link LAN and WAN networks.

▌42
CMGI INC.

100 Brickstone Sq.
Andover, MA 01810
PH: (978)684-3600
E-mail: jstevens@cmgi.com

URL: http://www.cmgi.com
Contact: Catherine Taylor, Investor Relations

Founded: 1986. **Annual Revenue:** US$1,238. **Employees:** 3584. **Description:** Services: Provider of direct marketing services, mailing list compilers and Internet service providers.

▌43
CNET NETWORKS INC.

235 2nd St.
San Francisco, CA 94108
PH: (415)344-2000
URL: http://www.cnet.com

Founded: 1992. **Annual Revenue:** US$286. **Employees:** 2000. **Description:** Services: Developer of World Wide Web sites and producer of television programming.

▌44
COBALT GROUP INC.

2200 First Ave. S, Ste. 400
Seattle, WA 98134-1408
PH: (206)269-6363
E-mail: info@cobaltgroup.com
URL: http://www.cobaltgroup.com

Founded: 1995. **Annual Revenue:** US$55. **Employees:** 602. **Description:** Services: Designs and maintains Internet sites for automobile dealerships, provider of e-commerce business-to-business site dealing in auto parts for new and used car dealers.

▌45
COLLECTORS UNIVERSE INC.

1936 E Deere Ave.
Santa Ana, CA 92705
PH: (949)567-1234
URL: http://www.collectors.com

Founded: 1986. **Annual Revenue:** US$45. **Employees:** 226. **Description:** Services: Internet-based auctions and premium auctions.

▌46
COMCAST CORP.

1500 Market St.
Philadelphia, PA 19102-2148
PH: (215)665-1700
URL: http://www.comcast.com

Founded: 1963. **Annual Revenue:** US$38,132. **Employees:** 38000. **Description:** Communications: Cable television and Internet and cellular communications services. Services: Professional ice hockey teams. Retail: Web-based shopping. Finance: Holding company.

▌47
CORIO INC.

959 Skyway Rd., Ste. 100
San Carlos, CA 94070
PH: (650)232-3000
E-mail: marketing@corio.com
URL: http://www.corio.com

Founded: 1988. **Annual Revenue:** US$50. **Employees:** 308. **Description:** Services: Remote application management service provider.

▌48
CROSSWALK.COM INC.

4100 LaFayette Center Dr., Ste. 110
Chantilly, VA 20151-1200
PH: (703)968-4808
E-mail: info@crosswalk.com
URL: http://www.crosswalk.com

Founded: 1993. **Annual Revenue:** US$5. **Employees:** 30. **Description:** Services: Developer of Christian web sites.

▌49
CYBERIAN OUTPOST INC.

PO Box 636
Kent, CT 06757
PH: (860)927-2050
E-mail: press@outpost.com
URL: http://www.outpost.com

Founded: 1995. **Annual Revenue:** US$355. **Employees:** 345. **Description:** Retail: Retailer of computers and accessories, software, consumer electronics, cameras.

▌50
CYBERSOURCE CORP.

1295 Charleston Rd.
Mountain View, CA 94043
PH: (650)965-6000
URL: http://www.cybersource.com
Contact: Jennifer Jennings

Founded: 1994. **Annual Revenue:** US$31. **Employees:** 178. **Description:** Services: Provider of Internet commerce services.

▌51
DELL COMPUTER CORP.

807 Las Cimas Pkwy.
Austin, TX 78746
PH: (512)338-4400
E-mail: info@dell.com
URL: http://www.dell.com
Contact: Elizabeth Helle Allen, Vice President, Corporate Communications

Founded: 1984. **Annual Revenue:** US$31,888. **Employees:** 40000. **Description:** Manufacturing: Computers and printers.

∎ 52

DELTA AIR LINES INC.

PO Box 20706
Atlanta, GA 30320-6001
PH: (404)715-2600
URL: http://www.delta.com
Contact: Thomas J. Slocum, Corporate Communications

Founded: 1924. **Annual Revenue:** US$13,879. **Employees:** 76273. **Description:** Transportation: Scheduled air carrier for both passengers and freight.

∎ 53

DENNIS INTERACTIVE

1040 Ave. of the Americas, 22nd Fl.
New York, NY 10018
PH: (212)372-3884
E-mail: cherry@dennisinter.com
URL: http://www.dennisinter.com

Employees: 10. **Description:** Manufacturing: The company develops software for third party kiosks, CD-ROMs, DVDs and web sites.

∎ 54

DIGITAL IMPACT INC.

177 Bovet Rd.
San Mateo, CA 94402
PH: (650)356-3400
E-mail: info@digitalimpact.com
URL: http://www.digitalimpact.com

Founded: 1997. **Annual Revenue:** US$39. **Employees:** 389. **Description:** Services: provider of online direct marketing solutions.

∎ 55

DIGITAL INSIGHT CORP.

26025 Mureau Rd.
Calabasas, CA 91302
TF: 888-344-4674
URL: http://www.digitalinsight.com

Founded: 1995. **Annual Revenue:** US$95. **Employees:** 738. **Description:** Services: Internet banking services to credit unions, banks and savings and loans.

∎ 56

DIGITAL ISLAND

45 Fremont St., 12th Fl.
San Francisco, CA 94105

PH: (415)738-4100
E-mail: info@digitalisland.net
URL: http://www.digitalisland.net

Founded: 1995. **Annual Revenue:** US$59. **Employees:** 900. **Description:** Services: Digital Island's services includes global content distribution and hosting, the localization of end user online experiences, and a reliable Intelligent Network. They are a provider of network services for globalizing e-Business applications.

∎ 57

DIGITAL RIVER INC.

9625 W 76th St.
Eden Prairie, MN 55344-3765

Description: Services: Electrical and scientific apparatus

∎ 58

DIGITALTHINK INC.

601 Brannan St.
San Francisco, CA 94107
TF: 888-686-8817
E-mail: info@digitalthink.com
URL: http://www.digitalthink.com

Founded: 1996. **Annual Revenue:** US$43. **Employees:** 464. **Description:** Services: Provider of Web-based training courses and technology.

∎ 59

DOUBLECLICK INC.

450 W 33rd St.
New York, NY 10001
FX: (212)889-0062
E-mail: info@doubleclick.net
URL: http://www.doubleclick.net
Contact: Jennifer Blum

Founded: 1996. **Annual Revenue:** US$406. **Employees:** 1929. **Description:** Services: Internet advertising agency and developer of direct marketing software, online marketing site.

∎ 60

DOW CHEMICAL CO.

2030 Dow Ctr.
Midland, MI 48674-2030
PH: (989)636-1000
URL: http://www.dow.com
Contact: Leslie Hatfield, Global Media Relations

Founded: 1897. **Annual Revenue:** US$27,805. **Employees:** 50000. **Description:** Manufacturing: Organic and inorganic industrial chemicals, extruded, laminated, foam and thermoforming plastics, plastic pipes and valves. Finance: holding company.

∎ 61

DOW JONES AND COMPANY INC.

105 Madison Ave., 10th Fl.
New York, NY 10016
PH: (646)742-3504
E-mail: newswires@dowjones.com
URL: http://www.dowjones.com/corp

Founded: 1882. **Annual Revenue:** US$1,773. **Employees:** 8100. **Description:** Manufacturing: Financial and electronic newspaper and magazine publishing.

∎ 62

DRUGSTORE.COM INC.

13920 SE Eastgate Way, Ste. 300
Bellevue, WA 98005
PH: (425)372-3200
E-mail: info@drugstore.com
URL: http://www.drugstore.com

Founded: 1998. **Annual Revenue:** US$145. **Employees:** 379. **Description:** Retail: Health and beauty products, including prescriptions through a web-based service.

∎ 63

DYNEGY INC.

PO Box 4777
Houston, TX 77210
PH: (713)507-6400
E-mail: ir@dynegy.com
URL: http://www.dynegy.com
Contact: Deborah Fiorito, Executive Vice President and Chief Communications Officer

Founded: 1984. **Annual Revenue:** US$42,242. **Employees:** 61000. **Description:** Manufacturing: Power generation and wholesale and direct commercial and industrial marketing and trading of power, natural gas, coal, emission allowances and weather derivatives to transportation, gathering and processing of natural gas liquids. Communictions: Broadband.

∎ 64

E-FUNDS CORP.

1391 Warner Ave.
Tustin, CA 92780-6442
PH: (714)259-5266
Contact: Chris Duliga, Marketing & Sales Manager

Founded: 1993. **Annual Revenue:** US$4. **Employees:** 30. **Description:** Services: Developer of electronic banking software.

∎ 65

E-LOAN INC.

5875 Arnold Rd., Ste. 100
Dublin, CA 94568

TF: 888-356-2622
URL: http://www.e-loan.com

Founded: 1996. **Annual Revenue:** US$211. **Employees:** 436. **Description:** Services: Mortgage banking and related services.

∎ 66

EARTHLINK INC.

1375 Peachtree St., Level A
Atlanta, GA 30309
URL: http://www.earthlink.net
Contact: Debra Thomas, Media Relations

Founded: 1994. **Annual Revenue:** US$1,245. **Employees:** 6736. **Description:** Services: Internet provider.

∎ 67

EASTMAN CHEMICAL CO.

PO Box 511
Kingsport, TN 37662-5075
PH: (423)229-2000
E-mail: ebusiness@eastman.com
URL: http://www.eastman.com
Contact: Betty V. DeVinney, VP Communications

Founded: 1920. **Annual Revenue:** US$5,384. **Employees:** 15800. **Description:** Manufacturing: Manufacturer of polyester plastics and specialty chemicals for the pharmeceutical and agricultural industries.

∎ 68

EBAY INC.

2145 Hamilton Ave.
San Jose, CA 95125
PH: (408)558-7400
E-mail: investor_relations@ebay.com
URL: http://www.ebay.com

Founded: 1995. **Annual Revenue:** US$749. **Employees:** 2560. **Description:** Sevices: Provider of Internet marketplace for the sale/auction of goods and services by individuals and businesses.

∎ 69

EBENX INC.

605 N Hwy., 169, Ste. LL
Minneapolis, MN 55441-6465
PH: (763)614-2000
E-mail: info@ebenx.com
URL: http://www.ebenx.com

Founded: 1993. **Annual Revenue:** US$37. **Employees:** 495. **Description:** Services: Specialized technology-based solutions for the administration of health and welfare benefit programs.

▌70

ECOLLEGE.COM

10200 A E Girard Ave.
Denver, CO 80231
TF: 888-884-7325
URL: http://www.ecollege.com

Founded: 1996. **Annual Revenue:** US$20. **Employees:** 223. **Description:** Services: Technology that enables online environment for distance and on-campus learning.

▌71

EDGAR ONLINE INC.

50 Washington St., 9th Fl.
Norwalk, CT 06854
TF: 800-416-6651
URL: http://www.edgar-online.com

Founded: 1987. **Annual Revenue:** US$17. **Employees:** 99. **Description:** Services: Provider of stock information via electronic filings.

▌72

EGAIN COMMUNICATIONS CORP.

714 E Evelyn Ave.
Sunnyvale, CA 94086
PH: (408)212-3400
URL: http://www.egain.com
Contact: Anne Carr

Founded: 1997. **Annual Revenue:** US$53. **Employees:** 595. **Description:** Services: Developer of e-commerce customer service software solutions for the Internet.

▌73

EGGHEAD.COM INC.

1350 Willow Rd.
Menlo Park, CA 94025
PH: (650)470-2400
URL: http://www.egghead.com

Founded: 1994. **Annual Revenue:** US$479. **Employees:** 653. **Description:** Retail: Reseller of computer hardware, software, and peripherals through retail stores, the Internet and catalogs. Finance: Holding company.

▌74

ELECTRONIC ARTS INC.

209 Redwood Shores Pky.
Redwood City, CA 94065-1175
PH: (650)628-1500
URL: http://www.ea.com

Founded: 1982. **Annual Revenue:** US$1,725. **Employees:** 3500. **Description:** Services: Diversified interactive entertainment company, develops and publishes video and computer games.

▌75

EMERGE INTERACTIVE INC.

10315 102nd Ter.
Sebastian, FL 32958
TF: 877-578-2333
E-mail: info@emergeinteractive.com
URL: http://www.emergeinteractive.com
Contact: Juris Pagrabs, Exec VP, CFO

Founded: 1994. **Annual Revenue:** US$1,195. **Employees:** 287. **Description:** Services: Information and business tools for livestock producers via the internet, auction houses, livestock facilities design, livestock marketing.

▌76

ENGAGE INC.

100 Brickstone Sq., 2nd Fl.
Andover, MA 01810
TF: 877-836-4243
E-mail: info@engage.com
URL: http://www.engage.com
Contact: Kimberly A. Robinson

Founded: 1995. **Annual Revenue:** US$43. **Employees:** 279. **Description:** Services: Developer of online marketing software. Computer related services.

▌77

ENTERASYS NETWORKS INC.

PO Box 5005
Rochester, NH 03866
PH: (603)332-9400
E-mail: financial@enterasys.com
URL: http://www.cabletron.com

Founded: 1983. **Annual Revenue:** US$977. **Employees:** 2600. **Description:** Manufacturing: Manufactures computer communications equipment.

▌78

ENTRUST TECHNOLOGIES INC.

1 Hanover Pk., 16633 Dallas Pky., Ste. 800
Addison, TX 75001
TF: 888-690-2424
E-mail: entrust@entrust.com
URL: http://www.entrust.com

Founded: 1996. **Annual Revenue:** US$118. **Employees:** 792. **Description:** Services: Developer of security and privacy systems for data communications.

▌79

EPRISE CORP.

200 Crossing Blvd.
Framingham, MA 01702
PH: (508)661-5200
URL: http://www.eprise.com

Founded: 1992. **Annual Revenue:** US$19. **Employees:** 216. **Description:** Services: Software, professional services, and partnerships for web page design.

▌80

ESPEED INC.

135 E 57th St.
New York, NY 10022
PH: (212)938-5000
E-mail: info@espeed.com
URL: http://www.espeed.com

Founded: 1999. **Annual Revenue:** US$125. **Employees:** 312. **Description:** Services: Electronic securities trading. Manufactures: e-trading software.

▌81

E*TRADE GROUP INC.

4500 Bohannon Dr.
Menlo Park, CA 94025
PH: (650)331-6000
E-mail: ir@etrade.com
URL: http://www.etrade.com

Founded: 1982. **Annual Revenue:** US$1,275. **Employees:** 3495. **Description:** Finance: Online discount securities brokerage firm and holding company.

▌82

EUNIVERSE INC.

6300 Wilshire Blvd., Ste 1700
Los Angeles, CA 90048
PH: (310)215-1001
E-mail: ads@euniverse.com
URL: http://www.euniverse.com

Founded: 1999. **Annual Revenue:** US$33. **Employees:** 146. **Description:** Communications: Interactive Internet media entertainment.

▌83

EVOLVE SOFTWARE INC.

1400 65th St., Ste. 100
Emeryville, CA 94608
PH: (510)428-6000
E-mail: info@evolve.com
URL: http://www.evolve.com
Contact: Andrew Carothers

Founded: 1995. **Annual Revenue:** US$35. **Employees:** 258. **Description:** Services: Developer of professional services automation software.

▌84

EXPEDIA INC.

13810 SE Eastgate Way, Ste. 400
Bellevue, WA 98005
PH: (425)564-7200
URL: http://www.expedia.com

Founded: 1999. **Annual Revenue:** US$222. **Employees:** 896. **Description:** Transportation: Travel planning services, airline reservations, car rental and hotel reservations via the internet.

▌85

FAIRMARKET INC.

500 Unicorn Park Dr.
Woburn, MA 01801-3341
TF: 800-531-7871
E-mail: info@fairmarket.com
URL: http://www.fairmarket.com
Contact: Mark Sutton, Public Relations

Founded: 1997. **Annual Revenue:** US$9. **Employees:** 68. **Description:** Services: On-line auction host and e-commerce services.

▌86

FASTNET CORP.

3864 Courtney St., Ste. 130, Two Courntey Pl.
Bethlehem, PA 18017
PH: (610)266-6700
E-mail: corp@fast.net
URL: http://www.fast.com

Annual Revenue: US$13. **Employees:** 123. **Description:** Services: Fastnet is an Internet service provider offering Internet access and enhanced services to a broad range of business and individual customers. Their suite of business products is comprised of reliable dedicated Internet access - our core product - enhanced by other services including managed security, web hosting and colocation, unified messaging and Virtual Private Networks.

▌87

FEDERATED DEPARTMENT STORES INC.

7 W Seventh St.
Cincinnati, OH 45202
PH: (513)579-7000
URL: http://www.federated-fds.com
Contact: Susan Robinson, Investor Relations

Founded: 1929. **Annual Revenue:** US$15,651. **Employees:** 129000. **Description:** Retail: Department store chains, mail-order house, specialty and clearance stores.

▌88

FEDEX CORP.

942 S Shady Grove Rd.
Memphis, TN 38120

PH: (901)369-3600
E-mail: webmaster@fedex.com
URL: http://www.fedex.com
Contact: T. Michael Glenn, Executive Vice President,
Market Develop

Founded: 1971. **Annual Revenue:** US$20,607. **Employees:** 215000. **Description:** Transportation: Worldwide package delivery, courier services, long distance trucking and air chartering. Finance: Holding company.

∎ 89
FINDWHAT.COM INC.

121 W 27th St., 9th Fl.
New York, NY 10001
PH: (212)255-1500
URL: http://www.findwhat.com

Founded: 1999. **Annual Revenue:** US$20. **Employees:** 74. **Description:** Services: Internet search engine and web site enhancement services.

∎ 90
FREEMARKETS INC.

FreeMarkets Center, 210 6th Ave.
Pittsburgh, PA 15222
PH: (412)434-0500
URL: http://www.freemarkets.com

Founded: 1995. **Annual Revenue:** US$148. **Employees:** 1000. **Description:** Services: Provider of online marketplace for industrial parts and raw materials.

∎ 91
FROST AND SULLIVAN INC.

1040 E Brokaw Rd.
San Jose, CA 95131-2309
PH: (408)392-2000
E-mail: dfrigstad@frost.com
URL: http://www.frost.com

Founded: 1961. **Annual Revenue:** US$267. **Employees:** 700. **Description:** Services: Marketing consulting firm.

∎ 92
FTD.COM INC.

3113 Woodcreek Dr.
Downers Grove, IL 60515
PH: (630)724-6200
URL: http://www.ftd.com

Founded: 1993. **Annual Revenue:** US$130. **Employees:** 97. **Description:** Retail: Internet and telephone marketing company for same day delivery of florist arrangements.

∎ 93
GANNETT COMPANY INC.

1100 Wilson Blvd., 28th Fl.
Arlington, VA 22234
PH: (703)284-6000
URL: http://www.gannett.com

Founded: 1906. **Annual Revenue:** US$6,344. **Employees:** 51500. **Description:** Manufacturing: Newspaper and magazine publishing. Communications: Television broadcasting stations. Services: Informational retrieval, advertising, marketing and telemarketing. Finance: Holding company.

∎ 94
GAP INC.

2 Folsom St,
San Francisco, CA 94105
PH: (650)952-4400
URL: http://www.gap.com
Contact: Michele Weaver, Director, Investor Relations

Founded: 1969. **Annual Revenue:** US$13,848. **Employees:** 166000. **Description:** Retail: Men's, women's and children's casual and activewear store chain.

∎ 95
GENERAL ELECTRIC CO.

3135 Easton Tpk.
Fairfield, CT 06431-0001
PH: (203)373-2211
E-mail: gary.sheffer@corporate.ge.com
URL: http://www.ge.com
Contact: Beth Comstock, Corporate Vice President of Communications

Founded: 1892. **Annual Revenue:** US$125,913. **Employees:** 310000. **Description:** Manufacturing: Major appliances, lighting products, industrial automation products, medical diagnostic imaging equipment, motors, electrical distribution and control equipment, locomotives, power generation and delivery products, nuclear power support services and fuel assemblies, commercial and military aircraft jet engines, and engineered materials, such as plastics, silicones and superabrasive industrial diamonds Services: Consumer and business financing. Communications: Television broadcasting. Finance: holding company.

∎ 96
GENERAL MOTORS CORP.

300 Renaissance Ctr.
Detroit, MI 48265-3000
PH: (313)556-5000
E-mail: charles.licari@gm.com
URL: http://www.gm.com
Contact: Charles Licari, Public Relations

Founded: 1908. **Annual Revenue:** US$177,260. **Employees:** 365000. **Description:** Manufacturing: Designing, manufacturing, and marketing of vehicles, locomotives, and heavy-duty automatic transmissions. Finance: Motor vehicle financing and insurance. Services: Data processing firm., digital communications. Finance: holding company.

▮ 97

GETTY IMAGES INC.

601 N 34th St., Ste. 400
Seattle, WA 98103
PH: (206)925-5000
E-mail: feedback@gettyimages.com
URL: http://www.gettyimages.com
Contact: Rosanne Marks, VP Corp. Communications

Founded: 1995. **Annual Revenue:** US$451. **Employees:** 1845. **Description:** Services: Provider of imagery and related products and services to advertising agencies, graphic design firms, broadcasting and publishing companies, CD-ROM and online publishing.

▮ 98

GLOBALSCAPE INC.

6000 Northwest Pkwy., Ste. 101
San Antonio, TX 78249-3343
PH: (210)308-8267
E-mail: media@globalscape.com
URL: http://www.globalscape.com

Founded: 1996. **Annual Revenue:** US$5. **Employees:** 35.

▮ 99

HEADHUNTER.NET INC.

333 Research Court, Ste. 200
Norcross, GA 30092
PH: (770)300-9272
URL: http://www.headhunter.net

Founded: 1996. **Annual Revenue:** US$57. **Employees:** 377. **Description:** Services: Provides on-line recruiting services.

▮ 100

HEALTHEON WEB MD

400 The Lenox Bldg., 3399 Peachtree Rd NE
Atlanta, GA 30326
PH: (404)479-7600
URL: http://www.webmd.com

Annual Revenue: US$102. **Employees:** 1825. **Description:** Services: Designs internet based health information systems.

▮ 101

HEALTHEXTRAS INC.

2273 Research Blvd., 2nd Fl.
Rockville, MD 20850
PH: (301)548-2900

E-mail: info@healthextras.com
URL: http://www.healthextras.com

Founded: 1997. **Annual Revenue:** US$88. **Employees:** 82. **Description:** Insurance: Provider of pharmacy, health and disability benefits.

▮ 102

HEALTHGATE DATA CORP.

25 Corporate Dr., Ste. 310
Burlington, MA 01803-4245
PH: (781)685-4000
E-mail: info@healthgate.com
URL: http://www.healthgate.com

Founded: 1997. **Annual Revenue:** US$9. **Employees:** 79. **Description:** Services: Providing scientific, technical, and medical publishers the technology to present their information electronically.

▮ 103

HERTZ CORP.

225 Brae Blvd.
Park Ridge, NJ 07656
PH: (201)307-2000
URL: http://www.hertz.com

Founded: 1924. **Annual Revenue:** US$4,916. **Employees:** 29800. **Description:** Services: Passenger car and equipment rental and leasing.

▮ 104

HEWLETT-PACKARD CO.

3000 Hanover St.
Palo Alto, CA 94304-1185
PH: (650)857-1501
E-mail: randy_lane@hp.com
URL: http://www.hp.com

Founded: 1939. **Annual Revenue:** US$45,200. **Employees:** 88500. **Description:** Manufacturing: Manufacturer of computer servers, software, storage, services and support, PCs and workstations, personal information appliances and printers and supplies.

▮ 105

HOMESTORE.COM INC.

30700 Russell Ranch Rd.
Westlake Village, CA 91362
PH: (805)557-2300
E-mail: gary.gerdemann@homestore.com
URL: http://www.homestore.com

Founded: 1993. **Annual Revenue:** US$325. **Employees:** 2800. **Description:** Services: Provider of online media and technology to the real estate industry.

▌106

HOOVER'S INC.

5800 Airport Blvd.
Austin, TX 78752-3812
PH: (512)374-4500
URL: http://www.hoovers.com

Founded: 1990. **Annual Revenue:** US$32. **Employees:** 287. **Description:** Manufacturing: Reference books publishing. Services: Online business information and services.

▌107

HOT JOBS INC.

24 W 40th St., 12th Fl.
New York, NY 10018
E-mail: sales@hotjobs.com
URL: http://www.hotjobs.com

Description: Services: Developer of internet job placement and recruiting software.

▌108

HOTEL RESERVATIONS NETWORK INC.

8140 Walnut Hill, 1010
Dallas, TX 75231
PH: (214)369-1246
URL: http://www.hotels.com

Description: Services: Hotel reservation and car rental services.

▌109

HUGHES NETWORK SYSTEMS INC.

11717 Exploration Ln.
Germantown, MD 20876
PH: (301)428-5500
URL: http://www.hns.com

Founded: 1971. **Annual Revenue:** US$1,943. **Employees:** 3000. **Description:** Manufacturing: Communications equipment and systems.

▌110

IBASIS INC.

20 Second Ave.
Burlington, MA 01803
PH: (781)505-7500
E-mail: info@ibasis.net
URL: http://www.ibasis.net
Contact: Adam Banker, Manager Worldwide Public Relations

Founded: 1996. **Annual Revenue:** US$134. **Employees:** 441. **Description:** Communications: Provider of telecommunication technology.

▌111

IGO CORP.

9393 Gateway Dr.
Reno, NV 89511
PH: (775)746-6140
E-mail: TechSupport@igo.com
URL: http://www.igo.com

Founded: 1993. **Annual Revenue:** US$40. **Employees:** 193. **Description:** Wholesale: Specialty batteries.

▌112

IMANAGE INC.

950 Tower Ln., Ste. 500
Foster City, CA 94404
PH: (650)356-1166
E-mail: info@imanage.com
URL: http://www.imanage.com

Founded: 1995. **Annual Revenue:** US$39. **Employees:** 229. **Description:** Services: Developer of document and networking software.

▌113

IMPROVENET INC.

1286 Oddstad Dr.
Redwood City, CA 94063
PH: (650)701-8000
URL: http://www.improvenet.com

Founded: 1996. **Annual Revenue:** US$7. **Employees:** 111. **Description:** Services: Web-based home improvement.

▌114

INGRAM MICRO SA

Sant Ferran 52-68, Poligono Industrial Dolores Alameda
E-08940 Cornella de Llobregat Barc, Spain
PH: 93 474 90 90
E-mail: ingrammicro@ingrammicro.es
URL: http://www.ingrammicro.es

Annual Revenue: US$348. **Employees:** 280. **Description:** Wholesale trade in computer equipment

▌115

INSWEB CORP.

11290 Pyrites Way, Ste. 200
Gold River, CA 95670
PH: (916)853-3300
URL: http://www.insweb.com

Founded: 1996. **Annual Revenue:** US$23. **Employees:** 143. **Description:** Services: Electronic quotation and online purchasing of insurance on the Internet.

▌ 116

INTEL CORP.

PO Box 58119
Santa Clara, CA 95052-8119
PH: (408)765-8080
E-mail: support@cs.intel.com
URL: http://www.intel.com

Founded: 1968. **Annual Revenue:** US$26,539. **Employees:** 86100. **Description:** Manufacturing: Manufactures semiconductor devices, microcomputer chips, chipsets, motherboards and flash memory.

▌ 117

INTERCOMMERCE

Aksakov Str. 21
1000 Sofia, Bulgaria
PH: 02 87 93 64
E-mail: intcom@omega.bg
URL: http://intercommerce.hypermarket.net/

Founded: 1970. **Description:** Wholesale: Import and export of consumer goods and raw materials; barter trade; compensation deals; financial operations; provision of intermediary services; tourism; transport and insurance of goods

▌ 118

INTERNATIONAL BUSINESS MACHINES CORP.

1133 Westchester Ave.
White Plains, NY 10604
PH: (914)499-1900
E-mail: askibm@vnet.ibm.com
URL: http://www.ibm.com
Contact: Rob Wilson

Founded: 1911. **Annual Revenue:** US$85,866. **Employees:** 319876. **Description:** Manufacturing: Computer systems, networks and microelectronics. Services: Developer of computer-system and network software. Finance: holding company.

▌ 119

INTERNET AMERICA INC.

350 N St. Paul, Ste. 3000
Dallas, TX 75201
PH: (214)861-2500
E-mail: info@airmail.net
URL: http://www.airmail.net

Founded: 1995. **Annual Revenue:** US$35. **Employees:** 200. **Description:** Services: Internet service provider that provides an array of Internet services tailored to meet the needs of both individual and business subscribers.

▌ 120

INTERNET CAPITAL GROUP INC.

435 Devon Park Dr., Bldg. 600
Wayne, PA 19087
PH: (610)989-0111
URL: http://www.icge.com
Contact: Michelle Strykowski, Director, Corporate Communications

Founded: 1996. **Annual Revenue:** US$671. **Employees:** 31. **Description:** Services: Investment company for e-commerce business-to-businesse companies. Finance Holding company.

▌ 121

INTERNET PICTURES CORP.

1009 Commerce Park Dr., Ste 400
Oak Ridge, TN 37830
PH: (423)482-3000
E-mail: sales@ipix.com
URL: http://www.IPix.com
Contact: Stuart Roberson, SVP Marketing

Founded: 1986. **Annual Revenue:** US$29. **Employees:** 87. **Description:** Services: Developer of panoramic photo and digital video software.

▌ 122

INTERTRUST TECHNOLOGIES CORP.

4750 Patrick Henry Dr.
Santa Clara, CA 95054
PH: (408)855-0100
E-mail: info@intertrust.com
URL: http://www.intertrust.com

Founded: 1990. **Annual Revenue:** US$8. **Employees:** 188. **Description:** Services: Developer of secure electronic commerce and digital rights management software.

▌ 123

INTRAWARE INC.

25 Orinda Way, Ste. 101
Orinda, CA 94563
PH: (925)253-4500
E-mail: info@intraware.com
URL: http://www.intraware.com
Contact: Roman Reznicek

Founded: 1996. **Annual Revenue:** US$52. **Employees:** 200. **Description:** Services: Developer of enterprise software and online services to IT professionals.

▌ 124

INTUIT INC.

PO Box 7850
Mountain View, CA 94039-7850
PH: (650)944-6000

URL: http://www.intuit.com
Contact: Michael Runzler

Founded: 1983. **Annual Revenue:** US$1,262. **Employees:** 6100. **Description:** Services: Provider of small business, tax preparation and personal finance software.

∎ 125
ITXC CORP.

750 College Rd. E
Princeton, NJ 08540
PH: (609)750-3333
E-mail: itxc@itxc.com
URL: http://www.itxc.com
Contact: Mary Evslin, VP, Marketing

Founded: 1997. **Annual Revenue:** US$173. **Employees:** 224. **Description:** Communications: Internet telephony.

∎ 126
IVILLAGE INC.

500-512 7th Ave.
New York, NY 10018
PH: (212)600-6000
URL: http://www.ivillage.com

Founded: 1995. **Annual Revenue:** US$60. **Employees:** 262. **Description:** Services: On-line community for women.

∎ 127
J2 GLOBAL COMMUNICATIONS

6922 Hollywood Blvd., Ste. 800, 8th Fl.
Hollywood, CA 90028
PH: (323)860-9200
E-mail: sales@mail.j2.com
URL: http://www.j2.com
Contact: Jeff Adelman

Founded: 1995. **Annual Revenue:** US$33. **Employees:** 134. **Description:** Services: Developer of software allowing fax machine and phone to be connected to user's e-mail.

∎ 128
J.C. PENNEY COMPANY INC.

6501 Legacy Dr.
Plano, TX 75024-3698
PH: (972)431-1000
E-mail: jcpis@jcpenney.com
URL: http://www.jcpenney.net

Founded: 1902. **Annual Revenue:** US$32,004. **Employees:** 270000. **Description:** Retail: Department store chain and mail-order house.

∎ 129
JUNO ONLINE SERVICES

1540 Broadway, 27th Fl.
New York, NY 10036
PH: (212)597-9000
E-mail: pr@support.juno.com
URL: http://www.juno.com
Contact: Gary Baker

Founded: 1996. **Annual Revenue:** US$114. **Employees:** 332. **Description:** Services: On-line services.

∎ 130
KEYNOTE SYSTEMS INC.

777 Mariners Island Blvd.
San Mateo, CA 94404
PH: (650)403-2400
E-mail: info@keynote.com
URL: http://www.keynote.com
Contact: Jason Pfannenstiel, Public Relations Coordinator

Founded: 1995. **Annual Revenue:** US$46. **Employees:** 360. **Description:** Services: Developer of quality assurance internet software.

∎ 131
KMART CORP.

3100 W Big Beaver Rd.
Troy, MI 48084
PH: (248)463-1000
URL: http://www.bluelight.com
Contact: Steve Pagnani, Manager, Corporate Media Relations

Founded: 1899. **Annual Revenue:** US$37,028. **Employees:** 252000. **Description:** Retail: Discount general merchandise, family clothing, grocery and home improvement store chain.

∎ 132
L90 INC.

4499 Glencoe Ave.
Marina Del Rey, CA 90292
PH: (310)751-0200
URL: http://www.l90.com

Founded: 1997. **Annual Revenue:** US$52. **Employees:** 217. **Description:** Services: Online advertising and marketing company.

∎ 133
LANDACORP INC.

4151 Ashford Dunwoody Rd., Ste. 505
Atlanta, GA 30319
PH: (404)531-9956
URL: http://www.landacorp.com

Founded: 1980. **Annual Revenue:** US$16. **Employees:** 164. **Description:** Services: Developer of health services practice management software.

▌134
LANDS' END INC.
Lands' End Ln.
Dodgeville, WI 53595
PH: (608)935-9341
E-mail: mailbox@landsend.com
URL: http://www.landsend.com

Founded: 1963. **Annual Revenue:** US$1,569. **Employees:** 10200. **Description:** Retail: Direct merchant of traditionally styled casual clothing for men,women and children, accessories, shoes, soft luggage and home products.

▌135
LEARN2 CORP.
111 High Ridge Rd., Ste. 5
Stamford, CT 06905
PH: (203)975-9602
URL: http://www.learn2.com

Founded: 1995. **Annual Revenue:** US$4. **Employees:** 85. **Description:** Services: Providing learning and communications products over the Internet and intranets. Developer and publisher of interactive entertainment and educational products.

▌136
LENDINGTREE INC.
11115 Rushmore Dr.
Charlotte, NC 28277
PH: (704)541-5351
URL: http://www.lendingtree.com

Founded: 1996. **Annual Revenue:** US$28. **Employees:** 254. **Description:** Finance: Internet-based loan marketplace for consumers and lenders.

▌137
LIFEMINDERS INC.
13530 Dulles Technology Dr., Ste. 500
Herndon, VA 20171-3414
PH: (703)793-8210
E-mail: info@lifeminders.com
URL: http://www.lifeminders.com

Annual Revenue: US$54. **Employees:** 138. **Description:** Services: On-line direct marketing firm offering reminder service to subscribers and provides direct marketing products and services to companies.

▌138
LOG ON AMERICA INC.
One Cookson Pl, 6th Fl.
Providence, RI 02903
TF: 888-985-3668
URL: http://www.loa.com
Contact: Tom Towhill

Founded: 1992. **Annual Revenue:** US$13. **Employees:** 164. **Description:** Services: Provider of online services.

▌139
LOISLAW.COM INC.
105 N 28th St.
Van Buren, AR 72956
PH: (501)471-5581
E-mail: info@loislaw.com
URL: http://www.loislaw.com

Founded: 1987. **Annual Revenue:** US$57. **Employees:** 300. **Description:** Manufacturing: Legal CD-ROM publishing.

▌140
LOOKSMART LTD.
625 2nd St.
San Francisco, CA 94107
PH: (415)348-7000
E-mail: feedback@looksmart.net
URL: http://www.looksmart.com

Founded: 1996. **Annual Revenue:** US$85. **Employees:** 367. **Description:** Services: Category-based web directory.

▌141
LOUDEYE TECHNOLOGIES INC.
1130 Rainier Ave. S
Seattle, WA 98144
PH: (206)830-5300
E-mail: info@loudeye.com
URL: http://www.loudeye.com

Founded: 1997. **Annual Revenue:** US$10. **Employees:** 43. **Description:** Services: Provider of advanced digital media services, consulting, and applications through the Internet.

▌142
LUCENT TECHNOLOGIES INC.
600 Mountain Ave.
Murray Hill, NJ 07974
PH: (908)582-8500
E-mail: lucentir@lucent.com
URL: http://www.lucent.com

Founded: 1996. **Annual Revenue:** US$21,294. **Employees:** 77000. **Description:** Manufacturing: Manufacturer of communications systems and products. Services: Provider of software, which enable service providers to provide wire-line and wireless access, local, long distance and international voice, data and video and cable services.

▌ 143

MARRIOTT INTERNATIONAL INC.

10400 Fernwood Rd.
Bethesda, MD 20817
PH: (301)380-3000
URL: http://www.marriott.com

Founded: 1927. **Annual Revenue:** US$10,152. **Employees:** 143000. **Description:** Services: Hotels and resorts, food service and facilities management, operator of independent and assisted living retirement communities. Finance: Franchiser of hotels. Wholesale:Food.

▌ 144

MARTHA STEWART LIVING OMNIMEDIA INC.

11 W 42nd St.
New York, NY 10036
FX: (212)827-8204
URL: http://www.marthastewart.com

Founded: 1982. **Annual Revenue:** US$296. **Employees:** 610. **Description:** Manufacturing: Provider of "how to" content and related products for homemakers and other consumers.

▌ 145

MCAFEE.COM CORP.

535 Oakmead Pkwy.
Sunnyvale, CA 94085
PH: (408)992-8100
URL: http://www.mcafee.com

Founded: 1998. **Annual Revenue:** US$62. **Employees:** 160. **Description:** Services: Online services including virus protection and repair.

▌ 146

MEDINEX SYSTEMS INC.

806 W Clearwater Loop, Ste. N
Post Falls, ID 83854
PH: (208)777-4203
E-mail: info@medinex.com
URL: http://www.medinex.com

Founded: 1997. **Annual Revenue:** US$5. **Employees:** 83. **Description:** Services: Medinex Systems is a medical software, medical supply distribution and technology company.

▌ 147

MEDSITE INC.

330 7th Ave., Ste. 16N
New York, NY 10001
TF: 877-633-7483
E-mail: inquiries@medsite.com
URL: http://www.medsite.com

Founded: 1997. **Annual Revenue:** US$4. **Employees:** 81. **Description:** Services: Medical information website.

▌ 148

MERISEL INC.

200 Continental Blvd.
El Segundo, CA 90245-0984
PH: (310)615-3080
URL: http://www.merisel.com
Contact: Leslie J. Sinfield, Corporte Communications

Founded: 1980. **Annual Revenue:** US$2,094. **Employees:** 570. **Description:** Wholesale: Microcomputer hardware and software products. Finance: Holding company.

▌ 149

MICRON INC.

3815 Lancaster Pke.
Wilmington, DE 19805
PH: (302)998-1184
E-mail: micronanalytical@compuserve.com
URL: http://www.micronanalytical.com

Founded: 1966. **Employees:** 11. **Description:** Services: Provider of laboratory services including microstructural and microchemical analysis.

▌ 150

MICROSOFT CORP.

1 Microsoft Way
Redmond, WA 98052-6399
FX: (425)936-7329
URL: http://www.microsoft.com
Contact: Waggener Edstrom

Founded: 1975. **Annual Revenue:** US$28,370. **Employees:** 48030. **Description:** Services: Manufactures microcomputer software and hardware items, computer books and multimedia products.

▌ 151

MODEM MEDIA INC.

230 East Ave.
Norwalk, CT 06855
PH: (203)299-7000
URL: http://www.modemmedia.com

Founded: 1987. Annual Revenue: US$103. Employees: 500. Description: Communications: Digital marketing communications consulting.

▌ 152

MOORE MEDICAL CORP.

PO Box 1500
New Britain, CT 06050-1500
PH: (860)826-3600
URL: http://www.mooremedical.com

Founded: 1947. Annual Revenue: US$133. Employees: 275. Description: Wholesale: Brand-name and generic medical and surgical supplies.

▌ 153

MOTOROLA INC.

1303 E Algonquin Rd.
Schaumburg, IL 60196
PH: (847)576-5000
E-mail: invest1@email.mot.com
URL: http://www.mot.com
Contact: Scott Wyman

Founded: 1928. Annual Revenue: US$33,075. Employees: 147000. Description: Manufacturing: Automobile and industrial electronics, cellular radio telephones, semiconductor and radio communication products, computer and information systems. Finance: holding company.

▌ 154

MP3.COM INC.

4790 Eastgate Mall
San Diego, CA 92121-1970
PH: (858)623-7000
URL: http://www.mp3.com

Founded: 1997. Annual Revenue: US$80. Employees: 308. Description: Manufacturing: Music online.

▌ 155

MULTEX.COM INC.

100 Williams St., 7th Fl.
New York, NY 10038
PH: (212)607-2500
E-mail: multex@multex.com
URL: http://www.multex.com

Founded: 1993. Annual Revenue: US$94. Employees: 506. Description: Services: Research reports via the internet; subscription and pay-per-view services.

▌ 156

MYPOINTS.COM INC.

100 California St., Ste. 1200, 12th Fl.
San Francisco, CA 94111

PH: (415)676-3700
E-mail: sales@mypoints.com
URL: http://www.mypoints.com

Founded: 1996. Annual Revenue: US$64. Employees: 301. Description: Services: Direct marketing services via the internet.

▌ 157

NATIONAL SEMICONDUCTOR CORP.

PO Box 58090
Santa Clara, CA 95052
PH: (408)721-5000
E-mail: invest.group@nsc.com
URL: http://www.national.com
Contact: Bill Callahan

Founded: 1959. Annual Revenue: US$1,495. Employees: 10300. Description: Manufacturing: Manufactures intensive semiconductors and integrated circuits used in communication devices, networking equipment and automobiles.

▌ 158

NBC INTERNET INC.

225 Bush St.
San Francisco, CA 94104
PH: (415)375-5000
URL: http://www.nbci.com

Founded: 1999. Annual Revenue: US$36. Employees: 635. Description: Manufacturing: Television broadcasting.

▌ 159

NEOFORMA INC.

3061 Zanker Rd.
San Jose, CA 95134
E-mail: info@neoforma.com
URL: http://www.neoforma.com

Founded: 1996. Annual Revenue: US$28. Employees: 196. Description: Services: Provider of Internet marketplace for healthcare products, surgical instruments and supplies.

▌ 160

NETBANK INC.

PO Box 2368
Alpharetta, GA 30023
PH: (770)343-6006
URL: http://www.netbank.com

Founded: 1996. Annual Revenue: US$2,880. Employees: 140. Description: Financial: Internet online bank.

▌161
NETCENTIVES INC.
475 Brannan St., 3 Fl.
San Francisco, CA 94107
PH: (415)503-3930
URL: http://www.netcentives.com
Contact: Stacey Levitz, Senior Director, Corporate Communication

Founded: 1996. **Annual Revenue:** US$43. **Employees:** 494. **Description:** Services: Loyalty and e-mail direc-marketing marketing and related software.

▌162
NETCREATIONS INC.
379 W Broadway, Ste. 202
New York, NY 10012
PH: (212)625-1370
E-mail: contact@netcreations.com
URL: http://www.netcreations.com

Founded: 1995. **Annual Revenue:** US$21. **Employees:** 40. **Description:** Services: Prepackaged software for opt-in email marketing services.

▌163
NETZEE INC.
6190 Powers Ferry Rd., Ste. 400
Atlanta, GA 30339-2966
PH: (770)850-4000
URL: http://www.netzee.com

Founded: 1999. **Annual Revenue:** US$26. **Employees:** 127. **Description:** Services: Provides Internet and telephone access services to small banks, thrifts, and credit unions, Web site design and e-commerce services.

▌164
NEW FRONTIER MEDIA INC.
5435 Airport Blvd., Ste. 100
Boulder, CO 80301
PH: (303)444-0632
URL: http://www.noof.com

Founded: 1988. **Annual Revenue:** US$52. **Employees:** 137. **Description:** Services: Electronic distribution of adult entertainment through internet, cable television, and satellite.

▌165
NEW YORK TIMES CO.
229 W 43rd St.
New York, NY 10036
PH: (212)556-1234
URL: http://www.nytco.com

Founded: 1896. **Annual Revenue:** US$3,016. **Employees:** 12050. **Description:** Manufacturing: Media: Newspaper and magazine publishing, television broadcasting, Internet-based information services. Manufacturing: holding company.

▌166
NEWSEDGE CORP.
80 Blanchard Rd.
Burlington, MA 01803
PH: (781)229-3000
E-mail: invrel@newsedge.com
URL: http://www.newsedge.com

Founded: 1989. **Annual Revenue:** US$71. **Employees:** 309. **Description:** Services: Global provider of syndicated content services and electronic publishing technologies for business.

▌167
NEXTCARD INC.
595 Market St., Ste. 1800
San Francisco, CA 94105
PH: (415)836-9700
E-mail: investorrelations@nextcard.com
URL: http://www.nextcard.com

Founded: 1996. **Annual Revenue:** US$105. **Employees:** 930. **Description:** Finance: Consumer credit processing.

▌168
NIKU CORP.
350 Convention Way
Redwood City, CA 94063
PH: (650)298-4600
E-mail: info@niku.com
URL: http://www.niku.com
Contact: Marty Tacktill

Founded: 1997. **Annual Revenue:** US$66. **Employees:** 340. **Description:** Services: Provider of Internet software products and offer an online marketplace for the sourcing, management and delivery of professional services.

▌169
NORDSTROM INC.
1617 6th Ave., Ste. 500
Seattle, WA 98101-1742
PH: (206)628-2111
URL: http://www.nordstrom.com

Founded: 1901. **Annual Revenue:** US$5,634. **Employees:** 43000. **Description:** Retail: Men's, women's and children's apparel, shoe and accessory store chain.

▌170

NORTEL NETWORKS CORP.

8200 Dixie Rd., Ste. 100
Brampton, ON, Canada L6T5P6
PH: (905)863-0000
E-mail: investor@nortelnetworks.com
URL: http://www.nortelnetworks.com
Contact: David Chamberlin

Founded: 1895. **Annual Revenue:** US$17,511. **Employees:** 53600. **Description:** Services: Provider of optical, wireless, local, business and personal internet services. Manufacturing: Communications equipment.

▌171

OFFICE DEPOT INC.

2200 Old Germantown Rd.
Delray Beach, FL 33445
PH: (561)438-4800
E-mail: Investor.Relations@officedepot.com
URL: http://www.officedepot.com
Contact: Gary Schweikhart, PR Dir.

Founded: 1986. **Annual Revenue:** US$11,200. **Employees:** 48000. **Description:** Retail: Office supply chain stores. Manufacturing: Offset and letterpress printing, perfect, plastic and glue binding. Finance: holding company,

▌172

OFFICIAL PAYMENTS CORP.

3 Landmark Sq.
Stamford, CT 06901
PH: (203)356-4200
URL: http://www.officialpayments.com

Founded: 1996. **Annual Revenue:** US$31. **Employees:** 68. **Description:** Services: Electronic payment service for income, state, property taxes, tickets, fines.

▌173

ONVIA.COM INC.

1260 Mercer St.
Seattle, WA 98109
TF: 800-331-2822
URL: http://www.onvia.com

Founded: 1996. **Annual Revenue:** US$18. **Employees:** 97. **Description:** Services: On-line business-to-business marketplace offering variety of products and services.

▌174

OPENWAVE SYSTEMS INC.

800 Chesapeake Dr.
Redwood City, CA 94063
PH: (650)562-0200
E-mail: info@openwave.com
URL: http://www.phone.com

Founded: 1999. **Annual Revenue:** US$465. **Employees:** 2200. **Description:** Services: Provider of Internet-based communications in infrastructure software and applications.

▌175

ORACLE CORP.

500 Oracle Pkwy.
Redwood City, CA 94065
PH: (650)506-7000
E-mail: receive@us.oracle.com
URL: http://www.oracle.com
Contact: Jennifer Glass

Founded: 1980. **Annual Revenue:** US$9,673. **Employees:** 43000. **Description:** Services: Developer of management systems software.

▌176

ORBITZ INC.

200 S Wacker Dr., Ste. 1900
Chicago, IL 60606
PH: (312)894-4000
URL: http://www.orbitz.com

Annual Revenue: US$43. **Employees:** 187. **Description:** Services: Internet travel services.

▌177

OVERTURE SERVICES INC.

74 N Pasadena Ave., 3rd Fl.
Pasadena, CA 91103
FX: (626)685-5601
E-mail: feedback@Overture.com
URL: http://www.overture.com
Contact: Kasey Byrne, Chief Communications Officer

Founded: 1997. **Annual Revenue:** US$288. **Employees:** 559. **Description:** Services: Online marketplace that introduces consumers and businesses that search the Internet to advertisers who provide products, services and information.

▌178

PACIFIC CENTURY CYBERWORKS LTD.

39/F PCCW Tower, TaiKoo Place, 979 King's Road
Quarry Bay-Hong Kong, Hong Kong
PH: 852 2888 2888
E-mail: ir@pccw.com
URL: http://www.pccw.com

Founded: 1979. **Description:** Wholesale: Following the merger with Cable and Wireless HKT in August 2000 the company has restructured into four operating sectors: telecommunications services, global communications services, net enterprises, and infrastructure services

∎ 179
PAYPAL INC.
1840 Embarcadero Rd.
Palo Alto, CA 94303
PH: (650)251-1100
URL: http://www.paypal.com

Founded: 1999. **Annual Revenue:** US$105. **Employees:** 618. **Description:** Services: Electronic payment services.

∎ 180
PC CONNECTION INC.
730 Milford Rd., Rte. 101A
Merrimack, NH 03054
PH: (603)423-2000
URL: http://www.pcconnection.com

Founded: 1982. **Annual Revenue:** US$1,180. **Employees:** 1312. **Description:** Retail: Mail-order service of software, peripherals and computers.

∎ 181
PEAPOD INC.
9933 Woods Dr., Ste. 375
Skokie, IL 60077
PH: (847)583-9400
URL: http://www.peapod.com
Contact: Paula Wheeler, Corporate Communications Officer

Founded: 1989. **Annual Revenue:** US$100. **Employees:** 891. **Description:** Services: Internet-based grocery shopping and delivery.

∎ 182
PEGASUS SOLUTIONS INC.
3811 Turtle Creek Blvd., Ste. 1100
Dallas, TX 75219
PH: (214)528-5656
URL: http://www.pegsinc.com

Founded: 1989. **Annual Revenue:** US$180. **Employees:** 1518. **Description:** Services: Provider of end-to-end reservation distribution systems, reservation technology systems and hotel representation services for the global hospitality industry.

∎ 183
PFSWEB INC.
500 N Central Expy.
Plano, TX 75074
PH: (972)881-2900
E-mail: pfsinfo@Ppfsweb.com
URL: http://www.pfsweb.com

Founded: 1995. **Annual Revenue:** US$28. **Employees:** 575. **Description:** Services: Managment services for e-commerce.

∎ 184
PLAYBOY ENTERPRISES INC.
680 N Lake Shore Dr.
Chicago, IL 60611
PH: (312)751-8000
URL: http://www.playboyenterprises.com

Founded: 1965. **Annual Revenue:** US$291. **Employees:** 605. **Description:** Manufacturing: Magazine, calendar and catalog publishing, television and home video production, product marketing.

∎ 185
PORTERA SYSTEMS INC.
1688 Dell Ave.
Campbell, CA 95008
PH: (408)364-3600
E-mail: info@potera.com
URL: http://www.portera.com
Contact: Dave Jarrat

Founded: 1996. **Annual Revenue:** US$47. **Employees:** 300. **Description:** Services: Business web solutions for the services industry

∎ 186
PRICELINE.COM INC.
800 Connecticut Ave.
Norwalk, CT 06854
PH: (203)705-3000
E-mail: info@priceline.com
URL: http://www.priceline.com
Contact: Brian Ek, Press Contact

Founded: 1998. **Annual Revenue:** US$1,170. **Employees:** 359. **Description:** Services: Provider of e-commerce marketplace site, bid and accept system.

∎ 187
PRIMEDIA BUSINESS MAGAZINES AND MEDIA INC.
9800 Metcalf Ave.
Overland Park, KS 66212
PH: (913)341-1300
E-mail: inquiries@primediabusiness.com
URL: http://www.primediabusiness.com

Founded: 1886. **Description:** Manufacturing: One of the world's largest technical and trade publishing companies with nearly 100 publications, more than 30 trade shows, 450 books and directories and 100-plus Web sites.

▌188

PROMOTIONS.COM INC.

450 W 33rd St.
New York, NY 10001
PH: (212)971-9800
E-mail: info@promotions.com
URL: http://www.promotions.com
Contact: Larry Quartaro, Chief Financial Officer

Founded: 1996. **Annual Revenue:** US$11. **Employees:** 25.
Description: Services: Customized on-line promotions.

▌189

PSINET INC.

44983 Knoll Sq.
Ashburn, VA 20147
PH: (703)726-4100
E-mail: info@psi.com
URL: http://www.psi.com

Founded: 1989. **Annual Revenue:** US$996. **Employees:**
5000. **Description:** Services: Provider of corporate and private network internet access including dedicated and dial-up lines, web hosting and web security services and software, design of consulting solution systems and software.

▌190

PTEK HOLDINGS INC.

3399 Peachtree Rd. NE, Ste. 600
Atlanta, GA 30326
PH: (404)262-8400
URL: http://www.ptek.com
Contact: Trisha Harris, Vice President, Corporate Communications

Founded: 1991. **Annual Revenue:** US$423. **Employees:**
2240. **Description:** Communications: Provider of voice mail and email deliverys.

▌191

PURCHASE-PRO INC.

4650 Arville St., Ste F
Las Vegas, NV 89103

Description: Services: Electrical and scientific apparatus

▌192

QVC

Marco Polo House, Chelsea Bridge, 346 Queenstown Rd.
London SW84NQ, United Kingdom
PH: 020 77055600
E-mail: info@qvcuk.com
URL: http://www.qvcuk.com

Annual Revenue: US$304. **Employees:** 1680. **Description:**
Retail: Retail trade in a wide range of consumer goods via a home shopping channel broadcast on cable and satellite television

▌193

QWEST COMMUNICATIONS INTERNATIONAL INC.

1801 California St.
Denver, CO 80202
PH: (303)992-1400
E-mail: info@qwest.com
URL: http://www.qwest.com
Contact: Joan H. Walker, Senior vice president, corporate communications

Founded: 1988. **Annual Revenue:** US$16,610. **Employees:** 67000. **Description:** Communications: Facilities-based provider of communications services including long distance, pre-paid and credit calling cards, and conferencing equipment. Manufacturing: Fiber-optic networks.

▌194

REALNETWORKS INC.

PO Box 91123
Seattle, WA 98111-9223
PH: (206)674-2700
URL: http://www.realnetworks.com

Founded: 1994. **Annual Revenue:** US$189. **Employees:**
798. **Description:** Services: Develops and markets software products and services designed to enable users of personal computers and other consumer electronic devices to send and receive audio, video and other multimedia services using the Web.

▌195

RECREATIONAL EQUIPMENT INC.

6750 S 228th St.
Kent, WA 98032
PH: (253)395-3780
URL: http://www.rei.com

Founded: 1938. **Annual Revenue:** US$698. **Employees:**
7000. **Description:** Retail: Outdoor equipment, clothing store chain and mail-order catalog.

▌196

REGISTER.COM INC.

575 8th Ave., 11th Fl.
New York, NY 10018
PH: (212)798-9100
URL: http://www.register.com
Contact: Dawn Patrick, Directof of Customer Services

Founded: 1994. **Annual Revenue:** US$116. **Employees:**
360. **Description:** Services: Developer of Internet publishing software.

∎ 197
RIVERSTONE NETWORKS INC.

5200 Great America Pkwy.
Santa Clara, CA 95054
PH: (408)878-6500
E-mail: comments@riverstonenet.com
URL: http://www.riverstonenet.com

Founded: 1996. **Annual Revenue:** US$211. **Employees:** 472. **Description:** Services: Provide of solutions to deploy high-speed infrastructures.

∎ 198
ROWECOM INC.

725 Concord Ave.
Cambridge, MA 02138
PH: (617)495-5800
URL: http://www.rowe.com

Founded: 1994. **Description:** Services: Developer of web based services for management of knowledge resources.

∎ 199
SALESFORCE.COM INC.

1 Market St., Ste. 300
San Francisco, CA 94105
PH: (415)901-7000
E-mail: info@salesforce.com
URL: http://www.salesforce.com

Founded: 1999. **Annual Revenue:** US$81. **Employees:** 175. **Description:** Services: Provides online software applications for sales leads generation, maintaining customer information, and tracking customer interactions.

∎ 200
SCIQUEST INC.

PO Box 12156
Research Triangle Park, NC 27709-2156
PH: (919)659-2100
URL: http://www.sciquest.com

Founded: 1995. **Annual Revenue:** US$23. **Employees:** 132. **Description:** Services: Web-base, interactive marketplace. Wholesale: Scientific and laboratory products used by pharmaceutical, clinical, biotechnology, chemical, industrial and educational organizations worldwide.

∎ 201
SEARS, ROEBUCK AND CO.

3333 Beverly Rd.
Hoffman Estates, IL 60179
PH: (847)286-2500
E-mail: sears@sracweb.com
URL: http://www.sears.com
Contact: Peggy A. Palter

Founded: 1886. **Annual Revenue:** US$41,078. **Employees:** 323000. **Description:** Retail: Department store chain and mail-order house. Services: automobile repair, home appliance repair and maintenance services, opticians. Construction: Home improvement products and services such as siding, roofing, cabinet refacing, heating, ventilation and air conditioning.

∎ 202
SELECTICA INC.

3 W Plumeria Dr.
San Jose, CA 95134-2111
PH: (408)570-9700
E-mail: info@selectica.com
URL: http://www.selectica.com
Contact: Laurie Spoon, VP of Corporate Marketing

Founded: 1996. **Annual Revenue:** US$45. **Employees:** 753. **Description:** Services: Developer of systems utilities, including application development and system design.

∎ 203
SIMUTRONICS CORP.

1300 Piccard Dr., Ste. 102
Rockville, MD 20850
PH: (301)670-7935
E-mail: custserv@slmutronics.com
URL: http://www.simutronics.com

Founded: 1987. **Annual Revenue:** US$5. **Employees:** 42. **Description:** Services: Developer of online multiplayer games software.

∎ 204
SKILLSOFT CORP. (NASHUA, NH)

20 Industrial Park Dr.
Nashua, NH 03062
FX: (603)324-3009
E-mail: isr@skillsoft.com
URL: http://www.skillsoft.com

Founded: 1997. **Annual Revenue:** US$44. **Employees:** 230. **Description:** Services: Developer and provider of educational software.

∎ 205
SOUTHWEST AIRLINES CO.

PO Box 36611
Dallas, TX 75235-1611
PH: (214)792-4000
URL: http://www.southwest.com

Founded: 1971. **Annual Revenue:** US$5,565. **Employees:** 31580. **Description:** Transportation: Provider of scheduled air passenger service.

▌206

SPORTSLINE.COM INC.

2200 W Cypress Rd.
Fort Lauderdale, FL 33309
PH: (954)351-2120
URL: http://www.sportsline.com
Contact: Larry Wahl, Corporate Communications

Founded: 1994. **Annual Revenue:** US$65. **Employees:** 335. **Description:** Services: Online sports information service, sports merchandise ecommerce.

▌207

STAMPS.COM INC.

3420 Ocean Park Blvd., Ste. 1040
Santa Monica, CA 90405-3324
PH: (310)581-7200
E-mail: info@stamps.com
URL: http://www.stamps.com

Founded: 1996. **Annual Revenue:** US$19. **Employees:** 315. **Description:** Services: Provides e-mail site which allows users to calculate and prints postage from a PC, manage mailing expenses, access addressing information.

▌208

STANDARD REGISTER CO.

PO Box 1167
Dayton, OH 45401-1167
PH: (937)221-1000
URL: http://www.standardregister.com

Founded: 1912. **Annual Revenue:** US$1,196. **Employees:** 5692. **Description:** Manufacturing: Document management experts, responding with innovative and differentiated documents, systems and services.

▌209

STAPLES INC.

500 Staples Dr.
Framingham, MA 01702
PH: (508)253-5000
E-mail: investor@staples.com
URL: http://www.staples.com

Founded: 1985. **Annual Revenue:** US$10,744. **Employees:** 48458. **Description:** Retail: Office supplies store chain.

▌210

STARMEDIA NETWORK INC.

75 Varick St.
New York, NY 10013
PH: (212)905-8200
URL: http://www.starmedianetwork.net

Founded: 1996. **Annual Revenue:** US$23. **Employees:** 520. **Description:** Services: Internet service provider for South American countries.

▌211

STARWOOD HOTELS AND RESORTS WORLDWIDE INC.

777 Westchester Ave.
White Plains, NY 10604
PH: (914)640-8100
URL: http://www.starwoodlodging.com

Founded: 1970. **Annual Revenue:** US$3,967. **Employees:** 115000. **Description:** Services: Operator of hotels. Finance: Holding company.

▌212

STEELCASE INC.

PO Box 1967
Grand Rapids, MI 49501
PH: (616)247-2710
URL: http://www.steelcase.com

Founded: 1912. **Annual Revenue:** US$3,090. **Employees:** 19300. **Description:** Manufacturing: Metal and wooden office furniture: desks, files, chairs and modular panels.

▌213

SUN MICROSYSTEMS INC.

901 San Antonio Rd.
Palo Alto, CA 94303
PH: (650)960-1300
E-mail: investor-relations@sun.com
URL: http://www.sun.com
Contact: Beth Pampaloni

Founded: 1982. **Annual Revenue:** US$15,721. **Employees:** 38900. **Description:** Manufacturing: provider of network computing products, including desktop systems, servers, storage and network switches. Services: developer of operating system software, systems/network support and management, education.

▌214

SUPPORT.COM

575 Broadway
Redwood City, CA 94063
TF: 877-493-2778
URL: http://www.support.com

Annual Revenue: US$30. **Employees:** 155. **Description:** Services: Support is the leading provider of support infrastructure that automates and personalises user support over the internet, extranet and intranet.

▌215

SUTTER HEALTH

2200 River Plaza Dr.
Sacramento, CA 95833
PH: (916)733-8800
URL: http://www.sutterhealth.org

Founded: 1996. **Annual Revenue:** US$3,546. **Employees:** 33774. **Description:** Services: Provider of healthcare, education, research, and administration, including psychiatric hospitals, skilled nursing facilities, medical and fundraising foundations, health libraries, hospices, adult daycare and clinics.

▌216

SWITCHBOARD INC.

120 Flanders Rd.
Westboro, MA 01581
PH: (508)898-1122
URL: http://www.switchboard.com
Contact: Allie Burns

Founded: 1995. **Annual Revenue:** US$16. **Employees:** 80. **Description:** Services: Online national directory of U.S. listing information.

▌217

TARGET CORP.

1000 Nicollet Mall
Minneapolis, MN 55403
PH: (612)304-6073
URL: http://www.targetcorp.com
Contact: Douglas Kline

Founded: 1902. **Annual Revenue:** US$39,167. **Employees:** 192000. **Description:** Retail: Discount department and clothing store chains; web-based shopping. Finance: Holding company.

▌218

TECH DATA CORP.

5350 Tech Data Dr.
Clearwater, FL 33760
PH: (727)539-7429
URL: http://www.techdata.com
Contact: Chuck Miller, Director of Corporate Communications

Founded: 1974. **Annual Revenue:** US$17,200. **Employees:** 10500. **Description:** Wholesale: Microcomputers, computer hardware and software products.

▌219

TERRA LYCOS S.A.

Calle Nicuragua, 54
Barcelona, Spain
PH: 349 14523000
E-mail: investor.relations@corp.terralycos.com
URL: http://www.terralycos.com

Founded: 1995. **Annual Revenue:** US$27. **Employees:** 3196. **Description:** Services: Provider of Internet access and web content.

▌220

TESSCO TECHNOLOGIES INC.

11126 McCormick Rd.
Hunt Valley, MD 21031-1494
PH: (410)229-1200
E-mail: info@tessco.com
URL: http://www.tessco.com
Contact: L. Michelle Manfra, Corporate Communications

Founded: 1982. **Annual Revenue:** US$249. **Employees:** 528. **Description:** Manufacturing: Filtering systems, antennas, transmission lines, and other cellular base site infrastructure products and integration services, cell phone batteries, test andmaintenance equipment.

▌221

THEGLOBE.COM INC.

120 Broadway, 22nd. Fl.
New York, NY 10271
PH: (212)894-3600
URL: http://www.theglobe.com

Founded: 1994. **Annual Revenue:** US$30. **Employees:** 197. **Description:** Services: On-line advertising services. Manufacturing: Magazine publishing.

▌222

TICKETMASTER

3701 Wilshire Blvd., 9th Fl.
Los Angeles, CA 90010
PH: (213)639-6100
E-mail: info@citysearch.com
URL: http://www.ticketmaster.com

Founded: 1998. **Annual Revenue:** US$672. **Employees:** 4600. **Description:** Services: Provider of event ticketing services; provider of online personals, city guides, and camping reservations.

▌223

TICKETS.COM INC.

555 Anton Blvd.
Costa Mesa, CA 92626
PH: (714)327-5400
URL: http://www.tickets.com

Founded: 1988. **Annual Revenue:** US$56. **Employees:** 878. **Description:** Services: Developer of ticketing and box office management.

■ 224

TMP WORLDWIDE INC.

622 Third Ave., 39th Fl.
New York, NY 10017
PH: (212)351-7000
E-mail: corporate.communications@tmp.com
URL: http://www.tmpw.com

Founded: 1967. **Annual Revenue:** US$2,550. **Employees:** 11000. **Description:** Services: Advertising agency specializing in yellow pages, recruitment, and Internet advertising.

■ 225

TOYS "R" US INC.

225 Summit Ave.
Montvale, NJ 07645
PH: (201)262-7800
URL: http://www.tru.com
Contact: Rebecca A. Caruso

Founded: 1948. **Annual Revenue:** US$12,630. **Employees:** 71000. **Description:** Retail: Children's toy and clothing store chains; education specialty store chain.

■ 226

TRADESTATION SECURITIES INC.

2700 N Military Tr., Ste. 200
Boca Raton, FL 33431
PH: (561)995-1010
E-mail: Sales@TradeStation.com
URL: http://www.tradestation.com

Founded: 1991. **Description:** Services: Developer of pre-packaged financial software.

■ 227

TRAVELOCITY.COM INC.

15100 Trinity Blvd.
Fort Worth, TX 76155
PH: (817)785-8000
URL: http://www.travelocity.com
Contact: Judy Haveson

Founded: 1999. **Annual Revenue:** US$302. **Employees:** 1554. **Description:** Services: Provider of online travel services and television production. Transportation: Travel agency.

■ 228

UNITED ONLINE INC.

2555 Towngate Rd.
Westlake Village, CA 91361
PH: (805)418-2000
URL: http://www.unitedonline.net
Contact: Peter Delgrosso, Manager, Public Relations

Founded: 2001. **Annual Revenue:** US$176. **Employees:** 623. **Description:** Services: Internet service provider.

■ 229

UNITED PARCEL SERVICE INC.

55 Glenlake Pwy. NE
Atlanta, GA 30328-3498
TF: 800-742-5877
URL: http://www.ups.com
Contact: Joseph R. (Joe) Moderow, Senior Vice President of Legal & Public Affairs, General Counsel

Founded: 1907. **Annual Revenue:** US$30,646. **Employees:** 359000. **Description:** Transportation: Long-distance trucking.

■ 230

US SEARCH.COM INC.

5401 Beethoven St.
Los Angeles, CA 90066
PH: (310)302-6300
E-mail: corporate@ussearch.com
URL: http://www.1800ussearch.com

Founded: 1994. **Annual Revenue:** US$18. **Employees:** 117. **Description:** Services: Information search services.

■ 231

USINTERNETWORKING INC.

1 USi Plz.
Annapolis, MD 21401-7478
PH: (410)897-4400
URL: http://www.usinternetworking.com

Founded: 1998. **Annual Revenue:** US$150. **Employees:** 700. **Description:** Services: Internet communication services such as web-enabled customer service systems, sales force automation, supply chain systems and electronic commerce gateways.

■ 232

VALUECLICK INC.

4360 Park Terrace Dr., Ste. 100
Westlake Village, CA 91361
PH: (818)575-4500
E-mail: pr@valueclick.com
URL: http://www.valueclick.com
Contact: Elizabeth M. Lloyd, Press Contact

Founded: 1997. **Annual Revenue:** US$45. **Employees:** 107. **Description:** Services: Internet advertising firm.

■ 233

VANDYKE SOFTWARE INC.

4848 Tramway Ridge Dr. NE, Ste. 101
Albuquerque, NM 87111-2873

PH: (505)332-5700
E-mail: sales@vandyke.com
URL: http://www.vandyke.com
Contact: Marc Orchant, Customer Relations

Founded: 1995. Annual Revenue: US$5. Employees: 23. Description: Services: Developer of secure access and terminal emulation software.

▌234
VANTAGEMED CORP.

3017 Kilgore Rd., Ste. 180
Rancho Cordova, CA 95670
PH: (916)638-4744
URL: http://www.vantagemed.net

Founded: 1985. Annual Revenue: US$24. Employees: 290. Description: Services: Developer of health services and physician practice management software.

▌235
VERTICALNET INC.

300 Chester Field Pkwy.
Malvern, PA 19355
PH: (610)240-0600
E-mail: info@verticalnet.com
URL: http://www.verticalnet.com

Founded: 1995. Annual Revenue: US$126. Employees: 164. Description: Services: E-commerce provider, software related to direct materials procurement.

▌236
VIA RAIL CANADA INC.

PO Box 8116, Sta. A
Montreal, PQ, Canada H3C3N3
PH: (514)871-6000

Founded: 1977. Annual Revenue: US$525. Employees: 3013. Description: Transportation: Transportation

▌237
VICINITY CORP.

370 San Aleso Ave.
Sunnyvale, CA 94085
PH: (408)543-3000
URL: http://www.vicinity.com

Founded: 1995. Annual Revenue: US$20. Employees: 127. Description: Services: Internet and wireless services.

▌238
WAL-MART STORES INC.

702 SW Eighth St.
Bentonville, AR 72716-8611

PH: (479)273-4000
E-mail: cserve@wal-mart.com
URL: http://www.walmart.com
Contact: Robert Connolly, Executive vice president, marketing and consumer communication

Founded: 1962. Annual Revenue: US$217,799. Employees: 303000. Description: Retail: Operator of discount stores, supermarkets, specialty department stores and restaurants. Services: Family entertainment centers.

▌239
WALT DISNEY CO.

500 S Buena Vista St.
Burbank, CA 91521
PH: (818)560-1000
URL: http://www.disney.com
Contact: Andrea Marozas, The Walt Disney Company

Founded: 1938. Annual Revenue: US$25,256. Employees: 114000. Description: Services: Enterntainment company, including: motion picture film production for film, video and television industry, theme park operator. Retail: Gifts and novelty items. Finance: holding company.

▌240
WASHINGTON POST CO.

1150 15th St. NW
Washington, DC 20071
PH: (202)334-6000
URL: http://www.washpostco.com
Contact: Guyon Knight, VP Corporate Communications

Founded: 1877. Annual Revenue: US$2,417. Employees: 12300. Description: Manufacturing: Newspaper and magazine publishing, broadcast and cable television stations and networks. Services: electronic information services, test preparation, educational and career services.

▌241
WEBHIRE INC.

91 Hartwell Ave.
Lexington, MA 02421-3125
PH: (781)869-5000
E-mail: info@webhire.com
URL: http://www.webhire.com
Contact: Susan Chebookjian

Founded: 1982. Annual Revenue: US$22. Employees: 120. Description: Services: Developer of human resource staffing software.

▌242
WHEELS INC.

666 Garland Pl.
Des Plaines, IL 60016
PH: (847)699-7000

E-mail: info@wheels.com
URL: http://www.wheels.com

Founded: 1939. **Annual Revenue:** US$671. **Employees:** 603. **Description:** Services: Car and truck leasing.

▍243
WORLDCOM GROUP

500 Clinton Center Dr.
Clinton, MS 39056
PH: (601)460-5600
E-mail: info@worldcomgroup.com
URL: http://www.worldcom.com

Annual Revenue: US$35,179. **Employees:** 61800. **Description:** Communications: Long distance provider. Services: Web hosting services.

▍244
WORLDCOM INC.

500 Clinton Center Dr.
Clinton, MS 39056-5630
PH: (601)460-5600
URL: http://www.worldcom.com
Contact: Scott Hamilton, Investor Relations

Founded: 1983. **Annual Revenue:** US$35,179. **Employees:** 61800. **Description:** Communications: Provider of local and long distance telephone services. Finance: Holding company.

▍245
W.W. GRAINGER INC.

100 Grainger Pkwy.
Lake Forest, IL 60045-5201
PH: (847)535-1000
E-mail: postoffice@Grainger.com
URL: http://www.grainger.com
Contact: Edward J. Franczek, Senior Vice President, Marketing and Sales

Founded: 1927. **Annual Revenue:** US$4,754. **Employees:** 15385. **Description:** Wholesale: HVAC equipment, motors, hand and power tools and pumps.

▍246
XEROX CORP.

800 Long Ridge Rd.
Stamford, CT 06904-1600
PH: (203)968-3000
E-mail: webmaster@xerox.com
URL: http://www.xerox.com

Contact: Christa Carone, Director, Corporate Public Relations

Founded: 1906. **Annual Revenue:** US$16,500. **Employees:** 78900. **Description:** Manufacturing: Computer peripheral equipment and office machines. Services: Computer, data processing, and Internet services.

▍247
YAHOO! INC.

701 First Ave.
Sunnyvale, CA 94089
PH: (408)731-3300
URL: http://www.yahoo.com

Founded: 1994. **Annual Revenue:** US$717. **Employees:** 3000. **Description:** Services: Internet search engine, audio and video streaming, store hosting and management, and Web site tools and services.

▍248
YELLOW FREIGHT SYSTEM INC.

P. O. Box 7270
Shawnee Mission, KS 66207
PH: (913)344-3000
URL: http://www.yellowfreight.com/
Contact: J. Kevin Grimsley, Senior Vice President, Marketing and Sal

Founded: 1920. **Annual Revenue:** US$2,330. **Employees:** 24000. **Description:** Transportation: Long-distance trucking

▍249
ZILOG INC.

532 Race St.
San Jose, CA 95126
PH: (408)558-8500
E-mail: info@zilog.com
URL: http://www.zilog.com
Contact: Thomas C. Carson, Senior Vice President, Sales

Founded: 1974. **Annual Revenue:** US$172. **Employees:** 1000. **Description:** Manufacturing: Integrated circuits.

▍250
ZONES INC.

707 S Grady Way
Renton, WA 98055-3233
PH: (425)430-3000
URL: http://www.zones.com

Founded: 1986. **Annual Revenue:** US$541. **Employees:** 554. **Description:** Retail: Mail-order house specializing in computer software.

Ranking by Revenue

This list shows the leading e-commerce companies worldwide ranked by their annual revenue figures, in US$ millions. The basis for this list is Interactive Week magazine's annual ranking, the Interactive 500 (2001), and revenue figures were updated through original research.

Company	Rank	
Wal-Mart Stores Inc.	1	217,799
General Motors Corp.	2	177,260
General Electric Co.	3	125,913
International Business Machines Corp.	4	85,866
Hewlett-Packard Co.	5	45,200
Dynegy Inc.	6	42,242
Sears, Roebuck and Co.	7	41,078
Target Corp.	8	39,167
AOL Time Warner Inc.	9	38,234
Comcast Corp.	10	38,132
Kmart Corp.	11	37,028
WorldCom Inc.	12	35,179
Worldcom Group	12	35,179
Motorola Inc.	14	33,075
J.C. Penney Company Inc.	15	32,004
Dell Computer Corp.	16	31,888
United Parcel Service Inc.	17	30,646
BellSouth Corp.	18	29,589
Microsoft Corp.	19	28,370
Dow Chemical Co.	20	27,805
Intel Corp.	21	26,539
Walt Disney Co.	22	25,256
Lucent Technologies Inc.	23	21,294
FedEx Corp.	24	20,607
Cisco Systems Inc.	25	18,915
Nortel Networks Corp.	26	17,511
Tech Data Corp.	27	17,200
Qwest Communications International Inc.	28	16,610
Xerox Corp.	29	16,500
Sun Microsystems Inc.	30	15,721
Federated Department Stores Inc.	31	15,651
Delta Air Lines Inc.	32	13,879
Gap Inc.	33	13,848
Toys "R" Us Inc.	34	12,630
Office Depot Inc.	35	11,200
Staples Inc.	36	10,744
Marriott International Inc.	37	10,152
Arrow Electronics Inc.	38	10,128
Oracle Corp.	39	9,673
Burlington Northern Santa Fe Corp.	40	9,208
Cendant Corp.	41	8,950
Ashland Inc.	42	7,719
Boise Cascade Corp.	43	7,422
Gannett Company Inc.	44	6,344
Air Products and Chemicals Inc.	45	5,717
Nordstrom Inc.	46	5,634
Southwest Airlines Co.	47	5,565
Eastman Chemical Co.	48	5,384
Apple Computer Inc.	49	5,363
Blockbuster Inc.	50	4,960
Hertz Corp.	51	4,916
Barnes and Noble Inc.	52	4,870
W.W. Grainger Inc.	53	4,754
Alticor Inc.	54	4,100

Company	Rank	
Starwood Hotels and Resorts Worldwide Inc.	55	3,967
CDW Computer Centers Inc.	56	3,962
Sutter Health	57	3,546
Alltel Communications Co.	58	3,150
Amazon.com Inc.	59	3,122
Steelcase Inc.	60	3,090
New York Times Co.	61	3,016
NetBank Inc.	62	2,880
Charles Schwab and Co. Inc.	63	2,839
TMP Worldwide	64	2,550
Washington Post Co.	65	2,417
Yellow Freight System Inc.	66	2,330
Merisel Inc.	67	2,094
Hughes Network Systems Inc.	68	1,943
Dow Jones and Company Inc.	69	1,773
Alaska Airlines Inc.	70	1,751
Electronic Arts Inc.	71	1,725
CIENA Corp.	72	1,603
Lands' End Inc.	73	1,569
National Semiconductor Corp.	74	1,495
3Com Corp.	75	1,478
E*TRADE Group Ino.	76	1,275
Intuit Inc.	77	1,262
EarthLink Inc.	78	1,245
CMGI Inc.	79	1,238
Standard Register Co.	80	1,196
eMerge Interactive Inc.	81	1,195
PC Connection Inc.	82	1,180
Priceline.com Inc.	83	1,170
PSINet Inc.	84	996
Enterasys Networks Inc.	85	977
CFSB Bancorp Inc.	86	880
BUY.COM Inc.	87	788
eBay Inc.	88	749
Yahoo! Inc.	89	717
Recreational Equipment Inc.	90	698
Ticketmaster	91	672
Wheels Inc.	92	671
Internet Capital Group Inc.	92	671
Ameritrade Inc.	94	655
Zones Inc.	95	541
Via Rail Canada Inc.	96	525
1-800-Flowers.com Inc.	97	497
Egghead.com Inc.	98	479
Openwave Systems Inc.	99	465
Getty Images Inc.	100	451
PTEK Holdings Inc.	101	423
DoubleClick Inc.	102	406
Cyberian Outpost Inc.	103	355
Ingram Micro SA	104	348
Homestore.com Inc.	105	325
QVC	106	304
Travelocity.com Inc.	107	302
Martha Stewart Living Omnimedia Inc.	108	296
Playboy Enterprises Inc.	109	291
Overture Services Inc.	110	288
CNET Networks Inc.	111	286
Frost and Sullivan Inc.	112	267
Tessco Technologies Inc.	113	249
Expedia Inc.	114	222
Riverstone Networks Inc.	115	211
E-LOAN Inc.	115	211
Agency.com Ltd.	117	202
RealNetworks Inc.	118	189

Company	Rank		Company	Rank	
Pegasus Solutions Inc.	119	180	Engage Inc.	176	43
United Online Inc.	120	176	DigitalThink Inc.	176	43
ITXC Corp.	121	173	iGo Corp.	180	40
Zilog Inc.	122	172	iManage Inc.	181	39
Akamai Technologies Inc.	123	163	Digital Impact Inc.	181	39
USinternetworking Inc.	124	150	eBenX Inc.	183	37
FreeMarkets Inc.	125	148	NBC Internet Inc.	184	36
drugstore.com inc.	126	145	Internet America Inc.	185	35
iBasis Inc.	127	134	Evolve Software Inc.	185	35
Moore Medical Corp.	128	133	j2 Global Communications	187	33
FTD.com Inc.	129	130	eUniverse Inc.	187	33
VerticalNet Inc.	130	126	Hoover's Inc.	189	32
eSpeed Inc.	131	125	Official Payments Corp.	190	31
Beyond.com Corp.	132	120	CyberSource Corp.	190	31
Entrust Technologies Inc.	133	118	theglobe.com inc.	192	30
Register.Com Inc.	134	116	Support.com	192	30
Juno Online Services	135	114	Internet Pictures Corp.	194	29
PayPal Inc.	136	105	PFSweb Inc.	195	28
NextCard Inc.	136	105	Neoforma Inc.	195	28
Modem Media Inc.	138	103	LendingTree Inc.	195	28
Healtheon Web MD	139	102	Terra Lycos S.A.	198	27
Peapod Inc.	140	100	Netzee Inc.	199	26
Digital Insight Corp.	141	95	VantageMed Corp.	200	24
Multex.com Inc.	142	94	StarMedia Network Inc.	201	23
Avenue A Inc.	143	90	SciQuest Inc.	201	23
HealthExtras Inc.	144	88	InsWeb Corp.	201	23
LookSmart Ltd.	145	85	Bluefly Inc.	201	23
Salesforce.com Inc.	146	81	Be Free Inc.	201	23
MP3.com Inc.	147	80	Webhire Inc.	206	22
chinadotcom Corp.	148	76	NetCreations Inc.	207	21
NewsEDGE Corp.	149	71	BackWeb Technologies Ltd.	207	21
Ask Jeeves Inc.	150	67	Vicinity Corp.	209	20
Ashford.com Inc.	150	67	FindWhat.com Inc.	209	20
Niku Corp.	152	66	eCollege.com	209	20
SportsLine.com Inc.	153	65	Stamps.com Inc.	212	19
MyPoints.com Inc.	154	64	Eprise Corp.	212	19
McAfee.com Corp.	155	62	US Search.com Inc.	214	18
iVillage Inc.	156	60	Onvia.com Inc.	214	18
Digital Island	157	59	EDGAR Online Inc.	216	17
Loislaw.com Inc.	158	57	Switchboard Inc.	217	16
HeadHunter.NET Inc.	158	57	Landacorp Inc.	217	16
Tickets.com Inc.	160	56	Log On America Inc.	219	13
Cobalt Group Inc.	161	55	Fastnet Corp.	219	13
LifeMinders Inc.	162	54	Bertelsmann Inc.	221	12
eGAIN Communications Corp.	163	53	Promotions.com Inc.	222	11
New Frontier Media Inc.	164	52	Loudeye Technologies Inc.	223	10
L90 Inc.	164	52	HealthGate Data Corp.	224	9
Intraware Inc.	164	52	FairMarket Inc.	224	9
Autoweb.com Inc.	164	52	InterTrust Technologies Corp.	226	8
24/7 Real Media Inc.	164	52	ImproveNet Inc.	227	7
Corio Inc.	169	50	VanDyke Software Inc.	228	5
Portera Systems Inc.	170	47	Simutronics Corp.	228	5
Keynote Systems Inc.	171	46	Medinex Systems Inc.	228	5
ValueClick Inc.	172	45	Globalscape Inc.	228	5
Selectica Inc.	172	45	Crosswalk.com Inc.	228	5
Collectors Universe Inc.	172	45	Medsite Inc.	233	4
SkillSoft Corp. (Nashua, NH)	175	44	Learn2 Corp.	233	4
Orbitz Inc.	176	43	E-Funds Corp.	233	4
Netcentives Inc.	176	43	Bingo.com Inc.	236	2
			Aptimus Inc.	236	2

Ranking by Number of Employees

This list shows the leading e-commerce companies worldwide ranked by number of employees. The basis for this list is Interactive Week magazine's annual ranking, the Interactive 500 (2001), and figures were updated through original research.

Company	Rank	
General Motors Corp.	1	365,000
United Parcel Service Inc.	2	359,000
Sears, Roebuck and Co.	3	323,000
International Business Machines Corp.	4	319,876
General Electric Co.	5	310,000
Wal-Mart Stores Inc.	6	303,000
J.C. Penney Company Inc.	7	270,000
Kmart Corp.	8	252,000
FedEx Corp.	9	215,000
Target Corp.	10	192,000
Gap Inc.	11	166,000
Motorola Inc.	12	147,000
Marriott International Inc.	13	143,000
Federated Department Stores Inc.	14	129,000
Starwood Hotels and Resorts Worldwide Inc.	15	115,000
Walt Disney Co.	16	114,000
Blockbuster Inc.	17	89,700
Hewlett-Packard Co.	18	88,500
AOL Time Warner Inc.	18	88,500
BellSouth Corp.	20	87,875
Intel Corp.	21	86,100
Xerox Corp.	22	78,900
Lucent Technologies Inc.	23	77,000
Delta Air Lines Inc.	24	76,273
Toys "R" Us Inc.	25	71,000
Qwest Communications International Inc.	26	67,000
WorldCom Inc.	27	61,800
Worldcom Group	27	61,800
Dynegy Inc.	29	61,000
Nortel Networks Corp.	30	53,600
Cendant Corp.	31	53,000
Gannett Company Inc.	32	51,500
Dow Chemical Co.	33	50,000
Staples Inc.	34	48,458
Microsoft Corp.	35	48,030
Office Depot Inc.	36	48,000
Barnes and Noble Inc.	37	45,000
Oracle Corp.	38	43,000
Nordstrom Inc.	38	43,000
Dell Computer Corp.	40	40,000
Burlington Northern Santa Fe Corp.	41	39,000
Sun Microsystems Inc.	42	38,900
Comcast Corp.	43	38,000
Cisco Systems Inc.	43	38,000
Sutter Health	45	33,774
Southwest Airlines Co.	46	31,580
Hertz Corp.	47	29,800
Ashland Inc.	48	25,100
Boise Cascade Corp.	49	24,168
Yellow Freight System Inc.	50	24,000
Steelcase Inc.	51	19,300
Air Products and Chemicals Inc.	52	17,800
Eastman Chemical Co.	53	15,800
W.W. Grainger Inc.	54	15,385
Washington Post Co.	55	12,300

Company	Rank	
Arrow Electronics Inc.	56	12,200
New York Times Co.	57	12,050
Charles Schwab and Co. Inc.	58	12,000
Apple Computer Inc.	59	11,434
Alaska Airlines Inc.	60	11,025
TMP Worldwide Inc.	61	11,000
Tech Data Corp.	62	10,500
National Semiconductor Corp.	63	10,300
Lands' End Inc.	64	10,200
Alticor Inc.	65	10,000
Dow Jones and Company Inc.	66	8,100
Amazon.com Inc.	67	7,800
Recreational Equipment Inc.	68	7,000
EarthLink Inc.	69	6,736
Intuit Inc.	70	6,100
Standard Register Co.	71	5,692
PSINet Inc.	72	5,000
3Com Corp.	73	4,615
Ticketmaster	74	4,600
CIENA Corp.	75	3,778
CMGI Inc.	76	3,584
Electronic Arts Inc.	77	3,500
E*TRADE Group Inc.	78	3,495
Terra Lycos S.A.	79	3,196
Via Rail Canada Inc.	80	3,013
Yahoo! Inc.	81	3,000
Hughes Network Systems Inc.	81	3,000
Homestore.com Inc.	83	2,800
CDW Computer Centers Inc.	84	2,700
Enterasys Networks Inc.	85	2,600
Ameritrade Inc.	86	2,573
eBay Inc.	87	2,560
1-800-Flowers.com Inc.	88	2,400
PTEK Holdings Inc.	89	2,240
Openwave Systems Inc.	90	2,200
CNET Networks Inc.	91	2,000
DoubleClick Inc.	92	1,929
Getty Images Inc.	93	1,845
Healtheon Web MD	94	1,825
QVC	95	1,680
Travelocity.com Inc.	96	1,554
Pegasus Solutions Inc.	97	1,518
Agency.com Ltd.	98	1,500
PC Connection Inc.	99	1,312
Zilog Inc.	100	1,000
FreeMarkets Inc.	100	1,000
NextCard Inc.	102	930
Digital Island	103	900
Expedia Inc.	104	896
Peapod Inc.	105	891
Tickets.com Inc.	106	878
Akamai Technologies Inc.	107	841
RealNetworks Inc.	108	798
Entrust Technologies Inc.	109	792
Selectica Inc.	110	753
Digital Insight Corp.	111	738
USinternetworking Inc.	112	700
Frost and Sullivan Inc.	112	700
Egghead.com Inc.	114	653
NBC Internet Inc.	115	635
United Online Inc.	116	623
PayPal Inc.	117	618
Martha Stewart Living Omnimedia Inc.	118	610
Playboy Enterprises Inc.	119	605

Company	Rank		Company	Rank	
Wheels Inc.	120	603	Intraware Inc.	179	200
Cobalt Group Inc.	121	602	Internet America Inc.	179	200
eGAIN Communications Corp.	122	595	theglobe.com inc.	181	197
PFSweb Inc.	123	575	Neoforma Inc.	182	196
Merisel Inc.	124	570	iGo Corp.	183	193
Overture Services Inc.	125	559	InterTrust Technologies Corp.	184	188
Zones Inc.	126	554	Orbitz Inc.	185	187
Tessco Technologies Inc.	127	528	BackWeb Technologies Ltd.	186	180
StarMedia Network Inc.	128	520	CyberSource Corp.	187	178
Multex.com Inc.	129	506	Salesforce.com Inc.	188	175
Modem Media Inc.	130	500	Beyond.com Corp.	189	169
eBenX Inc.	131	495	Be Free Inc.	190	165
Netcentives Inc.	132	494	VerticalNet Inc.	191	164
Riverstone Networks Inc.	133	472	Log On America Inc.	191	164
DigitalThink Inc.	134	464	Landacorp Inc.	191	164
iBasis Inc.	135	441	McAfee.com Corp.	194	160
E-LOAN Inc.	136	436	Support.com	195	155
Ask Jeeves Inc.	137	416	Autoweb.com Inc.	196	152
Digital Impact Inc.	138	389	eUniverse Inc.	197	146
drugstore.com inc.	139	379	InsWeb Corp.	198	143
HeadHunter.NET Inc.	140	377	NetBank Inc.	199	140
LookSmart Ltd.	141	367	LifeMinders Inc.	200	138
Register.Com Inc.	142	360	New Frontier Media Inc.	201	137
Keynote Systems Inc.	142	360	j2 Global Communications	202	134
Priceline.com Inc.	144	359	SciQuest Inc.	203	132
Cyberian Outpost Inc.	145	345	Vicinity Corp.	204	127
Niku Corp.	146	340	Netzee Inc.	204	127
SportsLine.com Inc.	147	335	Fastnet Corp.	206	123
Juno Online Services	148	332	Webhire Inc.	207	120
Stamps.com Inc.	149	315	US Search.com Inc.	208	117
eSpeed Inc.	150	312	ImproveNet Inc.	209	111
NewsEDGE Corp.	151	309	ValueClick Inc.	210	107
MP3.com Inc.	152	308	EDGAR Online Inc.	211	99
Corio Inc.	152	308	Onvia.com Inc.	212	97
24/7 Real Media Inc.	152	308	FTD.com Inc.	212	97
MyPoints.com Inc.	155	301	Internet Pictures Corp.	214	87
Portera Systems Inc.	156	300	Learn2 Corp.	215	85
Loislaw.com Inc.	156	300	Medinex Systems Inc.	216	83
Alltel Communications Co.	156	300	HealthExtras Inc.	217	82
VantageMed Corp.	159	290	Medsite Inc.	218	81
Hoover's Inc.	160	287	Switchboard Inc.	219	80
eMerge Interactive Inc.	160	287	HealthGate Data Corp.	220	79
Ingram Micro SA	162	280	FindWhat.com Inc.	221	74
Engage Inc.	163	279	Official Payments Corp.	222	68
CFSB Bancorp Inc.	163	279	FairMarket Inc.	222	68
Moore Medical Corp.	165	275	Bluefly Inc.	224	66
iVillage Inc.	166	262	Bertelsmann Inc.	225	50
Evolve Software Inc.	167	258	Loudeye Technologies Inc.	226	43
BUY.COM Inc.	167	258	Simutronics Corp.	227	42
LendingTree Inc.	169	254	NetCreations Inc.	228	40
Ashford.com Inc.	170	234	Globalscape Inc.	229	35
SkillSoft Corp. (Nashua, NH)	171	230	Internet Capital Group Inc.	230	31
Avenue A Inc.	171	230	E-Funds Corp.	231	30
iManage Inc.	173	229	Crosswalk.com Inc.	231	30
Collectors Universe Inc.	174	226	Aptimus Inc.	233	28
ITXC Corp.	175	224	Promotions.com Inc.	234	25
eCollege.com	176	223	VanDyke Software Inc.	235	23
L90 Inc.	177	217	Micron Inc.	236	11
Eprise Corp.	178	216	Dennis Interactive	237	10
			Bingo.com Inc.	238	6

Collegis Inc.; O:1330
Collier & Markowitz; O:1331
Collins Center for Executive Education; O:2970; O:2952
CologneMesse; O:3585
Colony One Online, Inc.; O:3854
Colorado Association of Commerce and Industry; O:50
Colorado Idea Net, Inc.; O:3855
Colorado Software Summit, Java and XML Programming Conference; O:3350
Colorado State University; O:2800
Columbia University; O:3108
Comcast Corp.; C:46
COMDEX Executive Symposium; O:3351
COMDEX Technology Conference; O:3352
Comduit, Inc.; O:3856
Comergent C3 Configurator; O:378
Comergent Distributed E-Business System; O:379
Comergent Technologies Inc.; O:860; O:840; O:827; O:747; O:692; O:380; O:379; O:378
Comet Media; O:3857
Comino Group plc; O:1332
Comitnow; O:3858
Command Technology Solutions Inc.; O:4547
ComMark; O:3859
commerce application; T:51
Commerce Catalog; O:380
Commerce Creator; O:381
Commerce in the Digital Age; O:2448
Commerce Exchange Business Suite 4.0; O:382
Commerce Exchange Retail Suite 4.0; O:383
Commerce Gateway; O:384
Commerce Intelligence 4.0; O:385
Commerce Net; O:51
Commerce One; O:388; O:387; O:389; O:386
Commerce One 5.0; O:386
Commerce One Buy; O:387
Commerce One Collaborative Platform; O:388
Commerce One Source; O:389
Commerce Portal; O:390
Commerce Services Network; T:10
CommerceQuest Inc.; O:391
CommerceQuest RetailPack System; O:391
Commercial eCommerce Suite; O:392
Commercial Internet Exchange Association; O:52
Commercial-Resources.com; O:3860
commodity suppliers; T:82
common gateway interface (CGI) files; T:61
Common Vision; O:1333
ComMotion Interactive; O:3861
CommPact Digital Arts, Inc.; O:3862
CommSciences Inc.; O:1334
CommSpeed; O:4548
Communication
    Between Personal Computers; T:66
Communication Strategy Consultants; O:1335
Communication Technologies for E-Commerce; O:2449
Communications; O:3353
Communications Fraud Control Association; O:53
Communications and Show Management, Inc.; O:3666
Community Manager; O:393
Community model; T:27
CommVerge Conference and Exhibition; O:3354
COMNET Conference and Expo; O:3355
Company Information
    On Web Sites; T:59
Co. Post Newsweek Tech Media; O:3473
CompanyV.com Corp.; O:3863
CompareWebHosts.com; O:4549
compensation; T:33
Competition
    Isms And; T:10
    Transforming Business Strategies And; T:84
Competition in Electronic Commerce; O:2450

competitive advantage; T:84; T:23
Competitive Intelligence Executive Summit; O:3356
Competitive Strategies for E-Business; O:2451
Compilation of state and federal privacy laws; O:3169
Complete internet & world wide web programming training course; O:3170
Complete e-Commerce book : design, build & maintain a successful web-based business; O:3171
Complete idiot's guide to Internet privacy and security; O:3172
CompleteSource; O:394
CompleXero, Inc.; O:3864
Comprotex Web Development; O:3865
Compsaver Computers; O:3866
CompStar Technologies Inc.; O:1336
Compudoc; O:3867
CompuNerdz Web Creations; O:3868
CompUofC; O:2545; O:2746
Computer Audit Control and Security; O:3357
Computer Based Training; O:2848; O:3013; O:2395; O:3039
Computer Business Solutions, Inc; O:3869
Computer and Communications Industry Association; O:54
Computer Consulting from the Beach; O:1337
Computer Design and Integration, LLC; O:1338
Computer Evolutions, Inc.; O:3870
Computer Faire; O:3358
Computer Fest; O:3359
Computer Graphics Unlimited, Inc.; O:3871
Computer Horizons Corp.; O:1339
Computer, Internet and electronic commerce terms : judicial, legislative and technical definitions; O:3173
Computer Professionals for Social Responsibility; O:55
Computer Resource Team Inc.; O:1340
Computer Security for E-Business; O:2452
Computer Security Institute; O:3375; O:3600; O:56
Computer Security, Privacy and Policy; O:2453
Computer Software Industry Association; O:57
Computer Software Systems Inc.; O:1341
Computer Solutions Consulting; O:4550
Computer Techniques, Inc.; O:3872
Computer Technologies and Internet Solutions Inc.; O:1342
The Computer and Technology Showcase; O:3360
Computer Tutor; O:1343
computer viruses; T:77
ComputerJobs.com; T:41
computers; T:29
Computing Magic; O:3873
Computing Technology Industry Association; O:58
CompuTR Web Design; O:3874
Compuware Corp.; O:980; O:786; O:437; O:1344
ComSite Web Service; O:3875
Comtek; O:3361
Concentric Enterprises Inc.; O:1345
Concept Developers, LLC; O:3876
Concept Factory; O:3877
Concept Marketing Group Inc.; O:1346
Concepture Solutions; O:3878
Configuration Manager; O:395
Configurator; O:396
Connect; O:3362
Connect - IT; O:3363
ConnecTec Communications, Inc.; O:3879
Connected Customer; O:397
connected economy; T:9
Connected International Meeting Professionals Association; O:59
Connected Merchant; O:398
Connected Plan; O:399
Connected Store POS; O:400
Connected Supplier/Momentis; O:401
Connected.com; T:25; T:18
Connection; O:1347
Connectivity; T:84; T:9
Connelly Design; O:3880
Connexions.net; O:1348

933

937

953

ValueClick Inc.; T:2; T:3; T:232
Vandelay Enterprises; O:4469
Vanderbilt University; O:2757; O:2729
VanDyke Software Inc.; C:233
Vanguard Communications Corp.; O:2299
Vantage Architecture; O:4470
VantageMed Corp.; C:234
Vapor; O:2300
Varian,Hal R.; T:34
VBITS - Visual Basic Insiders' Technical Summit; O:3687
VCDC - Visual C Developers Conference; O:3688
Velocity 7; O:4471
Vencon Management Inc.; O:2301
Ventera; O:2302
venture capital; T:8; T:76
Venture Management (Entrepreneurship); O:3100
VentureNet Partners Ltd.; O:2303
Verdi Productions; O:4472
Verio Inc.; T:89
Verisign; T:74; T:68; T:65; T:4473
VeriSign Inc.; O:2304
Veritas; T:64
Veritech Corp.; O:4474
Verity Inc.; O:2305
Vermont Chamber of Commerce; O:219
Versatility Data Management; O:4475
version control; T:91
version-control software; T:73
Vertex Customer Management; O:2306
Vertical 360; O:4476
VerticalNet Inc.; C:235
Via Rail Canada Inc.; C:236
VIANT Corp.; O:4477; O:2307
Vicinity Corp.; C:237
Video; T:55; T:1262
VideoLink Mail; O:1029
VideoLink Pro; O:1030
Vietnam Telecomp - International Exhibition in Vietnam on Telecommunications, Electronics and Informatics; O:3689
Viewloclty Inc.; O:691; O:393; O:374; O:831; O:704; O:935; O:572; O:848; O:469
Vignette; O:1037; O:1032; O:1034; O:1031; O:1036; O:1035; O:1033
Vignette V6 Advanced Deployment Server; O:1031
Vignette V6 Content Collaboration Server; O:1032
Vignette V6 Content Suite; O:1033
Vignette V6 Multi-Channel Communication Server; O:1034
Vignette V6 Multisite Content Manager; O:1035
Vignette V6 Relationship Management Server Advanced Edition; O:1036
Vignette(R) V6 Enterprise Adapters; O:1037
Vigord Corp.; O:2308
Villa Julie College; O:2972
Village Principle Corp.; O:2309
Vine Technology; O:2310
VIP Communique; O:2311
Virginia Internet Service Providers Alliance; O:220
Virginia Tech; O:3000
Virginia.com; O:4630
Virtual business magazine; O:3277
Virtual Banks; T:32
Virtual Communications; O:2312
virtual communities; T:34
virtual contracts; T:43
Virtual Design Network; O:4478
Virtual Host Professionals; O:4631
The Virtual Institute of Information; O:3150
A Virtual Solution; O:221
Virtual Store; O:1038
Virtual Terminal; O:1039
Virtual Tribes Inc.; O:2313
VirtualCart; T:80; T:74
VirtualRep Inc.; O:2314
Virtuoso Web Design Services; O:4479
viruses; T:25; T:18

Insurance Against; T:39
Visinet; O:4480
Vision
    In Business Plans; T:9
VisionFactory Inc.; O:2315
VisionOne Inc.; O:2316
VisionPartner; O:2317
Vista 7 West Inc.; O:2318
Vista Plus; O:1040
Vista Trak Inc.; O:2319
Vistronix Inc.; O:2320
Visual Auction; O:1041
Visual Elk; O:1042
Visual FoxPro DevCon; O:3690
Visual Perspectives Internet Inc.; O:2321
VJ Studio; O:4481
VMEbus International Trade Association; O:222
VNU Business Media.; O:3345; O:3413; O:3616
VNU Expositions; O:3363; O:3456; O:3455
VocalPoint Technologies; T:86
Voice Commerce; T:86
voice portals; T:86
VoiceCentral; O:2322
Voicecon; O:3691
VoiceXML; T:86
Volaris Online; O:4482; O:4632
Volt Directory Marketing; O:3254
Voluntary Interindustry Commerce Standards Association; O:223
VON - voice on the net; O:3692
Voyager Collaborate; O:1043
Voyager Fulfill; O:1044
Voyager Select; O:1045
Voyager Strategy Consultants; O:2323
Voyager XPS; O:1046
Voyus Canada Inc.; O:2324
VPN Solutions; O:1047
VSLive!; O:3693
VS.NET Connections; O:3694
Vstore.com; T:74
VTweb.com; O:4633
W. Averell Harriman School for Management and Policy; O:2991
W. P. Corcoran and Ass., Inc.; O:4483
Wake Forrest University; O:3030; O:2855
Wal-Mart Stores Inc.; C:238
Walden University; O:2433; O:2535; O:2567
Walker Information; O:2325
Walker Interactive Systems Inc.; O:499; O:494; O:490; O:479
Wall Street Journal; T:36
Walt Disney Co.; C:239
Warehouse Management (DCS); O:1048
warehouse management systems (WMS); T:83
Warren WebWorks; O:4484
Warrington College of Business; O:2893
WAS Inc.; O:2326
Washington Association of Internet Service Providers; O:224
Washington Post Co.; C:240
Washington Software Alliance; O:225
Waterfall models; T:81
Waters Computer Consultants; O:2327
Waukesha Area Chamber of Commerce; O:226
Wave Design; O:4485
Waveset Lighthouse; O:1049
Waveset Technologies Inc.; O:1049
WCZ.com; O:4486
WD Net Inc.; O:2328
WDDG-New York City; O:4487
WE Concepts, Inc.; O:4488
Weaving a website : programming in HTML, JavaScript, Perl and Java; O:3278
Web sites built to last; O:3279; O:3281; O:3280; O:3282
    For Multilingual Users; O:54
    For Web Rings; O:88
Web 2 Market, Inc.; O:4489